Civil Actions Against the Police

AUSTRALIA AND NEW ZEALAND
The Law Book Company Ltd.
Sydney : Melbourne : Perth

CANADA AND U.S.A.
The Carswell Company Ltd.
Agincourt, Ontario

INDIA
N. M. Tripathi Private Ltd.
Bombay
and
Eastern Law House Private Ltd.
Calcutta and Delhi
M.P.P. House
Bangalore

ISRAEL
Steimatzky's Agency Ltd.
Jerusalem : Tel Aviv : Haifa

MALAYSIA : SINGAPORE : BRUNEI
Malayan Law Journal (Pte.) Ltd.
Singapore and Kuala Lumpur

Civil Actions Against the Police

by

Richard Clayton, B.A. (Oxon)

of Middle Temple, Barrister

and

Hugh Tomlinson, B.A. (Oxon), M.A. (Sussex), Dip. Law (City)

of Gray's Inn, Barrister

LONDON
SWEET & MAXWELL
1987

Published in 1987 by
Sweet & Maxwell Limited
11 New Fetter Lane, London
Computerset by Promenade Graphics Limited, Cheltenham
Printed in Great Britain by
Robert Hartnoll (1985) Limited, Bodmin, Cornwall

British Library Cataloguing in Publication Data
Clayton, Richard
Civil actions against the police.
1. Civil procedure,—England
I. Title II. Tomlinson, Hugh
344.207'5 KD7325

ISBN 0–421–34420–2

Preface

The immediate stimulus for writing this book came from the range of policing and civil liberties issues arising out of the 1984 miners' strike. The public order problems of mass picketing evoked a controversial police response. The *"Dartford Tunnel"* case was a startling, if abortive, attempt directly to involve the civil law in policing issues. In the absence of clearly defined "civil rights" in English law, the relationship between common law rights and police powers became increasingly important and the idea of a book on the "police and civil law" began to take shape in our minds.

We claim no originality in turning our attention to this area. The 1980s have seen a remarkable resurgence of what we were told as students is a central function of the civil law: the protection of the "civil rights" of citizens against police misconduct. As with all "new directions" in the law, there are many reasons for this resurgence. We mention, in no particular order: public dissatisfaction with "administrative remedies" such as police complaints; concern about policing methods after the riots of 1981, increasing awareness of "human rights" through the Strasbourg Court and the development of "civil liberties" courses within law degrees.

Although there has been a steady trickle of civil actions against the police for many centuries this seems almost to have dried up in the 1950s and 60s. It was perhaps the famous *White* case[1] which raised many from their "dogmatic slumbers" to the realisation that the civil law could be of assistance to victims of police misconduct. The work of a large number of lawyers and advice workers over recent years has been of great value in the writing of this book. We will be forgiven for only mentioning one by name: Tony Gifford Q.C. who wrote the first article on the subject[2] and spoke at a number of public meetings where civil actions against the police became a topic for lively debate.

The idea for a book in the present form crystallised when we realised that no one had attempted to set out the present law on the legal remedies of citizens for police misconduct.[3] On close examination, the considerable and ever-expanding literature on the police has almost no direct bearing on the questions facing practitioners who bring civil actions against the police. With few exceptions,[4] this literature can be divided into two broad categories. First, there are the sociological and political writings about the positions and roles of the police. Even when these address issues of misconduct they have no direct bearing on the availability of legal remedies. Secondly, there is a large body of work—some of which is very accomplished—covering the "powers of the police." Surprisingly little of this work overlaps with

[1] *White* v. *MPC, The Times,* April 24, 1982.

[2] "Civil Actions Against the Police" (1983) Legal Action 81.

[3] We subsequently became aware of John Harrison's project for a book on this area which was published as *Police Misconduct: Legal Remedies.*

[4] We are thinking in particular of Harry Street's pioneering work, *Freedom the Individual and the Law,* Geoffrey Marshall's important work on the legal status of the police and Laurence Lustgarten's recent book on the "governance of police": see Bibliography.

the present book.[5] It is interesting, for example, that none of the many discussions of the Police and Criminal Evidence Act 1984 directly addresses the question of the legal effect of a breach of the "safeguard" provisions by the police.[6]

Civil Actions Against the Police is, therefore, primarily an analysis for legal practitioners of the civil law rights and remedies for police misconduct. The title may give rise to a misunderstanding. The word "against" simply indicates that the defendants, against whom such civil actions are brought, will be police officers. The title is not intended to convey any "anti-police" bias. We are of the view—which we assume is shared by most people—that it is vital that the essential social function of policing is carried out within a clear and enforceable framework of rights and responsibilities. Indeed the book can be seen as part of a wider project: the examination of the legal remedies available to the citizen against abuses of power by public authorities.

During the course of writing a number of books were published which illuminated the subject area. David Feldman's book on entry, search and seizure was published when we were at an advanced stage of preparation. It introduces rigorous standards into this area of the law and we are indebted to it. John Harrison's useful guide to this area appeared while the book was in proof and we have only been able to include a small number of cross-references to it.

The transcript of the argument in the case of *Holtham* v. *MPC*[7] became available too late for substantial inclusion in the text. Counsel for the police argued that interest should not be awarded on damages for false imprisonment or malicious prosecution.[8] Peter Pain J. held that interest should be awarded but for a reduced period of three years to take into account delay by the plaintiffs in bringing the matter to court. It is believed that this ruling confirms the practice in police cases over a number of years.[9]

The Privy Council case of *Yuen Kuen-yeu* v. *Attorney General of Hong Kong*[10] was also reported too late for inclusion in the text. It represents another stage in the judicial retreat from the clarity of Lord Wilberforce's "two stage" test for determining the existence of a duty of care.[11] According to the Privy Council this test has "been elevated to a degree of importance greater than it merits."[12] The question of "neighbourhood" is now said to involve a close and direct relationship between the parties as well as foreseeability of likely harm. The second stage of the test will, therefore, rarely have to be applied.[13] The Privy Council expresses approval of some elements of the decision in *Hill* v. *Chief Constable of West Yorkshire*[14] but

[5] But see Hargreaves and Levenson, Chap. 12; Robilliard & McEwan, Chap. 7 and Feldman, Chap. 15.
[6] See Chap. 1, below at p. 28.
[7] (1986) December 15, Queen's Bench Division, Peter Pain J. and a jury. Transcript: W. H. Clarke.
[8] Relying on a note in relation to libel in *The Supreme Court Practice* 1988, 6/2/13; see also, McGregor, para. 470.
[9] See Chap. 3 below at p. 91.
[10] [1987] 2 All E.R. 705.
[11] See Chap. 10 below at p. 296.
[12] *Yuen Kuen-yeu* v. *Attorney General of Hong Kong* [1987] 2 All E.R. 705 at 710e.
[13] *Ibid.* at 710f–j and 712c–h.
[14] [1987] 2 W.L.R. 1126; see Chap. 10 below at pp. 305 *et seq.*

prefer not to give a final view of the "policy arguments" relieving public authorities such as the police from negligence liability.

The association which has led us to take on and endure the rigours of writing a book together goes back a number of years. We first met sitting in the Oxford University Examination Schools in November 1973. Since then we have followed widely divergent paths which, rather to our surprise, converged in the Middle Temple in 1984. Our discussions of the constitutional and political issues of policing developed into the project which finally matured into the present book.

We would like to thank our colleagues in both of our chambers for clarifying and sharpening our ideas by constant discussion and criticism. A large number of practitioners supplied us with details of unreported cases and copies of judgments. We would like to acknowledge the assistance of Kate Akester, Steve Bassam, Gabriel Black, Graham Cooke, Stephen Grosz, Carol Harlow, John Harrison, Ian Macdonald, Duncan Pratt, Stephen Sedley Q.C., Roger Smith and John Wardell. We would also like to thank His Honour Judge John Lord and His Honour Judge McDonnell for providing copies of unreported judgments. Mr. C. S. Porteous and various other members of the Metropolitan Police Solicitors' Department read parts of the manuscript and provided a "Schedule" of awards of damages in recent years. The staff of the Middle Temple Library were unfailing in their patience and courtesy. Many thanks to Rosalind Carne for preparing the index. Caroline Davidson laboured over some barely legible handwriting to convert several chapters to the digestible form of the ubiquitous floppy disc. Finally, we would like to thank all those who dealt with the book at Sweet and Maxwell, and in particular our editors.

The main brunt of a book of this length and complexity is inevitably borne by those closest to the authors. In the struggle between word processor and social life the former was too often victorious. We would therefore like to acknowledge the assistance and tolerance of our friends and families and, in particular, Anne and Caroline.

The ultimate responsibility for any errors or omissions is, of course, our own. The book endeavours to state the law as at May 1, 1987 but we have been able to include some later material.

Richard Clayton
Verulam Buildings,
Gray's Inn

Hugh Tomlinson,
New Court,
Middle Temple

July 14, 1987

Table of Contents

Table of Cases

Table of Statutes

Bibliography

Alderson, J., *Human Rights and the Police* (1984)

Alderson, J., *Policing Freedom: a Commentary on the Dilemmas of Policing in Western Democracies* (1979)

Aldous, G. and Alder, J., *Applications for Judicial Review* (1985)

Archbold, *Pleading, Evidence and Practice in Criminal Cases* (42nd ed., 1985 by Mitchell, S., Buzzard, J.H., Richardson, P.J.)

Atiyah, P.S., *Vicarious Liability in the Law of Torts* (1967)

Atkins Court Forms, Vol. 40 (2nd ed., 1979)

Brogden, M., *Police, Autonomy and Consent* (1982)

Bunyon, T., *The History and Practice of the Political Police in Britain* (1976)

Butler, D. and Halsey, A.H., *Policy and Politics* (1978)

Carr, A.P., *Criminal Procedure in Magistrates' Courts* (1984)

Clerk & Lindsell on Torts (15th ed., 1982, Dias, R.W.M.)

County Court Practice

Critchley, T.A., *A History of the Police in England and Wales* (the revised ed., 1978)

Crossley Vaines, *Personal Property* (5th ed., 1973)

Devlin, P., *The Judge* (1981)

Dicey, A.V., Introduction to the Study of the Law of the Constitution (10th ed., 1959)

Feldman, D., *The Law Relating to Entry, Search and Seizure* (1986)

Fleming, J., *Law of Torts* (6th ed., 1983)

Franks, M., *Limitation of Actions* (1959)

Goode, R., *Commercial Law* (Rev. ed., 1985)

Gordon, R.J.F., *Judicial Review: Practice and Procedure* (1985)

Gurry, F., *Breach of Confidence* (1984)

Halsbury's Laws of England, Vols. 36, 45 (4th ed.)

Hanbury and Maudsley, *Modern Equity* (12th ed., 1985)

Hargreaves, F., and Levenson, H., *A Practitioner's Guide to the Police and Criminal Evidence Act 1984* (1985)

Harlow, C., *Compensation and Government Torts* (1982)

Harrison, J., *Police Misconduct: Legal Remedies* (1987)

Hawkins, *Pleas of the Crown* (8th ed., 1824)

Hewitt, P., *A Fair Cop* (1982)

Jefferson, T. and Grimshaw, R., *Controlling the Constable* (1984)

Kemp, D.A. McL. and Kemp, M.S., *The Quantum of Damages*

Kenny, *Cases on Tort* (4th ed., 1926)

Kerr on Injunctions (6th ed., 1927)

Lea, J. and Young, J., *What is to be done about law and order?* (1984)

Leigh, L.H., *Police Powers in England and Wales* (1st ed., 1975)

Leigh, L.H., *Police Powers in England and Wales* (2nd ed., 1985)

Lenin, V.I., *The State and Revolution* (1956)

Lustgarten, L., *The Governance of Police* (1986)

McCormick, *Evidence* (3rd ed., 1984)

McGregor on Damages (14th ed., 1980, McGregor, H.)

Marshall, G., *Police and Government* (1965)

Meagher, R.P., Q.C., Gummow, W.M.C. and Lehane, J.R.F., *Equity* (2nd ed., 1984)

Mirfield, P., *Confessions* (1985)

Nozick, R., *Anarchy, State and Utopia* (1974)

Phipson on Evidence (13th ed., 1982, Buzzard, J.H., May, R. and Howard, M.N.)

Policing Studies Institute, *Police and People in London* (1983)

Pollock's Law of Torts (15th ed., 1952)

Pounder, C., *Police Computers and the Metropolitan Police* (1985)

Prosser, *Restatement of the Law of Torts* (2nd ed.)

Prosser and Keeton, *Handbook on Torts* (5th ed., 1984)

Radzinowicz, L. and King, J., *Growth of Crime: the International Experience* (1977)

Robiiliard, St.J. and McEwan, J., *Police Powers and the Individual* (1986)

Salmond, *The Law of Torts* (15th ed., 1969 by Heuston, R.F.V.)

Salmond and Heuston, *The Law of Torts* (18th ed., 1981 by Heuston, R.F.V. and Chambers, R.S.)

Scarman, Lord, *English Law: New Dimension* (1974)

Sharpe, R.J., *Habeas Corpus* (1976)

Smith, J.C., *The Law of Theft* (5th ed., 1984)

Stephen, H., *Malicious Prosecution* (1888)

Stephen, Sir J.F., *History of the Criminal Law* (1889)

Stevens, P. and Willis, C., *Ethnic Minorities and Complaints Against the Police* (1981)

Street, H., *Principles of the Law of Damages* (1962)

Street, H., *The Law of Torts* (7th ed., 1983)

Tapper, C., *Computer Law* (1983)

Tapper, C., *Computers and the Law* (1973)

Tapper, C., *Crime, Proof and Punishment—Essays for Sir Rupert Cross* (1981)

Taylor, I., *Law and Order: Arguments for Socialism* (1981)

The Supreme Court Practice

Wacks, R., *The Protection of Privacy* (1980)

Wilkinson's Road Traffic Offences (12th ed., 1985 by Halnan, P. and Spencer, J.)

Williams, G., *Joint Torts and Contributory Negligence* (1950)

Willis, C., *Ethnic Minorities and Complaints Against the Police* (1981)

Winfield and Jolowicz on Tort (12th ed., 1984, Rogers, W.V.H.)

Wolchover, D., *The Exclusion of Improperly Obtained Evidence* (1984)

Zander, M., *A Bill of Rights?* (1985)

Introduction: Policing and the Citizen

1. THE PURPOSE OF THE BOOK

This book sets out to provide a comprehensive treatment of the law and practice relating to civil actions against the police. It seeks to cover all the causes of action and remedies available under the present law of England and Wales to a citizen whose civil liberties are interfered with by police activity. It is, therefore, a legal textbook for practitioners and students and does not attempt to deal with the social and political context of actions against the police. Nevertheless, questions of technical law cannot properly be understood without some discussion of broader issues. In recent years the relationship between police and public has become the subject matter of intense political debate. This debate has had a direct influence on the law, when judges use the perceived crime wave to justify unprecedented extensions of common law police powers.

Civil Actions Against the Police is not intended to be a direct contribution to the various policing debates. It does, however, have a bearing on one of their central issues: the question of how police misconduct is to be controlled. In particular, it constitutes an extended examination of the proposition that the police are accountable to the law. This Introduction will provide a brief treatment of the broader context in which civil actions against the police take place. This may not be immediately relevant to the practitioner who can find out about the structure of the book by turning to the last section of this Introduction.[1]

2. THE LAW AND ORDER CRISIS

The increasing numbers of civil actions brought against the police reflects the radical changes in the relations between police and society in the post-war period. A central element in these changes is the perceived "crisis" in law and order.

There is no doubt that most people believe that crime is on the increase. A 1979 survey showed that 88 per cent. thought that there was more violence and lawlessness than ten years previously and 62 per cent. believed

[1] See p. 15, below.

that there would be even more ten years in the future.[2] The official crime statistics appear to support this perception: "notifiable" (that is, serious) offences per 100,000 of the population having increased from 1,094 in 1950 to 6,674 in 1984.[3] The public perception is of a crime wave and this has been reinforced by these official statistics.

A number of criminologists have pointed out that this crime wave is not all that it seems. The official statistics are a notoriously unreliable indicator of criminal activity. They give little indication of the amount of crime actually committed since the "dark figure" of unreported crime may be as high as 90 per cent.[4] Increases in recorded crime levels do not, of themselves, demonstrate the existence of a crime wave. The Home Office has recognised that the increased numbers of burglaries and thefts from dwellings recorded by the police between 1972 and 1980 is "largely due to an increase in the proportion of such offences committed which were recorded."[5] Additional police resources and efficiency themselves generate more reporting of crime. Declining social tolerance of casual violence in the street or the home has also led to increases in reported crime. Nevertheless, such considerations have had little impact on public perceptions. The crime wave or law and order crisis remains the starting point for recent policing debates.

Different approaches to the law and order "crisis" have led to very different views about policing. The conventional approach, which has often found favour with judges, is that there really is an unprecedented crime wave which results from a breakdown of values in our society. The police are seen as a neutral social agency, protecting the general interest of society as a whole against the actions of deviant elements. As early as 1947 a High Court judge took the crime wave into account in considering the standard of "reasonable cause to suspect" in a false imprisonment case.[6] Following this view, the solution to the crime problem lies in more effective policing. This is seen as involving "technical questions" to be solved by experts. If the police ask for more powers and equipment then they should be given them and allowed to get on with the job.[7]

At the other end of the spectrum is a view associated with the "radical criminologists" of the 1970s which has more recently been characterised as "left idealism"[8] On this view, the crime wave is greatly exaggerated and not really a social problem at all.[9] Crime is seen as deriving from economic deprivation and the reaction of deprived groups to an unjust society. The police are seen as instruments of the "dominant class." Their role is not a technical one of solving crime but a directly political one of buttressing exploitation. All extensions of police powers are, therefore, viewed with suspicion and hostility. The task is not to improve policing but to bring the police under democratic control and, as far as possible, neutralise them as an instrument of political repression.

[2] See I. Taylor, *Law and Order: Arguments for Socialism* at p. 2.

[3] *Criminal Statistics* (1984) Cmnd. 9621, Table 2.2, p. 33.

[4] L. Radzinowicz & J. King *Growth of Crime: the International Experience.*

[5] Criminal Statistics in England and Wales, Cmnd. 8376, (1981) p. 28.

[6] See *Wright* v. *Sharp* (1947) 176 L.J. 308 at 311.

[7] *Cf.* M. D. A. Freeman, "Law and Order in 1984" (1984) Current Legal Problems 175 at 177ff.

[8] J. Lea and J. Young, *What is to be done about law and order?* at pp. 93–104.

[9] *Ibid.*, at pp. 11–26.

In recent years, a third view of the "problem" of law and order has become influential.[10] It seeks to be more realistic than radical criminology whilst going behind the platitudes of the conventional view. It acknowledges that crime is an important social problem for working class and ethnic communities as well as for the middle classes. Crime control is also taken seriously with the emphasis on deterrence, the demarginalisation of criminals and the minimal use of prison.[11] In particular, a "realistic attitude" is adopted towards policing. The emphasis is on the police as providing a service to the community, a service which should be under clear democratic control and working with the close co-operation of the community.

These different responses to the law and order "crisis" have been accompanied by a number of debates on policing methods. There has been criticism of the high technology "fire brigade" tactics of some police forces. Mr John Alderson, the one time Chief Constable of Devon and Cornwall became a well known advocate of an alternative approach known as community policing.[12] There has, in turn, been criticism from the left of community policing as a confidence trick, "the iron fist in the velvet glove."[13] These issues remain of central importance with the Commissioner of the Metropolitan Police, Sir Kenneth Newman, claiming that the distinction between "hard" and "soft" policing is an unreal one.[14]

The standard police view remains that greater police resources and powers are needed to combat the crime wave. They have consistently argued for substantial increases in police numbers and funding. Partly through their efforts the police establishment in England and Wales has risen from 60,190 in 1948 to 124,600 in 1980. The last 20 years has also seen a new willingness by the police to intervene directly in the political processes which shape the law. This has covered both the criminal law and the question of police powers. Police criticism of the right to silence found support in the Eleventh Report of the Criminal Law Revision Committee in 1972. Many of the proposals of the then Commissioner of the Metropolitan Police, Sir David McNee, to the Philips Commission[15] eventually became enacted in the Police and Criminal Evidence Act 1984. In his evidence to the commission Sir David suggested that "unwillingness to make the law more effective . . . will increase pressure on the police to use more arbitrary methods."[16]

In the face of such suggestions from senior police officers it is perhaps not surprising that the 1984 Act substantially increased police powers. This was the culmination of a steady increase in police powers over the post-war period. Before the Act the police could only lawfully hold a suspect without charge for 48 hours.[17] They can now hold suspects for up to 72 hours for

[10] See, I. Taylor, *Law and Order: Arguments for Socialism* at pp. 123–212 and J. Lea and J. Young, *What is to be done about law and order?* at pp. 262–273.

[11] See J. Lea and J. Young, *What is to be done about law and order?* at pp. 266–267.

[12] See John Alderson, *Policing Freedom: a Commentary on the Dilemmas of Policing in Western Democracies.*

[13] See I. Taylor *Law and Order: Argument for Socialism* at pp. 147–148.

[14] Report of the Commissioner of Police for the Metropolis, Cmnd. 9790 (1985).

[15] Report of the Royal Commission on Criminal Procedure, Cmnd. 8092 (1981).

[16] Written Evidence to the Royal Commission on Criminal Procedure, 1978.

[17] Although this period was often ignored: see generally *R.* v. *Holmes, ex. p. Sherman* [1981] 2 All E.R. 612.

questioning, albeit subject to certain safeguards.[18] There is now a general stop and search power,[19] a general power to arrest for any offence[20] and a power to set up road blocks.[21]

3. THE POLICE AND CIVIL RIGHTS

The law and order "crisis" has, therefore, given rise to a **substantial** increase in police numbers and powers. This has been justified by an appeal to an overriding interest of the community in social order and harmony. The rights and liberties of people suspected or accused of crime have, in the wake of the crime wave, become increasingly subordinated to the interest of the community in bringing offenders to justice. The delicate balance between the two has been disturbed. This is an important factor in calls for the enactment of a Bill of Rights.

The modern position can be contrasted with the earlier view that the existence of a professional police force constituted an unacceptable threat to individual liberties. As a Select Committee said in 1822

> "It is difficult to reconcile an effective system of police with that perfect freedom of action and exemption from interference which are the great privileges and blessings of society in this country; and your Committee think that the forfeiture or curtailment of such advantages would be too great a sacrifice for improvement in police or facilities in detection of crime, however desirable in themselves if abstractly considered."[22]

Nevertheless, the first significant steps towards the modern police force were taken a mere seven years later with the establishment of the Metropolitan Police Force.

Although most participants in policing debates have usually paid lip service to notions of the balancing of interests[23] there has been an increasing polarisation between advocates of "effective policing" and "civil liberties." The Philips Commission attempted to break down this polarisation by adopting the criterion that the law governing police powers should be "fair, open and workable."[24] Nevertheless, its recommendations led to an unprecedented extension of police powers in the Police and Criminal Evidence Act 1984.

The courts have also had to consider the balancing of individual rights against the interest of the community in cases dealing with police powers. In *Ghani* v. *Jones*[25] Lord Denning M.R., in substantially extending police

[18] See Chap. 5 at pp. 157 *et seq.* below.
[19] See Chap. 5, p. 129, below.
[20] See Chap. 5, at p. 141, below.
[21] See Chap. 7 at p. 241, below.
[22] Report of the Select Committee on the Police of the Metropolis, June 7, 1822.
[23] For dissenting voices, from the right, see R. Nozick, *Anarchy, State and Utopia*; from the left, see V. I. Lenin, *The State and Revolution.*
[24] Above, para. 2.8.
[25] [1970] 1 Q.B. 693 at 708F–G.

powers of seizure[26] dealt with the relation between freedom and police powers as follows

> "We have to consider, on the one hand, the freedom of the individual. His privacy and his possessions are not to be invaded except for the most compelling reasons. On the other hand, we have to consider the interest of society at large in finding out wrongdoers and repressing crime. Honest citizens should help the police and not hinder them in their efforts to track down criminals."

In line with the overall trend, the balance in this case was resolved in favour of the interest of society at large.

The role of the English courts in this balancing exercise is extremely limited. The courts cannot override statutory extensions of police powers in favour of the rights of the individual because of the lack of fundamental constitutional rights in English law.

The unwritten English constitution gives no recognition to positive individual rights which could take precedence over common law or statutory police powers. In English law such rights are "residual": they consist of what remains after taking into account all the legal restraints that impinge upon them. They can be swept aside by judges as in *Elias* v. *Pasmore*[27] where it was held that "the existence of the State must excuse the seizure of documents which seizure would otherwise be unlawful." More important, if parliament chooses to give the police exorbitant powers (as, for example, in section 62 of the Police and Criminal Evidence Act 1984),[28] these necessarily supersede an individual's common law rights.

Thus, English law knows no notion of human rights or civil rights. The general position was described by Dicey as follows:[29]

> "most foreign constitution makers have begun with declarations of rights. For this they have often been in nowise to blame . . . On the other hand, there remains through the English constitution that inseparable connection between the means of enforcing a right and the right to be enforced which is the strength of judicial legislation. The saw *ubi jus ibi remedium* . . . means that the Englishmen whose labours gradually framed the completed set of law and institutions which we call the Constitution, fixed their minds more intently on providing remedies for the enforcement of particular rights . . . than upon any declaration of the Rights of Man or of Englishmen."

This situation will continue unless Britain enacts a Bill of Rights[30] or incorporates the European Convention on Human Rights[31] and confers powers on the judiciary to make broad political value judgments.

Thus it is through a mish mash of remedies in actions brought in ancient torts such as trespass to the person, conversion or defamation that the common law protects particular interests such as bodily integrity, integrity of property, or interest in reputation. Obvious areas of civil rights such as the

[26] See Feldman, Chap. 10.
[27] [1934] 2 K.B. 164 at 173.
[28] See Chap. 5 at p. 172, below.
[29] See Dicey, *The Law and the Constitution* at pp. 198–199.
[30] See the discussion of Lord Scarman, *English Law: New Dimension*.
[31] See, *e.g.* M. Zander, *A Bill of Rights?*; for the Convention itself, see Chap. 14 at p. 424, below.

right to privacy or freedom from surveillance are not protected by the English law because no tort action corresponds to them.[32] As long as the police act bona fide and in accordance with their powers, an English court can give no remedy against them however distasteful it may find their actions.[33]

The one way in which the extent of police powers has been limited by the courts in the past is by the use of civil juries. This has allowed ordinary citizens to decide whether the police have acted lawfully. Until the last century civil juries had a crucial role in deciding whether an individual's rights had been breached. It was the jury who decided whether an arrest was based on "reasonable and probable cause" and it was open to them to reject the judge's direction on the law and to return a "general verdict."[34] In the words of one of the greatest of 20th century judges, trial by jury

> "has been a bulwark of liberty, the shield of the poor from the oppression of the rich and powerful. Anyone who knows the history of our laws knows that many of the liberties of the subject were originally established and are maintained by the verdicts of juries in civil cases. Many will think that at the present time the danger of attack by powerful private organisations or by encroachments of the executive is not diminishing."[35]

Nevertheless, the last 50 years have seen the almost total disappearance of the civil jury. In the centuries old struggle between judge and jury, the judge has been almost totally victorious in the civil law.[36] Although juries are still common in some police cases[37] their province has, in effect, been restricted to that of deciding "incidental matters of fact."[38] Their role as the "last defence of civil liberties" has declined almost to vanishing point in civil actions. The civil rights of the citizen are now in the hands of judges who are obliged to apply the law as enacted by parliament.

4. CONTROLLING THE POLICE

As police powers and resources have increased there have been increasing numbers of complaints about police misconduct. These partly reflect increased police activity, especially in situations of high social tension. The tendency of some police officers to abuse their powers[39] may itself be a reflection of the same social changes which have led to increases in crime.

The recent increase in the involvement of the civil courts in dealing with police misconduct is a direct consequence of the perceived failure of other mechanisms of control. Three areas are relevant here:

(1) the lack of direct political control over the police;

[32] See Chap. 9 at p. 273, below.
[33] See *Malone* v. *M.P.C.* [1979] Ch. 344.
[34] See Patrick Devlin, *The Judge* at pp. 117–148.
[35] *Per* Atkin L.J. in *Ford* v. *Blurton* (1922) 38 T.L.R. 801 at 805.
[36] See Chap. 11 at p. 000, below for a discussion of one aspect of this.
[37] For the availability of juries see Chap. 3 at p. 80.
[38] For juries in false imprisonment cases, see Chap. 5 at p. 152, below; for juries in malicious prosecution cases, see Chap. 8 at p. 256, below.
[39] See, *e.g.*, Policy Studies Institute, *Police and People in London*.

(2) the refusal of criminal courts to become involved in the control of police misconduct;
(3) the perceived lack of an effective police complaints procedure.

When the modern policing system was brought into being by the Municipal Corporations Act of 1835 the control of local police forces was firmly in the hands of local politicians.[40] Local watch committees exercised day-to-day policing control well into the 20th century. As late as 1936 it was authoritatively stated in the House of Commons that orders to the provincial police "are given by the statutory authority.[41] They have absolute control."[42]

The history of the modern police is full of examples of direct political control over policing. In the first 11 years after the Liverpool Watch Committee was established, a sub-committee met daily to supervise operations and on average issued an order a week in response to requests from local property owners concerning where police should be dispersed.[43] Between 1852 and 1870 brewers on watch committees controlled all prosecutions concerning publicans in Liverpool, Cambridge and Carlisle. In Norwich the Chief Constable was under instructions not to prosecute without the watch committee's approval. When he defied the rule he was dismissed.[44] In 1881 the Birmingham Chief Constable was prohibited from instituting certain proceedings without prior approval from the watch committee. He then asserted his independent right as the "guardian of public morality and order" and refused to comply unless ordered to do so by the Home Secretary and justices. The Home Secretary referred the Chief Constable to a section in the Municipal Corporations Act which empowered watch committees to make regulations "for preventing neglect or abuse and for rendering constables efficient in the discharge of their duties." The Chief Constable gave way. In 1902 the Chief Constable of Margate tendered his resignation in the face of conflicting instructions from justices and the watch committee over the prosecution of publicans whose licences had been extended on Boer War peace night.[45] It appears, however, that local political control began to weaken after the First World War as the influence of the Home Secretary grew. This has an explicit political dimension; at least part of the intention appears to have been to offset the influence of Labour councillors on watch committees.[46] By the 1950s, the doctrine of the "operational independence" of chief constables had become the conventional wisdom.[47]

This lack of local political control was clearly established by the famous 1958 dispute between the Nottingham Watch Committee and their Chief Constable. The Home Secretary refused to confirm a watch committee

[40] See Critchley at p. 124.
[41] *i.e.*, the police authorities.
[42] 314 H.C.Deb., 5s, c. 15; see generally, Marshall, Chap. 4; for the position concerned the Metropolitan Police over which the Home Secretary seems to have exercised unlimited authority, see R. Plehwe, "Police and Government in the Metropolis" (1974) P.L. 316.
[43] M. Brogden, *Police and Autonomy and Consent* at p. 62.
[44] C. H. Parris, "The Home Office and the Provincial Police in English & Wales 1856–70" (1961) P.L. 230 at 251.
[45] See Critchley, at p. 132.
[46] See Tony Bunyan, *The Political Police in Britain* at p. 72.
[47] See Chap. 13 at p. 411, below.

instruction to their chief constable.[48] These events contributed to the setting up of a Royal Commission on the Police in 1960. The Police Act 1964 followed the recommendations of the Commission's Report[49] and established the modern "tripartite" structure for control over the police.[50] The Act was silent on the crucial question of "operational control"[51] but the conventional wisdom is that this vests exclusively in chief constables. As Lord Chesham said on behalf of the government in 1958:

> "no police authority or any one else has any authority to interfere in relation to the enforcement of the law by the police. Naturally there is normally good co-operation between the police authority and their chief constable but the full responsibility for enforcement is a matter which is reserved entirely to the chief officer of the police. In the exercise of this responsibility he is answerable to the law alone and not to any public authority."[52]

The view that the police are independent of all political control when carrying out their "operational functions" has always had its critics. Many observers have suggested that the lack of explicit provision for political control means that this control is simply exercised surreptitiously. Thus, it was argued in evidence to the Royal Commission:

> "The present fiction that because (the Home Secretary) . . . does not control (the police forces) . . . he should not be answerable for them seems to result in us having the worst of both worlds, in that control is in effect exercised by anonymous Home Office officials whose conduct cannot be examined or questioned."[53]

In recent years the demands for greater political accountability of the police have become stronger. The politicisation of law and order issues (in part encouraged by the activities of the police themselves) has led to a demand that the community or its representatives should exercise a role in policing decisions at a general operational level. The relative merits of "reactive" or "community" policing in the inner city or the profile of the police in industrial disputes are not ultimately matters of technical policing expertise. Where the impact of policing decisions have wider social consequences the police alone are not competent to gauge them.

In the wake of the 1981 "inner city riots" which, in part, arose from perceptions of insensitive policing[54] the Police and Criminal Evidence Act 1984 set up "consultative committees" to obtain the view of local people on policing matters.[55] Despite continuing "accountability debates" the police still exercise complete operational independence—subject to the consider-

[48] See Critchley, at pp. 270 *et seq.*

[49] Royal Commission on the Police, Cmnd. 1728 (1962).

[50] See Chap. 1, at p. 30.

[51] See Chap. 13 at p. 411, below.

[52] 213 H.L.Deb., 5s, c. 47; see also the Evidence of the Association of Chief Police Officers to the Willink Commission, *Royal Commission on the Police*, 1960–1962, Minutes of Evidence 15 at p. 849.

[53] Inns of Court Conservative and Unionist Society, Royal Commission, Minutes of Evidence, 11–12 at p. 691.

[54] See Lord Scarman, *The Brixton Disorders, 10th–12th April 1981*, Cmnd. 8427 (1981), paras. 4.61 to 4.99.

[55] See Police and Criminal Evidence Act 1984, s.106.

able "advisory powers" of the Home Office. Thus allegations of police misconduct cannot be directly dealt with through the political process.

The second way in which police conduct might be subject to independent control is through the criminal courts. In common law jurisdictions such as the United States the courts have sought to deal with police misconduct by rejecting any evidence obtained as a result of breaches of the law.[56] The position is similar in Scotland. The English courts have never favoured such an approach. Although police investigations were, for many years, subject to "Judges Rules," a breach of these rarely resulted in the exclusion of evidence.[57] In general, outside the special area of confessions,[58] the English courts have refused to take police conduct into account when assessing the admissibility of evidence. It has therefore become established that a criminal trial will not be used as a means of dealing with police wrongdoing. As Lord Diplock put it in the leading case of *R.* v. *Sang*[59]:

> "the function of the judge at a criminal trial as respects the admission of evidence is to ensure that the accused has a fair trial according to law. It is no part of a judge's function to exercise disciplinary powers over the police or prosecution as respects the way in which evidence to be used at trial is obtained by them. If it was obtained illegally there will be a remedy in civil law; if it was obtained legally but in breach of the rules of conduct for the police, this is a matter for the appropriate disciplinary authority to deal with. What the judge at the trial is concerned with is not how the evidence sought to be adduced by the prosecution has been obtained but with how it is used by the prosecution at the trial."

During parliamentary discussion of the Police and Criminal Evidence Bill, Lord Scarman attempted to introduce a provision which would have excluded illegally obtained evidence in most circumstances.[60] He suggested that such a provision would have an important effect in deterring police misconduct.[61] This provision was replaced in the final Bill by what became section 78 of the Act. This only allows the court to exclude evidence if its admission would have "such an adverse effect on the fairness of the proceedings that the court ought not to admit it."[62] Although section 78 does provide the courts with a discretion to exclude evidence obtained as a result of police misconduct the "disciplining of police misconduct" is not a relevant consideration in applying the section. The test for admissibility is whether the evidence will have an adverse effect on the fairness of the trial.[63]

The third and most important mechanism for the control of police

[56] See *Mapp* v. *Ohio* (1961) 367 U.S. 643; see generally, McCormick, *Evidence* at pp. 384–409.

[57] See Phipson, at para. 22–39.

[58] For a general account of the rules in relation to confessions see Peter Mirfield, *Confessions.*

[59] [1980] A.C. 402 at 436.

[60] See H. L. Hansard, Vol. 455, cols. 635–675, July 31, 1984.

[61] See H. L. Hansard, Vol. 454, col. 932, July 11, 1984.

[62] s.78(1).

[63] For a general discussion see David Wolchover, *The Exclusion of Improperly Obtained Evidence.*

misconduct is the system of "police complaints." This administrative remedy which initiates the police disciplinary procedure was established on a formal basis in 1964 following recommendations by the Willink Commission.[64] The majority of the Commission felt that these matters should be left in the hands of chief constables because any whittling down of their administration of discipline would weaken their command.[65] By section 49 of the Police Act 1964 chief constables were under a duty to record and investigate complaints. However, public dissatisfaction about the lack of an independent element in the police complaints procedure continued to grow.[66] Following the report of a Home Office working party in March 1974[67] the Police Act 1976 brought an independent element into the procedure. Most complaints[68] were referred to an independent "Police Complaints Board" which could recommend the making of disciplinary charges.[69]

Notwithstanding these reforms, criticism of the complaints procedure continued. In particular, concern was expressed about the fact that the police investigated themselves when establishing the substance of a complaint and that the Police Complaints Board had insufficient powers in relation to questioning or extending investigations.[70] In its Triennial Review[71] the Police Complaints Board rejected these criticisms,[72] but did recommend a specialist body of investigating officers to investigate complaints arising from serious injury.[73] This recommendation was rejected by a Home Office Working Party.[74] Instead it suggested an extension of the existing system under which investigating officers were drawn from an outside police force and were subject to "independent supervision." Nevertheless, Lord Scarman in his report into the 1981 Brixton disorders felt that public confidence in the complaints procedure would not be increased unless there was a system of independent investigations for all complaints.[75] In 1982 the Home Secretary put forward a new scheme[76] which was further revised in 1983[77] and eventually enacted by the Police and Criminal Evidence Act 1984. This

[64] Cmnd. 1728 (1962), paras. 450–469.

[65] *Ibid.* paras. 428–433; but see the minority's view at paras. 472–479 and Appendix 5.

[66] See, *e.g.*, the Select Committee on Race Relations and Immigration Report (1972) 1971–2 H.C. 471–I and for a discussion of the resulting private members' bill on the subject see D. Paling, "Police Acts (Amendment) Bill 1973" (1973) Crim.L.R. 282.

[67] *The Handling of Complaints Against the Police* Cmnd. 5582 (1974).

[68] For the exceptions see s.2(2) and s.5(1) of the Police Act 1976.

[69] s.3(2).

[70] See, *e.g.*, P. Hewitt, *A Fair Cop.*

[71] Cmnd. 7966 (1980).

[72] *Ibid.* paras. 64–67; for a reply to their arguments see Alec Samuels, "Complaints against the Police" (1981) 131 New L.J. 28.

[73] Cmnd. 7966, (1980) para. 57–76.

[74] *The establishment of an independent element in the investigation of complaints against the police* Cmnd. 8193 (1981); see also Report of Working Group of the Police Advisory Board, 1981/2 H.C. 98–II iv Appendix E; and the "Fourth Report of the House of Commons Home Affairs Committee" Session 1981/2 H.C. 98–I.

[75] Cmnd. 8427 (1981), paras. 7.18 to 7.21.

[76] *Police Complaints Procedures* Cmnd. 8681 (1982).

[77] *Police Complaints and Discipline Procedures* Cmnd. 9072 (1983).

replaced the Police Complaints Board with a "Police Complaints Authority" with some new powers of supervision over complaints.[78]

Given the lack of independent investigation of complaints, it is doubtful whether the new system will overcome the criticisms of its predecessors. Lord Scarman's view has received broad support:

> "My own view is that if public confidence in the police complaints procedure is to be achieved, any solution falling short of a system of independent investigation, available for all complaints (other than the frivolous) which are not withdrawn, is unlikely to be successful."[79]

These criticisms centre on the performance of the present system. In its Final Report the Police Complaints Board stated that there had been a total of 17,245 complaints in 1984, but disciplinary charges were preferred in only 194 cases. In another 1,425 cases officers had "received advice."[80] In 1985 there were 5,462 complaints made against the Metropolitan Police of which 150 were found to be substantiated.[81] Furthermore, Home Office research shows that for every successful complaint made by a black person there are three successful complaints made by white people.[82]

Whatever the reasons for these statistics, there is little doubt that the apparent ineffectiveness of the complaints procedure is an important reason for the growing number of civil actions against the police. Increasing numbers of lawyers are advising clients who are aggrieved by police misconduct not to bother with complaints but to proceed immediately to a civil claim.[83] There is no doubt that civil actions have a much higher success rate than complaints. Thus, of the 126 actions against the Metropolitan police included in 1986, 52 settled out of court and the courts awarded damages in another 10, giving a success rate of 49 per cent. This can be contrasted with the most recent complaints figures, which show a success rate of 3 per cent.[83a]

5. CIVIL ACTIONS AGAINST THE POLICE

In response to criticism that they are not politically accountable the police often claim that it is through the legal process itself that they are

[78] For a detailed treatment of the present system, see Chap. 2 at pp. 41 *et seq.*

[79] *The Brixton Disorders* Cmnd. 8427 (1981), para. 7.21; the Police Federation have now been converted to this view: see 1981/2 H.C. 98–I, para. 32.

[80] Police Complaints Board, *Final Review Report: 1977–1985* Cmnd. 9584 (1985), Table 5; see Harrison at p. 8 for a full table.

[81] Report of the Commissioner of Police for the Metropolis Cmnd. 9790 (1985) at p. 139, Appendix 6iii.

[82] See P. Stevens and C. Willis, *Ethnic Minorities and Complaints Against the Police*; see Harrison at p. 9.

[83] See for example, the National Council for Civil Liberties spokesman quoted in *The Guardian*, December 23, 1985; Mr Tony Banks MP, quoted in *The Times*, July 31, 1985.

[83a] These are the 1985 complaints figures. For the figures relating to civil actions see Table 1, at p. 17, below. Civil actions are "filtered" by solicitors and the Legal Aid authorities so that obviously hopeless claims will not be pursued. The burden of proof in disciplinary actions is higher than in civil cases, see Chap. 2 at p. 49 below.

accountable to the community: that they are responsible to the law and to the law alone. It is true that the civil courts can adjudicate on the lawfulness of police conduct either in private law actions relating to the rights of individual citizens or in public law cases where their policy decisions and general performance of their duties can be subject to judicial "review." From the earliest reported cases, wronged citizens have sought to bring erring constables to book through the civil courts.[84] The police were given statutory protection against certain types of civil action as long ago as 1750, in a statutory provision which remains in force today.[85] The steady stream of such actions continued throughout the 19th and 20th centuries. In a landmark case in 1930[86] the High Court ruled that local authorities were not vicariously liable for the torts of their police forces. Nevertheless, actions against individual police officers were brought successfully throughout post-war period.[87]

The 1970s saw a large increase in such cases. The first year for which full figures are available for the Metropolitan Police is 1976. In that year 52 civil actions were initiated and 27 were concluded. The figures for 1985 are 175 cases initiated and 65 cases concluded.[88] The damages figures are even more striking. In 1973 the Metropolitan Police paid out £200 in damages in civil actions, in 1986 they paid out £377,000.[89] A survey of seven police authorities[90] showed that a total of 1,399 cases were initiated against them between 1980 and 1984.[91] Although there are large variations in the numbers of actions commenced against different forces the average is 65 actions per year, per force between 1980 to 1984. This gives an average annual figure for eight police forces, including the Metropolitan Police, of 583 actions initiated. Even assuming that many of the 42 police authorities in England and Wales had very small number of actions initiated against them it seems likely that well over 1,000 civil actions a year are now brought against the police. It is reasonable to assume that the large majority of these actions would be classified in the Judicial Statistics under the head of "nuisance, trespass, fraud, malicious prosecution, assault, conspiracy." Actions against the police therefore represent a substantial proportion of the total of 4170 such actions commenced in the High Court and the county court in 1985.[92]

There is little doubt that the apparent ineffectiveness of the complaints procedure has been an important reason for the growing numbers of civil actions against the police. Many lawyers now regard civil actions as the main forum in which the police can be brought to account for their misconduct. However, serious questions can be raised as to the usefulness of this

[84] For an early example see *Ward's* case (1636) Clay 44.

[85] See the Constables Protection Act 1750, s.6 of which remains in force; see Chap. 3 at p. 64 and Chap. 5 at p. 153 below.

[86] *Fisher* v. *Oldham Corp.* [1930] 2 K.B. 364.

[87] For some case in the 1950s and 1960s see the cases in Chap. 11, Appendix at p. 367, below.

[88] See *Policing London*, No. 24, November/December 1986; the comparable 1984 figures are 181 cases initiated and 107 concluded.

[89] For full details see Table 2 at p. 18, below. See also, *The Observer*, April 5, 1987.

[90] Merseyside, Lancashire, Greater Manchester, Derbyshire, West Yorkshire, Northumbria and Sussex; for full details, see Table 1 at p. 17, below.

[91] See *Policing London*, No. 19, August/September 1985.

[92] See *Judicial Statistics*, Annual Report, 1985, Cmnd. 9864 at p. 35 and p. 84.

form of accountability. The civil law is a blunt and imperfect instrument for exerting day-to-day control over police misconduct. There are four areas to be considered: the nature of police powers, the attitude of the courts, the time scales involved and the nature of the remedies available.

First, the way in which police powers are framed in English law gives rise to substantial difficulties in making individual officers accountable. Many police powers are exercisable on "reasonable suspicion." The standard applied here has been a relatively low one.[93] Where parliament has, apparently, made powers exercisable only on the commission of an offence the courts have extended them to situations where there were "reasonable grounds to suspect" that the offence was committed.[94] Furthermore, in many cases, the police act under the authority of warrants.[95] When they are acting "in obedience" to a warrant they are protected against civil actions by the Constable's Protection Act 1750.[96] Despite the draconian powers given by warrants, English law provides no effective procedure for checking whether the preconditions for their issue have been properly fulfilled. The Police Complaints Board expressed concern over the ease with which magistrates appear to grant warrants.[97] England differs from other common law jurisdictions in not requiring full written record of the grounds relied on for the issue of the warrant. This means that, in stark contrast to, for example, Canada, applications for the judicial review of warrants, are virtually impossible.[98] Thus, police activities under warrant are, in effect, legally unchallengeable.[99]

Secondly, the courts have long been wary of impeding legitimate policing activities. This has led to the applicable causes of action becoming unnecessarily complex and obscure. For example, the "checks and balances" built into the action for malicious prosecution mean that someone who is prosecuted as a result of police misconduct will only recover compensation in the very clearest of cases.[1] The courts have also shown extreme reluctance to interfere with "policing discretions." This can be seen with particular clarity in "judicial review" cases where their reluctance to interfere with chief constable's decisions contrast sharply with the judicial interventionism displayed in other areas. As Lawton L.J. said in *R.* v. *Metropolitan Police Commissioner, ex p. Blackburn (No. 4)*[2]:

> "The intention of the relevant statutes was to leave the commissioner to do his job as he thought best and to empower the Home Secretary to remove him if he was not doing his job efficiently. I can

[93] See Chap. 5 at p. 148, below.
[94] See *Wills* v. *Bowley* [1983] 1 A.C. 57.
[95] See Chap. 1 at p. 29, below; Chap. 5 at p. 153, below and Chap. 7 at p. 220, below.
[96] See Chap. 3 at p. 64, below; Chap. 5 at p. 153, below.
[97] Police Complaints Board, Triennial Review, Cmnd. 8853 (1983), para. 4.9; see also, K. W. Lidstone, "Magistrates, the police and search warrants" [1984] Crim.L.R. 449–458.
[98] See Chap. 7 at p. 235, below; and see Feldman at 4.36 and generally at 4.24 to 4.53.
[99] In the absence of proper documentation the action for "malicious procurement of a search warrant" is almost impossible to prove, the entire history of the common law revealing only one successful reported case: see Chap. 8 at p. 264, below.
[1] See Chap. 8 at p. 267, below.
[2] *The Times*, March 6, 1980, C.A.; reported in part.

see no justification for the courts meddling with the way in which he performs his duties."

This refusal to "meddle" has led to the courts declining to interfere with police discretion even in the clearest of cases.[3]

Thirdly, the well-known delays of the civil courts mean that civil actions against the police do not give a speedy or accessible remedy. The assault, false imprisonment and malicious prosecution claims by Mr and Mrs White for which Mars-Jones J. awarded £51,000 damages in April 1982 arose out of an incident which took place in September 1976.[4] The average period between the date of the misconduct and the date of resolution in seven representative cases against the Metropolitan Police Commissioner in 1985 and 1986 was over three and a half years.[5]

Finally, even when successful, civil actions against the police provide a very inadequate control mechanism for dealing with misconduct. A victim of police misconduct will usually want to see the officers involved brought to book and measures taken to prevent a repetition. These remedies are not provided by a successful civil action. The judgment of a civil court provides an individual plaintiff with "after event vindication" by way of damages. Such an award of damages will have no impact on the finances of the individual officers whose misconduct is in issue as they are paid from public funds. There is no reported case in which a remedy has been granted against the police to prohibit the recurrence of wrongdoing.

Even when officers are found by the civil courts to have acted illegally and abused their powers disciplinary action will not necessarily be taken against them. There are a number of notorious cases in which officers found guilty of misconduct by the civil courts have not been disciplined and have continued to operate in the same way. The award of damages for malicious prosecution made against P.C. Weller in 1964[6] did not prevent him from engaging in activities which led to another award of malicious prosecution damages to different plaintiffs some two years later.[7] The Court of Appeal in the case of *R.* v. *Steadman Thompson*[8] held that the evidence of an officer who had been found to have abused his powers in a civil case was "so tainted" as to be worthless.[9] It is noteworthy that the officer in question was still on duty several months after his actions had been condemned in forthright terms by a civil court.[10] Between 1980 and 1985 despite numbers of successful civil actions brought against the Metropolitan Police,[11] officers were only subject to disciplinary proceedings as a result in one case.[12] The rationalisation for this inactivity is startling:

"Regard is to be had to the time that has elapsed since the incident on

[3] See Chap. 13 at p. 410, below.
[4] See *White* v. *M.P.C.*, *The Times*, April 24, 1982.
[5] See *Policing London*, No. 24, Nov/Dec 1986, p. 52.
[6] *Blaker* v. *Weller* [1964] Crim.L.R. 311.
[7] *Allum and Hislop* v. *Weller and Jackson*, *The Times*, February 25, 1966.
[8] (1986) Legal Action, 146.
[9] See Chap. 3 at p. 88, below.
[10] See *Leon* v. *M.P.C.* [1986] C.L.Y. 2538.
[11] For some examples, see Chap. 11, Appendix, p. 367.
[12] See the written answer in H. C. Hansard, 6s, Vol. 94, Col. 279w.

which the civil action was based, to the effect of the passage of time on the witness's ability to recall events and on the officer's ability to defend himself and to the difference in the standards of proof in civil proceedings and disciplinary proceedings."[13]

The contention, from a Minister of the Crown, that a judicial finding of abuse of power is to be ignored because of a lapse of three or four years is as indefensible as it is shocking.

In general, civil actions are not a proper or effective mechanism for dealing with police misconduct. All they can do is provide an individualised remedy for a specific instance of police wrongdoing. As Lustgarten says:

> "(the) legal outlook is inherently negative, individualistic and orientated towards sanctions. Rewards and incentives, and measures devoted to altering misguided group values and solidarities which reinforce objectionable conduct are beyond its capabilities. It does not concern itself directly with the organisational context which stimulates misconduct."[14]

In short, it is clear that civil actions cannot be used as a device to discipline the police and make them more accountable. Although someone who is assaulted or maliciously prosecuted gains some reassurance from an award of damages, his successful claim will have minimal direct impact on policing practices. The extra-judicial remarks of Lord Fraser of Tullybelton about the illegal obtaining of evidence are of general application: one "only has to mention" the idea that civil actions can provide an adequate remedy to victims of police misconduct "to see how ridiculous it is in real life in most cases."[15]

The aims of this book are, therefore, limited. It does not suggest a strategy for making the police more accountable. It simply sets out to provide a comprehensive treatment of the civil law which might be invoked to deal with police misconduct. Although there are a number of areas which remain unexplored by practitioners,[16] the problems of police misconduct will not be solved by bringing legal action. Police accountability is a political problem which cannot be solved through the courts. At best legal action will provide solace to some wronged individuals and ammunition for those who are working for wider political reform.

6. THE STRUCTURE OF THE BOOK

The book is divided into three sections. The first deals with the background required for any civil action against the police: the legal position and organisation of the police (Chapter 1), complaints against the police

[13] *Ibid.*; for the standard of proof see Chap. 2 at p. 49.
[14] Lustgarten at p. 127.
[15] H. L. *Hansard*, Vol. 454, col. 940 (July 11, 1984).
[16] See Chap. 10 at p. 295.

(Chapter 2) and practice and procedure (Chapter 3). Discovery is dealt with in Chapter 3 and there is an Appendix to the chapter covering "Documents to look for in police cases."[17]

The second and central section of the book deals with the traditional tort actions against the police. English law gives everyone a range of rights over their own person, land and goods. These areas are dealt with in separate chapters covering interference with the person—assault, battery, false imprisonment, intimidation, intentionally causing nervous shock and "harassment" (Chapter 4)—and interference with land and goods—trespass to land, trespass to goods and conversion (Chapter 6). Police "powers" areas provide them with "defences" to these tort actions and are dealt with in two separate chapters covering "Powers over the Person" (Chapter 5) and "Powers in Relation to Land and Goods" (Chapter 7). The final chapter in this section deals with malicious abuse of legal procedure (Chapter 8). The main tort considered under this heading is malicious prosecution but the chapter also covers the limited case law on little used torts such as "malicious arrest" and "malicious procurement of a search warrant."

The third section of the book deals with "Other Actions and Remedies." It begins with a discussion of the law relating to police surveillance and information gathering (Chapter 9). The English law in this area suffers from a number of well known inadequacies and victims of improper surveillance usually find themselves without remedy. The applicability of a number of other tort actions to the police is then considered (Chapter 10). Actions for breach of statutory duty and for negligence are common in other spheres. They are potentially of broad application in relation to the police. Actions for conspiracy and defamation are less common and of limited relevance to civil actions against the police. The neglected common law action for "misfeasance in a public office" is, by contrast, of great potential importance in relation to the police. Chapters 11 and 12 deal with the remedies available in actions against the police. Chapter 11 seeks to provide a comprehensive coverage of the difficult and important area of the law of damages. The assessment of damages often leads to very serious practical problems in police cases. No proper assessment principles have been set out in the reported cases and the chapter seeks to fill this gap. An Appendix of the awards of damages made in police cases is provided.[18] Chapter 12 deals with the remedies of injunctions, declarations, habeas corpus and the various remedies available in relation to unlawfully seized goods under the Torts (Interference with Goods) Act 1977, the common law action in replevin and the Police (Property) Act 1897. Chapter 13 discusses the law of judicial review as it relates to the police. Although there have been a number of important cases in this area in recent years these have been subject to very little critical analysis. This chapter also deals with the law in relation to the "operational independence" of chief constables and the practice and procedure of judicial review. Chapter 14 covers the European Convention on Human Rights insofar as it may be relevant to actions against the police. The Convention is of limited application to the central areas of assault, arrest and prosecution but is potentially of great importance in areas such as privacy and surveillance which are inadequately covered by the law of torts.

[17] See at p. 96, below.
[18] See at p. 367, below.

Table 1: GLC Police Committee survey of police authority damage claims 1980–84

Police Authority	*No. of cases received*	*Yrs*	*Total paid in damages (£)*
Merseyside	368	1982–84	N/A
Lancashire	123	1983–84	9,638
Greater Manchester	245	1983–84	13,000
Derbyshire	13	1980–84	4,900
West Yorkshire	435	1980–84	29,042
Northumbria	192	1980–85	6,702
Sussex	23	1983	6,000
Total	**1,399**		**69,282**

Source: *Policing London*, August/September 1985, Vol. 3, p. 76.

Table 2: Civil Actions against the Metropolitan Police 1973–86[1]

Year	*No. of cases initiated*	*No. of cases settled*	*No. of cases in which damages were awarded*	*No. of cases concluded[2]*	*Amount paid in damages* £	*Amount paid in settlements* £	*Total amount paid* £
1973	NA	NA	NA	27	NA	NA	200
1974	NA	NA	NA	27	NA	NA	725
1975	NA	NA	NA	30	NA	NA	2,668
1976	52	NA	NA	34	NA	NA	7,521
1977	71	NA	NA	53	NA	NA	1,500
1978	105	NA	NA	12	NA	NA	50,945[3]
1979	95	NA	NA	7	NA	NA	1,991
1980	86	NA	4	11	4,896	3,397	9,035
1981	92	NA	7	21	14,693	10,385	31,871
1982	148	23	9	33	63,639	23,686	87,325
1983	135	33	5	83	2,855	60,455	63,310
1984	181	NA	7	107	15,617	162,986[4]	178,603
1985	175	56	7	68	13,951	193,049	207,000
1986	188	52	10	126	46,836	330,333[5]	377,169

Source: *Policing London*, August/September, 1985, Vol. 3, p. 76.
Hansard, February 20, 1986, col. 297; February 21, 1987, col. 348; March 25, 1987, col. 161.
The Observer, April 5, 1987.

Notes: [1] These figures are drawn from Parliamentary Answers given over a number of years and there are a number of small discrepancies.
[2] This figure covers cases which were struck out or discontinued as well as those settled and dealt with at court The only year for which a complete breakdown of this figure is available is 1986, as follows: 52 settled; 41 dealt with at court, 22 struck out, 11 discontinued.
[3] This figure includes the award of £37,000 to Police Sergeant Paling, see p. 375, below.
[4] This figure includes the sum of £120,000 paid to Stephen Waldorf who was mistakenly shot by police officers.
[5] This figure includes the sum of £236,000 paid to Barry Carlell who was left almost blind after an assault by a police constable who was

Part 1: The General Law

1. The Legal Status and Organisation of the Police

1. INTRODUCTION

The legal status of the British police is complex and suffers from many obscurities. Modern statutes governing the position have, according to the familiar pattern, been constructed on common law assumptions which have never been fully clarified. Despite the central importance of the police in the legal system there are considerable doubts as to such fundamental matters as their precise duties, the legal status of the organised "police force" and the extent to which they are obliged to follow the orders of police authorities.

Many civil actions against the police turn on the extent of their powers. These powers flow partially from statute and partially from their status as "constables" at common law. An understanding of the "office of constable" and the duties which flow from it remains fundamental to any analysis of the legal position of the police. The powers which the law gives to the police are, almost always, vested in individual constables. It is important to distinguish between the different types of powers involved. These areas dealt with in the first section of this chapter.

Although the law has taken very little direct cognisance of the fact that the police operate in "forces" an understanding of police organisation and hierarchy is sometimes of great importance in considering the civil law position of police officers. In the second section of this chapter, therefore, the organisation and structure of the police is considered. This involves not only the organisation of individual police forces but the relationship of forces to police authorities and to the Home Secretary. The police are regulated by a tri-partite system designed by the Police Act 1964. The present constitutional arrangement is that the police (outside London) are supervised by an ill-defined co-ordination of chief constables, police authorities and the Home Secretary.

The relationship between police officers can give rise to practical problems in relation to "vicarious liability." Difficult and unresolved questions arise concerning the circumstances in which chief constables are liable for the torts of officers in their force and the precise legal relationship between officers. These questions are considered in the fourth section of the chapter. In the final section police ranks, appointment and promotion are briefly discussed.

2. THE CONSTABLE: OFFICE, DUTIES AND POWERS

Introduction

From the point of view of most citizens the police appear to be one more branch of the government. They seem to be a nationally organised, hierarchical and disciplined body of men, under the ultimate control of the Home Secretary. In strict law, however, their position is very different. Although they are public servants in the broadest sense, they have a unique legal status. A police constable is an officer of the Crown and holds a public office. He is said to exercise an original discretion in keeping the Queen's peace which derives from the office of constable and the swearing of the constable's oath. He is said to be answerable to the law and to the law alone.

The position of chief constables and the Metropolitan and City of London Police Commissioners is also unique. The conventional view of their position is that they have complete "operational independence" from national and local government. It is said that the responsibility for maintaining law and order belongs solely to chief officers and no minister of the Crown or locally constituted police authority is entitled to interfere with the way in which they carry out these functions. This doctrine is discussed and criticised in Chapter 13.[1]

The roots of the unique constitutional status of the police are to be found in the gradual evolution of the common law system of part-time, unpaid, "parish constables" into the modern professional police force. The first organised "police force" along modern lines was, of course, established in London by the Metropolitan Police Act of 1829. This force was always under the ultimate direction of the Home Secretary although the precise limits of his powers over it have never been clearly established.[2] Outside London, local authorities were empowered to set up police forces by the Municipal Corporations Act 1835 (in the boroughs) and the County Police Act 1839 (in the counties). The next century saw the slow development of the present policing system with the number of police forces declining (from 237 in 1856 to 43 today), chief constables gradually asserting their "operational independence" and the Home Office taking on an increasing range of regulatory and supervisory functions.[3] The modern policing system was substantially in place after 1945 and was confirmed and regularised by the Police Act 1964. Although this legislation clarified the relationships between police authorities, chief constables and the Home Office[4] the basic "element of policing" is the same as it has been for many centuries: the common law constable. Despite the increasing numbers of statutory functions given to the constable over the past 150 years, there has been no comprehensive statutory definition of his duties. His basic legal status is still defined by the common law.

[1] See at p. 411, below.
[2] See R. Plehwe, "Police and Government in the Metropolis" [1974] P.L. 316–335.
[3] For a detailed history see Critchley.
[4] See at p. 30, below.

The office of constable

The 1929 Royal Commission[5] described the police in the following terms:

> "The police of this country have never been recognised either in law or tradition as distinct from the general body of citizens. Despite the imposition of many extraneous duties on the Police by legislation and administrative action, the principle remains that a Policeman, in the view of the common law is only "a person paid to perform, as a matter of duty, acts which if he were so minded he might have done voluntarily."[6]

Although these remarks are often quoted they do not recognise crucial differences between the common law powers of constables and those of private citizens. At common law a constable could arrest a person whom he had "reasonable and probable cause to suspect" was guilty of treason or felony (both of which at common law were capital offences). Furthermore, the common law also gave constables, but not ordinary citizens, a range of powers of entry and search.[7]

Although the distinctive role of the individual police constable was recognised by the common law, the police force as an organisation of constables, was not. Thus, *Halsbury's Laws of England* states that:

> "notwithstanding that the police have numerous statutory powers and duties, in essence a police force is neither more or less than a number of individual constables whose status derives from the common law, organised together in the interests of efficiency."[8]

A member of the police force when carrying out his duties as a constable acts as an officer of the Crown and a public servant.[9] Consequently, as a public officer, a constable commits a common law offence if he wilfully and culpably neglects to perform any duty which he is bound to perform (either at common law or by statute) unless the discharge of the duty would involve greater danger than a man of ordinary firmness and authority might expect to encounter.[10]

By virtue of the office itself, a constable acts on his own responsibility when exercising his powers (unless executing a lawfully issued warrant).[11] Therefore, although a chief constable commands his force, he cannot give an officer under his command an order to do acts which can only be lawfully done if the officer himself forms a suspicion on reasonable grounds.[12]

5 Royal Commission on Police Powers and Procedure, Cmnd. 3297 (1929).

6 Para. 15 quoting Sir James Fitzjames Stephen, *History of the Criminal Law*.

7 See generally, L. H. Leigh, *Police Powers in England and Wales* (1st ed., 1975) which deals with police powers before many of them were codified by the Police and Criminal Evidence Act 1984.

8 Vol. 36, para. 201.

9 *MacKalley's Case* (1611) 9 Co.Rep. 65b, 68b; *Lewis* v. *Cattle* [1938] 2 K.B. 454.

10 *Stephen's Digest of Criminal Law* at p. 114; *R.* v. *Dytham* [1979] Q.B. 722.

11 *Enever* v. *R.* [1936] 3 C.L.R. 969 at 977.

12 *R.* v. *Chief Constable of Devon and Cornwall, ex.p. C.E.G.B.* [1982] Q.B. 458 at 474, *per* Lawton L.J.

Similarly, he cannot divest policemen of their powers of arrest and any attempt to do so would be unlawful.[13]

A distinctive feature of the "office of constable" is the swearing of the constable's oath. Every constable upon his appointment must be attested as a constable by making a declaration that he does—

> "solemnly and sincerely declare and affirm that . . . (he) will well and truly serve Our Sovereign Lady, the Queen, in the office of constable without favour or affection malice or ill will; and that . . . (he) will to the best of his power cause the peace to be kept and preserved and prevent all offences against persons and properties of Her Majesty's subjects; and while . . . [he] will to the best of his skill and knowledge, discharge all the duties thereof faithfully according to the law."[14]

The declaration must be made before the Commissioner or Assistant Commissioner of the Metropolis or in any other case, a justice of the peace with jurisdiction within the police area.[15] The Royal Commission on the Police suggested that the constable's claim to be independent from outside control is reflected in the terms of the constable's oath.[16] However, it is difficult to see how such a suggestion can be supported by an examination of the words of the attestation itself.[17]

The "independence" of the constable

Lustgarten has suggested that the precise nature of the constable's "original authority" and "independence" can be subjected to further analysis.[18] He argues that "discretion" plays a central role. Perhaps the most important aspect of a constable's discretion is whether or not to invoke the criminal law in the first place.[19] Yet, the obvious dangers inherent in selective law enforcement have not troubled the courts. In *Arrowsmith* v. *Jenkins*[20] the Divisional Court dismissed such a complaint. Lord Parker C.J. said:

> "I think the defendant feels that she is under a grievance because—and one may put it this way—she says: 'Why pick on me? There have been many meetings in this street from time to time. The police, as on this occasion have attended these meetings and assisted to make free passage, and there is no evidence that anybody else has ever been prosecuted. Why pick on me?' That of course has nothing to do with this court. The sole question here is whether the defendant has contravened [the statute].[21]"

13 *R.* v. *Metropolitan Police Commissioner, ex p. Blackburn (No. 4), The Times*, December 1, 1979.
14 Police Act 1964, s.18, Sched. 2.
15 *Ibid.*
16 Cmnd. 1728 (1962), para. 32.
17 Marshall, at p. 18.
18 See Lustgarten, Chap. 1.
19 J. Goldstein "Police Discretion not to invoke the Criminal Process" (1959) 69 Y.L.J. 543.
20 [1963] 2 Q.B. 561.
21 In that case what is now s.137 of the Highways Act 1980.

It is also entirely within the constable's discretion what particular legal power he exercises and what particular charge he arrests for, where several are available to him.

At the same time the constable works within an organisational hierarchy which imposes substantial limitations on his "independence." He is subject to numerous standing orders which he is bound to obey as duly arising out of the chief constable's power and obligation to control the police force.[22] His decision to arrest is reviewed by his superiors who may reject his charge. It has, therefore, been argued that the only sense in which the police constable is "independent" is that he alone must assess whether or not the factual pre-conditions for making an arrest exist.[23]

The duties of the constable

The duties of constable derive from his office and have long been thought to be common law duties. However, in *George* v. *Garland*[24] it was held that the obligations of a police officer had become statutory duties because they are now expressed in the form of delegated legislation.[25] In any event, the question of whether the constable's duties are statutory or exist at common law is irrelevant for the purposes of enforcing them by way of judicial review.[26] The House of Lords made it clear in *C.C.S.U.* v. *Minister for the Civil Service*[27] that judicial review will apply to a power derived from the common law or the royal prerogative just as much as it does to a statutory power.

The primary function of the constable is the preservation of the Queen's Peace.[28] The leading case of *Glasbrook Bros.* v. *Glamorgan County Council*[29] concerned the payment of the police by colliery owners during a coal miners strike. Viscount Cave stated that

> "No doubt there is an absolute and unconditional obligation binding the police authorities to take all steps which appear to them necessary for keeping the peace, for preventing crime or for protecting property from criminal injury."[30]

In *Rice* v. *Connolly*[31] Lord Parker C.J. described the duties of the police as follows:

> "it is part of the obligations and duties of a police constable to take all steps which appear to him to be necessary for keeping the peace, for

[22] *Hawkins* v. *Bepey* [1980] 1 W.L.R. 419.
[23] Lustgarten, at p. 11.
[24] [1980] R.T.R. 77.
[25] Under Regulation 22 of the Police Regulations (1979), S.I. 1979 No. 1470.
[26] See Chap. 13 at p. 000, below.
[27] [1985] A.C. 374.
[28] *Halsbury's Laws of England* Vol. 36 at para. 320.
[29] [1925] A.C. 270.
[30] See above at p. 27.
[31] [1966] 2 Q.B. 414.

preventing crime or for protecting property from criminal injury. There is no exhaustive definition of the powers and obligations of the police but they are at least these and they would further include the duty to detect crime and to bring offenders to justice."[32]

Thus, it is a constable's duty to prevent breaches of the peace that he reasonably apprehends[33] but not to protect an individual against "a mere apprehension of future crime."[34] He is under a general duty to protect life and property[35] and to execute in his area a warrant issued by a justice of the peace.[36]

There is an important discretionary element in these duties. As Sir John Donaldson M.R. has put it:[37]

> "There is no doubt about the duty of the Chief and other Constables to keep the peace and enforce the law . . . However, Chief Constables have the widest possible discretion in their choice of the methods whereby they will discharge this duty (*R.* v. *Commissioner of Police for the Metropolis, ex. p. Blackburn* [1968] 2 Q.B. 118)."[38]

Cases such as *Glasbrook Bros.* v. *Glamorgan County Council*[39] and *Rice* v. *Connolly*[40] express this discretion in subjective terms: a constable must do what appears to him to be necessary. Nevertheless, it has been established by a number of important judicial review cases over the past two decades that, however subjective a discretion is, its exercise is subject to objective principles. The discretion must be exercised bona fide in accordance with the law, relevant matters must be taken into account and irrelevant matters must be excluded.[41] Furthermore, in the Scottish case of *Wilson* v. *Chief Constable of Lothian & Borders*[42] it was held that, in exercising their discretion, the police owed a duty of care to someone who would, foreseeably, be affected by its exercise.

In general, a constable's duties:

> "must be carried out in a fair and even-handed manner. Because his resources are finite he will not be able to provide perfect protection for all. Even if he has available resources his public duty is not boundless. He has a duty to protect against crime or threatened crime, particularly threatened violent crime. It is not his public duty to protect against the mere apprehension of possible crime. There is no absolute standard of duty and no definition of the exact amount of police protection to

[32] See above at p. 419.
[33] *Duncan* v. *Jones* [1936] 1 K.B. 218.
[34] *Per* Boreham J. in *Harris* v. *Sheffield United Football Club Ltd.* (1986) March 26; Reported in part *The Times*, April 4, 1986 approved, C.A., [1987] 3 W.L.R. 305.
[35] *Haynes* v. *Harwood* [1935] 1 K.B. 146.
[36] Magistrates' Courts Act 1980, s.125(2).
[37] *R.* v. *Oxford, ex p. Levey* (1986) October 30, C.A.; reported in part, *The Times*, November 11, 1986.
[38] *Ibid.*
[39] See above.
[40] See above.
[41] See Chap. 13 at p. 400, below.
[42] [1986] November 26, Court of Session, Lord McCluskey, unreported.

which an individual is entitled. Each case must depend upon its own circumstances."[43]

The nature of police powers

In order to be able to carry out their various duties in an effective manner the law gives constables a number of special "powers." Under these powers the police are "authorised" to do things which would otherwise be unlawful. If an ordinary citizen attempted to stop and search people in the street, to arrest them on suspicion of having committed crimes, or to enter and search their houses he would usually be liable to civil action. Police powers provide constables with a defence of "lawful justification" against civil actions in respect of actions carried out in pursuance of their duties.

In invoking their powers the police are seeking to justify activity which is, prima facie, an unlawful interference with another's interests.

As a general principle of statutory construction, statutes which justify such activity must be strictly construed against those seeking to reply on them. To cite the words of Lord Diplock:

> "if the statutory words relied upon as authorising the acts are ambiguous or obscure, a construction should be placed upon them that is least restrictive of individual rights which would otherwise enjoy the protection of the common law."[44]

The comments of Lord Scarman on the importance of express statutory provision are also relevant here:

> "it is not the task of judges, exercising their ingenuity in the field of implication, to go further in the invasion of private rights and liberties than Parliament has expressly authorised. The importance of express provision is that it affords the citizen the opportunity, if he chooses to use it, to read and understand the extent to which his rights and liberties have been curtailed."[45]

Police powers are of three basic types: common law powers, without warrant powers and with warrant powers. Different considerations apply to defences of "lawful justification" based on different types.

(1) *Common law powers.* Despite increasing trends towards the statutory codification of police powers the common law position remains of crucial importance in many cases. This is in part due to parliament's strange reluctance to abolish common law powers, even when enacting statutory powers covering the same ground. An example of this is the failure of the Police and

[43] *Per* Boreham J. in *Harris* v. *Sheffield United Football Club Ltd.* (1986) March 26; reported in part *The Times*, April 4, 1986.

[44] *I.R.C.* v. *Rossminster*, above at 1008 C–D; see also *Wills* v. *Bowley* [1983] 1 A.C. 57.

[45] *Morris* v. *Beardmore* [1981] A.C. 446 at 463.

Criminal Evidence Act 1984 to abolish common law powers of seizure.[46] Police powers at common law have been refined and adapated by judicial decision over the centuries. The courts continue to play a creative role in this field. The most recent example being the extension of the *Mareva* jurisdiction to the police.[47] As a matter of general principle such extensions should be limited in scope because the powers in question represent invasions of the common law rights of citizens.

Common law police powers are usually such that they can only be exercised if certain preconditions of fact and belief are fulfilled. Thus a constable has a common law power to arrest someone whom he sees breaking the peace or who so conducts himself that he causes a breach of the peace to be reasonably apprehended. If no breach of the peace has taken place and none is reasonably apprehended then the constable has no common law power of arrest and any arrest made will be unlawful.

(2) *Without warrant powers.* Many of the most important police powers of arrest, search, entry and seizure are statutory "without warrant" powers. In other words, they can only be exercised if particular preconditions of fact or belief laid down by the statute are fulfilled. The majority of such powers are now to be found in the Police and Criminal Evidence Act 1984. If the preconditions of fact or belief laid down by the Act are not met then an arrest, search or entry will have been done without "lawful justification" and an action in tort will lie. It is important to note that the lawfulness of the exercise of a police power must be justified **at the time of its exercise**, "It cannot be made lawful or unlawful according to what happens afterwards."[48]

The Police and Criminal Evidence Act 1984 contains a number of "procedural safeguards" in relation to "without warrant" powers. It is submitted that the proper approach when examining such provisions is as follows:

(a) It is first necessary to consider whether the police conduct *at the time* they are obliged to follow a particular provision is prima facie tortious: are they detaining or searching a person, entering land or holding goods at that time? If not then no action in tort will lie simply for a breach of the procedural safeguards. A failure to carry out a procedure that must be followed *after* the prima facie tortious conduct has occurred will not retrospectively render otherwise lawful actions unlawful.[49] Thus, for example, the police will not be guilty of false imprisonment solely because they fail to comply with a duty which arises after the suspect has been subjected to a "stop and search."[50]

[46] See Chap. 7 at pp. 212 *et seq.*, below.

[47] See Chap. 12 at pp. 383 *et seq.*, below; see also Feldman, Chap. 10 on the expansion of seizure powers by *Ghani* v. *Jones*, above.

[48] *Per* Lord Denning M.R. in *Chic Fashions (West Wales)* v. *Jones* [1968] 2 Q.B. 299 at 312.

[49] As Mr Douglas Hurd MP said in reply to a question on the subject during the Committee stage of the Police and Criminal Evidence Bill, "I am advised . . . that it would be extraordinary if a court decided that an action for trespass to the person . . . could be founded not on anything that happened on the occasion but on a subsequent failure to supply a piece of paper," quoted in Robilliard and McEwan, at p. 67, n. 79.

[50] See, *e.g.*, Chap. 5 at p. 131, below.

(b) If the conduct is prima facie tortious it is necessary to identify the police power in the Act which "justifies" the conduct and consider whether the police have acted "in accordance" with it;

(c) If the police have not acted in accordance with their statutory power it is necessary to consider whether or not, on a true construction of the statute, the provision casts a *mandatory duty* on the police. A procedural safeguard which gives the suspect an entitlement but which places the police under no duty to implement it will not render them liable in tort if they fail to do so (although an action for breach of statutory duty may lie).[51]

(d) If the police were acting in a way which was prima facie tortious and are in breach of a mandatory duty laid down by the statute then, it is submitted, they will be deprived of the defence of "lawful justification" and an action in tort will lie.[52]

Under section 66 of the 1984 Act the Secretary of State has a duty to issue codes of practice in connection with "searches of premises by police officers" and "the seizure of property found by police officers on persons or premises."[53] Any breach of the provisions of these codes of practice will render a police officer liable to disciplinary proceedings.[54] But, by section 67(10) a failure of a police officer to comply with any provision of a code "shall not of itself render him liable to any criminal or civil proceedings." Nevertheless, it is provided by section 67(11) that

> "In all criminal and civil proceedings any such code shall be admissible in evidence; and if any provision of such a code appears to the court or tribunal conducting the proceedings to be relevant to any question arising in the proceedings it shall be taken into account in determining that question."

In other words, the provisions of a code can be taken into account in civil proceedings. They will, it is submitted, be relevant to the "reasonableness" of police conduct in particular situations. Rather like the Highway Code they will not be definitive of this but will provide a basic framework within which reasonableness can be assessed.[55]

(3) *"With warrant" powers.* Police arrests, entries, searches and seizures are often conducted under the authority of a legal authorisation or "warrant."[56] A warrant gives the person to whom it is issued lawful authority to do acts which would otherwise be unlawful. A warrant provides a complete defence to a civil action in respect of things done "in obedience to it." Even if a warrant is, in fact, invalid the police will have a statutory defence under the Constables Protection Act 1750 provided they act "in obedience" to it.[57]

[51] See Chap. 10 at p. 310, below.

[52] For an example of this under a statute in force before the 1984 Act, see *Millington* v. *M.P.C.*, *The Times*, May 28, 1983. Forbes J., this discussion only appears in the full transcript.

[53] s.66(*c*) and (*d*).

[54] s.67(8).

[55] See Hargreaves and Levenson at p. 4.

[56] Research for the Royal Commission on Criminal Procedure showed that 30 per cent. of police searches are conducted under the authority of warrants, Cmnd. 8092 (1981), I Appendix 7.

[57] See Chap. 3 at pp. 64 *et seq*. and Chap. 5 at p. 153, below.

3. THE INSTITUTIONAL FRAMEWORK

Introduction

Modern police forces are large organisations with complex support structures and considerable budgets. Like all branches of government they are now subject to a complex network of rules and regulations. Most of these are not relevant to civil actions and are, therefore, outside the scope of this book. It is important, however, to be clear about the basic "institutional framework" within which police forces now operate. This involves three elements: chief officers, police authorities and the Home Secretary. Each element in the framework has different responsibilities under statute and common law. This section deals with the basic functions and responsibilities of the three elements. In some civil cases the internal organisation of a police force may be of importance. Each force has slightly different arrangements and, if such a case arises, it will be necessary to make enquiries into the specific organisational details which affect the case. By way of example the organisation of the Metropolitan Police is considered in the final part of this section.

The functions of chief officers

The chief officer of police for a county or combined police force[58] is the chief constable. The chief officer of the Metropolitan Police is the Commissioner of Police for the Metropolis whereas the chief officer for the City of London is the Commissioner of Police for the City of London.[59]

The direction and control of a county or combined police force is vested in the chief constable.[60] All chief officers have functions in relation to the control of street collections, the issue of firearms certificates, the registration of firearms dealers, public order (under the Public Order Act 1936) and may object to the grant or renewal of certain permits and licences.

Appointments and promotions in county or combined police forces (other than assistant chief constable's rank) are made by the chief constable in accordance with regulations made by the Home Secretary.[61] He performs duties in respect of probationary policemen (under Police Regulations)[62] and in formulating and conducting disciplinary proceedings.[63] He may also provide special police services at any premises or locality in his police area at the request of any person, subject to payment.[64]

Both the Commissioner of Police of the Metropolis and the Commissioner of Police for the City of London have certain special powers

[58] See at p. 31, below.
[59] Police Act 1964, s.62(6); Sched. 8.
[60] *Ibid.* s.5.
[61] *Ibid.* s.7(2).
[62] S.I. 1979 No. 1470.
[63] See above Chap. 2, at p. 48.
[64] Police Act 1964, s.15(1).

which are exercised by local authorities outside London. For example, the Commissioner of Police for the Metropolis is responsible for school crossing patrols[65] whereas the Commissioner of the Police for the City of London may grant, vary or revoke special orders of exemption for licensed premises or clubs with the approval of the Lord Mayor.[66]

The functions of police authorities

The police authority for the Metropolitan Police District is the Home Secretary whereas the police authority for the City of London is the Common Council of the City of London.[67] Every county constitutes a police area (unless the county is part of a combined police area or is part of a metropolitan county police authority). The police authority is the police committee of the county council of which two-thirds must be councillors appointed by the county council and one-third are magistrates.[68] For the ten combined police areas, two-thirds must be members of the constituent county councils and one-third magistrates.[69] As a result of the abolition of the metropolitan councils under the Local Government Act 1985, the metropolitan county police authorities have now been created.[70] These metropolitan county police authorities consist of councillors appointed from the constituent councils and magistrates appointed by the joint magistrates committee.[71]

It is the duty of a police authority to secure the maintenance of an adequate and efficient police force for its area.[72] It may provide, maintain or alter buildings, structures and premises provided the Home Secretary's consent is obtained.[73] It may provide vehicles, clothing and other equipment required for police purposes subject to complying with the Home Secretary's regulations.[74] The police authority must determine the overall budget of the force provided that the costs incurred under government regulations and statute are met.[75]

The police authority of a county or combined police force also performs certain personnel functions. Subject to the Home Secretary's approval and any regulations made by him, the authority decides how many policemen of each rank there are to be in the force and is empowered to appoint the chief constable.[76] After consulting with the chief constable and with the approval

[65] Road Traffic Regulation Act 1967, s.24(2)(*c*).
[66] Licensing Act 1964, s.74(6)(*b*).
[67] Police Act 1964, s.62(6), Sched. 8.
[68] *Ibid.* s.2.
[69] *Ibid.* s.3.
[70] With the exception of Tyne and Wear which became part of the combined police authority with the Northumberland county council, s.25 of the Local Government Act 1985.
[71] Local Government Act 1985, s.24 and Sched. 11.
[72] Police Act 1964, s.4(1).
[73] *Ibid.* s.4(3).
[74] *Ibid.* s.4(4).
[75] *Ibid.* s.8(4).
[76] *Ibid.* s.4(2).

of the Home Secretary, the authority must make appointments and promote to the rank of deputy chief constable.[77] With the approval of the Home Secretary the authority may call upon the chief constable, deputy chief constable or assistant chief constable to retire in the interests of efficiency.[78] However, before seeking such approval, the authority must give the officer an opportunity to make representations.[79] Finally, the police authority discharges certain functions when disciplining senior officers.[80]

In addition, the police authority may acquire land for police purposes[81] and may employ civilian staff for police purposes.[82] It has a number of other miscellaneous functions including duties in relation to street collections, civil defence, school crossing patrols and compensation for riot damage.

The Police Act 1964 imposes certain duties on the chief constable in relation to the police authority. He is under a duty to provide a general written report on policing in his area to be submitted to the police authority as soon as possible at the end of every calendar year.[83] The authority may also require the chief constable to submit a written report on such police matters as it specifies.[84] However, if it appears to the chief constable that his report would contain information which, in the public interest ought not to be disclosed or is not needed for the discharge of the authority's functions, he may request the authority to refer the requirement to the Home Secretary. Unless the Home Secretary confirms the requirement it will have no effect.[85]

New obligations have been created by the Police and Criminal Evidence Act 1984. Section 106(1) provides that:

> "Arrangements shall be made in each police area for obtaining the views of people in that area about matters concerning the policing of the area and for obtaining their co-operation with the police in preventing crime in the area."

The police authorities may consult with their chief constables about what arrangements will be appropriate.[86] In London, however, the Home Secretary will issue guidance to the Metropolitan Police Commissioner which he must take into account.[87] The Commissioner must make separate arrangements with each London borough and consult with each borough council.[88] The Common Council of the City of London must issue guidance to the Commissioner concerning the arrangements which he must take into account.[89] The Home Secretary may require the persons whose duty it is to

[77] Police Act 1964, s.6(4) as amended by Police and Criminal Evidence Act 1984, s.108(1) and (2).

[78] Police Act 1964, s.5(4) and 6(5).

[79] *Ibid.* ss.5(5) and 6(5).

[80] Police (Discipline) (Senior Officer) Regulations [1985] S.I. 1985 No. 519.

[81] Police Act 1964, s.9.

[82] *Ibid.* s.10(1).

[83] *Ibid.* s.12(1).

[84] *Ibid.* s.12(3).

[85] *Ibid.* s.12(3).

[86] Police and Criminal Evidence Act 1984, s.106(2).

[87] *Ibid.* s.106(3).

[88] *Ibid.* s.106(4), (5), (6), (7).

[89] *Ibid.* s.106(8).

make the arrangements for consultation to submit a report if he thinks they are inadequate.[90]

The functions of the Home Secretary

The functions of the Home Secretary are set out in the Police Act 1964. He is required to exercise his powers in such a manner and to such an extent as appears to him best calculated to promote the efficiency of the police.[91] Perhaps the most important power exercised by the Home Secretary in practice is his power to make regulations concerning the "government, administration and conditions of service of police forces." He is, therefore, able to impose uniform practices over an enormous range of policing matters such as pay scales, rank and promotion criteria, discipline, leave and even the issue, use and return of police clothing.[92]

He may order a local enquiry to be held by someone he appoints into any matter connected with the policing of any area.[93] He may require the chief constable or Commissioner of Police for the City of London to submit a report on any matter he specifies.[94] He has the power to make grants to police authorities for expenses incurred for police purposes,[95] makes regulations on police terms and conditions[96] and appoints H.M. Inspectors of the Constabulary who report to him on the efficiency of local forces.[97] He may direct a chief constable to assist another chief constable meet any special demand on his resources.[98] He may require a police authority to call upon a chief constable to retire in the interests of efficiency.[99]

The Home Office can give guidance on recommended police procedures by issuing circulars, and has issued circulars in relation to cautioning, the use of surveillance devices and the issue and use of firearms and baton rounds.

In addition to his specific statutory powers over the police, the Home Secretary has powers under the royal prerogative to maintain the peace.[1] It has been held that, under this prerogative power the Home Secretary can maintain a central store of equipment such as plastic bullets and CS gas to supply to chief constables.[2] The decision whether or not to use such equipment is a matter for the chief constable alone.[3]

[90] *Ibid.* s.106(10), (11).
[91] Police Act 1964, s.28.
[92] *Ibid.* s.32.
[93] *Ibid.* s.32.
[94] *Ibid.* s.30.
[95] *Ibid.* s.31.
[96] *Ibid.* s.33.
[97] *Ibid.* s.38.
[98] *Ibid.* s.14.
[99] *Ibid.* s.29(1).
[1] See *Harrison* v. *Bush* (1855) 5 E.&B. 354 at 363, *per* Lord Campbell C.J.
[2] *R.* v. *Secretary of State for the Home Department, ex.p. Northumbria Police Authority*, [1987] 2 W.L.R. 998.
[3] *Ibid.*

The structure of police forces: the example of the Metropolitan Police

The Metropolitan Police force is the largest in the country with an annual budget of nearly £800 million.[4] In November 1985 it consisted of 26,844 police officers and over 13,000 full-time civilian staff.[5] The force is divided into eight areas which are themselves sub-divided into a total of 75 divisions.[6]

The Commissioner of Police for the Metropolis is in overall command of the force.[7] In making decisions about policy and strategy he acts with the "Policy Committee" which consists of the Deputy Commissioner, four Assistant Commissioners, the Receiver[8] and the Deputy Receiver.

The new Metropolitan Police "areas" are under the command of a Deputy Assistant Commissioner, assisted by a Commander. The working unit of the force is the "Division" and recent reorganisations have aimed at decentralisation to divisional level. A metropolitan police "division" is commanded by a chief superintendent, assisted by a superintendent. A typical division will contain at least two police stations, one of which will be the "Divisional Station" and will have facilities for charging, police cells, a communications room and a C.I.D. Office. One outer London division in 1985 contained, in addition, two chief inspectors, eight inspectors, 37 sergeants and 206 constables, 128 of whom were "relief officers" who go out on the beat. These officers are divided into four "reliefs" and thus, at any one time, the theoretical maximum number of constables available for "beat duties" in this division was 32.[9] This division had four sub-divisions with their own police stations and one "police office." In 1985 it had a total of 27 police vehicles, 11 of which were ordinary "beat cars."[10]

4. THE VICARIOUS RESPONSIBILITY OF CHIEF OFFICERS

Introduction

At common law neither chief officers of police nor watch committees were vicariously liable for torts committed by officers in their force.[11] This

[4] 1985–96 estimate £770.849 million, *Hansard* November 20, 1986.
[5] G.L.C. *Guide to the Met.* at p. 11.
[6] As from 1987, previously, the force was divided into 24 districts: *ibid.* at p. 13.
[7] There were originally two commissioners but the modern practice is to appoint only one.
[8] Who is responsible for finance and is in charge of the "civilian departments" of the Metropolitan Police.
[9] In practice because of sickness and other duties the average strength of the relief in 1985 was 19 officers.
[10] The Bexleyheath Division, see G.L.C., *Guide to the Met.* at pp. 16 *et seq.*
[11] *Fisher* v. *Oldham Corpn.* [1930] 2 K.B. 364.

was because police constables were not "servants" of the watch committee or the chief constable but independent "officers of the Crown." The position was summarised as follows:

> "A constable . . . when acting as a peace officer, is not exercising a delegated authority, but an original authority, and the general law of agency has no application."[12]

It is submitted that, on the narrow question of whether police officers are "servants" of their watch committees or police authority this conclusion was legally sound.[13] Nevertheless, it gave rise to considerable practical difficulties as members of the public would bring civil actions against individual constables who had no right to recompense from public funds against awards of damages. The practice seems to have been to give financial support on an ad hoc case by case basis. The use of public funds by the Home Office to settle a civil action in 1959 gave rise to stormy parliamentary debates and was one of the factors which led to the setting up of the Royal Commission on the Police.[14]

The Royal Commission recommended that statutory provision be made for vicarious liability and this was enacted by section 48(1) of the Police Act 1964. This provides that the chief constable of a particular police force (or, in London, the Metropolitan Police Commissioner) is vicariously liable—

> "in respect of torts committed by constables under his direction and control in the performance or purported performance of their functions in like manner as a master is liable in respect of torts committed by his servants in the course of their employment."

If the officers committing the tort were being "lent" by one police force to another under the provisions of section of the Police Act 1964 then, by section 14(3) they are deemed to be under the direction and control of the chief officer to whom they are lent.

If a chief officer is found to be vicariously liable for a tort committed by a constable under his direction and control then damages are payable out of the police fund.[15] If an action against a chief officer is settled then the damages are payable out of the police fund only if the settlement is approved by the police authority.[16]

The provisions of section 48 give rise to a number of potential practical problems. First, it applies unclear common law provisions to the vicarious liability of chief constables without dealing with possible differences between police officers and ordinary employees. Secondly, instead of deeming constables to be servants for all purposes it confines this to actions in tort. This may give rise to difficulties in questions of vicarious responsibility outside the law of tort. These problems are considered in the next two sections.

[12] *Enever* v. *The King* [1906] 3 C.L.R. 969 at 977, *per* Griffith C.J., quoted with approval, *Fisher* v. *Oldham Corpn.* [1930] 2 K.B. 364 at 372; see also at p. 23 above and also Chap. 13 at pp. 413 *et seq.* below.

[13] See Marshall, at pp. 35 *et seq.*

[14] See Critchley at pp. 273 *et seq.*

[15] See Police Act 1964, s.48(2)(*a*): for "police fund" see s.62 and Sched. 8.

[16] *Ibid.* s.48(2)(*b*).

Vicarious liability and the law of tort

The effect of section 48 is to fix a chief constable with liability in all situations in which a "master is liable in respect of torts committed by his servants in the course of his employment." The situations in which a master is so liable depend on the very considerable case law in this area. Only the briefest of guidelines can be given here.[17]

The question to be asked in all vicarious liability cases is whether, at the time the tort was committed, the servant was "acting within the scope of his employment."[18] This does not mean that the servant must, in fact, be acting in performance of his master's purposes in an authorised way. If a servant is doing an authorised act then the master will be liable even if it is being done in an unauthorised manner.[19] If a servant is doing an act which is expressly forbidden by his master then the master will still be liable if the prohibition deals with conduct within the sphere of his employment. If, on the other hand, the prohibition limits the sphere of employment itself then the master will not be liable in respect of the prohibited acts.[20] The common law position is explicitly recognised in section 48 by the words "in the purported performance of their functions."

It is submitted that if a constable is on duty and is bona fide purporting to carry out policing functions then there is no doubt that his chief constable will be vicariously liable for any torts committed by him. If, however, a constable is acting so outrageously that it could not possibly be thought that he was "purporting to perform policing functions" then his chief may be in a position to deny vicarious liability. Thus, for example, if a police officer goes shoplifting whilst on duty it is difficult to see how his chief officer could be vicariously liable for wrongful interference with goods. As in all such cases liability will depend on all the circumstances of a particular case.

A difficult which is peculiar to the vicarious liability of police officers concerns torts committed by "off duty" police officers. In ordinary master and servant cases there can be no question of vicarious liability if the servant is not actually working for the master at the time the tort is committed. The position in relation to the police is less clear.

Police constables hold office under the Crown and it can be argued that they continue to have responsibilities of such office whether or not they are formally on duty. This is a problem which must often arise in practice in relation to the criminal offence of "assaulting a constable in the execution of his duty" contrary to section 51(1) of the Police Act 1964: is a person who assaults an off-duty constable guilty of the offence? Surprisingly enough, there is no direct authority on this point. The indirect authorities point in different directions. In the case of *McLorie* v. *Oxford*[21] Donaldson L.J. treats an officer's being on duty as a necessary condition for his acting "in the execution of his duty."[22] On the other hand, the defendant in the case of

[17] The fullest discussion is to be found in P. S. Atiyah, *Vicarious Liability in the Law of Torts*.

[18] See *Heatons Transport* v. *TGWU* [1973] A.C. 15 at 99, *per* Lord Wilberforce.

[19] See, *e.g.*, *Century Insurance* v. *N.I.R.T.B.* [1942] A.C. 509; and see the discussion in *Irving* v. *Post Office, The Independent*, April 3, 1987.

[20] See *Plumb* v. *Cobden Flour Mills* [1914] A.C. 62 at 67.

[21] [1982] Q.B. 1290.

[22] As he also does in *Coffin* v. *Smith* (1980) 71 Cr.App.R. 221.

Albert v. *Lavin*[23] was convicted of the section 51 offence in relation to an off-duty police officer. Although the point was not explicitly considered by either the Divisional Court (which included Donaldson L.J.) or the House of Lords the conviction was upheld.

It is submitted that, in strict law, police constables are always on duty. Thus, a chief constable will be liable for any torts committed by a police officer "in purported performance of" policing functions whether or not the officer was on duty for police pay purposes at the time.

Although there are a number of potential difficulties in this area there is no reported case in which a chief officer has sought to contend that he was not vicariously liable for the actions of one of his constables.

Agency and the police

The case of *Fisher* v. *Oldham*[24] not only denies that constables are "servants" of watch committees but goes on to hold that they exercise "original authority" and are that the "law of agency has no application."[25] If this were correct then it would mean that one police officer, exercising his functions as a "peace officer," could never be regarded as "acting on behalf" of the chief constable and senior officers who were giving him orders. This could have some impact on civil actions where questions of police knowledge are at stake.

It is submitted, however, that police officers must now be regarded as agents of their chief officer. The contrary dicta in *Fisher* v. *Oldham*[26] are, strictly, *obiter* as the case was directly concerned only with the relationship of master and servant. In any event, the position has now, arguably, been altered by the effect of section 5 of the Police Act 1964 which places a police force under the direction and control of the chief constable. Such direction and control suggests a subordination of the original authority of individuals constables to that of the chief constable.[27] This contention is supported by the case of *Hawkins* v. *Bepey*[28] in which it was held that a police officer instituting a prosecution was, in effect, doing so "on behalf of" his chief constable.

It is submitted, therefore, that police officers are properly regarded as agents of chief officers of police. It would follow that the usual principles of the law of agency apply. In particular, information which is given to a police officer within the scope of his authority is effective as if it were given to his principal, the chief officer. Matters which are known by any constable would therefore, be deemed to be known by the chief officer, and hence by all officers under his command as his agents.

The impact of this conclusion in police cases is limited by the fact that many police powers depend on the state of knowledge of the individual constable concerned. In deciding whether an arrest is lawful the knowledge and beliefs of the arresting officer (or the officer who supplied the information

[23] [1982] A.C. 546.
[24] [1930] 2 K.B. 364.
[25] See above at 372.
[26] See above.
[27] *Cf.* Atiyah, *Vicarious Liability in the Law of Torts* at p. 77.
[28] [1980] 1 W.L.R. 419.

for arrest)[29] must be considered. A chief officer cannot direct a constable to make an arrest.[30] The lawfulness of continued detention depends on what was known to the custody officer.[31] Whenever a statute requires *a constable* to have reasonable grounds then principles of agency will be irrelevant.

5. POLICE ORGANISATION

Introduction

Police forces now share many common organisational features as a result of the Home Secretary's powers to make regulations covering their administration.[32] In particular, the ranks of police forces, and the qualifications for the appointment and promotion of officers are laid down centrally and are dealt with in this section.

Police ranks

Police forces outside London are divided into eight separate ranks. The highest rank is the Chief Constable followed by Assistant Chief Constable (or Commander), Chief Superintendent, Superintendent, Chief Inspector, Inspector, Sergeant and Constable.[33] In the Metropolitan Police there are three additional ranks so that the top six ranks are: Commissioner, Deputy Commissioner, Assistant Commissioner, Deputy Assistant Commissioner, Commander and Chief Superintendent. Police Cadets are appointed by chief officers of police to undergo training as police officers.[34] They are not police constables and are not vested with the statutory or common law powers of constables.

Appointment of police officers

The office of constable cannot be held by a person born outside the United Kingdom unless he is British subject or a citizen of the Republic of Ireland.[35] People applying to be constables must be between the ages of 18 years six months and 30.[36]

[29] See Chap. 5 at pp. 151 *et seq.*, below.
[30] See at p. 23, above.
[31] See Chap. 5 at pp. 158 *et seq.*, below.
[32] Police Act 1964, s.33(1); see above at p. 33.
[33] Regulation 9 of the Police Regulations [1979] S.I. 1979 No. 1470.
[34] Police Act 1964, s.17(1); see also, *Wiltshire Police Authority* v. *Wynn* [1981] 1 Q.B. 95.
[35] See *Halsbury's Laws of England*, Vol. 36, para. 203, note 18.
[36] Unless they have had previous service in the police or the armed forces; regulation 14 of the Police Regulations [1979] S.I. 1979 No. 1470.

A police officer is on "probation" for the first two years of his service.[37] On promotion to sergeant and, again, to inspector there are further probationary periods of one year.[38]

Promotion of police officers

In order to quality for promotion from constable to sergeant and from sergeant to inspector an officer must serve a qualifying period and must pass the appropriate examination.[39] In general a candidate who has qualified for promotion must then go through a process of selection[40] but in the Metropolitan Police promotion between these ranks is based on the results of competitive examinations.[41] Promotion above the rank of inspector is determined entirely by selection. Transfer to plain clothes work with the C.I.D. is also entirely by selection. In the first instance, constables are given temporary transfers to the C.I.D. and are considered for permanent appointment after 12 months. The Metropolitan Police operate a system known as "Interchange" for C.I.D. promotions. Thus, when a C.I.D. officer is promoted he must return to the uniformed branch for a least 12 months. Return to the C.I.D. after this period is not automatic.[42]

Promotion to sergeant and inspector is not, therefore, based on "results" in terms of arrests, convictions and so on. Nevertheless, it does appear that initial appointments to the C.I.D. and reappointments to the C.I.D. under "interchange" may well depend on "results."[43]

[37] Regulation 16(2), Police Regulations [1979] S.I. 1979 No. 1470.
[38] See Police (Promotion) Regulations [1979] S.I. 1979 No. 991, regulations 3 and 7.
[39] See generally, Police (Promotion) Regulations [1979] S.I. 1979 No. 991 as amended by the Police (Promotion) (Amendment) Regulations [1981] S.I. 1981 No. 919 and [1982] S.I. 1982 No. 1602.
[40] See regulation 5 of the Police (Promotion) Regulations [1979] S.I. 1979 No. 991.
[41] *Ibid.* regulation 6.
[42] See Wolchover and Cogan, "Police Promotion" (1987) 137 New L.J. 155 at 157.
[43] *Ibid.* at 158.

2. Complaints against the Police

1. INTRODUCTION

When a member of the public is aggrieved by police misconduct he has a statutory remedy under the police complaints procedure. This procedure can be used to pursue allegations against the police whether or not civil proceedings are brought. Its primary purpose is to investigate such allegations in order to establish whether criminal or disciplinary charges should be laid against individual police officers.

The complaints procedure designed by the Police and Criminal Evidence 1984 is considerably more elaborate than its predecessors. It has established a three-tier system introducing conciliation and informal resolution of complaints. Serious complaints must now be referred to an independent body who will supervise their investigation. Presiding over the new scheme is the Police Complaints Authority. Its powers are greater than the Police Complaints Board set up under the Police Act 1976 since it has a role in the investigation process. It therefore has two divisions: one concentrating on the supervision of investigations, the other supervising disciplinary cases.

The current complaints system is, however, unlikely to survive unchanged in future years. Public concern about the disciplining of police officers is longstanding. A 1957 public enquiry into whether a complaint had been properly investigated[1] was one of the factors leading up to the establishment of the Royal Commission on the Police in 1960.[2] The Commission was specifically asked to consider the "means of ensuring that the complaints by the public are effectively dealt with" and made various recommendations which were implemented by the Police Act 1964. However, public dissatisfaction continued and parliament made further reforms in the Police Act 1976. Although this Act created a Police Complaints Board—which could recommend and ultimately direct the laying of disciplinary charges against policemen—the pressure for reform continued. The substantial and concerted campaign to introduce an independent element into what was once a matter of internal police discipline has not run its course. Even the Police Federation now supports independent investigation of all complaints.[3]

In this chapter the various elements of the complaints procedure and

[1] *The Allegation of Assault on John Walters*, Cmnd. 718 (1959).

[2] Cmnd. 1728 (1962).

[3] See Intro at p. 11, n. 79, above.

related preliminary matters are examined. Further, two specific aspects of the way in which complaints relate to civil proceedings are considered. First, where public policy prohibits material obtained in the course of the complaints investigation from being used in a civil claim, the justification and extent of this legal principle is analysed in some detail. Secondly, the question of whether to run a police complaint in tandem with a civil case has generated considerable debate and the arguments involved when making this tactical decision have therefore been included.

2. THE COMPLAINTS PROCEDURE: PRELIMINARY MATTERS

Introduction

The first area to consider is the proper subject matter of a complaint, how a complaint can be made and the informal resolution procedure. Secondly, the investigation stage is considered. This involves the standard procedure where the investigation is conducted internally and the circumstances in which the Police Complaints Authority itself will supervise the investigation. Finally, various matters which arise after the investigation has been completed need to be discussed. These cover points such as the referral of various reports of the investigation, the use of independent disciplinary hearings and the disciplinary rules including, in particular, the application and operation of the "double jeopardy" rule.

The proper subject matter of a complaint

The complaints procedure is designed to obtain redress against a police officer who misconducts himself. Its object as described by Lord Denning in *Neilson* v. *Laugharne*[4] is to ensure that if a policeman had done anything wrong the appropriate proceedings should be taken against him: criminal proceedings if it was a criminal offence or disciplinary proceedings if it was a disciplinary offence. The complaints procedure is not intended to cover broad policy issues which relate to the direction or control of the police by the chief constable.[5] The procedure is not a substitute for taking civil or criminal proceedings.[6] Indeed, complaints which involve allegations of criminal conduct by an officer are governed by special rules.[7]

The primary function of the complaints system remains a determination of whether a police officer is guilty of breaking the police discipline regulations.[8] The offences contained in the Disciplinary Code include discreditable conduct, neglect of duty, falsehood or prevarication, improper disclosure of information, corrupt or improper practice, abuse of authority,

[4] [1981] 1 Q.B. 736 at 744.
[5] Police and Criminal Evidence Act 1984, s.84(5).
[6] See at p. 57, below.
[7] See at p. 50, below.
[8] S.I. 1985 No. 518 and S.I. 1985 No. 519.

racially discriminatory behaviour, drunkenness and criminal conduct.[9] A police officer will also be liable for disciplinary proceedings for breaking the Codes of Practice.[9a]

Making a complaint

The 1984 Act contemplates that a complaint can be made orally although it is more conventional and desirable to make a complaint in writing. A complaint may be submitted either by a member of the public himself or by someone acting on his behalf provided it is submitted with his written consent.[10]

The question of what constitutes a complaint arose in *Peach* v. *Commissioner of Police of the Metropolis*.[11] Proceedings were brought as a result of the death of Blair Peach in the Southall riots in 1979. An extensive police inquiry followed both because of complaints made against the police and because the police initiated their own general inquiry into how the death occurred. When disclosure of witness statements taken in the investigations was sought in a subsequent civil action, the police objected on the grounds that statements taken during a complaints procedure are immune from disclosure on public interest grounds.[12] The issue, therefore, became whether a complaint had been received from a member of the public at the time the investigations began. An anonymous complaint was recorded at 1.30 am after which the police investigations commenced. At 11.00 am a witness accompanied by her solicitors made a statement to the police alleging that she saw an officer strike Blair Peach on the head with a truncheon. She did not, however, express herself specifically in terms of a complaint.

Unfortunately the comments made by the Court of Appeal are rather difficult to interpret. Although their remarks concerned the Police Acts of 1964 and 1976, they remain relevant to the present legislation. The Court of Appeal observed that there are no statutory provisions as to the mode of making complaints. Fox L.J. held that the fact that the police treat a statement as being a complaint does not establish that it is. Whether or not a complaint has been made is a question of fact and seems to turn on whether the allegations made amount to a complaint about police behaviour; the absence of the formal terms of a complaint is not determinative of the question.[13] Purchas L.J. doubted that it is open to a senior police officer to elect whether a communication involving a member of the public should be treated as a complaint.[14] The Court of Appeal appear to have ruled that a complaint does not come into existence unless it is made by an identifiable member of the public.

A complaint should be sent to the police and addressed to the Chief Offi-

[9] See reg. 5 and Sched. 1 Police (Discipline) Regulations [1985] S.I. 1985 No. 518 and reg. 4, Police (Discipline) Senior Officers Regulations [1985] S.I. 1985 No. 519; see also, Harrison, pp. 4–5 and pp. 133–135.

[9a] s.67(8); see Chap. 1, p. 29, above.

[10] s.84(4).

[11] [1986] Q.B. 1064.

[12] See at pp. 53 *et seq.*, below.

[13] [1986] Q.B. 1064 at 1075A–1076B.

[14] *Ibid.* at 1085E–H.

cer[15] of the relevant police force. A complaint can be sent to the Police Complaints Authority itself but it will then be transmitted to the appropriate authority[16] unless the Authority is satisfied that this would be contrary to the Complainant's wishes or in all the circumstances unnecessary. Furthermore, the Authority can transmit the complaint against the wishes of the complainant if it is satisfied that the general public interest requires it.[17]

Where a complaint is submitted to the chief officer of the police area, his first duty is to take any steps he feels are desirable to obtain or preserve evidence relating to the conduct complained of.[18] He must then decide whether he is the "appropriate authority" in relation to the officer complained against. The "appropriate authority" is, for an officer of the Metropolitan Police, the Commissioner, and for an officer of any other police force, the chief constable. However, if the officer complained about is above chief superintendent's rank the appropriate authority is the police authority.[19] If the chief officer decides he is not the "appropriate authority" he must send the complaint (or particulars of it if it was oral) to the appropriate authority and inform the complainant (or the person acting on his behalf).[20]

Once the chief officer has decided that he is the appropriate authority in respect of a complaint, he must record it[21] and then consider whether the complaint is suitable for informal resolution; he may appoint an officer from his force to assist him for this purpose.

The informal resolution procedure

One of the innovations made by the 1984 Act is the informal resolution procedure. Its purpose is to filter complaints and to provide a flexible and informal approach to minor allegations of misconduct. However, a complaint will only be suitable for informal resolution if the complainant consents and if the chief officer is satisfied that the misconduct alleged—even if proved—will not amount to a criminal or disciplinary charge.[22] If it does appear suitable, the chief officer must seek to resolve it informally and may appoint an officer from his own force (of at least chief inspector's rank) or the rank of the officer complained of[23] to do so on his behalf.[24]

The appointed officer must as soon as practicable seek the views of the complainant and the officer involved and take such steps as appear to him appropriate. If it appears to him that the complaint has already been satisfactorily dealt with by the time it was brought to his notice, he may, subject

[15] *i.e.*, the Chief Constable or Commissioner of the Metropolitan or City of London Police.
[16] See above.
[17] Reg. 3, Police (Complaints) (General) Regulations [1985] S.I. 1985 No. 520.
[18] s.84(1).
[19] s.84(4).
[20] s.84(3).
[21] s.85(3).
[22] s.85(10).
[23] s.85(8).
[24] s.85(4).

to any representations made by the complainant, treat the complaint as informally resolved. However, the appointed officer cannot resolve a complaint by apologising on behalf of the officer unless that officer admits his misconduct.[25]

Where a complaint is dealt with by informal resolution, a record must be made of the outcome and the complainant is entitled to a copy of it from the chief officer if he applies within three months of the day his complaint is informally resolved or of the day when it is decided the complaint shall no longer be handled by informal resolution.[26]

After attempts have been made to resolve the complaint informally, the chief officer must instigate a formal investigation if it appears to him that informal resolution of the complaint is impossible or it is for any other reason unsuitable for informal resolution.[27]

It should be noted that no statement which is made for the purpose of informal resolution and which results in an informal resolution will be admissible in any subsequent criminal, civil or disciplinary proceedings.[28] This provision seems to reproduce the position regarding admissions in the formal complaints procedure. Admissions made during the formal complaints investigation will be inadmissible because of the "public interest immunity" protecting all statements made during the investigations from disclosure.[29] The Act, therefore, confirms that a similar immunity applies to admissions made in the informal resolution procedure.

3. THE COMPLAINTS PROCEDURE: THE INVESTIGATION STAGE

The standard complaints procedure

If the chief officer decides that a complaint against a junior officer is unsuitable for informal resolution or that informal resolution has not been achieved despite attempts to do so[30] he must appoint an officer (either from his own force or another one) to investigate the complaint formally.[31] The investigating officer must be of at least chief inspector's rank or the rank of the officer complained against.[32] He cannot be the same officer as the one appointed to achieve an informal resolution of the complaint[33]; nor can the investigating officer serve in the same sub-division or branch as the officer under investigation.[34] If the chief officer requests another chief officer to

[25] Police (Complaints) (Informal Resolution) Regulations [1985] S.I. 1985 No. 671, reg. 4.
[26] *Ibid.* reg. 5.
[27] Police and Criminal Evidence Act 1984, s.85(5).
[28] *Ibid.* s.104(3) and (4).
[29] See at pp. 53 *et seq.*, below.
[30] See, above at p. 43.
[31] Police and Criminal Evidence Act 1984, s.85(3) and (5).
[32] *Ibid.* s.85(8).
[33] *Ibid.* s.85(6).
[34] Police (Discipline) Regulations, [1985] S.I. 1985 No. 518, para. 5(*b*).

provide the investigating officer, the second officer is under a duty to do so.[35]

Unless the investigation is being supervised by the Police Complaints Authority[36] the investigating officer must submit his report to the chief officer supervising the complaint.[37]

Complaints against senior officers

The 1984 Act has introduced a special procedure for senior officers. These are defined as officers above chief superintendent's rank.[38] For such a complaint the appropriate authority is now the police authority itself.[39]

The police authority is under a duty to record the complaint and to investigate it.[40] However, if the police authority is satisfied that the conduct complained of, even if proved, would not justify criminal or disciplinary charges, it has a complete discretion as to how the complaints should be handled.[41]

In other cases, the investigating officer must be appointed either from the police authority's own force or from another one.[42] The investigating officer must be of at least the same rank as the officer under investigation[43] and cannot be serving in the same sub-division or branch.[44]

Unless the investigation is supervised by the Police Complaints Authority[45] the investigating officer must submit his report to the police authority.[46]

Referrals to the Police Complaints Authority

A complaint must be referred to the Police Complaints Authority if the misconduct alleged:

(a) resulted in death or serious injury (*i.e.* a fracture, damage to an internal organ, impairment of bodily function or deep cut or laceration[47] to some other person);
(b) constitutes an assault occasioning actual bodily harm;

[35] Police and Criminal Evidence Act 1984, s.85(7).
[36] See below at p. 46.
[37] Police and Criminal Evidence Act 1984, s.85(9).
[38] *Ibid.* s.83(4).
[39] *Ibid.*
[40] *Ibid.* s.86(1).
[41] *Ibid.* s.86(2).
[42] *Ibid.* s.86(3).
[43] *Ibid.* s.86(5).
[44] Police (Discipline) (Senior Officer) Regulations [1985] S.I. 1985 No. 519, reg. 5.
[45] See below at p. 46.
[46] Police and Criminal Evidence Act 1984, s.86(6).
[47] *Ibid.* s.87(4).

(c) constitutes an offence under section 1 of the Prevention of Corruption Act 1916;
(d) constitutes a serious arrestable offence.[48]

These referrals must be notified to the Police Complaints Authority not later than the end of the day following the day it first becomes clear to the appropriate authority[49] that the complaint requires a mandatory referral.[50]

In addition, there is a discretionary power to refer complaints to the Police Complaints Authority. Even if misconduct is not the subject of a complaint, it may be referred to the Police Complaints Authority if it appears to the appropriate authority[51] that the officer may have committed a criminal or disciplinary offence and it ought to be referred because of its gravity or because of exceptional circumstance.[52]

The Police Complaints Authority itself can require a complaint to be submitted even though it has not been referred by the appropriate authority.[53] The complaint must then be submitted not later than the end of the day following the day notification of the referral is made.[54]

The Police Complaints Authority can also be written to by the appropriate authority if it thinks a complaint is anonymous, repetitious or if it is not reasonably practicable to complete an investigation[55] and it thinks that the statutory complaints procedure should be dispensed with.[56] If the Police Complaints Authority shares this opinion, it can dispense with the complaints procedure and will notify the authority of its decision and notify the complainant unless this is not reasonable practicable.[57]

Investigations supervised by the Police Complaints Authority

Although the 1984 Act did not create an independent body to investigate complaints, it has now given a role to the Police Complaints Authority to supervise certain complaints. Investigation may be supervised if a complaint was mandatorily referred to the Police Complaints Authority.[58] Moreover, it can supervise a complaint investigation if it is desirable in the public interest to do so in relation to any complaint or where it is referred a matter which is not subject to a complaint.[59] If a decision to supervise is

[48] See Chap. 5 at p. 139, s.87(1), para. 4(1) Police (Complaints) (Mandatory Referrals, etc.) Regulations [1985] S.I. 1985 No. 673.
[49] See at p. 43, above.
[50] Police and Criminal Evidence Act 1984, s.87(3), reg. 4(*b*) *ibid.*; Mandatory Referrals, reg. 10(1) Police (Complaints) (General) Regulations [1985] S.I. 1985 No. 520.
[51] See at p. 43, above.
[52] Police and Criminal Evidence Act 1984, s.88.
[53] *Ibid.* s.87(2).
[54] Reg. 10(*b*) Police (Complaints) (General) Regulations [1985] S.I. 1985 No. 520.
[55] As defined in the Schedule of Police (Anonymous Repetitious, etc. Complaints) Regulations [1985] S.I. 1985 No. 672.
[56] *Ibid.* reg. 3(1), (2)
[57] *Ibid.* paras. 3(3) and 3(4).
[58] See at p. 45, above.
[59] See above and s.89(1)(2).

made, the Police Complaints Authority must notify the appropriate authority.[60]

In these circumstances no investigating officer can be appointed unless the Police Complaints Authority notify their approval of him; if one has already been appointed and the Police Complaints Authority is not satisfied with the officer, another one must be selected after its approval has been notified. The Police Complaints Authority may also issue directions imposing any additional requirements about the conduct of the investigation as appears to it necessary.[61]

At the end of the investigation, a report will be submitted to the Police Complaints Authority and a copy sent to the appropriate authority.[62] The Police Complaints Authority must then issue a statement stating whether or not the investigation was conducted to its satisfaction, specifying the respects in which it was not, any other respects that its satisfaction with the investigation ought to be recorded, and any other matters which it considers ought to be brought to the attention of the appropriate authority, the complainant or the officer under investigation or which ought to be dealt with in the public interest.[63] This statement should be submitted to the appropriate authority[64] and if practicable to the officer under investigation and the complainant.[65] Unless the Director of Public Prosecutions thinks there are exceptional circumstances, no criminal proceedings can be brought by the Director or the appropriate authority (see above) unless this statement has been submitted to the appropriate authority.[66] Similar provisions apply to disciplinary charges.[67]

4. THE COMPLAINTS PROCEDURE: THE POST INVESTIGATION STAGE

The referral of reports

Where a complaint concerns a senior officer[68] the police authority on receiving a report (whether submitted to it direct or via the Police Complaints Authority) must send a copy to the Director of Public Prosecutions unless it is satisfied that no criminal offence has been committed.

For junior officers the first consideration for the chief officer is whether a criminal offence may have been committed and whether the officer should

[60] See at p. 43, above.
[61] Reg. 5(2) Police (Complaints) (Mandatory Referrals, etc.) Regulations [1985] S.I. 1985 No. 673.
[62] Police and Criminal Evidence Act 1984, s.89(7).
[63] *Ibid.* s.89(7) (10), reg. 7 Police (Complaints) (General) Regulations [1985] S.I. 1985 No. 520.
[64] See at p. 43, above.
[65] Police and Criminal Evidence Act 1984, s.89(7), (8), (9).
[66] *Ibid.* s.89(13), (14).
[67] *Ibid.* s.89(12).
[68] See at p. 45, above.

be charged.[69] If he decides on both, the report will be sent to the Director of Public Prosecutions to consider launching criminal proceedings.[70] If the chief officer decides not to charge the officer despite deciding that a criminal offence may have been committed he must send a memorandum to the Police Complaints Authority, stating whether he is laying disciplinary charges and if not why not.[71] Similarly, if the chief officer decided no criminal proceedings may be appropriate, he must send a memorandum stating whether he has laid disciplinary charges and if not why not[72] to the Police Complaints Board together with a copy of the complaint and report.[73] However, no memorandum need be sent if the officer admits the disciplinary charges laid against him.[74]

Where the chief officer's memorandum states that he proposes to lay disciplinary charges (or has laid charges) he is under a duty to lay them and proceed with them.[75]

The Police Complaints Authority is likewise under a duty to consider first whether a criminal offence may have been committed and whether the officer should be charged.[76] If it considers that criminal charges should be laid, it must direct the chief officer to send the report to the Director of Public Prosecutions and may direct that the memorandum and complaint also be sent.[77]

On the other hand, where the memorandum states the chief officer has not laid charges (or does not propose to do so), the Police Complaints Authority may recommend and ultimately direct him to lay such charges as it specifies.[78] The chief officer must lay and proceed with the charges specified in the direction unless the Police Complaints Authority gives him leave not to do so.[79]

The use of independent disciplinary hearings

The fundamental principle remains that the chief officer is responsible for the disciplining of his police force. However, a hearing will be heard before a disciplinary tribunal if charges are laid as a result of a direction by the Police Complaints Authority or because the Police Complaints Authority feel it is desirable because of any exceptional circumstances affecting the case.[80] The tribunal will comprise a chairman who is the chief officer (or the person nominated by the Commissioner of the Metropolitan Police)[81] and two

[69] Police and Criminal Evidence Act 1984, s.90(3).
[70] *Ibid.* s.90(5).
[71] *Ibid.* s.90(6).
[72] *Ibid.* s.90(7).
[73] *Ibid.* s.90(9).
[74] *Ibid.* s.91(1).
[75] *Ibid.* s.90(10).
[76] *Ibid.* s.92(1).
[77] *Ibid.* s.92(2), (3), (4).
[78] *Ibid.* s.93(1), (3).
[79] *Ibid.* s.93(5), (6).
[80] *Ibid.* s.94(1), (2).
[81] *Ibid.* s.94(4).

members of the Police Complaints Authority.[82] The chairman will impose any punishment after consulting the members.[83]

The disciplinary rules

Although a complaint may lead to disciplinary proceedings concerning whether an officer has breached the disciplinary rules, the ambit of the rules and the procedure to be adopted in proving a complaint are outside the scope of this book. Nevertheless, some general points may be noted.

The officer hearing a disciplinary charge is obliged to allow the complainant to attend the disciplinary hearing while witnesses are being examined or cross-examined. The officer may also permit the complainant to be accompanied by a personal friend or relative if he considers it appropriate whether because of his age or otherwise.[84] Thus, the complainant is not entitled to be accompanied by his legal advisor at a police discipline hearing. Furthermore, he may be excluded in certain circumstances. If he is a witness against the officer, he and his friend or relative may not attend before he gives evidence. He may be required to leave if a witness is giving evidence which should not be disclosed to a member of the public or if he behaves in a disorderly or abusive manner or misconducts himself.[85]

If the complainant is a witness against the officer, he may be cross-examined.[86] In any serious complaint against a junior officer, the complainant may be cross-examined by a lawyer since the officer is entitled to seek legal representation.[87] However, after the officer against whom the complaint is made gives his evidence, the officer conducting the hearing may put forward questions from the complainant provided they are proper ones and may allow him to cross-examine.[88]

Regardless of the disciplinary charge preferred the standard of proof in establishing it is formidable; the charge must be proved beyond reasonable doubt.[89] This standard is significantly higher than the normal burden in civil proceedings of the balance or probabilities. It has been said that it is desirable that this civil standard is used in disciplinary hearings[90] so that the standard applied in police disciplinary hearings is anomalous. Furthermore, the standard in ordinary unfair dismissal proceedings is even lower.

[82] Police and Criminal Evidence Act 1984, s.94(3)(*a*).

[83] *Ibid.* s.94(3)(*b*).

[84] Police (Discipline) Regulations [1985], above; regulation 22(2); Police (Discipline) (Senior Officers) Regulations [1985], above.

[85] Reg. 22 Police (Discipline) Regulations 1985, above; Reg. 17, Police (Discipline) (Senior Officer) Regulations 1985, above.

[86] Reg. 18(7) Police (Discipline) Regulations 1985, above; Reg. 13(6), Police (Discipline) (Senior Officer) Regulations 1985, above.

[87] s.102.

[88] Reg. 22, Police (Discipline) Regulations 1985, above; Reg. 17, Police (Discipline) (Senior Officer) Regulations 1985, above.

[89] Reg. 23(2), Police (Discipline) Regulations [1985], above; Reg. 18(2), Police (Discipline) (Senior Officer) Regulations [1985], above; *R.* v. *Police Complaints Board, ex p. Madden* [1983] 1 W.L.R. 447 at 467.

[90] *R.* v. *Hampshire C.C, ex. p. Ellerton* [1985] 1 W.L.R. 749.

The employer simply has to show reasonable grounds for believing that misconduct has been committed.[91]

The "Double Jeopardy" rule

The Police and Criminal Evidence Act 1984 preserves the "double jeopardy" rule so as to ensure that officers should not be tried in disciplinary proceedings for offences which have already been subject to criminal proceedings. Section 104 provides as follows

> "(1) Where a member of police force has been convicted or acquitted of a criminal offence he shall not be liable to be charged with any offence against discipline which is in substance the same as the offence of which he has been convicted or acquitted.
> (2) Subsection (1) above shall not be construed as applying to a charge in respect of an offence against discipline which consists in having been found guilty of a criminal offence."

The section itself does not, therefore, prohibit bringing disciplinary proceedings where the charge itself is being guilty of a criminal offence. For the purposes of this provision "being guilty of a criminal offence" simply involves a finding of guilt so that disciplinary charges can be brought where the guilty officer is sentenced to an absolute or conditional discharge or receives a probation order.[92]

The section does not apply so as to prohibit disciplinary proceedings if an officer is not tried on criminal charges because the Director of Public Prosecutions considers the evidence insufficient to convict.[93] It is also submitted that section 104 will not prohibit disciplinary proceedings where the plea of *autrefois convict* or *acquit* would not apply in criminal cases; therefore, where a Crown Court judge directs a not guilty verdict in accordance with section 17 of the Criminal Justice Act 1967 but fails to follow its provisions,[94] (where a plea of not guilty is entered and the indictment, or count on the indictment, is marked "not to be proceeded with without the leave of this court or the Court of Appeal")[95]; the withdrawal of the summons in magistrates court proceedings[96] the dismissal of an information for non-appearance of the prosecutor (under section 15 of the Magistrates Courts Act 1980)[97]; the issuing of a certificate under section 44 of the Offences Against the Person Act 1861[98] and a ruling that there is no case to answer in committal proceedings.[99]

The other issue to be considered concerning the application of section

91 *Fearodo* v. *Barnes* [1976] I.R.L.R. 302.
92 *R.* v. *Secretary of State for the Home Department, ex p. Thornton* [1986] 3 W.L.R. 158.
93 *R.* v. *Police Complaints Board ex p. Madden* [1983] 1 W.L.R. 447.
94 *R.* v. *Griffiths* (1981) 72 Cr.App.Rep. 307.
95 *Connelly* v. *DPP* [1964] A.C. 1254.
96 *Brooks* v. *Bagshaw* (1904) 68 J.P. 514.
97 *R.* v. *Bennett & Bond* (1908) 72 J.P. 362.
98 *Reed* v. *Nutt* (1890) 54 J.P. 597; see Chap. 4 at pp. 109 *et seq.* below.
99 *R* v. *Manchester City Magistrates, ex p. Snelson* [1977] 1 W.L.R. 911.

104(1) is whether the disciplinary offence is in substance the same as the criminal one. Some assistance may be gleaned from the guidance issued by the Home Secretary on the double jeopardy rule.

The Police and Criminal Evidence Act 1984 specifically enjoins the Police Complaints Authority to take account of such guidance. Section 105(4) provides that:

> "In discharging their functions under section 93 above the Authority shall have regard to any guidance given to them by the Secretary of State with respect to such matters affecting the preferring and withdrawal of disciplinary charges as are for the time being the subject of guidance under section 104(1) and shall have regard in particular, but without prejudice to the generality of this subsection, to any such guidance as to the principles to be applied in cases that involve any question of criminal proceedings are not governed by section 104 above."

It was established by *R.* v. *Police Complaints Board, ex p. Madden*[1] (examining a parallel provision in the Police Act 1976) that the Police Complaints Authority is not obliged to comply with the Home Secretary's guidance since this amounts to a fetter on its own discretion whether to institute disciplinary procedures under section 83(1) of the Police and Criminal Evidence Act 1984. The guidance itself[2] states:

> "A police officer is subject to the criminal law and to a discipline code. As a result, alleged misconduct may render him liable to both criminal and disciplinary proceedings. It is necessary that where both these systems may apply, they are operated in ways which are neither unfair to the officer nor offensive to the public interest. In deciding whether to prefer a disciplinary charge the effect of any criminal proceedings which have already taken place has to be distinguished from the effect of any decision by the Director of Public Prosecutions that criminal proceedings should not be brought.
>
> **Where criminal proceedings have already taken place**
>
> Here it has to be examined whether . . . (section 104(1) operates. The section provides that an officer brought before the courts on a criminal charge should not, whether acquitted or convicted, thereafter be charged with a disciplinary offence which is in substance the same (save that criminal conduct itself constitutes a disciplinary offence). This is because, since the required standard of proof in disciplinary proceedings is the same as that in criminal proceedings, to bring a disciplinary charge following a criminal charge would be in effect to try the officer twice for the same offence. This is the only statutory bar to discipline proceedings and the sole situation in which it is appropriate to say that "double jeopardy" obtains.
>
> In considering whether . . . (section 104(1)) operates, close attention should be paid to the similarity in the elements of the criminal charge and the possible disciplinary charge. In some cases they may not be as similar as appears at first sight: the mental element of the criminal offence may be lacking in the disciplinary offence, or the conduct involved may differ. Where this is so, there is no bar to disciplinary

[1] [1983] 1 W.L.R. 447.

[2] Appendix B, Police Complaints and Disciplinary Procedures, Cmnd. 9072 (1983).

proceedings, because the two offences are not in substance the same. As examples, in criminal proceedings against a police officer for corruption it is necessary to establish that the officer agreed to show favour to the person from whom he agreed to accept a gift or consideration, but this element is absent from the disciplinary offence of accepting a gratuity; a criminal charge of perjury involves proof that an allegedly false statement was material to the proceedings in which it was made, but a disciplinary charge of falsehood does not; and a Theft Act charge will require proof of an intention permanently to deprive a person of his property or permanently to evade payment of a debt, whereas these elements are absent from disciplinary offences relating to the care of property or failure to discharge debts. By contrast, the criminal charge of assault and the disciplinary charge of unnecessary violence is the most common example of such charges being in substance the same.

There will also be cases where an acquittal on a criminal charge may be very relevant to the question whether to prefer a disciplinary charge, notwithstanding that the charges are not in substance the same so that . . . (section 104(1)) does not operate. This will be so, in particular, where a matter essential to the proof of the disciplinary charge was in issue in the criminal proceedings and was apparently resolved in the officer's favour. In the first example quoted . . . (above), if the essential issue in a trial for corruption was whether the officer received a gift, rather than whether he showed favour in return for the gift, it may not be appropriate to prefer a disciplinary charge of accepting a gratuity following an acquittal in the criminal proceedings.

Where the Director has decided that criminal proceedings should not be brought

Here . . . (section 104(1)) does not operate and all cases fall to be considered individually on their merits. However, account should be taken of such a decision by the Director if the criminal offence which he has considered is in substance the same as the disciplinary offence under consideration (*i.e.* the sort of examination outlined . . . [above] will be relevant here also) and his decision is on the grounds that the available evidence is insufficient: if the Director has decided that the evidence is insufficient for criminal prosecution it is for consideration whether it is sufficient for disciplinary proceedings. Ultimately, however, having considered each case on its merits, the disciplinary authority is free to bring proceedings if it thinks in all the circumstances that it is fair and appropriate to do so.

In a separate category are cases where the alleged misconduct is fairly trivial when regarded as a criminal offence, but far more serious in the context of a disciplined service. Cases of common assault, minor thefts of police property and the use of bad language to a member of the public might fall within this category. In such cases, the Director may decide that the offence is not such as to merit prosecution (he may use the expression that it would not be in the public interest to bring a criminal charge). If this is so, his decision is not relevant to the question whether disciplinary proceedings should be brought, since he has not expressed the view that the evidence is insufficient to justify criminal proceedings. It follows, therefore, that the disciplinary authority is free to take what action it thinks appropriate in such instances without further regard to the Director's decision."

The wording of section 105(4) indicates that the guidance given by the Home Secretary under the Police Act 1976 is still applicable. As the guidance itself says, the fact that a decision is made not to prosecute a police officer does not inevitably result in deciding not to lay disciplinary charges: this must depend on the circumstances of every case.

It is submitted that the double jeopardy rule and the effect of the Home Secretary's guidance place the police in an anomalous position when compared with ordinary employees charged with criminal offences at work. The unfair dismissal legislation does not confer any right upon the employee to wait for the result of the criminal proceedings but entitles the employer to dismiss the employee beforehand.[3] Furthermore, a dismissal will be fair if an employer dismisses two men even if he had reasonable grounds to believe that only one of them is guilty of theft but cannot identify which one.[4] In misconduct cases involving police officers criminal proceedings must be considered and determined before hearing disciplinary proceedings can be taken. It is difficult to appreciate the justification for making one rule for police officers and another rule for everyone else.

5. THE RELATIONSHIP OF COMPLAINTS TO OTHER PROCEEDINGS

Introduction

The complaints procedure can be used to pursue allegations of police misconduct regardless of whether civil or criminal proceedings are contemplated by the complainant and regardless of whether the misconduct would be illegal under the civil or criminal law. However, where a civil action is brought it is likely to raise the same issues of fact as are involved in the complaint and may be dealt with by the police in tandem with the complaint. Indeed, it seems to have become the practice of the police to treat the letter before action in a civil case as being a formal complaint.

Complaints are, therefore, relevant to a possible civil claim in at least two respects. The investigations into complaints which are carried out by the police could provide considerable assistance to a civil action but will not be disclosed because they attract public interest immunity. Furthermore, the institution of an investigation under the complaints procedure may have important implications for the conduct of a civil action. It follows that the question of whether the complaints procedure will help or hinder a civil action requires careful consideration.

Complaints and Privilege

At one stage it was the practice of police solicitors to advise their clients in civil proceedings to disclose all relevant documents (except those clearly

[3] *Harris (Ipswich)* v. *Harrison* [1978] I.C.R. 1256.
[4] *Monie* v. *Coral Racing* [1981] I.C.R. 109.

subject to public interest immunity such as statements made by informers). The Solicitor to the Metropolitan Police advised that investigations conducted under the complaints procedure should be disclosed so that the plaintiff would have copies of any statements made by the police officer against whom he was complaining and would be cross-examined on any statement made by him.[5]

However, the position was reversed by *Neilson* v. *Laugharne*[6] on the basis of public interest immunity.[7] According to Lord Denning M.R.[8]:

> "On the one hand we have a man who is suing the police for damages. He has got legal aid and demands to see all the statements taken by the police. He—or rather his solicitors—want to see the police statements so as to find out something, if they can, to back him up. On the other hand, there are the police who, for aught that appears apart from this man's complaint, have acted perfectly properly. Statements were taken on the basis they were to be used for the private investigations—to see if the police acted improperly in any way: and, if they had acted improperly, to be used in criminal or disciplinary proceedings against the police. No improper conduct by the police was disclosed at all.
> Yet now the plaintiff wants to see the statements for another purpose altogether—to help him make out a case for damages. I cannot think it would be right to let him do this. Some of the statements may contain the names of informers which should be kept secret anyway. I cannot think it incumbent on the police—or the court—to go through all these statements or to consider the contents of them—so as to assert a 'contents' privilege. It is in the public interest that the whole 'class' should be privileged from disclosure by the plaintiff."

Oliver L.J. expressed the principle involved somewhat more narrowly. He decided that the statements attracted public interest immunity because disclosure in civil proceedings would adversely affect the attainment of the legislation's purpose of ensuring complaints against the police are fully and properly investigated.[9]

Although Lord Denning M.R. suggested *obiter*[10] that the public interest immunity of statements taken by complaint investigations could be waived, his views were not followed in *Hehir* v. *MPC*.[11] In that case the police claimed privilege for police reports, statements and documents relating to a complaint investigation and then sought leave at trial to cross-examine the plaintiff on the statement he made in the investigation. The Court of Appeal ruled that all the statements were protected by public interest immunity and that the plaintiff could not, therefore, be cross-examined. They also observed that if such an immunity could be waived, it was the maker and not the recipient who was entitled to do so.

However, Lord Denning MR has reasserted the view that public interest immunity can be waived and that *Hehir* v. *MPC* is not a decision binding on

[5] *Hehir* v. *MPC* [1982] 1 W.L.R. 715 at 718.

[6] [1981] 1 Q.B. 736.

[7] See Zuckerman, "Privilege and Public Interest" in *Crime Proof and Punishment*, ed. C. F. H. Tapper.

[8] *Neilson* v. *Laugharne* [1981] 1 Q.B. 748.

[9] *Ibid.* at p. 752.

[10] *Ibid.* at p. 747.

[11] [1982] 1 W.L.R. 765.

the Court of Appeal.[12] There have, in fact, been instances in which such privilege has been waived[13]; and there are powerful arguments in favour of this course.[14] Nevertheless, it is submitted that the weight of authority is to the effect that public interest immunity cannot be waived[15] although it may evaporate by consent in limited circumstances.[15a] It is further submitted that the doctrine of waiver is not strictly applicable when it is sought to admit evidence of a statement without the consent of its maker and that the decision in *Hehir* v. *MPC* has the benefit of avoiding giving a manifestly unfair advantage to a police defendant. Whereas the police will have a copy of the plaintiff's statements, the plaintiff will not have sight of those made by the officers since they will not have been disclosed on public policy grounds.[16]

Although the conclusion reached in *Hehir* v. *MPC* prevented one obvious unfair advantage being given to police defendants, the Court of Appeal did not query the peculiar anomaly which allowed the issue to arise in the first place. If it is in the public interest that complaints investigations should not be disclosed then it is submitted that there can be no conceivable justification for them being supplied to a police defendant for the purposes of a civil action. They cannot be examined by the court or the plaintiff and it should follow that they should not be examined by the defendant either. The fact that the complaint investigation documentation is in the custody, possession or control of a chief officer defendant in civil proceedings is an entirely accidental result of the complaints investigation procedure and the fact that the chief officer is vicarously liable for the actions of his officer.[17] It is submitted that the "public interest" which prevents the plaintiff seeing the complaint investigation documents should also prevent them being revealed to whoever is conducting the defence of a civil action on the chief officer's behalf. Of course, the individual police officer being complained against is entitled to know the case against him but this does not mean that he or his solicitors (if he is being sued as an individual) should have the complaint investigation documentation for the purposes of a civil action. Bearing in mind the fact that complaints are usually not determined until after civil actions are over such a course would be most unlikely to cause any injustice to the officer complained about. By contrast, there is little doubt that the present system, which can, in effect, give police defendants the advantage of having the plaintiff's proof of evidence, causes considerable injustice to complainants.

Considerable reservations about the correctness of the decision in *Neilson* v. *Laugharne* continue to be expressed and subsequent cases have limited its scope. Thus in *Conerney* v. *Jacklin*[18] it was held that the immunity does not extend to the complaint itself. This decision has been

[12] See *Campbell* v. *Thameside Council* [1982] 1 Q.B. 1065 at 1072.

[13] See, *e.g.*, *Ellis* v. *Home Office* [1953] 2 Q.B. 135, 141; *Bearmans* v. *Metropolitan Police Receiver* [1961] 1 W.L.R. 634.

[14] See Zuckerman, "Balancing Justice and the Public Interest" (1983) 99 Law Quarterly Review 14.

[15] See *R* v. *Lewes JJ., ex. p. Home Secretary* [1973] A.C. 388, 407; *Air Canada* v. *Secretary of State for Trade (No. 2)* [1983] A.C. 394 at 436.

[15a] *Multi Guarantee* v. *Cavalier Insurance, The Times*, June 24, 1985.

[16] *Hehir* v. *MPC* [1982] 1 W.L.R. 719.

[17] Under s.48 of the Police Act 1964.

[18] [1985] Crim.L.R. 234.

criticised on the ground the same policy considerations which protect informers of child abuse from disclosure[19] should also apply in the case of those reporting police misconduct.[20] Nevertheless, its effect is that a police officer who is complained against can have sight of the complaint in order to sue in defamation. The blanket immunity covering statements in complaints investigations was further restricted in *Peach* v. *MPC*.[21] In that case the Court of Appeal decided that where statements were taken both because of a complaint and because there was a police inquiry into the death of a member of the public, the right to discovery depended upon what was the dominant purpose of obtaining them and discovery was ordered. It is submitted that, on the present state of the authorities, this principle will only apply where an investigation has in fact been commenced at the time when the complaint was made. In all other cases, the statements made in the course of the complaint investigation will be covered by public interest immunity. It follows that the extension of the *Peach* principle in the county court case of *Mason* v. *Chief Constable of Essex*[22] was unwarranted. In that case, pre-action discovery of complaints documents was ordered on the basis that had the police become aware of the plaintiff's allegations that he had received serious burns in a police station "whether or not there was a complaint . . . the Chief Constable would have caused an inquiry to be made"[23] and therefore the investigation of the complaint was not the "dominant purpose" of the investigation. But the "other purpose" in this case was not an actual inquiry but a hypothetical one and it is difficult to see how it is possible to say that this was the dominant purpose of the investigation which actually took place. It is submitted, therefore, that if *Neilson* v. *Laugharne*[24] is good law, *Mason's* case is wrongly decided.

There are, however, strong grounds for arguing that *Neilson* v. *Laugharne* is wrong in principle and should be reversed if the issue came before the House of Lords.[25] The broadbrush approach of "balancing public interest" whenever a public policy objection is taken[26] runs together two distinct principles: the law preventing disclosure on the ground that the functioning of government will be harmed by disclosing material relating to high level policy discussions or national security and the "immunity" of informers who supply information to public bodies and people in analogous situations.[27] The assertion of a generalised public interest immunity where the court must balance the public interest in favour of non-disclosure against the public interest in the administration of justice involves a misreading of *D* v. *NSPCC*.[28] In that case the House of Lords unanimously rejected the broad proposition that in every case where it is claimed that "public interest immunity" attaches to documents, a "balancing exercise" must be carried

[19] *D* v. *NPCC* [1973] A.C. 173.
[20] Robilliard & McEwan at pp. 248–249.
[21] [1986] Q.B. 1064.
[22] (1986) October 2, Southend County Court, unreported.
[23] *Ibid. per* H.H. Judge Rice.
[24] [1981] 1 Q.B. 736.
[25] See Price, "Public Interest Privilege and Section 49 Statements" (1981) 97 Law Quarterly Review 525.
[26] *cf. Medway* v. *Doublelock* [1978] 1 W.L.R. 710; *Gaskin* v. *Liverpool City Corp.* [1980] 1 W.L.R. 1549; *R* v. *Birmingham City Council, ex p. D* [1982] 1 W.L.R. 679.
[27] See Chap. 3, below at pp. 75 *et seq.*
[28] [1978] A.C. 171.

out. Instead, they extended the "informer immunity" principle.[29] The narrow grounds on which disclosure was refused in *Burmah Oil* v. *Bank of England*[30] and *Air Canada* v. *Secretary of State for Trade (No. 2)*[31] are also inconsistent with the *Neilson* v. *Laugharne* approach. In that case Lord Denning M.R. appeared to be swayed by the fact that the complaint disclosed no police wrongdoing. The reasoning of Oliver L.J. was based on the claim that the disclosure of complaints investigation materials would discourage candour and co-operation with such investigations. However, it has been said that the claim that the disclosure of documents will inhibit candour from witnesses because their statements might sometimes see the light of day is no longer arguable.[32] Furthermore, statements made in the course of a complaint investigation may be used in disciplinary or even criminal proceedings. Although Oliver L.J. purported to distinguish between giving evidence at these hearings and disclosure for the "quite alien purpose of use in civil litigation" as the basis for inhibiting co-operation with the complaints investigation[33] it is respectfully submitted that this is a distinction without a difference. It is difficult to see how the determination of the question of whether police conduct was unlawful under the civil law can be described as a "quite alien" purpose. Furthermore, it should be remembered that statements taken during complaints' investigations were, in fact, disclosed until the decision in *Neilson* v. *Laugharne*[34] without any apparent adverse consequences. The Court of Appeal did not refer to any empirical evidence to support the contention that disclosure would be inhibited.

Complaints and civil actions

Before bringing a civil action against the police it will always be necessary to consider whether or not an official complaint should be made. The chances of an aggrieved person being vindicated through a complaint are considerably lower than his chances of succeeding in a civil action.[35] Furthermore, the successful complainant is not entitled to compensation.[36] Nevertheless, decisions will have to be made about whether or not to make a complaint before issuing proceedings and whether or not to delay civil proceedings until the complaints procedure is exhausted. It must be borne in mind that in default of a plaintiff taking appropriate steps his letter before action will be usually be treated as complaint in any event. The Director of the Metropolitan Police Complaints Investigation Bureau observed, in 1983, that:

> "We now consider that all civil claims alleging assault, wrongful imprisonment or malicious prosecution should be treated as complaints

29 See Chap. 3, below at p. 76.
30 [1980] A.C. 1090.
31 [1983] A.C. 394.
32 *Campbell* v. *Tameside Council* [1982] 1 Q.B. 1065, *per* Ackner and O'Connor L.JJ. at pp. 1077 and 1079.
33 See above at p. 44.
34 [1981] 1 Q.B. 736.
35 See the figures in the Introduction, above at p. 11.
36 Robilliard & McEwan at p. 256.

under section 49 of the 1964 Police Act, although in the past this has not always been the case."[37]

Making a complaint will always expose the complainant to a number of risks. An officer who is the subject of a complaint is entitled to a copy of it and can then sue the complainant for defamation.[38] Under regulation 9 of the Police (Complaints) (General) Regulations[39] an officer (who is not a senior officer)[40] is entitled to a copy if no disciplinary charges are preferred. If a complaint is oral, the officer is entitled to a copy of its reduction to writing, extracts from the statements made to the police which themselves amount to complaints and any fresh complaints made.[41] The chief officer must supply this unless it might prejudice any criminal investigations or proceedings or is otherwise contrary to the public interest. If the request is refused it can be repeated after six months. A complaint does not attract the absolute privilege in defamation proceedings which attaches to pleadings in civil cases.[42] Instead, complaints against the police appear to be protected by qualified privilege since it is the duty of everyone in the interests of public efficiency and order to bring any misconduct or neglect of the public duty to the attention of the proper authorities for investigation. This point was expressly made by the Court of Appeal in *Conerney* v. *Jacklin*.[43] In addition, a complainant may be prosecuted for the offence of wasting police time.[44]

Opinion is strongly divided as to whether a civil action is helped or hindered by setting the complaints procedure in motion at the same time. Experience shows that judges and juries look unfavourably upon litigants suing for damages when they have failed to bring police misconduct to the attention of the authorities by instituting a complaint.

But utilising the complaints procedure in fact produces very few advantages for a plaintiff.[45] The first step that the police will take in a complaints investigation will be to interview the complainant. This will, therefore, give the intended defendant in a civil action the opportunity to take an extensive proof of evidence from the plaintiff. This will give the defendant an advantage which would not normally arise in the course of conventional civil proceedings and this statement may become part of the defendant's counsel's brief. In *Neilson* v. *Laugharne*[46] Oliver L.J. suggested that it could form the basis of cross-examination of the plaintiff although the statements

[37] Letter to Chief Executive of Camden Council, quoted in *Policing London*, No. 24, Nov/Dec 1986 at p. 52.

[38] *Conerney* v. *Jacklin* [1985] Crim.L.R. 234.

[39] *Ibid.*

[40] As defined by the Police (Discipline) (Senior Officer) Regulations, above.

[41] *R* v. *Commissioner of the Police for the Metropolis, ex p. Ware, The Times*, July 31, 1985.

[42] *Seaman* v. *Netherclifft* (1876) 1 C.P.D. 540 at 544; *Conerney* v. *Jacklin* [1985] Crim.L.R. 234.

[43] Although it does not appear in the report at [1985] Crim.L.R. 234 but only in the full transcript; see also *Cassidy* v. *Cunnochie* (1907) 9 F 112 which held that qualified privilege attached to a letter written to the chief constable of a county about the conduct of a police sergeant; see Chap. 10, below at pp. 319 *et seq.*

[44] Criminal Law Act 1967, s.5(7).

[45] See Harrison, "Police Complaints: Pitfalls for the Unwary Litigant" (1985) 136 New L.J. 239.

[46] [1981] 1 Q.B. 736 at 753.

itself could not be tendered as evidence to contradict his answers.[47] Furthermore, the complainant will be asked about his witnesses who will then also be interviewed by the police. These interviews will also be available to the police solicitors in the civil action.

However, initiating a complaint is unlikely to result in a disciplinary hearing before the civil action is concluded. The practice of the Metropolitan Police is to investigate the complaint but then to adjourn any disciplinary hearing until the outcome of the civil action is known.

Nevertheless, it may be said, against a plaintiff who does not complain, that he is under a "civic duty" to bring evidence of police wrongdoing to the attention of the authorities. So it is suggested that a complaint alleging police misconduct should be made—if the circumstances warrant it—when contemplating civil proceedings. The plaintiff's letter before action should state that the allegations made against the police officers should be treated as a complaint against the police but that the plaintiff wishes to pursue his civil claim before co-operating with the complaints investigation.[48] The letter before action must be accompanied by the written consent of the plaintiff that he wishes to make a complaint.[49] Such a letter gives the plaintiff the tactical advantage of saying in court that a complaint has been made but does not produce the tactical disadvantage of giving the police his proof of evidence at an early stage.

[47] Because they are covered by public interest immunity.

[48] As a matter of practice, any disciplinary action resulting from the complaint would be held over until after the determination of the civil action in any event.

[49] Police and Criminal Evidence Act 1984, s.84(4).

3. Practice and Procedure

1. INTRODUCTION

Civil actions against the police are a relatively new field of litigation. Many of the causes of action are difficult and unfamiliar. Nevertheless, the plaintiff will be dealing with police solicitors with considerable experience in the field. Difficult issues arise at every stage of the procedure. Although some of these will be familiar from other areas of litigation, police cases give rise to a number of special problems.

For example, problems with discovery due to the operation of the doctrine of "public interest immunity" may arise. Once an action is underway a plaintiff may be faced with a payment into court. Many police solicitors have evolved sophisticated "payment in" strategies which are difficult to counter because there are considerable problems in the estimation of the likely quantum of damages. Further complications arise at trial because police cases frequently involve civil juries.

2. BEGINNING AN ACTION

Introduction

Despite the very large increase in civil actions against the police over recent years, only a tiny fraction of police activity will give rise to potential civil liability. The large majority of people who are arrested, detained or prosecuted will have no cause of action against the police. Nevertheless, any allegations of excessive force, unreasonable or malicious behaviour by police officers should be carefully considered by legal advisors to discover whether a civil action is potentially available.

Relationship with criminal proceedings against the plaintiff

If the police activity in question led to a prosecution then, in general, it will not be prudent to commence a civil action until the criminal proceedings have been resolved. It is unlikely that civil legal aid will be granted until the resolution of the criminal matters.

The verdict of the criminal court will, of course, have an important bearing on the civil action. An acquittal may be of considerable assistance to the potential plaintiff, especially if the issues involved are similar to those which will be raised in the civil proceedings. A conviction will, in general, be an absolute bar to a malicious prosecution action—although an action may still be possible if an accused was acquitted on part of the indictment or only convicted of a lesser offence.[1]

Although a conviction will not necessarily be a bar to other civil proceedings in, for example, assault or false imprisonment, the plaintiff is not allowed to use civil proceedings to mount a "collateral attack" on the decision of a criminal court. It is a "collateral attack" to bring a civil action which seeks to reopen an issue which has already been decided in a previous criminal trial. Such an action is liable to be struck out as an abuse of the process of the Court.

The limits of this doctrine are unclear. It was, however, given a very wide interpretation by the House of Lords in *Hunter* v. *Chief Constable of West Midlands Police*.[2] The plaintiff brought an action against police officers who he alleged assaulted him in order to obtain confessions in the "Birmingham pub bombings" case. At the plaintiff's trial for murder the issue of the admissibility of the confession was raised and after a trial within a trial the judge held that the confessions had not been obtained by violence. It was held that the civil action should be struck out as an abuse of the process as it was a collateral attack on the decision of the criminal court. The trial judge's ruling on the confession could only be attacked by an appeal to the Court of Appeal (Criminal Division).

Thus, it will be an abuse of the process of the Court to bring a civil action which involves an attack on any **decision** made in the course of a criminal trial. It is submitted, however, that an action should only be struck out if it **necessarily** involves the reopening of a matter which was **expressly decided** by a criminal court. If no express ruling on the issue was made in the course of the criminal trial the civil action should be allowed to proceed. Any doubt should be resolved in the plaintiff's favour.

If, however, a clear decision was made in a criminal case a civil action which directly challenges it will be struck out as a matter of course unless "fresh evidence" has become available. The fresh evidence in question must be such as "entirely changes the aspect of the case."[3]

Relationship with criminal proceedings against the police

In some cases the police misconduct alleged will attract criminal as well as civil liability. At common law, under the rule in *Smith* v. *Selwyn*,[4] a civil

[1] See Chap. 8, below at p. 253.
[2] [1982] A.C. 529.
[3] *Ibid.* at 545C.
[4] [1914] 3 K.B. 98.

action alleging misconduct which amounted to a felony would be stayed until a prosecution had been brought or sufficient reason had been shown why this had not been done. There was no need for an impecunious plaintiff to prosecute a defendant if all the facts had been reported to the police and they had decided not to prosecute.[5] This rule has now been abolished by section 1 of the Criminal Law Act 1967 which abolishes the distinction between felonies and misdemeanours and provides that the law and practice applicable to misdemeanours shall apply to all offences.

A victim of a police assault may wish to bring a private prosecution before a civil action. If such a prosecution is successful section 11 of the Civil Evidence Act 1968 allows the conviction to be pleaded as evidence that the assault in fact took place.[6] It is presumed that the assault took place unless the defendant proves the contrary.[7] In addition, a successful prosecutor who was injured by a police assault will be entitled to compensation under the Criminal Injuries Compensation scheme.[8]

Nevertheless, there are considerable problems with a criminal prosecution of police officers. First, legal aid is not available for private prosecutions and the costs may be substantial, particularly if the offence is an indictable one and the officer in question elects jury trial. Secondly, the high criminal burden of proof means that a conviction is likely to be difficult to obtain unless there is compelling independent evidence of the assault. Thirdly, a prosecution of police officers will, of necessity, involve disclosure of the plaintiff's case to the police and will be of great assistance to them in subsequent civil proceedings. Fourthly, a conviction for common assault may be a bar to subsequent civil proceedings for assault.[9] Finally, although the failure of a prosecution is not a bar to subsequent civil proceedings on the same issue (because of the lower civil burden of proof) the police officer's acquittal may well influence a civil jury in his favour.

Experience shows that juries are extremely reluctant to convict police officers of serious crimes—particularly when the alleged victims are people with criminal records. The result of this is that the Director of Public Prosecutions appears to operate the controversial 50 per cent. rule: he will not institute criminal proceedings against police officers unless he is advised that there is more than a 50 per cent. chance of obtaining a conviction.

It is suggested, therefore, that there will seldom be circumstances in which it will be prudent to commence a private prosecution of a police officer. Nevertheless, if such a prosecution is successful the police will have considerable difficulties challenging the conviction in subsequent civil proceedings. Any defence which involves a "collateral attack" on the findings of a criminal court will be struck out as an abuse of the process of the Court.[10]

If an officer is prosecuted by the Crown Prosecution Service then a plaintiff will, of course, be entitled to rely on any conviction in subsequent civil proceedings. An acquittal or a refusal by the D.P.P. to prosecute will not be a bar to a civil action.

[5] *Oloro* v. *Ali* [1965] 3 All E.R. 829; *Gouldbourne* v. *Magnus* [1959] C.L.Y. 2661.

[6] R.S.C., Ord. 18, r. 17A.

[7] See below at p. 89.

[8] See Donald B. Williams, *Criminal Injuries Compensation.*

[9] See Chap. 4, below at p. 109.

[10] See above at p. 61.

Initial Steps and Complaints

The important first step is to take detailed instructions from the client. It is vital that a full statement be taken as early as possible. The police will have their notes of the events in question and possibly records of interviews with the client as well. Any inconsistencies between these interviews, the pleaded case and the plaintiff's evidence at trial will be harmful to his case. It is also vital to gather "corroborating evidence" at the earliest possible opportunity. In assault cases medical reports will often be required. Photographs of any injuries or property damage should be prepared. Statements should be taken as soon as possible from any available witnesses.[10a]

The question of making a complaint before an action is commenced was discussed in Chapter 2.[11] The first direct contact with the defendant's legal advisers will be a letter before action. This letter should be kept short: only setting out the plaintiff's case in the barest outline. Plaintiffs should avoid becoming involved in protracted correspondence with police solicitors before action as this may involve disclosure of too much of the plaintiff's case. There is a danger of this being taken to be a complaint unless it is drafted in the form suggested.[12]

The next step is the actual commencement of the action. Difficult questions often arise as to the appropriate court in which to begin the action. The plaintiff's advisers must consider the likely quantum of damages recoverable. The county court limit for damages in tort is at present £5,000[13] and a plaintiff who recovers less than £3,000 in the High Court is only entitled to costs on the county court scale. A plaintiff who recovers less than £600 in a High Court action is not entitled to any costs of the action.[14]

The estimation of the likely quantum of damages is an extremely difficult problem in all police cases. As a general rule any claim involving both malicious prosecution and false imprisonment will potentially attract damages of more than the county court limit of £5,000. The quantum of damages in a false imprisonment case is largely dependent on the length of time for which the plaintiff was detained: a detention of more than eight or nine hours could produce an award of damages over the county court limit. If the claim is for assault then normal personal injury principles are the starting point for any assessment of damages. If the police have behaved "outrageously" or "oppressively" an allowance of at least £1,000–1,500 should be made for exemplary damages.[15] If there is any doubt the proceedings should be commenced in the High Court—the case can always be transferred down to the county court at a later stage.

It is important to decide whether to join individual police officers as defendants in a civil action against the police.[15a] By section 48(1) of the Police Act 1964 the chief constable of a particular police force (or, in London, the Metropolitan Police Commissioner) is vicariously liable for torts

[10a] See generally, Harrison, Chap. 2 and Chap. 6, pp. 91–94.

[11] See above at pp. 58 *et seq.*

[12] See above at p. 59.

[13] County Courts Act 1984, s.15.

[14] *Ibid.* s.20.

[15] For a detailed discussion see Chap. 11.

[15a] See generally, John Harrison, "Suing the police: choosing the defendant" [1987] Legal Action 20.

committed by officers under his direction and control as if they were his employees.[16]

A potential action will, therefore, always lie against the Chief Officer of police in respect of the actions of police officers in his area. If the plaintiff is able to ascertain the identity of the police officers involved there will, therefore, be two possible defendants: the individual police officer or officers involved and the Chief Officer.

There are two clear disadvantages in suing the individual officers in relation to the Chief Officer. First, an increase in the number of defendants is likely greatly to increase the difficulties of settling a case. Experience suggests that individual police officers, advised by the Police Federation, are considerably more reluctant to settle than police solicitors' departments. Secondly, if the individual officers are parties to an action then they are entitled to remain in court throughout the trial and an application cannot be made to have them leave court during the plaintiff's case.[17]

On the other hand, there is always the possibility that the Chief Officer may seek to avoid vicarious liability by claiming that the officers were not acting "in the performance or purported performance of their duties." If this point is raised in the Chief Officer's Defence then consideration should be given to joining the individual officers.

If the officers committing the tort were being "lent" by one police force to another under the provisions of section of the Police Act 1964 then, by section 14(3) they are deemed to be under the direction and control of the chief officer to whom they are lent. He is, therefore, the appropriate defendant.

Actions in "warrant" cases

If the police actions which gave rise to the potential civil claim were purportedly done under the authority of a search or arrest warrant then procedural difficulties may arise. A valid warrant provides the police with the defence of lawful justification in respect of actions which would otherwise be tortious. The Constables Protection Act 1750 extends that protection to actions which are "in obedience" to an **invalid** justices' warrant.

If the police actions were done under a warrant then the plaintiff must either comply with the provisions of the 1750 Act or specifically allege in his pleadings that the actions were not done "in obedience" to the warrant in question.

By section 6 of the 1750 Act it is provided that no action shall be brought against any constable for any thing done "in obedience" to a justice's warrant—

> "until demand hath been made or left at the usual place of his abode by the party or parties intending to bring such action, or by his, her, or their attorney or agent, in writing signed by the party demanding the same, of the perusal and copy of such warrant, and the same hath been refused or neglected for the space of six days after such demand; and in case after such demand and compliance therewith, by shewing the said

[16] See Chap. 1 above at pp. 34 *et seq.*

[17] See below at p. 85 n. 68.

warrant to and permitting a copy to be taken thereof by the party demanding the same."

A precedent of such a formal demand can be found in *Atkins Court Forms*.[18]

If an action is brought without such a formal demand being made then it can be struck out as an abuse of the process. If the demand is made and complied with, then the constable (and presumably, the chief constable) will have a complete defence, notwithstanding "any defect of jurisdiction" in the justice who issued the warrant. The section applies to all civil actions with the exception of an action in replevin.[19]

The section only applies to "justices" warrants." Thus, a constable acting under an invalid warrant issued by the Secretary of State,[20] a High Court Judge,[21] or, presumably, a circuit judge, will not be protected.

If the police actions were "in obedience" to the warrant then the plaintiff must make a "formal demand" under section 6. If this demand is substantially complied with[22] then his only course is to bring an action against the justice who issued it. If the demand is not complied with, a civil action can be brought but the warrant can, nevertheless, be pleaded in the police officer's defence. If it can be shown that the officer's actions were done "in obedience" to the warrant then he will have a complete defence to any civil action in relation to them.[23]

Pre-commencement orders

In three special situations discovery of relevant facts and documents can be obtained before the commencement of proceedings. A plaintiff can obtain pre-action discovery in personal injury cases, an order for the inspection of property in any case[24], or an order for discovery against a non-party who has "facilitated" a tort against him.[25]

The most common pre-action applications in police cases are likely to be under R.S.C., Ord. 24, r. 7A. This allows a person whose is "likely to be a party" to a subsequent action in respect of personal injuries or death to apply for an order for discovery against any other person "likely to be party" to that action. This provision is applied in the county court by C.C.R. Ord. 13, r. 7(1)(g).[26] An action for "personal injury or death" has been broadly construed.[27] All that is necessary is that there be some connection or relation between the plaintiff's claim and personal injuries. This would clearly include any action against the police for assault which had resulted

[18] (2nd ed., 1979) Vol. 40, at p. 11.
[19] *Fletcher* v. *Wilkins* (1805) 6 East 283.
[20] *Entick* v. *Carrington* (1765) 2 Wils. 275.
[21] *Gladwell* v. *Blake* (1834) 1 Cr.M. & R. 636.
[22] "substantial compliance" will be sufficient, see *Atkins* v. *Kilby* (1840) 11 Ad. & El. 777.
[23] Except an action for replevin, see above.
[24] R.S.C., Ord. 29, r. 7A.
[25] See *Norwich Pharmacal* v. *Customs & Excise* [1974] A.C. 133 and *B.S.C.* v. *Granada Television Ltd.* [1981] A.C. 1096.
[26] The relevant statutory provisions are Supreme Court Act 1981, s.33 and County Courts Act 1984, s.53.
[27] *Paterson* v. *Chadwick* [1974] 1 W.L.R. 890.

in injury to the plaintiff. "Likely to be" has been construed as "may well be," dependent on the outcome of the discovery application.[28] In the High Court the application is made by originating summons. The potential plaintiff must satisfy the court that the discovery will virtually decide whether litigation would or would not be begun.[29]

It appears that orders for discovery under this provision have been made against the police in a number of unreported cases.[30]

Under R.S.C., Ord. 29, r. 7A the Court may make a pre-action order for the inspection of "property which may become the subject-matter of subsequent proceedings . . . or as to which any question may arise in any such proceedings." In *Taylor* v. *Anderton*[31] the applicant sought pre-action inspection—under R.S.C., Ord. 29, r. 7A—of the documents on the strength of which a search warrant had been granted. Scott J. held that documents were not "property" for the purposes of this rule and that there was no jurisdiction to grant the application. However, he did not wish to hold that the court's inherent jurisdiction to order pre-action discovery "can no longer be invoked." Nevertheless, in the circumstances of that case he ruled that public interest immunity attached to the documents in question because a decision whether or not to prosecute the applicant was imminent. The question of whether there is an inherent jurisdiction to obtain pre-action discovery of the documents behind a search warrant if a decision not to prosecute has already been made, therefore remains open.

3. THE PLEADINGS

Introduction

Pleadings are a key part of any civil action and it is important to have them in order at an early stage. If facts are not properly pleaded then the plaintiff should not be allowed to raise them at the trial of the action. This rule is more honoured in the breach, especially in the county court, but it still provides a dangerous trap for the unwary. Although the court has wide discretion to allow amendments these may be refused at a late stage and the plaintiff may well find himself debarred from raising important issues. Lord Edmund-Davies has summarised the position as follows:

> "pleadings continue to play an essential part in civil actions, and although there has been since the Civil Procedure Act 1833, a wide power to permit amendment, circumstances may arise where the grant of permission would work injustice or, at least, necessitate an adjournment which may prove particularly unfortunate in trials with a jury. To shrug off a criticism as "a mere pleading point" is therefore bad law and bad practice. For the primary purpose of pleadings remains and it can still prove of vital importance. The purpose is to define the issues and

[28] *Dunning* v. *United Liverpool Hospitals Board* [1973] 1 W.L.R. 586 at 590E.

[29] *Shaw* v. *Vauxhall Motors* [1974] 1 W.L.R. 1035.

[30] *E.g.*, *Mason* v. *Chief Constable of Essex* (1986) October 2, Southend County Court, unreported.

[31] *The Times*, October 21, 1986; see also, *Huddleston* v. *Control Risks Ltd.* [1987] 1 W.L.R. 701.

thereby to inform the parties in advance of the case they have to meet and so enable them to take steps to deal with it."[32]

The Statement of Claim—pleading the causes of action

The Statement of Claim must set out all the material facts on which the plaintiff intends to rely. Which facts are "material" depends on the cause of action involved. In some cases the burden of proof is entirely on the plaintiff. In others, once the plaintiff has raised the basic facts the burden shifts onto the defendant to justify his conduct.

An essential element in almost all police cases will be the vicarious liability of the Chief Officer of Police for the actions of his police constables. The Chief Officer of Police will often be the only defendant. It should be specifically pleaded that the defendant was, at all material times, the Chief Officer of Police for a particular area. The tortious acts should then be pleaded—either as the acts of a named individual, a police constable, or simply as the acts of "a police constable." Vicarious liability is then established by pleading that: "The said police constable was at all material times under the direction and control of the defendant in the performance or purported performance of his functions."

If the officers were being "lent" by one district to another, the "borrowing" chief officer is liable for their torts.[33] This should be specifically pleaded. If the officer involved in the matter has been convicted of a relevant criminal offence then this should be specifically pleaded. The statement of claim must give particulars of the offence involved, the court which made the conviction and the date on which it was made. If it is not obvious the statement of claim should state the issue in the case to which the conviction is relevant.[34]

The following pleading points should be noted in relation to the main causes of action which are likely to relevant in police cases[35]:

(1) *"Assault and battery."* In an action for assault and battery the Statement of Claim should allege that the conduct complained of was "intentional," otherwise it is possible that it will be struck out as disclosing no cause of action.[36] If, however, the act "speaks for itself as being plainly intentional, wilful or deliberate" then it will not be necessary to specifically allege that it was "intentional."[37] If, for example, the plaintiff's case is that he was struck repeatedly by a police officer with a truncheon then it is clear that such an act must have been "intentional" in the required sense. It is not necessary to plead that the **infliction of injury** was intentional.[38] It may be necessary to plead that a particular assault was "hostile."[39] The plaintiff may be ordered to give particulars of the facts on which he relies to show

[32] *Farrell* v. *Secretary of State for Defence* [1980] 1 W.L.R. 172 at 180A–B.
[33] Police Act 1964, s.14(3).
[34] See R.S.C., Ord. 18, r. 7A; C.C.R., Ord., r. 9.
[35] For pleading other causes of action see *Atkins Court Forms* (2nd ed.).
[36] See *Fowler* v. *Lanning* [1959] 1 Q.B. 426; see also Chap. 4 below at p. 107.
[37] *Bullen Leake & Jacob's Precedents of Pleadings* at p. 224.
[38] See *Wilson* v. *Pringle* [1987] Q.B. 237.
[39] *Ibid.*

that the acts alleged were intentional.[40] Matters relied on as aggravating the injury must be specifically pleaded.[41]

(2) *"False imprisonment."* It is not necessary to plead facts relied on in support of a claim that the detention was unlawful because, once a detention is alleged, the burden of proving it was lawful shifts to the defendant. The plaintiff only need plead that he was "unlawfully detained" by police officers (either particular named officers or, if the identities of the officers involved is not known, by "police constables"), at a particular place for a particular period of time. There are, however, three situations in which it will be appropriate for a plaintiff to plead specific facts in a false imprisonment case. First, if the claim is that an arrest was not lawfully made then the relevant facts should be pleaded. For the sake of clarity in the pleading this could be pleaded as a "wrongful arrest."[42] Secondly, if it is admitted that the initial detention was lawful, but is alleged that it later became unlawful because, for example the period of time involved was excessive, then this should be specifically pleaded. Thirdly, if it is claimed that the detention of a lawfully arrested plaintiff became unlawful by reason of some failure to comply with the relevant provisions of the Police and Criminal Evidence Act 1984[43] then the relevant facts should be specifically pleaded.

(3) *"Malicious prosecution."* The tort of malicious prosecution involves five elements, all of which must be specifically pleaded. These are as follows:

(a) that there was a prosecution which was initiated or continued by the defendant;
(b) that the prosecution terminated in the plaintiff's favour;
(c) that the defendant acted maliciously;
(d) that the defendant acted without reasonable or probable cause for the prosecution and;
(e) that the prosecution caused the plaintiff loss and damage.

If any of these elements are not specifically alleged then the Statement of Claim is liable to be stuck out as disclosing no reasonable cause of action. The plaintiff may be ordered to give particulars of malice under R.S.C., Ord. 18, r. 12(1)(*b*).

(4) *"Trespass to land."* The essential element to be pleaded are, first the plaintiff's entitlement to possession of the land in question and secondly, the acts of the defendant which are alleged to constitute the trespass, for example, wrongfully entering or remaining on the land.

(5) *"Interference with Goods."* In an action for trespass to goods or conversion, the writ (and presumably the Statement of Claim) must contain a statement showing the value of the goods in question.[44] The goods must be described with sufficient detail in order to enable them to be identified by

[40] R.S.C., Ord. 18, r. 12(1)(*b*); see below at p. 72.
[41] See below at p. 69.
[42] See Chap. 4 below at p. 115.
[43] See Chap. 5 below at p. 165.
[44] R.S.C., Ord. 6, r. 2(1)(*d*).

the defendant. The Statement of Claim should state the acts which are said to constitute the trespass or conversion.

(6) *"Misfeasance in a public office."* This involves four elements. The Statement of Claim should, therefore, allege:

(a) that the defendant was a "public officer";
(b) that he "misconducted himself in his office," in that he **either**, knowingly acted knowing that he had no power to do so, **or** he maliciously abused his office (particulars of malice should be given);
(c) that it was foreseeable that the plaintiff would be injured by this misconduct; and
(d) that, as a result of it, the plaintiff was caused damage.

The Statement of Claim—pleading damages

The plaintiff does not have to give particulars of any "general damages" beyond the facts relied on as the basis of his general damages claim. Thus, it is sufficient, in an assault and battery case to give particulars of the injuries caused. On the basis of those injuries the court will award general damages for pain, suffering and loss of amenity. Similarly, in false imprisonment or malicious prosecution, once the detention or the prosecution is pleaded the court can award damages for loss of liberty, damage to reputation and so on without further details being given. The plaintiff will never be ordered to give particulars of general damage.[45] Nevertheless, it is advisable specifically to plead anything which makes the injury or damage to the plaintiff worse than it might otherwise have been. If the damage claimed is of a kind which is not a necessary and immediate consequence of the tort alleged then particulars of the nature and extent of the damage should be pleaded so as to inform the defendant of the case which he has to meet.[46] Thus, for example, if it is claimed that the plaintiff suffered nervous shock as a result of a wrongful arrest, this should be specifically pleaded. The plaintiff should also plead particulars of any unusual circumstances leading to future losses.[47] The Rules of Court also specify a number of other matters relating to damages which must be specifically pleaded.

(1) *Aggravated damages.* If the plaintiff intends to rely on any circumstances of aggravation then these should be pleaded. These can cover matters such as the defendant's conduct or motives and the circumstances in which the tort took place. Thus, for example, if a wrongful arrest is accompanied by racial or sexual abuse, if it happens publically in front of a large number of people, these will all be circumstances of aggravation. A failure by the defendant to acknowledge that a detention was unlawful or that a

[45] *London & Northern Bank Ltd.* v. *Newnes* (1900) 16 T.L.R. 433.

[46] *Perestrello e Companhia* v. *United Paint Co. Ltd.* [1969] 1 W.L.R. 570—failure to plead loss of profit in a breach of contract case meant that this could not be recovered.

[47] *Domsalla* v. *Barr* [1969] 1 W.L.R. 630.

prosecution was baseless will also aggravate the damages payable to the plaintiff.[48]

(2) *Exemplary damages.* In the High Court a claim for exemplary damages must be specifically pleaded "together with the facts on which the party pleading relies."[49] Thus, exemplary damages should be claimed in the body of the Statement of Claim and not just in the prayer and the facts relied on to show that the police conduct was "arbitrary, oppressive or unconstitutional" should be set out. It has been held that, in the county court, it is not necessary to plead exemplary damages specifically[50]: this also applies in cases involving the police.[51]

(3) *Special damage.* "Quantifiable pre-trial pecuniary loss" must be specifically pleaded otherwise the plaintiff will not be allowed to give evidence of it at trial.[52] Thus any damage to property, loss of earnings, expenses or obtaining a release from custody, should be set out in the Statement of Claim. If the action involves a claim for loss of earnings then the plaintiff should disclose any benefits accrued in his pleadings.[53]

(4) *Interest.* Interest must be specifically pleaded in the body of the Statement of Claim[54] and in the prayer. The statute under which the interest is being claimed should be pleaded. These rules also apply in the county court.[55] In the case of *Ward* v. *Chief Constable of Avon & Somerset*[56] a claim for interest which was not specifically pleaded was disallowed by the Court of Appeal. Interest is recoverable on damages for false imprisonment or malicious prosecution.[56a]

The defence

The plaintiff's case should be set out in the Statement of Claim with sufficient particularity to enable the defendant to know what allegations he has to meet.

The function of the defence is to set out the case which the defendant will seek to establish at trial. Under R.S.C., Ord. 18, r. 8(1), it is provided that:

> "A party must in any pleading subsequent to a statement of claim plead specifically any matter, for example, performance, release, any relevant statute of limitation, fraud or any fact showing illegality . . .
> (b) which, if not specifically pleaded might take the opposite party by surprise; or
> (c) which raises issues of fact not arising out of the preceding pleading."

[48] See Chap. 11 below at p. 344.
[49] R.S.C., Ord. 18, r. 3.
[50] *Drane* v. *Evangelou* [1978] 1 W.L.R. 455.
[51] *Bryning* v. *Oxford* [1983] C.A. Transcript 847.
[52] *Ilkiw* v. *Samuels* [1963] 1 W.L.R. 991 at 1006, *per* Diplock L.J.
[53] *Cheeseman* v. *Bowaters United Kingdom Paper Mills Ltd.* [1971] 1 W.L.R. 1773.
[54] R.S.C., Ord. 18, r. 8(4).
[55] C.C.R., Ord. 6, r. 1A.
[56] *The Times*, July 17, 1985.
[56a] See *Holtham* v. *M.P.C.* (1986) December 15, unreported, in which Peter Pain J. awarded interest on false imprisonment damages after hearing argument on the point.

Thus if the police are seeking to rely on the defence of "lawful justification" this must be specifically pleaded. According to the *Supreme Court Practice*:

> "When a defendant seeks to justify a prima facie unlawful act, he must show his authority or excuse with precision. If he seeks to justify his act by a warrant . . . he must state the date and nature of the document and name the person who signed or otherwise issued it . . . "[57]

It is important to note that the effect of Ord. 18, r. 8(1)(*c*) is that if the defendant wishes to raise any new issue of fact this must be pleaded in the defence. A simple denial will not allow the defendant to raise any positive case at trial. If, on a particular issue, defendants simply deny a plaintiff's case and put him to proof—

> "it is not even permissible for them to proceed to put forward some affirmative case which they had not pleaded or alleged; and it is not, therefore, right that they should, by cross-examination of the plaintiffs or otherwise, suggest such an affirmative case."[58]

If there is any doubt as to whether the defence, as pleaded, raises any positive case, this can be resolved by a Request for Particulars. It should be borne in mind, however, that the effect of such a request may be simply to put the defendant on notice of defects in his case which he can then remedy. If such defects only emerge at trial it may be too late for them to be corrected.

Requests for Particulars

The Request for Further and Better Particulars is a key part of any civil action. The function of particulars is described in *The Supreme Court Practice*[59] as follows:

> "(1) to inform the other side of the nature of the case they have to meet as distinguished from the mode in which that case is to be proved . . .
> (2) to prevent the other side being taken by surprise at the trial . . .
> (3) to enable the other side to know what evidence they ought to be prepared with and to prepare for trial . . .
> (4) to limit the generality of the pleadings . . . or of the claim or the evidence . . .
> (5) to limit and define the issues to be tried, and as to which discovery is required . . .
> (6) to tie the hands of the party so that he cannot without leave go into any matters not included . . . But if the opponent omits to ask for particulars, evidence may be given which supports any material allegation in the pleadings."

Thus, a properly formulated Request for Particulars can force the defendant to set out his case in some detail. Once this is done, the defendant is then tied to the case as particularised. The same principles, of course, apply to the plaintiff. In many civil cases, therefore, considerable tactical manoeuvring takes place with each side trying to give as little detail as possible of

[57] 1988, 18/12/17.
[58] *per* Lord Evershed M.R., *Regina Fur Co. Ltd.* v. *Bossom* [1958] 2 Lloyd's Rep. 425 at 428.
[59] 1988 ed., para. 18/12/2—we have omitted the authorities cited in support of these propositions.

their own case while tying the other side down to as much detail as possible.

Particulars of the Statement of Claim will not be ordered before the Defence has been served unless "in the opinion of the court, the order is necessary or desirable to enable the defendant to plead or for some other special reason."[60]

The usual practice is to serve a formal "Request for Particulars" setting out the paragraphs of the pleading required to be particularised and the particulars being asked for. If such a request is not complied with then an application can be made for particulars to be ordered under R.S.C., Ord. 18, r. 12(3) or C.C.R., Ord. 6, r. 7 (further particulars of claim) or C.C.R., Ord. 9, r. 11 (particulars of defence).

The particulars to which a party is entitled are partly dependent on the Rules of Court and partly dependent on case law. The position in the High Court is governed by R.S.C., Ord. 18, r. 12. If either party alleges any condition of mind, except knowledge, than particulars must be given "of the facts on which the party relies" as establishing that condition of mind.[61] Thus, if a plaintiff alleges malice or an intentional act then particulars must be given. Similarly, if a defendant sets up the defence of "lawful justification" in circumstances which require that a constable believed something on reasonable grounds then particulars must be given of the facts which are relied on as establishing the belief.

It has been held that, when the defence raised is that the defendant had reasonable cause for suspecting that an offence had been committed he must give particulars of the alleged offence and or the cause for suspicion, but not of the names of those who had provided the information.[62] Where "knowledge or notice" is alleged then the court **may** order particulars of the facts relied on.[63] When a plaintiff simply alleges that a detention was "unlawful" the defendant is not entitled to particulars of "unlawfulness' because the burden of showing that the detention was "lawful" is on the defendant.[64]

A defendant does not have to give particulars of a simple denial. This principle was applied in the police case of *Stapeley* v. *Annetts*[65] when the allegation was of malicious prosecution and the Defence simply denied that there was a lack of reasonable and probable cause. The Court of Appeal refused to order particulars of this denial. If, however, a denial, though negative in form "is pregnant with an affirmative"—for example, a denial that an officer did not give reasons for an arrest—then particulars of this affirmative must be given.[66] A failure to give particulars of a pregnant negative will render it liable to be struck out as embarrassing.[67] If there is any doubt whether a denial is a pregnant negative or not then, to force the defendant to "pin his colours to the mast," the following form of request has been suggested:

[60] R.S.C., Ord. 18, r. 12(5).
[61] R.S.C., Ord. 18, r. 12(1)(*b*).
[62] *Green* v. *Garbutt* (1912) 28 T.L.R. 575.
[63] R.S.C., Ord. 18, r. 12(4).
[64] See Chap. 4 below at p. 121.
[65] [1970] 1 W.L.R. 20.
[66] *per* Stable J., *Pinson* v. *Lloyd's & National Provincial Foreign Bank Ltd.* [1941] 2 K.B. 72 at 85.
[67] *Ibid.* at 88.

"Stating with the particularity with which the plaintiff will be met at the trial, the substance of the defendant's factual case and without prejudice to the generality thereof, further stating:
(*a*) Whether the defendant intends to make any affirmative allegations at trial, and
(*b*) If yes, particularising the same."[68]

4. DISCOVERY

What is discoverable?

Within 14 days of the close of pleadings in a High Court action each party must make and serve: "a list of the documents which are or have been in his possession, custody or power relating to any matter in question between them in the action."[69]

It is important to note that **all** documents must be included on the list—even if they are no longer in the possession, custody or power of the party or if privilege is claimed for them. The list should give a complete picture of all the relevant documents that a party has ever had, whatever their nature.

The category of "relevant" documents is extremely wide. The classic definition is that it includes any document which it is reasonable to suppose "contains information which may enable the party to advance his own case or to damage that of his adversary" or which might fairly lead him to a train of inquiry which may have either of these consequences.[70] Thus, there is no need for the document to have immediate relevance to the case if it "might" lead to inquiries which "may" help the party who is seeking discovery. On the other hand, discovery cannot be used for a mere "fishing expedition."[71]

It is submitted that (subject to questions of privilege)[72] other complaints against an officer in a particular case are relevant and discoverable. Thus, in the personal injury case of *Board* v. *Hedley (Thomas) Co. Ltd.*[73] the plaintiff complained that she had suffered dermatitis as a result of using the defendant's product "Tide." It was held that letters of complaint from other purchasers were relevant because "they may fairly lead to a train of inquiry enabling the plaintiff to advance her case" and should, therefore, be disclosed.[74] Similarly, any documents relating to an officer's involvement in other civil actions against the police will be discoverable.

A tape recording which records relevant information or evidence is a

[68] Iain S. Goldrein, "Personal Injury Litigation: How to Keep the Plaintiff in the Saddle—III" (1986) 136 New L.J. 147 at 150.
[69] R.S.C., Ord. 24, r. 2(1).
[70] *Compagnie Financiere* v. *Peruvian Guano Co.* (1882) 11 Q.B.D. 55.
[71] See *Barham* v. *Lord Huntingfield* [1913] 2 K.B. 193; *Gaskin* v. *Liverpool City Council* [1980] 1 W.L.R. 1549.
[72] See Chap. 2 above at pp. 53 *et seq.*
[73] [1951] 2 All E.R. 431.
[74] *Ibid.* at 432H; see also *Marshall* v. *Goulston Discount (Northern) Ltd.* [1967] Ch. 72.

"document" and must be disclosed on discovery.[75] Personal diaries and other notes are discoverable. A document is discoverable whether or not it is admissible in evidence.[76]

Privilege in police cases

Although discovery must be given of **all** relevant documents a party can object to the production for inspection of certain documents on the ground that they are "privileged." If a claim to privilege is to be made the **existence** of the documents in question is made known to the other side but it is indicated that privilege is being claimed. If the claim to privilege is successful then, unless the privilege is waived, the other party is not entitled to see the documents in question. There are four types of privilege which may be relevant in police cases:

(1) *Legal professional privilege.* Communications between a client and his legal advisors are privileged from disclosure if they are made in relation to the giving of legal advice. This applies to communications with salaried legal advisors such as police solicitors departments.[77] The privilege also covers communications with third parties provided these are "for the purposes" of actual or contemplated litigation. There must, however, be a "definite prospect" of such litigation[78] but it is not essential that a cause of action has arisen.[79] The "dominant purpose" of the communication must be the seeking of advice for the contemplated litigation.[80] Thus, reports of internal police investigations into particular police actions will only attract legal professional privilege if the main purpose of bringing them into existence was an actual or contemplated civil action. Any statements or reports made before litigation was contemplated will not be privileged under this head. The privilege does not attach to a communication which is "intended to facilitate or to guide the client in the commission of a crime or fraud."[80a]

The privilege is that of the client and not of the legal advisor. It may be waived by the client either expressly or by implication. Waiver may be implied, for example, from the use of the document in cross-examination,[81] or from the disclosure of part of a document on discovery[82] or by counsel in open court.[83] The mistaken inclusion of a privileged document in a list for inspection can be corrected at any time until inspection actually takes place, but not afterwards.[84] Where one party to an action has obtained docu-

[75] *Grant* v. *Southwestern Properties* [1975] Ch. 185.

[76] *O'Rourke* v. *Darbishire* [1920] A.C. 581.

[77] *Crompton (Alfred) Amusement Machines Ltd.* v. *Customs & Excise Commissioners (No. 2)* [1974] A.C. 405.

[78] *Ibid.*

[79] *Bristol Corp.* v. *Cox* (1884) 26 Ch.D. 678.

[80] *Waugh* v. *British Railways Board* [1980] A.C. 521.

[80a] *R.* v. *Cox and Railton* (1884) 14 Q.B.D. 153; see also, *Chandler* v. *Church, The Independent,* April 30, 1987.

[81] *Nea Karteria Maritime Co.* v. *Atlantic & Great Lakes Steamship Co. (No. 2)* [1981] Com.L.R. 138.

[82] *Pozzie* v. *Eli Lilly & Co., The Times,* December 3, 1986.

[83] *Great Atlantic Insurance* v. *Home Insurance* [1981] 1 W.L.R. 529.

[84] *Re Briamore* [1986] 3 All E.R. 132.

ments covered by legal professional privilege which belong to another party, an injunction will be granted to restrain the use of information derived from the documents whether or not they were improperly obtained.[85]

(2) *Privilege against self-incrimination.* No one is bound to answer any question or produce any document or thing which would have a tendency to expose him to any criminal charge which is reasonably likely to be preferred.[86] It is possible that this privilege could be invoked by individual police officers when there is an allegation, such as an assault, which could possibly lead to criminal proceedings.

(3) *Public interest immunity.* The basis of the modern law in this area—which is sometimes known as Crown Privilege—is to be found in the police case of *Conway* v. *Rimmer.*[87] This involved a malicious prosecution action by a former probationary police officer against a police superintendent. The Home Secretary objected to the production of probationary reports about the plaintiff and a report for the D.P.P. about the alleged offence on the grounds of Crown Privilege. This claim of privilege was rejected by the House of Lords. The test to be applied to decide whether a particular document should not be disclosed in the public interest is: "whether the withholding of a document because it belongs to a particular class is really necessary for the proper functioning of the public service."[88]

The present police practice in relation to public interest immunity claims was laid down by the Lord Chancellor in 1962 who announced two important changes.

> "The first is that privilege will not be claimed in proceedings for malicious prosecution, wrongful arrest and other proceedings against the police where the justification for the prosecution, arrest or other police action is at issue in the proceedings, unless the disclosure of the statement would reveal the identity of a police informer. The second modification relates to the manner of claiming privilege for statements made to the police. The claim of privilege will still be made on the ground of public interest, but it is proposed that in future the claim should be made without a Minister's certificate or affidavit and that the court should be left to decide, having regard to the principles laid down in the cases whether the statements should be produced."[88a]

Public interest immunity covers anything which might be material in a pending prosecution. This immunity continues to apply until either the decision not to proceed with the prosecution or the end of the criminal trial.[89] If there is unreasonable delay in making the decision to prosecute then a continuation of the immunity may no longer be justified.[90]

[85] See *English & American Insurance* v. *Herbert Smith & Co.* (1987) 137 New L.J. 148.

[86] *per* Goddard L.J., *Blunt* v. *Park Lane Hotel Ltd.* [1942] 2 K.B. 253 at 257.

[87] [1968] A.C. 910.

[88] *per* Lord Reid, *ibid.* at 952G.

[88a] Viscount Kilmuir, H.L. Deb. Vol. 237, No. 46, cols. 1191–1192, March 8, 1962; see Harrison at pp. 18–19.

[89] *Conway* v. *Rimmer* [1968] A.C. 910 at 953–954, *per* Lord Reid; *IRC* v. *Rossminster* [1980] A.C. 952 at 1012, *per* Lord Diplock.

[90] *IRC* v. *Rossminster* [1980] A.C. 952 at 1012; see also *per* Scott J. in *Taylor* v. *Anderton, The Times*, October 21, 1986; October 16, 1986; Transcript: D Sellers.

If the police carry out an investigation for the sole purpose of investigating a police complaint then the documents so obtained are covered by public interest immunity.[91] However, the complaint itself is not privileged.[92] If the investigation is made for more than one purpose then public interest immunity will only apply if the investigation of the complaint is the "dominant purpose."[93] This area is discussed in detail in Chapter 2.

If an issue of public interest immunity arises, the procedure to be followed is a four stage one:

(a) the court must determine whether the claim for immunity is, *prima facie* a valid one. If it is valid, then;

(b) the court must determine whether the party seeking production of the document can show that the public interest in the administration of justice requires its production. It must be shown that the document is discoverable, that is, that it is relevant and would assist the case of the party claiming production;

(c) the judge should then compare the two public interests. If there is a doubt about the immunity or he is in favour of disclosure then;

(d) he should inspect the documents in question to make the final decision.[94]

(4) *Informer immunity.* It has long been accepted that "in a public prosecution a witness cannot be asked such questions as will disclose the identity of the informer.[95] The exact nature of this immunity is unclear. It extends to the identity of premises used for surveillance.[96] It may cover the actual information provided by an informer as well as the identity of the informer himself.[97] This information may not be disclosed in any subsequent civil action.[98] It is likely that the immunity will apply to all informers who furnish information to the police in the course of the performance of their duties, whether or not a "public prosecution" results.[99] The New Zealand case of *Tipene* v. *Apperley*[1] suggested a distinction between "informers" and ordinary witnesses:

> "A member of the public making a statement to the police in the course of a criminal investigation usually expects and is expected to give evidence at the trial if anyone is charged . . . He is not an informer whose identity must be kept secret at all costs."

It is submitted that this distinction is also applicable in English law. Thus, in a civil action, the police would not be able to rely on this immunity to

[91] See *Neilson* v. *Laugharne* [1981] Q.B. 736.

[92] *Conerney* v. *Jacklin* (1985) Crim.L.R. 234.

[93] *Peach* v. *M.P.C.* [1986] Q.B. 1064.

[94] See *Air Canada* v. *Secretary of State for Trade (No. 2)* [1983] 2 A.C. 394 at 398–9, *per* Bingham J.

[95] *Att.-Gen.* v. *Briant* (1846) 15 M.&W. 164, at 185; *Marks* v. *Beyfus* (1890) 25 Q.B.D. 494.

[96] *R* v. *Rankine* [1986] Q.B. 861.

[97] *Marks* v. *Beyfus* (1890) 25 Q.B.D. 494 at 498, *per* Lord Esher M.R.

[98] *D* v. *N.S.P.C.C.* [1978] A.C. 171 at 218C, *per* Lord Diplock; see also *Solicitor-General of Canada* v. *Royal Commission* (1981) 128 D.L.R. (3d) 193; Supreme Court of Canada.

[99] See *Solicitor-General of Canada* v. *Royal Commission*, above at 224–225.

[1] (1978) 1 N.Z.L.R. 761 at 767.

justify a refusal to disclose the identity or the information given by "ordinary witnesses" which were given in relation to criminal investigations.

This "immunity" is different from "public interest immunity" and need not actually be claimed by the police.[2] The judge should prevent such information being disclosed and has no discretion to allow its disclosure in civil cases.[3]

Interrogatories and Notices to Admit

Interrogatories are usually requested at the Summons for Directions or Pre-Trial Review stage. Interrogatories may be asked in relation to any matter which is in question in the action. In other words, they can be asked about: "any facts the existence or non-existence of which is relevant to the existence or non-existence of the facts directly in issue."[4]

They must be asked in relation to facts, not to evidence.[5] In general "fishing interrogatories" are not allowed and interrogatories should be confined to facts which there is some reason to think are true.[6]

Interrogatories will only be allowed if they are "necessary either for disposing fairly of the cause or matter or for saving costs."[7] They will not, therefore, be allowed where it is clear that no admission will be obtained or where the admission of fact required can be proved by a witness who will be called in any event.[8] Whether or not interrogatories are allowed is a matter of discretion.[9]

The party interrogated must answer to the best of his knowledge, information and belief after making all necessary inquiries of his servants or agents.[10] He may object to answering on the ground of privilege in his answer to the interrogatories.[11] If his answers are insufficient the court may order further answers either by affidavit or oral examination.[12]

In a malicious prosecution case the defendant can administer interrogatories on circumstances which relate to reasonable and probable causes on all matters which are relevant and which the party interrogated would be bound to answer if in the witness box.[13] On the other hand, in the absence of special circumstances, interrogatories asking for the defendant's sources of information will not be allowed.[14]

The purpose of a Notice to Admit facts is to narrow the areas of factual dispute between parties to a civil action in order save costs at trial. A notice to admit may be served at any point up to trial without the leave of the

[2] *Bisaillon* v. *Keable* (1983) 2 D.L.R. (4th) 193 at 222.
[3] *Marks* v. *Beyfus* (1890) 25 Q.B.D. 494.
[4] *per* Lord Esher M.R., *Marriott* v. *Chamberlain* (1886) 17 Q.B.D. 154 at 163.
[5] See above at note 4.
[6] *The Supreme Court Practice* 1988, para. 26/1/3.
[7] *Ibid.* para. 26/1/4.
[8] *Griebart* v. *Morris* [1920] 1 K.B. 659.
[9] *Codd* v. *Delap* [1906] W.N. 57.
[10] *Anderson* v. *Bank of Columbia* (1876) 2 Ch.D. 644.
[11] R.S.C., Ord. 26, r. 4.
[12] R.S.C., Ord. 26, r. 5.
[13] *Zychlinski* v. *Maltby* (1861) 10 C.B.N.S. 838.
[14] *Maas* v. *Gas Light & Coke Co.* [1911] 2 K.B. 543.

court. Such a Notice specifies the fact or facts, the admission of which is required. Any admission is made for the purposes of the action only.[15] If the admission is refused and the matter is subsequently proved at trial then the party who refused to admit it will bear the costs of proving it, whatever the outcome of the trial.[16]

Notices to Admit can be of considerable tactical value in putting pressure on defendants to give serious consideration to weaknesses in their case, or face costs penalties.

5. GENERAL INTERLOCUTORY MATTERS

Introduction

Once the pleadings are closed directions must be given for the further progress of the action. In the High Court this is done at the hearing of a "Summons for Directions,"[17] in the county court there is a "Pre-Trial Review."[18] The following areas for directions will commonly arise:

(1) discovery, inspection and interrogatories;
(2) transfer to another court;
(3) further and better particulars and amendment;
(4) orders relating to the preservation of property;
(5) expert evidence;
(6) directions for trial.

Discovery, inspection and interrogatories have already been considered.

If an action is commenced in the High Court the court can, either of its own motion or on the application of any party to the proceedings, order the transfer of the whole or part of any High Court proceedings to the county court under section 40 of the County Courts Act 1984. This can be done if the parties consent; or if the amount recoverable is within the county court limit or if:

> "the High Court considers that the proceedings are not likely to raise any important question of law or fact and are suitable for determination by a County Court."

The third of these grounds enables the High Court to transfer actions which involve claims over the county court limit if they are legally and factually straightforward. Assault claims against the police may well be transferred on the this ground. Malicious prosecution or false imprisonment cases are often not "legally straightforward" and should not, it is submitted, be transferred under this head.

Under section 42 of the County Courts Act 1984 the county court may order the transfer of the whole or part of proceedings to the High Court if:

(1) the court considers that some important question of law or fact is likely to arise; or

[15] See generally R.S.C., Ord. 27, r. 2: C.C.R., Ord. 20, r. 2.
[16] R.S.C., Ord. 62, r. 6(7).
[17] R.S.C., Ord. 25.
[18] C.C.R., Ord. 17.

(2) the court considers that the plaintiff is likely to be entitled to a sum exceeding the amount recoverable in the county court; or
(3) any counterclaim involves matters beyond the jurisdiction of the county court.

An application for such a transfer should be made to the registrar of the county court, on notice.

At the Summons for Directions (or Pre-Trial Review) an order can be made for the supply of Further and Better Particulars which have not been supplied voluntarily. As Requests for Further and Better Particulars almost invariably ask for particulars to which the party is not, in fact, entitled, such an order should never be agreed by consent unless subject to the proviso that only those particulars which counsel advises should be given will be supplied. If a plaintiff does consent to a Request for Particulars he waives his right to argue that the defendant is not entitled to some of the particulars requested.[19]

If the discovery given by the police is not adequate then further discovery can be sought at the Directions stage. The plaintiff may make an application for specific discovery under R.S.C., Ord. 24, r. 7. This should be supported by an affidavit describing the document or class of documents discovery of which is being sought and stating reasonable grounds for believing the document or class of documents is relevant and is likely to be or have been in the defendant's possession, custody or power. If a sufficient case has been made out then an order may be made that the defendant file an affidavit stating whether or not he has the document or class of documents in question.

Interrogatories will usually be requested at the Directions stage.[20]

If orders for the preservation and inspection of property have not already been dealt with then they should be determined at the Directions stage.

Under R.S.C., Ord. 29, r. 9, a plaintiff can make an application for an "interim payment" on account of any damages which a defendant may be held liable to pay at trial. Interim payments are available in the county court where the sum claimed is more than £500.[21] Such payments are most unlikely in police cases.

Expert evidence

Unless the court gives leave, or all the parties agree, expert evidence cannot be adduced at trial.[22] These rules apply in both High Court and county court cases.[23] An application for leave to adduce expert evidence will usually be made at the Summons for Directions or Pre-Trial Review stage. The rules distinguish between "personal injury actions" and "other actions."

[19] *Fearis* v. *Davies, The Times,* June 5, 1986.
[20] See above at p. 77.
[21] C.C.R., Ord. 13, r. 12.
[22] R.S.C., Ord. 38, r. 36.
[23] C.C.R., Ord. 20, r. 27.

In personal injury actions there is, in effect, a presumption in favour of disclosure of expert evidence, so that: "unless the Court considers that there is sufficient reason for not doing so, it shall direct that the substance of the evidence be disclosed in the form of a written report or reports.[24]

The court may, if it thinks fit, treat the following circumstances as sufficient reasons for not giving such direction, namely,

> "that the expert evidence may contain an expression of opinion—
> (i) as to the manner in which the personal injuries were sustained; or
> (ii) as to the genuineness of the symptoms of which the complaint is made."[25]

In assault cases the police may well seek to resist disclosure on the first of these two grounds. A plaintiff should also give consideration to resisting disclosure on this ground.

In other actions the burden is on the party seeking disclosure to show that this is "desirable" to direct that the substance of any expert evidence be disclosed in the form of a written report.[26] In deciding whether to give such a direction the Court must have regard to all the circumstances and may treat any of the following circumstances as affording a sufficient reason for not giving such a direction:

> "(a) that the expert evidence is or will be based to any material extent upon a version of the facts in dispute between the parties; or
> (b) that the expert evidence is or will be based to any material extent upon facts which are neither—
> (i) ascertainable by the expert by the exercise of his own powers of observation, nor
> (ii) within his general professional knowledge and experience."[27]

In practice, the court should normally make an order for the exchange of non-medical experts' reports.[28] If there are "technical issues" in a case it is now "axiomatic" that "all cards be on the table" before the trial begins.[29]

When the court takes the view that only part of the evidence should not be disclosed then it may direct disclosure of the remainder.[30]

Directions for trial—judge or jury?

False imprisonment and malicious prosecution are among the rare civil actions which are still regularly tried by jury. In the High Court an application for trial by jury must be made before the place and mode of trial is

24 R.S.C., Ord. 38, r. 37(2).
25 R.S.C., Ord. 37, r. 37(3).
26 R.S.C., Ord. 38, r. 38(1).
27 R.S.C., Ord. 38, r. 38(2).
28 *Ollett* v. *Bristol Aerojet Ltd.* [1979] 1 W.L.R. 1197.
29 *per* Mustill L.J., *Wilsher* v. *Essex A.H.A.* [1986] 3 All E.R. 801 at 830f.
30 R.S.C., Ord. 38, r. 39.

fixed.[31] In the county court the application may be made at any time before the trial.[32]

The right to jury trial in civil cases is now governed by section 69(1) of the Supreme Court Act 1981 which provides that:

> "Where, on the application of any party to an action to be tried in the Queen's Bench Division, the court is satisfied that there is in issue—
> (a) a charge of fraud against that party; or
> (b) a claim in respect of libel, slander, malicious prosecution or false imprisonment; or
> (c) any question or issue of a kind prescribed for the purposes of this paragraph,
> the action shall be tried with a jury unless the court is of opinion that the trial requires any prolonged examination of documents or accounts or any scientific or local investigation which cannot conveniently be made with a jury."

The effect of section 69(1)(*c*) is that there is a "right to jury trial" so long as a case involves "some issue" of fraud, libel, slander, malicious prosecution or false imprisonment. The right it not lost simply because the case also involves other causes of action such as assault or wrongful interference with goods. The length or complexity of a case does not, of itself, take away the right to trial by jury.

The **right** is only lost when the named causes of action arise if the case involves the "prolonged examination of documents or accounts." The section should not be read as if the word "prolonged" were not there.[32a] Even if such examination is required the court still has discretion to order trial by jury, for example, when the honour or reputation of the applicant is at stake.[33]

Other cases "shall be tried without a jury unless the court in its discretion orders it to be tried with a jury."[34] The position in the county court is governed by the identical provisions of section 66(3) of the County Courts Act 1984.

Where there is no statutory right to jury trial the usual rule is that cases should be tried by a judge alone.[35] It has been said that jury trial should be ordered in cases in which:

> "for one reason or another it is specially important to one or other of the parties that he should have a judgment that fits the merits of a particular case."[36]

Issues of integrity and honour will be a weighty consideration in ordering a trial by jury on the application of the party whose integrity or honour is impugned.[37] The belief of the applicant that judges as a class might be

[31] R.S.C., Ord. 33, r. 5.
[32] C.C.R., Ord. 14, r. 10.
[32a] *Viscount De L'Isle* v. *Times Newspapers Ltd, The Times,* April 16, 1987.
[33] *Rothermere* v. *Times Newspapers* [1973] 1 W.L.R. 448.
[34] s.69(3).
[35] *Williams* v. *Beesley* [1973] 3 All E.R. 144 at 146j.
[36] Lord Devlin, *Trial by Jury* at p. 158, approved by Lord Denning M.R., *Rothermere* v. *Times Newspapers*, [1973] 1 W.L.R. 448 at 449.
[37] *Williams* v. *Beesley* [1973] 3 All E.R. 144 at 147a.

prejudiced against him or in favour of his opponent will not be a consideration in deciding whether or not to order trial by jury.[38]

Whether or not an application should be made for a jury trial will depend on all the circumstances of the particular case. The role of the civil jury is limited to decisions on issues of fact: the beliefs of an officer making an arrest or beginning a prosecution. The issue of whether there was a reasonable cause for the arrest or prosecution is a matter for the judge.[39] Juries do, however, have the important role of assessing general, aggravated and exemplary damages.[40]

The verdicts of juries are often difficult to predict—particularly on the quantum of damages—and, in a clear cut case, it may be to the plaintiff's advantage to have the matter tried by a judge alone. If the plaintiff's case appears to involve "technicalities"—for example, a failure to comply with the formalities of arrest—then, again, trial by a judge alone may be preferable from the plaintiff's point of view. If, on the other hand, the plaintiff's case involves a simple conflict of evidence with police officers, experience suggests that a jury trial is likely to be to his advantage.

Even when there is no right to a jury trial a plaintiff can of course, make an application for trial by jury, for example, on the ground that "honour and integrity" are at stake. In making such an application the stirring words of Lord Atkin should perhaps be borne in mind:

> "Trial by jury . . . is an essential principle of our law. It has been the bulwark of liberty, the shield of the poor from the oppression of the rich and powerful. Anyone who knows the history of our law knows that many of the liberties of the subject were originally established and are maintained by the verdicts of juries in civil cases. Many will think that at the present time the danger of attack by powerful private organisations or by encroachments of the executive is not diminishing."[41]

The plaintiff in the assault case of *Pascal* v. *M.P.C.*[42] successfully applied for jury trial (and was successful in the action). If the plaintiff does not apply for trial by jury it is unlikely that the police solicitors will make the application.

Payments into court

A payment into court is designed to force a plaintiff to accept an offer of settlement. A defendant can pay a sum of money into court in settlement of some or all of the plaintiff's causes of action, at any time up to judgment. If the plaintiff refuses to accept the payment in and, at trial, recovers damages which are less than or equal to the sums paid into court then he is liable to pay the defendant's costs after the date of payment in. As these costs will usually include the costs of the trial itself it is likely that a plaintiff who

[38] *Williams* v. *Beesley* [1973] 3 All E.R. 144 at 147a.
[39] For false imprisonment see Chap. 5 below at p. 152.
[40] See Chap. 11 below at pp. 349 *et seq.*
[41] *Ford* v. *Blurton* (1922) 38 T.L.R. 801 at 805.
[42] (1986) Clerkenwell County Court, unreported.

does not beat a payment in will lose most, if not all, of his damages in costs. Because of the unpredictability of damages awards in police cases it is often very difficult to decide whether or not to accept a payment in.

In a High Court case the plaintiff has 21 days to decide whether or not to accept a payment in. In the county court, the plaintiff has only 14 days to accept a payment in and this must be not less than three days before the hearing of the action begins.[43] After the appropriate period has expired the plaintiff can only accept with the leave of the court.[44] If he does not obtain such leave he may be required to pay the defendant's costs incurred between the date of payment in and the date of acceptance. The plaintiff cannot apply for leave to accept a payment in once the trial of the action has begun.[45] If a payment in is made during the trial then the plaintiff has two days to accept and can do so without leave.

The defendant usually pays into court a lump sum to cover all the plaintiff's causes of action.[46] A plaintiff who wishes to accept a payment in can request an amendment of the notice of payment in so as to apportion the lump sum between the different causes of action.[47] A payment in should include an amount for interest.[48]

A payment in will be late if made less than 21 days before trial in the High Court and 14 days before trial in the county court. A payment in must not be disclosed to the trial judge.[49]

In normal circumstances, so long as the plaintiff had sufficient time to consider whether or not to accept the payment in then a "costs penalty" will be incurred if he fails to "beat" the payment in. However, even when a payment in has been made the court retains a discretion as to costs. In particular, the judge can taken into account the fact that the defendant's case is an untrue one supported by untrue evidence or that he was guilty of "disgraceful conduct" in relation to the proceedings.

In police cases whether or not the police have been guilty of "oppressive conduct" in "abuse of their powers" will be an important consideration in deciding whether a plaintiff who fails to beat a payment in should receive his costs. Thus, for example, in the case of *Wilson & Farbridge* v. *M.P.C.*[50] Tudor Price J. initially awarded costs to the police when the plaintiff had failed to beat their payment in but later called for the costs issue to be reargued and awarded costs against the police. As Tudor Price J. said:

> "the Jury were of the opinion, on the balance of probabilities . . . that the case put forward on behalf of the Defence in this Court was an untrue one supported by untrue evidence. In those circumstances, it seems to me, on further consideration to be quite wrong to order Mr Wilson to pay any part of the Defence costs . . . In my view Mr Wilson was entitled to be vindicated by a jury's verdict and to have a jury express the view, as they undoubtedly have done, that the conduct of the individual police officers towards him was oppressive and abusive

[43] C.C.R., Ord. 11, r. 3.
[44] R.S.C., Ord. 22, r. 3(1).
[45] *Gaskins* v. *British Aluminium* [1976] Q.B. 564.
[46] R.S.C., Ord. 22, r. 1; C.C.R., Ord. 11, r. 1.
[47] *Townsend* v. *Stone Toms & Partners* (1984) 128 S.J. 659.
[48] R.S.C., Ord. 22, r. 1(8); C.C.R., Ord. 11, r. 1(8).
[49] R.S.C., Ord. 22, r. 7; C.C.R., Ord. 11, r. 7.
[50] (1985) December 10, unreported.

of their powers, and on reconsideration, therefore, I order that the costs of Mr Wilson should be paid by the Defendants."

6. THE TRIAL

The jury

If the case is to be tried by a judge and jury the first step will be the swearing in of the jury—12 people in the High Court and eight in the county court. Neither party has a right to peremptory challenge in a civil case.[51] Both parties do, however, have the same right to challenge for cause as the parties in a criminal case.[52] A party can either make a challenge "to the array" or "to the polls":

(1) *A challenge to the array.* This is a challenge of the whole panel of jurors. The only ground on which such a challenge can be made is that the officer appointed to summon the jurors was "biased" or had "acted improperly". If both parties challenge the array it must be quashed.[53] The array can also be challenged for favour.[54]

(2) *A challenge to the polls.* This is a challenge to an individual juror. A juror can be challenged because he is not qualified (*propter defectum*) or because he is biased or reasonably suspected of bias (*propter affectum*).[55] If there is some *prima facie* evidence of bias the juror who is challenged can be examined on oath (the *voir dire*) as to his bias.[56] The burden of proving bias is on the challenging party.[57] A direct professional or personal relationship with one of the parties will be a sufficient ground for challenge for cause[58] and, it is submitted, a juror who was or had been a police officer could be successfully challenged in a police case.

In the High Court the judge can accept a majority verdict of 11–1 or 10–2 as in a criminal case.[59] In the county court a majority verdict of 7–1 can be accepted.[60] Such a majority verdict must not be accepted unless it appears to the court that the jury have had such period of time for deliberation as the court thinks reasonable having regard to the nature and complexity of the case.[61] In addition the parties can agree to accept the verdict of a differently constituted majority, or of an incomplete jury.[62] Thus, for example, the parties could agree to accept a 5–3 majority verdict in a county court jury trial.

[51] *Creed* v. *Fisher* (1854) 9 Exch. 472.
[52] Juries Act 1974, s.12(2).
[53] Co.Litt 156a.
[54] See generally, Archbold, *Criminal Pleading Evidence & Procedure* para. 4–156.
[55] *Ibid.* para. 4–161.
[56] *R.* v. *Chandler* [1964] 2 Q.B. 322.
[57] *R.* v. *Savage* (1824) 1 Mood. 51.
[58] See, *e.g.*, *Bailey* v. *Macaulay* (1849) 13 Q.B. 815 in which a new trial was granted because a juror was a fellow committeeman of one of the parties.
[59] Juries Act 1974, s.17(1)(*a*).
[60] Juries Act 1974, s.17(2).
[61] Juries Act 1974, s.17(4).
[62] Juries Act 1974, s.17(5).

Trial procedure

The plaintiff's counsel will open the case unless, on the pleadings, the burden of proof on all issues lies on the defendant. Even if on the pleadings there are no issues on the plaintiff, he is entitled to begin in all actions in which substantial and unliquidated damages are claimed because he must still prove the damage.[63] Thus even if the plaintiff's only claim is for false imprisonment and the actual fact of the detention is admitted, the plaintiff has the right to open although, apart from damages, the only issue is that of the lawful justification for the detention the burden of proving which is on the defendant.[63a] In opening a case to a jury it appears that counsel should not mention the amount of damages claimed.[64]

If the case is tried with a jury questions of the admissibility of evidence and matters of law may be discussed in the absence of the jury. There is, however, no strict rule on this subject in civil cases. In the libel case of *Riches* v. *News Group Newspapers*[65] the Court of Appeal approved the trial judge's decision (made without objection) to hear submissions on the law in the presence of the jury.[66]

In civil trials there is no general rule that witnesses should be kept out of court until they have given their evidence. But an application can be made by either party, at any time—

> "for an order that all witnesses on both sides than the one under examination, to withdraw and not to leave the Court again after giving evidence so as to communicate with other witnesses before they give evidence."[67]

This does not apply to the parties, their expert witnesses or their solicitors.[68] In police cases it will usually be appropriate to exclude witnesses and if the defendant will not agree to such a course an application should be made for an order.

At the close of the plaintiff's case the defendant may submit that there is no case to answer. The test to be applied (whether or not the case is being tried with a jury) is whether there is any evidence "that ought reasonably to satisfy the jury that the fact sought to be proved is established."[69] When the case is heard by a judge alone the defendant must elect to call no evidence before a submission of no case to answer will be heard.[70] The judge must

[63] *Chapman* v. *Rawson* (1846) 8 Q.B. 673; see Phipson at pp. 33–28; McGregor at p. 1521.

[63a] Thus counsel for the police should not have opened in the false imprisonment case of *Holtham* v. *M.P.C.* [1986] unreported; reported on a different point *The Times*, January 1, 1987.

[64] See (1896) 41 S.J. 204, which refers to Hawkins J. stopping an action because this was done; *Watt* v. *Watt* [1905] A.C. 115, 118, *per* Lord Halsbury.

[65] [1986] Q.B. 256.

[66] *Ibid.* at 857d, *per* Stephenson L.J.

[67] *Supreme Court Practice*, 1988, 38/1/5 approved in *Tomlinson* v. *Tomlinson* [1980] 1 W.L.R. 322.

[68] *Tomlinson* v. *Tomlinson* [1980] 1 W.L.R. 322 at 327A.

[69] *Ryder* v. *Wombwell* (1868) L.R. 4 Ex. 32, 39.

[70] *Alexander* v. *Rayson* [1936] 1 K.B. 169, at 178–180.

put the election to the defendant's counsel expressly. If this is not done then the election will not be implied.[71] If the defendant elects to call no evidence and the submission fails then he is bound to lose. When the case is heard by a judge and jury then the defendant cannot make a submission of no case to answer until after his evidence has been called.[72] It has been suggested that the verdict of the jury could be taken, in any event, to save expense if the Court of Appeal overturns the judge's acceptance of a submission of no case to answer.[73] The general view, however, is that this procedure is unsatisfactory and that, if it is held that there is no case to answer the jury should be discharged without being asked for a verdict.[74]

In a jury trial the jury can intervene and stop the case at any point but this is a matter between the judge and the jury and it is not a course which should be suggested by counsel.[75] It has been said that it is "not the duty of the judge to sit quietly day after day. If he had formed the view that the jury had heard enough he was entitled to ask them."[76] If the jury gives a verdict for one party before they have heard all the evidence of the other then the judge can decide whether to discharge the jury and order a new trial or whether the trial should continue with the same jury.[77]

At the close of the defendant's evidence, the defendant's counsel has the right to make a speech to the jury. The plaintiff's counsel then makes a speech and the judge sums up. The judge must explain to the jury the effect of the evidence and the nature of the issues which they have to try. Counsel is entitled to draw the judge's attention to mistatements of fact in his direction but not to errors of law.[78] In almost all civil cases the jury will not simply be asked to give a "general" verdict—"for the plaintiff" or "for the defendant"—but a "special" verdict consisting of answers to a series of questions. They are not obliged to give such a special verdict and may confine themselves to a general verdict.[79] It is unknown for a modern jury to refuse a special verdict.

Counsel is entitled to ask the judge to put a specific questions to the jury, but unless they are distinctly raised on the record a refusal to put them does not amount to a misdirection.[80] If possible, the questions to be put to the jury should be agreed between the judge and counsel, in the absence of the jury, before the closing speeches. Even if both counsel agree on a question the judge may decide that, as a matter of law, it should not be put to the jury.[81]

If the jury have difficulty in agreeing and the parties will not agree to an appropriate majority verdict then the judge is entitled to direct the jury that it is their duty to do their utmost to reach agreement. It will be a misdirec-

[71] *Yuill* v. *Yuill* [1945] P. 15 at 17.

[72] *Payne* v. *Harrison* [1961] 2 Q.B. 403 at 413.

[73] *Halliwell* v. *Venables* [1930] L.J.K.B. 353.

[74] *Young* v. *Rank* [1950] 2 K.B. 510.

[75] *Beevis* v. *Dawson* [1957] 1 Q.B. 195 at 214.

[76] *per* Singleton L.J., *McCann* v. *Collins, The Times*, March 1, 1986.

[77] See *De Freville* v. *Dill* (1927) 43 T.L.R. 431; *Hobbs* v. *Tinling* [1929] 2 K.B. 1.

[78] *Payne* v. *Ibbotson* (1858) 27 L.J.Ex. 341; *R.* v. *Mowbray* (1912) 8 Cr.App.Rep. 8.

[79] *Devizes Corporation* v. *Clark* (1835) 3 Ad. & El. 506.

[80] *Walton* v. *Potter & Horsfall* (1841) 3 Man. & G. 411 at 433; *Weiser* v. *Segar* [1904] W.N. 93.

[81] See *Beeby* v. *Chief Constable of Nottingham* [1986] unreported, C.A. October 3; Transcript: Association.

tion, however, if the judge suggests that it is the duty of the minority to give up their independent judgment in the interests of agreement.[82]

If the jury fail to agree and the parties will not agree to an appropriate majority verdict then the case should be set down for a new trial. This is distinct from the situation in which an "order for a new trial" and is done by the trial judge as soon as the failure to agree is clearly irresolvable.[83]

Matters of evidence

Police cases are, of course, governed by the same rules of evidence as all civil cases. Hearsay can be admitted under the provisions of the Civil Evidence Acts 1968 and 1972.[84] However, a number of difficult issues may arise.

(1) *Bad character of parties of witnesses.* Unlike criminal cases, there are no special rules relating to the disclosure of previous convictions. The character of the plaintiff is material if it affects his credit.[85] Similarly, the character of the plaintiff's witnesses, the defendants and their witnesses are relevant if they go to credit. A judge has no discretion to prevent cross-examination as to previous convictions if they are relevant to a witness's credibility.[86] Previous convictions may be put to the plaintiff, the defendants or to any witnesses, in cross-examination and, if they are denied, they may be proved.[87] If, however, a plaintiff or a witness has convictions which are "spent" under the Rehabilitation of Offenders Act 1974 then he—

> "shall not . . . be asked, and if asked, shall not be required to answer, any question relating to his past which cannot be answered without acknowledging or referring to a spent conviction or spent convictions or any circumstances ancillary thereto."[88]

However, under section 7(3) of the 1974 Act, a judge may order that spent convictions be admitted if he—

> "is satisfied, in the light of any consideration which appear to . . . [him] to be relevant (including any evidence which has been or may thereafter be put before . . . [him]), that justice cannot be done in the case except by admitting or requiring evidence relating to a person's spent convictions or to circumstances ancillary thereto."

The effect of this section was considered by the Court of Appeal in the police case of *D* v. *Yates, Lettice & the Chief Constable of Lancashire.*[89] The plaintiff's claim was for assault, battery, wrongful arrest, false

[82] *Re Wright* [1936] 1 All E.R. 877.
[83] See *Davidson* v. *Rodwell* [1955] 1 W.L.R. 654.
[84] See R.S.C., Ord. 38, r. 20–34 and C.C.R., Ord. 20, rr. 14–26.
[85] See *R.* v. *Richardson & Longman* [1969] 1 Q.B. 299 at 304.
[86] See *D.* v. *Yates, The Times,* December 3, 1986; *Clifford* v. *Clifford* [1961] 1 W.L.R. 1274 at 1276.
[87] Criminal Procedure Act 1865, s.6.
[88] s.4(1)(*a*).
[89] November 27, 1986; Transcript; Association; reported in part, *The Times,* December 3, 1986.

imprisonment and malicious prosecution. The defendant police officers sought leave to cross-examine him on a three convictions (all three of which were spent by the time the appeal was heard). The Court of Appeal upheld the trial judge's ruling that such cross-examination should not be permitted. Although emphasising that this was, ultimately, a matter for the judge's discretion, they clarified a number of points in relation to section 7. They rejected the argument that the test under section 7 should be the same as that under section 1(*f*)(ii) of the Criminal Evidence Act 1898.[90] The test is a strict one: in the words of the section 7, it must be shown "that justice cannot be done." The fact that the "spent" convictions were for offences of violence made the jury's task very difficult because:

> "They would have to shut their minds to the fact that there was violence on three previous occasions, but could accept in deliberation the fact that there were convictions recorded against the plaintiff."

This led Purchas L.J. to the view that he would have exercised his discretion in the same way as the trial judge (although Nourse L.J. reserved his position on this point). Both judges emphasised that, in considering whether to exercise his discretion under section 7 the judge had to direct himself in accordance with the words of the section, taking into consideration the fact that the case was being heard by a jury, looking at all the evidence likely to be heard and only allowing cross-examination if justice could not otherwise be done.

In the malicious prosecution case of *Lawton* v. *Charles*[91] the defendant sought to cross-examine the plaintiff on a previous conviction on an occasion when the defendant had given evidence for the prosecution. Oliver J. ruled that this cross-examination was permissible on three grounds

> "first, reduction of damages[92]; secondly, the plaintiff's relationship with the defendant; and thirdly, because the plaintiff is a witness in a civil action and his word is being disputed. The jury are entitled to know the character of the plaintiff when assessing credibility."

(2) *Evidence in other proceedings.* When a plaintiff has given a Civil Evidence Act notice in relation to statements made in previous court proceedings then any party may apply to the court for directions and there is a wide discretion whether or not to exclude the statement.[92a] The fact that a police officer has been disbelieved on oath in a previous case is admissible and may be highly material. In the case of *R* v. *Steadman Thompson*[93] the Court of Appeal (Criminal Division) had to consider the correct direction in a criminal trial regarding the evidence of an officer who had been found guilty of a 'flagrant abuse of power" in a civil case,[94] Lawton L.J. giving the judgment of the Court, was of the view that the officer's evidence was "so tainted that the jury ought not to have relied upon it" and that they should have been directed accordingly (the conviction was, therefore, quashed).

[90] See Archbold at paras. 4–342 *et seq.*
[91] [1957] C.L.Y. 1328.
[92] See Chap. 11 below at p. 342.
[92a] RSC Order 38 rule 28; see generally, Harrison, pp. 17–18.
[93] [1986] *Legal Action*, 186.
[94] The officer had been involved in *Leon* v. *M.P.C.* [1986] C.L.Y. 2538.

(3) *Evidence and damages.* The good character of a party is presumed by law and may not, strictly, be proved in aggravation of damages. However, if a party's character is under attack, he may lead evidence of good character.[95] There is considerable doubt as to whether a defendant can lead evidence of the plaintiff's bad character in mitigation of damages in anything other than defamation cases.[96] However, if the party gives evidence then bad character can be brought out in cross-examination as to credit.[97]

(4) *Similar fact evidence.* Either party may wish to lead "similar fact evidence," for example previous misconduct of a similar nature by the police officers involved or previous unfounded allegations by the plaintiff. It is unclear whether the rules as to the reception of such evidence which apply in criminal cases are also applicable in civil cases.[98] According to Lord Denning M.R.:

> "In civil cases the courts will admit evidence of similar facts if it is logically probative, that is if it is logically relevant in determining the matter which is in issue; provided that it is not oppressive or unfair to the other side; and also that the other side has fair notice of it and is able to deal with it."[99]

Evidence of "dissimilar facts" can be admitted to prove the main fact. Thus, for example, a plaintiff who had been arrested for alleged drunkeness, could call evidence to demonstrate that he was not a heavy drinker.[1]

(5) *The effect of previous convictions.* Under section 11 of the Civil Evidence Act 1968, if a conviction is proved then the person against whom it is proved "shall be taken to have committed that offence unless the contrary is proved."[2] In other words, the party must prove, "on the balance of probabilities,"[3] that the offence was not, in fact, committed. This will, of course, be very difficult in the face of the criminal conviction. It seems that the conviction, once proved, is "a weighty piece of evidence of itself" in the proceedings.[4]

(6) *Excluding evidence in civil cases.* It has been held in an Australian case that there is no discretion to exclude admissible evidence in civil cases.[5] On the other hand, in the case of *Berger* v. *Raymond & Son Ltd.*[6] Warner J. assumed that he had such a discretion in relation to similar fact evidence if the admission of the evidence was "oppressive or unfair" to the other side. It is likely that, in civil jury cases at least, judges will continue to

[95] Phipson, para. 13–61.
[96] *Ibid.*
[97] *Watt* v. *Watt* [1905] A.C. 115 at 118.
[98] See Phipson, para. 12–07 ff.
[99] *Mood Music Publishing Co. Ltd.* v. *de Wolfe* [1976] Ch. 119 at 127; *Sattin* v. *National Union Bank* (1978) 122 S.J. 367.
[1] See generally Phipson, paras. 12–59–12–71.
[2] s.11(2).
[3] *per* Lord Diplock, *Hunter* v. *Chief Constable* [1982] A.C. 529.
[4] *per* Lord Denning M.R., *Stupple* v. *Royal Insurance* [1971] 1 Q.B. 50 at 72; see generally, Phipson, para. 28–95.
[5] *Manenti* v. *Melbourne Tramways* [1954] V.L.R. 115 at 118.
[6] [1984] 1 W.L.R. 625.

exercise an exclusionary discretion, at least in relation to similar fact evidence and probably more generally.

Costs

The general principles relating to the award of costs were summarised in the case of *Scherer* v. *Counting Instruments Ltd.*[7] The judge has "an unlimited discretion to make what order as to costs he considers the justice of the case requires."[8] But this discretion must be exercised "judicially" and in accordance with settled principles. The basic rule is that costs "follow the event."

> "That party who turns out to have unjustifiably either brought another party before the court, or given another party cause to have recourse to the court to obtain his rights is required to recompense that other party is costs."[9]

The successful party, therefore, has a "reasonable expectation" of obtaining his costs.

However, in the exercise of his discretion, the judge can refuse an award of costs to the successful party.

> "This discretion cannot be well exercised unless there are relevant grounds for its exercise . . . The grounds must be connected with the case. This may extend to any matter relating to the litigation and the parties' conduct in it, and also to the circumstances leading to the litigation, but no further."[10]

The successful party may be deprived of his costs if he presents a false case or false evidence or acts oppressively in the action.[11]

If the plaintiff recovers at least £3,000 in High Court proceedings, he is still entitled to High Court costs.[12] If he recovers less than £3,000 he may nevertheless obtain High Court costs if the High Court feels that there were reasonable grounds for supposing he might recover more than £5,000 damages or if it is satisfied that there was sufficient reason for bringing the action in the High Court.[13]

When a payment in has been made then the court must take this into account in exercising its discretion on costs.[14] If the amount paid into court exceeds the sum awarded to the plaintiff at trial then the defendant is the "successful party" and should, in the absence of other considerations, be awarded his costs from the date of payment in.[15] If the amount recovered and the amount paid in are exactly the same the defendant has not "beaten" the payment in and, in the ordinary course, the plaintiff will recover his

[7] [1986] 1 W.L.R. 615n at 621.
[8] *Ibid.* at 621D; S.C.A. 1981, s.51.
[9] *Ibid.* at 621D.
[10] *Ibid.* at 621 E–F.
[11] *Baylis Baxter Ltd.* v. *Sabath* [1958] 1 W.L.R. 529.
[12] County Courts Act 1984, s.20(2).
[13] County Courts Act 1984, s.19(2) and (3).
[14] R.S.C., Ord. 62, r. 9; applied in the county court by C.C.R., Ord. 38, r. 1.
[15] *Findlay* v. *Railway Executive* [1950] W.N. 570.

costs.[16] The fact that a jury have found that the police have acted "oppressively" and in abuse of their powers will be a strong ground for awarding costs against them.[17]

7. APPEALS

Introduction

The Court of Appeal has statutory jurisdiction to hear appeals from the High Court and the county court. Under R.S.C., Ord. 59, r. 3(1), an appeal to the Court of Appeal is "by way of rehearing." When the order appealed from is a "final order" of a High Court judge then no leave is required except in the case of a consent order or an order relating only to costs.

The same rules apply to appeals from the county court with the further qualification that if the claim was for an amount not exceeding one half the county court limit then leave of either the trial judge or the Court of Appeal is required. Thus, if the plaintiff claims damages in any sum above £2,500 (on the current limits) no leave is required.

Interlocutory appeals

When an interlocutory order is made by a Master or a District Registrar, for example in relation to discovery or expert evidence, there is an appeal as of right to a High Court judge (usually sitting in chambers). In the county court an appeal from any decision of the registrar lies, as of right, to the judge. Such appeal is by way of re-hearing and the judge considers the matter *de novo* and, therefore, has a "fresh discretion" to exercise. In both the county court and the High Court it is necessary to obtain leave from either the judge or the Court of Appeal to appeal against an interlocutory order to the Court of Appeal.

Appeals from "judge-only" cases—the order

After the trial by a judge alone he will make an order and, if the plaintiff is successful, assess the appropriate quantum of damages. Appeals against the quantum of damages are considered below. The order that is made will be based on (*a*) rulings on the law; (*b*) findings of fact; and possibly, (*c*) the exercise of discretion.

If the judge is wrong about the law on which his order is based then the Court of Appeal can correct him and alter any order accordingly. No special principles apply here.

[16] As happened in the police case of *Ward* v. *Chief Constable of Avon & Somerset*, *The Times*, July 17, 1985.

[17] See *Wilson & Farbridge* v. *M.P.C.* (1985) unreported, see above at p. 83.

The position relating to findings of fact is more complex. The burden of showing that the trial judge was wrong on a decision of fact is on the appellant. Nevertheless, it is the duty of the Court of Appeal to reconsider all the materials before the trial judge.[18] But, the trial judge has seen the witnesses and the appellate courts should not interfere unless it can be shown that the judge has failed to use his advantage of having seen the witnesses.[19] Thus, the Court of Appeal is reluctant to reject the judge's "primary findings of fact"—especially if these were based on an assessment of the credit of witnesses. The court will, however, form an independent assessment of the proper inferences to be drawn from the primary facts.[20]

It is even more difficult to overturn the exercise of a discretion by a first instance judge. It will not be overturned by the Court of Appeal unless it was based on a mistake of law or fact, or irrelevant matters were taken into account.[21]

Appeals from "judge-only" cases—quantum

The assessment of damages contains two elements: (*a*) rulings of law; (*b*) a "factual" assessment of damages. In cases tried by juries the former element is the province of the judge and the latter the province of the jury. In "judge-only" cases the trial judge must, of course, deal with both elements.

If the trial judge is mistaken about the applicable law of damages then this mistake can be simply corrected by the Court of Appeal. Such a mistake of law could involve, for example, the correct "remoteness rules" to apply, or whether compensatory damages should be reduced because of the plaintiff's character or behaviour.[22] An error of law will permit a reduction or an increase in the quantum of damages awarded.[23]

When it comes to the "factual" assessment of damages the Court of Appeal (perhaps in deference to the fact that this was, at common law, always a "jury function") has traditionally been more reluctant to interfere with the judge's assessment. The classic statement of the principles applied by the Court of Appeal to judge only awards of damages is found in the case of *Flint* v. *Lovell*.[24]

> "In order to justify reversing the trial judge on the question of the amount of damages it will generally be necessary that this court should be convinced either that the judge acted upon some wrong principle of law, or that the amount awarded was so extremely high or so very small as to make it, in the judgment of this court, an entirely erroneous estimate of the damage to which the plaintiff is entitled."

Although this rule is no longer strictly applied in personal injuries cases it

[18] *Coghlan* v. *Cumberland* [1898] 1 Ch. 704.

[19] See *The Supreme Court Practice* 1988, para. 59/1/18 and the cases cited there.

[20] *Benmax* v. *Austin Motor Co. Ltd.* [1955] A.C. 370.

[21] *The Supreme Court Practice* 1988, para. 59/1/19.

[22] See Chap. 11 below at p. 342.

[23] See, *e.g.*, *Dingle* v. *Associated Newspapers* [1964] A.C. 371.

[24] [1935] 1 K.B. 354 at 360.

still represents the law and the Court of Appeal will not interfere if the judge's award of damages falls within the appropriate range.[25]

Appeals from "jury cases"

Appeals from cases tried by a judge and jury are considerably more complex than those in "judge-only" cases. This is because the "constitutional position" of the jury is such that the judges in the appellate courts have traditionally felt extreme reluctance in substituting their own view of the facts for that of the jury.

There are two basic routes to challenging the decision of a jury on the facts. The first is to show that the judge made a mistake of law in allowing a particular issue to go to the jury at all. If this can be established the Court of Appeal can simply overturn the jury's finding without in any sense substituting its own view. An example of this is to be found in the case of *Middleweek* v. *Chief Constable of Merseyside*[26] in which the Court of Appeal held that the trial judge had wrongly left the issue of false imprisonment to the jury. The defendant's appeal was, therefore, upheld and the jury's award of £500 damages was overturned.

If, however, an issue was properly left to the jury then its decision can only be challenged by seeking an order for a new trial under R.S.C., Ord. 59, r. 11. The issues decided and the rulings given in the first trial are not binding in the new trial.[26a] A new trial may be granted if it can be established either that the jury was in some way misled, or that the jury was in some way at fault.

In certain circumstances the Court of Appeal has a discretion as to whether a new trial should be ordered. The position is governed by R.S.C., Ord. 59, r. 11(2) which states that:

> "The Court of Appeal shall not be bound to order a new trial on the ground of misdirection, or of the improper admission or rejection of evidence, or because the verdict of the jury was not taken upon a question which the judge at the trial was not asked to leave to them, unless in the opinion of the Court of Appeal some substantial wrong or miscarriage has been thereby occasioned."

There will have been a "substantial wrong or miscarriage" if a party is not permitted to have their real case presented to the jury. It is immaterial that, properly directed, the jury might well have arrived at the same conclusion.[27]

The grounds on which a new trial may be granted can be grouped under six heads:

(1) *Misdirection.* The most common ground for granting a new trial will be a misdirection of the jury by the judge. It is fairly common for new trials to be directed on this ground in libel cases. In the police case of *Shaper* v. *Robinson*,[28] the Court of Appeal directed a new trial because the trial judge

[25] See McGregor, para. 1567ff.

[26] *The Times*, August 1, 1985.

[26a] See *Bobolas* v. *Economist Newspaper*, *The Times*, June 16, 1987.

[27] See *Bray* v. *Ford* [1896] A.C. 44; *Hobbs* v. *Tinling* [1929] 2 K.B. 1; and, generally, McGregor, paras. 1554–1557.

[28] [1985] October 9, unreported; see [1987] 2 C.L. 47 for the resulting new trial.

had misdirected the jury on the burden of proof in false imprisonment.[29] A new trial can even be granted when the point in question was not taken at trial.[30] Misdirection includes a failure by the judge to direct the jury on an issue which he should have directed them.[31] But, in general, if a party did not raise the point at trial a new trial will not be granted.[32] Thus, it was held in a police case that when the question of exemplary damages was not pleaded and was not taken at trial a new trial would not be granted on the ground of non-direction on the point.[33] Although the usual misdirections complained of concern matters of law, a new trial may also be granted if the judge has misled the jury as to the matters they have to consider or the evidence.[34]

(2) *Improper admission or rejection of evidence.* The improper admission or rejection of evidence is a ground for a new trial. This is, however, subject to the "substantial wrong or miscarriage" rule. Thus, a new trial will not be ordered on this ground if the evidence in question could not have had a legitimate effect on the verdict.[35] No new trial will be ordered if the objection was not taken at trial and, if it had been taken, it might have been dealt with by calling other evidence.[36]

(3) *Improperly withdrawing the case from the jury.* A new trial will be ordered if the judge incorrectly removes a case from the jury and non-suits the plaintiff.[37]

(4) *Misleading the jury in other ways.* A new trial may be ordered because the jury has been misled in a wide range of other ways. It will be available, for example, if the judge refused to take the verdict of the jury on a particular issue. If the matter was not raised at trial, then a new trial will only be granted if there was some substantial wrong or miscarriage of justice.[38] A new trial may be ordered if the judge left to the jury a question which was, in fact, a matter for him.[39]

(5) *"Perverse Verdicts."* A new trial will be ordered if the verdict is one which no reasonable jury, properly directed **could** (not ought) have come to on the evidence. If reasonable men **might** find the verdict which has been found a decision of fact by a jury cannot be disturbed.[40] The question is: was the verdict such as to show that the jury have failed in their duty.[41]

[29] See also *Holden* v. *Chief Constable of Lancashire* [1986] 3 W.L.R. 1107 in which the Court of Appeal also ordered a new trial in a false imprisonment case.
[30] *Knight* v. *Egerton* (1852) 7 Ex. 407.
[31] See, *e.g.*, *Cooper* v. *Swadling* [1930] 1 K.B. 403.
[32] *Nevill* v. *Fine Art & General Insurance* [1897] A.C. 68 at 76.
[33] *Bryning* v. *Oxford* [1983] C.A., U.B. Transcript 847.
[34] *Jefferson* v. *Powell* [1916] 1 K.B. 57 at 74–75.
[35] *Manley* v. *Palache* (1895) 73 L.T. 98.
[36] *Bradshaw* v. *Widdrington* [1902] 2 Ch. 430 at 449.
[37] *Brearley* v. *L.N.W.R.* (1899) 15 T.L.R. 237.
[38] R.S.C., Ord. 59, r. 11(2).
[39] *Abrahams* v. *Dimmock* [1915] 1 K.B. 662.
[40] See *Metropolitan Ry. Co.* v. *Wright* (1886) 11 App.Cas. 152 at 156, *per* Lord Halsbury.
[41] *Mechanical & General Inventions Co.* v. *Austin* [1935] A.C. 346 at 375.

(6) *Misconduct of the jury generally.* A new trial will be ordered if it can be shown that the jury was guilty of misconduct of some kind. Thus, if their answers are mutually contradictory a new trial will be ordered.[42] A new trial may be ordered if a stranger was in the jury room for a substantial period while the jury were considering their verdict.[43]

Appeals from "jury cases"—quantum

Where there is an appeal on quantum alone in a case which was tried by a jury the same rules apply as to an appeal against a verdict on the facts. The Court of Appeal will not substitute its own view of the appropriate quantum of damages for that of the jury. The jury's award of damages will only be overturned if there are grounds for granting a new trial.

The Court of Appeal can, however, substitute its own view of the appropriate award of damages for that of the jury with the consent of both parties.[44] The consent of the plaintiff alone is insufficient.[45] If the jury have erroneously included or excluded any distinct head of damages then "with the consent of the party entitled to receive or liable to pay the damages as the case may be," the Court of Appeal may reduce or increase the damages award appropriately.[46] If the parties do not consent, the usual course is to order a new trial solely on the issue of damages under R.S.C., Ord. 59, r. 11(3).

The most important ground for awarding a new trial is that of the "perversity" of the jury's award of damages. On the traditional view the Court of Appeal would only grant a new trial if the damages were so excessive or so small that no jury could reasonably have given them.[47] In the iconoclastic case of *Ward* v. *James*[48] Lord Denning M.R. said that:

> "In the future this court will not feel the same hesitation in upsetting an award of damages by a jury. If it is "out of all proportion to the circumstances of the case" (that is, if it is far too high or far too low) this court will set it aside."

It is unclear whether this statement in fact represents the law. In cases where damages are "at large" the Court of Appeal has, traditionally, been extremely reluctant to interfere with jury awards.[49] This principle has was reaffirmed by the House of Lords in *Broome* v. *Cassell Co.*[50] As Lord Hailsham L.C. said:

> "I know of no principle of reason which would entitle judges, whether of appeal or at first instance, to consider that their own sense of the proprieties is more reasonable than that of a jury, or which would entitle

[42] *Vowles* v. *Armstrong Siddeley Motors Ltd.* [1938] 4 All E.R. 796.
[43] *Goby* v. *Wetherill* [1915] 2 K.B. 674.
[44] R.S.C., Ord. 59, r. 11(4)(*a*); see, *e.g.*, *Beckett* v. *Walker* [1986] unreported, C.A., U.B. Transcript 86–134.
[45] *Watt* v. *Watt* [1905] A.C. 115.
[46] R.S.C., Ord. 59, r. 11(4)(*b*).
[47] *per* Greer L.J., *Smith* v. *Schilling* [1928] 1 K.B. 429 at 440.
[48] [1966] 1 Q.B. 273 at 301 C–D.
[49] See McGregor, paras. 1563–1566.
[50] [1972] A.C. 1027.

> them to arrogate to themselves a constitutional status in this matter which Parliament has deliberately withheld from them, for ought we know, on the very ground that juries can expect to be more generous on such matters than judges."[51]

In the police case of *Reynolds* v. *MPC*,[52] the court of appeal refused to interfere with a jury award of £12,000 for a period of 14 hours false imprisonment because, although it was higher than they would have awarded it was not "so excessive that no reasonable jury ought to have made that award." The only recorded case of the Court of Appeal overturning a jury award because it was too small appears to be the false imprisonment case of *Beckett* v. *Walker*[53] in which the jury had awarded £200 for a period of imprisonment of 53 hours. The Court of Appeal were of the view that the award was one which "no reasonable jury could properly have reached."[54] An award of £500 was substituted!

APPENDIX: THE DOCUMENTS TO LOOK FOR IN POLICE CASES

In addition to the usual documents that a litigant would expect to see on discovery there are a large number of police documents which may assist a plaintiff's case and which are, therefore, discoverable. It is important to note that the police are compulsive record keepers and large numbers of relevant documents will usually be brought into existence in relation to any major incident. However, many of these documents are likely to be destroyed in the ordinary course of events within a few months of the incident taking place. So, it is important to give prompt notification of the possibility that such documents may be required for the purposes of a civil action.

Potentially discoverable police records can be considered under six heads:

(1) documents kept by officers on duty;
(2) documents kept at the police station to record day to day police activities;
(3) records of individual cases;
(4) records required by the Codes of Practice under the Police and Criminal Evidence Act 1984;
(5) records relating to individual officers;
(6) computerised records relating to incidents.

The documents mentioned in this Appendix are those held by the Metropolitan Police, but similar documents are held by other forces.

(1) *Documents kept by officers on duty.* All police officers on duty will, of course, have **notebooks** which will contain records of their activities. The difference between the police case, as pleaded, and the record of an incident may often provide valuable support to a plaintiff's case. Uniformed officers

[51] *Ibid.* 1066B–C.
[52] *The Times*, May 5, 1982.
[53] [1986] unreported, C.A. 86–134; [1986] II C.L.3.
[54] *Ibid. per* Nourse L.J.

will keep an **incident report book**. An **accident report book** will be completed in respect of all road traffic accidents. The **traffic process** book contains details of people charged with road traffic offences and occasionally other matters for which summonses are required.

(2) *Documents to record day to day activities.* The **duty state** is a book which records which officers are on duty, where they are on duty, and when they came on and will go off. The **parade book** is read out when officers are being briefed at the start of their tour of duty. It contains items of information which may be of use to constables before they go on duty. The **occurrence book** is kept by the station officer and provides an overall summary record of the station's activities forming a kind of index to officers notebooks and other "primary records." Reports of important incidents may be typed up and kept in an "occurrence file." There are large numbers of other records kept in the front office of a police station including records covering: missing persons; minor meetings and processions; police doctors' attendances ("the doctor's book"), firearms certificates issued; firearms found; property lost and found; stray dogs; production of documents, and verbal warnings given to motorists; and a "licensing register" dealing with inquiries made into licensed premises.

When telephone messages are received in a police station communications room then they should be recorded on the **message pad.** A **log of radio messages** from officers on duty will only be kept at higher levels of a police force. Thus, in the Metropolitan Police, tapes are kept of wireless messages and phone calls going through the "central force system" at Scotland Yard. Routine personal messages will not be recorded at a Divisional level. Tapes of radio messages are usually destroyed after three months. Many police forces now have computer "command and control" systems for 999 calls under which details of calls are typed directly into the computer.[54a]

Each "divisional" police station will have a "collator" whose job is to collate and file the information which comes into the station. These are usually kept in card indexes. Basic information is stored on suspects on index cards, covering matters such as name, address, description, ethnic identity code, date of birth, offences charged and any other relevant pieces of intelligence. These records are, increasingly, being computerised.

(3) *Records of individual cases.* If the plaintiff was charged and prosecuted there will, of course, be a charge sheet, notes of interview, statements and so on. There will also be all the records required to be made by the Codes of Practice.[55]

The police draw up a **crime report** in relation to every reported crime. This will be entered on a standard computer form, and will record matters such as details of the offence, victims, witnesses, suspects, comments and records of any arrests. This may provide useful information as to the state of the police beliefs before someone is arrested. These records are filed in "crime books," depending on the type of offence. There will be "major crime book," a "beat crime book" and possibly a "burglaries book."

[54a] See generally, British Society for Social Responsibility in Science, Technology of Political Control Group, *TechnoCop: new police technologies.*

[55] See below at p. 98.

(4) *Records required under the Codes of Practice.* Whenever a person is stopped and searched in the street the searching officer must make a record on the form provided ("the national search record").[56] This must include the prescribed information: the name or description of the person searched, their ethnic appearance, the object of the search, the grounds for making it, the date and time it was made, its result, any resultant inquiry or damage to property and the identity of the officer.[57] These records may be collated in the **person stopped** book at every police station.

Whenever premises are searched the officer in charge must make a **record of the search** on arrival at police station. This must include: the address of the premises; the date, time and duration of the search; the authority under which the search was made; the names of the searching officers; a list of any articles seized and, if not covered by warrant, the reason for their seizure; whether force was used and the reason for this; details of any damage caused during the search and the circumstances in which it was caused.[58] When premises are searched under a warrant then details of the following matters should be endorsed on the warrant: the articles seized; the time of execution of the warrant; the officers executing the warrant; whether a copy was handed to the occupier or left on the premises.[59] A **search register** must be maintained at each sub-divisional police station.

When a person is taken into police custody a separate custody record must be opened in relation to him as soon as practicable.[60] The person detained has a right to request a copy of this record for a period of 12 months after his release.[61] The custody record should show the matters such as the grounds for the person's detention, the person's property, any requests made to communicate with a person "who is known to him or who is likely to take an interest in his welfare," any letters or messages sent or received, any requests for legal advice and so on. If a person is charged then this will be recorded in the **charge book** or in the **persons at station register**. If the person was interviewed then an accurate record must be made of each interview.[62] Records relating to identification parades are kept by the "identification officer."[63]

(5) *Records relating to individual officers.* Like any large organisation the police force keeps detailed personnel records on individual police officers. Each constable will have a **personnel file.** This will contain the full records of each officer's probationary period and annual "qualification reports" and other documents. In addition, full records of disciplinary actions taken will be included, even when disciplinary penalties are "spent" for internal disciplinary purposes. A **discipline book** showing any formal disciplinary actions against officers in a force will be kept in every local police headquarters.[64] A **complaints register** is kept for each police force.[65]

[56] *Code of Practice on Stop and Search,* para. 4.
[57] *Ibid.* para. 4.5.
[58] *Code of Practice for Searching of Premises,* para. 7.1.
[59] *Ibid.* para. 7.2.
[60] *Code of Practice for Detention etc.,* para. 2.1.
[61] *Ibid.* para. 2.4.
[62] *Ibid.* paras. 11 and 12.
[63] *Code of Practice for Identification of Persons by Police Officers,* paras. 2.13–2.15.
[64] Police (Discipline) Regulations [1985] S.I. 1985 No. 518, reg. 29.
[65] Police (Complaints) (General) Regulations [1985] S.I. 1985 No. 520, reg. 12.

Previous complaints against an officer involved in a case are, it is submitted, relevant and discoverable documents. If an officer has been complained about previously there should be notes of the evidence at any relevant criminal or civil trials. If there have been previous civil actions involving a particular officer then, it is submitted, the documents relating to such cases are relevant and discoverable. This would include copies of the judgments and any documents relating to comments made about the officer by the judge.

(6) *Computer Records.* Police records are now increasingly computerised. Many of the records which are computerised will simply be versions of the written records already mentioned. Nevertheless, as an ever increasing number of police stations use their own computer terminals more information is placed directly on computer without a corresponding written record being brought into existence. Thus, at some police stations radio messages are now directly entered onto computer without being noted in writing. Such computer records may contain important information such as, for example, the exact times of such messages, which is not available elsewhere.

Part 2: Traditional Tort Actions

4. Intentional Torts to the Person

1. INTRODUCTION

The most common actions alleging police misconduct are based on the ancient torts of assault, battery and false imprisonment. Although such cases are often straightforward, a close examination of the torts is important for a large number of borderline assaults and detentions. It is through actions in trespass against the person that the courts have considered some fundamental questions concerning the liberty of the subject. Moreover, outside the simple "assault" and false imprisonment cases the law covers a broad area of "interferences" with the subject which often involve difficult legal issues.

It is perhaps surprising that so many important issues of principle remain unresolved. Fragmentary remarks and elliptical judgments derived from some very old authorities can present a misleading picture of a coherent and immutable body of law. In fact, crucial points remain unclear and developments occuring in other jurisdictions suggest new directions which could be taken by the English courts.

In this chapter the torts of assault, battery, false imprisonment and intimidation are examined. In addition, the implications of an apparently new tortious action of "harassment" are considered. Finally, the tort of intentionally causing nervous shock is discussed. This cause of action has its roots in English law but has become reformulated and elaborated in the United States.

2. ASSAULT AND BATTERY

Definition

Battery is the intentional and direct application of force to another person whereas assault is an act of the defendant which causes the plaintiff reasonable apprehension of the infliction of a battery on him by the defendant.[1] Consequently, throwing water at someone is an assault and only becomes battery if drops fall upon him.[2] The absence of the plaintiff's consent is not

[1] See Winfield & Jolowicz at p. 54.
[2] *Pursell* v. *Horn* (1838) 3 N & P 564.

an element of the tort. Consent is only relevant as a defence.[2a] It is necessary to consider the nature and character of the defendant's acts and the defendant's state of mind.

Battery: the nature and character of the defendant's act

Because applying force to another constitutes a battery, all of the following are tortious: spitting in a man's face,[3] touching another in anger,[4] taking an object someone is holding[5] (or wearing)[6] by force, taking someone's finger prints,[7] or cutting his hair.[8] In fact, it seems that a person may recover substantial damages for injury to his personal dignity from a battery which does him no physical harm.[9]

However, very slight and accidental contact is not tortious. Thus, "if two or more meet in a narrow passage and without any violence or design of harm, the one touches the other gently, it will not be a battery."[10] This rule has been explained on the basis that the courts cannot and should not be expected to give protection against the unavoidable incidents of everyday life.[11] However, the traditional justification for it is the doctrine of "implied consent"[12] a person consents to minor accidental contact but not to deliberate force or roughness which renders actual harm at all likely.[13] The modern approach was set out by Robert Goff L.J. in *Collins* v. *Wilcock*[14] as follows:

> "The fundamental principle, plain and incontestable, is that every person's body is inviolate. It has long been established that any touching of another person, however slight, may amount to a battery. So Holt C.J. held in *Cole* v. *Turner* (1704) 6 Mod. 149 that 'the least touching of another in anger is a battery.' The breadth of the principle reflects the fundamental nature of the interest protected. As Blackstone wrote in his *Commentaries* (17th ed. 1830) Vol. 3 at 120;
>
> > 'the law cannot draw the line between different degrees of violence, therefore totally prohibits the first and lowest stage of it; every man's person being sacred, and no other having a right to meddle with it, in any the slightest manner.'
>
> "The effect is that everybody is protected not only against physical injury but against any form of physical molestation. But so widely drawn a principle must inevitably be subject to exceptions. For

2a See below at p. 122.
3 *R.* v. *Cotesworth* (1704) 6 Mod.Rep. 172.
4 *Cole* v. *Turner* (1704) 6 Mod.Rep. 149.
5 *Green* v. *Goddard* (1704) 2 Salk. 641.
6 *Humphries* v. *Connor* (1864) 17 Ir CLR 1.
7 *Dumbell* v. *Roberts* [1944] 1 All E.R. 326 at 330.
8 *Forde* v. *Skinner* (1830) 4 C. & P. 239.
9 *Stenant* v. *Stonehouse* [1926] 2 D.L.R. 683.
10 *Cole* v. *Turner* (1704) 6 Mod.Rep. 149; *Tuberville* v. *Savage* (1669) 1 Mod.Rep. 3.
11 Street at p. 19.
12 See *Collins* v. *Wilcock* [1984] 1 W.L.R. 1173.
13 Winfield & Jolowicz at p. 56; and see *Coward* v. *Badderly* (1859) 4 H. & N. 478.
14 [1984] 1 W.L.R. 1172.

example, children may be subjected to reasonable punishment; people may be subjected to the lawful exercise of the power of arrest; and reasonable force may be used in self-defence or for the prevention of crime. But, apart from these special instances where the control or constraint is lawful, a broader exception has been created to allow for the exigencies of everyday life. Generally speaking, consent is a defence to battery; and most of the physical contacts of ordinary life are not actionable because they are impliedly consented to by all who move in society and so expose themselves to the risk of bodily contact. So nobody can complain of the jostling which is inevitable from his presence in, for example, a supermarket, an underground station or a busy street; nor can a person who attends a party complain if his hand is seized in friendship, or even if his back is slapped; see *Tuberville* v. *Savage* (1669) 1 Mod. 3. Although such cases are regarded as examples of implied consent, it is more common nowadays to treat them as falling within a general exception embracing all physical contact which is generally acceptable in the ordinary conduct of daily life. Although in the past it has sometimes been stated that a battery is only committed where the action is 'angry, revengeful, rude, or insolent' (see *Hawkins, Pleas of the Crown* (8th ed. 1824) Vol. 1, Chap. 15); nowadays it is more realistic and indeed more accurate, to state the broad underlying principle, subject to the broad exceptions."[15]

This principle was applied in the dubious decision of *Donnelly* v. *Jackman*[16] where it was held that a police officer who tapped another on the shoulder committed so trivial an interference with another's liberty that it did not take him outside the course of his duty. Nevertheless, where a police officer (who is not lawfully exercising a power of arrest) uses physical contact in the face of non-co-operation which persists beyond socially accepted standards of contact such as gripping an arm or shoulder, such contact will be unlawful.[17]

The interference with another must be directly caused by the defendant's act in the sense that it follows so directly from it that it may be described as part of the act. But no liability will arise if the interference results from some intervening cause so that it is not part of the defendant's act but merely a consequence of it. Thus, if a man throws a log on to the road, there will be a trespass if it hits someone but not if someone walking down the road trips over it as it lies there.[18]

At the same time the defendant need not have actual and immediate physical contact with the plaintiff to commit a battery. He will be liable if he removes a chair[19] or strikes a horse[20] so that the plaintiff falls to the ground and is injured. However, the defendant must have done some positive act; mere inaction as by passively obstructing the plaintiff will not render him liable.[21]

[15] *Collins* v. *Wilcock* [1984] 1 W.L.R. 1172.
[16] [1970] 1 W.L.R. 562; but see *Rawlings* v. *Till* (1837) 3 M. & W. 28.
[17] *Kenlin* v. *Gardner* [1967] 2 Q.B. 510; *Collins* v. *Wilcock* [1984] 1 W.L.R. 1172; see Chap. 5 below at p. 128.
[18] *Leame* v. *Bray* (1803) 3 East 593 at 602.
[19] *Hopper* v. *Reeve* (1817) 7 Taunt. 698.
[20] *Dodwell* v. *Burford* (1669) 1 Mod. 24.
[21] *Innes* v. *Wylie* (1844) 1 C. & K. 257.

Battery: the defendant's state of mind

To prove a battery it is not necessary to show an intention to injure the plaintiff.[22] A battery will be committed if force is applied intentionally or if the defendant knew his act was substantially certain to result in the application of force.

It has been said that a battery involves not only the application of force but a "hostile intent" on the part of the defendant. The Court of Appeal in *Wilson* v. *Pringle*[23] expressed it in the following terms:

> "in a battery there must an intentional touching or contact in one form or another of the plaintiff by the defendant. That touching must be proved to be a hostile touching. That still leaves unanswered the question 'when is a touching to be called hostile?' Hostility cannot be equated with ill-will or malevolence. It cannot be governed by the obvious intention shown in acts like punching, stabbing or shooting. It cannot be solely governed by an expressed intention although that may be strong evidence. But the element of hostility, in the sense in which it is now to be considered, must be a question of fact for the tribunal of fact. It may be imported from the circumstances. Take the example of the police officer in *Collins* v. *Wilcock* [1984] 1 W.L.R. 1172. She touched the woman deliberately but without an intention to do anything more than restrain her temporarily. Nevertheless, she was acting unlawfully and in that way was acting with hostility. She was acting contrary to the woman's legal right not to be physically restrained. We see no more difficulty in establishing what she intended by means of question and answer, or by inference from the surrounding circumstances, than there is in establishing whether an apparently playful blow was struck in anger. The rules of law governing the legality of arrest may require strict application to the facts of appropriate cases, but in the ordinary give and take of everyday life the tribunal of fact should find no difficulty in answering the question 'was this, or was it not, a battery?' Where the immediate act of touching does not itself demonstrate hostility, the plaintiff should plead the facts which are said to do so.[24]"

It is respectfully submitted, however, that this analysis is not supported by the authorities and that the Court of Appeal have imposed an unjustified gloss on the tort. In numerous cases of unchallenged authority it has been held that batteries were committed by trivial and apparently non-hostile touching such as tapping on the shoulder to attract attention,[25] or holding by the arm.[26] To say, that the police officer in *Collins* v. *Wilcock*[27] was, by touching the suspect, "acting unlawfully and in that way was acting with hostility"[28] is to fall into circularity as, according to the Court of Appeal, the only thing that makes such a touching unlawful is its "hostility."

22 *Wilson* v. *Pringle* [1987] Q.B. 237.
23 *Ibid.*
24 *Ibid.* at 11 A-D.
25 *Rawlings* v. *Till* (1837) 3 M. & W. 28.
26 *Kenlin* v. *Gardner*, [1967] 2 Q.B. 510.
27 [1984] 1 W.L.R. 1172.
28 *Wilson* v. *Pringle* [1987] Q.B. 237 at 252–253.

It is submitted, therefore, that any intentional application of force to another is a battery unless it which falls within what is generally accepted in the ordinary conduct of everyday life or is consented to by the plaintiff.[28a] It is not "generally accepted" for a person to be tapped on the shoulder or seized by the arm by a stranger. Such conduct will, therefore, be tortious. Consent may be express or it may be implied from the circumstances as where a sportsman is slapped on the back by enthusiastic spectators or an unconscious patient is given emergency treatment to save his life. If in such circumstances, the sportsman or the patient had expressly forbidden the conduct in question—by, for example, making a public announcement or carrying a card forbidding emergency treatment—then batteries would be committed. *Clerk and Lindsell* suggests, therefore, "that the true test is not whether a hostile intent on the part of the defendant, but whether an absence of consent on the part of the plaintiff can be inferred."[29]

It is also submitted that battery can be committed negligently as where a third party is accidentally injured when two people are fighting one another.[30] Thus—

> "if the injury is done by the act of the party himself at the time or he is the immediate cause of it, though it happens accidentally or by misfortune yet he is answerable in trespass."[31]

This obviously means that where an individual is accidentally battered by the police lawfully arresting someone else he may take proceedings.

There are tactical advantages in pursuing an action framed in negligent trespass (as opposed to negligence); this is because of the difference in the burden of proof. Whereas in an action in trespass the defendant has to prove he has not acted negligently, in negligence the plaintiff has to prove the allegation.[32] The one exception to this long established principle concerned accidents on or adjoining the highway when the plaintiff in trespass still had to prove negligence.[33] However, the exception may arise from a confusion, does not seem justified on historical grounds,[34] and was disputed in Australia as recently as 1980.[35]

Nonetheless in *Fowler* v. *Lanning*[36] Diplock J. ruled that the exceptional rule for highways should be applied generally so that the plaintiff must prove negligence whether he sues in trespass or negligence. In *Letang* v. *Cooper*[37] Lord Denning went a stage further and claimed that:

> "if one person intentionally applies force direct to another, the plaintiff

[28a] See *In Re T., The Independent*, July 14, 1987.

[29] Clerk & Lindsell, para. 14–05; it also follows that the ingredients of the tort of assault may be different from those of the crime; *per* Pollock C.B., in *Coward* v. *Baddeley* (1859) 4 H. & N. 478 at 480.

[30] *James* v. *Campbell* (1832) 5 C. & P. 372.

[31] *Leame* v. *Bray*, (1803) 3 East 593 at 600, *per* East J; *Cf.* Winfield, "The Myth of Absolute Liability" (1926) 42 L.Q.R. 37.

[32] Winfield & Jolowicz at pp. 116–119.

[33] *Holmes* v. *Mather* (1875) L.R. 10 Ex. 261; *River Wear Commissioner* v. *Adamson* (1877) L.R. 2 App.Cas. 743 at 767, *per* Lord Blackburn; *Phillips* v. *Britannic Hygienic Laundry* [1923] 1 K.B. 539.

[34] Winfield & Goodhart, "Trespass and Negligence" (1933) 49 L.Q.R. 359.

[35] *Lord* v. *The Nominal Defendant* (1980) 24 S.A.S.R. 456.

[36] [1959] 1 Q.B. 426.

[37] [1965] 1 Q.B. 232 at 239.

has a cause of action in assault and battery . . . If he does not inflict injury intentionally but only unintentionally, the plaintiff has no cause of action in trespass. His only cause of action is in negligence and then only on proof of want of reasonable care."

However it is submitted that negligent trespass remains as a tort distinct from negligence. The precise status of *Fowler* v. *Lanning* is unclear since it was approved *obiter* in *Letang* v. *Cooper*, and more recently, in *Wilson* v. *Pringle*.[38] Furthermore, the traditional rule that a defendant in trespass must still disprove his negligence continues to prevail in Australia where the High Court declined to follow Diplock J.'s decision[39] and in Canada where the courts have felt bound to follow a judgment of the Canadian Supreme Court[40] which applied the law as it was before *Fowler* v. *Lanning*.

In some circumstances an action framed in negligent trespass will be preferable to one based in negligence. For example, a plaintiff who suffers a direct injury inflicted by the defendant can succeed in trespass when the defendant owes him no duty. Negligent trespass is actionable without proof of actual damage. Contributory negligence will usually not be a defence to an action in trespass.[41] Finally the test for remoteness of damage differs between the two torts so that the plaintiff can recover if the damage was caused directly[42] even though it was not reasonably forseeable.

Assault

The law of assault substantially follows the law of battery except that assault involves the reasonable apprehension of force rather than the application of it.

It is often assumed that mere words without some kind of bodily movement cannot amount to an assault.[43] However, this principle has never been unqualified.[44] The normal justification for the principle seems to derive from obiter dicta in *R.* v. *Meade & Belt*[45] where Holroyd J. stated that "no words or singing are equivalent to an assault nor will they authorise an assault in return" and this dictum has been applied in Canada.[46]

At the same time it was said obiter in *R.* v. *Wilson*[47] that the words "Get out knives" themselves constituted an assault. In Australia threats to attack and kill the plaintiff made over the telephone some distance away were held to be an assault.[48] It is therefore submitted that the English

[38] [1987] Q.B. 237; see *Salmond on Torts* at p. 114.

[39] *McHale* v. *Watson* (1964) 111 C.L.R. 384, affirmed without reference to this point, (1966) A.L.J.R. 458.

[40] *Cook* v. *Lewis* (1952) 1 D.L.R. 1; *Halton* v. *Webb* (1977) 81 D.L.R.(3d) 377; Linden, *Canadian Tort Law* at pp. 284 *et seq.*

[41] See Chap. 11 at p. 339 below.

[42] *Allan* v. *New Mount Sinai Hospital* (1980) 109 D.L.R.(3d) 635 at 643; *Bettel* v. *Yim* (1978) D.L.R.(3d) at 543; see Chap. 11 at p. 338 below.

[43] Clerk & Lindsell, para. 14–10.

[44] "Notwithstanding the many ancient opinions to the contrary, it seems agreed at this day that no words whatsoever can amount to an assault," Hawkins, *Pleas of the Crown*, at p. 110.

[45] (1823) 1 Lew. 184.

[46] *R.* v. *Byrne* (1968) 3 C.C.C. 179.

[47] [1955] 1 W.L.R. 493 at 494.

[48] *Barton* v. *Armstrong* (1969) 2 N.S.W.R. 451.

courts could adopt the American view[49] that words do not make the actor liable for assault unless together with other acts or circumstances they put the other in reasonable apprehension of an imminent harmful or offensive contact with the person.[50] This approach did not appeal to Scott J. in the case of *Thomas* v. *NUM*[51] although it appears that he was referred only to the leading textbook and not to the authorities themselves. He stated that:

> "Assault is defined in *Clerk & Lindsell on Torts*, (15th ed.) (1982) para. 14–10 as 'an overt act indicating an immediate intention to commit a battery coupled with the capacity to carry that intention into effect.' The tort of assault is not, in my view, committed unless the capacity in question is present at the time the overt act is committed. Since the working miners are in vehicles and the pickets are held back from vehicles, I do not understand how even the most violent of threats or gestures could be said to constitute an assault."[52]

In any event, a movement otherwise constituting an assault may be negatived by the words preceding or accompanying them as in the famous case of *Tuberville* v. *Savage*[53] when the defendant placed his hand on a sword and said "were it not assize time I would not take such language from you."

Not every threatening act will be an assault. To shake a fist is not an assault if the victim is not near enough to be struck[54] but if he might be, it matters not that the actual blow is interrupted by a third party[55] or the victim makes an escape.[56] Whether pointing an unloaded pistol is an assault is unclear on the authorities; *Blake* v. *Barnard*[57] ruled that it would not, while *R.* v. *George*[58] suggested that it would.

It is sometimes claimed that in order to commit an assault the defendant must have the immediate means to carry out the act he threatens.[59] However, it is submitted that this is not relevant to the tort; the crucial issue is whether the act puts a reasonable person in fear of a battery.[60]

The relationships with criminal proceedings

Assault and battery are of course crimes as well as torts. The Offences Against the Persons Act 1861 provides that in certain circumstances

[49] Handford, "Tort Liability for threatening or insulting words" [1976] Can.B.R. 563.

[50] Prosser, *Second Restatement on Torts*, section 31.

[51] [1986] Ch. 20.

[52] *Ibid.* at 62B.

[53] [1669] 1 Mod.Rep. 3.

[54] *Cobbett* v. *Grey* (1849) 4 Ex. 729 at 744.

[55] *Stephens* v. *Myers* (1830) 4 C. & P. 483.

[56] *Martin* v. *Shopper* (1828) 3 C. & P. 375.

[57] (1840) 9 C. & P. 626.

[58] (1840) 9 C. & P. 483.

[59] *Steven* v. *Myers* (1830) 4 C. & P. 483, *per* Tindall C.J. at 349–50; *Osborn* v. *Veitch* (1858) 1 F. & F. 317, *per* Willes J. at 318; and *Thomas* v. *NUM* [1986] Ch. 20 at 62B.

[60] In *Logdon* v. *D.P.P.* [1976] Crim.L.R. 121 the defendant was guilty of a criminal assault where he did not intend to apply force but the victim believed she would be assaulted; see also *Smith* v. *Chief Superintendent of the Woking Police Station* (1983) 76 Cr.App.R. 234.

summary criminal proceedings operate as a bar against subsequent civil proceedings[61] although the Criminal Law Revision Committee has recommended that the provisions be repealed.[62] In practise, these provisions will not be very relevant to police cases since it is seldom desireable to bring criminal proceedings against the police as an alternative to a civil action.[63]

By sections 42 and 43 of the 1861 Act magistrates have power to convict summarily individuals charged with common assault or certain assaults on women and children under 14. Section 44[64] provides:

> "If the justices upon the hearing of any such case of assault or battery upon the merits where the [information] was preferred by or on behalf of the party aggrieved under either of the last two preceding sections shall deem the offences not to be proved, or shall find the assault or battery to have been justified or so dismiss the [information], they shall forthwith make out a certificate under their hand stating the fact of such dismissal, and shall deliver such a certificate to the party against whom the information was preferred."

Section 45[65] provides:

> "If any person against whom any such [information] as in either of the last three preceding sections mentioned shall have been preferred by or on behalf of the party aggrieved shall have obtained such a certificate or, having been convicted, shall have paid the whole amount adjudged to be paid or shall have suffered the imprisonment or imprisonment with hard labour, in every such case he shall be released from further or other proceedings, civil or criminal for the same cause."

The provisions will, therefore, apply if the defendant is acquitted and obtains a certificate or if he is convicted but has paid the fine imposed or served his sentence or imprisonment.

In order that a certificate be issued, the hearing must be upon the merits so one cannot be obtained if the defendant pleads guilty,[66] or if the prosecution withdraws the summons.[67] However, if the charge is dismissed, the magistrates are bound to issue a certificate upon an application being made and may be compelled to do so by mandamus.[68] The certificate itself is only valid if it shows that the information was dismissed on one of the three grounds prescribed in section 44.[69]

A defendant must prove the conviction either by the production of the original record, an examined copy,[70] or by a copy of the conviction purport-

[61] North, "Civil and Criminal Proceedings for Assault" (1966) 29 M.L.R. 16.
[62] Fourteenth Report, Report on Offences Against the Person, Cmnd. 7844, (1980) paras. 163–164.
[63] Chap. 3 above at p. 61.
[64] As amended by s.50 of the Magistrates' Courts Act 1980.
[65] As amended by the Criminal Justice Act 1948 and the Magistrates' Court Act 1980, s.50.
[66] *Ellis* v. *Burton* [1975] 1 W.L.R. 386.
[67] *Reed* v. *Nutt* (1890) 24 Q.B.D. 669.
[68] *Hancock* v. *Somes* (1859) 1 E. & E. 795.
[69] *Skuse* v. *Davies* (1839) 10 A. & E. 635.
[70] *Hartley* v. *Hindmarsh* (1866) L.R. 1 C.P. 553.

ing to by signed by a justice or proper officer of the court or by a copy of the entry in the register[71] certified by the clerk as a true copy.

If the magistrates order the defendant to enter a recognisance, there is no conviction for the purposes of the Act.[72] It is uncertain whether all proceedings are barred if the sentence given is not either a fine or imprisonment. Although a county court has held that there was no bar to civil proceedings when the defendant was bound over,[73] it was suggested obiter in *R.* v. *Miles*[74] that a defendant could invoke the Act where he was bound over after conviction.

Criminal proceedings will prevent a civil action even where it is brought by someone other than the original complainant.[75] However, if a final civil judgment has been given before criminal proceedings are instituted, a later civil appeal is not barred.[76]

The conviction[77] or dismissal[78] of a charge against an employee does not debar proceedings against his employer alleging that he is vicariously liable. Thus, it seems that the Chief Constable could not raise the Act as a bar in relation to assaults committed by constables under his direction.[79]

In addition to the obstacles created by the 1861 Act, there is a rule of public policy that civil proceedings are an abuse of process if they are used to initiate a collateral attack on a final decision made by a criminal court of competent jurisdiction.[80]

3. FALSE IMPRISONMENT

Definition

False imprisonment may be defined as intentionally but without lawful justification subjecting another to total restraint of movement either by actively causing his confinement or preventing him exercising his privilege of leaving the place where he is.[81]

The nature and character of the defendant's act

The term "false" is misleading since it is not being used in the ordinary sense of mendacious or fallacious but in the less common sense of erroneous or wrong such as false step.[81a]

[71] Under r.68 of the Magistrates' Court Rules 1981.
[72] *Hartley* v. *Hindmarsh* (1866) L.R. 1 C.P. 553.
[73] *Gibbons* v. *Harris* [1956] C.L.Y. 8611.
[74] (1890) 24 Q.B.D. 423 at 430.
[75] *Masper* v. *Brown* (1876) 1 C.P.D. 97.
[76] *Magee* v. *Storey* [1929] N.I. 134.
[77] *Dyer* v. *Munday* [1895] 1 Q.B. 742.
[78] *Corney* v. *Ministry of Labour* [1958] C.L.Y. 2656.
[79] Police Act 1964, s.48.
[80] *Hunter* v. *Chief Constable of West Midlands* [1982] A.C. 529; see Chap. 3 above at p. 61.
[81] *Fleming on Torts* at p. 26.
[81a] *Salmond on Torts* at p. 116, n. 46.

The classic definition of imprisonment is found in the 16th century work, *Termes de la Ley*:

> "Imprisonment is no other thing but the restraint of a man's liberty, whether it be in the open field or the stocks, or in the cage in the streets or in a man's own house as well as the common goal; and in all places the party so restrained is said to be the prisoner as long as he hath no liberty freely to go at all times to all places, whether without bail[82] or mainprise[83] or otherwise."[84]

An individual may therefore be confined in a house,[85] in a car driven at such speed that he cannot alight[86] or even in a large area within which he is free to move.[87]

The area of confinement must be fixed by the defendant and must constitute a total rather than partial restraint on his liberty. Consequently, it is not a false imprisonment to prevent someone going along any part of the highway and compelling him to go back; he is not imprisoned if he is free to go in some directions but not others.[88] Thus, where the police set up road blocks, they are not liable for false imprisonment by refusing to allow anyone to pass. However, the statements they make or the actions they take in barring the highway may make them guilty of assaults or batteries unless they can rely on the defence of "lawful justification."

The constraint imposed upon the plaintiff may be actual physical force but can include asserting legal authority to confine him[89] or dissuading him from leaving confinement[90] or restraining him through the plaintiff's desire to avoid public embarrassment.[91] Merely making a charge against the plaintiff without actually confining him does not constitute false imprisonment.[92] The plaintiff must actually be arrested[93]

The tort can also be committed if an individual is initially lawfully detained but his detention later becomes unlawful for some reason. At common law a constable could only detain a felon, arrested without warrant, for a reasonable time,[94] after this time had elapsed the detention would become unlawful. However, the police will now be liable for false imprisonment if they exceed their statutory powers to detain suspects. The difference between this statutory test of false imprisonment and the old common law

[82] The granting of bail releases a person from imprisonment; *Syed Mahamud Yusuf-ud-Din* v. *Secretary of State for India* [1903] 19 T.L.R. 496.

[83] A person mainprised is at large.

[84] Approved *Bird* v. *Jones* (1845) 7 Q.B. 742 and *Meering* v. *Grahame-White Aviation Co.* (1919) 122 T.L.R. 44.

[85] *Warner* v. *Ruddiford* (1858) 4 C.B.(NS) 180.

[86] *Burton* v. *Davies* [1953] Q.S.R. 26.

[87] *Kuchenmeister* v. *Home Office* [1958] 1 Q.B. 496; the plaintiff was prevented from proceeding from the airport to an aeroplane by immigration officers who were not authorised to prescribe the area within which he had to remain.

[88] *Bird* v. *Jones* (1845) 7 Q.B. 742.

[89] *Warner* v. *Riddiford* (1858) 4 C.B. (NS) 180 at 204, *per* Willes J.

[90] *Harnett* v. *Bond* [1925] A.C. 669.

[91] *Conn* v. *David Spencer* (1930) 1 D.L.R. 805.

[92] *Simpson* v. *Hill* (1795) Esp. 431.

[93] Chap. 5 below at p. 132.

[94] See *Wright* v. *Court* (1825) 4 B. & C. 596; *John Lewis & Co.* v. *Tims* [1952] A.C. 676 at 682.

test of whether the period of detention was "unreasonable" was analysed in *Millington* v. *MPC*.[95] In this case it was necessary to consider police powers of detention as they were prior to the Police and Criminal Evidence Act 1984. Forbes J. described the position as follows:

> "There seems no doubt, therefore, that at common law a constable had power to detain for a reasonable time. Has the position been altered by statute? Section 38(4) (of the Magistrates' Court Act 1952) requires 'where a person is taken into custody for an offence without a warrant and is retained in custody, he shall be brought before a magistrates' court as soon as practicable. . . . ' Section 38(4) had its origin in a similarly worded provision in section 22 of the Criminal Justice Administration Act 1914, so that at least since that time there has been a statutory duty to bring a detained person before justices as soon as practicable, but this of course is a duty only in relation to persons arrested without warrant. It seems to me inevitable that Parliament intended in such a case that the statutory duty to bring a man before justices as soon as practicable was intended to override the common law power of a constable to detain for a reasonable period."

It is submitted that the "detention provisions" of the Police and Criminal Evidence Act 1984 must also been taken an intended to override the common law. It follows that it is no longer appropriate to ask whether a person's detention by the police became unlawful because he was held for an unreasonably long time. An initially lawful detention will become unlawful if the relevant provisions of the 1984 Act are not complied with.[96]

The police may also become liable for false imprisonment if the conditions of detention become so intolerable that they are seriously prejudicial to the plaintiff's health by, for example, a cell becoming flooded or containing a leaking gas pipe, the subsequent detention will be unlawful.[97]

It is unclear if false imprisonment can arise from an ommission to carry out a duty[98] (as opposed to positive action). In *Herd* v. *Weardale Steal Coal and Coke Co.*[99] it was held by the Court of Appeal that a mere ommission cannot ground an action for false imprisonment. However, the House of Lords[1] seem to have proceeded on the narrower ground that the plaintiff could not establish his employer's breach of contract in failing to operate a lift to take him up from a coal mine after he wrongly refused to undertake certain work. It is therefore said that in such cases the plaintiff's right to be released depends (in the absence of unforseen circumstances) upon the terms of the agreement as a result of which he became confined.[2]

Nonetheless, it is well established that except under statute, a person

95 Reported in part (1983) 133 N.L. 806, *The Times*, May 28, 1983.

96 See Chap. 5 below at pp. 157 *et seq*.

97 *Middleweek* v. *Chief Constable of Merseyside, The Times*, August 1, 1985; Chap. 5 below at p. 162.

98 See *Mee* v. *Cruikshank* (1902) 186 L.T. 708 and see also, *Morriss* v. *Winter* [1930] 1 K.B. 243 where an action based on failing to discharge a prisoner at the termination of his sentence failed on other grounds and the point was not argued.

99 [1913] 3 K.B. 771; *per* Buckley and Hamilton L.JJ. and see also, *Burns* v. *Johnston* [1916] 2 Ir.R. 444.

1 [1915] A.C. 67.

2 *Fleming on Torts* at p. 28.

cannot be imprisoned to enforce a civil claim without due process of law.[3] Furthermore the other leading case of *Robinson* v. *Balmain New Ferry*[4] seems to have been decided on an altogether different basis[5]; it seems to have turned on whether or not the plaintiff was entitled to withdraw his consent to his continuing imprisonment.[6] It is accordingly submitted that the question of whether an ommission to carry out a duty (which may be contractual or otherwise) can ground an action for false imprisonment remains open.

The defendant's state of mind

There is no authority on this point although the tort is normally committed intentionally in the sense that the defendant intends to do an act which is substantially certain to effect (or continue)[7] the confinement[8]

The plaintiff's state of mind

False imprisonment can be committed even though the plaintiff is too ill to move[9] or where he is not suspicious that he is being restrained as in *Meering* v. *Grahame White Aviation Co.*[10] In that case Atkins L.J. suggested *obiter* that:

> "a person can be imprisoned, while he is asleep, while he is in a state of unconsciousness and while he is a lunatic."[11]

Unfortunately, these remarks were made without reference to *Herring* v. *Boyle*[12] which held that false imprisonment cannot arise where the plaintiff is unaware of the restraint.

The liability of a third party for false imprisonment by a police officer

It is of course possible for someone to be liable for false imprisonment where he does not personally commit the tort. A principal will be liable for acts of his agent acting within the scope of the authority which he con-

[3] See Amos, "A note on contractual restraint of liberty" (1928) 44 L.Q.R. 464.
[4] [1910] A.C. 295.
[5] *Cf. Herd* v. *Weardale Steel* [1915] A.C. 67 at 72, *per* Lord Haldane.
[6] Tan, "A misconceived issue in false imprisonment" (1981) 44 M.L.R. 166.
[7] *Griffin* v. *Coleman* (1859) 4 H. & N. 265.
[8] Street at p. 23.
[9] *Grainger* v. *Hill* (1838) 4 Bing.N.C. 212.
[10] (1919) 122 T.L.R. 44.
[11] *Ibid.* at 53–54.
[12] (1834) 1 Cr. M. & R. 377.

ferred.[13] However, he will not be liable if his agent exercises an independent judgment.

A third party will, therefore, not be held responsible for false imprisonment by an arresting police officer if the decision to make an arrest is entirely within the discretion of the officer and he simply gave information upon which the officer made his own judgment.[14] However, if a third party takes it upon himself to direct a police constable to arrest the plaintiff, then he will make himself liable for the false imprisonment.[15]

Signing a charge sheet is only evidence that the third party authorised an arrest; unless the third party actually directed the imprisonment, signing the charge sheet merely makes him the prosecutor.[16] Therefore, if he signs it at the request of a constable who has made his own independent inquiries, he will not be liable.[17] On the other hand, he will be liable, if the constable states the plaintiff will not be detained unless the third party signs it.[18] Indeed, it has been held that a statement from a third party that he took the plaintiff in charge was sufficient to make him liable for false imprisonment.[19]

Furthermore, where a third party knowingly makes a false statement which provides the basis for a constable's independent investigations, he may still be liable in false imprisonment (in addition to defamation).[20] This suggestion arises from the case of *Flewster* v. *Royle*[21] where the defendant falsely imprisoned the plaintiff by causing him to be seized by a press gang to which she had given false information. The decision has been explained as proceeding upon a finding that the defendant acted maliciously.[22] However, malice is not a necessary ingredient of false imprisonment; nor has it any relevance to the question of a principal's liability for his agent. Nevertheless, it has been argued that providing false information to a prosecutor should impose liability for false imprisonment in the same way as it does for malicious prosecution.[23]

False imprisonment and wrongful arrest

As a matter of practice it is often assumed that there is a tort of wrongful arrest which is distinct from false imprisonment and malicious arrest. This tort is regarded as having been committed when a purported arrest is, in fact, unjustified in law and therefore "wrongful." Such a view presupposes

[13] *Launchbury* v. *Morgans* [1973] A.C. 127; *Heaton's Transport* v. *T.G.W.U.* [1973] A.C. 15.
[14] *Sewell* v. *National Telephone Co.* [1907] 1 K.B. 557.
[15] *Hopkins* v. *Crowe* (1836) 4 A. & E. 774.
[16] *Sewell* v. *National Telephone Co.* [1907] 1 K.B. 557 at 560, *per* Collins M.R.
[17] *Grinham* v. *Willey* (1859) 4 H. & N. 496.
[18] *Austin* v. *Dowling* (1870) L.R.5C.P. 534.
[19] *A Chubb* v. *Wimpey & Co.* [1936] 1 All E.R. 69. The precise basis for Charles J.'s ruling is unclear and the Court of Appeal ordered a new trial at [1936] 3 All E.R. 148 without commenting upon it.
[20] See Chap. 10 below at p. 315.
[21] (1808) 1 Camp. 187.
[22] *Gospen* v. *Elphick* (1849) 4 Ex. 445; *Grinham* v. *Willey* (1859) 4 H. & N. 496 at 498.
[23] See Chap. 8 below at p. 251 and Kodlinger, "False Imprisonment through ministerial officers: the Commonwealth experience" (1979) I.C.L.Q. 766 at 772.

that whether or not a person is "arrested" depends not on the legality of what was done but on whether or not the suspect was deprived of his liberty to go as he pleases.[24] Nevertheless, it is clear from the authorities that there is no separate tort of wrongful arrest.[25] What the plaintiff in such an action is complaining about is the restriction on his liberty. It is difficult to see how a failed attempt at arrest could be called an "arrest" at all. As Lord Edmund-Davies said in *Spicer* v. *Holt*[26]:

> "where a man has quite unlawfully been physically restrained and is (however temporarily) detained in a condition which automatically invests him with a right to sue for damages for the tort of false imprisonment it is in strictness inaccurate to describe him as ever having 'been arrested' or 'under arrest'."

Thus, "wrongful arrest" is simply a form of false imprisonment and the onus is on the defendant to justify the arrest in the usual way. There may be situations in which, for the sake of clarity in pleadings, "wrongful arrest" would be pleaded instead of "false imprisonment."[27]

The distinction between false imprisonment and malicious prosecution

Where an imprisonment is effected through judicial proceedings, liability for false imprisonment virtually disappears:

> "The distinction between false imprisonment and malicious prosecution is well illustrated by the case where the parties being before a magistrate, one makes a false charge against another, whereupon the magistrate orders the person to be charged and taken into custody until the matter is investigated. The person making the charge is not liable for the action because he does not set a ministerial officer in motion but a judicial officer is interposed between the charge and the imprisonment."[28]

Consequently, where the plaintiff is wrongfully arrested without a warrant and remanded into custody by the magistrates he can only maintain an action for false imprisonment for the period up to the time of the remand. Thereafter, he must sue for malicious prosecution. Even if the court acts without jurisdiction the instigator of the complaint cannot be liable for false imprisonment.[29] However, the magistrates themselves may be liable for false imprisonment.[30] Where a valid order of the court has been obtained, the third party may again become liable for his agent's wrongful acts in executing that order. Whether the principal directed the act (rather

[24] This was the definition advanced by Viscount Dilhorne in *Spicer* v. *Holt* [1977] A.C. 987 at 1000.

[25] *cf.* Street at p. 24.

[26] [1977] A.C. 987.

[27] See Chap. 3 above at p. 68.

[28] *Austin* v. *Dowling* (1870) L.R.5 C.P. 534 at 540, *per* Willes J.

[29] *West* v. *Smallwood* (1838) 3 M. & M. 418; *Browne* v. *Chapman* (1848) 6 C.B. 365.

[30] See the Justices of the Peace Act 1979, s.45 and 52; *O'Connor* v. *Isaacs* [1956] 2 Q.B. 288; *R* v. *Waltham Forest JJ, ex p. Solanke* [1986] 1 W.L.R. 315.

than providing information for which he will escape liability)[31] is a question of fact.[32]

4. OTHER INTENTIONAL TORTS AFFECTING THE PERSON

"Harassment"

In the case of *Thomas* v. *National Union of Mineworkers (South Wales Area*[33] it was held that it was tortious for pickets to abuse workers entering their place of work even though there was no assault because the capacity to carry out the intention to commit a battery was not present (the workers being in buses and under police protection).[34] The pickets' conduct was held to be unlawful because:

> "the law has long recognised that unreasonable interference with the rights of others is actionable in tort. The law of nuisance is a classic example and was classically described by Lindley M.R. in *J Lyons & Sons* v. *Wilkins* [1899] 1 Ch. 255 at 267. I have already cited the passage. It is, however, not every act of interference with the enjoyment of an individual of his property rights that will be actionable in nuisance. The law must strike a balance between conflicting rights and interests. The point is made in *Clerk & Lindsell on Torts* at para. 23–01:
>
> > 'a variety of different things may amount to a nuisance in fact but whether they are actionable as the tort of nuisance will depend upon a variety of considerations and a balancing of conflicting interests.'
>
> Nuisance is strictly concerned with, and may be regarded as confined to, activity which unduly interferes with the use or enjoyment of land or of easements. But there is no reason why the law should not protect on a similar basis the enjoyment of other rights. All citizens have the right to use the public highway. Suppose an individual were persistently to follow another on a public highway, making rude gestures or remarks in order to annoy or vex. If continuance of such conduct were threatened no one can doubt but that a civil court would, at the suit of the victim, restrain by injunction the continuance of the conduct. The tort might be described as a species of private nuisance, namely unreasonable interference with the victim's rights to use the highway. But the label for the tort does not, in my view, matter."[35]

The case, therefore, appears to give recognition to a wider tort of "harassment," at least in relation to the user of the highway. It will have obvious application to cases involving allegations of police harassment. However, it is submitted that the existence of such a tort must remain open to argument. It is questionable whether a new tort may be deduced from an alleged

[31] *Crimshaw* v. *Chapman* (1862) 7 H. & N. 911.
[32] *Morris* v. *Salbery* (1889) 22 Q.B.D. 614.
[33] [1986] Ch. 20.
[34] *Ibid.* at 62B.
[35] *Ibid.* at 64 A-E.

general principle of tortious liability.[36] At the very least, the exact limits of the tort remain to be worked out. In *News Group Newspapers* v. *Society of Graphical and Allied Trades*[37] Stuart-Smith J. had this to say about the new tort:

> "[the Defendants] submit that Scott J. should not have invented a new tort and that it was not sufficient to found liability that there was an unreasonable interference with the rights of others, even though when a balance is struck between conflicting rights and interests the scale comes down in favour of the plaintiffs, unless those rights are recognised by the law and fall within some accepted head of tort. I am bound to say that, with all respect to Scott J., I think there is a force in these criticisms, especially where it does not appear that damage is a necessary ingredient of the tort."

Intimidation

It is a tort if a person by threatening another that he will commit an unlawful act causes him to do something (or refrain from doing something) which is to his own detriment.[38]

The origins of the tort involved threats of violence. Thus in the leading case of *Tarleton* v. *M'Gawley*[39] the defendant, a ship's captain, fired guns at an African canoe in order to prevent the occupants from trading with the plaintiff's ship and was successfully sued for damages. Although the tort is, in modern times, most commonly used in trade union cases it remains of general application.

The threats used must be coercive and must be distinguished from mere "warnings." A "threat" means:

> "an intimation by one to another that unless the latter does or does not do something the former will do something the latter would not like."[40]

The tort is only committed if the defendant threatens to commit a wrongful act.[41] Anything that a man can do lawfully he can also lawfully threaten to do.[42] This position may be contrasted with the tort of conspiracy in which a combination from the purpose of damaging the plaintiff will be actionable even though no lawful acts are involved.[43]

The tort will, therefore, be committed if the defendant threatens violence, or an unlawful detention or seizure of goods. It will also be committed if a police officer threatens to misuse his public office.[44]

In order for there to be a complete cause of action in intimidation the per-

[36] Benedictus, "The Use of the Law of Tort in the Miner's Dispute" 14 I.L.J. 176 at 181 *et seq*.
[37] [1986] I.R.L.R. 377 at 348.
[38] See *Rookes* v. *Barnard* [1964] A.C. 1129.
[39] (1794) Peake. 270.
[40] *Hodges* v. *Webb* [1920] 2 Ch. 70 at 89.
[41] *Ware & De Freville* v. *Motor Trade Association* [1921] 3 K.B. 40.
[42] See *Allen* v. *Flood* [1898] A.C. 1; *Rookes* v. *Barnard* [1964] A.C. 1129 at 1169.
[43] See Chap. 10 below at p. 323.
[44] See *David* v. *Abdul Cader* [1963] 1 W.L.R. 834, P.C.

son threatened must actually comply with the threats and suffer damage as a result. If someone is threatened with violence and decides to resist there is no action in intimidation.[45] Nevertheless, he may obtain a *quia timet* injunction[46] to restrain the threat to commit an unlawful act where he has not yet succumbed to the threats and suffered damage, provided the threats are serious and taken seriously by those to whom they are made.[47]

The tort of intimidation is likely to be of very limited application in relation to civil actions against the police. Nevertheless, it may be relevant where a person is unlawfully threatened by a police officer, for example, to make a confession or give information against a third party. The police may have sufficient evidence (independent of the confession) to provide a complete defence to an action for false imprisonment or malicious prosecution. If there are threats of violence then an action for assault would lie but if the threats are against another person, for example a threat that a child will be taken into care, then intimidation will be the only cause of action available. If the plaintiff has succumbed to the threat then he would have to show some financial loss or nervous shock. If he has not succumbed then, in an appropriate case, a *quia timet* injunction would be available.

Intentionally causing nervous shock

Illness or injury induced by nervous shock which does not arise from a physical impact or a threat to apply force is nevertheless tortious. This extension to the traditional forms of trespass to the person was considered in *Wilkinson* v. *Downton*.[48] The defendant told the plaintiff, as a practical joke, that her husband had had a serious accident and had broken his legs. This statement was false but had been made with the intention that it would be believed. Wright J. held that:

> "The defendant has wilfully done an act calculated to cause physical harm to the plaintiff—that is to say, to infringe her legal right to personal safety and has in fact, thereby caused physical harm to her. The proposition without more appears to me to state a good cause of action, there being no justification alleged for the act."[49]

The principle was approved by the Court of Appeal in *Janvier* v. *Sweeney*,[50] and in the recent case of *Burnett* v. *George*[51] where the Court of Appeal had to consider whether a non-molestation injunction expressed in general terms was too widely drawn. A narrower formulation was substituted and it was held that where:

> "there be evidence that the health of the plaintiff is being impaired by molestation or interference calculated to create such impairment . . . relief would be granted by way of an injunction to the extent that it would be necessary to avoid the impairment of health."

[45] See *Stratford* v. *Lindley* [1965] A.C. 269 at 283.
[46] See Chap. 12 below at p. 379.
[47] *News Group Newspapers* v. *SOGAT 82* [1986] I.R.L.R. 337.
[48] [1897] 2 Q.B. 57.
[49] *Ibid.* at 58–59.
[50] [1919] 2 K.B. 316.
[51] March 6, 1986 unreported.

However, the precise limits of the tort require clarification. It has been suggested that because there was no evidence that the defendants intended the plaintiffs in these cases to be ill, liability will arise simply if a defendant intends the act which induces the nervous shock.[52] Nevertheless, proof of the intention to cause the physical harm is a necessary ingredient of the tort. The decided cases may be explained on a different basis. On general principle, proof may be established by inferring that a person intends the natural consequences of his acts and it seems that this principle was applied to prove the intention to cause physical harm.[53]

If the defendant merely intends to frighten his victim, this will be sufficient if his conduct is of a kind reasonably capable of terrifying a normal human being or was known or ought to have been known to the defendant to be likely to terrify the plaintiff for reasons special to him.[54] On the other hand, firing a revolver after threatening to shoot someone has been held not to be acts which are calculated or likely to cause harm to another.[55]

No action will lie for mere mental suffering and it is necessary for the plaintiff to suffer from some recognisable psychiatric illness.[56] The tort may be committed if the defendant intentionally conducts himself so as to cause nervous shock and is not limited to statements alone.[57]

The tort of inflicting mental distress has become highly developed in the United States. By about 1930 liability for conduct exceeding all bounds usually tolerated by decent society of a nature which is especially calculated to cause and does cause mental distress of a very serious kind became recognised although its ultimate limits have yet to be determined.[58] Thus, for example, bullying a school girl with threats of prison and public disgrace unless she signed a confession of immoral conduct was tortious[59] as was prolonged and extreme hounding by insurance adjusters to effect a settlement.[60] Liability will also arise if the defendant knows that the plaintiff is especially sensitive and vulnerable to injury,[61] a principle which has been applied to sick persons, children and pregnant women.

In the United States there is no need to establish that the mental distress has resulted in physical illness. Intention will be proved if the plaintiff can show the defendant desired to cause it or knew that it was substantially certain to follow from his conduct or where there is a high degree of risk that mental distress will follow and the defendant goes ahead in conscious disregard of it. Liability will extend to conduct directed at third party where the plaintiff is not only present at the time but is known by the defendant to be present so that the mental distress can be reasonably anticipated; it seems that the recovery is not limited to near relations of the person attacked or close associates.

52 Goodhart (1944) 7 M.L.R. 88.

53 *Wilkinson* v. *Downton* [1897] 2 Q.B. 57 at 59; *Shapiro* v. *La Morta* (1924) 130 L.T. 622 at 625.

54 *Bunyan* v. *Jordan* (1936) 36 S.R. 350 at 353.

55 *Bunyan* v. *Jordan* (1936) 57 C.L.R. 1.

56 *Lynch* v. *Knight* (1861) 9 H.L. 577 at 598; although once some special damage is proved then mental suffering can be recovered as aggravated damages.

57 *Purdy* v. *Woznesensky* (1937) 2 W.W.R. 116.

58 Prosser, *Torts*, at pp. 49 *et seq.*

59 *Johnson* v. *Sampson* (1926) 167 Min. 203.

60 *Continental Car* v. *Garrett* (1933) 173 Miss. 676.

61 *Nickerson* v. *Hodge* (1920) 146 La. 735.

This tort may provide a suitable cause of action in relation to certain types of police misconduct. For example, if the police threatened the wife of a suspected criminal that her children would be taken into the care of a local authority unless she divulged information, she would have a right to damages if the threat induced nervous shock.

5. GENERAL DEFENCES TO TRESPASS TO THE PERSON

Introduction

Once it is proved or admitted that a trespass has occured, the burden is on the defendant to prove that it was justified.[62] The police can rely on the general defences available to all members of the public in addition to any special defences arising from police powers at common law or under statute. In this section the general defences are considered and in Chapter 5 police powers over the person are examined.

There are five general defences which are relevant to an action brought against the police[63]:

(1) that the plaintiff is a wrongdoer;
(2) consent;
(3) the statutory defence under section 45 of the Offences Against the Person Act 1861[64];'
(4) self-defence;
(5) the prevention of a crime or a breach of the peace.

The last two defences involve justifying—as being committed under the authority of law—acts which would otherwise be unlawful. Consequently, if that authority is abused, it may be argued that the defendant is liable for everything he did whilst exercising it[65]: in other words that he is a trespasser *ab initio*.[66] However, it should be noted that if a person is in lawful custody which then becomes unlawful, the false imprisonment will arise at the time of the unlawfulness and not at the time of the initial imprisonment.[67]

The plaintiff is a wrongdoer

The extent of this defence or its underlying justification has been uncertain. Sometimes it is claimed that a rule of public policy which debars a plaintiff who is guilty of wrongdoing from recovery arises from the maxim *ex turpi causa non oritur actio*. However, it would seem preferable to

[62] *Holroyd* v. *Doncaster* (1826) 3 Bing. 492; *Dallison* v. *Caffrey* [1965] 1 Q.B. 348 at 365.
[63] For defences to trespass generally see Clerk & Lindsell at pp. 14–29 *et seq.*
[64] See above at p. 109.
[65] See, *e.g. Ward's Case* (1636) Clay 44.
[66] See Chap. 7 below at p. 184.
[67] *Smith* v. *Egginton* (1873) 7 A. & E. 167.

confine this maxim to the law of contract.[68] Nonetheless, public policy grounds have led to decisions that no duty of care exists between joint participants to a burglary[69] or that no action for trespass lay for contracting venereal disease from an extra-marital relationship with a man who misrepresented his condition.[70] On the other hand, the principle does not extend to breaches of the health and safety legislation of which the plaintiff is guilty.[71]

In *Murphy* v. *Culhane*[72] Lord Denning M.R. suggested that a man who takes part in a criminal affray may be guilty of such a wicked act that he is deprived of the right to sue in trespass. He expressed similar views in *Lane* v. *Holloway*[73] where he also said that even if a fight is unlawful a participant can sue if he is struck with a blow out of proportion to the occasion.

It may now be argued that a plaintiff's misconduct may have implications beyond extinguishing his claim for aggravated and exemplary damages.[74] The plaintiff's wrongdoing may be relied upon as providing a complete defence to an action in tort. According to *Thackwell* v. *Barclay's Bank*[75] the court will look at the quality of the illegality relied upon and the proximity of the illegal conduct to the plaintiff's claim in order to determine:

(1) whether there has been illegality of which the court should take notice; and
(2) whether giving relief to the plaintiff is contrary to public policy because it would be indirectly assisting or encouraging him in his criminal act.

Thus, in *Barnes* v. *Nayer*[75a] the Court of Appeal upheld it as a defence in an action for trepass to the person. Consequently, the allegation that the plaintiff is a wrongdoer is likely to provide a fertile defence to actions brought against the police, particularly where they arise from incidents such as riots or from mass picketing and the plaintiff can be shown to have been a participant in the riot or picket.

Consent

The defence of consent (whether express or implied) raises a number of legal issues which are not directly relevant to alleged trespasses by the police.[76] However, if it is argued that the plaintiff has acted unlawfully, consent will provide an alternative to a defence based on *ex turpi causa*.[77]

In *Freeman* v. *Home Office*[78] it was held that the burden of proving the absence of consent lies on the plaintiff. This decision arose from the fact

[68] *Smith* v. *Jenkins* (1970) 119 C.L.R 397; *cf. Gordon* v. *M.P.C.* [1910] 2 K.B. 1080.
[69] *Ashton* v. *Turner* [1981] Q.B. 147.
[70] *Hegarty* v. *Shine* (1878) 14 Cox C.C. 345.
[71] *National Coal Board* v. *England* [1954] A.C. 403.
[72] [1977] 1 Q.B. 94 at 98.
[73] [1968] 1 Q.B. 379.
[74] See Chap. 11 at pp. 343 *et seq.*
[75] [1986] 1 All E.R. 676.
[75a] *The Times*, December 19, 1986.
[76] See Clerk & Lindsell, paras. 14–06 to 14–09.
[77] See *Murphy* v. *Culhane* [1977] 1 Q.B. 94; *Woh* v. *Martin*)1955) 3 D.L.R. 635.
[78] [1984] Q.B. 524.

that the court accepted the definition of battery as "the unconsented to intrusion of another's bodily integrity." It is submitted that this is not the correct definition of battery and that, once an "intentional touching" is shown by the plaintiff the burden of proving consent lies on the defendant.

Self-defence

A person may use reasonable force either to defend himself or to do what is reasonably necessary to rescue another person from attack.[79] In some circumstances an assault will justify a battery.[80] A defendant is not bound to wait until someone has landed a blow and may repel an attack rather than simply defend himself.[81]

The force used in self-defence must be proportionate to the aggressor's act:

> "A man cannot justify a maim for every assault: as if A strikes B, B cannot justify drawing his sword and cutting off his hand: but be such an assault whereby probably his life may be in danger."[82]

Thus, a person may possess petrol bombs if he believes it to be no more than is reasonably necessary to meet an imminently expected attack[83] but not, it would seem, to prevent the police from getting out of hand by invading the Catholic area of the Bogside.[84] A person may also use force to resist an unlawful arrest. He may use as much force as is reasonable in the circumstances to avoid it.[85]

Preventing a crime or breach of the peace

At common law every citizen in whose presence a breach of the peace is being committed (or reasonably appears to be about to be committed) may take reasonable steps to make the person who is breaking (or threatening to break) the peace from doing so. These steps may include detaining him against his will.[86] In order to justify any preventive action the possibility of a breach of the peace must be real. The imminence or immediacy of the threat to the peace determines what action is reasonable.[87] However, unlike an ordinary citizen, a police officer may rely on information from another as founding the reasonable grounds for his belief.[88] Once the danger of the breach of the peace is over, the common law right of arrest will cease.[89]

There is a surprising lack of an authoritative definition of a breach of the

[79] *R.* v. *Duffy* [1967] 1 Q.B. 63.
[80] *Titley* v. *Foxall* (1758) 2 Ld.Ken. 308; *Dale* v. *Wood* (1822) 7 Morre 33.
[81] *Palmer* v. *R.* (1971) 55 Cr.App.R. 223; *R.* v. *Bird* [1965] 1 W.L.R. 816.
[82] *Cook* v. *Beal* (1697) 1 Ld.Raym. 176 at 177.
[83] *Attorney-General's Reference (No. 2 of 1983)* [1984] Q.B. 456.
[84] *Devlin* v. *Armstrong* [1971] N.I. 13.
[85] *R.* v. *Jones* [1978 R.T.R. 137.
[86] *Albert* v. *Lavin* [1982] A.C. 546.
[87] *Moss* v. *McLachlan* [1985] I.R.L.R. 76.
[88] *Timothy* v. *Simpson* (1835) 1 C.M. & R. 755 at 761–3.
[89] *Baynes* v. *Brewster* (1841) 2 Q.B. 375; *R.* v. *Walter* (1854) Dears. 358.

peace.[90] It arises where harm is actually done or is likely to be done to a person or where he is put in fear of such harm or where his property is harmed through an assault, affray, riot, unlawful assembly or other disturbance.[91] Behaving in a disorderly manner[92] or using abusive language[93] will constitute a breach of the peace only if a crowd collects so a riot ensues. Therefore, conduct which is annoying but which does not involve violence, a threat of violence, or an incitement to violence will not amount to a breach of the peace.[94] However, the police have a statutory power of arrest against any person reasonably suspected of using threatening, abusive, insulting or disturbing words or displaying any written representation which is threatening, abusive or insulting under the Public Order Act 1986.[95]

Section 3(1) of the Criminal Law Act 1967 permits a person to use such force as is reasonable in all circumstances either to prevent a crime or assist in the lawful arrest of offenders, suspected offenders or people at large. Section 3(2) provides that these rules replace the common law rules regarding the force to be used for such purposes. More force than is reasonable will render a lawful arrest unlawful.[96] The circumstances to be taken into account under section 3(1) are those in which the defendant is placed when making an arrest; they therefore would not include defects in the planning of that arrest which was made by others.[97]

The force to be used when effecting an arrest should be proportionate to the mischief it is intended to prevent. Therefore, arms can fired only if it is the last resort to preserve life.[98] The justification for doing so would fail if no reasonable man with the knowledge of the facts known to the officer or reasonably known by him in the circumstances and the time for reflection could think that the prevention of harm if a suspect escaped justified exposing him to the risk of harm.[99] Yet it has been held to be reasonable for a soldier to shoot an escaping suspect in the back who he reasonably believed to be involved in terrorist activities.[1]

6. LIMITATION

The length of the limitation period depends on the nature of the damages claimed. If they include damages for personal injuries proceedings must be brought within three years; if they do not, the limitation period is six years.

Thus proceedings for intentional[2] and for non-intentional[3] trespass be

[90] See generally, Glanville Williams, "Arrest for Breach of the Peace" [1954] Crim.L.R. 578.

[91] *R.* v. *Howell* [1982] Q.B. 416.

[92] *Ingle* v. *Bell* (1836) 1 M. & W. 516.

[93] *Cohen* v. *Huskisson* (1837) 2 M. & W. 477.

[94] But see *R.* v. *Chief Constable of Devon & Cornwall, ex p. CEGB* [1982] 1 Q.B. 458 at 471, *per* Lord Denning M.R.

[95] ss. 4, 5, 6.

[96] *Allen* v. *M.P.C.* [1980] Crim.L.R. 441.

[97] *Farrell* v. *Secretary of State for Defence* [1980] 1 W.L.R. 172.

[98] *Lynch* v. *Fitzgerald* [1938] I.R. 382.

[99] *Attorney-General for Northern Ireland's Reference* [1977] A.C. 105.

[1] *R.* v. *McNaughton* [1975] N.I. 203.

[2] *Long* v. *Hepworth* [1968] 1 W.L.R. 1299.

[3] *Letang* v. *Cooper* [1965] 1 Q.B. 232.

brought within the three year period stipulated by section 11 of the Limitation Act 1980 since the damages claimed include damages for personal injuries. The same limitation also applies to intentionally causing nervous shock because the broad statutory definition of personal injuries in the Limitation Act 1980, section 38(1).

Time begins to run either on the date the cause of action accrues or on the date of knowledge of the person injured if this is later.[4] The date of knowledge is that time at which the plaintiff actually or constructively knows that the injury is significant, that the injury is wholly or partly attributable to the act or omission on which the cause of action is based, the identity of the defendant, and if the act or ommission was of a person other than the defendant, the identity of that person and additional factors supporting bringing an action against the defendant.[5] An injury is significant if the plaintiff would reasonably have considered it sufficiently serious to justify the institution of proceedings against a defendant who did not dispute liability and was able to satisfy a judgment.[6] Moreover, the plaintiff's knowledge includes knowledge he might reasonably be expected to acquire from the facts observable or ascertainable by him or with the help of a medical or other expert whose advice it was reasonable for him to seek. However, if he took all reasonable steps to obtain (and act upon, if appropriate) the advice, he will not be fixed with knowledge of a fact only ascertainable with expert advice.[7]

However, damages for personal injuries can be sought even though the claim is time barred. Section 33 of the Act confers a wide discretion upon the court to allow an action to proceed despite the fact that the three year limitation period has expired. It will permit a late claim if it is equitable to do so, taking account of the extent to which the three year period prejudices the plaintiff and the extent to which exercising the discretion prejudices the defendant.[8] In addition to considering all the circumstances of the case, the court must take six specific factors into account: the length of the plaintiff's delay and the reasons for it, the extent to which the evidence adduced or likely to be adduced by either party is likely to be less cogent than if the claim was made within three years, the conduct of the defendant after the cause of action accrued (including his response to requests for information or inspection that are reasonably made), the extent of any disability suffered by the plaintiff since the cause of action accrued, the extent to which the plaintiff acted promptly and reasonably once he knew whether the defendant's act or omission might give rise to an action in damages and the steps if any taken by the plaintiff to obtain medical, legal or other expert advice and the nature of the advice received.[9] The discretion is therefore framed extremely broadly; the only circumstances in which it cannot be invoked is where a second set of proceedings is commenced after proceedings were begun within the limitation period but then dropped.[10]

If the plaintiff dies the Law Reform (Miscellaneous Provisions) Act 1934

[4] Limitation Act 1980, s.11(4).
[5] Limitation Act 1980, s.14(1).
[6] *Ibid.* s.14(2).
[7] *Ibid.* s.14(3).
[8] *Ibid.* s.33(1).
[9] *Ibid.* s.33(3).
[10] *Walkley* v. *Precision Foundings* [1979] 1 W.L.R. 606.

allows his cause of action to survive for the benefit of his estate. If the plaintiff dies after the limitation period has expired, his personal representatives may seek to override the three year period under the discretion provided by section 33. If the death is within the limitation period, his personal representatives have three years, either from the date of death or from the date of their knowledge, whichever is the later, to commence proceedings[11] although they may again apply to the court to override the limitation period if the claim becomes statute barred under section 33(1). The position concerning intentional torts which do not result in personal injury is quite different. The period of limitation is six years from the accrual of the cause of action.[12] In an assault which does not cause personal injuries, or in false imprisonment the cause of action will accrue at the date of the assault or imprisonment, not at the date damage occurs. However, where false imprisonment begins more than six years before the claim is brought but continues within that period the plaintiff is entitled to recover such damages in respect of the imprisonment which does fall within the limitation period.[13] It also seems that the limitation period in the an action for "harassment" begins to run at the date of the interference (because the tort seems to be actionable without proof of special damage). On the other hand, actions for intimidation or intentionally causing nervous shock are actions on the case and time runs from the date on which the plaintiff suffers damage.

[11] Limitation Act 1980, s.11(5).
[12] *Ibid.* s.2.
[13] *Coventry* v. *Aspley* (1691) 2 Salk. 420.

5. Police Powers over the Person: Arrest, Detention and other Miscellaneous Powers

1. INTRODUCTION

This chapter deals with the specific police powers which justify what would otherwise be trespasses against the person. These powers have been radically re-cast by the Police and Criminal Evidence Act 1984. Some powers have been modified and a whole range of new powers have been introduced. These are based on the report of the Phillips Commission[1] which recommended that a number of police practices be defined in terms of a general legal framework, subject to safeguards by means of formal recording procedures. The 1984 Act strives to achieve these two purposes.

The procedural safeguards contained in the 1984 Act raise difficult questions as to whether or not a breach of a specific provision makes the police liable for trespass to the person. Any interference with the person—whether by assault, battery or detention—is prima facie unlawful and any such interference by the police will, therefore, be tortious unless it can be shown to be "justified." The general approach that should be taken when examining "procedural safeguards" of the type found in the 1984 Act is discussed in Chapter 1.[2]

2. DETENTION SHORT OF ARREST

Introduction

In *R.* v. *Brown*,[3] Shaw L.J. said that while every arrest involves a deprivation of liberty, not every deprivation of liberty involves an arrest. However,

[1] Report of the Royal Commission on Criminal Procedure, Cmnd. 8092, 1981.
[2] See above at p. 28.
[3] (1976) 64 Cr.App.R. 231 at 234.

in every instance it is incumbent upon the police to justify their conduct as being lawful. Whether the justification involves demonstrating that they effected a lawful arrest or detained a person lawfully without arresting him is not relevant for the purposes of an action in tort.

The power to stop for questioning

It is sometimes suggested that the police have legal power to detain a suspect on the street in order to question him.[4] However, the common law gives an officer no special power to commit what would otherwise be a trespass in this situation. If a police officer attracts someone's attention and goes beyond the physical contact generally accepted by all who move in society[5] he will be liable for battery. In *Collins* v. *Willcox*[6] Goff L.J. explained the position as follows:

> "Of course, a police officer may subject another to restraint when he lawfully exercises his power of arrest; and he has other statutory powers, for example, the power to stop, search and detain persons under . . . [s.1 of the 1984 Act]. But, putting such cases aside, police officers have for present purposes no greater rights than ordinary citizens. It follows that, subject to such cases, physical contact by a police officer with another person may be unlawful as a battery, just as it might be if he was an ordinary member of the public. But a police officer has his rights as a citizen as well as his duties as a policeman. A police officer may wish to engage a man's attention, for example if he wishes to question him. If he lays his hand on the man's shoulder for the purpose he commits no wrong. He may even do so more than once; for he is under a duty to prevent and investigate crime, and so his seeking further, in the exercise of that duty, to engage a man's attention in order to speak to him, may in the circumstances, be regarded as acceptable; see *Donnelly* v. *Jackman* [1970] 1 W.L.R. 562. But if, in taking into account the nature of his duty, his use of physical contact in the face of non-cooperation persists beyond generally acceptable standards of conduct, his action will become unlawful; and if a police officer restrains a man, for example by gripping his arm or his shoulder, then his action will also be unlawful, unless he is lawfully exercising his powers of arrest. A police officer has no power to require a man to answer him, though he has the advantage of authority, enhanced as it is by the uniform which the state provides and requires him to wear, in seeking a response to his inquiry. What is not permitted, however, is the unlawful use of force or the unlawful threat, actual or implicit, to use force: and, excepting the lawful exercise of his powers of arrest, the lawfulness of a police officer's conduct is judged by the same criteria as are applied to the conduct of any ordinary citizens of the country."

Furthermore, the police have no legal right to detain a suspect for questioning.[7] A person is not under a legal duty to answer questions from the

[4] See, *e.g.* Leigh at p. 53.
[5] See above Chap. 4 at p. 105.
[6] [1984] 1 W.L.R. 1172 at 1178.
[7] *Kenlin* v. *Gardiner* [1967] 2 Q.B. 510.

police; he has every right to remain silent or to refuse to answer.[8] He cannot, in the absence of some specific police power, be detained for questioning without expressly consenting to that detention.[9] A refusal to answer questions may amount to the offence of obstructing a police officer in the execution of his duty[10] if it is part and parcel of conduct deliberately aimed at rendering the performance of their duties more onerous.[11] This offence does not, of itself, give the police a power of arrest.[12] It is accordingly submitted that detaining an uncooperative suspect to assist police inquiries will amount to false imprisonment.[13]

The statutory power to stop and search

New stop and search powers which significantly increase police powers were introduced by the 1984 Act. Section 1(2) states that a police officer:

> "(a) may search
> (i) any person or vehicle;
> (ii) anything which is on or in a vehicle,
> for stolen or prohibited articles; and
> (b) may detain a person or vehicle for the purpose of such a search."

The 1984 Act repealed all stop and search powers for stolen or unlawfully obtained goods under Local Acts such as the Metropolitan Police Act 1839, section 66. The Code of Practice on the exercise of powers of stop and search states that the procedure stipulated in the 1984 Act should also apply to other stop and search powers such as section 47 of the Firearms Act 1968.[14]

(1) The scope of the power. This power to detain only arises if the police are acting lawfully in making their search. The power to search is exercisable if the police have "reasonable grounds to believe" that they will find stolen or prohibited articles.[15] If nothing suggests that the goods are stolen the search will be unlawful.[16]

An officer may also seize an article discovered in the course of his search if he has reasonable grounds for suspecting it to be stolen or prohibited.[17] However, an officer who detains a suspect or vehicle under this statutory power or by some other power which permits a search without making an arrest need not conduct the search if it subsequently appears to him that no

[8] *Rice* v. *Connolly* [1966] 2 Q.B. 414 at 419.
[9] *Bentley* v. *Brudsinski* (1982) 75 Cr.App.R. 217.
[10] Police Act 1964, s.51(3).
[11] *Ricketts* v. *Cox* (1982) 74 Cr.App.R. 298.
[12] *Wershof* v. *MPC* [1978] 3 All E.R. 540; *Gelberg* v. *Miller* [1961] 1 W.L.R. 153, but see *Marsh* v. *Arscott*, *The Times*, March 3, 1982.
[13] See generally, J. Gibbons and K. W. Lidstone, "The Offence of Obstruction: (1) Obstructing a Constable—the emergence of a new duty to cooperate with the police; (2) Obstructing Freedom?" [1983] Crim.L.R. 21.
[14] See para. 1.3 and Annex A.
[15] s.1(3).
[16] *R.* v. *Prince* [1981] Crim.L.R. 638.
[17] s.1(6).

search is required or that a search is impracticable.[18] If he decides not to conduct a search it seems that this will not render the initial detention unlawful.[19]

Moreover, a person or vehicle may only be detained for such time as is reasonably practicable to permit the search either at the place where the person was first stopped, or nearby.[20] The power (or any power to search without making an arrest) does not permit an officer to require a suspect to remove clothing in public other than an outer coat, jacket or gloves, or permit an officer out of uniform to stop a vehicle.[21]

(2) The goods that may be seized. The Act does not define "stolen." It would obviously cover theft itself[22] but does not extend to cover goods obtained as a result of other offences under the Theft Act. An article is prohibited if it is an offensive weapon made or adapted for use to cause injury or intended for such use.[23] Alternatively, the article may be made or adapted for use or intended for use for burglary, theft, taking a motor vehicle without authority or obtaining property by deception.[24]

(3) Where the search may be carried out. The police can utilise this power in any place to which the public (or a section of the public) has access as of right (upon payment or otherwise or by virtue of express or implied permission).[25] It can also be invoked in relation to any other place where people have ready access which is not a dwelling.[26] If the suspect is in a garden or a yard occupied with and used for a dwelling he may not be searched unless the police officer has reasonable grounds to believe he does not reside at the dwelling or has permission to be there from the resident of the dwelling[27] (although if the officer himself enters the garden, off the garden path, he will become a trespasser). Similarly, if an officer wishes to search a vehicle in the garden or yard of a dwelling, he must have reasonable grounds to believe that the person in charge of it does not reside at the dwelling or that the vehicle is not there with the permission of the resident of the dwelling.[28]

(4) The duty of the officer to identify himself. If an officer contemplates a search other than of an unattended vehicle either under this statutory power or another power to search without making an arrest,[29] he is under a duty before beginning his search to take reasonable steps to provide documentary evidence that he is an officer if he is not in uniform and (whether in uniform or not) to inform the suspect of his name and police station, the object of the proposed search, his grounds for proposing it and

[18] s.2(1).
[19] *David* v. *Morrison* (1979) 70 Cr.App.R. 142.
[20] s.2(8).
[21] s.2(9).
[22] See Theft Act 1968, s.1.
[23] s.1(7)(*a*).
[24] s.1(7)(*b*) and s.1(8).
[25] s.1(1)(*a*).
[26] s.1(1)(*b*).
[27] s.1(4).
[28] s.1(5).
[29] Other than s.27(2) of the Aviation Security Act 1982.

the suspect's right to a record[30] of the search[31] unless he feels that this will not be practicable.[32] It is submitted that a failure by a police officer to identify himself will make a subsequent search unlawful.

(5) The duty to provide records. The Act obliges an officer to make a record of the search in writing unless it is not practicable to do so.[33] If it is not practicable to make the record on the spot, the officer must make it as soon as practicable after the search is completed.[34]

The record itself must include the suspect's name if the officer knows it but the officer is not empowered to detain the suspect to discover his name[35]; otherwise, the record must describe the person stopped.[36] The record of the search of the vehicle must also describe the vehicle.[37]

The record must also state the object of the search, the grounds for making it, the date and time when it was made, the place where it was made, whether anything (and if so, what) was found, and whether and what injury or damage appears to the officer to have resulted from the search. The record must also identify the officer making the search.[38]

A person searched is entitled to a copy of this record within 12 months of the search being made.[39] The owner (or person in charge) of a vehicle searched is likewise entitled to a copy of the record within this time period provided that the record was made.[40]

However, the officer need not mention the right to have a copy of this record to the person searched (or in charge of a discarded vehicle) if it is not practicable.[41] Nevertheless, if an unattended vehicle is searched, the officer must leave a notice stating that he has searched it, the name of his police station, an application for compensation for any damage caused and informing of the right to a copy of the record.[42] The notice must be left inside the vehicle unless it is not reasonably practicable to do so without damaging it.[43] It is submitted that a failure by the police to provide the necessary records will not make the prior detention of a suspect or vehicle unlawful.

Records showing the use of stop and search powers[44] must be detailed in the annual report of the chief officer of police of every area.[45]

(6) Assisting the police with their inquiries. Apart from the power to stop and search the police have no power to detain a person short of arrest. In particular, they have no right to detain a suspect "to help them with their

[30] Under s.3(7) or s.3(8), see below.
[31] s.2(2) and s.2(3).
[32] s.2(4).
[33] See s.3(1). This provision does not apply to a search by a statutory undertaker under s.6 of the 1984 Act or under s.27(2) of the Aviation Security Act 1982.
[34] s.3(2).
[35] s.3(3).
[36] s.3(4).
[37] s.3(5).
[38] s.3(6).
[39] s.3(7) and s.3(9).
[40] s.3(8) and s.3(9).
[41] s.2(4) and s.2(5).
[42] s.2(6).
[43] s.2(7).
[44] As well as in relation to road blocks, see Chap. 7 below at p. 241.
[45] s.5.

inquiries."[46] The 1984 Act recognises this when it deals with the practice of holding suspects to assist the police with their inquiries. According to section 29, a person who voluntarily attends at the police station or other place where an officer is present (or accompanies him there) without being arrested in order to assist with an investigation is entitled to leave at will unless he is arrested. If an officer prevents a person who is voluntarily at a police station from leaving at will he must be informed at once that he is being arrested. Thus, if a person who goes voluntarily to the police station is prevented from leaving without being arrested then an action for false imprisonment will lie.

3. ARREST: DEFINITION AND PROCEDURE

The definition of arrest

Arrest itself generally involves the notion of taking someone into custody and is the first step in a criminal proceeding on a charge which is intended to be judicially investigated.[47] An arrest takes place where the suspect is not free to go as he pleases or has been told that he is in a state of custody.[48] It must be made quite plain to him that he is no longer free but there is no magic formula which applies and different procedures may be appropriate depending on the suspect's age, ethnic origin, knowledge of English, intellectual powers or mental or physical disabilities.[49] However, in *Alderson* v. *Booth*[50] it was suggested that the simplest words to use were "I arrest you." In that case the Divisional Court held that the words "I shall ask you to accompany me to the police station" were capable of being understood by the suspect as a request that he attend voluntarily.

The mere words "I am arresting you" not accompanied by an act of touching by the police or an act of submission by the suspect[51] does not constitute an arrest.[52] Thus, if the suspect does not acquiesce or submit to his arrest some degree of contact is essential.[53] However, where the arrest involves touching the suspect, it is not necessary for him to submit or to be brought under control for the arrest to be complete.[54]

On the other hand, an arrest will be effected by the suspect's submission if there is so great a constraint upon his will that he feels compelled to submit. Thus, he will be arrested if he is shown a warrant for his arrest and submits to orders when threatened with its execution[55] or if it is obvious that if he refuses to accompany the constable he will be compelled to do so.[56] "In

[46] See *R.* v. *Lemsatef* [1977] 1 W.L.R. 812 at 816.
[47] *Leachinsky* v. *Christie* [1946] K.B. 124 at 130.
[48] *Spicer* v. *Holt* [1977] A.C. 987 at 1000, *per* Viscount Dilhorne.
[49] *R.* v. *Inwood* [1973] 1 W.L.R. 647.
[50] [1969] 2 Q.B. 216.
[51] *Alderson* v. *Booth* [1969] 2 Q.B. 216 at 220.
[52] *Nicholls* v. *Bulman* [1985] R.T.R. 236.
[53] *Clowser* v. *Chaplin* [1981] R.T.R. 317.
[54] *Hart* v. *Chief Constable of Kent* [1983] R.T.R. 484.
[55] *Grainger* v. *Hill* (1838) 4 Bing.N.C. 212.
[56] *Chinn* v. *Morris* (1826) 2 C. & P. 361.

such cases . . . though little may be said much is meant and perfectly understood."[57] However, if the constable has no intention to apprehend the plaintiff and the plaintiff has no intention to submit to the warrant so that it is effectively being used as a summons to indicate that he is required to answer a charge, there is no arrest.[58] Similarly, where a person volunteers to go to a police station he cannot contend that he has been detained, although the position is different if he has a charge against him and therefore volunteers to meet it at the police station.[59]

The obligation to give reasons for an arrest

At common law no arrest will be lawful unless the person arrested is told both that he is under arrest and of the ground for his arrest at the time he is arrested or as soon as is practicable afterwards. This fundamental principle is now given statutory force by the 1984 Act.[60] If the information is not given then the arrest is unlawful.[61] The duty applies even if the fact of the arrest or ground of the arrest is obvious.[62] These duties do not apply if it is not reasonably practicable to inform him because he has escaped before he can be informed.[63]

The information to be conveyed under the 1984 Act appears to be the same as at common law. The leading case is *Christie* v. *Leachinsky*.[64] Lord Simonds stated the position as follows:

> "The arrested man is entitled to be told what is the act for which he is arrested. The 'charge' ultimately made will depend on the view taken by the law of his act. In ninety nine cases out of a hundred the same words may be used to define the charge or describe the act nor is any technical precision necessary: for instance, if the act constituting the crime is the killing of another man, it will be immaterial that the arrest is for murder and at a later hour the charge of manslaughter is substituted. The arrested man is left in no doubt that the arrest is for that killing. This I think is the fundamental principle viz that a man is entitled to know what in, the apt words of Lawrence L.J. are 'the facts which are said to be the crime on his part.' "[65]

It is necessary for the suspect to be told the true ground for his arrest[66] and sufficient detail of the allegations involved; thus, the arrest will be unlawful if the suspect is told he is arrested for burglary without informing

[57] *Bird* v. *Jones* (1845) 7 Q.B. 742 at 748, *per* William J.
[58] *Arrowsmith* v. *Le Mesurier* (1806) 2 B. & P. N.R. 211; *Cf. Wood* v. *Lane* (1834) 6 C. & P. 774; *Warner* v. *Riddiford* (1858) 4 C.B. (N.S.) 180 at 205, *per* Willes J.
[59] *Peters* v. *Stanway* (1835) 6 C. & P. 737.
[60] s.28(1) and (3).
[61] s.28(3).
[62] s.28(2) and (4).
[63] s.28(5).
[64] [1947] A.C. 573.
[65] *Ibid.* at 593.
[66] *R.* v. *Holah* [1973] 1 W.L.R. 127.

him of where and when it was committed.[67] Furthermore, it has been held in Canada that the officer should listen to any statement that the suspect seeks to make,[68] this may be relevant to the question of whether the officer carried out sufficient investigations before making the arrest.[69]

The need to give detailed information regarding the ground for an arrest was emphasised by the Court of Appeal in *Murphy* v. *Oxford*[70] where the plaintiff's claim for false imprisonment succeeded because he was merely told, on being arrested in Liverpool, that he was being arrested for a burglary in Newquay. Sir John Donaldson M.R. said:

> "It is clear from [*Christie* v. *Leachinsky*] that one of the reasons why an arrested person is entitled to be informed of the ground for the arrest—to use the words of the statute—is in order that he may be able to give more than a bare and unconvincing denial if he is in fact innocent. To tell a man that he is arrested for murder without any details of who he is said to have murdered and when and where, puts the citizen in the very difficult position that all he can do is to say 'Well, I did not.' That is not likely to be particularly convincing to anybody. On the other hand, the more details he is given the better his opportunity to give a convincing answer and, therefore, the better his chances of being speedily released from arrest . . . [To] say 'You are wanted on suspicion of burglary in Newquay' . . . presupposes that the accused is likely to be able to say, 'But I have never been to Newquay' or give some answer of that sort. But that is an unreasonable approach. The man may very well have been to Newquay on holiday or for any other reason and he is entitled to much fuller details in order that he may be able to deny the charge, if he is innocent, with conviction."

It is submitted that where the police utilise a general arrest power, they must state both the appropriate details of the offence they are alleging and the ground upon which they rely on as making the service of a summons impracticable or inappropriate. Otherwise the suspect has not been informed of the act for which he was arrested.[70a]

The officer should inform the suspect that he is a police officer[71] and should produce a warrant card if he is not in uniform.[72] However, there is no obligation to inform the suspect whether the arrest is made with a warrant or without a warrant.[73]

The 1984 Act makes it clear that an invalid arrest cannot be cured by subsequently explaining the ground for the arrest[74] since the ground for it must be given at the time of arrest or as soon as practicable afterwards. The obligation to give reasons for the arrest applies even where a suspect has been arrested for one offence is held at the station as a result and is then arrested

[67] *R.* v. *Telfer* [1976] Crim.L.R. 562.
[68] *R.* v. *Long* (1969) 8 C.R.N.S. 298.
[69] See below at p. 150.
[70] (1985) February 15, unreported. Transcript: Association.
[70a] But see *Nicholas* v. *DPP* [1987] Crim.L.R. 474.
[71] *Christie* v. *Leachinsky* [1947] A.C. 573 at 586.
[72] Glanville Williams, "Requisites of a Valid Arrest" (1954) Crim.L.R. 6 at p. 16.
[73] *R.* v. *Kulynycz* [1971] 1 Q.B. 367; but see the remarks of Scott L.J. in *Leachinsky* v. *Christie* 124 at 130 which, according to Robilliard & McEwan places a common law obligation on the police to read out warrants, p. 127, n. 170.
[74] Reversing the decision in *R.* v. *Kulynycz* [1971] 1 Q.B. 367.

for another offence[75]: the police are under a duty to give reasons on both occasions he is arrested.

Dealing with the suspect after arrest

The 1984 Act does not affect the obligations which arise after the making of a citizen's arrest. The citizen is under a common law duty to hand the suspect to a constable or to take him to the police station or before a magistrates' court as soon as he reasonably can. But so long as he does so within a reasonable time, he cannot be criticised because he holds the suspect for a time to consider the position.[76]

On the other hand, the 1984 Act does codify the duties of police officers when they make arrests outside a police station. If someone is arrested by an officer or is taken into police custody after a citizen's arrest anywhere other than at a police station he must be taken to a police station as soon as practicable.[77] However, this principle does not prevent an officer delaying taking a person to the station if his presence elsewhere is necessary to carry out such investigations as it is reasonable to carry out immediately.[78] The suspect may therefore be taken to his own home to see if stolen property is there, he may be kept in custody while an alibi is investigated or he may be subjected to an identification parade.[79] The fact that an officer is entitled to take a suspect to his home to search for stolen property does not oblige the police to take him there in order for his arrest to be lawful.[80] Where there is such a delay, the reasons for it must be recorded as soon as the suspect arrives at the police station.[81]

The police station to which he must be taken must be a designated police station[82] subject to certain exceptions.[83] If a suspect is taken to the wrong type of police station and detained there he may recover damages for false imprisonment.[84] Any police station will be appropriate unless the officer thinks it may be necessary to keep the arrested person in police detention for more than six hours[85] or if he works in a locality which has no designated police station and to an officer belonging to a body of policemen who are not maintained by a police authority.[86] Any police station may also be used if the officer arrested the suspect without assistance from another officer and no other officer is available or the suspect is taken into custody after a citizen's arrest by a police officer without the assistance of another officer and no other officer is available. In either case the suspect may be taken to any police station if it appears to the officer that he cannot take the suspect

[75] Under s.31.
[76] *John Lewis* v. *Tims* [1952] A.C. 676; *Dallison* v. *Caffrey* [1965] 1 Q.B. 348.
[77] s.30(1).
[78] s.30(10).
[79] *Dallison* v. *Caffrey* [1965] 1 Q.B. 345 at 366, 367.
[80] *McCarrick* v. *Oxford* [1983] R.T.R. 117.
[81] s.30(11).
[82] Under s.35.
[83] s.30(2).
[84] See *Cobbett* v. *Grey* (1849) 4 Ex. 729.
[85] s.30(3).
[86] s.30(4).

to a designated police station without the suspect injuring himself, the officer or some other person.[87] However, where the suspect is taken to a police station which is not designated he must be taken to a designated one within six hours if he is not released beforehand.[88]

Alternatively, an officer is entitled to release the suspect before he reaches the station if he is satisfied that there are not grounds for keeping him under arrest.[89] If he does so, he must record this as soon as practicable after the release.[90]

The duty under the 1984 Act does not affect the power to authorise detention at a port or on board a ship or aircraft or elsewhere under the Prevention of Terrorism Acts or the Immigration Act 1971 or to take someone found drunk and disorderly or incapable to an intoxication centre under section 34 of the Criminal Justice Act 1972.[91] Nor does it affect the power under Schedule 2, paragraph 18(3) of the Immigration Act 1971 to take a detained person to a place in order to ascertain his nationality and citizenship or for making arrangements to admit him to another country or any other purpose connected with that Act.[92]

The police will therefore be guilty of false imprisonment after making an arrest in the following circumstances:

(1) if they fail to take a suspect to the station as soon as practicable;
(2) if they fail to take a suspect to the appropriate police station;
(3) if they fail to release him before reaching the station although they believe there are no grounds for keeping him under arrest.

Search on arrest

At common law the police have no right to search a person to see if he has committed a crime.[93] However, they are under a duty to preserve the evidence of a crime for use at court[94] and have the power to take goods which they reasonably believe are material evidence against a suspect arrested for a serious offence (or those implicated in the same crime) if the goods are in his possession or immediate control at the time the arrest takes place.[95] In order for the search to be lawful the arrest itself must be lawful.[96] An officer conducting a search must inform the suspect of the reasons for it unless giving the reasons is unnecessary or impracticable.[97]

The 1984 Act gives the police a statutory power of search upon arrest. If a suspect is arrested other than at a police station the police have the power to

[87] s.30(5).
[88] s.30(6).
[89] s.30(7).
[90] s.30(8) and (9).
[91] s.30(2).
[92] s.30(13).
[93] *Ghani* v. *Jones* [1970] 1 Q.B. 693 at 706.
[94] *R.* v. *Lushington, ex. p. Otto* [1894] 1 Q.B. 420 at 423 but see *R.* v. *Uxbridge JJ. ex p. Sofer, The Times*, December 4, 1986.
[95] *Mellor* v. *Leather & Clough* (1853) 1 E. & E. 619.
[96] *Dillon* v. *O'Brien & Davis* (1887) 20 L.R. Ir. 200; but see *Field* v. *Sullivan* [1923] V.L.R. 70.
[97] *Brazil* v. *Chief Constable of Surrey* [1983] 1 W.L.R. 1115.

search him if they have reasonable grounds to believe that he is a danger to himself or others.[98] In addition, they have a general power to search for anything which they suspect might be used to help him escape or might be evidence relating to the offence.[99] They also have power to enter and search premises where the suspect was when arrested (or immediately before being arrested) for evidence relating to the offence for which he was arrested.[1] Both these powers oblige the police to have reasonable grounds for their belief.[2] This power of search only permits a search to the extent that it is reasonably required to discover the items in question.[3] It does not allow the police to require the suspect to remove any clothing in public other than an outer coat, jacket and gloves.[4] Moreover, the power to search premises is limited if the premises comprise two or more separate dwellings to that dwelling where the arrest took place (or where the suspect was, immediately before arrest) together with the common parts.[5]

An officer relying on this power may seize or retain anything he finds if he has reasonable grounds for believing that the suspect may use it to injure himself or another.[6] If the officer searches for anything to assist in an escape or which might be evidence relating to the offence, he may seize and retain anything he finds (other than items subject to legal privilege) or where he has reasonable grounds for believing[7] that the suspect might be able to use it to escape from custody or that it is evidence of an offence or has been obtained as a result of an offence.[8] The length of time that a suspect can be detained is discussed below. The power contained in the 1984 Act does not affect police powers under the Prevention of Terrorism Act.[9] It should also be noted that the police have an additional power to search suspects who are in detention.[10]

Because a personal search involves a significant restraint on individual freedom, important limitations have been imposed on police powers. As Donaldson L.J. put it in *Lindley* v. *Rutter*[11]:

> "It is the duty of the courts to be ever zealous to protect the personal freedom, privacy and dignity of all who live in these islands. Any claim to be entitled to take action which infringes these rights is to be examined with great care. But such rights are not absolute. They have to be weighed against the rights and duties of police officers acting on behalf of society as a whole. It is the duty of any constable who lawfully has a prisoner in his charge to take all reasonable measures to ensure that the prisoner does not escape or assist others to do so, does not injure himself or others, does not destroy or dispose of evidence and does not

[98] s.32(1).
[99] s.32(2)(*a*).
[1] s.32(2)(*b*); see Chap. 7 below at p. 210.
[2] s.32(6) and (7).
[3] s.32(3).
[4] s.32(4).
[5] s.32(7).
[6] s.32(8).
[7] See below at p. 145.
[8] s.32(9).
[9] s.32(10).
[10] See below at p. 170.
[11] [1981] 1 Q.B. 128 at 134.

commit further crime such as, for example, malicious damage to property. This list is not exhaustive but it is sufficient for present purposes. What measures are reasonable in the discharge of this duty will depend on the likelihood that the particular prisoner will do any of these things unless prevented. That in turn will involve the constable in considering the known or apparent disposition and sobriety of the prisoner. What can never be justified is the adoption of any particular measures without regard to all the circumstances of the case."

Therefore, a failure to justify the search, whether it is made under the common law powers or under the 1984 Act will result in an actionable battery. The reasons for a search must be given to the person searched unless giving them is unnecessary or impracticable.[12] Conducting a search without a power to do so will be unlawful. It has been held that a routine search to establish a suspect's identity was unlawful.[13] Even where the general power exists, the police must consider whether it is appropriate to invoke it in a particular case and must not conduct a search as matter or routine.[14] The same considerations apply when a search is conducted solely because of the Chief Constable's standing orders.[15] The power relied on will be strictly construed. Thus, for example, a search will be held to be unjustified when the police claim searching for objects which a prisoner might use to injure herself if they are, in fact, incapable of causing injury.[16] Any article seized from a suspect remains his property and he is entitled to demand their return subject to the police justifying their retention.[17]

4. THE POWER TO MAKE AN ARREST: WITHOUT WARRANT

Introduction

The powers to make an arrest without a warrant are now contained in the Police and Criminal Evidence Act 1984. All other previous statutory powers whether in local or general Acts have now been abolished (except those expressly preserved by the 1984 Act).[18] On the other hand, the Act does not affect common law powers of arrest—such as arrest for breach of the peace.[19]

The Act defines three classes of offences which allow an arrest without a warrant in addition to conferring a power to arrest an offender for fingerprinting.[20] These are: first, "arrestable offences," second a general power of arrest for lesser offences where certain restrictive criteria are met and, third the preserved powers of arrest under Schedule 2 to the Act.

[12] *Brazil* v. *Chief Constable of Surrey* [1983] 1 W.L.R. 1115.
[13] *R.* v. *Eeet* [1983] Crim.L.R. 806.
[14] *Brazil* v. *Chief Constable of Surrey* [1983] 1 W.L.R. 1115.
[15] *Lindley* v. *Rutter* [1981] 1 Q.B. 128.
[16] *R.* v. *Naylor* [1979] Crim.L.R. 532.
[17] See Chap. 7 below at p. 217.
[18] s.26.
[19] See Chap. 4 above at p. 123.
[20] See below at p. 171.

The definition of an arrestable offence

Section 24 of the Act enlarges the definition of arrestable offence which was previously contained in the Criminal Law Act 1967. The following offences are now arrestable offences: offences for which the sentence is fixed in law (such as murder), offences for which a previously unconvicted person over 21 could be sentenced to a term of imprisonment of five years or more under statute or common law and offences specifically listed in section 24(2).[21] The following offences are specifically listed:

(1) offences for which an arrest may be made under the customs and excise Acts as defined by section 1(1) of the Customs and Excise Management Act 1979;
(2) offences under the Official Secrets Acts 1911 and 1920 where the maximum term of imprisonment is under five years;
(3) offences under the Sexual Offences Act 1956—section 14 (indecent assault on a woman), section 22 (causing prostitution of a woman) or section 23 (procuration of a girl under 21);
(4) offences under the Theft Act 1968—section 12(1) (taking a motor vehicle or other conveyance without authority, etc.) or section 25(1) (going equipped for stealing etc.);
(5) offences under the Public Bodies Corrupt Practices Act 1889, section 1 (corruption of an official) or the Prevention of Corruption Act 1906, section 1 (corrupt transactions with agents).

Furthermore, section 24(3) provides that the powers of summary arrest in relation to arrestable offences also apply to conspiracy and attempts to commit such arrestable offences as well as inciting, aiding, abetting, counselling or procuring the commission of an arrestable offence.

It should be noted that a large number of offences are not arrestable offences and therefore cannot justify an arrest unless one of the "general arrest conditions" apply.[22] Examples of common offences which are not arrestable include, for instance, obstructing or assaulting police officers in the execution of their duty,[23] making off without payment,[24] or carrying an offensive weapon.[25]

The power to make an arrest for an arrestable offence

Section 24 confers certain powers of arrest on ordinary citizens. The police can rely on these powers to make "citizens' arrests" in addition to arrests justified by the powers of arrest specifically granted to police officers.

Section 24(4) provides that:

[21] See s.24(1).
[22] See below at p. 142.
[23] Police Act 1964, s.51.
[24] Theft Act 1978, s.3.
[25] Prevention of Crime Act 1953, s.1.

"Anyone may arrest without warrant—
(a) anyone who is in the act of committing an arrestable offence;
(b) anyone whom he has reasonable grounds for suspecting to be committing such an offence."

Therefore, such an arrest will be unlawful if the person arrested is not "in the act" and there are no grounds for reasonable suspicion.[26] Sometimes it is difficult to ascertain whether a criminal "act" is complete, particularly if it is unclear whether the offence consists of a single act or a continuing one. For example, the moment of appropriation in a shoplifting case will vary with the circumstances of each case.[27]

Section 24(5) provides that:

"Where an arrestable offence has been committed, any person may arrest without warrant—
(a) anyone who is guilty of the offence;
(b) anyone whom he has reasonable grounds for suspecting to be guilty of it."

In order to rely on this power it is essential that an actual offence has been committed. Thus, in the leading case of *Walters* v. *W. H. Smith & Sons*[28] damages for false imprisonment were awarded when the plaintiff was arrested because he was reasonably suspected of stealing a book which was not, in fact, stolen.

The powers of arrest without warrant which are only available to police officers are set out in section 24(6) and (7). Their additional powers permit them to make an arrest if they have reasonable grounds for believing an offence was committed even when it was not (so that had a police officer made the arrest in *Walters* v. *W. H. Smith & Sons* he would not have been liable in damages) and enable them to make an arrest before an offence has been committed. Section 24(6) provides that:

"Where a constable has reasonable grounds for suspecting that an arrestable offence has been committed he may arrest without warrant anyone whom he has reasonable grounds for suspecting to be guilty of the offence."

Section 24(7) provides that:

"A constable may arrest without warrant—
(a) anyone who is about to commit an arrestable offence;
(b) anyone whom he has reasonable grounds for suspecting to be about to commit an arrestable offence."

The police will therefore be guilty of trespass for making an arrest without warrant in the following circumstances:

(1) if they suspect he is about to commit an arrestable offence when they do not have reasonable grounds for doing so;
(2) if they suspect he is in the act of committing an arrestable offence when they do not have reasonable grounds for doing so;

[26] See above at p. 145.
[27] *R.* v. *Morris* [1984] A.C. 320.
[28] [1914] 1 K.B. 595.

(3) if they suspect someone on reasonable grounds to be guilty of committing an arrestable offence when they do not have reasonable grounds for suspecting the offence itself has been committed;
(4) if they do have reasonable grounds for suspecting an arrestable offence has been committed but do not have reasonable grounds for suspecting that it was committed by the person they in fact arrest.

General powers of arrest

Section 25 of the 1984 Act allows the police to make an arrest for any offence, however minor, provided that one of the general arrest conditions is satisfied and the service of a summons is impracticable or inappropriate. However, the power is subject to important limitations when compared with the power to arrest for arrestable offences.

Section 25(1) provides:

> "Where a constable has reasonable grounds for suspecting that any offence which is not an arrestable offence has been committed or is being committed or attempted, he may arrest the relevant person if it appears to him that service of a summons is impracticable or inappropriate because any of the general arrest conditions is satisfied."

A relevant person is defined by section 25(2) as any person whom the constable has reasonable grounds to suspect of having committed or having attempted to commit the offence or of being in the course of committing or attempting to commit it.

Unlike the power to arrest for arrestable offences a constable will be acting unlawfully if he arrests a person without reasonable grounds[29] even if the person committed an offence.[30] Furthermore, the general power does not cover arrests where a person is about to (or is reasonably suspected of being about to) commit an offence[31] or inciting, aiding or abetting or procuring another to do that offence.[32]

It is implicit in section 25(1) that the police should utilise the procedure for issuing a summons rather than make an arrest, all other things being equal. The wording of the section suggests that the test of whether a decision is lawful is purely subjective so that he has acted lawfully if he forms the belief bona fide. Nevertheless, the general arrest conditions either refer to reasonable grounds or to the existence of certain facts. Accordingly, it is submitted that the test is objective and is in addition subject to general administrative law principles that he must consider all relevant considerations and exclude irrelevant ones in forming the view that it is impracticable or inappropriate to serve a summons.

Any officer may exercise his general power of arrest if he feels that any one of the general arrest conditions make the service of a summons imprac-

[29] See at p. 145.
[30] *Cf.* s.24(5).
[31] *Cf.* s.24(7).
[32] *Cf.* s.24(3).

ticable or inappropriate. These "general arrest conditions" are set out in section 25(3) as follows:

> "The general arrest conditions are—
> (a) that the name of the relevant person is unknown to and cannot be readily ascertained by the constable;
> (b) that the constable has reasonable grounds for doubting whether a name furnished by the relevant person as his name is his real name;
> (c) that—
> (i) the relevant person has failed to furnish a satisfactory address for service; or
> (ii) the constable has reasonable grounds for doubting whether an address furnished by the relevant person is a satisfactory address for service;
> (d) that the constable has reasonable grounds for believing that an arrest is necessary to prevent the relevant person—
> (i) causing physical harm to himself or any other person;
> (ii) suffering physical injury;
> (iii) causing loss or damage to property;
> (iv) committing an offence against public decency; or
> (v) causing an unlawful obstruction of the highway;
> (e) that a constable has reasonable grounds for believing that an arrest is necessary to protect a child or other vulnerable person from the relevant person."

A number of the arrest conditions require a police officer to act reasonably; whether he has done so is a question of fact to be tested objectively. For example, the power to arrest where there are doubts about a person's name could be exercised if he had inconsistent identification documentation but not because he had a foreign name.

Section 25(4) makes it clear that the address furnished to the officer need not be the suspect's own. An address is satisfactory for service if it appears to the officer either that the person arrested at it will be there for a sufficiently long time for it to be possible to be served or that some other person who he specifies will accept service for him. It will, therefore, be sufficient for the suspect to give a business address or the address of his parents if this is nearby.

The power to arrest for offences against public decency is qualified by section 25(5). An arrest is prohibited unless members of the public going about their normal business cannot reasonably be expected to avoid the person arrested. Thus, if the police come across a couple committing an act of gross indecency in a car in a secluded spot, they would not be entitled to make an arrest without warrant.

Finally, section 25(6) makes it clear that the existence of these general powers of arrest do not affect any other powers of arrest either under the 1984 Act or at common law.

Preserved powers of arrest

Although section 26(1) repeals all previous statutory powers of arrest, section 26(2) expressly preserves those contained in Schedule 2 to the Act.

They primarily concern the power to arrest persons unlawfully at large, offences relating to animals, terrorist offences and immigration offences.[33]

The important "power of arrest" which can be attached to "domestic violence injunctions" appears to be impliedly preserved by section 26. This is because section 26(1) only repeals powers "to arrest a person otherwise than for an offence" when these are "without warrant or an order of the court." It has been suggested that, as such powers are made by court order they are unaffected by the 1984 Act.[34]

Such a power of arrest can be attached to an injunction granted under the Domestic Violence and Matrimonial Proceedings Act 1976. This power entitles a police officer to arrest without warrant anyone whom he has reasonable cause to suspect of being in breach of the injunction.[35] It is submitted that the arrested person should be given the reason for his arrest.[36] He must be brought before the judge within 24 hours (although Christmas Day, Good Friday or any Sunday are to be disregarded for this purpose) and he must not be released before this period ends, except at the discretion of the judge.[37] A power of arrest subject to the same conditions may be attached to an injunction in divorce proceedings.[38]

A similar power may be exercised by magistrates under the Domestic Proceedings and Magistrates' Courts Act 1978. Magistrates can attach a power of arrest to various orders that can be made under the Act.[39] The police may then arrest a person who they have reasonable cause to suspect is in breach of the order.[40] It is again submitted that the reason for the arrest must be given.[41] The arrested person must be brought before the magistrates within 24 hours (although Christmas Day, Good Friday or any Sunday are disregarded for this purpose).[42] In addition, magistrates may issue a warrant of arrest if the application is made to them concerning the breach of an order under section 16 of the Act.[43]

[33] The powers are: s.17(2) of the Military Lands Act 1892 (the power to arrest for byelaw offences); s.12(1) of the Protection of Animals Act 1911; s.2 of the Emergency Powers Act 1920; s.7(3) Public Order Act 1936 (the powers to arrest for wearing a uniform, carrying an offensive weapon at a public meeting or for threatening words or behaviour); s.49 of the Prison Act 1952; s.13 of the Visiting Forces Act 1952; ss.186 and 190B of the Army Act 1955; ss.104 and 105 of the Naval Discipline Act 1957; s.1(3) of the Street Offences Act 1959; ss.28(2) and 32 of the Children and Young Persons Act 1969; s.24(2) of the Immigration Act 1971 and paras. 17, 24 and 33 of Sched. 2 and para. 7 of Sched. 3 to that Act; ss.5(5), 7 and 100 of the Road Traffic Act 1972; s.7 of the Bail Act 1976; ss.6(6), 7(11), 8(4), 9(7) and 10(5) of the Criminal Law Act 1977; s.16 of the Child Care Act 1980; Sched. 5 to the Reserve Forces Act 1980; ss.60(5) and 61(1) of the Animal Health Act 1981; ss.18, 35(10), 36(8), 38(7), 136(1) and 138 of the Mental Health Act 1983; ss.12 and 13 of the Prevention of Terrorism (Temporary Provisions) Act 1984; s.5(5) of the Repatriation of Prisoners Act 1984.

[34] See Leigh at p. 86.

[35] D.V.M.P.A., s.2(3).

[36] *Christie* v. *Leachinsky* [1947] A.C. 567.

[37] D.V.M.P.A., s.2(4).

[38] *Lewis* v. *Lewis* [1978] Fam. 60.

[39] D.P.M.C.A., s.16.

[40] D.P.M.C.A., s.18(2).

[41] *Christie* v. *Leachinsky* [1947] A.C. 567.

[42] D.P.M.C.A., s.18.

[43] D.P.M.C.A., s. 18(4).

The police will be liable for false imprisonment if they do not have reasonable grounds to execute the power of arrest or if the power of arrest has expired.[44] It also seems that the police will be liable for false imprisonment in relation to a warrant under the 1976 Act if the order granting the power of arrest is made without jurisdiction or is otherwise unlawful since they cannot claim the protection of the Constables Protection Act 1750 if the warrant was not issued by a justice.[45] The circumstances in which a police officer will be liable in respect of an arrest under an invalid warrant issued under the 1978 Act are the same as in relation to any arrest warrant.[46]

The discretion to make an arrest

Even though the police have reasonable grounds for any belief that could justify an arrest, they still have a discretion whether or not to actually carry one out. The principles governing the exercise of this discretion (under what was section 2(4) of the Criminal Law Act 1967 and is now section 24(6)) were considered by the House of Lords in *Mohammed-Holgate* v. *Duke*[47] In that case it was decided that the police were not acting unlawfully at common law in making an arrest in the belief that the arrested suspect would be more likely to confess and tell the truth when in custody. Lord Diplock stated the general principles as follows:

> "So the condition precedent[48] . . . was fulfilled; and since the wording of the subsection under which he acted is may arrest without a warrant this left him with an executive discretion whether to arrest her or not. Since this is an executive discretion expressly conferred by statute upon a public officer, the constable making the arrest, the lawfulness of the way in which he has exercised it in a particular case cannot be questioned in a court of law except upon those principles laid down by Lord Greene M.R. in *Associated Provincial Picture Houses Ltd.* v. *Wednesbury Corporation* [1948] 1 K.B. 223 that have become too familiar to call for repetitious citation. The *Wednesbury* principles, as they are usually referred to, are applicable to determining the lawfulness of the exercise of the statutory discretion of a constable under . . . ,[49] not only in proceedings for judicial review but also for the purpose of founding a cause of action at common law for the species of trespass to the person known as false imprisonment."

Thus, the discretion to make an arrest must be exercised in good faith. In addition the arresting officer will be acting unlawfully if he takes into account matters which ought not to be considered or disregards any matters which ought to be taken into account.[50]

[44] See, *e.g.*, *Felicien* v. *MPC* (1985) unreported, see Chap. 11 below at p. 372.
[45] But see *Webb* v. *Batchelor* (1675) 1 Ventr. 273.
[46] See below at p. 157.
[47] [1984] A.C. 437.
[48] *i.e.*, that the constable had reasonable grounds to suspect a person to be guilty of an arrestable offence.
[49] s.24(6) of the 1984 Act.
[50] See, in general, Ryan and Williams, "Police Discretion" [1986] Public Law 285.

5. THE MEANING OF "REASONABLE GROUNDS"

Introduction

In many police cases the fundamental issue at trial will be whether the police had reasonable grounds for their belief or suspicion which was the basis of the power they were purporting to exercise. This will arise, for example, where they exercise their statutory power to stop and search,[51] where they make an arrest without warrant[52] and where they enter and search premises without warrant.[53] In contrast to the position in an action for malicious prosecution[54] the burden in a false imprisonment case is on the defendant to show that he did, in fact, have such reasonable grounds.[55] It is submitted that the burden of proof is on the police whenever they seek to justify trespass to the person, goods or land by relying on a "police power" involving the need for "reasonable grounds" for suspecting or believing. What is essential is that the officer has reasonable grounds for the suspicion or belief on which the power is based. Honest and reasonable belief in the existence of the power is not, of itself, sufficient and such a mistake of law will mean that the arrest will be unlawful.[56]

What constitutes "reasonable grounds" depends on the circumstances of every case and no complete judicial or statutory definition has been attempted.[57] Nevertheless a number of basic legal principles can be derived from the authorities and must be borne in mind in every case where the issue arises. There are four areas to be considered. First, the difference between "suspicion" and "belief" in the context of reasonable grounds. Secondly, the "subjective" and "objective" elements of "reasonable grounds." Thirdly, the partial guidelines and suggestions as to what may constitute "reasonable grounds" which have been suggested in the case law. Fourthly, the respective functions of judge and jury in deciding "reasonable grounds" cases (outside the sphere of malicious prosecution).[58]

The difference between "suspicion" and "belief"

The 1984 Act seems carefully to distinguish between instances where the police have to have reasonable grounds for their suspicion and those where they have to have reasonable grounds for their belief. For most powers over the person the police must show reasonable grounds for "suspecting"; for example, when they make an arrest without warrant or stop and search someone. However, a number of other powers depend upon reasonable grounds for "believing"; for example, when the police are entering and

[51] See above at p. 129.
[52] See above at p. 138.
[53] See Chap. 7 below at p. 204.
[54] See Chap. 8 below at p. 255.
[55] *Allen* v. *Wright* (1835) 8 C. & P. 522.
[56] See *Wershof* v. *MPC* [1978] 3 All E.R. 540.
[57] *Cf.* Robilliard & McEwan at pp. 68 *et seq.*
[58] See Chap. 8 below at pp. 256 *et seq.*

searching premises or searching a person upon arrest. It is necessary to look at the wording of each specific power.

The courts have recognised that there is a difference in meaning between "belief" and "suspicion" in this context[59] although the question of whether the correct standard is applied does not depend on whether the police officer exercising the power says he "suspects" rather than "believes."[60] In *Johnson* v. *Whitehouse*[61] Nolan J. stated that "the greater force of the word 'believe' is an essential part of the law" and in Canada it was said that a;

> "suspicion and belief cannot exist together. Suspicion is much less than belief; belief includes and absorbs suspicion."[62]

The House of Lords have described the distinction as "a fine one" but have insisted on its importance.[63]

It has been suggested that "suspicion" may arise from conjecture whereas "belief" can only exist when one is firmly persuaded of the truth of a particular fact[64] and that a reasonable person may suspect something although he would withhold his belief until further evidence appears which finally convinces him.[65]

The subjective and objective elements

The question of determining whether or not an officer has reasonable grounds for his suspicion or belief involves a two-part test[66]:

(1) **The subjective question**: did the police officer actually have the relevant suspicion or belief?
(2) **The objective question**: were there, in fact, reasonable grounds for that suspicion or belief?

The two questions are entirely separate although, as a matter of evidence, the objective presence of reasonable grounds will make it easier to infer the existence of the subjective belief.[67]

The significance of the subjective test is illustrated by *Siddique* v. *Swain*.[68] In that case an officer arrested a suspect for refusing to provide a breath test. The officer had received information about a traffic accident, had reason to believe that the defendant was the driver of the car in the accident and that the defendant had had nothing to drink since coming home. However, the Divisional Court held that the arrest was unlawful on the ground that there was no evidence that the officer in fact suspected that the suspect had alcohol in his body. The officer had never stated such a suspi-

[59] See *Baker* v. *Oxford* [1980] R.T.R. 315 at 320.
[60] *Johnson* v. *Whitehouse* [1984] R.T.R. 38.
[61] *Ibid.* at 47.
[62] *Gifford* v. *Kelson* (1943) 51 Man.R. 120.
[63] See *per* Lord Bridge, *Wills* v. *Bowley* [1983] 1 A.C. 57 at 103.
[64] Ryan & Williams, "Police Discretion" [1986] *Public Law* 285.
[65] Feldman at 4.18.
[66] See *King* v. *Gardner* (1980) 71 Cr.App.R. 13.
[67] See Feldman at 8.12.
[68] [1979] R.T.R. 474.

cion when requiring a blood test and all the surrounding circumstances did not necessarily establish that he had the relevant suspicion.

This two part test can be further refined. At common law a constable could justify arrest without warrant for a felony if he could show that a reasonable man, in his position would believe that there was a "reasonable and probable cause" for the arrest.[69] The burden was on him to show "reasonable and probable cause." There was a clear connection with malicious prosecution in which the burden of showing a lack of "reasonable and probable cause" is on the plaintiff. The substitution of the statutory words "reasonable cause" for the common law "reasonable and probable cause"[70] has not led to any alteration of substance in the applicable test. It follows, therefore, that assistance as to the meaning of "reasonable cause" and its cognates in relation to police powers can be gained from the malicious prosecution cases. The elaborate case law on malicious prosecution[71] suggests that the "subjective" and "objective" questions can be further sub-divided to give a "four part test" for reasonable and probable cause. It is submitted that this test is equally applicable to "police powers cases." The test is as follows:

(1) did the officer honestly have the requisite suspicion or belief?
(2) did the officer, when exercising the power, honestly believe in the existence of the "objective" circumstances which he now relies on as the basis for that suspicion or belief;
(3) was his belief in the existence of these circumstances based on reasonable grounds?
(4) did these circumstances constitute reasonable grounds for the requisite suspicion or belief?

The first two questions are "subjective" and the second two are "objective." If the answer to any one of these questions is "no" the officer will not have had "reasonable grounds."

The operation of this test can be illustrated by an example. If a police officer, D, claims to have been justified in arresting a suspect, P, without warrant, for a particular burglary on the grounds that he believed P had been seen in the vicinity of the burgled premises shortly after they had been broken into, the questions will be as follows: (1) did D honestly suspect that P had committed the burglary? (2) did he honestly believe that P had been seen in the vicinity? (3) was his belief that P had been seen in the vicinity based on reasonable grounds? (4) was the fact that P had been seen in the vicinity sufficient to constitute reasonable grounds for the suspicion that he had committed the burglary? The answer to any one of these questions may be "no."

Of course, D will not have "reasonable grounds" to suspect P whatever the objective situation and whatever his other beliefs if the answer to question (1) was "no" and he did not, in fact, suspect P of committing the burglary. But it is also possible that although D honestly suspected that P had committed the burglary and that he had been seen in the vicinity because he had been told this by a superior he did not himself believe that P was in the

[69] *Dallison* v. *Caffrey* [1965] 1 Q.B. 348 at 371, *per* Diplock L.J.
[70] By s.2 of the Criminal Law Act 1967 and s.24 of the Police and Criminal Evidence Act 1984.
[71] For a full discussion see Chap. 8 below at pp. 255 *et seq.*

vicinity at the time of the offence, perhaps because he believed that the burglary was committed earlier. In such a case, an arrest would be unlawful because the answer to question (2) was "no." The fact an arrested officer does not genuinely rely on grounds, at the time of the arrest, which he subsequently puts forward will make that arrest unlawful. A further alternative is that D honestly suspected that P committed the burglary and honestly believed he was seen in the vicinity of the burgled premises at the time because of information given by a notoriously unreliable informer. Once again, the arrest would be unlawful, this time because the answer to question (3) was "no." The fact that an arresting officer forms a suspicion on grounds which it is not reasonable to believe exist will make that arrest unlawful. Finally, the answer to question (4) will be "no" if the information relied upon is too weak to justify a suspicion. Thus, if the burglary was alleged to have taken place in a building in a busy street, in the middle of the day, the mere fact that a person was in the vicinity would not be sufficient ground for a reasonable suspicion.

In the majority of cases on "reasonable grounds" it will be unnecessary to consider these four questions in detail. The questions are usually run together because the central issue in the case will often be a simple factual dispute, for example, did the police officer in fact see the plaintiff running away from the scene of the crime?

The standard required

Even though a police officer genuinely suspects that, for example, someone has committed an arrestable offence, an arrest will be unlawful if reasonable grounds for it do not exist.[72] It is submitted that the basic guidelines as to what constitutes a standard of reasonableness given in cases of arrest without warrant apply, *mutatis mutandis*, to all police powers which require "reasonable grounds" as a precondition.

In relation to arrest without warrant the test:

> "whether there was reasonable and probable cause for the arrest . . . is an objective one, namely whether a reasonable man assumed to know the law and possessed of the information which in fact was possessed by the defendant would believe there was reasonable and probable cause."[73]

Any facts which arise after the arrest are irrelevant to the question of whether the original arrest was lawful. Nevertheless, if the officer has reasonable grounds for his suspicion he cannot be blamed afterwards because he is proved wrong and the plaintiff is acquitted.[74] Similarly, if the officer does not have reasonable grounds at the time of the arrest, that arrest will be unlawful even though it turns out that the suspect had, in fact, committed the offence.[75]

The standard against which the actions of the officer will be measured is

[72] See *Nakkuda Ali* v. *Jayaratne* [1951] A.C. 66 at 77; *Allen* v. *Wright* (1835) 8 C. & P. 522.

[73] *Dallison* v. *Caffrey* [1965] 1 Q.B. 348 at 371, *per* Diplock L.J.

[74] *Wright* v. *Sharp* (1947) 176 L.T. 308.

[75] *R.* v. *Dadson* (1850) 4 Cox. C.C. 358.

most fully discussed in the Privy Council decision of *Hussein* v. *Chong Foo Kam*.[76] It is a lower criterion than having sufficient information for a prima facie case. Lord Devlin stated that:

> "suspicion in its ordinary meaning is a state of conjecture or surmise where proof is lacking: "I suspect but I cannot prove." Suspicion arises at or near the starting point of an investigation of which the obtaining of prima facie proof is at the end. When such proof is obtained the police case is complete; it is ready for trial and passes on to its next stage."[77]

Furthermore, Lord Devlin held[78] that whereas prima facie proof consists of admissible evidence, suspicion can be based upon matters which could not be put in evidence at all.

If what is necessary are "reasonable grounds to suspect" then

> "the constable is justified if the facts, as they appeared to him at the time, were such as to warrant him . . . thinking that the man was probably guilty."[79]

If, however, as in some "entry and search" provisions, reasonable grounds for belief are required then the test is more stringent.[80] It is submitted that the officer must believe that the state of affairs in question does exist (rather than "probably" exists).

The meaning of reasonable grounds for suspicion was also canvassed by Scott L.J. in the case of *Dumbell* v. *Roberts*[81]:

> "The duty of the police when they arrest without warrant is no doubt to be quick to see the possibility of crime, but equally they ought to be anxious to avoid mistaking the innocent for the guilty. The British principle of personal freedom, that every man shall be presumed innocent until proved guilty, applies also to the police function of arrest—in a very modified degree it is true, but at least to the extent of requiring them to be observant, receptive and open minded and to notice any relevant circumstances which point either way, either to innocence or guilt. They may have to act on the spur of the moment and have no time to reflect and be bound, therefore, to arrest to prevent escape; but where there is no danger of the person who has *ex hypothesi* aroused their suspicion, that he is probably an 'offender' attempting to escape, they should make all presently practicable enquiries from persons present or immediately accessible who are likely to be able to answer their enquiries forthwith. I am not suggesting a duty on the police to try to prove innocence; that is not their function: but they should act on the assumption that their prima facie suspicion may be ill founded. That duty attaches particularly where slight delay does not matter because there is no possibility in the circumstances of the arrest or intended arrest, of the suspected person running away. The duty attaches, I think simply, because of the double-sided interest of the public in the liberty of the individual as well as in the detection of crime."

[76] [1970] A.C. 942.
[77] *Ibid.* at 948.
[78] *Ibid.* at 949.
[79] *Per* Lord Denning M.R., *Wiltshire* v. *Barrett* [1966] 1 Q.B. 312 at 322.
[80] *Per* Lord Bridge, *Wills* v. *Bowley* [1983] 1 A.C. 57 at 103.
[81] [1944] 1 All E.R. 326 at 329.

The opposite approach was taken in *McArdle* v. *Egan*[82] where it was said[83] that once the police have formed a reasonable suspicion they are not obliged to make further inquiries. The extent to which the police must take steps to investigate a suspect's assertion of his innocence is, therefore, uncertain. In *Hogg* v. *Ward*[84] a police officer who arrested a suspect who gave a reasonable explanation which circumstances did not contradict was held to have no reasonable cause for suspicion. Similarly, in *Warre* v. *Matthews*[85] a failure to run a check on the police national computer resulted in a finding that the officer did not have reasonable cause. In contrast, in *McCarrick* v. *Oxford*[86] there was reasonable cause where a police officer arrested a suspect for driving whilst disqualified verified the disqualification by radio and then took him to the police station without first going to the suspect's house to confirm his story that he was not, in fact, disqualified. However, in the recent case of *Holtham* v. *M.P.C.*,[87] Peter Pain J. held that reasonable grounds for suspicion:

> "was a good deal more than suspicion. That meant that the police were required, when in the course of investigation some new factor emerged that threw doubt on the suspicion that existed already, to re-examine the suspicion to see whether it could be reasonably maintained.
>
> In the present case there were two new factors: the plaintiffs were not hostile to the police as they had expected but had been open and co-operative, and the police search had revealed nothing. That required the police to re-examine their suspicion."

The limited burden of proving a reasonable cause is illustrated by the case of *Ward* v. *Chief Constable of Avon & Somerset*.[88] An officer searched a house for a list of stolen items including Easter eggs. He found 11 eggs in the plaintiff's bedroom and two downstairs. The plaintiff said the eggs were hers, that she had bought them at a named supermarket at a cost of 37 pence each. He was suspicious of the number of eggs and the fact they they had no price labels nor did they appear ever to have had price labels fixed which were later removed. The price stated by the plaintiff was too cheap and this suspicion was justified because later at the police station the plaintiff stated a higher price. The plaintiff complained that the police inquiries prior to the arrest were not detailed enough. However, the Court of Appeal confirmed that it is unnecessary for the police to probe every explanation. They ruled that looking objectively at what the officer did he had reasonable cause for making the arrest. He had found the eggs in circumstances which aroused his suspicion and which called for an explanation. He was given an explanation which was apparently untrue and he had disbelieved it on good grounds.

Whether or not a police officer has reasonable cause will, of course, depend on the facts of each case. Indeed, the circumstances that may be taken into account are so various that the Phillips Commission[89] decided

[82] (1934) 150 T.L.R. 412.
[83] *Ibid. per* Lord Wright at 413 and *per* Slesser L.J. at 414.
[84] (1858) 3 H. & N. 417.
[85] (1978) unreported, Transcript Association, 1978 W. No. 1780 at 34.
[86] [1983] R.T.R. 117.
[87] *The Times*, January 8, 1987.
[88] *The Times*, June 26, 1986.
[89] Royal Commission on Criminal Procedure, Cmnd. 8092, (1981) para. 3.25.

against proposing a statutory definition of the grounds of reasonable suspicion. Nevertheless, the Code of Practice on Stop and Search does attempt to "provide guidance." It is submitted that, with appropriate amendments, this guidance applies to all police powers requiring reasonable suspicion or belief. The guidance is in the following terms[90]:

> "1. Reasonable suspicion does not require **certainty** . . . nor does the officer concerned have to be satisfied . . . beyond reasonable doubt. Reasonable suspicion, in contrast to mere suspicion must be founded on fact. There must be some concrete basis for the officer's suspicion, related to the individual person concerned, which can be considered and evaluated by an objective third person. Mere suspicion, in contrast, is a hunch or instinct which cannot be explained or justified to an objective observer. An officer who has such a hunch or instinct may well be justified in continuing to keep the person under observation or speak to him, but additional grounds which bring up mere suspicion to the level of reasonable suspicion are needed before he may exercise [the appropriate] . . . powers . . .
>
> 2. Reasonable suspicion may arise from the nature of the property observed or being carried or suspected of being carried coupled with other factors including the time, the place or the suspicious behaviour of the person concerned or those with him. The decision to search must be based on all the facts which, to a careful officer, bear on the likelihood that [what is suspected will be true] . . . and not only on what can be seen at the time. So an officer with prior knowledge of the behaviour of someone he sees in a certain situation, or acting on information received (such as a description of a suspected offender) may have reasonable grounds for searching him although another officer would not.
>
> 3. Reasonable suspicion cannot be supported simply on the basis of a higher than average chance that the person has committed or is committing an offence, for example, because he belongs to a group within which offenders of a certain kind are relatively common, or because of a combination of factors such as these. For example, a person's colour of itself can never be a reasonable ground for suspicion. The mere fact alone that a person is carrying a particular kind of property or is dressed in a certain way or has a certain hairstyle is likewise not of itself sufficient. Nor is the fact that a person is known to have a [relevant] previous conviction . . .
>
> 4. The degree of suspicion required to establish the reasonable grounds justifying the exercise of powers of stop and search is no less than the degree or level of suspicion required to effect an arrest without warrant for any of the suspected offences to which these powers relate."

The case law also deals with some of the issues that may arise:

(1) A police officer can rely on hearsay evidence from a fellow officer[91] provided that the information he relies upon itself affords reasonable grounds for suspicion.[92] Where one officer acts upon information from

[90] Annex B; the specific references to stop and search have been deleted.

[91] *Moss* v. *Jenkins* [1975] R.T.R. 25 at 30; *McKee* v. *Chief Constable of Northern Ireland* [1984] 1 W.L.R. 1358.

[92] *Siddique* v. *Swain* [1979] R.T.R. 474.

another officer by, for example, relying upon information in the police computer, the officer who must have reasonable grounds for his suspicion is the one who originally put the information into the computer. The officer who acts on the basis of that information is a "mere conduit."[93]

(2) An officer can rely on hearsay evidence from a member of the public[94] or from an informer, provided he is known to be sensible and trustworthy[95];

(3) The police may take account of a suspect's criminal record[96] but mere association with someone that the police suspect has committed an offence will not be sufficient[97];

(4) A false alibi will be a very suspicious circumstance and will provide strong grounds for suspicion.[98]

The role of judge and jury

In the early 19th century the determination of whether a police officer had reasonable cause to suspect or whether a person had been detained for an unreasonably long period were questions of fact to be decided by the jury.[99] However, it is now well-established that the question of whether particular grounds for suspicion are reasonable involves questions of law to be decided by the judge.[1] This is inconsistent with the general position that questions of reasonableness are for the jury, but is also true of malicious prosecution.[2] Nevertheless, it does have the result that the judge's decision on reasonableness is fully open to review on appeal.[3]

The role left to the jury in false imprisonment cases brought against the police is, therefore, rather limited. The way in which the judge should approach these issues was discussed by the Court of Appeal in *Dallison* v. *Caffrey*.[4] According to Diplock L.J. the position is as follows:

(1) The judge alone decides the question of relevance: he must decide what facts given in evidence are relevant to the question of whether the suspicion or belief was a "reasonable" one;

(2) The judge decides if there is a case to go to the jury: he decides if the evidence on a relevant matter raises an issue of fact to be left to the determination of the jury and should not put the case to the jury if there is no real conflict of evidence;

(3) The jury must decide what happened if there is a conflict of evidence between the plaintiff's version of events and the police version; sometimes problems may arise about finding an accurate and simple question to put to the jury and in *Green* v. *De Havilland*[5]

[93] See *per* Forbes J., *Millington* v. *MPC The Times*, May 28, 1983; in the unreported part of the case, Transcript: Counsell & Co.

[94] *Monaghan* v. *Corbett* (1983) 147 J.P. 545 at 547.

[95] *Lister* v. *Perryman* (1870) L.R. 4 H.L. 521 at 531; *Isaacs* v. *Brand* (1817) 2 Stark 167.

[96] *McArdle* v. *Egan* (1934) 150 T.L.R. 412 at 413.

[97] *Reynolds* v. *MPC* (1982) unreported, Transcript Association, CAT 977 p. 7.

[98] *Hussein* v. *Chong Fook Kam* [1970] A.C. 942 at 949.

[99] See *Beckwith* v. *Philby* (1827) 6 B. & C. 635 at 638.

[1] *Lister* v. *Perryman* (1870) L.R. 4 H.L. 521; *McArdle* v. *Egan* (1934) 150 L.T. 412.

[2] See Chap. 8 below at p. 247.

[3] *Lister* v. *Perryman* (1870) L.R. 4 H.L. 521; see Chap. 3 above at p. 93.

[4] [1965] 1 Q.B. 348 at 372.

[5] (1968) 112 S.J. 766.

Geoffrey Lane J. ruled that they be asked "was the defendant's account substantially accurate and if not in what respects?"

(4) The jury must also decide the factual question of whether the police had an honest suspicion or belief if there is sufficient evidence to raise the issue; however the judge should not allow the jury to consider the question of an officer's bona fides except in the unlikely situation of there being some positive evidence that, despite the existence of reasonable grounds, the officer himself did not honestly believe that the grounds existed;

(5) It is for the jury to decide whether the suspect has been detained for an unduly long period. Although this question has normally been left for the determination of the jury[6] the Court of Appeal in *McCarrick* v. *Oxford*[7] suggested that the judge should decide it. It is submitted that these remarks which seem to have been made without the issue being argued cannot be justified by the decision in *Lister* v. *Perryman*[8] which was solely concerned with whether reasonable grounds for suspicion involved a question of law for the judge to decide.

6. THE POWER TO MAKE AN ARREST: WITH A WARRANT

Introduction

Effecting an arrest which would otherwise be a trespass will be authorised if it is made under a warrant.[9] However, the circumstances under which the police may be held liable when acting under a warrant are very limited. An arrest warrant in principle might fail to provide a complete defence if it were issued without jurisdiction or improperly executed; unlike a search warrant it cannot be challenged as being formally defective in some way.[10] The Constables Protection Act 1750 protects officers who make an arrest under a warrant issued without jurisdiction.

The protection of constables for warrants issued without jurisdiction

Police constables were given protection for acts done in obedience to warrants issued without jurisdiction by the Constables Protection Act 1750. It has been suggested that the act does not protect the officer where the form of the warrant is grossly defective.[11] Section 6 of this Act (the only section which remains in force) lays down a procedure to be followed in any action:

[6] See, *e.g.*, *Lawrence* v. *Chief Constable of Dyfed-Powys Police* [1983] C.L.Y. 973; *Peacock & Hoskyn* v. *Musgrove & Porter* [1956] Crim.L.R. 418.
[7] [1983] R.T.R. 117.
[8] (1870) L.R. 4 H.L. 521.
[9] As to the force which may be used in making the arrest see Chap. 4 above at p. 124.
[10] See Chap. 7 below at p. 232.
[11] See Feldman at 15.60.

> "brought against any constable, headborough, or other officer, or against any person or persons acting by his order or in his aid, for any thing done in obedience to any warrant under the hand or seal of any justice of the peace."

The procedure is as follows:

First, a demand must be "made or left at the usual place of his abode by the party or parties intending to bring such action, or by his, her or their attorney or agent, in writing signed by the party demanding the same, of the perusal and copy of such warrant";

Second, **either** this demand must be "refused or neglected for the space of six days," in which case the constable can be sued; **or**, if the demand is complied with by showing the warrant and permitting the party to make a copy, in which case if an action is brought against the constable then on the producing and proving of the warrant at trial "the jury shall give their verdict" for the constable "notwithstanding any defect of jurisdiction" in the justice or justices who signed or sealed it.

Thus a constable who acts in obedience to a warrant is protected from an action in tort even though the warrant is unlawful.[12] "Substantial compliance" with the terms of the warrant is sufficient.[13] Nevertheless, the constable must act strictly in obedience to the terms of the warrant. In the case of *Hoye* v. *Bush*[14] a constable applied for a warrant for the arrest of one Richard Hoye. The justice mistakenly issued it in the name of his father, John Hoye. The constable was liable for false imprisonment when he arrested Richard Hoye. Tindal C.J. said that it would be wrong to allow a constable to decide whether or not the warrant was mistaken because:

> "It would be dangerous if a person whose office is wholly ministerial, were allowed to sit in judgment and say who is the unnamed person intended by the warrant which he is required to execute."[15]

If a warrant is issued without jurisdiction and then executed, the person on whom it was executed is confined to his remedy against the issuing justice.[16] The procedure here is now governed by Justices of the Peace Act 1979. Where the issue of the warrant has been followed by a conviction or order in the same matter no action shall be brought against the justice until the conviction or order has been quashed.[17] No action shall be brought if, before the issue of the warrant, a summons was issued and served and the person on whom it was served did not appear in accordance with it.[18] When a discretionary power is granted to a justice by an enactment no action shall be brought against him "by reason of the manner in which he exercises his discretion in the exercise of the power."[19] Although there is no authority on this section it is submitted that a justice who exercises a discretion capriciously or maliciously is acting outside his jurisdiction and is not acting in "execution of the power" and so cannot pray this section in aid. When an

[12] See *Atkins* v. *Kilby* (1840) 11 Ad. & El. 777.
[13] *Ibid.*
[14] (1840) 1 Man. & G. 775.
[15] *Ibid.* at 786.
[16] See *Price* v. *Messenger* (1800) 2 B. & P. 158, *per* Lord Eldon C.J. at 161.
[17] s.45(4)(*a*).
[18] s.45(4)(*b*).
[19] s.47.

action is brought against a justice in the county court he may object and all subsequent county court proceedings are null and void.[20] Furthermore, even though he acts outside his jurisdiction his liability for damages is limited to one penny if he is acting "in the execution of his office."[21]

The circumstances in which a warrant will be issued without jurisdiction

As a result of the statutory protection conferred by the 1750 Act a police officer will not be held liable for an arrest made under a warrant issued without jurisdiction; only the issuing Justices of the Peace are potentially liable.[22] Consequently, the circumstances in which a warrant can be lawfully issued are strictly speaking outside the scope of this book. However the situations when an arrest warrant is properly issued will be briefly outlined.[23]

The most important statute authorising an arrest warrant is section 1 of the Magistrates' Courts Act 1980. This states that upon an information being laid before a justice that any person has (or is) suspected of committing an offence, the justices may issue a summons or a warrant. A warrant cannot be issued unless the information is in writing and substantiated on oath. In addition, section 13 of the Magistrates' Courts Act permits an arrest warrant to be issued where a defendant fails to attend after receiving a summons. Section 1(4) restricts the court's power to issue a warrant for offenders under 17.

Similar provisions apply to the Crown Court. Section 81 of the Supreme Court Act 1981 provides that a summons or warrant may be issued where an indictment has been signed but the defendant is not yet committed. The section also empowers the arrest of a person who fails to appear in breach of a recognisance for his appearance of the Crown Court.

There are numerous other statutes empowering the issue of arrest warrants including, for example, the Army Act 1955, the Insolvency Act 1986 and the Extradition Act 1870.[24]

Executing a warrant improperly

The principal statute concerned with the execution of an arrest warrant is section 125 of the Magistrates' Courts Act 1980[25] which provides:

> "(1) A warrant of arrest issued by a Justice of the Peace shall remain in force until it is executed or withdrawn;

[20] s.51.
[21] s.52; *R.* v. *Waltham Forest J.J., ex p. Solanke* [1986] 1 W.L.R. 315.
[22] See *O'Connor* v. *Isaacs* [1956] 2 Q.B. 288.
[23] For a further discussion see Leigh at pp. 91–93.
[24] See Leigh at pp. 91 *et seq.*
[25] As amended by s.33 of the Police and Criminal Evidence Act 1984.

(2) A warrant of arrest, warrant of commitment or search warrant issued by a justice of the Peace may be executed anywhere in England and Wales by any person to whom it is directed or by any constable acting within his police area. This subsection does not apply to a warrant of commitment or warrant of distress issued under Part VI of the General Rate Act 1967;

(3) A warrant to which this subsection applies may be executed by a constable notwithstanding that it is not in his possession at the time; but the warrant shall, on the demand of the person arrested, be shown to him as soon as practicable;

(4) The warrants to which subsection (3) above applies are:

(a) a warrant to arrest a person in connection with an offence;

(b) without prejudice to paragraph (a) above, a warrant under section 186(3) of the Army Act 1955, section 105(3) of the Naval Discipline Act 1957 or Schedule 5 to the Reserve Forces Act 1980 (desertion etc);

(c) a warrant under;

(i) section 102 or 104 of the General Rate Act 1967 (insufficiency of distress);

(ii) section 18(4) of the Domestic Proceedings and Magistrates' Courts Act 1978 (protection of parties to marriage and children of the family); and

(iii) sections 55, 76, 93 or 97 above."

An arrest warrant may, therefore, be executed anywhere in England and Wales by any person to whom it is directed or any constable acting within his police area. It is submitted that section 125(2) must be read in conjunction with rule 96 of the Magistrates' Court Rules.[26] If a person is specifically named in the warrant as the person to whom it is directed, that person may execute the warrant anywhere in England or Wales. If it is instead directed to the officers of the police area in which it is issued, they may execute it anywhere in England and Wales. Moreover, an officer may execute the warrant in his own police area although it is not directed to him or to the officers of his area.[27] It should also be noted that the warrant may be served on any day, including Sunday.

Section 125(3) states that it is not necessary for the person executing a warrant to have the warrant itself in his possession when making an arrest.[28] However, when making the arrest the officer must inform the person arrested of the reason for his arrest[29] but is not obliged to inform him that he is acting under a warrant.[30]

If an arrest warrant is issued under a statute other than the Magistrates' Courts Act 1980 the provisions of section 125 will still apply.[31] However, the word "offence" seems to import an act or omission punishable under the criminal law, so that the section does not apply, for example, to a warrant

[26] S.I. 1981 No. 552.

[27] See generally, D. A. Thorne, "The Execution of Warrants of Arrest," [1962] Crim.L.R. 520 at 597.

[28] *Cf.* warrants to which the section does not apply; and see *R.* v. *Purdy* [1975] Q.B. 288.

[29] See above at p. 133.

[30] *R.* v. *Kulynycz* [1967] 1 Q.B. 367.

[31] *Magee* v. *Morris* [1954] 1 W.L.R. 806.

issued for non-payment of maintenance[32] or to proceedings for breach of a recognisance.[33]

Thus the circumstances in which an officer will be liable in trespass for improperly executing an arrest warrant are limited. He will be liable:

(1) if he executes it on a person different from the person named or described in the warrant[34] although he would be protected if he reasonably suspected the man he took into custody to be guilty of an arrestable offence[35];
(2) if he uses unreasonable force in making the arrest[36];
(3) if the arresting officer is not the person to whom the warrant is directed and is not within his police area;
(4) if the arresting officer fails to give notice of the grounds of the arrest.[37]

Even if he is liable for false imprisonment by reason of the improper execution of the warrant, he will not be responsible for any subsequent detention of the person arrested if the warrant is directed at such a detention because he is then entitled to the protection of the Constables Protection Act 1750.[38]

7. THE DETENTION OF SUSPECTS— GENERAL PRINCIPLES

Introduction

The 1984 Act has erected a new legal framework for the detention of suspects. Not only does it for the first time make a legal distinction between assisting police with their enquiries voluntarily and being arrested[39]; it also prescribes the conditions under which and the length of time for which a person can be detained. The extension of the power to detain for up to 96 hours without charge was one of the most controversial introduced by the Act.

Part IV of the Act sets out the statutory scheme.[40] The basic principle is that a suspect may be detained for up to 24 hours at which time he must either be released or charged. If the police wish to detain him further without charge a police officer of at least superintendent's rank can authorise detention to last up to 36 hours in all. Detention without charge up to the maximum of 96 hours can only be obtained by applying to the magistrates' court.

Various procedures must, therefore, be carried out within strict time

[32] *Horsfield* v. *Brown* [1932] 1 K.B. 355.
[33] *R.* v. *Marlow JJ., ex p. O'Sullivan* [1984] Q.B. 381.
[34] *Hoye* v. *Bush* (1840) 1 Man. & G. 775.
[35] s.24(6) of the Police and Criminal Evidence Act 1984.
[36] See Chap. 4 above at p. 124.
[37] See above at p. 133.
[38] See *Horsfield* v. *Brown* [1932] 1 K.B. 355.
[39] See above at p. 131.
[40] s.34(1).

limits. However, the impact of these safeguards appears to be reduced by section 45(2) which provides that: "Any reference in this Part of the Act to a period of time or a time of day is to be treated as approximate only." This provision will clearly prevent the police becoming liable for false imprisonment when they fail to comply with some duty by a matter of minutes. The extent to which it might undermine the safeguards created by the Act will depend on the attitude of the courts.[41]

It should be noted that none of the provisions of the 1984 Act concerning detention apply to children (*i.e.* to persons under 14)[42] who are arrested without a warrant other than for homicide.[43] Instead, the arresting officer must ensure an inspector or officer in charge of the police station investigates the matter who may, on completing his inquiries either release the child or make arrangements for his detention in a place of safety.[44]

The custody officer

The supervision of suspects is the responsibility of the "custody officer." The intention of the Act is that he is independent of arresting police officers. Consequently, the basic rule is that none of his functions shall be performed by an officer involved in investigating the offence for which the person has been detained.[45]

The custody officer must be of at least a sergeant's rank unless there is no such officer at the station.[46] There must be at least one officer available to perform the functions of a custody officer at any police station which is regularly used for detention.[47]

It is the custody officer who ensures that those who are detained are treated in accordance with the provisions of the 1984 Act and the Codes of Practice, and that proper custody records[48] are kept.[49] Moreover, if the suspect is transferred to an investigating officer or an officer in charge of him outside the police station in accordance with any of the Codes of Practice, that officer must give an account to the custody officer of the manner in which he discharged his various responsibilities.[50] In addition, custody officers' duties cease if an arrested juvenile is transferred to the care of a local authority.[51]

Where an officer of higher rank than the custody officer gives directions concerning detention which is at variance with how the custody officer would have performed his duties, the custody officer must refer the matter

[41] Robilliard & McEwan at pp. 164–165.
[42] s.70 of the Children and Young Persons Act 1969.
[43] s.52.
[44] s.28(4) and (5) of the Children and Young Person's Act 1969.
[45] s.36(5).
[46] s.36(3).
[47] s.36(1).
[48] See below at p. 160.
[49] s.39(1).
[50] s.39(2) and (3).
[51] s.39(3).

at once to an officer of superintendent rank or above who is responsible for the station.[52]

The power to detain, charge and release

(1) The custody officer's first duty—whether to charge. If someone is arrested for an offence (either without a warrant or under a warrant not endorsed for bail), the custody officer at the station where he is detained must decide if there is sufficient evidence to charge him for that offence.[53] He must decide this as soon as is practicable after the arrested person arrives at the station or if he is arrested there, as soon as practicable afterwards.[54] A person may be detained at the station for as long as necessary for the officer to discharge this function.[55]

The crucial decision once a suspect is detained, therefore, is whether to charge him. Once he is charged continued detention must be justified on different and narrower grounds than if he remains uncharged. It is submitted that a custody officer's decision to detain but not to charge is potentially open to three challenges:

(1) on the ground that it was not made bona fides;
(2) on the ground that it was not made within the requisite time periods;
(3) on the ground that, looking objectively at the evidence available to the custody officer, the suspect should in fact have been charged.

The custody officer has a duty to consider charging "as soon as practicable" which probably means as soon as is feasible.[56] In the case of *R.* v. *Holmes, ex p. Sherman*[57] the Divisional Court considered the common law principle that a police officer who has enough evidence to charge a person should do so without delay. It was pointed out that if there is sufficient evidence to charge the police would be acting unlawfully if they delayed charging in order to seek advice from superior officers, legal advice or corroborative evidence.

In *Ex p. Sherman*, the Divisional Court also stated that the common law duty to charge without delay could not be restricted by setting an unduly high standard of "sufficient evidence." In *R.* v. *Hudson*[58] it was said that once a suspect had broken down and confessed, it was difficult to say that there was not sufficient evidence to charge him. Nonetheless, it is not clear what standard the court should apply in considering the objective question of whether there is sufficient evidence to charge a suspect at a particular time. The evidence required must be stronger than that required to justify an arrest without warrant. Thus, the police will not be under an obligation to charge simply because they reasonably believe the suspect is "probably

[52] s.39(6).
[53] s.37(1).
[54] s.37(10).
[55] s.37(1).
[56] See *Palmer* v. *Southend Council* [1984] 1 W.L.R. 1129.
[57] [1981] 2 All E.R. 612.
[58] (1980) 72 Cr.App.R. 163.

guilty" of an offence.[59] If, however, they are in possession of admissible evidence showing that the suspect is probably guilty then, it is submitted that they are under an obligation to charge.[60]

When a suspect is arrested and detained he is entitled upon request to have someone informed of his arrest[61] and to consult privately with a solicitor.[62] These rights are expressed as an entitlement of the suspect (subject to certain defined limitations) as opposed to a duty cast upon the police which they are obliged to carry out. It is, accordingly, submitted that any breach of the suspect's rights in this regard will not render subsequent detention unlawful—although they may give rise to an action for breach of statutory duty.[63]

Once a suspect is held in detention the Code of Practice lays down the procedure to be followed. Its relevance for our purposes is that the Code requires the custody officer to open a custody record for the arrested person "as soon as practicable."[64] This record must show both that the arrested person has acknowledged receipt of a written notice setting out his rights—to have someone informed of his arrest, to consult a solicitor and to consult the Codes of Practice.[65] The custody record must also record whether the arrested person has waived his right to legal advice.[66] When the suspect leaves detention he (or his lawyers) must be supplied with a copy of the custody record as soon as practicable if it is requested. This entitlement lasts for 12 months.[67]

If the custody officer decides he has sufficient evidence to charge a suspect for the offence for which he was arrested he must either charge that person or release him without charge (either on bail, or without bail).[68] If the decision to prosecute has not been taken when the suspect is released, he must be informed of this,[69] although a failure to do so will not make the detention retrospectively unlawful. It should be noted that a person not in a fit state to be charged or released may be kept in police custody until he is fit to leave the police station.[70]

(2) The custody officer's duty when the suspect is charged. If the custody officer does in fact decide to charge the suspect (unless the offence is under a warrant endorsed with bail), he must order his release either on bail or without bail except where the following conditions apply. He can continue to detain an adult suspect:

(1) if he cannot ascertain the suspect's name or address or has reasonable grounds for doubting that the name and address supplied are the real ones; or
(2) if he has reasonable grounds for believing the suspect's detention is

[59] See above at p. 148.
[60] This contrasts with the position on an arrest without warrant. See above at p. 149.
[61] s.56.
[62] s.58.
[63] See Chap. 10 below at p. 313.
[64] Para. 2.1.
[65] Para. 3.2.
[66] Para. 3.4.
[67] Para. 2.4.
[68] s.37(7).
[69] s.37(8).
[70] s.37(9).

necessary for his own protection or to prevent him physically injuring another or causing loss or damage to property; or

(3) if the custody officer has reasonable grounds for believing the suspect will fail to answer his bail; or

(4) if the custody officer has reasonable grounds to believe that his detention is necessary to prevent him from interfering with the administration of justice or with the investigation of offences or of a particular offence.

By contrast the custody officer can only detain an arrested juvenile if he cannot ascertain the suspect's name or address or has reasonable grounds for doubting that the name and address are the real ones or if he has reasonable grounds for believing that the juvenile ought to be detained in his own interest.[71]

If continued custody is authorised, a written record of the grounds for the detention must be made as soon as practicable[72] in the presence of the suspect who must at that time be told of the grounds for his detention.[73] This latter requirement does not apply if the suspect is incapable of understanding what is said to him, violent or likely to be violent or in urgent need of medical attention.[74]

Where the suspect is both charged and kept in detention he must be brought before the magistrates' court in the petty sessional division where the police station is situated as soon as is practicable. The police are obliged to bring him before the court no later than the first sitting after he is charged.[75] If no sitting is due on the day of the charge or the next day, the custody officer must inform the clerk to the justices of the situation[76] and he must arrange for a court to sit no later than the day next following the relevant day.[77]

(3) The custody officer's duty where there is insufficient evidence to charge. Where the custody officer decides that he does not have sufficient evidence to charge a person, the arrested person must be released (either on bail, or without bail) unless he has reasonable grounds to believe that the suspect's continued detention without charge is necessary either to secure or preserve evidence relating to the offence for which he was arrested or to obtain such evidence by questioning him.[78] If the custody officer becomes aware that there are grounds for arresting or detaining someone for another offence, he may be arrested at the station[79] when the procedures for detention will again apply.

If the custody officer authorises a person who is not charged to remain in police detention, he must as soon as practicable, make a written record of the grounds for the detention.[80] The written record must be made in the

[71] s.38(1)(2).
[72] s.38(3).
[73] s.38(4).
[74] s.38(5).
[75] s.46(1) and (2).
[76] s.46(3).
[77] s.46(6).
[78] s.37(2).
[79] s.31(1).
[80] s.37(4).

presence of the arrested person who will then be informed by the custody officer of the grounds for his detention[81] unless at the time the arrested person is incapable of understanding what is said to him, is violent or likely to become violent or in urgent need of medical attention.[82] It is submitted that a failure to comply with these procedures will make the suspect's detention unlawful. The obligations appear to impose a duty on the police and are analogous to the common law obligation to provide reasons upon arrest.[83]

As soon as the custody officer becomes aware that the grounds for detention have ceased to apply and is not aware of any other ground which would justify the detention continuing, he must release the suspect immediately[84] (unless the suspect appears to be unlawfully at large).[85] If the custody officer has released a suspect because the grounds for detention have ceased to apply, he must be released without bail unless it appears that there is a need to investigate further any matter for which he was detained or to take proceedings in relation to these in which case he must be released on bail.[86] An arrest for a breath test is regulated by the Act[87] so that the police are entitled to hold an arrested person until he is fit to leave the police station.[88]

(4) The conditions of detention. The Code of Practice makes numerous recommendations about the conditions of detention. So far as practicable, not more than one person should be detained in each cell. The cells must be adequately heated, cleaned and ventilated. Blankets, mattresses, pillows and other bedding must be of a reasonable standard and in a clean and sanitary condition. Toilet and washing facilities must be provided. The suspect must be offered two light meals and one main meal every 24 hours.[89] A failure to comply with the Code of Practice will not make the detention unlawful[90] and it seems that the conditions must become intolerable before an action for false imprisonment will become available: for example, if the prison conditions seriously prejudice the plaintiff's health by becoming flooded or containing a leaking gas pipe.[91]

(5) Police Bail. At various stages after the arrest the police have to decide whether to release the suspect on bail. Except where a suspect released on bail is re-arrested because new evidence justifying an arrest has come to light since the arrest, release on bail is to be regarded as being granted in accordance with the Bail Act 1976.[92] Depending on the decision of the custody officer the suspect is under a duty to appear either before the magistrates' court at the approved time or at the police station at the appointed

[81] s.37(5).
[82] s.37(6).
[83] *Christie* v. *Leachinsky* [1947] A.C. 573.
[84] s.34(2).
[85] s.34(4).
[86] s.34(5).
[87] s.34(6).
[88] s.37(9).
[89] See generally, para. 8, above.
[90] See Chap. 1 above at p. 29.
[91] See *Middleweek* v. *Chief Constable of Merseyside, The Times*, August 1, 1985.
[92] s.47(1) and (2).

time.[93] If a suspect who is not charged reports to the station, the custody officer can detain him for the purposes of charging him if there is sufficient evidence to charge him.[94] If he is in fact charged, the only grounds which justify his detention are those applicable if he had been arrested and charged at the outset.[95] On the other hand, if there is not sufficient evidence to charge, the suspect may be detained for as long as the custody officer has reasonable grounds for believing[96] that his detention is necessary to secure or preserve evidence relating to the offence or to obtain evidence by questioning.[97] If he is detained without charge, any earlier period when he was detained before being released on bail will count towards the total period of time for which the police are permitted to detain him.[98]

(6) The position of juveniles. When a juvenile is arrested and detained and grounds exist which justify laying an information against him, the custody officer must inform him that a decision concerning his being charged is to be taken and must specify the offence.[99] In addition, he must take such steps as are practicable to identify the person responsible for the juvenile's welfare[1] and give to the person (if it is practicable to do so) the same information he must give to the juvenile as soon as is practicable.[2] It is submitted that a failure to comply with these procedures will make the detention unlawful. There seems to be a duty on the police which is, again, analogous to the common law obligation to give reasons on arrest.[3]

How to calculate the period of detention

Unless continued detention is authorised[4] a suspect cannot be detained for more than 24 hours[5] (which may be approximate)[6] at which time he must (if he has not been charged)[7] be released either on bail or without bail.[8] He cannot then be re-arrested without a warrant unless new evidence justifying that further arrest has come to light since his release.[9] Although the statute is not clear, it would appear that this evidence need not be admissible in a court of law since there is no such requirement that it be so when making an arrest.[10]

If a suspect is arrested in a particular police area and is dealt with there,

93 s.47(3).
94 s.37(1).
95 s.38; see above at p. 160.
96 See above at p. 145.
97 s.47(5).
98 s.47(6).
99 s.37(1).
1 s.37(13).
2 s.37(12).
3 See *Christie* v. *Leachinsky* [1947] A.C. 573.
4 See below at p. 165.
5 s.41(1).
6 See above at p. 158.
7 See p. 160.
8 s.41(7).
9 s.41(9).
10 See above at p. 149.

time begins to run as soon as he is brought to the station.[11] If he attended voluntarily at the station (or accompanied a police officer to the station without being arrested) and is then arrested, time runs from the arrest.[12]

On the other hand, where the suspect is arrested in a police area other than where he is sought, and is not questioned there, time runs either from the moment he arrives at the station where he is sought or from 24 hours after the time of his arrest whichever is earlier.[13] If someone is already in the custody of a police station in England or Wales and is wanted in another police area and is taken there to investigate the offence, time will run from 24 hours after he leaves the place of detention in the first police area or from the time he arrives at the first station in the second area, whichever period is the shorter.[14]

When someone is arrested outside England or Wales time runs either from the time he arrives at the first police station in England or Wales or 24 hours after his entry into England or Wales, whichever is earlier.[15]

Review of detention

Under the 1984 Act detention at a police station must be reviewed by the "review officer." For persons arrested and charged, the custody officer conducts a review. For person arrested but not charged, the review is carried out by an officer of at least the rank of an inspector who is not involved in the investigation.[16]

The first review shall take place no later than six hours after detention was first authorised; the second no later than nine hours after the first and subsequent reviews at intervals of no more than nine hours.[17] These time periods may be approximate.[18]

A review may be postponed if at the latest time that review must occur, it is not practicable to carry it out.[19] A postponement of a review is permitted in two specific situations: if the suspect is being questioned and the review officer is satisfied that interrupting would prejudice the investigation or if at that time no review officer is available.[20] If the review is postponed, it must be carried out as soon after the latest period specified as practicable[21]; however, the review officer is required to record the reasons for the postponement on the custody record.[22] The fact that a review is carried out after a postponement does not have the effect of extending the time at which any later review must be carried out.[23]

11 s.41(2)(*d*).
12 s.41(2)(*c*).
13 s.41(2)(*a*) and (3).
14 s.41(5).
15 s.41(2)(*b*).
16 s.40(1)(2).
17 s.40(3).
18 See above at p. 158.
19 s.40(3)(*a*).
20 s.40(3)(*b*).
21 s.40(5).
22 s.40(7).
23 s.40(6).

If a suspect is not yet charged at time of a review, the review officer must decide whether to charge him, release him on bail or otherwise or to detain him further. The principles he applies are the same as those that the custody officer[24] implements in making his decision whether or not to charge a person or hold him in custody.[25] Similarly, if the suspect is charged, the review officer when considering whether to order his release on bail applies the same principles as those used by the custody officer.[26]

If an officer of higher rank than the review officer gives directions which are at variance with the review officer's decision, the review officer must refer the matter at once to an officer of superintendent rank or above who is in charge of the station.[27]

Before deciding whether to authorise continued detention, the review officer must give either the detained person (unless he is sleeping) or any solicitor representing him who is available at the time an opportunity to make representations about the detention.[28] These representations may be made orally or in writing.[29] However, the review officer may refuse to hear oral representations if he considers him unfit because of his condition or behaviour.[30] It is probable that a failure to follow these procedures will make the detention unlawful. The Act imposes obligations on the police and is analagous to the duty to listen to any statements made by a suspect when he is given the reason for his arrest.[31]

8. THE DETENTION OF SUSPECTS: EXTENDING THE PERIOD

The power to authorise continued detention

Detention may be extended for up to 36 hours (which may be approximate)[32] if:

(1) a police officer of superintendent's rank (or above) who is responsible for the police station at which the suspect is detained has reasonable grounds for believing that such detention is necessary to secure or preserve evidence relating either to the offences for which the suspect was arrested or to obtain such evidence from questioning; and

(2) the offence for which the suspect is a "serious arrestable offence"; and

[24] See above at p. 161.
[25] s.40(8).
[26] See above at p. 160; s.40(10).
[27] s.40(11).
[28] s.40(12).
[29] s.40(13).
[30] s.40(14).
[31] See above at p. 134.
[32] See above at p. 158.

(3) the investigation is being conducted diligently and expeditiously.[33]

A "serious arrestable offence" is one of several serious offences set out in the Act[34] such as murder or causing an explosion likely to endanger life or property. Alternatively, it can be an arrestable offence[35] which has led to certain specified consequences, is intended to lead to such consequences or is likely to lead to such consequences.[36] The consequences are: serious harm to the security of the State or to public order; serious interference with the administration of justice or investigation of any offence or offences; serious injury[37] to any person or any substantial financial gain (or loss) to any person.[38]

If all these conditions are met, the officer may authorise holding the suspect for 36 hours from the commencement of the detention. If he authorises detention for less than 36 hours, then he may authorise detention for up to the 36 hour maximum provided the conditions still apply.[39] Furthermore, if it is proposed to transfer the suspect to another police area, the officer when deciding to keep him in detention must take account of the distance and time the journey would take.[40]

However, no authorisation may be made more than 24 hours after detention began or before the second review by the review officer (which occurs 15 hours after detention began).[41] When an officer first authorises extended detention he must inform the suspect of the grounds for his continued detention and record them on his custody record.[42] As with a review of detention the suspect (and his solicitor) must be given the opportunity to make oral or written representations[43] although the officer may decline to hear oral representations from the suspect if he considers his condition or behaviour renders him unfit.[44] It is submitted that the failure to follow these procedures will make the suspect's detention unlawful. The Act imposes an obligation on the police which is analogous to the common law duty to give reasons on arrest.[45]

Every person detained has the right to contact his family, friend or solicitor.[46] If a suspect's extended detention has been authorised and he does not at the time exercise those rights, the officer must inform him of his rights, decide whether they can be exercised, he must record his decision in the custody record and record his reasons for his refusal if he does so.[47] In contrast to the same duties imposed when the suspect is first detained, these duties are stipulated in the Act rather than merely in the Code of Practice. A failure by the officer to follow these procedures will make the detention

[33] s.42.
[34] Sched. V, Pts. I and II.
[35] See above at p. 139.
[36] s.116(3).
[37] As defined by s.116(8).
[38] s.116(6).
[39] s.42(2).
[40] s.42(3).
[41] s.42(4).
[42] s.42(5).
[43] s.42(7).
[44] s.42(8).
[45] *Christie* v. *Leachinsky* [1947] A.C. 573.
[46] See ss.56 and 58 and p. 160.
[47] s.42(9).

unlawful. The Act imposes obligations on the police which are, again, analogous to the common law duty to give reasons on arrest.[48]

After 36 hours has expired under this procedure, the suspect must be released either with or without bail unless he is charged with the offence or his further detention ordered by a magistrates' court.[49] Moreover, he cannot be released and then re-arrested unless new evidence justifying the decision comes to light.[50]

The power to apply for further detention

Detention beyond 36 hours up to a maximum of 96 hours (which may be approximate)[51] may be ordered by a magistrates' court (defined as a court of two or more justices not sitting in open court).[52] As we have already indicated, detention will normally not exceed 24 hours unless a superintendent authorises detention up to 36 hours.

Thereafter, an application can be made on oath by an officer supported by an information. If the magistrates' court has reasonable grounds to believe that further detention is justified, it can issue a warrant of further detention.[53] The hearing is *inter partes*. The suspect must be given a copy of the information and must be brought before the court for the hearing.[54] He is entitled to be legally represented and if he is not represented but wishes to be so, the hearing will be adjourned during which time he is kept in detention.[55]

Further detention will only be justified under the following conditions:

(1) the suspect's detention without charge is necessary to secure or preserve evidence relating to the offence for which he is under arrest or to obtain such evidence by questioning;
(2) he is under arrest for a serious arrestable offence[56];
(3) the investigation is being conducted diligently and expeditiously.[57]

In general, an application for a warrant must be made within 36 hours of when detention commenced.[58] If it is not practicable for the court to sit within this period, the application must be made within the next six hours.[59] However, if the period is so extended, the suspect may be kept in police custody and a note must be made on his custody record of the fact that he was detained for the extra period and the reasons why.[60] However, if the application is made outside the 36 hour period, the court may dismiss it if it appears that it would have been reasonable to have made the

[48] *Christie* v. *Leachinsky* [1947] A.C. 573.
[49] s.42(10).
[50] s.42(11).
[51] See above at p. 158.
[52] s.43.
[53] s.43(1).
[54] s.43(2).
[55] s.43(3).
[56] See above at p. 166.
[57] s.43(4).
[58] s.43(5)(*a*).
[59] s.43(5)(*b*).
[60] s.43(6).

application before the period expired.[61] This provision is mandatory so that if it would have been reasonable for the police to draft on information within the 36 hour period, the application to extend detention must be dismissed.[61a]

The suspect must be informed of the reasons why further detention is sought. The information submitted must, therefore, state the general nature of the evidence upon which the arrest is based, the inquiries that have been made, the further inquiries to be made and reasons why continued detention is necessary for such inquiries.[62]

If the magistrates are not satisfied by the case for further detention they may either dismiss the application or adjourn the hearing to a time no later than 36 hours when the detention began.[63] If the application is dismissed the suspect can still be lawfully detained until the end of the 24 hour period (or to the end of the 36 hour period of further detention if this is or has been authorised)—he need not be released immediately.[64] Otherwise, the suspect must be released on bail or without bail.[65]

A warrant for further detention can be obtained from the magistrates' court if a further application is made supported by an information.[66] The period of extension may be for as long as the court thinks fit taking into account the evidence before it[67] but it shall not exceed 36 hours or mean that the total period for which the suspect is in detention exceeds 96 hours.[68] Moreover, a further extension can be sought provided the total period of detention does not exceed 96 hours.[69]

The court must be provided with the same particulars required in the original application[70] and the suspect has the same right to representation.[71] If the extension is refused, the suspect must either be released either with or without bail or charged[72] unless the application is refused when he is already being lawfully detained under a warrant and the warrant has not expired.[73] Once the suspect's detention has been authorised by the magistrates they might be potentially liable for the false imprisonment, but the police will not.

Detention and false imprisonment

The detailed provisions concerning detention in the 1984 Act have increased the grounds for claiming false imprisonment. In addition to being

[61] s.43(7).
[61a] *R.* v. *Slough Justices, ex p. Stirling, The Times*, March 24, 1987.
[62] s.43(14).
[63] s.43(8).
[64] s.43(16).
[65] s.43(15).
[66] s.44(1).
[67] s.44(2).
[68] s.44(3).
[69] s.44(4).
[70] See above at p. 167.
[71] s.44(6).
[72] s.44(7).
[73] s.44(6).

liable for damages where the conditions of detention are so intolerable as to render it unlawful, the police will fail to justify a detention in the following circumstances:

(1) if the custody officer fails to decide to charge the suspect as soon as practicable after he arrives at the station;
(2) if the custody officer does charge the suspect but detains him in custody when he is not entitled to do so;
(3) if the custody officer decides not to charge the suspect but continues to detain him when he is not entitled to do so;
(4) if the custody officer becomes aware that the grounds for detention have ceased to apply but fails to release the suspect;
(5) if the suspect's detention was not reviewed within the correct time period and the police cannot show that it was not practicable to conduct such a review;
(6) if the review officer does not apply the correct principles when deciding whether to charge the suspect, release him or to continue detaining him;
(7) if the suspect's detention is extended beyond 24 hours by an officer below superintendent's rank or where an officer of superintendent's rank authorises extended extension on incorrect grounds;
(8) if the suspect's properly authorised detention exceeds 36 hours without an application to a magistrates' court;
(9) if the suspect is released on police bail and attends at a police station where he is improperly detained.

It is further submitted that a failure by the police to provide information to the suspect in accordance with their various statutory duties will make the detention unlawful under the principles of *Christie* v. *Leachinsky*.[74] The police will, therefore, be liable for false imprisonment:

(10) where the custody officer fails to inform a suspect where he has not been charged; of the grounds of his detention;
(11) where the custody officer fails to inform a juvenile (and the person responsible for his welfare, if practicable) that he is being charged, specifying the offence;
(12) if the custody officer reviewing detention fails to give the suspect or his solicitor an opportunity to make representations about the detention when they are entitled to do so;
(13) where the officer authorising extended detention fails to inform the suspect of the grounds of extended detention or fails to give the suspect or his solicitor an opportunity to make representations when they are entitled to do so;
(14) where the officer responsible for extended detention fails to inform the suspect of his rights to contact friends, family or a solicitor.

However, no action for false imprisonment can be pursued if the police fail to comply with certain procedures once the suspect ceases to be detained or where they fail to inform him of his right to contact friends, family or a solicitor. In these circumstances the only remedy available will be an action for breach of statutory duty.[75]

[74] [1947] A.C. 573.
[75] See Chap. 10 below at p. 313.

9. OTHER POWERS OVER THE PERSON IN DETENTION

Powers of search in detention

Searches by the police of suspects in detention are regulated by the 1984 Act unless it is a search arising out of an arrest for "terrorism."[76]

The custody officer at the station must ascertain and record everything a person has with him when he is brought to the station after being arrested or when he is arrested at the station after attending there voluntarily or accompanying an officer without being arrested.[77] The record will be made as part of the arrested person's custody record.[78] Anything may be seized and retained[79] although clothes and personal effects may only be seized if the officer believes the suspect may cause physical injury to himself or others, may damage property, may interfere with evidence or assist him to escape or if the officer has reasonable grounds to beleve that they may be evidence relating to an offence.[80] When anything is seized the suspect must be told the reason for the seizure unless he is (or is likely to become) violent or is incapable of understanding what is said to him.[81]

Moreover, the custody officer may, if he thinks it necessary in performing his duties of securing and recording articles, order the suspect to be searched; it is up to the custody officer to decide how extensive a search to carry out.[82] Such a search may be conducted by a constable of the same sex as the suspect.[83]

The Code of Practice states that a strip search may take place only if the custody officer considers it necessary to remove an article which the suspect is not allowed to keep.[84] However, a strip search would not be unlawful so long as the officer honestly believes that it is necessary to remove the article.

It seems that the reason for all searches of arrested suspects in detention should be given to the suspect unless giving them is unnecessary or impracticable.[85] Although the suspect's clothes or personal effects may be seized in certain prescribed situations, the police consider the particular circumstances of every case[86] and cannot invoke these powers or apply the chief constable's standing orders[87] as a matter of course.

The custody officer is not entitled to order an intimate search. An inti-

76 s.53(1)(2).
77 s.54(1).
78 s.54(2).
79 s.54(3).
80 s.54(4).
81 s.54(5).
82 s.54(6).
83 s.54(9).
84 Code of Practice for Detention, Treatment and Questioning of Persons by Police Officers, Annex A.
85 *Brazil* v. *Chief Constable of Surrey* [1983] 1 W.L.R. 1155.
86 *Ibid.*
87 *Lindley* v. *Rutter* [1981] 1 Q.B. 128.

mate search means a search which consists of a person's body orifices.[88] Such a search may constitute degrading treatment in contravention of the European Convention on Human Rights.[89]

An intimate search may be made if an officer of at least the rank of superintendent has reasonable grounds for believing that the arrested suspect may have concealed on him anything he could use to cause physical injury to himself or others which he might use in detention (or in court custody) or that he has concealed on him a Class A drug which he had with an intent to supply to another or to export with an intent to evade a prohibition or restriction.[90] However, the officer cannot authorise an intimate body search unless he has reasonable grounds for believing it cannot be found without an intimate body search being conducted.[91]

If the officer authorises such a search he may do so orally or in writing; if authorisation is only oral he must confirm it in writing as soon as practicable.[92] Furthermore, if an intimate search is carried out, the custody record must state which parts of his body were searched and why.[93] This information must be recorded as soon as practicable after the search is completed.[94] The Act also requires the annual reports made under the Police Act 1964 contain information about the intimate searches carried out in the police area to which they refer.[95]

An intimate search must be carried out by a suitably qualified person unless an officer of at least the rank of superintendent considers this not to be practicable[96]; in such a case the intimate search must be carried out by a constable of the same sex as the suspect.[97] However, intimate searches for drug offences can only be done by a suitably qualified person.[98] Intimate searches must be carried out at police stations, hospitals, a doctor's surgery or some other place used for medical purposes[99] except for searches relating to drug offences which cannot take place at the station.[1–2]

Fingerprinting

The 1984 Act permits the police to fingerprint a suspect with his consent.[3] Someone of 17 or over must consent personally whereas if he is 14 he may consent but so must his parent or guardian.[4] If consent is given in the

[88] s.118(1).
[89] Van Bueren, "Once more unto Strasbourg," L.A.G. Bulletin, May 1983; see Chap. 14 below at p. 431.
[90] s.55(1).
[91] s.55(2).
[92] s.55(3).
[93] s.55(10).
[94] s.55(11).
[95] s.55(14), (15) and (16).
[96] s.55(5).
[97] s.55(6) and (7).
[98] s.55(4).
[99] s.55(8).
[1–2] s.55(9).
[3] s.61(1).
[4] s.65.

police station, it must be in writing.[5] It should be noted that the police can, in certain circumstances, require a suspect to attend the station for the purposes of fingerprinting.[6]

In addition to their power in relation to immigration and terrorist offences,[7] the Act does allow the police to fingerprint without consent. An officer of at least the rank of superintendent may authorise fingerprinting at the station if he has reasonable grounds for suspecting the involvement of a person whose fingerprints are to be taken in a criminal offence and for believing the fingerprints will prove or disprove his involvement.[8] Such an authorisation can be given orally or in writing, but if given orally it must be confirmed in writing as soon as practicable.[9]

Moreover, if a suspect has been charged with a recordable offence (as defined by the regulations made under section 27(4)) or has been informed he will be reported for such an offence and he has not had fingerprints taken in the course of the investigation of the offence, his fingerprints can be taken at the station without his consent.[10] Again no consent is required if the suspect is convicted of a recordable offence.[11]

Where fingerprinting is obtained without consent, the suspect must be told the reason for taking them which must be recorded as soon as practicable after they are taken.[12] If he is in police detention the reason must be recorded on his custody record.[13]

Fingerprints are defined as including palm prints.[14] It is a question of fact for the police to decide whether the part of the hand of which the police wish to take prints is a palm print.[15]

If the police fail to comply with the statutory procedures for obtaining fingerprints, they will be liable for battery.

Intimate samples

The 1984 Act allows the police to take intimate samples (which are defined as a sample of blood, semen or any tissue fluid, urine, saliva or pubic hair or a swab taken from someone's body orifice.[16] Intimate samples can only be taken from a person in police detention if they are authorised by an officer of at least superintendent's rank and the consent of the suspect is given[17] in writing.[18] The officer can give authorisation if he has reasonable grounds for suspecting the involvement of that person in a serious arres-

[5] s.61(2).
[6] s.27.
[7] s.61(9).
[8] s.61(3)(*a*) and s.61(4).
[9] s.61(5).
[10] s.61(3)(*b*).
[11] s.61(6).
[12] s.61(7).
[13] s.61(8).
[14] s.65.
[15] *R.* v. *Tottenham JJ., ex p. L., The Times*, November 11, 1985.
[16] s.65.
[17] s.62(1).
[18] s.62(4).

table offence[19] and believing that the sample will tend to confirm or disprove that involvement.[20] Authorisation can be given orally or in writing but if it is oral, it should be confirmed in writing as soon as is practicable.[21]

Where authorisation is given and an intimate search is proposed, the officer must inform the suspect that authorisation has been given and the grounds for it[22] (including the nature of the offence suspected).[23] If the sample itself is taken the authorisation, grounds and consent must be recorded as soon as is practicable after the sample is taken.[24] These facts will be recorded on his custody record if he is in police detention.[25] Samples other than urine or saliva must be taken by a registered medical practitioner.[26]

If the police fail to comply with the statutory provisions for obtaining intimate samples, they will be liable for battery. However, the mere fact that from the point of view of the suspect, the battery is oppressive will not entitle him to exemplary damages although he may recover aggravated damages if appropriate.[27]

This power to take intimate samples is quite draconian. Although a suspect need not consent, the fact that adverse inferences can be drawn from a refusal to provide a sample is plainly inconsistent with the right to remain silent and the privilege against self-incrimination. In Canada taking blood without consent for non-therapeutic purposes has been held to be unconstitutional as a breach of the Canadian Charter of Rights and Freedoms.[28] It is difficult to dissent from Feldman's verdict that there is "little of principle" to support the powers under sections 62 and 63 and that their abolition is to be looked forward to.[29]

Non-intimate samples

Non-intimate samples (which are defined as a sample of hair other than pubic hair, a sample taken from or under a nail, a swab taken from any part of a suspect's body other than a body orifice or a footprint or similar impression from any part of the body other than the hand)[30] can also be taken under the Act.

Non-intimate searches cannot be taken without the consent of the suspect which must be given in writing.[31] However, they can be taken without consent if the suspect is in police detention or court custody and an officer of at least superintendent's rank authorises it.[32] Authorisation can be given

[19] See above at p. 166.
[20] s.62(3).
[21] s.62(3).
[22] s.62(5).
[23] s.62(6).
[24] s.62(7).
[25] s.62(8).
[26] s.62(9).
[27] *Barbara* v. *Home Office* (1984) 132 New L.J. 888: Chap. 11 below at p. 343.
[28] *R.* v. *Dyment* (1984) 9 D.L.R. (4th) 614.
[29] Feldman at 9.30 and 9.34.
[30] s.65.
[31] s.63(2).
[32] s.63(3).

if the officer has reasonable grounds for suspecting the suspect of being involved in a serious arrestable offence[33] and for believing that the sample will tend to confirm or disprove his involvement.[34] Authorisation can be given orally or in writing, but if it is oral, it must be confirmed in writing as soon as is practicable.[35]

Where authorisation is given and a non-intimate sample is proposed, the officer must inform the suspect that he is giving the authorisation and of the grounds for giving it[36] (including the nature of the offence suspected).[37] If a non-intimate sample is taken, the authorisation and its grounds must be recorded as soon as is practicable after the sample is taken.[38] These will be recorded on the custody record if the suspect is in police detention.[39]

If the police fail to comply with the statutory procedures for obtaining non-intimate samples they will be liable in battery. However, the mere fact that, from the point of view of the suspect, the battery is oppressive will not entitle him to exemplary damages although he may recover aggravated damages if appropriate.[40]

This power to take non-intimate samples is even more remarkable than the power to take intimate ones. A police officer without reference to any judicial officer can take a person's hair or fingerprints to use as evidence against him. It has been suggested that this power breaches the guarantee of bodily integrity under the European Convention on Human Rights.[41]

[33] See above at p. 166.
[34] s.63(4).
[35] s.65(5).
[36] s.65(6).
[37] s.65(7).
[38] s.65(8).
[39] s.65(9).
[40] See *Barbara* v. *Home Office* (1984) 132 New L.J. 888; see also Chap. 11 below at p. 343.
[41] Feldman at 9.34; Chap. 14 below at p. 431.

6. Interfering with Land and Goods

1. PROTECTING LAND AND GOODS

Police powers and the law of tort

In the course of their duties the police often search houses or cars. If they find property which they suspect is relevant to some criminal activity then they may have power to seize it. A wide range of different activities are involved. The police may cross the threshold of a house or enter it for a short period to carry out investigations. On the other hand, they may take over premises and remain there for a considerable period, obstructing their use for other purposes. They may search a car or they may go through substantial business premises with a fine-tooth comb. They may seize a small item of property or a substantial income earning chattel such as a large lorry. A large segment of the complex range of civil remedies relating to land and goods is brought into play.

The English law provides land and property owners with powerful protection against the encroachments of others. Anyone who interferes with the land or goods of another must justify their actions. There are a range of "lawful justifications" for such interference which are available to everyone, including the police. In addition, the police have wide powers of entry, search and seizure when they suspect that the occupiers or owners are involved in crime. Although these powers have recently been clarified and partially codified by the Police and Criminal Evidence Act 1984 they remain complex and often unclear. Certain of them can be exercised by a police officer acting on "reasonable suspicion." Others require a magistrate's or judge's warrant.

These powers, in effect, provide police constables with a defence to tort actions for interfering with land and goods. Thus, although an interference is proved and none of the ordinary defences are available, the police will not be liable if they are acting within their powers.

The approach for someone who feels that his land or goods have been unlawfully interfered with by the police consists of two parts.

(1) Was the interference itself unlawful? This involves consideration of the torts of trespass to land and wrongful interference with goods and the defences (including that of "lawful justification") which are

available to all citizens; if the answer to this question is "yes" then the second question arises:

(2) Do the police have a special "lawful justification" for their apparently unlawful actions? In other words: do they have a defence to the tort action due to the fact that they were acting within their statutory or common law powers?

The first question will be considered in this chapter, the second in Chapter 7.

The civil law in relation to land and goods is one of the most ancient and complex areas of the English law. It is beyond the scope of this book to give a comprehensive coverage of the law, especially in relation to goods. Many of the famous obscurities of the tort of conversion, for example, have little or no relevance to civil actions against the police.[1]

First the elements of the tort of trespass to land and the ancient doctrine of trespass *ab initio* are considered. Secondly, the tort of trespass to goods which covers any direct physical interference with the possession of goods is considered. Thirdly, the tort of conversion, which covers the dealing with goods in a manner inconsistent with the rights of their owner (or the person in possession of them) is dealt with. The final section deals with the situations in which the different torts apply. The various remedies which are available to a person who wishes to obtain the return of seized goods are considered in Chapter 12.[2]

Land or goods: the position of fixtures

It is sometimes important to know whether a particular action relates to interference with land or interference with goods. The distinction between the two is usually plain and obvious: a field is land, a watch is goods. Difficulties arise, however, when goods are, in some way, "attached" to land. The general rule is that "whatever is attached to the soil becomes part of it" (*quicquid plantatur solo, solo cedit*). Goods which are attached to land are, for legal purposes, land rather than goods. Anyone who damages them must be sued in trespass to land rather than for interference with goods.

This doctrine has effects which, at first sight, appear paradoxical. Thus a door in a timber yard is a chattel but when it is fixed in a door frame it becomes land. If it is later removed from the frame it becomes a chattel again. It may sometimes be difficult to tell whether a particular object, such as a kitchen fitting, is a chattel or land. The present day position was summarised by Scarman L.J. in the case of *Berkley* v. *Poulett*[3] as follows;

> "The answer today to the question whether objects which were originally chattels have become fixtures, that is to say part of the freehold, depends upon the application of two tests: (1) the method and degree of annexation; (2) the object and purpose of the annexation."

If, for example, it is alleged that police officers have damaged a flat in the course of a search then, it is likely that some of the things will be chattels

[1] For a comprehensive treatment see Clerk & Lindsell, Chap. 21.

[2] See below at p. 387.

[3] (1976) 242 E.G. 39.

(for example, furniture) and some will be land (for example, doors or windows). In practice the main difference between the two is likely to be the different limitation periods which apply.[4]

2. TRESPASS TO LAND

Introduction—Who can sue?

Trespass to land can be defined as any direct physical intrusion by one person onto land in the possession of another which cannot be justified by law. It is important to note that what the law protects is not the "ownership" of the land but the "possession" of it. Only the person in possession can bring a trespass action.

Possession, in general, is simply the occupation or physical control of the land in question. This is sometimes known as "possession in fact" or "*de facto*" possession. The person claiming possession must have the power to use the land and keep others off it and this must be accompanied by an intention to keep it as his own (an *animus possidendi*).[5]

Thus, in order to be able to sue in trespass a person must be in possession of the land trespassed upon. It appears that such possession must be "clear and exclusive,"[6] in other words the possessor must be able to exclude the whole world (except anyone having a joint right to such possession). Thus a freeholder or a tenant can sue in trespass—no matter what the period of the tenancy. On the other hand, lodgers, visitors or servant licensees cannot sue for trespass unless, on a true interpretation of things, they are in fact subtenants.[7]

The position of squatters is more complicated. When a squatter enters land he does not immediately gain possession.[8] This only happens when the rightful owner acquiesces in his physical occupation of the land. At this point the squatter can exclude the whole world, except the owner, from the land. He can bring a trespass action against anyone who enters the squatted premises without lawful justification except the true owner.[9] In other words, *jus tertii*, the right of a third person, is no defence in an action for trespass to land. In such a situation it is no defence for the person who enters to say that the squatters were not the true owners of the premises and were not in lawful occupation unless he can show that his actions were done with the authority of the true owner.[10]

In practice, the question of who is entitled to sue in trespass will usually be straightforward. In the case of a house or flat which is occupied, the person or persons in occupation will be able to sue. If the owner(s) are in

[4] See below at p. 300.

[5] See below at p. 187.

[6] *per* Best C.J., *Revett* v. *Brown* (1828) 5 Bing. 7 at 9; but see *Bristow* v. *Cormican* (1878) 3 App.Cas. 641 at 657.

[7] See *Allan* v. *Liverpool* (1874) L.R. 9 Q.B. 180; *Bertie* v. *Beaumont* (1812) 16 East. 33; *Mayhew* v. *Suttle* (1854) 4 E. & B. 347.

[8] See *per* Lord Denman, *Brown* v. *Dawson* (1840) 12 A. & E. 624 at 629.

[9] *Delaney* v. *T. P. Smith Ltd.* [1946] K.B. 393.

[10] *Graham* v. *Peat* (1801) 1 East. 244.

occupation then they will be the proper plaintiffs. If the premises are occupied by tenants or sub-tenants then they can sue rather than the landlord.[11] The sub-lessee of a particular room can maintain a separate action for trespass against the whole world, including the sub-lessor.[12] A person who is in occupation as a statutory tenant under the Rent Acts can also sue for trespass.[13]

In the case of an unoccupied building the person entitled to sue is the one who has the means of obtaining entry such as the key.[14] If there are no buildings on the land then the person in possession will be the one who can show "acts of enjoyment of the land."[15] There is a general presumption that the person having title to the land is in possession of it.[16]

What is a trespass?

A trespass is classically defined as an unjustifiable intrusion onto land in the possession of another. More precisely trespass, as unjustifiable interference with the possession of land, can take three forms. A person can be liable in trespass in relation to land in possession of another if he wrongfully:

(1) enters onto it;
(2) remains on it;
(3) places objects on it.

(1) Trespass by entry. This is the most straightforward form of trespass: the slightest entry will be sufficient. In the stirring words of Lord Camden C.J.:

> "by the laws of England every invasion of private property, be it ever so minute, is a trespass. No man can set his foot upon my ground without my licence, but he is liable to an action, though the damage be nothing."[17]

The extent of the entry is irrelevant to the question of whether or not a trespass has actually taken place. As Lord Coleridge C.J. said:

> "if the defendant places a part of his boot on the plaintiff's land unlawfully it is as much a trespass as if he had walked half a mile on it."[18]

[11] *Cooper* v. *Crabtree* (1882) 20 Ch.D. 589.
[12] *Lane* v. *Dixon* (1847) 3 C.B. 776.
[13] See, *e.g.* *Keeves* v. *Dean* [1924] 1 K.B. 685 at 694; *Brown* v. *Brash & Ambrose* [1948] 2 K.B. 247.
[14] *Jewish Maternity Society's Trustees* v. *Garfinkle* (1926) 95 L.J.K.B. 766.
[15] *Jones* v. *Williams* (1837) 2 M. & W. 326 at 331.
[16] *Hebbert* v. *Thomas* (1835) 1 C. M. & R. 861 at 864; *Ramsay* v. *Margrett* [1894] 2 Q.B. 18 at 27. If there are two people asserting the right to possession and both doing some act in assertion of that right "the person who has title is in actual possession and the other person is a trespasser" *Jones* v. *Chapman* (1849) 2 Ex. 803 at 821.
[17] *Entick* v. *Carrington* (1765) 19 State Trials 1066G.
[18] *Ellis* v. *Loftus Iron* (1874) 10 L.R. C.P. 10 at 12.

Thus it will be trespass if a police officer places his foot inside a door. It also seems to be trespass to touch the boundary walls of a house or land.[19]

It is no defence to a trespass action that the defendant honestly believed that he had a right to enter.[20] Thus a constable who enters premises as the result of an honest mistake as to his powers can be a trespasser. There is no "authority of necessity" allowing a man to enter onto another's land.[21] In other words, it is no defence to an action in trespass for a police officer to say that the entry was necessary in order to enable him to chase a fugitive or prevent a crime. Any *voluntary* entry will be a trespass.[22] However, the defence of "inevitable accident" is probably available.[23]

In all these situations there is only a trespass if there is no lawful justification for the entry. The police may enter premises under their various powers.[24] In addition, their entry may be justified in the same ways as that of any other citizen. The usual justifications for entry are considered in the next section.

Considerable legal difficulties arise when someone has permission to enter onto land for one purpose but in fact enters for another. Two situations can be distinguished. First, where a person has permission to enter land for a limited purpose and **acts** in excess of his permission when he is on the land. Secondly, where a person with a limited permission enters with the **intention** of exceeding that permission but does not actually act in excess of it.

There is no doubt that a person who enters lawfully under a limited permission becomes a trespasser from the moment that he **acts** in excess of his permission. As Lord Atkin said, if I have invited someone onto my premises

> "so far as he sets foot on so much of the premises as lie outside the invitation or uses them for purposes which are alien to the invitation he is . . . a trespasser."[25]

The position regarding entry with intent to exceed a limited permission is more complex. In *Byrne* v. *Kinematograph Renters Society*[26] Harman J. decided that a person who had gained entry to a cinema for the purpose of counting patrons rather than watching films was not a trespasser. This decision was distinguished by the Court of Appeal (Criminal Division) in

[19] "a single stone put against the wall . . . would have been sufficient" for trespass; *per* Parke J., *Gregory* v. *Piper* (1829) 9 B. & C. 591 at 594; see also, *Westripp* v. *Baldock* [1938] 2 All E.R. 779.

[20] *Hewlitt* v. *Bickerton* (1947) 150 E.G. 421; or that the land was his, *Basely* v. *Clarkson* (1681) 3 Lev. 37.

[21] See *Hewlitt* v. *Bickerton* (1947) 150 E.G. 421.

[22] For cases of involuntary entry see *Smith* v. *Stone* (1647) Style 65; *Braithwaite* v. *South Durham Steel* [1958] 1 W.L.R. 986; *Public Transport Commission of N.S.W.* v. *Perry* (1977) 14 A.L.R. 273.

[23] See *NCB* v. *Evans* [1951] 2 K.B. 861; and the dicta in *Mann* v. *Saulnier* (1959) D.L.R. (2d) 130 at 132.

[24] See Chap. 7 below at p. 204.

[25] *Hillen* v. *ICI* [1936] A.C. 65 at 69. Many of the old cases relate to the common law distinction between "invitees" and "licensees," but are still good law on the trespass point. This doctrine is distinct from that of trespass *ab initio*, see below at p. 184.

[26] [1958] 1 W.L.R. 762 at 776.

the case of *R.* v. *Jones & Smith*[27] in which the defendant S was held to be a trespasser in his father's house because he entered with intent to steal, despite the fact that he had his father's unreserved permission to enter. This was because entry to steal was clearly in excess of his permission. In an Australian case a police officer who entered premises intending to commit a tort (misfeasance of public office) was held, for that reason to be a trespasser.[28]

It is submitted that a person who enters onto another's land with a limited permission with the intention of exceeding that permission is a trespasser at the moment of entry. It would follow that a police officer who has permission from the occupier to enter a house to discuss a road traffic accident is a trespasser if his true purpose was to conduct a surreptitious search for stolen goods.[29]

(2) Trespass by remaining on land. When a person enters lawfully there may come a time when his presence on the land is no longer lawful and at that point he becomes a trespasser.[30] The most common situation is that of a bare licensee[31] whose licence is revoked. When this happens the law allows the licensee a reasonable time to leave the land[32] and to remove his goods.[33] If he does not leave after a reasonable time has elapsed the person in possession of the land is entitled to use reasonable force to eject him.[34] It is clear that this doctrine applies to constables as much as to ordinary citizens. Thus, in the well known case of *Davis* v. *Lisle*[35] a constable, believing that an offence had been committed by a lorry, followed it into Mr Davis' garage. On being told to leave he started to take out his "warrant card" and was then hit by Mr Davis. The Divisional Court held that the constable was a trespasser at the time when he was hit because instead of leaving he was, by reaching for his warrant card, asserting an unjustified claim to stay.

(3) Trespass by placing objects onto land. The direct placing of any physical object onto the land will be a trespass. Throwing a person onto another's land is trespass.[36]; It is probably trespass to cause gas to go on to land.[37] An action can also be based on the defendant having allowed or encouraged animals to run on to the plaintiff's land.[38]

Trespass, however committed, does not produce a single "one-off" cause

27 [1976] 1 W.L.R. 672.

28 *Farrington* v. *Thomson & Bridgland* [1959] V.R. 286.

29 This approach is supported by the Commonwealth authorities; see *Gross* v. *Wright* [1923] 2 D.L.R. 171 at 189; *Barker* v. *R.* (1983) 7 A.L.J.R. 426; *Strang* v. *Russell* (1905) 24 N.Z.L.R. 916; see also J. C. Smith, *The Law of Theft* at p. 338 and see Feldman at 2–08 – 2–12; and the discussion of licences obtained by fraud, below at p. 181.

30 *Minister of Health* v. *Bellotti* [1944] K.B. 298; *Cottreau* v. *Rodgerson* (1966) 53 D.L.R. (2d) 549 at 557.

31 See below at p. 181.

32 See *Robson* v. *Hallett* [1967] 2 Q.B. 939 at 953A.

33 *Ministry of Health* v. *Bellotti* [1944] K.B. 298 at 306.

34 See *Green* v. *Goddard* (1702) 2 Salk. 641; and see below at p. 184.

35 [1936] 2 K.B. 434.

36 *Smith* v. *Stone* (1647) Style 65.

37 See the dicta in *McDonald* v. *Associated Fuels* [1954] 3 D.L.R. 775 at 783.

38 *Beckwith* v. *Shordike* (1767) 4 Burr. 2092.

of action when the trespass occurs. Rather, there is a new trespass every moment that the defendant remains on the plaintiff's land.[39]

Justifying intrusions onto land—the doctrine of licences

To be a trespass any "intrusion" onto land must be wrongful. In addition to their special powers of entry[40] the police can also rely on the same justifications for entry as ordinary citizens. There are a wide range of these, the majority of which are unlikely to have any relevance to actions in relation to the police.[41] The most important "lawful justification for entry" is the licence. A constable who enters premises without a warrant and not under his general statutory powers will usually have to justify his entry in terms of a licence.

A licence, in this sense, is a permission to enter. Some licences, like theatre tickets, are contractual. These are unlikely to be relevant to the position of police officers.[42] The most common form of licence to enter is the bare or gratuitous licence. This can be express or implied.

An express licence to enter is given, for example, when the occupier or his agent, invites someone to enter the land in question. Whether or not a particular non-occupier can grant an express licence to enter depends on whether he has the actual or ostensible authority of the occupier to grant such a licence.[43] It is clear that an occupier's wife may, by conduct or expressly, permit entry.[44] It is generally accepted that a child of the occupier may give an express licence to enter.[45] A police officer is entitled to assume that guests have authority to invite him into their host's home when he has got into difficulties and invites them in to clear his name.[46] In *McGowan* v. *Chief Constable of Kingston upon Hull*[47] it was held that a **former** co-habitee could grant a licence to police officers to enter premises although she was no longer resident there because the occupier had impliedly invited her by taking their child as a "bait" to entice her back.

The position is unclear if an express licence was in fact obtained by fraud or duress. If the person seeking entry makes a fraudulent statement as to his identity and this is relied on then he will be a trespasser because the permission given was not given to him but to the person he fraudulently misrepresented himself to be.[48] If the person seeking entry makes fraudulent statements on other matters, such as the purposes for which entry is being sought, then, it is submitted, whether or not he is a trespasser depends on whether the "misapprehension of the consenting party goes to the root of

39 *Holmes* v. *Wilson* (1839) 10 A. & E. 503.
40 See Chap. 7.
41 For a complete treatment see Clerk & Lindsell, paras. 22–26 to 22–40.
42 For a general discussion of licences see Hanbury and Maudsley, *Modern Equity*, Chap. 27.
43 See Feldman, at 2.03–2.07.
44 *Faulkner* v. *Willetts* [1982] Crim.L.R. 453.
45 As happened in *Morris* v. *Beardmore* [1981] A.C. 446.
46 *Jones & Jones* v. *Lloyd* [1981] Crim.L.R. 340.
47 [1968] Crim.L.R. 34.
48 By analogy with the famous contract case of *Cundy* v. *Lindsey* (1878) 3 App.Cas. 459.

the whole transaction."[49] Thus, if a police officer obtains permission to enter by saying, untruthfully, that he is investigating a murder, the consent will be vitiated and the officer will be a trespasser. On the other hand, if the officer is untruthful about his rank or status then the consent will be effective, unless these matters were material and operative on the mind of the person who gave the consent. Duress will clearly negative consent[50] as will a material misrepresentation as to the purposes of entry.

When an express licence is not granted, the law will sometimes imply one. The situations in which a constable has such an implied licence to enter has been discussed in a number of authorities. The general position was stated by Atkin L.J. as follows:

> "it appears to me quite impossible to suggest, merely because a constable may suspect there is something wrong, that he has a right to enter a dwelling house either by opening a door or by entering an open door or an open window and go into the house."[51]

Thus, if a constable cannot enter under a statutory or common law power he has no special licence implied by virtue of his office. He can, however, take advantage of the licences which the law implies in favour of any citizen. A licence will be implied when land is habitually entered by people who have no express permission to do so.[52] For present purposes the most important of these is the implied licence to go to the front door of a house or flat. As Lord Widgery C.J. put it:

> "anyone who has any genuine reason for wishing to enter the house or garden has implied licence from the occupier to approach the front or nearest door and ask whether he may be given permission for what he wishes to do."[53]

The activation of a burglar alarm at police headquarters gives the police an implied licence to enter the premises which it relates to in order to make investigations.[54]

Two points should be noted here. First, an implied licence is of strictly limited extent. Thus in *Brunner* v. *Williams*,[55] a weights and measures inspector who entered a garden for the purpose of checking on a coal dealer was outside his implied licence and therefore a trespasser because he did not enter simply for the purpose of approaching the front door. Secondly, because this is a licence implied by law it is perfectly possible for the person in possession to override it either by keeping the garden gate locked or by express provision. Donaldson L.J. summarised the position as follows:

> "There can be no doubt that, in the absence of a locked gate or some

[49] See Clerk & Lindsell, para. 14–07 on consent in cases of battery; see also Feldman at 2.08–2.12.
[50] See *Jeffrey* v. *Black* [1978] Q.B. 490.
[51] *Great Central Railway* v. *Bates* [1921] 3 K.B. 578 at 581–2.
[52] *e.g.*, a field which is habitually used as a short cut, *Lowery* v. *Walker* [1911] A.C. 10.
[53] *Brunner* v. *Williams* (1975) 73 L.G.R. 266 at 272; see also, *Robson* v. *Hallett* [1967] 2 Q.B. 939.
[54] *Kay* v. *Hibbert* [1977] Crim.L.R. 226.
[55] (1975) 73 L.G.R. 266.

> other notice such as 'Police keep out,' police officers, like all other citizens, have an implied licence to enter upon a driveway and to approach the door of a dwellinghouse if they have, or reasonably think they have, legitimate business with the occupier."[56]

Both express and implied licences can, of course, be revoked by the occupier or his agent and, after the licensee has been given a reasonable time to leave the premises, he becomes a trespasser.[57] Whether or not particular words are to be regarded as revoking the licence is a matter of fact in each case. An implied licence must, however, be "expressly refused" and words such as "fuck off" will not, in general, be sufficient to bring it to an end.[58]

The question of who is entitled to revoke a licence is, again, a matter of actual or ostensible authority. Thus in *McArdle* v. *Wallace (No. 2)*[59] a police officer who had entered a café to make enquiries about stolen goods was held to be a trespasser when he did not leave after being told to do so by the café proprietor's son.

When permission to enter is given by an agent of the occupier, such as a member of his family or an invitee, the occupier can revoke the licence and require the licensee to leave in exactly the same way as he could if he had given the licence himself.[60]

It was suggested in the case of *R.* v. *Thornley*[61] that a licence given by one of two co-occupiers cannot be unilaterally revoked by the other. In that case police officers were invited into premises by a wife who alleged that she was being assaulted. It was held that the licence could not be unilaterally revoked by her husband. This case appears to have been decided without reference to the civil law authorities. In *Robson-Paul* v. *Farrugia*[62] the Court of Appeal held that a licence granted by one of two co-owners could be validly revoked by the other. As Davies L.J. said:

> "If one can grant a licence . . . then . . . the other can revoke the licence. Otherwise, the licensee would remain in the premises *ad infinitum*."[63]

Thus, it is submitted, whoever grants a licence, it can be validly revoked by the clear words of one co-occupier.

The two most common circumstances in which a constable can enter premises without a "power" to do so are, therefore, as follows:

(1) if the person in possession, or his agent, has given him permission;
(2) if he is acting within an "implied licence" to enter.

"Express revocation" brings either type of licence to an end and, after a reasonable time has expired, the constable becomes a trespasser.

[56] *Lambert* v. *Roberts* [1981] 2 All E.R. 15; see also, *per* Diplock L.J., *Robson* v. *Hallett* [1967] 2 Q.B. 939 at 954A.
[57] *Ministry of Health* v. *Bellotti* [1944] K.B. 298.
[58] *Snook* v. *Mannion* [1982] Crim.L.R. 601; *Gilham* v. *Breidenbach* [1982] R.T.R. 328 n.
[59] (1964) 108 S.J. 483; following on from *McArdle* v. *Wallace* [1964] Crim.L.R. 467.
[60] See *e.g.*, *Morris* v. *Beardmore* [1981] A.C. 446 H.L.
[61] [1981] Crim.L.R. 637.
[62] (1969) 20 P. & C.R. 820.
[63] See also, *Annen* v. *Rattee* [1985] 1 E.G.L.R. 136 C.A.

Trespassers and the use of force

The person in possession of land[64] may use reasonable force to eject a trespasser from his land.[65] If the person is a trespasser because of the express revocation of a licence he must, first, be allowed a reasonable time to leave.[66] The person in possession can also use reasonable force to prevent a trespasser from entering or to control his movements when he is on the land.[67]

Reasonable force can also be used to retake land which has been occupied by another. This right is, however, subject to section 6 of the Criminal Law Act 1977 which makes it an offence for anyone other than a displaced residential occupier to use or threaten violence for the purpose of securing entry to premises occupied by another.

The force used in all these circumstances must be reasonable and must not, in the first instance, include beating, wounding or physical injury.[68] If, however, the trespasser resists with excessive force the occupier is entitled to use further reasonable force in self-defence.[69]

Trespass *ab initio*

Someone who lawfully enters land but then acts in excess of his authority becomes a trespasser.[70] If that person has entered under an authority given by law (as opposed to a permission given by the occupier) there has long been an additional remedy to discourage abuse of legal authority. This is provided by the ancient doctrine of trespass *ab initio*. The most famous formulation is that in the *Six Carpenters'* case[71];

> "when entry, authority or licence is given to any one by the law and he doth abuse it, he shall be a trespasser *ab initio*."

In other words, he is a trespasser not just from the moment of the abuse but from the moment of entry. The subsequent misconduct renders the initial entry unlawful. This means that the occupier of the land can recover damages for the whole period that the wrongdoer is on the land and not just for the period after the abuse.[72] It may also be that the occupier is entitled to use reasonable force to eject the wrongdoer from the land without waiting for a reasonable time to elapse.[73]

What this doctrine means is that an authority given **by law**, without the owner's consent protects the person exercising it so long, and only so long, as the authority is not abused. If it is abused then it is as if the law had never

[64] *Holmes* v. *Bagge* (1853) 1 E. & B. 782.
[65] *Green* v. *Goddard* (1702) 2 Salk. 641.
[66] See above at p. 183.
[67] *Harrison* v. *Rutland (Duke of)* [1893] 1 Q.B. 142.
[68] *Collins* v. *Renison* (1754) Sayer 138.
[69] See generally, Clerk & Lindsell; Chap. 4 above at p. 123.
[70] See above at p. 179.
[71] (1610) 8 Co.Rep. 146a.
[72] *Shorland* v. *Govett* (1826) 5 B. & C. 485.
[73] See Street at p. 57, n. 18.

given such authority.[74] It might be thought that this doctrine could be of considerable use to protect the citizen from abuses of police power.[75] It is, however, very rarely used today and very narrow in its application. This is partially explained by two substantial limitations on the doctrine which operate to restrict its scope considerably.

The first of these formed the *ratio* of the *Six Carpenter's* case; the "abuse" must amount to a positive wrongful act, a misfeasance rather than a mere omission or non-feasance.[76] Furthermore, the abuse must itself be a trespass, other forms of wrongdoing being insufficient.[77] A trespass to goods[78] or to the person[79] will be sufficient, but malice alone will not make someone a trespasser *ab initio*.[80]

The second limitation concerns the situation where a person entering under the authority of the law seizes a quantity of goods but only part of the seizure is unlawful. He is only a trespasser *ab initio* as to the part wrongfully seized.[81] This obscure doctrine has been affirmed in a number of cases.[82] These include the notorious case of *Elias* v. *Pasmore*[83] in which police officers lawfully entered the plaintiff's premises and seized a large number of documents, some of which were used at various criminal trials and others of which were not. It was held that the police were trespassers *ab initio* in respect of the wrongfully seized documents only and not in respect of the entire transaction. This case has been widely criticised, but does appear to represent the law. More recently the Court of Appeal have doubted whether any unlawful seizure of goods would make a police entry onto premises wrongful *ab initio*.[84]

It appears that if a person entering under the authority of the law commits a trespass to the person then his entire entry is unlawful. Thus in *Ward's Case*[85] a constable was searching the Plaintiff's house for stolen goods under a search warrant and

> "upon the evidence it appeared the Defendant in this search did pull the clothes from off a womans bed then in her bed, to search under her Smock, and this was holden to be a misdemeanor in the Constable, and all with him and did make all their proceedings in this place illegal from the beginning."

The fact that the constable was a trespasser *ab initio* meant that the arrest of the Plaintiff was unlawful and he appears to have recovered damages for trespass to the person.

[74] See *Pollock's Law of Torts*, at p. 298.
[75] See Clerk & Lindsell, para. 22–29.
[76] See also *Delta Holdings* v. *Magnum* (1975) 59 D.L.R. (3d) 126 at 130.
[77] *Shorland* v. *Govett* (1826) 5 B. & C. 485.
[78] *Elias* v. *Pasmore* [1934] 2 K.B. 164.
[79] *Ward's Case* (1636) Clay 44.
[80] *Birt* v. *Magnay* (1843) 7 Jur. 127.
[81] *Harvey* v. *Pocock* (1843) 11 M. & W. 770 at 774, *per* Lord Abinger C.B.; see also *Dod* v. *Monger* (1704) 6 Mod.Rep. 215.
[82] See *Canadian Pacific Wine* v. *Tuey* [1921] 2 A.C. 417, P.C.; *Owen & Smith* v. *Reo Motors* (1934) 151 L.T. 274.
[83] [1934] 2 K.B. 164.
[84] *Chic Fashions* v. *Jones* [1968] 2 Q.B. 299.
[85] (1636) Clay 44.

In the *Chic Fashions* case Lord Denning M.R. had this to say about the whole doctrine;

> "at one time a man could be made a trespasser *ab initio* by the doctrine of relation back. But that is no longer true. The *Six Carpenter's Case* was a by-product of the old forms of action. Now that they are buried it can be interred with their bones."[86]

This view has been criticised.[87] It is perhaps not surprising that more recent judicial support for the doctrine has come from Lord Denning M.R. himself. In the case of *Cinnamond* v. *British Airports Authority*[88] in which, referring to the position of car hire drivers at Heathrow Airport, and after citing the *Six Carpenter's Case* he said;

> "These car-hire drivers abused the authority given to them by the law by hanging about and 'touting.' So they became trespassers from the beginning and can be turned out."[89]

There is little doubt, therefore, that the doctrine remains good law. If a police officer who has entered under an authority conferred by law—whether this is conferred by statute, common law or a search warrant—commits an act of trespass then he becomes a trespasser *ab initio*. At this point he will no longer be acting "in the execution of his duty" and the occupier will be entitled to use reasonable force to eject him. If the police officer seizes more goods than he is entitled to then he is only a trespasser *ab initio* in relation to those goods. On the other hand, it appears that if there is a trespass to the person—such as battery on the occupier by pushing or otherwise—on the course of a lawful search, then the searching officers will be trespassers *ab initio* and the entire search will be unlawful.

3. WRONGFUL INTERFERENCE WITH GOODS

Introduction

From the earliest times the common law has provided strong protection for those whose goods are taken, damaged or otherwise interfered with. Over the centuries the courts have refined and developed the law to cover a huge range of situations. Many of the difficulties with this area of law stem directly from this long history. The Law Reform Committee did produce some recommendations for reform[90] which were given limited effect by the Torts (Interference with Goods) Act 1977. This introduced the term "wrongful interference with goods" to cover tortious damage to goods or interests in goods[91] and a number of procedural reforms.[92] It also "abol-

[86] [1968] 2 Q.B. 299 at 313F-G; see also *per* Diplock L.J. at 317 and *per* Salmon L.J. at 320.
[87] See, *e.g.*, Winfield & Jolowicz, at p. 347.
[88] [1980] 1 W.L.R. 582 at 588.
[89] *Ibid.* at p. 588H.
[90] 18th Report, Conversion and Detinue, Cmnd. 4774 (1971).
[91] Torts (Interference with Goods) Act 1977, s.1.
[92] *Ibid.* s.3.

ished" the tort of detinue.[93] Nevertheless, many of the old complexities remain and "interference with goods" is therefore treated under two heads, trespass and conversion.

Trespass is a wrong to possession of goods while conversion is a wrong to rights over them. Atkin L.J. put the difference like this:

> "An act of conversion differs from a mere trespass inasmuch as the former must amount to a deprivation of possession to such an extent as to be inconsistent with the right of the owner and evidence of an intention to deprive him of that right, whereas the latter includes every direct forcible injury or act disturbing the possession of the owner, however slight the act may be."[94]

There are, therefore, two important differences between the torts;

(1) in trespass to goods, as in other forms of trespass, the defendant's act must be **direct**, in conversion it can be indirect;

(2) any interference with possession is a trespass, to be conversion the defendants acts must be serious enough to constitute some kind of attack on the plaintiff's **rights** to the goods.

Ownership and possession

It is important to be clear about the "rights" over goods that the law protects from "wrongful interference." Two basic concepts are relevant: ownership and possession.

The owner of goods can be broadly defined as the person in whom the "absolute legal title" to those goods is vested. It is extremely difficult to provide a full theoretical clarification of this definition.[95] In practice, however, the analysis of ownership is unlikely to cause problems in police cases. A person who has acquired the goods from the person with absolute legal title by sale or gift will become their owner.

The concept of "possession" is also very complex. Three "types" of possession must be distinguished:

(1) Custody. This is the simple physical control over an object (sometimes called *de facto* possession) and does not, of itself, give legal rights over the goods. Thus, the fact that a dinner guest has physical control over his host's knife and fork does not give him any legal rights over them. For a person to have custody of goods it is not necessary for him to have them directly under his control—it is enough for him to have indirect control, through another person, or through control of the place where the goods are kept. Thus, he can have custody of the goods in his house or car even if he is away from home or has parked his car.

(2) Legal possession. This is the crucial concept for the purposes of wrongful interference with goods. A person will have legal possession of goods if he has custody of them plus the intention to exercise sole and

[93] Torts (Interference with Goods) Act, s.2.
[94] *Sanderson* v. *Marsden and Jones* (1922) 10 Ll.L.R. 467 at 472.
[95] See Goode, *Commercial Law* at pp. 52–54.

exclusive dominion over them (an *animus possidendi*) against the whole world.

(3) The right to possession. A person with an interest in goods—whether as owner, or a limited interest such as that of a hirer or a person holding the goods as a pledge—will have a "right to possession" of them. Nevertheless he may not actually have them in his custody. This can happen, for example, when the period of hire of a car comes to an end and the car is not returned. In this case, the person with the interest has a "right to possession" of the goods and may sue for wrongful interference with them.

Where possession is doubtful—because, for example, the goods are kept in a house occupied by several different people—possession follows title.[96]

For various historical and practical reasons, the common law did not take the route of protecting the rights of owners. What the law protected were rights of possession.[97]

The basic rule in both trespass[98] and, more controversially, conversion[99] is that the person who must sue for a wrongful interference with goods is the person with either legal possession or "the right to possession" at the time of the interference. In other words, there is no need for a plaintiff to show ownership of the goods; a "possessory title" will be sufficient. Thus, whoever has control over goods and the intention of asserting sole and exclusive control over them is entitled to protect those goods against interference from the whole world, except the true owner.[1]

When there is a bailment of goods the question of who has legal possession and therefore the right to sue depends on whether the bailee has an interest in the goods. A bailee who has an interest, for example a person who hires a car, is in legal possession of the goods although he is, of course, not their owner. A bailee who does not have an interest, for an example a person who has borrowed a car from a friend, has joint legal possession with the owner. In the first case only the hirer can bring an action for wrongful interference with the car. In the second case, both the owner and the bailee can bring actions. This has led to problems of "double recovery" which have now been dealt with by statute.[2]

One immediate result of the law protecting of possession rather than ownership concerns the position of the thief. It appears that a thief who has control over goods and an *animus possendi* has a "possessory title" to the goods and can sue anyone who wrongfully interferes with them unless he is their owner, or is acting with their owner's authority. There is no reported case in which a thief has successfully sued in trespass or conversion but there are dicta to the effect that a thief will be able to sue someone who wrongfully removes the goods from his possession.[3] The general view is that the thief does acquire a possessory title over the goods but that the

[96] See *French* v. *Gething* [1972] 1 K.B. 236.

[97] See Pollock and Wright, *Possession in the Common Law*; for general accounts see Goode, *Commercial Law*, Chap. 2; and Crossiey Vaines, *Personal Property*.

[98] See below at p. 190.

[99] See below at p. 194.

[1] Special problems arise, however, if he is a thief: see below at p. 189 and p. 199.

[2] See below at p. 193.

[3] See *per* Blackburn J., *Buckley* v. *Gross* (1863) 3 B. & S. 566 at 574.

courts will not assist him in enforcing his rights:[4] in other words, if the police can show that goods seized by them were stolen then they can rely on the defence of *ex turpi causa* in an action for wrongful interference.

Possession in police cases

When goods are seized by the police difficult problems arise as to the effect of such a seizure on the "possessory title" of the person from whom they are seized.

If the police seizure was unlawful then the person from whom goods were seized can rely on his possessory title to bring an action for wrongful interference.[5] He does not need to prove that he is the owner of the goods. The fact that the police suspect that the goods are stolen will not, of itself, provide them with a defence to such an action. In order to rely on the defence of *ex turpi causa* the burden is on the police to prove, on the balance of probabilities, that the goods were stolen or were otherwise the fruits of wrongdoing.

The position is more complex if the goods are **lawfully** seized from the person in possession. In the unreported county court case of *Benson* v. *MPC*[6] it was decided that the fact that the police had taken lawful possession of the chattels deprived the plaintiff of his possessory title and he could not found an action upon it,

> "the police officers obtained lawful possession of the chattels which are the subject matter of this action and that . . . [they] are entitled to retain possession unless and until the Plaintiff can establish a better claim."[7]

Thus, it was suggested that lawful seizure of goods by the police destroys a possessory title and, in order to bring an action for wrongful interference with those goods the plaintiff must establish ownership.[8]

This case was, however, decided without reference to the important Australian case of *Field* v. *Sullivan*[9] in which these matters were analysed in some detail. Macfarlan J. pointed out that when a person is lawfully deprived of possession of goods his right to possession (that is, his possessory title) may be destroyed entirely, as in the case of sale, or it may be merely suspended, as in the case of bailment.[10] He applies this distinction to seizure by the police as follows;

> "A's property and right to possession are made subject to the right of the police or other person seizing under the authority of the law to

[4] See Goode, *Commercial Law*, at p. 53, n. 16; and *Benson* v. *MPC*, Westminster County Court, Unreported. Case No. 83 35143, H.H. Judge McDonnell. The authors would like to thank His Honour for providing them with a copy of his judgment; see also below at p. 199.

[5] See *Field* v. *Sullivan* [1923] V.L.R. 70 at 84, SC of Victoria.

[6] Westminster County Court (1983), Unreported. Case No. 8335143.

[7] Judgment at p. 7.

[8] This is the same as the position under the Police (Property) Act 1897; see *Raymond Lyons* v. *MPC* [1975] Q.B. 321 and Chap. 12 below at p. 390.

[9] [1923] V.L.R. 70; SC of Victoria.

[10] *Ibid.* at 84.

> detain them during the period during which the detention is authorised; when that time expires,[11] and no lawful order has been made for their disposition,[12] his right to possession, if nothing more appears, again operates. I say "if nothing more appears," for it may appear by evidence that A never had a right of possession . . . and that therefore there was no suspended right of possession to revive or again operate."[13]

Thus, if the police can show that the person from whom the goods were seized had, in fact, no right to possession of the goods, then his possessory title will not revive. In the absence of such evidence, once the police right to retain the goods has lapsed, the former possessor can rely on his original possessory title to sue for wrongful interference. He does not need to prove ownership and, the dicta to the contrary in *Benson's* case[14] should not be followed.

The definition of goods

It will usually be a simple matter to decide whether what has been interfered with are "goods" for legal purposes. In section 14(1) of the Torts (Interference with Goods) Act 1977 "goods" are defined as including all chattels personal other than things in action or money. It is clear that an action in trespass or conversion will not lie if there is an interference with a thing in action such as a debt. The position of money is more difficult. At common law, a particular "sum of money" could only be recovered by suing for a debt or for money had and received. But specific coins or banknotes could be recovered in action for trespass or conversion.[15] The general view is that section 14(1) has not affected the common law position.[16] In *Malone* v. *MPC*[17] it was assumed by both sides that an action for the delivery up of specific banknotes could be made under the 1977 Act.

The only other difficulty which is likely to arise relates to the position of items on land which may, in law, be "fixtures" and therefore "real property" as opposed to chattels.[18]

4. TRESPASS TO GOODS

Introduction

Trespass to goods can be defined as any wrongful act of direct physical interference with goods which are in the possession of another. It is gener-

[11] See Chap. 7 below at p. 217, for the periods of time for which the police are entitled to hold goods.
[12] *e.g.*, under the Police (Property) Act 1897, see Chap. 12 below at p. 390.
[13] *Ibid.* at 85.
[14] Westminster County Court (1983), Unreported. Case No. 8335143.
[15] *Burn* v. *Morris* (1834) 2 Cr. & M. 579.
[16] See Clerk & Lindsell, paras. 21–36; Feldman at 15.44.
[17] [1980] Q.B. 49.
[18] See above at p. 176.

ally assumed that many of the same rules which apply to other forms of trespass are equally applicable to trespass to goods.

Thus, following the general rule for trespass, trespass to goods is actionable *per se*. There is old authority to the effect that touching animals is not actionable *per se*.[19] Nevertheless, it is difficult to see how there could be said to have been special damage in several of the reported cases.[19a] *Kirk* v. *Gregory*[20] is direct authority for the view that trespass to goods is indeed actionable *per se*.[21] There are also good policy arguments in favour of this view—in relation to situations where large numbers of people might touch a chattel, each touch causing no damage but the cumulative effect, over a period, being very serious.[22]

The defendant's acts

A trespass to goods must, like other forms of trespass, be **direct**. Thus if poison is fed to the plaintiff's dog there is a trespass, while if poison is left in such a position that the plaintiff's dog will eat it there is not.[23] Locking someone's goods in a room will not be trespass[24] but moving them to a room and then locking them in will be.[25]

It would seem that any direct physical contact will be sufficient. The well-known dictum of Alderson B. is often quoted here—"stratching the panel of a carriage would be a trespass"[26]—but it appears that it is not necessary to actually to damage someone else's goods to commit a trespass. As Lord Diplock has put it "the act of handling a man's goods without his permission is prima facie tortious."[27] It is well established that moving another's goods will be a trespass.[28] Picking up and putting down will be sufficient for, "in trespass . . . a party is liable if he takes the thing only for an instant."[29] A mere touch is sufficient to found an action in trespass.[30] Damages have been awarded in a wide range of situations. These include:

19 *Slater* v. *Swann* (1731) 2 Stra. 872.

19a See below.

20 (1876) 1 Ex.D. 55.

21 See also, the argument of counsel set out by Lord Blanesburgh in *Leitch & Co.* v. *Leydon* [1931] A.C. 90 at 106.

22 *e.g.*, paintings in art galleries; see Street at p. 53.

23 See, *e.g. Hutchins* v. *Maughan* [1947] V.L.R. 131—mixing poison with a racehorse's feed.

24 *Hartley* v. *Moxham* (1842) 3 Q.B. 701.

25 *Kirk* v. *Gregory* (1876) 1 ExD. 55.

26 *Fouldes* v. *Willoughby* (1841) 8 M. & W. 540 at 549.

27 *IRC* v. *Rossminster* [1980] A.C. 952 at 1011.

28 "a simple asportation of a chattel, without any intention of making further use of it" may well be sufficient for an action in trespass *Fouldes* v. *Willoughby* (1841) 8 M. & W. 540, *per* Lord Abinger C.B. at 544–5; see also *Kirk* v. *Gregory* (1876) 1 ExD. 55; and *Penfold Wines* v. *Elliott* (1946) 74 C.L.R. 204 at 214–215.

29 *per* Best C.J., *Price* v. *Helyar* (1828) 4 Bing. 597.

30 See *Hesperides Hotels* v. *Sermet, The Times*, March 15, 1982.

removing car tyres,[31] taking down an election poster,[32] erasing a tape recording,[33] and even showing a private letter to an unauthorised person.[34]

The defendant's state of mind

It is not clear what the mental state of the trespasser must be for his direct interference with the plaintiff's goods to be a trespass. There is no doubt that there is a trespass if the interference is "intentional." At the other end of the spectrum there is undoubtedly a defence of "inevitable accident."[35] It seems that "inevitable" in this context means merely "not negligent."[36] There are dicta in the New Zealand case of *Everitt* v. *Martin*[37] to the effect that a purely accidental contact is not actionable. This does not appear to be the English law and it is certainly not the case in Australia or Canada.[38]

It is submitted that a negligent trespass is still a "trespass."[39] There is some doubt as to whether the burden of proving negligence lies with the plaintiff or with the defendant. According to *Fowler* v. *Lanning*[40] it lies with the plaintiff but the Australian High Court has taken the opposite view.[41] The rules appear to be the same as in trespass to the person.[42]

Who can sue?

As the wrong is to **legal possession** not ownership the plaitiff must be in possession of the goods at the time of the interference, and ownership is irrelevant,[43] "mere possession in the plaintiff is enough against a wrong-doer."[44] Any person who can prove actual possession or the immediate right to possession can bring an action.[45]

When the action is founded on "mere possession" such possession should be "clear and unequivocal."[46] There is no possession until the plaintiff has

[31] *GWK* v. *Dunlop* (1926) 42 T.L.R. 376.
[32] *Yelloly* v. *Morley* (1910) 27 T.L.R. 20—damages of £1 were awarded.
[33] *Flegan* v. *Hayward*, Thame County Court, see the news report in *The Times*, October 1, 1966; £200 damages; 1986 value: £1,274.
[34] *Thurston* v. *Charles* (1905) 21 T.L.R. 659—£400 damages.
[35] See *NCB* v. *Evans* [1951] 2 K.B. 861.
[36] See *per* Diplock J., *Fowler* v. *Lanning* [1959] 1 Q.B. 426 at 433.
[37] [1953] N.Z.L.R. 298.
[38] See *Williams* v. *Milotin* (1957) 97 C.L.R. 465; *Bell Canada* v. *Beaumont* (1974) 35 D.L.R. (3d) 367.
[39] Despite the dicta of Lord Denning M.R. to the contrary in *Letang* v. *Cooper* [1965] 1 Q.B. 232; s.11(1) of the Torts (Interference with Goods) Act 1977 says that contributory negligence is no defence to proceedings founded on "intentional trespass to goods."
[40] [1959] 1 Q.B. 426.
[41] *McHale* v. *Watson* (1964) 111 C.L.R. 384.
[42] See Chap. 4 below at p. 107.
[43] *Ward* v. *Macaulay* (1791) 4 T.R. 489 at 490.
[44] *Carter* v. *Johnson* (1839) 2 Mood & R. 263 at 265, *per* Lord Abinger C.B.; see also *Field* v. *Sullivan* [1923] V.L.R. 70; *Bird* v. *Fort Frances* [1949] 2 D.L.R. 791.
[45] *Wilbraham* v. *Snow* (1669) 2 Wms Saunders 47a.
[46] *Peachey* v. *Wing* (1826) 5 L.J.(OS)K.B. 55.

"actual power" over the thing he claims to possess.[47] It remains unclear whether a thief can maintain an action for trespass to goods.[48]

Possession can be either actual or constructive,[49] in other words, on a bailment of goods which does not exclude the right to immediate possession the bailor can sue for trespass to goods.[50] If the owner gives a third party "gratuitous permission" to use his chattel "he may maintain trespass for any injury done to it while it is so used"[51] because he retains legal possession.

When the bailment does exclude the right to immediate possession by the owner (as, for example, in a contract of hire purchase of a car) the bailor cannot sue in trespass. The proper plaintiff is the bailee as the person in legal possession. It has been said that an owner with the right to immediate possession can bring an action[52] but probably only if there is a wrong to the possession of the actual legal possessor.[53]

Justifications for trespass to goods

Trespass is defined as **wrongful** direct physical interference with another's goods. Not all direct physical interferences will be wrongful.

The fact that the plaintiff had given the defendant permission to interfere with the goods in question will plainly be a defence[54] as will the fact that the interference took place in the exercise of a legal right. As we have said, a police officer will have a good defence if he can show that he touched or removed the goods under a statutory or common law power.

Other defences present more difficulty. It will probably be a good defence to an action for trespass to goods to show that the interference was reasonably necessary for the preservation of the goods[55] or the prevention of serious crime.[56] In the case of unintentional trespass, contributory negligence will be a defence.[57] It is possibly a defence for the defendant to show that the interference was caused by the plaintiff's own wrongful act.[58]

It has been suggested that there will only be a trespass if the plaintiff's possession is **lawful**.[59] There is no direct authority on the point and it is

[47] *Young* v. *Hitchens* (1844) 6 Q.B. 606 at 611.

[48] See Clerk & Lindsell, para. 21–60; see above at p. 189.

[49] *Topham* v. *Dent* (1830) 6 Bing 515 at 516.

[50] And so can the bailee *Nicolls* v. *Bastard* (1835) 2 Cr.M. & R. 659; *The Winkfield* [1902] P. 42—but the relief given shall be such as to avoid double liablity of the wrongdoer; see the 1977 Act, s.7(2).

[51] *Loton* v. *Cross* (1810) 2 Camp. 464 at 465, *per* Lord Ellenborough.

[52] *Johnson* v. *Diprose* [1893] 1 Q.B. 512 at 515.

[53] See *per* Dixon J., *Penfold Wines* v. *Elliott* (1946) 74 C.L.R. 204.

[54] The position is similar to that relating to land, see above at p. 181.

[55] *per* Bramwell B., *Kirk* v. *Gregory* (1876) 1 ExD. 55 at 58; see also *Cope* v. *Sharpe (No. 2)* [1912] 1 K.B. 496.

[56] *Handcock* v. *Baker* (1800) 2 Bos. & P. 260—prevention of a felony.

[57] See s.11(1) of the Tort (Interference with Goods) Act 1977.

[58] According to *Knapp* v. *Salsbury* (1810) 2 Camp. 500 the plaintiff's own negligence will be a defence.

[59] See *Halsbury's Laws of England* Vol. 45, para. 1491; the authority cited is *Davis* v. *Nest* (1833) 6 C. & P. 167 which does not provide direct support for the proposition in the text.

unclear whether a thief has sufficient possession to support an action in conversion.[60] It is submitted that the lawfulness of possession makes no difference to an action in trespass subject to a possible defence of *ex turpi causa*.[61]

In common with other forms of trespass it is no defence for a defendant to show that he had a reasonable, though mistaken, belief that he was the true owner of the goods[62] or that he had a right to remove them. On the other hand, "inevitable accident" will be a defence.

5. CONVERSION

Introduction

Conversion is a wrong to the plaintiff's rights over goods. It covers a wide range of interferences and the difficulties of giving it a comprehensive definition are notorious[63]—that great common lawyer Bramwell L.J. going so far as to say that he "never did understand with precision what was a conversion."[64] Nevertheless, the basic outlines of the tort are fairly clear.

The Common Law Procedure Act 1852, in laying down forms of pleading, provided a kind of statutory definition of conversion as follows: "That the defendant converted to his own use, or wrongfully deprived the plaintiff of the use and possession of the plaintiff's goods."[65] The essence of someone "converting goods to his own use" is a denial of the plaintiff's rights to those goods or the assertion of some other rights which are inconsistent with them. The Law Reform Committee adopted Salmond's definition in the following terms:

> "A conversion is an act (or complex series of acts) of wilful interference without lawful justification, with any chattel in a manner inconsistent with the right of another, whereby that other is deprived of the use and possession of it. Two elements are combined in such interference: (1) a dealing with the chattel in a manner inconsistent with the right of the person entitled to it, and (2) an intention in so doing to deny that person's right or to assert a right which is in fact inconsistent with such right. But where the act done is necessarily a denial of the other's right or an assertion of a right inconsistent with it, the tort may have been committed. For conversion may consist in an act deliberately done

[60] See Clerk & Lindsell, para. 21–60 and *Buckley* v. *Gross* (1863) 3 B. & S. 566 at 574, *per* Blackburn J.; see the discussion of this point in relation to conversion below at p. 193.

[61] See below at p. 200.

[62] *Wilson* v. *Lombank* [1963] 1 W.L.R. 1294; *Colwill* v. *Reeves* (1811) 2 Camp. 575.

[63] See *e.g.*, *Sanderson* v. *Marsden & Jones* (1922) 10 Lloyd's Rep. 467, *per* Bankes L.J. at 470, Atkin L.J. at 472; and most recently *Howard Perry & Co.* v. *British Railways* [1980] 1 W.L.R. 1375 at 1380B, *per* Megarry V.-C., endorsing the statement of Clerk and Lindsell that "It is perhaps impossible to frame a definition which will cover every conceivable case."

[64] *Hiort* v. *London & NW Ry.* (1879) 4 ExD. 188 at 194.

[65] See *Howard Perry & Co.* v. *British Railways* [1980] 1 W.L.R. 1375 at 1380 E-F.

inconsistent with another's right, though the doer may not know or intend to challenge the property or possession of that other."[66]

There are three central questions arising out of this basic notion of conversion:

(1) what rights does the plaintiff have to have over the goods in question?
(2) to what extent does the defendant have to **intend** to deny the plaintiff's rights?
(3) what kinds of acts will constitute a denial of those rights?

It should also be noted that, although conversion is an action on the case it does seem to be actionable without proof of special damage.[67] Thus, it appears that if the plaintiff can show that his goods were converted but the goods are not damaged and he cannot show any loss or damage resulting from the conversion he is still entitled to succeed in conversion, although he will only be entitled to nominal—and perhaps aggravated and exemplary[68]—damages.

Who can sue in conversion?

It is a common mistake to assume that conversion is a wrong to title to goods and that only an owner can sue in conversion. Indeed, there are a number of authorities which appear to support this view.[69] But the common law has never been directly concerned with ownership in this area. All that really matters is possession.[70] As Slade J. said:

> "the general rule is that the title which must be established . . . (in an action in conversion) consists of proof not so much of absolute ownership, as proof that he had at the time of detention or conversion, either actual possession of the goods or the immediate right to possession of them."[71]

It follows that anyone who is in possession of goods, with the intention of exercising dominion over them, can bring an action in conversion—whether or not he is the lawful "owner" of the goods. The position of the thief is more complex.[72] The defendant who is sued by someone who is not

[66] 18th Report of Law Reform Committee, Cmnd. 4774 (1971), para. 38, quoted from *Salmond on Torts*, at p. 125.
[67] *Hiort* v. *London NW Ry.* (1879) 4 ExD. 188.
[68] See Chap. 11 below at pp. 343 *et seq.*
[69] See, *e.g.*, *Crocker* v. *Molyneux* (1828) 3 C. & P. 470; *Halsbury's Laws* takes this view, see Vol. 45, para. 1433.
[70] The position may have been different in detinue: see *Singh* v. *Ali* [1960] A.C. 167 at 176.
[71] *Winkworth* v. *Christie, Manson and Woods Ltd.* [1980] Ch. 496 at 499; see also *per* Ackner L.J. in *The Playa Larga and Marble Islands* [1983] 2 Lloyd's Rep. 171 at 187; and the 18th Report of the Law Reform Committee Cmnd. 4774 (1971), para. 9.
[72] See above at p. 189.

the owner of the goods can now set up the rights of the true owner as a defence.[73] He may also be able to set up a defence of *ex turpi causa.*[74] The action can, of course, also be brought by the person with the right to immediate possession.

The defendant's state of mind

Conversion involves a denial of the plaintiff's right to goods. In many cases, the intention of the defendant in interfering with those goods will be of crucial importance in determining whether that interference is a conversion. This is particularly so in cases involving the police because officers will usually not be claiming goods as their own but purportedly retaining them for police purposes. The intentions of the officers will often be central to the question of whether an action for conversion will lie.

In *Lancashire and Yorkshire Railway Company* v. *MacNicoll*[75] it was argued that there was no conversion without *mens rea*. Atkin L.J. dealt with the point in a well known passage as follows:

> "It appears to me plain that dealing with goods in a manner inconsistent with the right of the true owner amounts to a conversion, providing it is also established that there is an intention on the part of the defendant in so doing to deny the owner's right or to assert a right which is inconsistent with the owner's right. But that intention is conclusively proved if the defendant has taken the goods as his own or used the goods as his own."[76]

In other words, the defendant's dealing with the plaintiff's goods must show an intention to convert them but this intention can often be inferred from the fact that the defendant did a deliberate act "the effect of which would be to deprive the owner of . . . dominion over a particular chattel."[77] In other cases there is no need to establish any intention as it is clear that the act itself deprives the plaintiff of possession and ownership of his goods. The obvious example of this is when the goods are destroyed.[78]

There is, however, another sense in which the defendant's acts must be intentional. The particular acts of the defendant which are said to constitute conversion must be "intentional." There is no such thing as "negligent conversion" at common law.[79] This is, of course, subject to the principle that a man is presumed to intend the natural and probable consequences of his actions.[80]

[73] See the Torts (Interference with Goods) Act 1977, s.8 and below at p. 199.

[74] See below at p. 200.

[75] (1918) 118 L.T. 596.

[76] *Ibid.* at 598.

[77] *per* Bankes L.J., *Sanderson* v. *Marsden & Jones* (1922) 10 Lloyd's Rep. 467 at 470.

[78] *per* Bankes L.J., *ibid.*; see also Salmond's definition of conversion above at p. 194.

[79] See *e.g. Ashby* v. *Tolhurst* [1937] 2 K.B. 242. There was, however, negligent detinue, when a bailee, in breach of his duty, allowed goods to be lost or destroyed. This is now a form of conversion by reason of s.2(2) of the 1977 Act.

[80] See, *e.g. Moorgate Mercantile* v. *Finch & Read* [1962] 1 Q.B. 701.

The nature of the defendant's acts

What constitutes a sufficient "assertion of rights" over goods will depend on the kind of dealing the plaintiff's goods which the defendant has engaged in. The simplest approach is to consider a number of common "situations of dealing" in which the police are likely to be involved.

(1) Conversion by taking. Anyone who takes goods from the possession of another is, of course, prima facie guilty of a trespass. But, on its own, a taking will not be a conversion.[81] There must be an intention on the part of the taker to assert a right over the goods.[82] There need not be an intention to claim ownership of the goods, it is enough that the taker does something which is inconsistent with the rights of dominion of the owner. The usual way in which this is proved is if the goods are taken for the use of the defendant or a third party.[83] Simply moving a chattel without any intention to convert is not conversion[84] but if it is moved to an unreasonable place and is consequently lost an action does lie.[85] This form of conversion has limited application in police cases.

(2) Conversion by keeping. This is the mode of conversion which is likely to be most relevant in relation to civil actions against the police. There must be "some definite or deliberate act or witholding as being a necessary preliminary to this cause of action"[86] which is adverse to the rights of the plaintiff. This is usually proved by the defendant refusing to return the goods after the plaintiff or some person in his name and with his authority[87] has demanded their return.[88] The demand must be unconditional[89] and specific.[90] The refusal must also be unconditional[91] and the person who refuses must have had it in his power to deliver up the article demanded.[92] The refusal is only **evidence** of conversion,[93] it is necessary to consider whether the refusal is justifiable. It is not necessary to establish a demand and a refusal if it can be shown that the detention itself is wrongful.[94]

81 *per* Lord Abinger C.B., *Fouldes* v. *Willoughby* (1841) 8 M. & W. 540 at 547.
82 *Lancashire and Yorkshire Railway Company* v. *MacNicoll* (1918) 118 L.T. 596 at 598.
83 See *Fouldes* v. *Willoughby* (1841) 8 M. & W. 540 at 547.
84 *Ibid.* at 547.
85 *Forsdick* v. *Collins* (1816) 1 Stark 173.
86 *per* Fletcher Moulton L.J., *Clayton* v. *Le Roy* [1911] 2 K.B. 1031 at 1048.
87 *Gunton* v. *Nurse* (1821) 2 Brod. & Bing. 447.
88 This was the essence of the action in detinue, the whole of which is now covered by conversion.
89 *Rushworth* v. *Taylor* (1842) 3 Q.B. 699—a demand that the goods be returned in their original state was insufficient.
90 *Abington* v. *Lipscomb* (1841) 1 Q.B. 776.
91 *Alexander* v. *Southey* (1821) 5 B. & Ald. 247.
92 *Smith* v. *Young* (1808) 1 Camp. 439 at 440.
93 See, *e.g.*, *Clark* v. *Chamberlain* (1836) 2 M. & W. 78 at 84—despite powerful dicta to the contrary by Holt C.J. in *Baldwin* v. *Cole* (1704) 6 Mod.Rep. 212.
94 *London Jewellers* v. *Sutton* (1934) 50 T.L.R. 193 at 194; *Clayton* v. *Le Roy* [1911] 2 K.B. 1031 does not establish the contrary.

If the defendant, while not denying the plaintiff's right to the goods, seeks to detain them for an indefinite period this will be a conversion, for a

> "denial of possession to the plaintiffs does not cease to be a denial by being accompanied by a statement that the plaintiffs are entitled to the possession that is being denied to them."[95]

Thus, British Railways refusing to release steel to its owners because they were afraid of industrial action by rail workers in support of the steel strike was a conversion.[96] This will be one of the most important forms of conversion in police cases. If, having seized goods in the course of their investigations, the police refuse to return them despite having no lawful justification for their retention[97] an action in conversion will lie.

(3) Conversion by destruction. If the defendant destroys the identity of the plaintiff's chattel then he will be guilty of conversion.[98] But damage to a chattel, by itself, is not conversion.[99] The negligent destruction of goods was not conversion at common law but it is now conversion by section 2(2) of the 1977 Act if done by a bailee. The police will, therefore, be liable in conversion if, as bailees they negligently destroy goods belonging to the plaintiff without lawful justification.

(4) Conversion by using. If the defendant has used the plaintiff's goods as his own then there will be a conversion. In the words of Holt C.J., "The wearing of a pearl is a conversion."[1] It is a conversion to take someone's car for a joy-ride.[2]

(5) Conversion by wrongful delivery. It is a conversion to deliver another's goods to a third party with the intention of transferring title or some other right in the goods. This form of conversion is committed by someone who has lawfully come into possession of the goods but then attempts to transfer property in them to someone other than the lawful owner. For example, in the important police case of *Winter* v. *Bancks*[3] the plaintiff's gig was stolen and subsequently recovered by the police from one Broderick. The prosecution of Broderick for theft failed, whereupon the police officer who had taken possession of the gig, acting on the instructions of his superior, refused to return it to the plaintiff but, instead, gave it to Broderick. The plaintiff successfully sued the officer in question for coversion of the gig. It was also held that it was no defence that the defendant police officer was acting on the orders of his superiors.

(6) Conversion by other acts. There are a whole range of other acts which may constitute a conversion. It is unlikely that forms of conversion such as misdelivery by a carrier or wrongful sale in a market overt without delivery

[95] *Howard Perry & Co.* v. *British Railways Board* [1980] 1 W.L.R. 1375 at 1380E.
[96] *Ibid.*
[97] See Chap. 7 below at p. 217.
[98] *Heald* v. *Carey* (1852) 11 C.B. 977.
[99] *Simmons* v. *Lillystone* (1853) 8 Ex. 431.
[1] *Petre* v. *Heneage* (1701) 12 Mod. 519 at 520; see also *Mulgrave* v. *Ogden* (1590) Cro.Eliz. 219.
[2] *Aitken Agencies* v. *Richardson* [1967] N.Z.L.R. 65.
[3] (1901) 17 T.L.R. 446.

will have much application to civil actions against the police. The basic principle—that the defendant must do something which amounts to a denial of the plaintiff's rights over the goods—runs through all these forms.[4]

Defences

As in the case of trespass to goods it is a defence to an action for conversion that the defendant acted with the leave and licence of the plaintiff[5] or that he has dealt with them under a power conferred by law.[6] If goods are taken by a thief and then come into the hands of the police they cannot be sued in conversion if they are holding the goods for the purpose of a prosecution, the goods are in *custodia legis*.[7] Ignorance of the plaintiff's interest in the goods is, however, in general no defence.[8]

Difficult problems arise when the "legal possessor" of goods is not the owner and has therefore no "right to possession." Under the Tort (Interference with Goods) Act 1977 it is now a defence to show that a third party has a better right than the plaintiff as respects all or any part of the interest claimed by the plaintiff.[9] This must be done in accordance with the Rules of Court which require the plaintiff to give particulars of his title and to identify any person who, to his knowledge, has or claims any interest in the goods.[10] The defendant can then apply for directions as to whether any person should be joined with a view to establishing whether he has a better right to the goods than the plaintiff or has a claim as a result of which the defendant might be doubly liable.[11] The court has jurisdiction to join a person who, at the time of the application has no right to the goods, with a view to determining whether, at the time of the alleged tort, he had a better right to the goods than the plaintiff.[11a]

It is unclear whether the title of an unknown person can be set up as a defence under the 1977 Act. In *Benson* v. *MPC*[12] Judge McDonnell, *obiter*, expressed the view that "it is highly arguable that a Defendant may now defeat a Plaintiff's claim by showing a superior title in a person unknown."

If the goods are **unlawfully** taken from him, the "legal possessor" will have a right of action against the "taker" even though he cannot show any "right to possession."[13] It is submitted that this is also the position when goods are lawfully taken for a limited purpose which has been achieved (for

[4] See Clerk & Lindsell.

[5] *Unwin* v. *St. Quintin* (1843) 11 M. & W. 277.

[6] See Chap. 7.

[7] *Tyler & Witt* v. *London & SW Ry.* (1884) Cab. & El. 285.

[8] See *Marfani & Co.* v. *Midland Bank Ltd.* [1968] 1 W.L.R. 956 at 970–971.

[9] s.8(1).

[10] R.S.C., Ord. 15, r. 10A(1).

[11] R.S.C., Ord. 15, r. 10A(2).

[11a] See *de Franco* v. *Commissioner of Police for the Metropolis. The Times*, May 8, 1987.

[12] Westminster County Court (1983), Unreported. Case No. 83 35143 at p. 7 of the judgment.

[13] See *Bird* v. *Fort Frances* [1949] 2 D.L.R. 791; High Court of Ontario.

example, use of the goods in evidence) unless the "taker" can show that the original possession was unlawful.[14]

It appears that the police are entitled to rely on the maxim *ex turpi causa non oritur actio* as a defence to an action for conversion. This maxim has been explained as follows:

> "All that the Rule means is that the courts will not enforce a right which would otherwise be enforceable if the right arises out of an act committed by the person asserting the right . . . which is regarded by the court as sufficiently antisocial to justify the courts refusing to enforce that right."[15]

It is well established that the maxim will have no application when good title to the property claimed by the plaintiff has actually passed to him despite the illegality. Thus, in the case of *Gordon* v. *MPC*[16] the police were unable to rely on the maxim to prevent a plaintiff from recovering seized money which represented the proceeds of illegal betting.[17]

It is submitted that this maxim will provide the police with a defence to a claim for conversion (or trespass) if they can show that the goods in question were stolen goods, or bought with the proceeds of stolen goods.[18] Thus in *Solomon* v. *MPC*[19] a claim for conversion by the police of a car which had been bought with the proceeds of theft was dismissed because it was contrary to public policy to permit the plaintiff to use the courts to recover property which was deemed, by statute, to be stolen.[20] In the New Zealand case of *Gill* v. *A.-G.*[21] an action for the conversion of banknotes which were admitted to be the proceeds of sale of illegal drugs was dismissed on the basis of the rule of public policy that: "a man is not to be allowed to have recourse to a court of justice to claim a benefit from his crime."

6. LIMITATION

Trespass to land

No action can be brought for the recovery of land after the expiration of 12 years from the date on which the cause of action first accrued.[22] Thus, although there is a new trespass every moment that the unjustifiable intrusion onto the plaintiff's land continues[23] the limitation period is calculated from the first moment of a particular defendant's trespass. This limi-

[14] See *Field* v. *Sullivan* [1923] V.L.R. 70; and see above at p. 189.
[15] *per* Diplock L.J., *Hardy* v. *Motor Insurers Bureau* [1964] 2 Q.B. 745.
[16] [1910] 2 K.B. 1080.
[17] See also, *Major* v. *A.-G. of British Columbia* [1982] 4 W.W.R. 359.
[18] Such goods being "stolen goods" by reason of the provisions of s.24(2) of the Theft Act 1968.
[19] [1982] Crim.L.R. 606.
[20] See also, *Benson* v. *MPC* (1983) Westminster County Court, unregistered, judgment, pp. 8–9.
[21] [1982] N.Z. Recent Law 71.
[22] Limitation Act 1980, s.15.
[23] *Holmes* v. *Wilson* (1839) 10 A. & E. 503.

tation period will apply to actions for damage to fixtures as well as to actions for entry onto land by the defendant.

Interference with goods

The general rule is that an action "founded on tort" may not be brought after the expiration of six years from the date on which the cause of action accrued.[24] If any fact relevant to the plaintiff's right of action is deliberately concealed by the defendant, his agent or any person through whom he claims then time does not begin to run until the plaintiff has discovered the concealment or could, with reasonable diligence have discovered it.[25]

The basic "tort limitation period" of six years will apply to an action for trespass to goods. As this is a tort which is actionable *per se* the cause of action will accrue, and hence time will begin to run, from the moment there is a direct physical interference with the plaintiff's goods, regardless of when he suffers damage.

The basic "tort limitation period" of six years also applies to action in conversion. As conversion is probably actionable *per se*[26] time, again, runs from the date of the conversion. However, where a cause of action in conversion accrues to a particular person and, before he recovers possession of the chattel, a further conversion takes place, no action can be brought in respect of the further conversion after six years from the accrual of the cause of action in respect of the original conversion.[27] If, six years after the original conversion, possession of the goods has not been recovered, the title of the original possessor is extinguished.[28]

If the conversion in question amounts to theft then the rights of the person from whom they are stolen is not subject to the time limits in the Limitation Act.[29]

7. ACTIONS AGAINST THE POLICE IN RELATION TO LAND AND GOODS

The causes of action discussed in this chapter may be available in a wide range of situations of police activity. This section provides an overview of common situations in which the different actions may be used. It should be read in conjunction with the discussion of "Remedies in Relation of Goods" in Chapter 12.

(1) Trespass to land. Many police trespasses to land will be limited in extent and of a "technical nature." Nevertheless, the "integrity of the home" is seen as a fundamental interest deserving of strict protection and substantial damages can be recovered even for "technical" trespasses, particularly if

[24] Limitation Act 1980, s.2.
[25] Limitation Act 1980, s.32(1).
[26] See above at p. 195.
[27] Limitation Act 1980, s.3(1).
[28] *Ibid.* s.3(2).
[29] *Ibid.* s.4.

the police have acted in an oppressive manner, or have caused substantial upset or anxiety to the occupier.

An action for trespass to land would be appropriate in the following situations:

(1) where police officers have entered a house or garden without permission or a warrant or any other "lawful justification." Any entry, however slight, will be sufficient—for example, a foot in the door or perhaps even leaning against a door or a wall;
(2) where police officers refuse to leave premises after they have been given permission to enter and that permission has been expressly withdrawn;
(3) where fixtures—for example doors or windows are damaged in the course of a police search—if the search is a lawful one the police will only be liable if unreasonable force was used;
(4) where the police, having purported to enter premises for one purpose have in fact entered for another.

(2) Wrongful interference with goods. When a person's goods are interfered with the appropriate cause of action will be either trespass to goods or conversion.[30]

Trespass to goods will be the appropriate cause of action in the following situations:

(1) where goods are unlawfully removed from the plaintiff's possession by the police;
(2) where goods are damaged by the direct and deliberate actions of police officers, for example, during a police search;
(3) where the plaintiff's goods are unlawfully moved around, or possibly just touched, by police officers.

Damages can be recovered for loss of use and possibly for the cost of hiring an alternative. In some circumstances aggravated or exemplary damages may be awarded.[31]

Conversion will be appropriate in situations such as the following.

(1) where the plaintiff is wrongly prevented from gaining access to his goods, the goods not having been touched;
(2) where the police lose or damage goods which are in their possession lawfully (having been seized under warrant, for example);
(3) where the police refuse to return goods which are lawfully in their possession when they are no longer needed for the purpose for which they were seized (for example, goods seized as evidence in relation to a line of inquiry which is subsequently abandoned);
(4) where the police deliver goods owned by the plaintiff to a third party with the intention that the third party should take the goods as owner;
(5) where the police, having come into the possession of goods lawfully (for example, after they are handed in as found) use them as their own.

[30] "Replevin" is best regarded as an additional "remedy" rather than a separate cause of action; see Chap. 12 below at p. 387.

[31] See Chap. 11 below at pp. 343 *et seq.*

7. Lawful Justifications for Entry, Search and Seizure

1. INTRODUCTION

It is an important part of police work to enter and search premises and to collect evidence, seize stolen goods and so on. If the police do this without the consent of the occupier or the person in possession of the goods[1] such activity is prima facie unlawful and an action in tort will lie. As Lord Diplock put it in the *Rossminster* case:

> "entering a man's house, searching it and seizing his goods against his will are tortious acts against which he is entitled to the protection of the court unless the acts can be justified either at common law or under some statutory authority."[2]

This chapter deals with the common law and statutory authorities which allow the police to enter premises and seize goods.

Whether or not a particular police activity gives rise to an action in tort depends on a close examination of the facts of the situation and the power on which they are seeking to rely as "justifying" their activities. Police powers can be divided into three types: "common law," "without warrant" and "with warrant" powers. Powers of the first two types depend on the existence of particular preconditions of fact and belief, while "with warrant" powers depend on the existence of a formally valid legal authorisation or warrant.[3] Powers of all three types have now been partially codified by the Police and Criminal Evidence Act 1984.

The most important police powers over land and goods are likely to be those which enable them to enter premises in the first place without a warrant. Police powers of entry and search without warrant are, therefore, considered first. Once they have entered premises the police may then seek to seize goods which they find there and police powers of seizure without warrant are dealt with next. A person whose goods have been seized will want to have them back, or at least to have access to them, as soon as possible. The various common law and statutory rights in this area are then examined

[1] Or some other general defence: see Chap. 6 above at p. 199.
[2] *IRC* v. *Rossminster* [1980] A.C. 952 at 1008.
[3] See generally, Chap. 1 above at p. 27.

Police powers under warrants are considered in the next three sections of the chapter. These deal with the general procedure for the issue and execution of warrants, the circumstances in which warrants are available and the procedure for challenging warrants. The final section of the chapter examines police powers over motor vehicles.

2. ENTRY AND SEARCH WITHOUT WARRANT

Introduction

The 1984 Act abolishes "all the rules of common law under which a constable has power to enter premises without a warrant"[4] with one exception[5] and provides for entry and search by "a constable" in seven different situations. It does not affect the other 23 statutory provisions under which constables can enter and search without a warrant.

The police have no general power to enter or remain on premises simply for the purposes of making inquiries or questioning suspects.[6] If, therefore, they cannot rely on one of these powers or some other general "justification" for a "without warrant" entry then such entry will be illegal and an action in trespass will lie.[7]

Entry and search at common law

The only common law power of entry and search which is preserved by the 1984 Act is "any power of entry to deal with or prevent a breach of the peace."[8] A breach of the peace takes place when an act is done or threatened "which either actually harms a person, or in his presence, his property, or is likely to cause such harm, or which puts someone in fear of such harm being done."[9] There is little doubt that the police have power to enter premises to deal with breaches of the peace which are actually in progress.[10] It seems that even if police officers are trespassers they are entitled to remain on premises to deal with a breach of the peace.[11]

The power to deal with "apprehended" breaches is more controversial. According to the case of *Thomas* v. *Sawkins*[12] if a constable "has reasonable grounds to apprehend a breach of the peace" taking place on private premises then he has lawful authority to enter or remain on the premises to stop

[4] s.17(5).
[5] s.17(6), see below.
[6] See, *e.g.*, *Great Central Railway* v. *Bates* [1921] 3 K.B. 578 at 581–582, *per* Atkin L.J. quoted in Chap. 6 above at p. 181.
[7] See above at p. 203 and Leigh, pp. 207 *et seq.*
[8] s.17(6).
[9] *per* Lawton L.J., *R.* v. *Howell* [1982] Q.B. 416 at 426G; see also *R.* v. *Chief Constable of Devon and Cornwall, ex p. CEGB* [1982] Q.B. 458.
[10] *R.* v. *Walker* (1854) Dears C.C. 358.
[11] *Robson* v. *Hallett* [1967] 1 Q.B. 939 at 954C.
[12] [1935] 2 K.B. 249.

or prevent that breach of the peace. This case has been strongly criticised as representing an unwarranted extension of police powers and a "constitutional innovation."[13] Its precise ratio is unclear and Feldman suggests that it should be confined to its own facts, namely power to enter a public meeting to prevent reasonably apprehended breaches of the peace.[14]

If the police are in fresh pursuit of someone who is suspected of a breach of the peace which has occurred elsewhere they may enter premises in pursuit. However, once the pursuit ends and if there is no likelihood of the breach of the peace recurring then there is no power to enter.[15]

Entry and search under 1984 Act: preliminary matters

The 1984 Act provides for seven separate powers to enter and search "premises." These powers are conferred on "constables." Provision is also made for the use of "reasonable force" in the exercise of these powers. These three preliminary matters will be considered in turn.

(1) Premises. A partial definition of premises is provided by section 23 as follows:

> "In this Act—
> 'premises' includes any place and, in particular, includes—
> (a) any vehicle, vessel, aircraft or hovercraft;
> (b) any offshore installation; and
> (c) any tent or movable structure."

"Place" is not defined but it must include any land or building. It follows that the powers of entry and search without warrant provided for by the 1984 Act permit the police to search vehicles as well as houses.

(2) Constables. The Act contains no definition of a constable, but the term clearly covers all police officers, of whatever rank, who have been "attested" constable before the proper authority.[16] If an officer is not in uniform when exercising these powers then the Code of Practice requires that he should show his warrant card[17] but this is not a statutory requirement and all these powers can be lawfully exercised by an officer in plain clothes who has not proved that he is a constable.

(3) Reasonable force. Under section 117 of the Act where any power is conferred on a constable by the Act he may use "reasonable force, if necessary, in the exercise of the power." Thus, a police constable is entitled to use such force in the exercise of any power of entry and search conferred by the Act.

"Force" means the application of energy to an obstacle with a view to removing it. This means that pushing open a door which is ajar is using

[13] A. L. Goodhart (1936) 6 C.L.J. 22.
[14] Feldman at 12–26.
[15] *R.* v. *Marsden* (1868) L.R. 1 C.C.R. 131.
[16] See Hargreaves and Levenson at pp. 6–8; Chap. 1 above at p. 22.
[17] Para. 5.5.

force.[18] If a constable applies more force than is necessary then he is liable in tort. The burden is on him to establish that the force really was necessary.[19] Thus, if in the course of a lawful entry and search the police break down doors or damage furniture, they will prima facie be liable in tort for the damage caused unless they can establish

(1) that it was necessary to use **some** force; and
(2) that the amount of force actually used was, in the circumstances "reasonable."

It is submitted that in ordinary circumstances it is unlikely to be reasonable to use force to break into premises without first requesting entry from the occupier. The Code of Practice provides that the officer in charge of a search shall first ask for consent unless he knows the premises to be unoccupied or the persons entitled to grant access are known to be absent or there are reasonable grounds for believing that alerting the occupier would frustrate the object of the search or endanger people.[20]

Entry and search under 1984 Act: the powers

The powers of entry and search without warrant provided for by the 1984 Act are all related to powers of arrest. There are five powers allowing "entry and search" to make an arrest and two which allow the search of premises for evidence after an arrest has been made. None of these powers allow the police to enter and search as part of general investigations before any arrest is contemplated. If the police wish to conduct such a search they must obtain the consent of the occupier, a search warrant or use some other statutory power of entry and search without warrant.

The first five entry and search powers are provided for by section 17 of the 1984 Act and share the "safeguard" provisions of section 17(2)–(4).

(1) To execute an arrest warrant. Under section 17(1)(*a*) a constable may enter and search any premises for the purpose

"of executing—
(i) a warrant of arrest issued in connection with or arising out of criminal proceedings; or
(ii) a warrant of commitment issued under section 76 of the Magistrates' Courts Act 1980."

Arrest warrants are considered in detail in Chapter 5. A warrant of commitment under section 76 of the Magistrates' Courts Act is issued for failure to pay a sum adjudged to be paid on conviction or by an order of the court.

(2) To arrest for an arrestable offence. By section 17(1)(*b*) a constable may enter and search premises for the purpose "of arresting a person for an arrestable offence." Arrestable offences are defined by section 24 and are

[18] See *Swales* v. *Cox* [1981] Q.B. 849; a case on force in relation to the old common law powers of entry.
[19] *Ibid.* at 855.
[20] Para. 5.4.

those for which a constable may arrest someone without warrant.[21] The person that the constable is seeking does not actually have to be on the premises. It will be sufficient if there are "reasonable grounds for believing" that he is there[22] Thus, the entry will be lawful even if no arrest, in fact, results. On the other hand, an entry for some other purpose will not be rendered lawful by a subsequent arrest for an arrestable offence.

It seems that an entry will only be lawful under this head if the arrestable offence for which the person has been sought has actually been committed. So, although a constable can lawfully arrest someone when no arrestable offence has actually been committed—provided he has reasonable grounds for suspecting that it has been committed[23]—he cannot lawfully search premises for the person he reasonably suspects of committing it unless the offence has actually been committed.

(3) To arrest for certain specified offences. By section 17(1)(*c*) a constable may enter and search any premises for the purpose of arresting a person for the following offences:

(a) under section 1 of the Public Order Act 1936—prohibition of uniforms in connection with political objects;

(b) under section 4 of the Public Order Act 1986—fear or prevention of violence;

(c) under sections 6 to 8 or 10 of the Criminal Law Act 1977—offences relating to entering and remaining on property. This power can only be exercised by a constable in uniform.[24]

(4) To recapture a person who is unlawfully at large. By section 17(1)(*d*) a constable may enter and search premises for the purpose of "recapturing a person who is unlawfully at large and whom he is pursuing."[25] A person is unlawfully at large if he has escaped from lawful arrest, prison, or detention centre.[26] The constable must actually be pursuing the person if he is to enter under this provision, so that it does not allow entry when he simply suspects that the person is on the premises if he is not actually in pursuit at the time.

(5) To save life, limb or property. By section 17(1)(*e*) a constable may enter and search premises for the purposes of "saving life or limb or preventing serious damage to property."[27]

Section 17 lays down various restrictions on the exercise of these five powers of entry and search:

(a) Powers 1 to 4 are only exercisable "if the constable has reasonable

[21] See Chap. 5 above at p. 139.
[22] s.17(2)(*a*); see Chap. 5 above at p. 145.
[23] s.24(6); see Chap. 5 above at p. 140.
[24] s.17(3).
[25] The police had a similar power at common law: see *Hart* v. *Chief Constable of Kent* [1983] R.T.R. 484.
[26] See Prison Act 1952, s.49(2) as amended.
[27] This is broader than the common law power in *Handcock* v. *Baker* (1800) 2 Bos. & P. 260 which was restricted to entry when there were reasonable grounds for suspecting that an unlawful killing was taking place.

grounds for believing that the person whom he is seeking is on the premises."[28] The test here is the objective one of "reasonable grounds for belief."[29] It follows that an honest belief by the constable is not, of itself, enough to make his entry lawful. To establish the defence of "lawful justification" here the police must show not only that the entry and search was for one of the above purposes but that what was known to the constable carrying out the entry and search, immediately before exercising the power, was sufficient to provide reasonable grounds for suspecting that the person being sought was on the premises entered. If the constable was, for example, carrying out a random check or acting on gossip or a "hunch," he will be liable in trespass, whether the person was there or not;

(b) When premises consist of two or more separate dwellings, such as a block of flats, powers 1 to 4 can only authorise entry into the common parts[30] and any dwelling in which the constable has "reasonable grounds for believing that the person whom he is seeking may be."[31]

(c) Powers 1 to 5 only permit the police "to search to the extent that it is reasonably required for the purpose for which the power of entry is exercised."[32] More generally, as the entry and search under section 17 is "for the purpose" of doing the various things set out it follows that once that purpose has been achieved (because, for example, the person named in the warrant has been arrested) the premises cannot be further searched under this section. For similar reasons it would seem that a search for goods cannot be carried out under this section (unless it is for the purpose of preventing serious damage to them or saving life or limb, under power 5).

The 1984 Act provides for two other important powers of entry and search without warrant:

(6) To search for evidence the premises of a person under arrest. Under section 18 of the Act:

> "a constable may enter and search any premises occupied or controlled by a person who is under arrest for an arrestable offence, if he has reasonable grounds for suspecting that there is on the premises evidence, other than items subject to legal privilege, that relates—
>
> (a) to that offence; or
>
> (b) to some other arrestable offence which is connected with or similar to that offence."[33]

The power depends, therefore, on the existence of five conditions: (i) the premises must be occupied or controlled by a person—it would not be sufficient, for example, that he simply had property stored there; (ii) who has

[28] s.17(2)(*a*).

[29] See the discussion in Chap. 5 above at p. 145.

[30] s.17(2)(*b*)(i).

[31] s.17(2)(*b*)(ii).

[32] s.17(4).

[33] s.18(1).

been arrested—it is submitted that the arrest must have been lawful[34]; (iii) for an arrestable offence[35]; (iv) the constable has reasonable grounds for suspecting[36] that there is evidence on the premises; (v) that relates either to the offence for which the person has been arrested or to a similar or connected offence.

This power to search is subject to a number of qualifications set out in the section:

(a) The power to search is only "to the extent that is reasonably required for the purpose of discovering such evidence"[37]:

(b) The power may only be exercised if authorised by an officer of the rank of inspector or above in writing.[38] Such an authorisation must be an independent document and a written record of an oral authorisation will not be sufficient.[39] The police officers going to search the premises should take such authority with them.[40] However, a search may be conducted before taking the person to a police station and without such authorisation

> "if the presence of that person [that is, the person arrested] at a place other than a police station is necessary for the effective investigation of the offence."[41]

It is submitted that this sub-section only covers the situation where the arresting officer cannot take the person arrested to the police station immediately. It does not appear to cover the situation in which a constable wishes to conduct an immediate search because of the danger that evidence will be destroyed. In such a situation the presence of the **person arrested** at a place other than a police station is not **necessary**—he could simply be taken there by another officer. If a search takes place under this latter provision the constable must "inform an officer of the rank of inspector or above that he has made the search as soon as practical after he has made it"[42];

(c) The officer who authorises the search or is informed of it must "make a record in writing" of the grounds for the search and the nature of the evidence that was sought[43];

(d) "If the person in occupation or control of the premises at the time of search is in police detention at the time the record is to be made, the officer shall make the record as part of his custody record."[44]

It is submitted that a search will be unlawful if it goes beyond what is reasonably required for the purpose of discovering evidence of the relevant offences. It will also be unlawful if requirement (b) is not complied with.

[34] See *Spicer* v. *Holt* [1977] A.C. 987 at 1005; see Chap. 5 above at pp. 132 *et seq*. for the conditions for a lawful arrest.

[35] See Chap. 5 above at p. 139.

[36] See Chap. 5 above at p. 145.

[37] s.18(3).

[38] s.18(4).

[39] See the Crown Court decision of *R.* v. *Badham* [1987] L.A.G. Bulletin, 12.

[40] *Ibid.*

[41] s.18(5).

[42] s.18(6).

[43] s.18(7).

[44] s.18(8): for "custody record" see Chap. 5 above at p. 160.

However, it is submitted that a failure to make the relevant records in accordance with (c) and (d) will not make an otherwise lawful search unlawful.

(7) To search premises where a person was when arrested. When a person is arrested at a place other than a police station a constable has power:

> "to enter and search any premises in which he was when arrested or immediately before he was arrested for evidence relating to the offence for which he has been arrested."[45]

This power covers both arrestable and non-arrestable offences. There is no need for the premises to be "occupied or controlled" by the person arrested. This section deals with "search on arrest" and does not allow the police to search premises after the person arrested has been taken to the police station.[46]

The power conferred by this section is limited in a number of ways:

(a) It is submitted that the person must have been **lawfully** arrested[47];
(b) He must actually have been on the premises;
(c) It is only a power "to search to the extent that is reasonably required" to discover such evidence[48];
(d) If the premises consists of two or more separate dwellings the power is limited to the dwelling in which the arrest took place or the person was immediately before his arrest and the common parts[49];
(e) The search can only relate to the offence for which the person was arrested, not for similar or connected offences.

It is submitted that a breach of any of these requirements will make a search unlawful.

It should be noted that there is no "without warrant" power to search premises occupied by third parties for evidence relating to a person under arrest if these conditions do not apply.[50]

Entry and search under other statutes

The police have a number of other statutory powers of entry without warrant. These include the important power under section 5 of the Road Traffic Act 1972 (as amended by the Transport Act 1981, section 25) to enter premises to arrest a person reasonably suspected to have been driving under the influence of drink or drugs. Other statutory provisions relate to matters such as the production and supply of controlled drugs,[51] licensed premises

[45] s.32(2)(*b*).
[46] See the Crown Court decision of *R.* v. *Badham* [1987] Crim.L.R. 202.
[47] See *Spicer* v. *Holt* [1977] A.C. 987 at 1005.
[48] s.32(3).
[49] s.32(7).
[50] See *McLorie* v. *Oxford* [1982] 1 Q.B. 1290.
[51] Misuse of Drugs Act 1971, s.23(1).

with special hours certificates,[52] premises where fire is reasonably believed to have broken out,[53] theatres,[54] cinemas,[55] betting offices and race tracks.[56] There are, in total, 23 police powers of entry without warrant contained in public general legislation.[57]

Entry and search without warrant: a summary

The police can only enter premises in the limited situations allowed for by statute. As Donaldson L.J. put it:

> " 'An Englishman's home is his castle' is one of the few principles of law known to every citizen . . . The rule is, of course, subject to exceptions, but they are few and it is for the police to justify a forcible entry."[58]

Apart from statutory provisions limited to specific situations the police can only enter and search premises in four situations:

(1) where a breach of the peace is taking place (or perhaps "reasonably apprehended") there[59];
(2) to save life, limb or property[60];
(3) where they are seeking to arrest someone in specified situations[61];
(4) to search for evidence after arrest.[62]

In the first three situations the only search that will be allowed is, in effect, a search for a person: whether it be the person breaching the peace, threatening life, limb or property or being sought for arrest. A search under these powers will, therefore, be unlawful if:

(1) the police are searching for property;
(2) the police do not, at the moment of entry, have reasonable grounds for believing that the person sought is there or there is no breach of the peace or threat to life, limb or property.

Any search for property under these powers will be a trespass by police officers, a wrongful interference with goods and will possibly make them trespassers *ab initio*. If the entry is not justified the police will be trespassers.

In the fourth situation the police can search the premises of a person arrested for evidence of the offence for which he was arrested or evidence of any "connected or similar" offence. They can also search the premises where he was arrested or where he was immediately before arrest for

[52] Licensing Act 1964, s.186 as substituted by the Licensing (Amendment) Act 1977, s.1.
[53] Fire Services Act 1947, s.30(1).
[54] Theatres Act 1968, s.15(3).
[55] Cinematograph (Amendment) Act 1982, s.5(1).
[56] Betting, Gaming and Lotteries Act 1963, ss.10(4) and 23.
[57] For a full list see Hargreaves and Levenson, Appendix V (*c*), pp. 413–414.
[58] *McLorie* v. *Oxford* [1982] 1 Q.B. 1290.
[59] See above at p. 204.
[60] See above at p. 207.
[61] See above at p. 208.
[62] See above at pp. 206 *et seq.* and 210.

evidence relating to the offence for which he was arrested. A search under these powers will be unlawful if:

(1) no lawful arrest has taken place;
(2) the suspect did not occupy or control the premises or was not there at the time of or immediately before his arrest;
(3) a search of premises occupied or controlled by the suspect is conducted for evidence in relation to unrelated offences committed by the suspect;
(4) premises where a suspect was arrested are searched for evidence of another offence committed by the suspect;
(5) a search is conducted for evidence of offences committed by third parties.

An action will lie for wrongful interference with goods and such a search may mean that the police officers are trespassers *ab initio*.

Although **searches** cannot be lawfully conducted outside the situations outlined police officers may seize evidence of other offences when they are lawfully on premises under either their common law[63] or statutory[64] powers.

3. SEIZURE WITHOUT WARRANT

Police powers of seizure at common law

The starting point of any consideration of police powers of seizure without warrant at common law is now the judgment of Lord Denning M.R. in *Ghani* v. *Jones*.[65] This judgment represented a substantial extension of the pre-existing law but must now be accepted as correct.[66] Lord Denning M.R. sets out the applicable principles which, for present purposes, can be summarised as follows[67]:

(1) the police must have reasonable grounds for believing that a "serious offence" has been committed;
(2) the police must have reasonable grounds for believing that the article to be seized is the "fruit," "instrument" or "material evidence" of the crime;
(3) the police must have reasonable grounds for believing that the person in possession has himself committed the crime or is implicated in it, or is an accessory to it "or at any rate his refusal (to hand over the property) must be quite unreasonable."

The lawfulness of the police conduct must be judged at the time of the seizure, not by subsequent events.[68]

The common law, therefore, only allows the seizure of a narrow range of

[63] See below.
[64] See below at p. 212.
[65] [1970] 1 Q.B. 693.
[66] See the full discussion in Feldman, Chap. 10.
[67] *Ghani* v. *Jones* [1970] 1 Q.B. 693 at 708–709.
[68] *Ibid.* at 709.

items from people who are reasonably suspected of committing or being implicated in "serious crime."[69] It seems that the police may seize goods which they reasonably suspect to have been stolen from someone they reasonably suspect to have stolen or dishonestly handled them.[70] It is important to note that the common law does not permit seizure from unimplicated third parties unless their refusal to hand over the property is "quite unreasonable."[71]

These common law powers of seizure have now been superseded, but not abolished, by the provisions of the Police and Criminal Evidence Act 1984.

Police powers of seizure under statute

The police have powers to enter premises and seize property under a number of statutes.[72] General police powers of seizure of goods have been partially codified by the 1984 Act. By section 23 every power of seizure conferred by an enactment passed before or after the 1984 Act shall be construed as including a power to require any information contained in a computer and accessible from the premises to be produced in a form in which it can be taken away and in which it is visible and legible. The 1984 Act itself provides for seven separate powers of seizure without warrant.

The first three powers are conferred by section 19 and are only exercisable "by a constable who is lawfully on any premises." The lawfulness of a constable's presence will depend on the general law of trespass and the availability of any defences based on powers of entry, whether with or without warrant. These provisions do not authorise the seizure of an item "which the constable exercising the power has reasonable grounds for believing to be subject to legal privilege."[73]

(1) Items obtained in consequence of crime which may be disposed of. Under section 19(2) a constable may seize anything which is on the premises if he has reasonable grounds for believing—

> "(a) that it has been obtained in consequence of the commission of an offence; and
> (b) that it is necessary to seize it in order to prevent it being concealed, lost, damaged, altered or destroyed."

Whether or not the item in question has been obtained "in consequence" of an offence must be a matter of fact depending on the nature of the offence and the nature of the item. It is submitted that if a constable has a mistaken belief about the meaning of "in consequence" the seizure will be unlawful even if the belief is reasonable.

(2) Evidence of crime which may be disposed of. Under section 19(3) a constable may seize anything which is on the premises if he has reasonable grounds for believing—

[69] This category was not given clear definition: see Feldman at 10.13.
[70] *Lodwick* v. *Sanders* [1985] 1 W.L.R. 382.
[71] *Wershof* v. *MPC* [1978] 3 All E.R. 540; and Feldman at 10.18.
[72] See Hargreaves and Levenson, Appendix V.
[73] s.19(6); for a discussion of "legal privilege" see below at p. 227.

"(a) that it is evidence in relation to an offence which he is investigating or any other offence; and
(b) that it is necessary to seize it in order to prevent the evidence being concealed, lost, altered or destroyed."

(3) Information on computer which may be disposed of. There is also a broad provision giving the police powers similar to (1) and (2) in relation to computers. Under section 19(4) a constable may require information on computer to be produced in a visible and legible form which can be taken away if he has reasonable grounds for believing—

"(a) that—
(i) it is evidence in relation to an offence which he is investigating or any other offence; or
(ii) it has been obtained in commission of an offence; and
(b) that it is necessary to do so in order to prevent it being concealed, lost, tampered with or destroyed."

Section 19 makes considerable alterations in the common law position. First, it allows seizure when there is reasonable suspicion of the commission of **any offence.** Secondly, the range of items liable to seizure is wider than that permitted by the common law—covering information on computer and anything "obtained in consequence" of an offence rather than just its "fruits." Thirdly, the section allows seizure from unimplicated third parties on the same basis as from those reasonably suspected of crimes. Fourthly, restrictions are placed on the common law position by only allowing seizure if this is "necessary" to avoid disposal of the items in question. Finally, the section 19 powers can only be exercised if the constable is "lawfully" on the premises.

The 1984 Act also confers a number of other powers of seizure.

(4) Evidence found on premises of person under arrest. When premises occupied or controlled by a person under arrest for an arrestable offence are searched for evidence by a constable under section 18(1)[74] he may "seize and retain anything for which he may search."[75] This power includes a power to require any information contained in a computer and accessible from the premises to be produced in a form in which it can be taken away and in which it is visible and legible.[76] It should be noted that, under this power, there is no need for the constable to believe that the evidence may be disposed of.

(5) Evidence found on stop and search. Under section 1 a constable has wide powers to search people and vehicles if "he has reasonable grounds for suspecting that he will find stolen or prohibited articles."[77] "Prohibited articles" are defined by section 1(7) as offensive weapons or made or adapted for use in the course of or in connection with various Theft Act offences.[78] By section 1(6):

[74] See above at p. 208.
[75] s.18(2).
[76] s.20.
[77] s.1(3).
[78] See Chap. 5 above at p. 130.

"If in the course of such a search a constable discovers an article which he has reasonable grounds for suspecting to be a stolen or prohibited article he may seize it."

(6) Evidence found after arrest. Under section 32(2)(*a*) a constable may search a person arrested at a place other than a police station for anything which he might use to assist him to escape from lawful custody or which might be evidence relating to an offence.[79] When a constable finds anything when searching a person under this power it may be seized and retained (other than an item subject to legal privilege)[80] if the constable

"has reasonable grounds for believing—
(a) that he (i.e. the person searched) might use it to assist him to escape from lawful custody; or
(b) that it is evidence of an offence or has been obtained in consequence of the commission of an offence."

(7) Property a person has with him at a police station. When a person is either arrested at a police station or brought to a police station after arrest the custody officer at the police station[81] "may seize and retain" any thing that the person has with him.[82] The custody officer may only seize clothes and personal effects if he

"(a) believes that the person from whom they are seized may use them—
(i) to cause physical injury to himself or another person;
(ii) to damage property;
(iii) to interfere with evidence; or
(iv) to assist him to escape; or
(b) has reasonable grounds for believing that they may be evidence relating to an offence."[83]

The person from whom the property is seized must be told the reason for the seizure unless he is violent, likely to become violent, or is incapable of understanding what is said to him.[84] The person may be searched if the custody officer considers it necessary to carry out his duty to ascertain and record everything that the person has with him.[85] Similar seizure provisions apply to property found on intimate body search.[86]

The relationship between common law and statutory powers of seizure

The Police and Criminal Evidence Act 1984 does not abolish the common law powers. The police will, therefore, be able to rely on common law

[79] See Chap. 5 above at p. 136.
[80] See below at p. 227.
[81] See Chap. 5 above at p. 158.
[82] s.54(1) and (3); and see Chap. 5 above at p. 170.
[83] s.54(4).
[84] s.54(5).
[85] s.54(6); see Chap. 5 above at p. 158.
[86] s.55(12); for intimate body searches see Chap. 5 above at p. 170.

powers as a defence to an action for trespass for goods when they are trespassers. They cannot rely on section 19 because this only applies when the police are "lawfully" on premises. Nevertheless, such seizures will be lawful at common law provided that the *Ghani* v. *Jones* principles are complied with.[87]

General restrictions on seizure

Any seizure of goods which is done without consent or warrant and which does not fall under one of these powers will be a trespass to goods. Problems often arise when the police seize large quantities of goods. This area was considered by the Court of Appeal in *Reynolds* v. *MPC*.[88] Although the case was directly concerned with police powers of seizure under a search warrant the discussion is of general application to all seizures. It is clear that, whether acting with or without warrant, the police are not entitled to seize property indiscriminately. As Waller L.J. put it:

> "Searching and taking away papers is an invasion of liberty and any such action must be carefully scrutinised . . . If there are only a few papers, no doubt they can be carefully scrutinised on the spot without too much disturbance to the household. If there are many papers, it may be in the best interests of the householder for the police to be broadly selective, ie. rule out documents which are clearly irrelevant, and take others which they reasonably believe to be of evidential value to examine more closely at the police station . . . In my judgment the question in every such case must be whether the police were acting reasonably or not."[89]

But it is clear that a constable who is seizing goods must have regard to the nature and contents of **each item** that he is considering seizing and decide whether or not there are reasonable grounds for believing that it is an item which falls under his powers to seize.[90] In *Reynolds'* case the trial judge directed the jury that they should consider the reasonableness of the search **as a whole.** This was held to be a misdirection. It was necessary to consider reasonableness in relation to every item seized. As Slade L.J. said:

> "The jury should be asked whether in regard to each file, book, bundle or separate documents, the officer in question, at the time of removal, had reasonable cause to believe that it was seizable."[91]

Nevertheless, where large quantities of documents are concerned, the police do not have to consider the "seizability" of every single page. Provided that he acts reasonably a constable is entitled to seize "files, books, bundles or documents which at the time of removal he reasonably believes" contain material which could be seized under one of his powers.[92] When files and bundles of papers are seized the items falling under the powers

[87] See above at p. 212.
[88] [1985] Q.B. 881.
[89] *Ibid.* at 889A–C.
[90] *per* Slade L.J. at 895.
[91] *Ibid.* at 897A.
[92] *Ibid. per* Slade L.J. at 896D.

should be sorted out with "reasonable expedition" and the "non-seizable" items should be returned "reasonably promptly" to the owner.[93]

If the police do not give proper consideration to each item seized then they will be liable for trespass to goods. Damages of £50 were awarded in *Reynolds'* case for the seizure of several sacks of papers without any proper sorting of the "seizable" from the "non-seizable."

4. RETENTION, ACCESS AND COPYING

Introduction

Although goods have been lawfully seized, the police will be guilty of wrongful interference with goods if they cannot justify their continuing retention. The owners of the goods also have common law and statutory rights of access to the goods and to copies of documents. The violation of these rights may also give rise to possible civil actions.

Retention of seized items

When the police seize an item under their common law seizure powers they:

> "must not keep (it) . . . nor prevent its removal for any longer than is reasonably necessary to complete their investigations or preserve it for evidence. If a copy will suffice it should be made and the original returned. As soon as the case is over, or it is decided not to go on with it, the article should be returned."[94]

The main reason, at common law, for retaining property is for use in court proceedings.[95] Police constables have an overriding duty to retain property which may be used as evidence[96] although this "desirable standard" cannot always be applied.[97] The property must be returned when charges are dropped or the proceedings have been disposed of. Further retention will be tortious[98] It appears that the police are entitled to retain property if it is likely to be a "reasonably necessary" part of the evidence.[99]

The common law position is supplemented (but not superseded) by the provisions of section 22 of the Police and Criminal Evidence Act 1984. Under that section, any material seized may be retained for "so long as is necessary in all the circumstances."[1]

[93] *Reynolds* v. *MPC* [1985] Q.B. 881, *per* Slade L.J. at 896E.
[94] *per* Lord Denning M.R., *Ghani* v. *Jones* [1970] 1 Q.B. 693 at 708.
[95] See generally, Feldman at 11.07–11.33.
[96] See *R.* v. *Lushington, ex p. Otto* [1894] 1 Q.B. 420 at 423–424.
[97] *R.* v. *Uxbridge JJ. ex p. Sofaer, The Times*, December 4, 1986.
[98] See *Elias* v. *Pasmore* [1934] 2 K.B. 164.
[99] *Malone* v. *MPC* [1980] Q.B. 49 at 60A, *per* Stephenson L.J. and 70C *per* Roskill L.J.; see Feldman at 11.12–11.14.
[1] s.22(1).

The length of time involved is, of course, a question of fact in each case. But without prejudice to the generality of this provision section 22 lays down a number of more specific rules regarding the retention of property:

(1) Anything seized for the purposes of criminal investigations may be retained for use as evidence at a trial for an offence or for forensic examination or investigation in connection with an offence[2];

(2) "anything may be retained in order to establish its lawful owner, where there are reasonable grounds for believing[3] that it has been obtained in consequence of the commission of an offence"[4];

(3) nothing seized on the ground that it may be used to cause physical injury to any person, to damage property, to interfere with evidence or to assist in escape from police detention or lawful custody may be retained:

> "when the person from whom it was seized is no longer in police detention or the custody of a court or is in the custody of a court but has been released on bail"[5];

(4) nothing may be retained for use as evidence at a trial or for investigation in connection with an offence "if a photograph or copy would be sufficient for that purpose."[6] It should be noted that whether or not a copy is sufficient for that purpose is purely an objective test and does not depend on the belief, reasonable or otherwise, of police officers.

It is also expressly provided that nothing in section 22 affects the power of any court to make an order under the Police (Property) Act 1897.[7]

Access and copying

The common law position regarding the supply of copies of seized documents was considered by the Court of Appeal in the case of *Arias* v. *MPC*[8] Certain commercial documents had been seized by the police. The owners admitted that the seizure was lawful but applied for an order for the delivery up of the goods or, alternatively, copies.[9] The police resisted the application on the ground that if copies were supplied there was a real danger that the investigation might be hampered and an opportunity provided to fabricate evidence.[10] The Court rejected the argument that "the mere statement by a responsible officer that he had reasonable grounds for belief that premature disclosure of information was contrary to the public interest was sufficient to justify the seizure and retention of the documents." Rather, it was a question of balancing the public interest in the "arrest, prosecution and convic-

[2] s.22(2)(*a*).
[3] See Chap. 5 above at p. 145.
[4] s.22(2)(*b*).
[5] s.22(3).
[6] s.22(4).
[7] s.22(5); see Chap. 12 below at p. 390.
[8] *The Times*, August 1, 1984; (1984) 128 S.J. 784.
[9] The cause of action entitling them to copies is unclear but this point was not taken by the police.
[10] This is the same as the statutory exception in s.21(4)—see below at p. 219.

tion" of criminals against the fact that the documents belonged to the plaintiffs. The court was of the view that the latter was the important consideration and granted the plaintiff's application, rejecting the police argument that the investigation might be hampered. According to Kerr L.J.—

> "What had been said on affidavit [by the police] amounted to no more than speculation, suspicion. That could be said in almost any case where the police were in possession of documents which could be regarded as incriminating."

Only in extreme cases could the police "not reveal their full reasons for refusing to give access to documents because that would in effect "give the game away."

When the police have seized material in exercise of a power conferred by an enactment, including one passed after the 1984 Act, section 21 confers certain rights of access and copying on specified people. These rights apply to goods seized both without and with a warrant.

(1) On a request made by someone showing himself to be the occupier of the premises on which it was seized or to have had custody or control of it immediately before the seizure, the constable must provide him with a record of what has been seized within a reasonable time of the request being made.[11]

(2) If a request for permission to be granted access to something which has been seized by a constable and "is retained by the police for the purpose of investigating an offence"[12] is made to the officer in charge of the investigation by a person who had custody and control of the thing immediately before it was seized or by someone acting on his behalf then the person who made the request shall be allowed access under the supervision of a constable.[13] But there is no such right of access:

> "if the officer in charge of the investigation for the purposes of which it was seized has reasonable grounds for believing that to do so would prejudice—
>
> (a) that investigation;
> (b) the investigation of an offence other than the offence for the purposes of investigating which the thing was seized; or
> (c) any criminal proceedings which may be brought as a result of—
> (i) the investigation of which he is in charge; or
> (ii) any such investigation as is mentioned in paragraph (b) above."[14]

The case of *Arias* v. *MPC*[15] indicates that the police must have substantial reasons and not just speculation and suspicion to justify reliance on this exception. Under paragraph 5.9 of the Code of Practice a record of the grounds for refusal of access must be made.

(3) If a request is made to the officer in charge of the investigation by a

[11] s.21(1) and (2).
[12] s.21(3)(*b*).
[13] s.21(3).
[14] s.21(8).
[15] *The Times*, August 1, 1984.

person who had custody or control of the thing immediately before it was so seized or by someone acting on behalf of such a person, the officer shall

(a) "allow the person who made the request access to it under the supervision of a constable for the purpose of photographing or copying it; or
(b) photograph or copy it, or cause it to be photographed or copied."[16]

When a constable photographs or copies a document under (b) the photograph or copy shall be supplied to the person making the request within a reasonable time.[17] The right to such a copy is limited in the same circumstances as the right to access.[18]

Retention and access: a summary

The owner of goods[19] retained by the police will have a potential action for wrongful interference in the following situations:

(1) if they are retained for longer than is "reasonably necessary" for the completion of investigations;
(2) if they are not returned when charges are dropped or proceedings disposed of;
(3) if they were seized because they might have been used to cause injury, etc., and the person from whom they were seized has been released;
(4) if a copy would have been sufficient for police purposes.

If the police lawfully retain documents but refuse to give copies then an action can be brought to compel the provision of copies.[20] In addition, section 21 casts duties on the police in relation to access and copying. If the police are in breach of these duties then a person with a right of access or a right to a copy could, it is submitted, enforce his rights by making an application for mandamus to compel the police to carry out their duty.[21] It is submitted that an action for breach of statutory duty will also lie and substantial damages would be recoverable if the failure to provide access or copies had caused loss to the plaintiff.

5. WARRANTS AND POLICE POWERS

Introduction

At common law, Justices of the Peace could issue warrants authorising constables to search for and seize stolen goods. They are also empowered by statute to issue search warrants in a wide variety of other cases. The 1984

16 s.21(4).
17 s.21(6) and (7).
18 s.21(8).
19 Whether with "absolute" or "possessory" title, see Chap. 6 above at p. 187.
20 See *Arias* v. *MPC, The Times*, August 1, 1984.
21 See Chap. 13 below at p. 417.

Act provides an additional power for Justices of the Peace to issue search warrants for evidence of "serious arrestable offences."

The 1984 Act now lays down the procedure for applying for warrants and for executing them. This is expressed to apply to the issue of warrants to constables "under any enactment, including an enactment contained in an Act passed after this Act."[22]

Pre-application procedures

There are no specific statutory procedures which must be gone through before an application for a warrant can be made. Nevertheless, a search warrant is a very considerable invasion of a citizen's rights and it must be used with considerable care. As Hirst J. put it in the case of *Bayliss* v. *Hill*[23]:

> "the institution of the search warrant procedure is a very serious matter, securing as it does a right of entry into a person's home. Consequently, it behoves the senior ranks of the police to proceed with special care before invoking the procedure and in particular to ensure that there is substantial and apparently reliable evidence to support the application for a warrant to a magistrate: equally it behoves the officers who actually execute the warrant to perform their duty with consideration and courtesy."

The Code of Practice on Search and Seizure sets out various steps to be taken before an application for a search warrant or production order is made. This covers the following areas:

(1) The checking of the information on which the application is to be made to ensure that it is accurate and recent and has not been provided maliciously or irresponsibly. In particular "An application may not be made on the basis of information from an anonymous source where corroboration has not been sought."[24]
(2) The officer should ascertain the nature and location of the articles concerned as specifically as possible.[25]
(3) The officer should make enquiries as to the occupier of the premises and should obtain any other information relevant to the application.[26]
(4) A search warrant application should be authorised by an officer of at least the rank of inspector (or in a case of urgency, the senior officer on duty), a production order application should be authorised by an officer of at least the rank of superintendent.[27]
(5) If there are reasons to believe that there will be adverse effects on

[22] s.15(1).
[23] (1984) unreported, Transcript: Association. A version of this paragraph is given in *The Times*, April 17, 1984.
[24] Para. 2.1.
[25] Para. 2.2.
[26] Para. 2.3.
[27] Para. 2.4.

community relations then, except in cases of urgency, the community liaison officer should be consulted.[28]

(6) The application should be accompanied by an information in writing stating: the enactment under which the application is made; as specifically as is reasonably practicable, the premises to be searched and the object of the search; and the ground on which the application is made.[29]

A breach of these procedures will not of itself make the search under warrant illegal but it may go to the question of whether the police officer was acting in good faith. It may also be evidence that the mandatory provisions of sections 15 and 16 were not properly complied with.

Applying for warrants

The procedure for applying for a warrant to enter and search premises is set out in section 15 of the Act. This makes it quite clear that:

> "an entry on or search of premises under a warrant is unlawful unless it complies with this section and section 16 below."

Thus any failure to comply with any of the "application" or "execution" provisions of the Act will mean that the subsequent entry and search will be a trespass. These procedural provisions relate to the invasion of common law rights and should be strictly construed.[30] Failures to follow the correct procedure are not "defects of jurisdiction in the justice" and so the Constables Protection Act does not apply and an action can be brought.

Section 15 sets out seven procedural requirements regarding applications for warrants and the form they should take:

(1) When the constable applies for the warrant it is his duty

> "(a) to state—
> (i) the ground on which he makes the application; and
> (ii) the enactment under which the warrant would be issued;
> (b) to specify the premises which it is desired to enter and search; and
> (c) to identify, so far as is practicable, the articles or persons to be sought."[31]

It should be noted that the premises **must** be specified. If it is not "practicable" to do this then the warrant cannot be lawfully issued.

(2) An application for such a warrant must be made *ex parte* and supported by an information in writing.[32] The Act does not make any specific requirements as to the contents of the information in writing but under the Code of Practice it should state: the enactment under which the application is made, as specifically as is reasonably practicable the premises to be searched and the object of the search and the ground on which the appli-

[28] Para. 2.5.
[29] Para. 2.6.
[30] See Chap. 1 above at p. 28.
[31] s.15(2).
[32] s.15(3).

cation is made (including, where the purpose of the proposed search is to find evidence of an alleged offence, an indication of how the evidence relates to the investigation).[33]

(3) The constable must answer on oath "any question that the justice of the peace or judge hearing the application asks him."[34] According to the Notes for Guidance to the Code of Practice the officer should be prepared to deal with any questions about the accuracy of previous information supplied by any informant (whose identity need not be disclosed) or other related matters.[35]

(4) The warrant can authorise "an entry on one occasion only."[36]

(5) Two copies must be made of the warrant.[37]

(6) The copies must be clearly certified as copies.[38]

(7) The warrant must contain a number of specific items of information. By section 15(6) a warrant

> "(a) shall specify—
> (i) the name of the person who applies for it;
> (ii) the date on which it is issued;
> (iii) the enactment under which it is issued; and
> (iv) the premises to be searched; and
> (b) shall identify, so far as is practicable, the articles or persons to be sought."

If the person whose premises the police are seeking to enter sees that any of these pieces of information are missing from the warrant he is entitled to refuse the police entry.[39]

In addition to these statutory requirements there are a number of possible common law requirements as to the contents of warrants[40]:

(1) It is generally accepted that a warrant will not be valid unless signed or sealed by the issuing authority[41];

(2) Although it is wise to add to the warrant a statement that the preconditions for its issue have been fulfilled this was held by a majority of the Law Lords in *IRC* v. *Rossminster*[42] not to be a requirement. However, English[43] and Commonwealth[44] authorities to the contrary were not cited and it is submitted that the matter remains unclear.[45]

(3) The House of Lords in *Rossminster* also rejected the argument that the warrant should state the offences to which it relates once again

33 Para. 2.6.
34 s.15(4).
35 Note 2A.
36 s.15(5).
37 s.15(7).
38 s.15(8).
39 *Syce* v. *Harrison* [1980] Crim. L.R. 649; see below at p. 232.
40 See, generally, Feldman, Chap. 5.
41 See Feldman at 5.06.
42 [1980] A.C. 952.
43 *Lindsay* v. *Leigh* (1848) 11 Q.B. 455 at 465.
44 See *R.* v. *Tillett, ex p. Newton* (1969) 14 F.L.R. 101.
45 Feldman argues that the dissenting speech of Lord Salmon is to be preferred on this point, Feldman at 5.12.

without the relevant authorities[46] being cited. It is submitted that the position here is also unclear.[47]

Once a police constable has obtained a formally valid warrant which complies with this section he can then proceed to execute it.

Procedural requirements for executing warrants

The requirements for the execution of all kinds of search warrants are set out in section 16 of the Act. Once again, they must all be complied with to enable the constable to rely on the warrant as a defence in an action for trespass.

Section 16 lays down seven requirements for the lawful execution of a search warrant:

(1) The warrant may be executed by **any** constable.[48] It may authorise "persons," that is non-constables, to accompany any constable who is executing it.[49] If the warrant does not provide such authorisation then such a person will be a trespasser.

(2) Entry and search under a warrant must be within one month from the date of its issue.[50]

(3) Entry and search under a warrant must be at a reasonable hour unless "it appears to the constable executing it that the purpose of a search may be frustrated on an entry at a reasonable hour."[51] It is difficult to see how, in the absence of evidence of bad faith, the police could be in breach of this requirement as the test is simply a subjective one of what "appeared" to the constable as "possibly" frustrating the purpose of the search.

(4) When the occupier of the premises to be entered and searched is present at the time when a constable seeks to execute the warrant the constable:

> "(a) shall identify himself to the occupier and, if not in uniform, shall produce to him documentary evidence that he is a constable;
> (b) shall produce the warrant to him; and
> (c) shall supply him with a copy of it."[52]

It is implicit in these provisions that a constable must have the search warrant in his possession when executing it.[53] When the occupier is not present and "some other person who appears to the constable to be in charge of the premises is present" then the same provisions apply.[54] If there is no person present who appears to the constable to be in charge of the premises then a copy of the warrant must be left in a prominent place.[55] Presumably the

[46] See, *e.g.*, *Re United Distillers Ltd.* [1947] 3 D.L.R. 900.
[47] See generally, Feldman at 5.26–5.30.
[48] s.16(1).
[49] s.16(2).
[50] s.16(3).
[51] s.16(4).
[52] s.16(5).
[53] See Feldman at 6.24–6.27; this can be contrasted with the position regarding arrest warrants, see Chap. 5 above at p. 156.
[54] s.16(6).
[55] s.16(7).

occupier or other person should be given an opportunity to examine the warrant and check its validity. If the warrant is found to be invalid then the occupier is entitled to refuse entry.[56]

(5) A search under a warrant may only be a search "to the extent required for the purpose for which the warrant was issued."[57] As the warrant must specify the enactment under which it is issued and "so far as it practicable, the articles sought" the purpose for which it was issued should usually be clear. A search for other items will be unlawful and an action for trespass to land and trespass to goods will lie in respect of such a search. It would follow that a "generalised search" for any incriminating items will be unlawful.[58]

If a warrant authorises the police to search for a specific item of stolen property, once they have found that item subsequent searches will be unlawful.[59] This is confirmed by paragraph 5.8 of the Code of Practice which states that:

> "A search under warrant may not continue under the authority of that warrant once all the things specified in it have been found."

Thus, if police officers enter other parts of the premises after finding the specific items such an entry will be a trespass and if anything else is taken away this will be trespass to goods. However, the police may be able to rely on one of their "without warrant" powers in such a situation. Thus, if they arrest the occupier they can rely on the power in section 18(1).[60] Furthermore, as they are, when executing a search warrant "lawfully on the premises," they can seize property under their section 19 powers.[61] The Code of Practice provides that:

> "Searches must be conducted with due consideration for the property and privacy of the occupier of the premises searched and with no more disturbance than necessary. Reasonable force may be used only where this is necessary because the co-operation of the occupier cannot be obtained or is insufficient for the purpose."[62]

(7) The constable who executes the warrant must make an endorsement on it stating—

> (a) "whether the articles or persons sought were found; and
> (b) whether any articles were seized, other than the articles which were sought."[63]

If the constable fails to make this endorsement, the entry and search is unlawful. It is not clear whether this unlawfulness relates back to the original entry and makes it a trespass *ab initio*.

A constable may use reasonable force, if necessary, in the execution of a warrant.[64]

[56] See below at p. 232.
[57] s.16(8).
[58] See Feldman at 7.12.
[59] *Crozier* v. *Cundey* (1827) 6 B.&C. 232.
[60] See above at p. 208.
[61] See s.3A, above.
[62] Para. 5.9.
[63] s.16(9).
[64] s.117; for a discussion of "force" see above at p. 205; see also Feldman at 6.41–6.57.

Acting "in obedience" to the warrant

Assuming that all the procedural requirements of sections 15 and 16 have been complied with a constable must still act "in obedience" to the warrant. The warrant will, of course, be "strictly construed." Thus a constable will be liable if he executes it on the wrong person[65] or the wrong premises. If the warrant give the wrong address for premises, it will not authorise a search of the correct flat.[66] It appears that if the constable is guilty of an unlawful act in the course of executing the warrant this does not render him a trespasser *ab initio*.[67]

A warrant does not authorise the police to engage in a general ransack of premises. Where the police are considering the seizure of large quantities of property under a warrant they must give separate consideration to each item seized. In particular, if large quantities of documents are seized, the police must consider the nature and content of each file, book or document seized.[68] The general principles here are the same as those for seizures without warrant.[69]

Actions against the police in warrant cases: a summary

When a search is conducted under the authority of a search warrant an action for trespass to land or goods will lie if:

(1) any of the "application" provisions of section 15 are not complied with;
(2) any of the "execution" provisions of section 16 are not complied with and in particular if a "generalised search" is conducted under a warrant authorising search for specific items;
(3) the searching officers do not have the warrant with them at the time of the search;
(4) the searching officers execute the warrant on the wrong premises.

Any unlawful act committed during the course of a search under warrant may render the officers trespassers *ab initio*.[70]

6. THE AVAILABILITY OF WARRANTS

Introduction

Because a constable who enters and searches premises and seizes material under warrant is not liable in respect of acts done in obedience to it provided all the correct procedural requirements are fulfilled, it follows that the cir-

[65] See *Hoye* v. *Bush* (1840) 1 Man. & G. 775.
[66] *R.* v. *Atkinson* [1976] Crim.L.R. 307.
[67] *Elias* v. *Pasmore* [1934] 2 K.B. 164; see Chap. 6 above at p. 184.
[68] *Reynolds* v. *MPC* [1985] Q.B. 881.
[69] See above at p. 216.
[70] See Chap. 6 above at p. 184.

cumstances in which a warrant can lawfully be issued are, strictly speaking, outside the scope of this book. If a warrant is issued without jurisdiction remedy lies against the issuing justice and not against the police. Nevertheless, an action under such a warrant is still unlawful although the constable has a defence in relation to acts done "in obedience" to it. The "lawfulness" of a constable's presence on premises is relevant to the lawfulness of other police powers.[71] The situations in which a warrant can be properly issued under the 1984 Act will, therefore, be briefly outlined.

As a precondition to this it is necessary to consider the different categories of potentially seizable "material" (that is, "evidence" in the widest sense) set out in the Act. The category of "legally privileged material" is relevant in cases of seizure without warrant because it is protected from seizure by section 19(6) of the Act.[72] Different provisions regarding search and seizure apply to each type of material.

Types of material

The 1984 Act divides the kind of material which the police may wish to search for and seize into four categories.

(1) Items subject to legal privilege. These are defined as:

> "(a) communications between a professional legal adviser and his client or any person representing his client made in connection with the giving of legal advice to his client;
> (b) communications between a professional legal adviser and his client or any person representing his client or any such representative and any other person made in connection with or in contemplation of legal proceedings and for the purposes of such proceedings; and
> (c) items enclosed with or referred to in such communications and made—
> (i) in connection with the giving of legal advice; or
> (ii) in connection with or in contemplation of legal proceedings and for the purposes of such proceedings, when they are in possession of a person who is entitled to possession of them."[73]

Items held with the intention of furthering a criminal purpose are not items subject to legal privilege.[74]

(2) Excluded material. This is defined by section 11 of the Act and covers various items "held in confidence."[75] These items are "personal records"[76] acquired or created in the course of any trade, profession, business, or occupation or for the purposes of any paid or unpaid office[77]; human tissue or

[71] *e.g.*, powers of seizure under s.19; see above at p. 213.
[72] See above at p. 213.
[73] s.10(1).
[74] s.10(2); see *Frank Truman Export Ltd.* v. *MPC* [1977] Q.B. 952; and see Feldman at 4.54–4.78.
[75] See Feldman at 4.79–4.99.
[76] As defined in s.12.
[77] s.11(1)(*a*).

tissue fluid taken for the purposes of diagnosis or medical treatment[78] and "journalistic material"[79] consisting of documents or records other than documents.[80] Personal records or human tissue or tissue fluid is held in confidence if it is subject to an express or implied undertaking to hold it in confidence or if it is subject to a restriction on disclosure or an obligation of secrecy contained in any enactment.[81] Journalistic material is held in confidence if it is subject to such an undertaking, restriction or obligation and it has been continuously so held since it was first acquired or created for the purposes of journalism.

(3) Special procedure material. This is defined by section 14 as including two kinds of material. First, "journalistic material" other than excluded material. Second, material other than items subject to legal privilege and excluded material which is in the possession of a person who acquired or created it in the course of a trade, business, profession, occupation or for the purpose of any paid or unpaid office which is held in confidence or subject to a restriction on disclosure or an obligation of secrecy contained in any enactment.[82]

(4) Other material. This is any "material" which does not fall into one of the other three categories.

Access to legally privileged material

The Act provides no power of police access to legally privileged material. Moreover, it expressly states that any previous Act which authorised search of premises under warrant for the purposes of criminal investigation shall cease to have effect so far as it related to the authorisation of searches for items subject to legal privilege.[83] Legally privileged items may not be sought for on arrest[84] and may not be seized.[85] It appears that such items may be sought for (but not seized) on arrest.[86]

Access to excluded material

Once again the Act provides that any previous Act which authorised the search for excluded material shall cease to have effect.[87] But it does lay

[78] s.11(1)(*b*).
[79] As defined in s.13.
[80] s.11(1)(*c*).
[81] s.11(2).
[82] s.14(2).
[83] s.9(2)(*a*).
[84] s.18(1).
[85] s.19(6).
[86] s.32(1).
[87] s.9(2)(*b*)—this does not apply to statutes which enable the police to seize such material under written authority other than a warrant: see Hargreaves and Levenson at p. 42.

down a procedure whereby the police can obtain possession of such material either by applying to a circuit judge for a production order or, in exceptional circumstances, a search warrant.

A circuit judge can only make a production order if he is satisfied that:

(1) there are reasonable grounds for believing that there is excluded material on the premises specified; and
(2) but for section 9(2) there would have been power under some other statute to issue a warrant to seize the material; and
(3) the issue of such a warrant "would have been appropriate."[88]

An application for such an order is made *inter partes*. The police must first give notice to the person who appears to be in possession of the material that he intends to apply for an order.[89] When the notice of application has been served the person shall not "conceal, destroy, alter or dispose of the material to which the application relates" except with the leave of a judge or the written permission of a constable, until the matter has been disposed of.[90] It is the duty of a police officer applying for an order under these provisions—

> "to set out in the notice which goes to the person whose assistance is required a description of all that it is sought to be produced or to be discovered."[91]

If this is not done then this "goes to the very root of the procedure properly to be applied for bringing effectively into being the power of the judge to make an order under Schedule 1" and any order made will be invalid.[92] The notice should contain further information:

> "(1) The general nature of the offence under consideration. It was not necessary to specify the precise offence or section. By way of example, "fraud" or "riot" or "wounding" would suffice.
> (2) The address of the premises where the material was alleged to be."[93]

When such an order is granted it is desirable for the judge to give the reasons why he was satisfied as to the grounds for the belief that the material was on the premises.[94]

Access to special procedure material

Any previous Act which authorised the obtaining of a warrant to search for special procedure material will only cease to have effect if the material

[88] Sched. 1, para. 3.
[89] Sched. 1, paras. 7 and 8.
[90] Sched. 1, para. 11.
[91] *per* Watkins L.J., *R.* v. *Central Criminal Court, ex p. Adegbesan* [1986] 3 All E.R. 112 at 118; see also *R.* v. *Central Criminal Court, ex p. Carr, The Independent,* March 5, 1987.
[92] *Ibid.*: the order was quashed in that case.
[93] *per* Glidewell L.J., *R.* v. *Central Criminal Court, ex p. Carr, The Independent,* March 5, 1987.
[94] *Ibid.*

consists of documents or records other than documents.[95] Thus, if the police already have statutory power to obtain such a warrant they can use it. If there is no existing power, or if the special procedure material is documentary, then they will have to apply to a circuit judge for a production order. Such an order may be granted if the police can satisfy one of two sets of "access conditions."

The first set of access conditions are as follows:

(1) there must be reasonable grounds for believing;
(a) that a serious arrestable offence has been committed; and
(b) that there is material on the premises which includes special procedure material but not excluded material; and
(c) the material is likely to be of substantial value to the investigation; and
(d) the material is likely to be relevant evidence.
(2) other methods of obtaining the material have been tried without success or appear bound to fail.
(3) it is in the public interest having regard to the benefit likely to accrue to the investigation and to the circumstances under which the person holds the material, that the material should be produced or that access to it should be given.[96]

Some guidance as to the way in which the courts will treat such applications is provided by the case of *Chief Constable of Avon and Somerset Constabulary* v. *Bristol United Press*.[97] In that case, Stuart-Smith J. (sitting as a circuit judge) ordered the production of photographs of public disorders taken for "journalistic purposes." Although the mere assertion that the material would be of substantial value was insufficient the court was entitled to draw inferences although the respondent could produce evidence to the court, without the police seeing it, to show that the material was not of substantial value. It was held that, to fulfil paragraph 2(*a*) of the access conditions in Schedule 1, it was not necessary for the material sought to relate to some particular criminal offence. The judge was prepared to draw the inference, in the absence of contrary evidence that photographers would take pictures of assaults and acts of violence and that their assaults would, therefore, be likely to provide evidence of "serious arrestable offences."[98] The judge was of the view that the public interest in the "impartiality and independence of the press" would not be undermined by making the order. Even if it was undermined in some people's eyes "that could not outweigh the great public interest in the conviction of those guilty of serious crime." An application for judicial review of this decision was refused.[99] It is submitted that the interpretation of paragraph 2(*a*) of Schedule 1 in this case is too wide and, in effect, allows the police to make "fishing" applications without any specific offence in mind. Furthermore, the decision reflects the low priority likely to be given to the public interest in the independence of the press in applications for the production of Special Procedure material.

[95] s.9(2)(*c*).
[96] Sched. 1, para. 2.
[97] *The Independent*, November 4, 1986.
[98] See the discussion in *Ex p. Bristol Press & Picture Agency, The Times*, November 11, 1986.
[99] *Ibid.*

The second set of access conditions are the same as those for excluded material.[1] The procedure for making such an application is identical to that for excluded material and the "Notice" should contain the same information about the documents, the nature of the offence and the address of the premises.[2]

In limited circumstances a search warrant can be obtained, from a circuit judge, in respect of special procedure material. The judge must be satisfied that the access conditions in Schedule 1 are satisfied and that "further conditions" relating to the impracticability of communication with the person entitled to grant access or to the prejudice to the investigation of a production order are fulfilled.[3] A search warrant can also be issued by a circuit judge if he is satisfied that the conditions in Schedule 1, paragraph 2 are fulfilled and a production order has not been complied with.[4]

Access to other material

The most important "with warrant" power involves access to material which does not fall into one of the three special categories in the 1984 Act. This will cover most of the items that the police will usually search for—items such as stolen goods or money, weapons, or fingerprints. Warrants can be applied for in relation to any premises; whether or not the occupier is himself suspected of involvement.

Section 8 of the Act gives a justice of the peace the power to authorise entry and search of premises for other material if he is satisfied that there are reasonable grounds for believing that the material in question does not fall into one of the three special categories and:

> "(a) that a serious arrestable offence has been committed; and
> (b) that there is material on premises specified in the application which is likely to be of substantial value (whether by itself or together with other material) to the investigation of the offences; and
> (c) that the material is likely to be relevant evidence."[5]

"Relevant evidence" is defined in section 8(4) as "anything that would be admissible in evidence at a trial for the offence."

In addition, the justice of the peace must be satisfied that one of four other conditions are fulfilled. These are set out in section 8(3) and are as follows:

> "(a) that it is not practicable to communicate with any person entitled to grant entry to the premises;
> (b) that it is practicable to communicate with a person entitled to grant entry to the premises but it is not practicable to communicate with any person entitled to grant access to the evidence;
> (c) that entry to the premises will not be granted unless a warrant is produced;

[1] Sched. 1, para. 3.
[2] See *R.* v. *Central Criminal Court, ex p. Carr, The Independent,* March 5, 1987.
[3] See Sched. 1, paras. 12(*a*) and 14.
[4] Sched. 1, para. 12(*b*).
[5] s.8(1).

(d) that the purpose of a search may be frustrated or seriously prejudiced unless a constable arriving at the premises can secure immediate entry to them."

In other words, a warrant should not be issued unless there are some grounds for believing that the evidence cannot be obtained without the use of the warrant.

7. CHALLENGING SEARCH WARRANTS

Introduction

When a search warrant has been issued the police are authorised to do things which would otherwise be unlawful. The occupier of the premises to which the warrant relates may wish to challenge its validity. In theory a warrant can be challenged for three types of reasons:

(1) because it is formally invalid on its face;
(2) because the factual preconditions for its issue were not fulfilled;
(3) because the issuing authority did not give the matter proper consideration.

Although challenges in respect of simple formal defects are straightforward, other challenges present considerable difficulties and the English case law in this area is extremely sparse.

In practice, the opportunities for making a challenge to the terms of warrants are very limited. In the unlikely event of an occupier being able to discover the existence of a warrant before execution he can, in an appropriate case, challenge it in judicial review proceedings. In the large majority of cases, however, the first that the occupier will know of the existence of a warrant is when police officers attempt to execute it. Before allowing this to happen the occupier is entitled to see the warrant.[6] A warrant should be carefully scrutinised. If it is clearly formally defective the occupier is entitled to refuse to allow a search to be carried out. If the warrant is formally valid but the occupier claims that there were, in fact, no grounds for its issue, he must allow the search to be made. If he refuses, the police can rely on their power to use reasonable force to execute a warrant.[7] He can then seek the return of all materials seized under the warrant. There is some doubt as to the correct legal procedure in this situation. Before dealing with the question of procedure it is necessary to analyse the three "heads of challenge" referred to.

Formal invalidity

The general requirements for the formal validity of warrants are set out in section 15 of the Police and Criminal Evidence Act 1984.[8] A warrant will be

[6] See above at p. 224.
[7] See above at p. 205.
[8] See above at p. 222.

formally invalid if it: is addressed to the wrong person or premises; does not specify its date of issue; does not specify the enactment under which it is issued; is not signed by a justice of the peace; or is more than one month old. In these circumstances, the police can be refused entry under the warrant at the outset.

Special difficulties arise in relation to the requirement that a warrant "shall identify, so far as is practicable, the articles or persons to be sought."[9] It is submitted that a warrant which fails to specify any articles or persons will be invalid. Similarly, it is submitted that, if the warrant specifies materials in vague general terms it will also be invalid.[10] If the warrant purports to specify the goods sought in more specific terms, its validity will depend on the facts of each case and what is "practicable." If, for example, an occupier is accused of the theft of one specific item then a warrant which fails to specify that item but is expressed in general terms will not comply with the statutory requirement. On the other hand, if an occupier is accused of a long and complex series of frauds, then a warrant in very general terms authorising a search for evidence relating to those frauds will be valid. In general, the more specific the terms of the warrant the more likely it is to be valid. In all but the very clearest cases, an occupier who believes the warrant to be too broadly framed should allow the search to take place and should then seek remedy through the courts. Thus, when the Special Branch seized materials from BBC Scotland under the terms of an excessively broad warrant, an order for their return was obtained from the Court of Session.[11] The precise form of such proceedings in England is a matter of some difficulty.[12]

Factual preconditions not fulfilled

Before a warrant is issued, the issuing authority must be satisfied that certain factual preconditions have been fulfilled. If the matters which were before the issuing authority were fully set out in documentary form **and** the occupier of the premises to which the warrant related had access to such documents then he would be in a position to question the basis on which the warrant was granted.

Unfortunately, documentary evidence of the full grounds on which the warrant was granted is rarely available. Although it has long been established that an application for a warrant had to be by "sworn information"[13] this did not have to be in writing. Even when an information was required

[9] Police and Criminal Evidence Act 1984, s.15(6)(*b*).

[10] *cf.* the Canadian case of *Re PSI Mind Development Institute and The Queen* (1977) 37 C.C.C. (2d) 263, where the words "materials of every nature" were struck out of a warrant, and see *Schumiatcher* v. *A-G for Saskatchewan* (1960) 34 C.R. 152 and *R.* v. *Johnson & Franklin Wholesale Distributors* (1971) 3 C.C.C. (2d) 484 where the issue turned on whether the wording left a wide open discretion to the officers as to how the warrant should be executed; see generally, Feldman at 15.13.

[11] See *The Guardian*, February 2, 1987.

[12] See below at p. 235.

[13] See *Wilkes* v. *Lord Halifax* (1763) 19 State. Tr. 981; *Caudle* v. *Seymour* (1841) 1 Q.B. 889 at 893.

by statute to be in writing, it did not usually contain the grounds for application because these would be given orally on oath.[14] All applications for search warrants must now be supported by an information in writing.[15] Under the Code of Practice an information should state "the ground on which the application is made" and an indication of how the evidence relates to the investigation.[16] It remains to be seen how much detail will, in fact, be included in such informations but past experience suggests that they will not condescend to particulars.

Even where an information does contain full details of the grounds on which the application was made the occupier will not be able to obtain immediate access to it. There is a general public interest immunity from disclosure[17] of the factual grounds on which the police rely in forming the belief that they must have when seeking a warrant. This immunity will apply until either the criminal trial is concluded or a decision is reached not to prosecute. This immunity may be lost if there is unreasonable delay in making a decision about prosecution.[18] While the immunity continues, the plaintiff (or applicant for judicial review) is not entitled to discovery or interrogatories aimed at ascertaining these factual grounds. Thus, in the case of *Taylor* v. *Anderton* pre-action discovery of informations behind four search warrants was refused on the ground of public interest immunity despite the fact that five months had lapsed since they were sworn without any decision having been made regarding the prosecution of the applicant.[19]

The court cannot oblige the police to disclose the grounds for their belief when they oppose a claim for interlocutory relief but must be satisfied by a statement in their affidavit that they have reasonable grounds for their belief unless the evidence on the application is strong enough to justify the inference that no reasonable person could have thought so.[20]

Once criminal proceedings have terminated there will be little point in the occupier challenging a warrant because the police will be under a duty to return seized property to him in any event[21] and they will be protected by the warrant from an action in trespass.[22] Thus, an occupier will only be able to challenge a warrant on the ground that the factual preconditions for its issue were not fulfilled in the clearest of cases where he can show, in effect, that the police cannot possibly have had any grounds for obtaining the warrant.

The situation in relation to search warrants can be contrasted to that of "production orders" in respect of "special procedure" or "excluded" material under Schedule 1 to the Police and Criminal Evidence Act 1984. Such applications are made *inter partes* and the occupier will therefore have full details of the grounds on which the application was made and be able to

[14] See Feldman at 4.09–4.12.

[15] Police and Criminal Evidence Act 1984, s.15(3).

[16] Para. 2.6.

[17] *Conway* v. *Rimmer* [1968] A.C. 910; see generally Chap. 2 above at p. 53, and Chap. 3 above at p. 75.

[18] See *IRC* v. *Rossminster* [1980] A.C. 952 at 1012, *per* Lord Diplock; see also *Taylor* v. *Anderton, The Times*, October 21, 1986; Transcript: D Sellers.

[19] See Chap. 3 above at p. 66.

[20] See *IRC* v. *Rossminster*, [1980] A.C. 952 at 1011–1013, *per* Lord Diplock.

[21] See above at p. 217.

[22] See above at p. 220.

challenge their adequacy. In *R.* v. *Central Criminal Court, ex p. Carr*[23] a production order made by a judge against two of the applicants was quashed by the Divisional Court after the prosecution conceded that the access conditions had not been fulfilled.

Lack of proper consideration by the issuing authority

In considering whether to issue a warrant the courts should act "judicially." They must exercise proper judgment and act fairly and reasonably.[24] The issuing justice or circuit judge ought to assess the material before him to see whether or not the statutory criteria have been made out.[25] If he fails to do this he will be acting without jurisdiction.[26] Applications for warrants are *ex parte* proceedings and, if they take place in the magistrates' court there is no transcript. It is therefore very unlikely that evidence will be available to enable an occupier to challenge a warrant on this ground. The position in Canada is very different because statute prescribes that the grounds contained in the information[27] or in the warrant itself must be set out in some detail.

Procedure

If a person whose goods have been removed under the authority of a warrant wishes to obtain their immediate return because he claims that the warrant was invalid there are two routes available to him. First, he can challenge the warrant itself in judicial review proceedings. He can seek an order of certiorari to quash the warrant and an injunction to obtain the return of the goods. Secondly, he can seek an order for interim delivery up of the goods in an ordinary action.

The first form of action presents no special procedural difficulties and has been attempted in two reported cases in the past decade. In *R.* v. *Justice of the Peace for Peterborough, ex p. Hicks*[28] an interim injunction was awarded before a separate application was made for certiorari to quash a warrant granted under the Forgery Act 1913. The application was rejected.[29] In the famous case of *IRC* v. *Rossminster*[30] judicial review was sought of search warrants granted to the Inland Revenue. The Court of Appeal granted the application and ruled that the warrants were invalid. It was ordered that

[23] *The Independent*, March 5, 1987.
[24] See the authorities cited in Feldman at 4.08, n. 1.
[25] See *Hope* v. *Evered* (1886) 17 Q.B.D. 338.
[26] See generally, Feldman, Chap. 4.
[27] See, *e.g.*, *Regency Realties* v. *Loranger* (1961) 36 C.R. 291 and *R.* v. *Bender* (1916) 36 O.L.R. 378.
[28] [1977] 1 W.L.R. 1371.
[29] See generally, Feldman at 4.62.
[30] [1980] A.C. 952.

all the documents be returned and all copies destroyed upon counsel's undertaking. This decision was reversed by the House of Lords. In Canada applications to challenge search warrants by certiorari are relatively common and a considerable body of case law has developed in this area.[31]

The second form of procedure was used in the case of *Frank Truman Export* v. *MPC*[32] and appears to have been fairly regularly employed in a number of unreported cases. There are, however, some difficulties with this approach as a result of the decision of the House of Lords in *O'Reilly* v. *Mackman*[33] that, as a general rule it would be contrary to public policy and an abuse of the process to seek "public law" redress in an ordinary action. It would follow that a direct challenge to a warrant in an ordinary action would be struck out as an abuse of the process.

The position is less clear, however, when the relief which the plaintiff is seeking is the return of goods seized under a warrant. One exception to the *O'Reilly* v. *Mackman* principle is where the invalidity of the public law decision arises as a "collateral issue" in a private law claim.[34] The court will, therefore, allow a case to proceed by writ where the primary claim is based in tort[35] or contract[36] or breach of statutory duty,[37] where the private law content of the claim is sufficiently great[38] or where the public law issue is raised as a defence.[39]

On the basis of these authorities, it could be argued that, because any entry and seizure by the police is prima facie a tortious invasion of private law rights, the correct procedure would be to seek an injunction and/or an order for delivery up in an ordinary action. The question of the validity of the search warrant could be said merely to arise as a collateral issue, being the defence which the police put forward to justify their tortious acts. On the other hand, it could be said that the primary purpose of such proceedings is to impugn the decision of a public authority, namely the justice's decision to issue the warrant. Accordingly, there is a real risk that an ordinary action would fail altogether if it was held, on a full hearing, that the correct procedure was an application for judicial review.

There is no reported case on the effect of *O'Reilly* v. *Mackman* on applications for the return of goods seized under a warrant. Under R.S.C., Ord. 53, r. 9(5), the court can order that a judicial review application continue as if it had been begun by writ but this will only be done if the application reveals some breach of a public law obligation.[40] There is no correlative power to convert a writ action into an application for judicial

[31] For a discussion, see Feldman at 15.12–15.15.

[32] [1977] Q.B. 952; see also *Roandale* v. *MPC* [1979] C.L.Y. 518.

[33] [1983] A.C. 237.

[34] *Ibid.* at 285, *per* Lord Diplock.

[35] *Davy* v. *Spelthorne Borough Council* [1984] A.C. 262.

[36] *Law* v. *National Greyhound Racing Club* [1983] 1 W.L.R. 1302; *R.* v. *BBC, ex p. Lavelle* [1983] 1 W.L.R. 23.

[37] *An Bord Bainne Co-operative Ltd.* v. *Milk Marketing Board The Times*, February 21, 1984.

[38] *Gillick* v. *West Norfolk AHA* [1986] A.C. 112 at 163, *per* Lord Fraser; at 178, *per* Lord Scarman.

[39] *Wandsworth LBC* v. *Winder* [1985] A.C. 461; see generally, Aldous and Alder Chap. 9.

[40] See *R.* v. *Secretary of State for Home Affairs, ex p. Dew, The Times*, March 6, 1987; *R.* v. *East Berkshire Health Authority, ex p. Walsh* [1985] Q.B. 152, *per* Purchas L.J.

review.[41] It may be that this dilemma could be resolved by judicial guidance being given at the initial application for the injunction.

Effect of a warrant being quashed

If a warrant is quashed in judicial review proceedings this will not necessarily lead to the seized goods being returned. First, it may be that the warrant is only partially invalid and that the invalid parts can be severed from the whole. This is the procedure in Canada.[42]

Secondly, even where the whole warrant is quashed the court may be reluctant to order return of the goods if their retention can be justified on other grounds. In a number of Canadian cases it has been held that return of the goods would only be ordered if the prosecution cannot show that the goods are required as evidence and the applicant's rights to the goods are clear[43] but the better view seems to be that return should be ordered if the warrant is quashed.[44]

Nevertheless, the police may rely in the alternative on their common law or statutory powers of seizure without warrant[45] and they may claim that they are entitled to retain articles seized under their common law duty to preserve evidence for a criminal trial.[46] Thus, in *Butler* v. *Board of Trade*[47] Goff J. refused to grant an injunction as a matter of discretion to prevent a letter obtained in breach of confidence[48] from being used in criminal proceedings.

It will, therefore, be necessary either to give the appropriate undertakings to the court so as to ensure that relevant evidence will not be destroyed if the articles seized are returned or to concede that the police are entitled to retain such evidence. If the police cannot show that the materials seized are relevant evidence. The court should require their immediate return as, for example, in *Ghani* v. *Jones*.[49]

In any event it is always open to the police to obtain a fresh warrant if the original one is successfully challenged.[50] In Canada it has been held that it is improper to issue a second warrant before the validity of the first one is determined[51] or for the police to return to the premises with the articles and a second warrant after the first one is quashed and claim they are entitled to re-seize the articles.[52]

[41] *O'Reilly* v. *Mackman* [1983] A.C. 237 at 284A–B, *per* Lord Diplock.
[42] See Feldman at 15.13.
[43] See *Re Black and The Queen* (1973) 13 C.C.C. (2d) 446.
[44] See *Bergeron* v. *Deschamps* (1977) 33 C.C.C. (2d) 234, S.C. of Canada.
[45] See above at pp. 212 *et seq.*
[46] See *R.* v. *Lushington, ex p. Otto* [1894] 1 Q.B. 430, as qualified by *R.* v. *Uxbridge JJ., ex p. Sofaer, The Times*, December 4, 1986.
[47] [1971] Ch. 690.
[48] See Chap. 9 below at p. 275.
[49] [1970] 1 Q.B. 693.
[50] As happened in the BBC Scotland case, see *The Guardian*, February 2, 1987.
[51] *Schumiatcher* v. *A-G for Saskatchewan* (1960) 34 C.R. 154.
[52] *Re Den Hoy Gin* (1965) 47 C.R. 89; *Alder* v. *A-G for Alberta* (1978) 5 Alta. L.R. (2d) 129.

8. POLICE POWERS IN RELATION TO VEHICLES

Introduction

Police powers in relation to vehicles are of considerable practical importance. The police often stop cars or lorries to check documents or to make enquiries about road traffic matters. Large numbers of vehicles are searched for stolen property, weapons or drugs. This is sometimes done under common law powers and sometimes under a controversial provision of the Road Traffic Act 1972. Although the police have a wide range of powers under the "breathalyser" legislation to administer "breath tests" to the drivers there are no specific "breathalyser" powers to stop motor vehicles. In addition to these "road traffic" powers there is a power to operate road checks under the Police and Criminal Evidence Act 1984. The powers of "entry and search" without warrant under the 1984 Act also apply to motor vehicles.

Common law powers to stop vehicles

Although there appears to be no direct authority on the point, it seems clear that, at common law, a constable has a power to stop a vehicle in any case where he would have a power to stop a person. Thus, there is no doubt that a constable would be able to stop a vehicle if he had a reasonable suspicion that an occupant had committed an arrestable offence. The police will now have power to stop a vehicle for a non-arrestable offence if the "general arrest conditions of section 25 of the Police and Criminal Evidence Act 1984 are fulfilled.[53] It is submitted that this will allow the police to stop vehicles when he reasonably suspects that any road traffic offence has been or is being committed. The police also have the power to stop motor vehicles if they apprehend on reasonable grounds that there is a "real possibility" of a breach of the peace being committed by their occupants.[54]

In *Lodwick* v. *Sanders*[55] Watkins L.J. appeared to suggest that a constable acting reasonably on a genuine inquiry into the suspected commission of crime had a common law power to require a motor vehicle to stop. It is probable that there is only such a power if a constable could make a lawful arrest. Just as a constable has no common law power to detain a person to make inquiries[56] it is submitted that he cannot require a vehicle to stop simply to assist in his inquiries.

A constable also has a right to control and regulate traffic on the roads which derives from his common law duty to protect life and property.[57] This:

"is not a right to regulate traffic for the police officer's own personal

[53] See Chap. 5 above at p. 141.
[54] *Moss* v. *McLachlan* [1985] I.R.L.R. 76.
[55] [1985] 1 W.L.R. 382 at 390E.
[56] *Ibid.* at 388G-H.
[57] *Hoffman* v. *Thomas* [1974] 1 W.L.R. 374 at 379; see Chap. 1 above at p. 26.

> motives or entertainment; it is fundamentally a right to regulate traffic because of the dangers to life and limb which unregulated traffic can present."[58]

It has, therefore, been held that a constable does not have the common law right to direct a motorist to take part in a traffic census.[59]

Once a motorist has been stopped then, at common law, the police have no general power to detain his vehicle[60] unless he reasonably suspects it to have been stolen[60a] in which case he

> "is entitled to take reasonable steps to detain it for such reasonable time as will enable him . . . to effect an arrest and explain to the driver the reason for the arrest."[61]

These limited common law powers are now supplemented by statute.

Statutory powers to stop motor vehicles

Under section 159 of the Road Traffic Act 1972,

> "A person driving a motor vehicle on a road and a person riding a cycle, not being a motor vehicle on a road shall stop the same on being so required by a constable in uniform, and if he fails to do so he shall be guilty of an offence."

A road is defined in the statute as including highways and roads other than highways "to which the public has access."[62] A car park is not a "road" for these purposes.[63]

It is not entirely clear whether this section actually confers on the police a new general power to stop a vehicle or simply places a driver under a duty to stop when a constable has required him to do so under some other power.

The former view has been expressed by the Divisional Court in a number of cases. Thus in *Beard* v. *Wood*[64] it was held that the section did confer a general power to stop vehicles on the police.[65] In the "breathalyser" case of *Chief Constable of Gwent* v. *Dash*.[66] Macpherson J. was of the view that section 159 conferred a general and unqualified power

> "provided there is no malpractice or oppression or caprice or

[58] *Hoffman* v. *Thomas* [1974] 1 W.L.R. 374 at 397F.
[59] *Ibid.*
[60] *R.* v. *Waterfield* [1964] 1 Q.B. 164; but see *Ghani* v. *Jones* [1970] 1 Q.B. 693; and see Feldman at 10.02–10.08 and 10.30.
[60a] *Lodwick* v. *Sanders* [1985] 1 W.L.R. 382.
[61] *Ibid.* at 390F.
[62] Road Traffic Act 1972, s.196.
[63] See *Griffin* v. *Squires* [1958] 1 W.L.R. 1106; see generally, *Wilkinson's Road Traffic Offences* at pp. 40–50.
[64] [1980] R.T.R. 98.
[65] See also *Lodwick* v. *Sanders* [1985] 1 W.L.R. 382 at 388E, *per* Watkins L.J.; but see *per* Webster J. at 392F.
[66] [1986] R.T.R. 41.

> opprobious conduct . . . there is no restriction upon the stopping of motorists by a policeman in the execution of his duty."[67]

However, the latter view was strongly supported by the Divisional Court in *Steel* v. *Goacher*.[68] According to Griffiths L.J. section 159

> "imposes a duty on a motorist to stop when required to do so by constable in uniform. It does not follow that a constable in uniform must be deemed to have acted lawfully when, for whatever reason, he requires a motorist to stop for purely practical reasons; there must be a rule that motorists stop when called upon to do so by a constable in uniform. The motorist must assume for the purpose of stopping that he is being lawfully required to stop, otherwise a dangerous and chaotic state of affairs would result. But once the motorist has stopped he can, thereafter, challenge the constable's right to stop him, for nothing in the wording of the section gives any power to the constable to stop the motorist. It is a section designed to ensure safety and good order rather than to confer any specific power on a police constable.

This view is also supported by the case of *Winter* v. *Barlow*.[69]

It is submitted that the latter view is to be preferred. On general principles, section 159 should be strictly construed in the way which makes least alteration to a citizen's rights at common law.[70] It would follow that a police officer can only lawfully require a vehicle to stop in the exercise of specific common law or statutory power although the driver is under a duty to stop in any event. It is submitted that when a constable requires a vehicle to stop he must give his reasons for doing so as he is required to give reasons for detaining a vehicle.[71]

In addition to the common law powers already mentioned, it is submitted that a constable has the power, by necessary implication, to require a motorist to stop to take a breath test if one of the "preconditions" for requiring a test set out in section 7 of the Road Traffic Act is fulfilled. The constable must be in uniform and have reasonable cause to suspect:

> "(a) that a person driving or attempting to drive or in charge of a motor vehicle on a road or other public place has alcohol in his body or has committed a traffic offence whilst the vehicle was in motion; or
> (b) that a person has been driving or attempting to drive or been in charge of a motor vehicle on a road or other public place with alcohol in his body and that that person still has alcohol in his body; or
> (c) that a person has been driving or attempting to drive or been in charge of a motor vehicle on a road or other public place and has committed a traffic offence whilst the vehicle was in motion."[72]

A constable who has lawfully stopped a vehicle has, by "necessary inference" a power to require it to remain at a standstill while he has a reason-

[67] *Chief Constable of Gwent* v. *Dash* [1986] R.T.R. 41 at 46J–K.
[68] [1983] R.T.R. 98.
[69] [1980] R.T.R. 209 at 213B, *per* Eveleigh L.J.
[70] But see s.4(2) of the Police and Criminal Evidence Act 1984 which refers to "the power conferred by section 159"; see below at p. 241.
[71] *per* Webster J., *Lodwick* v.*Sanders* [1985] 1 W.L.R 382.
[72] s.7(1) of the Road Traffic Act 1972, substituted by s.25 of the Transport Act 1981.

able opportunity of exercising the power under which he required it to stop.[73]

Road checks

The mystery surrounding section 159 is compounded by section 4 of the 1984 Act. Under this section the police have the power to carry out "road checks" which are defined as:

> "the exercise in a locality of the power conferred by section 159 of the Road Traffic Act 1972 in such a way as to stop during the period for which its exercise in that way in that locality continues all vehicles selected by any criterion."[74]

This section appears to confirm that section 159 confers a "power," but given the wide terms of section 159 itself it is unclear why this section is required unless it is accepted that no "power" is actually conferred. Section 4 prescribes detailed conditions for the exercise of this "road check" power.

(1) a road check can only be used to ascertain whether the vehicle is carrying a person who has committed or is intending to commit an offence other than a road traffic offence, or a person is a witness to such an offence or a person who is unlawfully at large[75];

(2) a road check must be authorised in writing by a police officer of the rank of superintendent or above[76] unless it appears to an officer below the rank of superintendent that a road check "is required as a matter of urgency"[77];

(3) a road check can only be authorised if the officer has reasonable grounds for believing that the offence in question is a "serious arrestable offence" and that the person in question "is, or is about to be, in the locality in which vehicles would be stopped if the road check were authorised."[78]

The written authorisation must specify the name of the officer giving it, its purpose, the locality in which vehicles are to be stopped and any relevant serious arrestable offence.[79] The officer who gives the authorisation must specify the locality in which vehicles are to be stopped,[80] and unless it is a case of urgency, must specify a period not exceeding seven days during which the road check may continue and may direct when it should take place during the period.[81] If it appears to the authorising officer above the rank of superintendent that the road check ought to continue he may specify a further period, not exceeding seven days during which it may

[73] *Lodwick* v. *Sanders* [1985] 1 W.L.R. 382 at 389E.
[74] s.4(2).
[75] s.4(1).
[76] s.4(3).
[77] s.4(5).
[78] s.4(4).
[79] s.4(13) and (14).
[80] s.4(10).
[81] s.4(11).

continue.[82] Where a person is stopped in a road check the person in charge of the vehicle is entitled to a written statement of the purpose of the road check if he applies within 12 months.[83]

Stopping and searching motor vehicles without warrant

The powers of entry and search without warrant conferred on the police by the 1984 Act[84] apply to motor vehicles as well as houses and flats. It is submitted that these imply a power to stop vehicles to carry out such searches.

The 1984 Act also provides a specific power for a constable to search a motor vehicle or anything in or on it for "stolen or prohibited articles" if he has reasonable grounds for suspecting that he will find such articles.[85] If the vehicle is in a garden or yard used with a dwelling then a constable may not search the vehicle or anything in or on it unless he has reasonable grounds for believing:

> "(a) that the person in charge of the vehicle does not reside in the dwelling; and
> (b) that the vehicle is not in the place in question with the express or implied permission of a person who resides in the dwelling."[86]

Any search of a motor vehicle which is not justified by these powers will be a trespass to goods even if nothing is damaged[87] and an action in damages will lie.

Police powers in relation to vehicles: a summary

It would seem then, that section 159 of the Road Traffic Act 1972 does not confer a general power to stop vehicles but that the police may do so for any one of the following reasons:

(1) to arrest any occupant for an arrestable offence;
(2) to arrest any occupant if the "general arrest conditions" of section 25 of the 1984 Act are fulfilled. This will allow a vehicle to be stopped if any road traffic offence is reasonably suspected;
(3) if it is reasonably suspected that the vehicle is stolen[88];
(4) to regulate traffic because of the dangers to life and limb[89];
(5) in order to carry out a breath test if the conditions of section 7 of the Road Traffic Act 1972 are fulfilled;
(6) to exercise any statutory power of search without warrant;
(7) in the exercise of their "road block" powers.[90]

[82] s.4(12).
[83] s.4(15).
[84] See above at p. 204.
[85] s.1(2) and (3); see Chap. 5 above at p. 129.
[86] s.1(5).
[87] See Chap. 6 above at p. 191.
[88] See *Lodwick* v. *Sanders* [1985] 1 W.L.R. 382.
[89] *Hoffman* v. *Thomas* [1974] 1 W.L.R. 374.
[90] See above at p. 241.

A driver who is required to stop is obliged to do so but the stop will not be lawful unless justified under one of these powers or some other express statutory provision. A failure to give the reason for the stop of the vehicle will, on the analogy of arrest, make it unlawful.[91] It is submitted that an unlawful stop will be a false imprisonment.[92] If the officer touches or searches the vehicle this will be a trespass to goods.[93] Exemplary damages will be available if the police act in an "arbitrary, unconstitutional and oppressive" manner.[94]

[91] See above at p. 240.
[92] See Chap. 4 above at p. 111.
[93] See Chap. 6 above at p. 190.
[94] See Chap. 11 below at p. 344.

8. Malicious Prosecution and Related Actions

1. INTRODUCTION

The scope of the torts

The culmination of much police work is the prosecution of a suspected offender. People who are prosecuted can suffer damage to their reputation, distress, inconvenience and expense. If the charges prove to be baseless and there is an acquittal they are likely to have a sense of grievance. They can of course make an official complaint against the police[1] but this will not provide any financial compensation. This is only available through an action in the tort of "malicious prosecution." If the police action falls short of an actual prosecution, compensation may still be available in one of the related "malicious process" torts, such as malicious arrest or malicious procurement of a search warrant. These actions protect the citizen's interest in freedom from unjustifiable litigation. They are obviously closely related to the action for defamation which protects a citizen's general reputation but they are in fact of much more ancient origin.[2]

Malicious prosecution is considered first and in most detail. It is the oldest and by far the most fully developed of the actions for abuse of legal procedure. The other actions are exceedingly rare and their exact extent—sometimes even their existence—is a matter of some dispute.

The action for malicious prosecution is of great antiquity, going back to the writ of conspiracy to abuse legal procedure which appears to have originated in the reign of Edward I. This fell into disuse in the sixteenth century and was replaced by an "action on the case," that is, an action in which actual damage had to be proved, which had the advantage of being available against a single defendant.

[1] See Chap. 2 above at p. 40.
[2] See generally: Winfield, *History of Conspiracy and Abuse of Legal Procedure.*

Policy considerations

In developing these civil actions the courts have always been concerned to balance two opposing policy considerations. On the one hand, there is a strong public interest in honest men bringing suspected criminals to justice and the judges have long been careful to avoid doing anything to discourage this. On the other hand, there is also a public interest in protecting the innocent citizen from baseless accusations brought out of malice or spite. The concern to balance these considerations continues up to the present day.

This balancing act has made malicious prosecution and the related actions very convoluted and complex torts. Too much weight has been given to the interests of prosecutors and not enough to those of the citizen. Malicious prosecution has become an extremely difficult tort to prove, requiring the proof of a negative. Without some hard evidence of a lack of honest belief in the charges made on the part of the prosecuting police officers a plaintiff faces an extremely difficult task.

There are strong grounds for arguing that the law in this area should be reformed. The power in the hands of police officers in relation to prosecutions is immense. Even though they are sifted by crown prosecutors, an unscrupulous police officer can simply manufacture evidence in the sure knowledge that, if this looks sufficiently strong, a prosecution will inevitably result. The innocent victim of such activities has the greatest difficulties in obtaining redress. This point has been made by a number of commentators, a Research Study for the Royal Commission on Criminal Procedure concluding that malicious prosecution is "no obstacle to the dishonest prosecutor and no real protection to the innocent who are prosecuted".[3] Several judges have also commented on the need for reform. As Lord Devlin pointed out in *Glinski* v. *McIver*[4] the present law evolved at a time when there was no police organisation and judges were anxious not to deter private prosecutors from coming forward. Higher standards should be applied to the police than to private citizens

> "Although . . . [the police officer] may be more exposed to attack from persons he has mistakenly prosecuted, he should not stand in need of as high a degree of protection as the private individual, for there can be no occasion on which in his case a mixture of motives could be accepted as excusable."

It is important that honest police officers should be fully protected against vexatious actions by disgruntled people they have unsuccessfully prosecuted. But it is equally important that innocent citizens are protected from the actions of the small minority of dishonest police officers who misuse the criminal law for their own ends.

[3] Lidstone, Hogg & Sutcliffe, *Prosecutions by private individuals and non-police agencies*, Royal Commission on Criminal Procedure Research Study No. 10, HMSO, 1980 at p. 106.
[4] [1962] A.C. 726 at 776–777.

Malicious process and false imprisonment

When legal procedures are used against someone it is likely that he will have been "imprisoned" in the legal sense, that is confined as a result of the operation of the process. Thus, when someone is prosecuted he may be "confined" whilst awaiting trial. A malicious arrest will mean that he is "detained" by the arresting officer. It is important to be clear as to when a malicious process action will lie and when the appropriate claim will be for false imprisonment.

The basic difference between the two has been expressed to be one of presumption. While imprisoning a man is prima facie wrongful, setting the law in motion is prima facie right and proper. Thus, in a malicious prosecution case the plaintiff must prove that the defendant lacked reasonable cause for the prosecution whilst in false imprisonment it is the defendant who must prove reasonable cause.

In practice, however, it is sometimes very difficult to decide which action is appropriate. In *Austin* v. *Dowling*[5] it was said that a person is liable to an action for false imprisonment if he sets a "ministerial officer" (for example, a policeman) in motion and liable for an action in malicious prosecution if he sets a "judicial officer" (for example, a magistrate) in motion. Thus a police officer who arrests someone out of malice will be liable for false imprisonment. On the other hand, if he lays an information before a magistrate which leads a second police officer to make the arrest he will be liable for malicious prosecution or malicious arrest although there would be no liability on the second officer. This distinction has been approved in a number of later cases.[6]

An action for malicious process presupposes that all the proper procedural formalities have been carried out while, in false imprisonment, it is of the essence that the initial act is itself wrongful.[7]

In practice, an action in false imprisonment will be appropriate if the plaintiff was "detained" by the police but released before the courts became involved. However, if some form of legal process such as a warrant or a summons is validly used against a plaintiff then his only available action is one for a malicious abuse of that legal process.

2. MALICIOUS PROSECUTION: INTRODUCTION

The elements of the tort

To succeed in an action for malicious prosecution, the plaintiff must prove five things:

(1) that there has been a prosecution which has caused him "damage";
(2) that the prosecution was instituted or continued by the defendant;
(3) that the prosecution was terminated in his favour;

[5] (1870) L.R. 5CP 534 at 540.
[6] See, *e.g. Sewell* v. *National Telephone Co.* [1907] 1 K.B. 557.
[7] Street at p. 401; see also *Sewell* v. *National Telephone Co.* [1907] 1 K.B. 557.

(4) that the defendant acted without reasonable and probable cause; and
(5) that the defendant acted maliciously.

These five elements and their special difficulties are considered in the next five sections.

The role of the jury

An action for malicious prosecution is one of the few remaining civil claims in which the plaintiff retains the right to jury trial.[8]

The concern of the judges not to discourage honest men from laying reasonable charges has made the role of a malicious prosecution jury an extremely complex one. This has further added to the difficulties of the action.

At common law all issues of fact are always for the jury, while matters of law are for the judge. This remains the situation in criminal trials. But in malicious prosecution actions a crucial matter of fact—whether or not the defendant had "reasonable or probable cause" for the prosecution—seems to have been a matter for the judge since at least the sixteenth century.[9] This was because it has long been believed, at least by judges, that juries were too ready to award damages against unsuccessful prosecutors.[10]

But the jury were not left without any function, even in relation to the question of reasonable and probable cause. If, "in the course of the judge's inquiry, he finds that it is necessary to resolve some disputed question of incidental fact, that question is a jury question."[11] The details of the role of the jury in relation to this element are discussed below.[12]

The question of malice is one for the jury alone.[13] But this too is not free from complications. The existence of the motive is a pure jury question. But, once the motive has been found, whether or not it is wrongful is a matter of law and therefore a question for the judge.

The existence of damage and a prosecution which has terminated in the defendant's favour will usually be questions of law, to be determined by the judge as preliminary issues if there is any dispute.

3. DAMAGE

Introduction

Malicious prosecution is an "action on the case" and "damage" is, therefore, a necessary ingredient of the action.[14] The fact that he has been

[8] See Chap. 3 above at p. 80.
[9] *Johnstone* v. *Sutton* (1786) 1 T.R. 545; or possibly, *Pain* v. *Rochester Whitfield* (1599) Cro.Eliz. 871.
[10] See *Leibo* v. *Buckman* [1952] 2 All E.R. 1057 at 1063, *per* Denning L.J.; *Glinski* v. *McIver*, [1962] A.C. 726 at 741–742 and 777–778.
[11] *per* Lord Devlin, *Glinski* v. *McIver* [1962] A.C. 726 at 768.
[12] See below at p. 256.
[13] *Mitchell* v. *Jenkins* (1833) 5 B. & Ad. 588.
[14] See Chap. 11 below at p. 347.

brought to court, inconvenienced and accused of a criminal offence is not necessarily sufficient. The damage suffered must be of a legally recognised kind. Once **some** damage is established, however slight, damages are "at large" and the plaintiff is not limited to recovering for the compensation for the damage he has actually proved.[15]

Types of damage

The law as to which types of damage are sufficient to establish a cause of action in malicious prosecution was laid down as long ago as 1698 by Holt C.J. in the famous case of *Saville* v. *Roberts*.[16] There were, he said, three kinds of damage which would be sufficient ground to support this action:

> "1. The damage to a man's fame, as if the matter whereof he is accused be scandalous . . .
> 2. The second sort of damages . . . are such as are due to the person; as where a man is put in danger to lose his life, or limb or liberty . . .
> 3. . . . damage to a man's property as where he is forced to expend his money in necessary charges to acquit himself of the crime of which he is accused . . . "[17]

It is now established that the word "scandalous" used under the first head is synonymous with the word "slanderous" as used in the law of defamation.[18] In other words, the accusation that the plaintiff was guilty of the crime of which he was subsequently not convicted must have been one which "tended to lower him in the estimation of right-thinking members of society generally."[19]

It can be seen that this definition of "damage" is an extremely wide one. It appears that if the crime of which the plaintiff had been accused was one punishable by imprisonment he has suffered sufficient damage under Holt C.J.'s first and second heads.[20] This will cover the majority of cases in which prosecutions are instigated by the police.

"Damage" in relation to minor offences

Potential difficulties arise when the offence for which the plaintiff was prosecuted was a minor, "regulatory" one, punishable only by a fine. This area was considered in some detail in the case of *Berry* v. *BTC*.[21]

[15] See Chap. 11 below at p. 341.

[16] 1 Ld.Raym. 374; 5 Mod. Reports 405. There are no less than ten reports of this case, including two completely different ones in the Modern Reports. The two for which references are given are the only ones which gave the passage cited.

[17] 1 Ld.Raym. 374 at 378.

[18] *Berry* v. *BTC* [1962] 1 Q.B. 306 at 335.

[19] See *Sim* v. *Stretch* [1936] 2 All E.R. 1237 at 1240.

[20] *Wiffen* v. *Bailey* [1915] 1 K.B. 600; although it appears that, originally, actual loss of liberty had to be proved to establish damage under the second head; see *Berry* v. *BTC* [1961] 1 Q.B. 149 at 161.

[21] [1962] 1 Q.B. 306.

Mrs Berry had been accused and convicted of wrongfully pulling the communication cord on a train. She was acquitted on appeal and awarded 15 guineas costs. This still left her £64 2s. out of pocket on legal expenses. She then brought an action for malicious prosecution. Diplock J. found against her on the preliminary issue of whether there was sufficient damage to found an action. He was bound by a previous Court of Appeal case to hold that the difference in costs was not sufficient "property damage." He considered whether or not the accusations were "scandalous" and said that the correct question was "Is the statement that the plaintiff was charged with the offence capable of a *non*-defamatory meaning?"[22] If a non-defamatory meaning is possible then there is no damage under the first head of *Saville* v. *Roberts*.[23]

The Court of Appeal did not comment on this analysis of "scandalous" but gave full consideration to the question of "property damage." It was held that, despite the rule in civil cases, in criminal cases a party's "taxed" costs were not presumed to be full compensation for costs actually incurred. It followed that any difference between awarded and actual costs was sufficient "property damage" to found an action in malicious prosecution.[24]

In summary, therefore, there is sufficient damage in law if either:

(1) the plaintiff was charged with a imprisonable offence; or
(2) the charge was necessarily defamatory to the plaintiff; or
(3) the plaintiff incurred any legal or other costs in defending the charge.

It is difficult to imagine many charges brought by the police which will not have one of these three consequences.

4. THE PROSECUTION

Introduction

The second element in the tort of malicious prosecution is the prosecution itself. This must have been "instituted or continued" by the defendant. The classic, but unhelpful statement of the law is that of Lopes J. in the case of *Danby* v. *Beardsley*[25] where he says that the question to be asked is, "Is there any evidence to show that the defendant was actively instrumental in putting the law in force?"

Two matters require further clarification. First, the actual point at which a prosecution is in fact commenced. Secondly, what role does the defendant in fact have to take to be "the prosecutor."

[22] [1961] 1 Q.B. 149 at 166; see also *Wiffen* v. *Bailey* [1915] 1 K.B. 600.
[23] 1 Ld.Raym. 374; 5 Mod. Reports 405.
[24] See the judgment of Devlin L.J. in *Berry* v. *BTC* [1962] 1 Q.B. 306.
[25] (1880) 43 L.T. 603.

The commencement of a prosecution

On the standard view, a prosecution consists in "setting a judicial officer in motion."[26] In theory, this is done by the "laying of an information" before a magistrate. In practice, however, proceedings often begin with the arrest or charging of a suspect and without a formal "information" being laid.

It is clear that, once a plaintiff is actually brought before a court a "judicial officer" is in motion and a prosecution has been instituted.[27] Difficult problems may arise when a prosecution comes to an end at a very early stage.

It has been held in Canada that the laying of an information before a magistrate is sufficient "institution" of proceedings even though it is withdrawn before a summons or a warrant have been issued.[28] It was suggested that the essential matter is not whether the magistrate has acted "judicially," but whether the informant has done all he can do to launch criminal proceedings.

In *Mohamed Amin* v. *Bannerjee*[29] the Privy Council held that a complaint made to a magistrate who held a public inquiry and then dismissed it was a sufficient "prosecution." It was emphasised that "prosecution" should not be taken in a technical sense. Thus, the test as to whether an actual "prosecution" has been instituted was not whether proceedings have reached a stage at which they may be correctly described as a "prosecution" but whether they have reached a stage at which damage to the plaintiff results.

Nevertheless, problems remain where matters are brought to an end without an information being laid or a court becoming involved. It is submitted that a prosecution will have begun if the plaintiff has been charged.[30] Thus, if the police decide not to proceed after having charged the plaintiff a potential action for malicious prosecution will lie.

The defendant's role

The prosecution must have been "instituted" by the defendant. He does not have to have conducted the entire prosecution himself. It is sufficient that he should have signed the charge sheet and expressed his willingness to give evidence.[31] Anyone who actually "makes a charge" before a magistrate or to the police will be potentially liable in an action for malicious prosecution.

[26] *Austin* v. *Dowling* (1870) L.R. 5 C.P. 534 at 540; *Sewell* v. *National Telephone Co.* [1907] 1 K.B. 557 (C.A.).

[27] See *R.* v. *Elliott* [1985] Crim.L.R. 310.

[28] *Casey* v. *Automobiles Renault* (1965) 54 D.L.R. (2d) 600.

[29] [1947] A.C. 322 at 331.

[30] See *R.* v. *Brentwood JJ., ex. p. Jones* [1979] R.T.R. 155; Prosecution of Offenders Act 1985, s.15(2); for a detailed discussion, see Andrew Sanders, "Malicious Prosecution—Further Problems" (1986) 83 L.S.Gaz. 1626.

[31] *Malz* v. *Rosen* [1966] 1 W.L.R. 1008; *Romegialli* v. *Marceau* (1963) 42 D.L.R. (2d) 481.

The situation is more complex if no actual "charge" is made but the facts are merely stated to a magistrate. If someone goes before a magistrate and gives an **honest** account of the facts as he believes them to be, leaving the decision as to whether or not to act to the magistrate then no action for malicious prosecution will lie.[32] The exact reasoning behind this is not entirely clear. On the other hand, if the accuser knows his story to be false then he is liable to be sued for malicious prosecution.[33]

It is clear that a defendant will be a "prosecutor" for these purposes even if, technically, the decision as to whether or not to proceed was taken by someone else. Thus, a private individual who goes to the police and makes false accusations as a result of which the police commence a prosecution can be sued directly.[34]

If an individual police officer "institutes" proceedings by making a report implicating the plaintiff in a crime then he will be potentially liable in malicious prosecution. He will be potentially liable even if the actual decision to prosecute was taken by his superior.[35] The police continue to institute proceedings under the Crown Prosecution Service and their liability in malicious prosecution remains unchanged.[36] It is submitted that if a prosecution is instituted by the Director of Public Prosecutions after false allegations made by police officers an action will lie against the officers.

The case of *Evans* v. *London Hospital*[37] must be treated with some care. The case involved an action against a hospital which had provided incorrect post-mortem information which had led to the prosecution of the plaintiffs for murder. The mistake was discovered before trial and no evidence was offered. The claim was struck out by Drake J. because the defendant was not the "prosecutor" in the required sense. The judge put the matter as follows:

> "It was for the police or the D.P.P. (in reality, clearly for the D.P.P.) to decide whether or not to prosecute and I think the proposed addition of a claim of malicious prosecution against the defendants or any of them is misconceived. That is sufficient to dispose of that proposed cause of action. However, I think there are other grounds for doubting whether the defendants can be said to have 'set the law in motion.' "[38]

These "other grounds" are, it is submitted, the correct ones. The reports provided by the defendants were requested by the police who were already investigating the offence. The law was, therefore, already in motion when the defendants became involved. The first ground suggested by Drake J. is not consistent with the authorities. It is not relevant that the defendant did not, technically, "make the decision to prosecute" as long as he, in fact, "set the law in motion."

32 *Pandit Gaya Parshad Tewari* v. *Sardar Bhagat Singh* (1908) 24 T.L.R. 884; *Cohen* v. *Morgan* (1825) 6 D. & R. 8.

33 *Pandit Gaya Parshad Tewari* v. *Sardar Bhagat Singh* (1908) 24 T.L.R. 884; *Farley* v. *Banks* (1885) 4 E. & B. 493 at 499; *Hope* v. *Evered* (1886) 17 Q.B.D. 338 at 340.

34 *Malz* v. *Rosen* [1966] 1 W.L.R. 1008; a malicious prosecution action against the police themselves would not succeed if they were acting honestly on the information supplied.

35 *Malz* v. *Rosen* [1966] 1 W.L.R. 1008.

36 See generally, R. Clayton and H. Tomlinson, "Police Malice and Crown Prosecutors," (1985) 84 L.S.Gaz. 3505.

37 [1981] 1 W.L.R. 184.

38 *Ibid.* at 189.

A defendant will be liable if, after having properly commenced proceedings, he subsequently learns of facts which mean that he has no reasonable cause for the prosecution but nevertheless carries on with it, as Lord Cockburn C.J. said in the case of *Fitzjohn* v. *Mackinder*.[39]

> "A prosecution, though in the outset not malicious, as having been undertaken at the dictation of a Judge or magistrate, or, if spontaneously undertaken, from having been commenced under a bona fide belief in the guilt of the accused, may nevertheless become malicious in any of the stages through which it has to pass if the prosecutor, having acquired positive knowledge of the innocence of the accused, perseveres *malo animo* in the prosecution, with the intention of procuring *per nefas* a conviction of the accused."

5. FAVOURABLE TERMINATION OF THE PROSECUTION

Introduction

The third element to be established by the plaintiff is that there was a "favourable termination" of the prosecution instituted or continued by the defendant. The usual situation will be an acquittal after a criminal trial. But "favourable termination" has much wider sense. The plaintiff does not have to show that there was an acquittal on the merits and there is no question of his having to show that he was, in fact, innocent of the charge.

It will be a "favourable termination" if the prosecution was discontinued with the leave of the court,[40] or if the indictment was quashed for formal reasons.[41] The same is true for a conviction which is quashed on appeal for whatever reason.[42]

If justices refuse to commit at the end of committal proceedings this is a "favourable termination" even though new proceedings could be brought.[43] If proceedings are abandoned without the leave of the court being sought then, on the balance of the authorities, there is a "favourable termination."[44] This is also the case when the proceedings are brought to an end with the plaintiff's consent and on agreed terms.[45] Thus, if the prosecution offer no evidence after the defendant has agreed to a bind over there is a

[39] (1861) 9 C.B.(N.S.) 505 at 531; see also, *per* Lord Goddard C.J., *Tims* v. *John Lewis* [1951] 2 K.B. 459 at 472. This is also the position in the United States, see *Prosser on Torts* at p. 836.

[40] *Watkins* v. *Lee* (1839) 5 M. & W. 270.

[41] *Jones* v. *Gwynn* (1712) 10 Mod. 148; *Wicks* v. *Fentham* (1791) 4 T.R. 247.

[42] *Herniman* v. *Smith* [1938] A.C. 305 at 315; *Reynolds* v. *Kennedy* (1748) 1 Wils. 232.

[43] See *R.* v. *Essex JJ., ex p. Churchill* (1933) 49 T.L.R. 283 which says that a refusal to commit is a "dismissal" for costs purposes.

[44] See *Pierce* v. *Street* (1832) 3 B. & Ad. 397; *Watkins* v. *Lee* (1839) 5 M. & W. 270; *Mills* v. *Kelvin & White* (1913) 50 Sc.L.R. 331, which are all civil cases: *cf.*, *Arundell* v. *Tregano* (1607) Yelv. 116; *Casey* v. *Automobiles Renault* (1965) 54 D.L.R. (2d) 600.

[45] *Craig* v. *Hasell* (1843) 4 Q.B. 481 at 492.

"favourable termination" even though the proceedings have been terminated with the plaintiff's consent. The position when proceedings are brought to an end by being stayed by a *nolle prosequi* from the Attorney-General is unclear. It seems likely that this will also be regarded as a "favourable termination."[46]

It is unclear whether there will be a "favourable termination" when the court directs that the charges or indictment should "lie on the file, not to be proceeded with without the leave of the Court or the Court of Appeal." This is common practice after a defendant has pleaded guilty to some counts on an indictment or has been found guilty on one indictment and there is another one outstanding. The effect of such an order is clear, it

> "starts off by having the same effect as an order for an adjournment but an adjournment which it is accepted may never result in a trial."[47]

In the majority of cases in which such an order is made there will be no further trial.[48] Such an order cannot be challenged by an application for judicial review.[49] It remains unclear whether such an order can be made without the consent of the accused but, in any event, he appears to have no remedy if an order is made without his consent.[50] Given that the order has the same effect as an adjournment it is submitted that it does not represent a favourable termination of the prosecution. If such an order were made in circumstances in which the accused is contemplating a malicious prosecution action then he could apply to the trial judge or the Court of Appeal for an order that the charges or the indictment be listed for hearing.

Malicious prosecution actions after convictions

There are two quite common situations in which a person who is actually convicted can, nevertheless, begin an action for malicious prosecution. The first is where he is acquitted as charged but convicted of a less serious offence. This appears to be sufficient "favourable termination." As Wills J. said in *Boaler* v. *Holder*[51] "To put a man on his trial for a much graver offence than you have any chance of convicting him is a legal wrong." Thus if a person is charged with grievous bodily harm but convicted of only common assault than a malicious prosecution action would lie.

The second situation concerns a person who is charged with a number of offences and is convicted on some counts but acquitted on others. According to *Reed* v. *Taylor*[52] this is a "favourable termination" in relation to the counts on which he was acquitted. In the later case of *Delisser* v. *Towne*[53] it was suggested that this decision appeared to be in conflict with the well

[46] See Winfield & Jolowicz at p. 554.
[47] *R.* v. *Central Criminal Court, ex p. Raymond* [1986] 1 W.L.R. 710 at 714H.
[48] *Ibid.* at 715A.
[49] *Ibid.*
[50] *Ibid.*
[51] (1887) 3 T.L.R. 546.
[52] (1812) 4 Taunt. 616.
[53] (1841) 1 Q.B. 333 at 339.

known case of *Johnstone* v. *Sutton*[54] It is submitted that the cases do not in fact conflict. The point in *Johnstone* v. *Sutton* is that there should be no action for malicious prosecution if the additional charges on the indictment (that is, the ones on which the plaintiff was acquitted) "created no additional trouble, vexation, or expenses" because the action "is not adapted to so trifling a complaint."[55] If the additional charges do create additional damage then, it would follow, an action would lie. *Reed* v. *Taylor* was followed in the first instance case of *Palmer* v. *Birmingham Manufacturing.*[56]

This line of authority was approved by the Court of Appeal in *Leibo* v. *Buckman*[57] which concerned a plaintiff who had worked for the defendant who had agreed to pay for some tools for him and had given him £35 towards these. The plaintiff submitted various receipts for tools, including one for £7 15s which the defendant discovered to be forged. The defendant prosecuted the plaintiff for theft of the whole sum. The plaintiff was acquitted and brought an action for malicious prosecution. The jury said that the defendant did not honestly believe his charge and the plaintiff's guilt and that he was acting maliciously. The judge ruled that there was no evidence on which a jury could find that the proceedings were not brought honestly and entered a verdict for the defendants. On appeal a majority of the Court of Appeal (Denning L.J. dissenting) held that the plaintiff was entitled to succeed because, although the defendant may have had reasonable and probable cause for preferring a charge in respect of the £7 15s he had none for the balance and therefore the whole charge was preferred without reasonable and probable cause.

These principles may be of some practical importance. Take for example a situation where it appears that the prosecution have, as a tactical manoeuvre designed to obtain pleas of guilty to lesser offences, charged an accused with a number of serious matters on which the evidence is slight. If a "deal" was finally arrived at whereby no evidence was offered on the serious charges in return for guilty pleas on the less serious ones then, it is probable that an action in malicious prosecution would lie in relation to the more serious charges.

In general, however, when the plaintiff has been convicted as charged, there can be no action for malicious prosecution even if he can show that it was grossly unjust or procured by fraud and there was no right of appeal.[58]

Thus if corrupt police officers fabricate evidence to procure a conviction, no action can be brought until the conviction is actually overturned. This rule has been criticised, and it is difficult to see why a plaintiff convicted on demonstrably perjured evidence cannot obtain redress in the civil courts without a formal quashing of his conviction. The view of Byles J. in *Basébé* v. *Matthews*[59] was that otherwise every case would have to be retried on its merits, but, this is surely an exaggerated fear. It is unlikely that large numbers of convicted criminals would start using the action for malicious

[54] (1786) 1 T.R. 493 at 547.
[55] *Ibid. per* Lord Mansfield and Lord Loughborough.
[56] (1902) 18 T.L.R. 552.
[57] [1952] 2 All E.R. 1057.
[58] *Basébé* v. *Matthews* (1867) L.R. 2 C.P. 684; *Metropolitan Bank* v. *Pooley* (1885) 10 App.Cas. 210; *Everett* v. *Ribbands* [1952] 2 Q.B. 198.
[59] (1867) L.R. 2 C.P. 684.

prosecution as a means of self-vindication. This could be avoided by requiring a plaintiff in such circumstances to show strong evidence to call the conviction into question before being allowed to proceed.[60]

6. LACK OF REASONABLE AND PROBABLE CAUSE

Introduction

The most difficult aspect to prove in any action for malicious prosecution is the lack of a reasonable or probable cause for the prosecution. "Reasonable" and "probable" appear to be synonyms and the general view is that the second word adds nothing to the first. The plaintiff's difficulty stems from the fact that he has the heavy burden of proving a negative. In line with the usual general principle, the court will not order a defendant to give further and better particulars of a simple denial of lack of reasonable and probable cause.[61] The plaintiff thus has very little to go on. He may well not know what, specifically, the defendant is alleging was the "reasonable and probable cause" for the prosecution but must prove that he did not have it. This difficulty is often considerably mitigated in practice by bringing a malicious prosecution action in tandem with one for false imprisonment. In the latter action the burden is on the defendant to show a justification for the imprisonment. This is likely to be closely related to the reasonable and probable cause which he implicitly relies on to justify his prosecution.

The question of whether there was a reasonable and probable cause is one for the judge[62] while incidental questions of fact are for the jury.

Such questions of incidental fact can, however, only be put to the jury if there is some affirmative evidence of the absence of reasonable and probable cause.[63] According to the Australian case of *Mitchell* v. *Heine & Sons*[64] it is not sufficient to suggest that, because the information before the prosecutor was very weak, an inference can be drawn that he lacked reasonable and probable cause for the prosecution. Some evidence must be led of his actual state of belief. It is submitted that this is incorrect and that, as in other cases, inferences as to belief can be drawn from all the circumstances of a case.

The meaning of "reasonable and probable cause"

The exact meaning of "reasonable and probable cause" has long caused difficulty. The standard explanation is that given by Hawkins J. in the case

[60] See Winfield & Jolowicz at p. 555.

[61] *Stapeley* v. *Annetts* [1907] 1 W.L.R. 70, although the courts will order particulars of a pregnant negative, see Chap. 3 above at p. 72.

[62] See, *e.g. Lister* v. *Perryman* (1870) L.R. 4 H.L. 521.

[63] *Ibid.*

[64] (1938) 38 S.R.(N.S.W.) 466.

of *Hicks* v. *Faulkner*[65] and approved by the House of Lords in *Herniman* v. *Smith*.[66]

> "an honest belief in the guilt of the accused based upon a full conviction, founded upon reasonable grounds, of the existence of a state of circumstances, which, assuming them to be true, would reasonably lead any ordinarily prudent and cautious man, placed in the position of the accuser, to the conclusion that the person charged was probably guilty of the crime imputed."

This involves four separate questions,[67] the first two being subjective and the second two objective. The questions are as follows:

(1) Did the prosecutor have an honest belief in the guilt of the accused?
(2) Did the prosecutor have an honest conviction of the existence of the circumstances relied on?
(3) Was this conviction based on reasonable grounds?
(4) Did the matters relied upon constitute reasonable and probable cause for the belief in the accused's guilt?

The first two questions are, in effect, for the jury, the second two are for the judge and are the nub of the issue of "reasonable and probable cause."

The questions for the jury

The questions relating to the defendant's beliefs are regarded as "incidental questions of fact" and are, therefore, for the jury.[68] But they do not arise in every case.[69]

The exact form of the question has long been a matter of dispute. In *Abrath* v. *N.E. Ry. Co.*[70] the House of Lords suggested that it should be in two parts: (1) Did the defendant take reasonable care to inform himself of the state of the case? (2) Did he honestly believe his case? These questions might seem eminently sensible, but unfortunately they leave nothing for the judge to do. As H. Stephen points out[71] if the answer to both is "yes" the plaintiff loses, if the answer to either is "no" the plaintiff wins.

These difficulties led to the Court of Appeal suggesting, in *Tempest* v. *Snowden*[72] that a single question be put to the jury "Did the defendant honestly believe in the plaintiff's guilt?" The approved formulation is now "Did the defendant honestly believe in the charges he was making?" or "Did the prosecutor honestly believe in his case?"[73]

[65] (1881) 8 Q.B.D. 167 at 171.
[66] [1938] A.C. 305.
[67] See the argument of counsel in *Abbott* v. *Refuge Ass. Co.* [1962] 1 Q.B. 432 at 443 and also the judgment of Upjohn L.J. at 453–454.
[68] *Glinksi* v. *McIver* [1962] A.C. 726 at 754, *per* Lord Radcliffe.
[69] *Ibid.* at 754; *Blachford* v. *Dod* (1831) 2 B. & Ad. 179.
[70] (1886) 11 App.Cas. 247.
[71] *Malicious Prosecution* at pp. 82–83.
[72] [1952] 1 K.B. 130.
[73] *Glinski* v. *McIver* [1902] A.C. 726 at 761, 767; *Dallison* v. *Caffrey* [1965] 1 Q.B. 348 at 368.

This form of the question will usually be sufficient to deal with both "subjective" questions although cases may arise in which the jury must be asked specifically whether the prosecutor believed in "the circumstances relied on." A number of points arise in relation to these questions.

First, it is necessary to consider whether a prosecutor must actually believe in the guilt of the accused. On a number of occasions Lord Denning has forcefully argued that the prosecutor's belief is irrelevant. Thus in *Tempest* v. *Snowden*[74] he states that "once the facts as known to the prosecutor are ascertained, the state of his belief goes only to malice, and not to reasonable and probable cause." He repeats the same view in *Glinski* v. *McIver* but the general view of the rest of the House is against him and his statements in the earlier case are disapproved.[75] The beliefs of the prosecutor **are** relevant to reasonable and probable cause and if the prosecutor personally does not believe the accused is guilty then he lacks reasonable and probable cause even if a reasonable man could have believed in the accused's guilt on the basis of the facts known to the prosecutor. As Lord Denman C.J. said in *Haddrick* v. *Heslop*[76]:

> "It would be quite outrageous if, where a party is proved to believe that a charge is unfounded, it were to be held that he could have reasonable and probable cause."

The second question concerns the strength of belief that is required of a prosecutor. It is clear that it is not necessary for him to believe that the accused **is guilty**,[77] or that he will probably be convicted.[78] Perhaps all that he has to believe is that there is a prima facie case against the accused. Overall, the law appears to be, as Dixon J. put it in an Australian case, that the prosecutor must believe that "the probability of the accused's guilt is such that upon general grounds of justice a charge against him is warranted."[79]

Thirdly, it is necessary to consider which "circumstances" are relevant to the prosecutor's beliefs. The relevant facts are those actually known to the defendant at the time he proceeded with the prosecution, not the facts as they actually existed.[80] More specifically, the relevant facts are those which are actually present to the defendant's mind and operating on it at the time when he instituted or continued the prosecution. Facts unknown to him at that time do not prevent the facts known to him from constituting a reasonable and probable cause.[81] Hence, as Lord Denman C.J. said in *Turner* v. *Ambler*[82]:

> "the reasonable and probable cause must appear not only to be deducible in point of law from the facts, but to have existed in the defendant's mind at the time of his proceeding."

[74] [1952] 1 K.B. 130 at 140.
[75] [1962] A.C. 726 at 770, *per* Lord Devlin.
[76] (1848) 12 Q.B. 268 at 274–275.
[77] *Tempest* v. *Snowden* [1952] 1 K.B. 130.
[78] *Dawson* v. *Vasandau* (1863) 11 W.R. 516 at 518.
[79] *Commonwealth Life Assurance Society* v. *Brain* (1935) 53 C.L.R. 343 at 382; approved *Glinski* v. *McIver* [1962] A.C. 726 at 766–767.
[80] *Herniman* v. *Smith* [1938] A.C. 305 at 315.
[81] *Delegal* v. *Highley* (1837) 3 B.N.C. 950; *Herniman* v. *Smith* [1938] A.C. 305; *Wright* v. *Sharp* (1947) 176 L.T. 308.
[82] (1847) 10 Q.B. 252.

The questions for the judge

The third and fourth, "objective questions," are for the judge. The law lays down certain factors to be taken into account. There will be no "reasonable and probable cause" if the circumstances before the prosecutor would not have led "an ordinarily prudent and cautious man" to conclude that the person charged was probably guilty of the offence."[83] This does not take us much further, but Upjohn L.J. has suggested a number of steps that such a man would take:

> "(1) he or his advisers would take reasonable steps to inform himself of his true state of the case, *Abrath* v. *N.E. Ry. Co.*[84]; (2) he or his advisers would finally consider the matter upon admissible evidence only[85]; (3) in all but the plainest cases, he would lay the facts before counsel of standing and experience in the relevant branch of the law and receive the advice that a prosecution is justified. . . . In addition, of course, the defendant must bona fide accept and act on the advice and, though that is part of a subjective test, it cannot be wholly removed from consideration at this stage."[86]

Failure to take any of these steps will be "evidence from which the judge may infer absence of reasonable and probable cause."[87]

In relation to the first of these requirements the prosecutor need only take "reasonable steps."

> "It is not required of any prosecutor that he must have tested every possible relevant fact before he takes action. His duty is not to ascertain whether there is a defence but whether there is a reasonable and probable cause for the prosecution."[88]

Nevertheless, if the prosecutor **knows** that the accused has a good defence—for example, that he did not have the necessary *mens rea* because he was acting under a claim of right—then he has no reasonable and probable cause for his prosecution.[89]

If the prosecutor is mistaken about some matter of fact which, if true, would have given him reasonable and probable cause for the prosecution the question is: was the mistake a reasonable one to make? Reasonable men can make mistakes.[90] It would appear that the "reasonableness" of such a mistake should be regarded as a disputed matter of fact to be left to the jury.[91]

If counsel advises that a prosecution is justified it is unclear whether this

[83] *Glinski* v. *McIver* [1962] A.C. 726 at 754.
[84] (1883) 1 Q.B.D. 440; see also, *Phillips* v. *Naylor* (1859) 4 H. & N. 565.
[85] *Meering* v. *Grahame-White Aviation Co. Ltd.* (1919) 122 L.T. 44; see also *Tims* v. *John Lewis* [1951] 2 K.B. 459 at 474.
[86] *Abbott* v. *Refuge Assurance Co.* [1962] 1 Q.B. 432 at 454.
[87] *Ibid.* at 454–455.
[88] *per* Lord Atkin, *Herniman* v. *Smith* [1938] A.C. 305 at 319; see also *Musgrove* v. *Newell* (1836) 1 M. & W. 582 at 586.
[89] See, *e.g.* *James* v. *Phelps* (1840) 11 A. & E. 483; Clerk & Lindsell at pp. 18–25.
[90] See *Hicks* v. *Faulkner* (1878) 8 Q.B.D. 167.
[91] *Douglas* v. *Corbett* (1856) 6 E. & B. 511.

is conclusive of the question "reasonable and probable cause." In the case of *Ravenga* v. *Mackintosh*[92] Bayley J. said that it was conclusive. This was said by Viscount Simonds in *Glinski* v. *McIver* to be "sound," so that;

> "a police officer who lays an information and prefers a charge, and at every step acts upon competent advice, particularly perhaps if it is the advice of the legal department of Scotland Yard, I should find it difficult to say that the officer acted without reasonable and probable cause."[93]

But this statement was *obiter* and was made without the benefit of the Court of Appeal decision in *Abbott* v. *Refuge Assurance Co. Ltd.*[94] decided some four weeks before *Glinski* was argued. In *Abbott's* case the Court of Appeal took the view that the advice of counsel was an important factor which a reasonable man was entitled to take into account in deciding whether to prosecute, but it was not conclusive and could not, of itself, furnish reasonable and probable cause for a prosecution. This view, it is submitted, represents the law.[95]

The fact that counsel or some other legal adviser has advised that a prosecution has a reasonable prospect of success will, of course, be of no great value if he was not experienced in that type of work or if the whole of the facts were not put before him.[96] Thus, a police officer will not be able to rely on such advice if it can be shown that he put false or incomplete evidence before his advisers.

It appears that there cannot be a lack of reasonable and probable cause if the Attorney-General has granted his *fiat* for a prosecution and it is not shown that the facts were put before him unfairly although authority on this area is sparse.[97]

An important practical point on reasonable and probable cause involves the common practice of an accused agreeing to be bound over to be of good behaviour and, in return, the prosecution offering no evidence against him. This will be a "favourable termination" of the prosecution but the fact of the plaintiff having given such an agreement may be led in evidence by the defendant as evidence of "reasonable and probable cause"; the argument being that the plaintiff would not have agreed to such a course if there had not been some basis for the allegations made. This is a weak argument as an accused may often be advised to agree to a bind over to limit the risk of a conviction and to produce a speedy disposal of the matter. This cannot be construed as an "admission" in relation to "reasonable and probable cause."

Whether or not there is a reasonable or probable cause depends on the particular facts of each case but there are a number of additional matters on which the courts have pronounced. First, the fact that the accused was committed for trial or convicted by a court of first instance does not appear to be decisive of the question of reasonable and probable cause. The point does not seem to have ever been argued but was assumed in cases such as

92 (1824) 2 B. & C. 693 at 697.

93 [1962] A.C. 726 at 745; see also Lord Denning at 759, Lord Radcliffe at 756, Lord Devlin at 777.

94 [1962] 1 Q.B. 432.

95 See Clerk & Lindsell at pp. 18–28.

96 See *Abbott* v. *Refuge Life Assurance Co.* [1962] 1 Q.B. 432 at 448–449, *per* Ormerod L.J.; and *Hewlett* v. *Cruchley* (1813) 5 Taunt. 277.

97 See *Bradshaw* v. *Waterlow & Sons* [1915] 3 K.B. 527.

Herniman v. *Smith*[98] and *Abbott* v. *Refuge Assurance*[99] in both of which the plaintiff had only been acquitted on appeal.

Secondly, there does not, despite some older judicial dicta to the contrary[1] appear to be any rule that no prosecutor can be made liable simply on the ground of a mistake in law. It is always a question of fact and degree. Thus, in *Wershof* v. *Metropolitan Police Commissioner*,[2] May J. held that a police sergeant lacked reasonable and probable cause to prosecute the plaintiff for wilful obstruction of a police officer because he had no grounds for believing that the obstruction was "wilful" in the requisite legal sense. The fact that the sergeant did not appreciate what the legal position was does not appear to be relevant (although the finding here was perhaps based on the judge's view that the sergeant never "applied his mind to the nature of what he considered to be the unnecessary recalcitrance of the plaintiff).[3] If a mistake was made on a difficult question of law this will not be evidence of a lack of reasonable and probable cause.[4] However, it has been held in an Australian case that there will be no reasonable and probable cause where a plaintiff has been prosecuted for an offence which is not known to the law—even if this was done on legal advice.[5]

Thirdly, it is clearly established that want of reasonable and probable cause can never be inferred from malice. As Viscount Simonds put it in *Glinski* v. *McIver*, "even from the most express malice, want of probable cause, of which honest belief is an ingredient, is not to be inferred."[6] He insists that "the importance of observing this rule cannot be exaggerated."[7] It should be noted, however, that an officer who maliciously prosecuted a plaintiff **with** reasonable and probable cause would arguably be guilty of the tort of misfeasance in a public office.[8]

The relationship between the jury and the judge questions

The position so far can be summarised as follows. The absence of reasonable and probable cause is a question for the Judge. The jury's role is the determination of incidental questions of fact. The primary question of fact for their determination is that of the prosecutor's honest belief in his charge. This does not arise in every case but must be asked if there is some evidence of lack of belief.

The relationship between these two sets of questions is now clear[9]:

98 [1938] A.C. 505.
99 [1962] Q.B. 432.
1 See, *e.g. Johnson* v. *Emerson* (1871) L.R. 6 Ex. 329 at 365.
2 [1978] 3 All E.R. 540.
3 *Ibid.* at 553f; May J. went on to find that there was no malice; see also Clerk & Lindsell at pp. 18–27.
4 *Phillips* v. *Naylor* (1859) 4 H. & N. 565.
5 *Mackenzie* v. *Hyam* (1908) 8 S.R.(N.S.W.) 587.
6 [1962] A.C. 726 at 744; see *Johnstone* v. *Sutton* (1786) 1 T.R. 510.
7 *Ibid.*
8 See Chap. 10 below at p. 324.
9 See Street at pp. 404–405.

(1) If the question of honest belief is properly left to the jury and they decide that this was not present, then the judge is bound to hold that there was a lack of reasonable and probable cause. As Lord Radcliffe says: "I take it to be settled law that if the defendant can be shown to have initiated the prosecution without himself holding an honest belief in the truth of the charge . . . he cannot be said to have acted upon reasonable and probable cause."[10]

(2) If, on the other hand, the question of honest belief does not arise **or** the jury decide that an honest belief was, in fact, present, then the judge must go on to consider the "objective" question. This is because "mere belief in the truth of his charge does not protect an unsuccessful prosecutor, given of course, malice, if the circumstances before him would not have led "an ordinarily prudent and cautious man" to conclude that the person charged was probably guilty of the offence."[11]

Thus a plaintiff in a malicious prosecution action can approach the proof of lack of reasonable and probable cause in one of two ways. If he can put forward some evidence that the prosecutor did not "believe his charge" he is entitled to have this question put to the jury.[12] If they find a lack of honest belief then the judge must find that there was no reasonable and probable cause for the prosecution. The second possibility is that he can try to show that, however honest the prosecutor was, a reasonable man would not have brought a prosecution in those circumstances. If a police officer who honestly believes that an accused is guilty initiates a prosecution against him in order to teach him a lesson, or in order to set him up as an example to others, he will be liable in malicious prosecution if the evidence before him would not have led a reasonable man to believe that the accused was probably guilty.

7. MALICE

Definition

The final element in the tort of malicious prosecution is malice. This does not mean spite or hatred but merely "wrongful motive."[13] It is wrongful to intend to use legal process for something other than its legally appointed and appropriate purpose.[14] As Alderson B. put it:

"Any motive other than that of simply instituting a prosecution for the

[10] *Glinski* v. *McIver* [1962] A.C. 736 at 753; see also, *per* Lindley J., *Shrosbery* v. *Osmaston* (1877) L.T. 792 at 794.

[11] *Glinski* v. *McIver* [1962] A.C. 726 at 754, *per* Lord Radcliffe.

[12] *Ibid.*

[13] *Mitchell* v. *Jenkins* (1833) 5 B. & D. 588 at 595; see also *Brown* v. *Hawkes* [1891] 2 Q.B. 718 at 723.

[14] *Pike* v. *Waldrum* [1952] 1 Lloyd's Rep. 431 at 451.

> purpose of bringing a person to justice, is a malicious motive on the part of the person who acts in that way."[15]

It will not, of course, be "malicious" to institute a prosecution because of the prosecutor's anger or indignation at the crime he believes to have been committed.[16]

Although there is no direct authority on the point, it appears that, when the prosecutor's motives are mixed, the prosecution is malicious unless his predominant motive is the vindication of the law.[17] In the case of police officers it has been said by Lord Devlin that "there can be no occasion on which . . . a mixture of motives could be accepted as excusable."[18]

The courts have been asked to rule, at various times, whether particular motives are malicious. Thus, it is well established that prosecuting someone to deter others "is not a motive of such a direct character as to afford a legitimate foundation for a criminal prosecution."[19] Similarly, it is "malicious" to prosecute someone because he gave evidence against the police on a previous occasion[20] or to keep him quiet in other legal proceedings.[21] But it is not malicious to prosecute someone in order to be able to take civil proceedings when the law required that to be done.[22]

The role of the jury

The burden of proving that the prosecution was actuated by a wrongful motive is on the plaintiff and the question of whether or not it existed is one for the jury.[23] But before the question of the defendant's motive can be put to the jury the plaintiff must show that there is a "case to answer." It is for the judge to decide whether there is any evidence of malice to go to the jury.[24] This burden can be discharged either by proving a particular "improper" motive or by showing that, in the circumstances, the prosecution must have been based on such a motive.[25]

The plaintiff's actual motive is a pure jury question. But once the motive has been found whether or not it is wrongful is a matter of law and therefore a question for the judge.

Lack of reasonable and probable cause is evidence from which the jury may infer malice.[26] For this purpose, they can form their own view of what is reasonable and should not be directed by the judge.[27] Thus, if it can be shown that a police prosecution was based on fabricated or perjured evi-

[15] *Stevens* v. *Midland Counties Ry.* (1854) 10 Ex. 352 at 356.
[16] *Brown* v. *Hawkes* [1891] 2 Q.B. 718 at 722.
[17] *Ibid.*; and see Winfield & Jolowicz at p. 519.
[18] *Glinski* v. *McIver* [1962] A.C. 726 at 777.
[19] *per* Alderson B., *Stevens* v. *Midland Counties Ry.* (1854) 10 Ex. 352 at 356.
[20] *Glinski* v. *McIver* [1962] A.C. 726.
[21] *Haddrick* v. *Heslop* (1848) 12 Q.B. 267.
[22] *Abbott* v. *Refuge Assurance Co.* [1962] 1 Q.B. 432.
[23] *Mitchell* v. *Jenkins* (1833) 5 B. & Ad. 588.
[24] *Brown* v. *Hawkes* [1891] 2 Q.B. 718.
[25] *Ibid.*
[26] *Johnstone* v. *Sutton* (1786) 1 T.R. 510; *Brown* v. *Hawkes* [1891] 2 Q.B. 718.
[27] *Hicks* v. *Faulkner* (1878) 8 Q.B.D. 167 at 175.

dence this will be sufficient to establish both lack of reasonable and probable cause, **and** malice. But the lack of reasonable and probable cause will not, of itself, be sufficient to show malice if the jury find that the prosecutor honestly believed in his charge. In such a case there must be further evidence of some indirect motive.[28] If a police officer maliciously prosecutes someone **with** reasonable and probable cause an action for misfeasance in a public office may lie.[29]

8. MALICIOUS PROCESS

Introduction

There are some types of police action which involve the courts but which stop short of actual prosecution. The most obvious examples are the procuring of search or arrest warrants. What civil remedy is available to someone against whom such warrants are issued and who may be put to distress and inconvenience thereby?

It has long been established that an action in tort will lie for the malicious use of legal process falling short of actual prosecution. As Crompton J. said in *Castrique* v. *Behrens*.[30]

> "There is no doubt, on principle, and on the authorities, that an action lies for maliciously and without reasonable and probable cause setting the law of this country in motion to the damage of the plaintiff. . . . But in such an action it is essential to show that the proceeding alleged to be instituted maliciously and without reasonable and probable cause has terminated in favour of the plaintiff, if from its nature it be capable of such a termination."

To succeed in an action for "malicious process" the plaintiff must prove, therefore, that the defendant:

(1) maliciously;
(2) instituted some process;
(3) without reasonable and probable cause;
(4) which caused him damage; and
(5) which, if capable of such termination, terminated in his favour.

If the proceedings are *ex parte* then they will not be capable of termination in the plaintiff's favour. This applies to the most important "malicious process" tort—the malicious procurement of a search warrant. In all cases;

> "The question is not: Was it a prosecution? It is: Were the proceedings capable of being terminated in the plaintiff's favour?"[31]

[28] See *per* Atkin L.J., *Meering* v. *Grahame-White Aviation* (1919) 122 L.T. 44 at 55.
[29] See Chap. 10 below at p. 324.
[30] (1861) 3 E. & E. 709; cited with approval in *Everett* v. *Ribbands* [1952] 2 Q.B. 198.
[31] *per* Somervell L.J., *Everett* v. *Ribbands* [1952] 2 Q.B. 198 at 203.

Malicious procurement of a search warrant

A police officer who maliciously obtains a search warrant without reasonable and probable cause will be liable in tort.[32] As Hirst J. put it in the case of *Bayliss* v. *Hill*[33]:

> "Although there is a paucity of concrete cases on the topic, it is well established . . . that if a person obtains a search warrant on information given by him maliciously and without reasonable and probable cause, the householder in respect of whose premises the warrant is obtained has a valid, although rarely used, cause of action akin to malicious prosecution."

This view was confirmed by the Court of Appeal in the case of *Reynolds* v. *MPC*.[34] Waller L.J. stated the position as follows:

> "There is no dispute that to procure the issue of a search warrant without reasonable or probable cause and maliciously is an actionable wrong (see *Clerk and Lindsell on Torts* (1982) at para. 18–08 and *Everett* v. *Ribbands* [1952] 1 All E.R. 823 at 826; [1952] 2 Q.B. 198 at 205, *per* Denning L.J.) and the burden of proof is on the plaintiff who is asserting that there was no reasonable or probable cause (see *Abrath* v. *North Eastern Rly. Co.* (1886) 11 App.Cas. 247). When the facts on which the application was based are established, it is then for the judge to decide whether it has been proved that there was no reasonable and probable cause for the issue of a search warrant."[35]

In other words, the principles of the tort of maliciously procuring a search warrant are identical to those for malicious prosecution—save that there is no need for a "favourable termination."

The only reported case in which such an action was successful appears to be the old case of *Elsee* v. *Smith*[36] which was approved by the House of Lords in *Roy* v. *Prior*.[37]

Other malicious process torts

There is a long established action known as "malicious arrest."[38] Its original application was to civil arrest but it also applies in criminal matters.[39] This was confirmed by the House of Lords in *Roy* v. *Prior*.[40] The defendant in that case was a solicitor who had issued a witness summons requiring the plaintiff to attend a criminal case. The plaintiff failed to turn up and the

[32] See *Elsee* v. *Smith* (1822) 1 D. & R. 97; *Wyatt* v. *White* (1860) 5 H. & N. 371;

[33] (1984), unreported Transcript: Association.

[34] [1985] Q.B. 881.

[35] *Ibid.* at 886A–B.

[36] [1822] 2 Chitty 304.

[37] [1971] A.C. 470 at 488A.

[38] *Norrish* v. *Richards* (1835) 3 Ad. & E. 733; *Churchill* v. *Siggers* (1854) 3 El. & Bl. 929.

[39] See *Foth* v. *O'Hara* (1959) 15 D.L.R. (2d) 332 at 336.

[40] [1971] A.C. 470.

defendant arranged for an application to be made for a warrant for his arrest. The plaintiff was arrested and held for nine and a half hours. The plaintiff's case was that the summons had never been served on him. The House of Lords held that a good cause of action was disclosed by this allegation.

There appears to be a tort of malicious detention[41] although its limits and application are unclear.

Maliciously procuring someone to be held to bail to keep the peace (that is, to be "bound over") was held to be actionable in *Steward* v. *Gromett*.[42] There was no need for a termination in favour of the plaintiff because, at that time, such proceedings were *ex parte*.

The present position is rather different. Although "bind overs" can be given after a conviction or as part of an agreement for the withdrawal of a charge,[43] "bind over" proceedings are civil in nature and are now brought by way of "complaint" under section 115 of the Magistrates' Courts Act 1980.[44] Such proceedings are *inter partes* and a favourable termination is therefore required. Thus, in *Everett* v. *Ribbands*[45] a police officer laid a complaint at the instance of a third party, for the plaintiff to be bound over to keep the peace. The plaintiff was bound over after a hearing. His action for malicious prosecution was dismissed because there was no "favourable termination."

It is, of course, plain that damages are the only remedy available in an action for malicious prosecution. It is obviously impossible to obtain an injunction to restrain the police from bringing future prosecutions which terminate in the plaintiff's favour! The position is not so clear in relation to malicious process. It is just conceivable that an injunction could be granted to restrain the police from maliciously obtaining unjustified search warrants in the future although it is difficult to see how such an injunction could be obtained in practice.

9. LIMITATION

By section 2 of the Limitation Act 1980, the limitation period for tort actions is six years. Time runs from the date at which the cause of action accrued. There is some doubt as to when a cause of action in malicious prosecution "accrues."

As a general rule when damage is part of the cause of action, the cause of action "accrues" when the damage occurs.[46] This suggests that, in an action for malicious prosecution, time would run from the date the plaintiff incurs damage by being threatened with imprisonment or the charge being made public. This approach is supported by the only reported English case directly on the subject, *Violett* v. *Sympson*.[47] In that case it was held that in

[41] *Crozer* v. *Pilling* (1825) 4 B. & C. 26; *Moore* v. *Gardner* (1847) 4 B. & C. 26.

[42] (1859) 7 C.B.(N.S.) 191.

[43] See above at p. 259.

[44] For "bind overs" generally, see A. P. Carr, *Criminal Procedure in Magistrates' Courts*, Chap. 11.

[45] [1952] 1 All E.R. 823.

[46] See *Whitehouse* v. *Fellowes* (1861) 10 C.B.N.S. 765.

[47] (1857) 8 E. & B. 344.

a case which involved the maliciously procuring of an order against a debtor time runs from the date of making of the order. This case is relied upon by Franks who states the position as follows:

> "in general the cause of action accrues upon the occurence of the damage, but if the damage is inferred not proved then from termination of the proceedings in the plaintiff's favour."[48]

In the case of *O'Connor* v. *Isaacs*,[49] Diplock J. said *obiter*, that although an action in malicious prosecution cannot be brought while the conviction still subsists:

> "Nevertheless, although that is a fact which would have to be proved in order to succeed, time runs in malicious prosecution from the date at which the loss, which is followed by special damage arose."[50]

This was, according to Diplock J. due to the fact that "favourable termination" is not an "essential part of the cause of action."

> "but is a requirement which has to be satisfied before the remedy for the already existing cause of action can be pursued."[51]

This distinction between an "essential part of the cause of action" and a "prior requirement" is an artificial one unsupported by authority. No cause of action in malicious prosecution exists unless the proceedings have terminated in the plaintiff's favour. If a prosecutor acts maliciously and without reasonable and probable cause but a court nevertheless finds the plaintiff guilty, no tort is committed. It is straining language too far to say that such a plaintiff has a "cause of action" but cannot bring an action because a "prior requirement" is not fulfilled. It would seem then that the cause of action in malicious prosecution only accrues when the prosecution has terminated in the plaintiff's favour.

This analysis is supported by the Canadian malicious prosecution case of *Crandall* v. *Crandall*[52] in which it was said that "This cause of action did not accrue, because it was not complete until (the plaintiff's) . . . acquittal." In another Canadian case it was held that, in an action for instituting malicious civil proceedings, time only begins to run when those proceedings are terminated.[53] This approach was not available in *Violett* v. *Sympson* because there was no question of the order being set aside and, therefore, no question of "favourable termination."

The case of *Riches* v. *D.P.P.*[54] involved the striking out of a malicious prosecution case on the ground that it was time barred, Proceedings were commenced against the plaintiff in 1963 and he was convicted in 1964 but his conviction was quashed on appeal on April 7, 1965. The writ was issued on March 6, 1972 thus, on either view, he was out of time. None of the three judges considered which was the correct approach but Davies L.J. said that:

[48] Franks, *Limitation of Actions* at p. 194.
[49] [1956] 2 Q.B. 288; Diplock J. and C.A.
[50] *Ibid.* at 325.
[51] *Ibid.* at 327–328.
[52] (1880) 30 U.C.C.P. 497.
[53] *Mayor of Montreal* v. *Hall* (1885) 12 S.C. 74.
[54] [1973] 1 W.L.R. 1019.

> "this whole case of the plaintiff's was at any rate, if not earlier, barred in 1971—and probably it was barred a good deal earlier."[55]

On the other hand, in the unreported case of *Wenlock* v. *Shimwell*[56] the Court of Appeal took the view that time ran from the date of favourable termination. In that case the prosecution was instituted in the summer of 1958, committal proceedings commencing on September 10, 1958. The plaintiff's conviction was quashed on appeal on February 2, 1960. He issued a writ on September 21, 1964. This contained allegations of "injurious falsehood" relating to statements made before September 1958. The Court of Appeal struck this part of the claim out as being statute barred but allowed the malicious prosecution claim to continue. In other words, it was clearly assumed that time ran from the date of favourable termination because, as Davies L.J. said:

> "You cannot start an action for malicious prosecution unless you can show that the proceedings have terminated in your favour."[57]

This approach would appear to be the correct one.

In an action for malicious arrest or malicious procurement of a search warrant there can be no question of "favourable termination." In such a case time must run from the date of the arrest or of the procurement of the warrant.

10. SOME CONCLUSIONS

The action for malicious prosecution and the related "malicious process" actions do provide a safety net for the citizen, albeit of a very broad mesh. Someone who is unsuccessfully prosecuted by the police in circumstances which lead them to believe that the police were acting improperly does have a right of action. In all serious cases it is likely that such actions would be best brought in the High Court as it is likely that the victim of a malicious prosecution for a serious criminal offence would receive damages in excess of the county court limit of £5,000.

The unsuccesfully prosecuted person should consider the following matters before beginning malicious prosecution proceedings:

(1) is there any evidence that the prosecuting officer did not believe that the charge was justified?;
(2) is there any evidence that they were being prosecuted for some extraneous reason, for example "to teach them a lesson," or to punish them for having impeded police investigations in the past?

An action for malicious prosecution would be pointless without some evidence under one of these headings. The most common situation will be where the police officers in the case have given false evidence in an attempt

[55] *Riches* v. *D.P.P.* [1973] 1 W.L.R. 1019 at 1024.
[56] (1966) April 27, C.A.T. 114A.
[57] *Ibid.* at pp. 4–5.

to obtain a conviction of the plaintiff. If it can be shown that crucial evidence was falsified by the officers who commenced the prosecution it follows that they did not "honestly believe in their case" and that the plaintiff is entitled to succeed in an action for malicious prosecution.

Part 3: Other Actions and Remedies

9. Police Surveillance and Information Gathering: Powers and Remedies

1. INTRODUCTION

The modern police force uses the full range of up to date technological devices to assist in the performance of its duties. Suspects are kept under observation, their houses may be subject to "bugging," mail may be opened and telephones tapped. In addition, large quantities of information about individual citizens are now stored on police computers. These activities are an essential policing function but are, of course, open to potential abuse. Although an interference with someone's privacy is less tangible than an interference with his person it may be just as distressing or damaging. Inaccurate information on police computers may do someone serious financial harm. This chapter deals with the limitations on police activities of this type and the remedies available for abuse.

It is, in strict law, inaccurate to speak of police "powers" of surveillance and information gathering. These activities are, in general, not carried out under any direct statutory or common law authority. They are, in effect, based on the common law principle that whatever is not expressly forbidden by law is permissible.[1] Such activities are not forbidden because they do not, in general, infringe interests of the citizen which are recognised by the common law. Furthermore, parliament has shown itself extremely reluctant to step in to assist the citizen. Although there is some skimpy protection provided by recent legislation[2] the most effective remedy remains an application under the European Convention on Human Rights.[3]

There are considerable legal difficulties in obtaining civil remedies for police misconduct in this area.[4] Furthermore, there are likely to be very serious practical problems in showing that surveillance has taken place at

[1] See *Malone* v. *MPC* [1979] Ch. 344 at 366.

[2] Data Protection Act 1984, see below at pp. 291 *et seq.*; Interception of Communications Act 1985, see below at pp. 286 *et seq.*

[3] See Chap. 14 below at p. 424.

[4] It may, however, be possible to make a complaint: see Chap. 2 above at p. 40.

all. It is of the essence of telephone tapping or "bugging" that the suspect is unaware of what is happening. Similarly, a person is unlikely to become aware of the contents of any police records which relate to him.

An application under the European Convention has thrown considerable doubt on the traditional British system of regulating powers of surveillance and information-gathering by "administrative guidelines." In the important case of *Malone* v. *United Kingdom*[5] the European Court ruled that telephone tapping violated the Convention because it was not "in accordance with the law." This decision led to a new statutory framework for the interception of communications.[6] Nevertheless, many police practices in this area are still governed by administrative guidelines. The guidelines indicating when the post office can assist the police[7] and for aural and visual surveillance[8] remain in the form of Home Office Circulars. No remedy lies for a breach of the guidance contained in such circulars and it is difficult to see how present British police practice is in accordance with the Convention.

Police surveillance and information gathering often involves serious intrusion into an individual's "privacy." The extent to which the English law recognises a "right to privacy" will, therefore, be considered. The doctrine of breach of confidence will then be discussed as a remedy where the police disclose information given to them in confidence and as possible remedy for surreptitious surveillance. The protection given at common law and the Interception of Communications Act 1985 in relation to spying, eavesdropping and interception of communications is then examined. Finally, the Data Protection Act 1984 is scrutinised in order to establish the extent to which it provides assistance to the citizen in relation to information held on police computers.

2. THE RIGHT TO PRIVACY

Introduction: privacy in the United States

The principle of a right to privacy emerged from a famous article published by Warren and Brandeis (who later became a justice of the U.S. Supreme Court) in 1890.[9] Drawing primarily on the law of intellectual property they argued that:

> "in very early times the law gave a remedy only for physical interference with life and property, for trespass vi et armis. Thus the 'right to live' served only to protect the subject from battery in its various forms; liberty meant freedom from actual restraint; and the right to property secured to the individual his lands and his cattle. Later there came a recognition of man's spiritual nature, of his feelings and his intellect. Gradually the scope of these legal rights broadened; now the right to

[5] (1984) 7 E.H.R.R. 14; see below at p. 285 and Chap. 14 below at p. 432.

[6] See below at pp. 286 *et seq.*

[7] Home Office *Consolidated Circular to the Police* s.1, paras. 1.69–1.70.

[8] H.C. Deb. December 19, 1984, Written Answer No. 169, Home Office Guidelines, appended.

[9] Warren & Brandeis, "The Right to Privacy," 4 Harv.Law Rev. 193.

life has come to mean the right to enjoy life—the right to be let alone; the right to liberty securing the exercise of extensive civil privileges; and the term 'property' has grown to comprise every form of possession—intangible, as well as tangible."[10]

Although the proposition that a right to privacy can be derived from preceding English case law is very difficult to support,[11] the article remains enormously influential and has grounded a whole new area of jurisprudence in the United States. Thus in the *Restatement of the Law of Torts*[12] it is stated that:

"(1) One who invades the right to privacy is subject to liability for the resulting harm to the interest of another.
(2) The right to privacy is invaded by
(a) the unreasonable intrusion upon the seclusion of another;
(b) the appropriation of the other's name or likeness;
(c) unreasonable publicity given to the other's private life;
(d) publicity that unreasonably places the other in a false light before the public."[13]

The common law position

Despite these developments in the United States, the English common law has never recognised a right to privacy as such[14] although "privacy" may be indirectly protected by other means.[15] The only occasion on which the courts have been directly asked to consider the existence or effect of such a right was in *Malone* v. *MPC (No. 2)*.[16] In that case the plaintiff issued proceedings after the prosecution had admitted tapping his telephone in a criminal trial brought against him in respect of alleged handling of stolen goods. He claimed that telephone tapping authorised by the warrant of the Home Secretary was unlawful on three main grounds: that it is unlawful to intercept or monitor a person's telephone conversations without his consent based on the right to property, the right to privacy and the right to confidentiality[17]; that the right to privacy contained in the European Convention on Human Rights[18] either conferred direct rights in English law or provided a guide in cases of ambiguity or lack of clarity in English law; and that the tapping was unlawful in the absence of any grant of powers to the executive either by statute or common law.[19] Sir Robert

[10] Warren & Brandeis, "The Right to Privacy," 4 Harv. Law Rev. 193.
[11] See W. F. Pratt, "The Warren and Brandeis Argument for a Right to Privacy" [1975] P.L. 161.
[12] Prosser, 2nd ed.
[13] *Ibid.*, para. 652A.
[14] See the remarks of Lord Denning M.R. in *In Re X (a minor)* [1975] Fam. 47 at 58 and *Turner* v. *Spooner* (1861) 30 L.J.Ch. 801 at 803.
[15] Winfield & Jolowicz at p. 566.
[16] [1979] Ch. 344.
[17] See below at pp. 275 *et seq.*
[18] See Chap. 14 below at pp. 430 *et seq.*
[19] See below at pp. 283–284.

Megarry V.-C. disposed of the claim based on the "right to privacy" in the following way:

> "the contention is that although at present no general right of privacy has been recognised by English law, there is a particular right of privacy, namely, the right to hold a telephone conversation in the privacy of one's own home without molestation. This, it was said, ought to be recognised and declared to be part of English law, despite the absence of any English authority to this effect. As I have indicated, I am not unduly troubled by the absence of English authority: there has to be a first time for everything, and if the principles of English law, and not least analogies from the existing rules, together with the requirements of justice and common sense, pointed firmly to such a right existing, then I think the court should not be deterred from recognising the right.
>
> On the other hand, it is no function of the courts to legislate in a new field. The extension of the existing laws and principles is one thing, the creation of an altogether new right is another. At times judges must, and do, legislate; but as Holmes J. once said, they do so only interstitially, and with molecular rather than molar motions: see *Southern Pacific Co.* v. *Jensen* (1917) 244 U.S. 205, at 221, in a dissenting judgment. Anything beyond that must be left for legislation. No new right in the law, fully-fledged with all the appropriate safeguards, can spring from the head of a judge deciding a particular case: only Parliament can create such a right."[20]

Unsuccessful attempts were made to enact a right of privacy in 1961 and 1967. The most ambitious proposal was put forward by Brian Walden M.P. in 1969 who agreed to withdraw his bill in the face of opposition from the Home Secretary. However, the Younger Committee on Privacy was appointed to consider whether legislation was needed to give further protection to the individual citizen and to commercial and business interests against intrusions into privacy by the private sector. When the Committee reported in 1972, they decided by a majority against creating a "general right to privacy" primarily because it would confer upon the courts too wide discretion in enforcing the law.[21] Instead, three principal recommendations were made: that a new crime and tort of unlawful surveillance be created[22]; that there be a new tort of disclosure or of the other use of information unlawfully acquired[23] and that the Law Commission review the law of breach of confidence so that it could be clarified and put into legislative form.[24] The Law Commission did conduct such a review[25] but no action has yet been taken on the Committee's first two proposals or on those of the Law Commission.

The main thrust for legislative change has in fact come from the need to comply with United Kingdom obligations under the European Convention. The legal controls on police surveillance and information gathering there-

[20] *Malone* v. *MPC (No. 2)* [1979] Ch. 344 at 372.

[21] Report of the Committee on Privacy, Cmnd. 5012 (1972), paras. 33–44 and 661–666.

[22] *Ibid.*, paras. 560–565.

[23] *Ibid.*, para. 632.

[24] *Ibid.*, para. 630.

[25] Law Commission Report 110, *Breach of Confidence* Cmnd. 8388 (1981).

fore have no direct link to a "right to privacy" that exists in English law. This approach may have some merit because the currency of "privacy" has become so devalued that it probably no longer warrants consideration as a legal term of art.[26]

3. BREACH OF CONFIDENCE

Introduction

The Younger Committee believed that the remedies available for breach of confidence provided "much greater protection of privacy than is generally realised."[27] Although the doctrine can be traced back earlier,[28] it is generally thought that breach of confidence derives from the famous case of *Prince Albert* v. *Strange*,[29] a decision which Warren and Brandeis relied heavily upon in arguing there was a general right of privacy.[30] In that case the Prince obtained an injunction on the basis of breach of confidence to prevent an exhibition of the royal couple's etchings against a defendant who had acquired copies without their consent. The doctrine has proved to be extremely flexible and protects not merely trade secrets but personal confidences such as marital secrets[31] and artistic confidences.[32]

The juristic basis of the breach of confidence doctrine is uncertain and controversial. The courts have frequently invoked the law of contract to protect confidential information, particularly in commercial disputes and master and servant cases. On other occasions, the doctrine has been held to arise out of an independent equitable jurisdiction,[33] that he who has received information in confidence shall not take unfair advantage of it.[34] Therefore, it has been said that the approach of the courts has been flexible and pragmatic so that considerations of conceptual neatness have been secondary to the question of whether the court should intervene in the case immediately to hand.[35]

Breach of confidence may provide some assistance where the police invade an individual's privacy. It is possible that the police may be guilty of a breach of confidence in the conventional sense of misusing information imparted "in confidence." The doctrine may also provide a remedy for complaints concerning surveillance devices (other than those involved in intercepting letters and telephone calls which are now governed by the Interception of Communications Act 1985[36]). The ingredients of the cause

[26] R. Wacks, *The Protection of Privacy* at pp. 10 *et seq.*
[27] *Ibid.* para. 630.
[28] See, *e.g. Thompson* v. *Stanhope* (1774) Amb. 737.
[29] (1848) 2 De.G. & Sm. 652.
[30] See above at p. 272.
[31] *Argyll* v. *Argyll* [1967] 1 Ch. 304.
[32] See, *e.g. Gilbert* v. *Star Newspapers* (1894) 11 T.L.R. 4.
[33] *Saltman Engineering* v. *Campbell Engineering* (1948) 65 R.P.C. 203; [1963] 3 All E.R. 413n.
[34] *Seager* v. *Copydex* [1967] 1 W.L.R. 923.
[35] F. Gurry, *Breach of Confidence* at p. 58.
[36] See below at pp. 286 *et seq.*

of action will be discussed in outline before examination of whether breach of confidence can be utilised if confidential information is acquired by police surveillance. Because the police may be able to escape liability altogether by relying on the defence of "just cause or excuse," the nature of this defence then falls to be considered.

The elements of breach of confidence

In order to prove a breach of confidence it is necessary to show all of the following:

(1) that the information is confidential;
(2) that there was a relationship of confidence regarding that information;
(3) that there has been or will be a breach of that relationship of confidence.

(1) Information. The types of information which qualify for protection were described by Megarry J. in *Coco* v. *A. N. Clarke Engineering*[37]:

> "something which is public property and public knowledge cannot *per se* provide any foundation for proceedings for breach of confidence. However confidential the circumstances of the communication, there can be no breach of confidence in revealing to others something which is already common knowledge."

Whether the publication of information has been so extensive as to destroy confidentiality is "a question of degree depending on the facts of the particular case."[38] So, what is confidential in one part of the country may not be in another.[39] How the confidential information is conveyed does not affect whether its publication will be restrained and the doctrine has been applied to information which was given orally,[40] pictorially, such as photographs[41] and possibly by telephone.[42]

(2) The relationship of confidence. A general test to discover if a relationship of confidence exists was put forward by Megarry J. in *Coco* v. *A. N. Clarke Engineering*[43]:

> "It seems to me that if the circumstances are such that any reasonable man standing in the shoes of the recipient of the information would have realised that upon reasonable grounds the information was being given to him in confidence, then this will suffice to impose upon him the equitable obligation of confidence."

Relationships of confidence have been found to exist in a wide variety of

[37] [1969] R.P.C. 41 at 47.
[38] *Franchi* v. *Franchi* [1967] R.P.C. 149 at 153, *per* Cross J.
[39] *Exchange Telegraph* v. *Central News* [1897] 2 Ch. 48.
[40] See *Fraser* v. *Thames Television* [1984] Q.B. 44.
[41] *Pollard* v. *Photographic* (1889) 40 Ch.D. 345.
[42] *Francome* v. *Mirror Group Newspapers* [1984] 1 W.L.R. 892.
[43] [1969] R.P.C. 41 at 48.

circumstances. A banker's obligation of confidence at the very least extends to any information derived from the customer himself.[44] However, the police might justify breaking that obligation by relying on the defence of just cause or excuse[45] and can in any event apply to the court for an order to inspect banker's books under the Bankers Books Evidence Act 1879.[46] A doctor is duty bound not to disclose information from his patient without consent except in the public interest. Thus, a doctor will be obliged, in the public interest, to identify a driver allegedly guilty of dangerous driving.[47] Similarly, the confidential nature of the relationship between a journalist and his informant has been acknowledged[48]; however, a journalist will be guilty of contempt of court if he refused to identify his source[49] although he may have a statutory defence if the information is published—unless the court is satisfied that disclosure is necessary in the interests of justice or national secuity or for the prevention of disorder or crime.[50] Nevertheless, the police may justify breaching a journalist's obligation of confidence by the defence of just cause and excuse[51] and may also apply to the court for production orders under the Police and Criminal Evidence Act 1984.[52]

A third party who acquires confidential information from one of the original parties to the confidence will be liable for breach of confidence. Even if he is unaware that he is receiving information in breach of confidence in the first place, he can be restrained from divulging the information once he knows it was originally given in confidence.[53]

(3) Breach. The final element in the cause of action is an actual "breach" of confidence. It must be proved that the person to whom the information was given by the plaintiff, used or disclosed it, in a manner which was inconsistent with the nature of the relationship in which the information was given.

Subject to any defence based on just cause or excuse[54] the police may be liable for breach of confidence in a wide range of situations. If they take documents which are held by someone in confidence and make them public then the person to whom the confidence is owed can take proceedings for breach of confidence.[55] Similarly, if someone gives confidential business or personal information to the police and they realise it is confidential but nevertheless make it public, they will again be liable for breach of confidence. Thus, the police might be liable for publishing confidential

[44] *Tournier* v. *National Provincial and Union Bank of England* [1924] 1 K.B. 461.
[45] See below at pp. 280 *et seq.*
[46] See Archbold para. 10–79–10–81.
[47] *Huneter* v. *Mann* [1974] 1 Q.B. 767.
[48] *Attorney-General* v. *Mulholland* [1963] 2 Q.B. 477; and see *In re an Inquiry under the Company Securities (Insider Dealing) Act 1985, The Times*, May 7, 1987, on appeal from; April 1, 1987.
[49] *Attorney-General* v. *Mulholland* [1963] 2 Q.B. 477; *Attorney-General* v. *Lumdin* (1981) 75 Cr.App.Rep. 90.
[50] s.10 of the Contempt of Court Act 1981; see *Defence Secretary* v. *Guardian Newspaper* [1985] A.C. 339; *Maxwell* v. *Pressdram Ltd., The Times*, November 12, 1986.
[51] See below at pp. 280 *et seq.*
[52] See Chap. 7 above at pp. 228 *et seq.*
[53] *Fraser* v. *Evans* [1969] 1 Q.B. 349 at 361, *per* Lord Denning M.R.
[54] See below at pp. 280 *et seq.*
[55] Although this may add little to an action for conversion; see Chap. 6 above at pp. 194 *et seq.*

information about a company's financial position and problems[56] or "secret and intimate personal confidences."[57] However, the most important potential application of breach of confidence against the police will be where they acquire confidential information surreptitiously.

Breach of confidence and surreptitious surveillance

The misuse of information obtained from eavesdropping, bugging or any form of surveillance device may render the police guilty of breach of confidence. The difficulty in applying the doctrine to this situation is that, on the traditional view, an action will only lie if there is a breach of confidence by a person to whom information was given in confidence; the action is based on a **relationship** of confidence between two people. If information is acquired by surveillance or eavesdropping, there is no such relationship and therefore no direct conceptual basis for a successful action in breach of confidence. Indeed, there appears to be no reported English case in which an action has succeeded where information has been acquired without there being a "relationship of confidence."

Several older authorities suggest that an action for breach of confidence might arise in any case where information has been acquired by reprehensible means. In *Webb* v. *Rose*[58], an injunction was granted to restrain the printing of conveyancing precedents taken from a conveyancing chambers while in *Millar* v. *Taylor*[59] it was said that an injunction would be granted to prevent

> "surreptitiously or treacherously publishing what the owner had never made public at all nor consented to the publication; . . . Ideas are free. But when the author confines them to his study, they are like birds in a cage which none but he can have a right to let fly."

It seems that these are early copyright cases which turn on the form in which an idea is expressed (rather than the idea as such which is the concern of breach of confidence).[60] In *Lord Ashburton* v. *Pape*[61] Swinfen Eady L.J. said, *obiter*:

> "The principle upon which the Court of Chancery has acted for many years has been to restrain the publication of confidential information improperly or surreptitiously obtained or of information imparted in confidence which ought not to be divulged."

Some commentators have suggested that breach of confidence covers all cases of industrial espionage: that once a plaintiff could show the defendant used information which the defendant knew he was not entitled to without

[56] *Jarman & Platt* v. *Barget* [1977] F.S.R. 260.
[57] *Argyll* v. *Argyll* [1967] 1 Ch. 304.
[58] (1732), cited (1769) 4 Burr. 2303 at 2330.
[59] (1769) 4 Burr. 2303 at 2378–2379.
[60] Law Commission Report 110, *Breach of Confidence* Cmnd. 8388 (1981), para. 4.8.
[61] [1913] 2 Ch. 469 at 475.

the plaintiff's consent an action will lie to restrain him.[62] It is submitted that such an unqualified assertion is not justified on the authorities. Nevertheless, it is difficult to understand a policy distinction which allows A to restrain B from disclosing confidential information which he has directly imparted to him but means that he can do nothing if B has acquired the information surreptitiously, by for example, breaking into his house. It has been suggested that the courts should restrain the publication of confidential information acquired by "reprehensible means."[63] However, the Law Commission thought it was very doubtful under the present law that information acquired by reprehensible means would be impressed with the obligation of confidence[64]; whereas the Commission initially favoured creating a new tort of disclosure or other use of information unlawfully obtained,[65] it eventually preferred dealing with the problem as part of a new statutory tort of confidence.[66]

The position has become somewhat clearer in the light of recent decisions. In the Australian case of *Franklin* v. *Giddins*[67] the defendant stole budwood embodying confidential information in the form of a new strain of nectarine tree from the plaintiff's orchard and was convicted of theft. The plaintiff subsequently brought an action for breach of confidence seeking delivery up for destruction. Dunn J. stated:

> "I find myself quite unable to accept that a thief who steals a trade secret with the intention of using it in commercial competition with its owner and so uses it is less unconscionable than a traitorous servant."[68]

The analogy brought the claim within the scope of the traditional doctrine but the decision has been criticised because the principle of "unconscionableness" is extremely broad.[69] In *ITC Film Distributors* v. *Video Exchange*[70] where documents were obtained in the courtroom by the defendant from the plaintiff by a trick Warner J. accepted *obiter* that:

> "where A has improperly obtained information belonging to B the court will at the suit of B order A to return the document to B and to deliver up any copies of it that A has made and will restrain A from making use of any such copies or of any information contained in the document."[71]

The two reported cases on telephone tapping also indicate that surreptitiously acquiring confidential information may be actionable as a breach of confidence. Curiously, however, in neither case was it argued that no action

[62] J. & R. Jacob "Confidential Communications" (1969) 119 New L.J. 133; but see R. Wacks, "Breach of Confidence and the protection of privacy" (1977) 127 New L.J. 328.

[63] G. Jones, "Restitution of Benefits obtained in breach of another's confidence" (1970) 86 L.Q.R. 463 at 482.

[64] Law Commission Report 110, *Breach of Confidence* Cmnd. 8388 (1981), para. 4.10.

[65] Law Commission Working Paper No. 58, *Breach of Confidence*, para. 134.

[66] Law Commission Report 110, *Breach of Confidence*, Cmnd. 8388 (1981), paras. 6.27–6.46.

[67] (1978) 1 Qd. 72.

[68] *Ibid.* at 80.

[69] F. Gurry, *Breach of Confidence* at p. 165.

[70] [1982] Ch. 431.

[71] *Ibid.* at 438.

would lie because information had been obtained without any party to the telephone conversation being in breach of confidence. In *Malone* v. *MPC (No. 2)*[72] the plaintiff's claim for breach of confidence failed in part on the ground that a right to confidentiality was negatived since:

> "a person who utters confidential information must accept the risk of any unknown overhearing that is inherent in the circumstances of communication . . . I do not see why someone who has overheard some secret in such a way should be exposed to legal proceedings if he uses or divulges what he has heard. No doubt an honourable man would give some warning when he realises what he is hearing is not intended for his ears; but I have to concern myself with the law, and not with moral standards. There are, of course, many moral precepts which are not legally enforceable."[73]

These remarks were disapproved by the Court of Appeal in *Francome* v. *Mirror Group Newspapers*[74] and purportedly distinguished on the footing that Sir Roberty Megarry V.-C. was only dealing with authorised telephone tapping by the police. The plaintiff who was a well-known jockey brought proceedings against the Daily Mirror for publishing an article based on a phone tap by eavesdroppers which allegedly recorded breaches of the racing rules. In upholding the interlocutory injunction restraining the publication, the Court of Appeal decided that there was a serious issue to be tried concerning whether eavesdropping amounted to a breach of confidence. Sir Robert Megarry V.-C. himself awarded an injunction for breach of confidence in similar circumstances in an unreported decision in 1981 preventing the publication of alleged transcripts of telephone conversations between the Prince of Wales and Lady Diana Spencer obtained by telephone tapping.[75]

Unfortunately, there is still no English decision which squarely addresses the question of whether an eavesdropper can be liable for a breach of confidence. Nevertheless, it is submitted that it is strongly arguable that such a cause of action exists and that proceedings may be brought against the police by individuals who are subject to unjustified surveillance.

The defence of just cause or excuse

It is well established that the courts will not intervene to protect a confidence if this would contravene the public interest. As Wood V.-C. put it in *Gartside* v. *Outram*,[76] "there is no confidence as to the disclosure of iniquity." The justification for this defence was explained by Lord Denning M.R. in *Initial Services* v. *Putterill*[77]:

> "It extends to any misconduct of such a nature that it ought to be in the public interest to disclose it to others . . . The exception should extend

[72] [1979] Ch. 344.
[73] *Ibid.* at 376.
[74] [1984] 1 W.L.R. 892.
[75] News Report, *The Times*, May 7 and 8, 1981.
[76] (1856) 26 L.J. Ch. 113.
[77] [1968] 1 Q.B. 398 at 405.

> to crimes, frauds, misdeeds, both those actually committed as well as those in contemplation provided always—and this is essential—that the disclosure is justified in the public interest. The reason is because "no private obligation can dispense with that universal one which lies on every member of society to discover every design which be formed contrary to the laws of society, to destroy the public welfare."[78]

The principle has been held to justify disclosure of fraudulent business practices,[79] alleged miscarriages of justice and corrupt and disgraceful police practices[80] and dangerous medical practices[81] provided they continue to endanger the public.[82] The defence does not depend on proving iniquity against the person claiming breach of confidence and involves balancing the public interest in favour of publication against the public interest in maintaining the right of confidentiality.[83]

In *Malone* v. *MPC (No. 2)*[84] Sir Robert Megarry V.-C. ruled that breaching a confidence by telephone tapping could be justified not only if iniquity was proved but if it was suspected. He stated:

> "If certain requirements are satisfied, then I think that there will plainly be just cause or excuse for what is done by or on behalf of the police. These requirements are, first, that there should be grounds for suspecting that the tapping of the particular telephone will be of material assistance in detecting or preventing crime, or discovering the criminals, or otherwise assisting in the discharge of the functions of the police in relation to crime. Second, no use should be made of any material obtained except for these purposes. Third, any knowledge of information which is not relevant to those purposes should be confined to the minimum number of persons reasonably required to carry out the process of tapping. If those requirements are satisfied, then it seems to me that there will be just cause or excuse for carrying out the tapping, and using information obtained for those limited purposes."[85]

These criteria cannot be said to place an onerous burden on the police; in particular it is suggested that although the police must have "grounds for suspicion" such grounds need not be reasonable or substantial. It is respectfully submitted that this formulation of the doctrine is far too wide and compares unfavourably with the more rigorous approach applied when newspapers attempt to justify the publication of material in breach of confidence.[86] If this test were adopted whenever the police acquire confidential information by surveillance devices, it would make it virtually impossible to envisage any circumstances where they would be acting unlawfully.

[78] See *Annesley* v. *Anglesea (Earl)*; (1843) L.R. 5 Q.B. 317n.
[79] *Gartside* v. *Outram* (1856) 26 L.J.Ch. 113.
[80] *Cork* v. *McVicar, The Times*, October 31, 1984.
[81] *Hubbard* v. *Vosper* [1972] 2 Q.B. 84.
[82] *Schering Chemicals* v. *Falkman* [1982] 1 Q.B. 1.
[83] *Lion Laboratories* v. *Evans* [1985] Q.B. 526; see also *Attorney-General* v. *The Observer, The Times*, July 26, 1986.
[84] [1979] Ch. 344.
[85] *Ibid.* at 380E–G.
[86] See, *e.g. Lion Laboratories* v. *Evans* [1985] Q.B. 526; but compare, *In re an Inquiry under the Company Securities (Insider Dealing) Act 1985, The Times*, May 7, 1987.

However, these dicta may be distinguished if the surveillance was not authorised by the Home Secretary[87] and are probably *obiter* in any event.

4. LIMITATIONS ON POLICE SURVEILLANCE

Introduction

The legal restraints on police surveillance are not extensive. The common law protects the citizen indirectly, if at all. The statutory protection conferred after the Government lost its case against Mr. Malone before the European Court of Human Rights[88] has altered little of substance. Furthermore, it does not extend to "visual" or "aural" surveillance by the police. Nevertheless, it is possible that the police activity in spying or eavesdropping or intercepting letters or tapping telephones can be shown to be unlawful at common law in a limited class of cases. After considering the position at common law the European Convention on Human Rights will be dealt with, before turning to the Interception of Communications Act 1985.

Spying and eavesdropping: the common law position

If an individual is kept under observation he might have a cause of action in assault,[89] intentionally inducing nervous shock[90] or the police may be guilty of harassment.[91] If he is subject to surveillance devices, he may have an action for breach of confidence.[92] However, the most obvious remedies lie in trespass to land and nuisance although these suffer from important limitations.

If a police officer enters onto a person's land to observe him or plant a listening device there, he will be guilty of trespass.[93] Thus damages for trespass were awarded where a defendant secretly installed a microphone in the plaintiff's flat[94] or under her marital bed.[95] If this were done by the police then aggravated and exemplary damages may be available. However, the highly sophisticated nature of surveillance devices has undermined the value of an action in trespass. It is easy to eavesdrop on a person's home without entering it to install the device.

A nuisance will be committed if a person's act or omission unreasonably interferes with another's enjoyment of land. However, in *Victoria Park Racing* v. *Taylor*[96] the High Court of Australia held that spying is not an action-

[87] See *Francome* v. *Mirror Group Newspapers* [1984] 1 W.L.R. 892.
[88] *Malone* v. *United Kingdom* (1984) 7 E.H.H.R. 14; see Chap. 14 below at p. 432.
[89] Chap. 4 above at p. 108.
[90] Chap. 4 above at p. 119.
[91] Chap. 4 above at p. 117.
[92] See above at pp. 275 *et seq.*
[93] Chap. 6 above at pp. 177 *et seq.*
[94] *Greig* v. *Greig* [1966] V.R. 376.
[95] *Sheen* v. *Clegg, The Daily Telegraph,* June 22, 1961.
[96] (1937) 58 C.L.R. 479; petition refused by the Privy Council January 20, 1938.

able nuisance. They refused to prevent racing broadcasts from a high platform built to gain an unimpeded view over the plaintiff's race track since the defendant's activities did not interfere with or intend to interfere with the plaintiff's land but merely made the business less profitable. An action in nuisance also failed where a dentist in Balham sought an injunction against neighbours who installed large mirrors to observe his study and surgery.[97]

The limited usefulness of an action for nuisance in cases of "spying" is confirmed by *Bernstein* v. *Skyways*.[98] In that case, it was held that flying over the plaintiff's land to take photographs did not constitute a trespass to land because an owner's rights in the airspace above his land are limited to such a height as is necessary for the ordinary use and enjoyment of the land. Furthermore, since taking photographs without consent is not unlawful[99] it could not render the aeroplane a trespasser *ab initio*[1] and transform the act into a trespass. However, Griffiths J. went on to say, *obiter*, that:

> "if the circumstances were such that the plaintiff was subjected to the harassment of constant surveillance of his house, accompanied by the photographing of his every activity, I am far from saying that the court would not regard such a monstrous invasion of his privacy as an actionable nuisance for which they would give relief."[2]

It has been pointed out that such behaviour would be a straightforward action in nuisance for disturbing an individual's enjoyment of his land and owes nothing to an "invasion of privacy."[3] Similarly, persistent and protracted harassment by telephone has been held to constitute a nuisance.[4] It is therefore submitted that police observation of a person's house will only be actionable in nuisance if it could be said to constitute an unreasonable interference with his enjoyment of his house or flat. It may, however, be tortious on the basis that the police are guilty of "harassment," intentionally inducing nervous shock or possibly assault.[5]

Intercepting correspondence and telephone tapping: the common law position

The interception of a letter would not be a trespass unless the letter is actually touched; "the eye cannot by the laws of England be guilty of a trespass."[6] Nevertheless, the practice of intercepting letters under the Home

[97] Kenny, *Cases on Tort* at p. 367; cited in the Younger Committee Report Appendix I, p. 291.
[98] [1978] 1 Q.B. 479.
[99] *Sports and General Press Agency* v. *"Our Dogs" Publishing* [1916] 2 K.B. 880 at 884, *per* Horridge J.
[1] See Chap. 6 above at p. 184.
[2] *Ibid.* at 489.
[3] R. Wacks, *The Protection of Privacy* at p. 34.
[4] *Motherwell* v. *Motherwell* (1976) 73 D.L.R. (3d) 62.
[5] Photographing a person against his will is not an assault; see *Murray* v. *Ministry of Defence* [1985] 12 N.I.J.B. 1. See also Chap. 4 above at p. 103.
[6] *Entick* v. *Carrington* (1765) 19 St.Tr. 1030 at 1066 *per* Lord Camden C.J.

Secretary's warrant is of very long standing although the authority for doing so is obscure. The issue was considered by the Birkett Committee which was appointed in 1957 following the disclosure of transcripts of telephone conversations between a barrister and a criminal in connection with professional disciplinary proceedings, by the Home Secretary to the Chairman of the Bar Council. The Committee thought that the Home Secretary's powers were recognised by a statutory exemption from criminal proceedings for post office employees who open or delay letters while acting under his warrant.[7] The Committee also considered the question of whether the Home Secretary's powers emanated from the Royal Prerogative but did not express a concluded view. Their overall conclusion was somewhat tentative:

> "It is difficult to resist the view that if there is a lawful power to intercept communications in the form of letters or telegrams, then it is wide enough to cover telephone communications as well."[8]

The Committee also established that since 1951 the Home Secretary granted warrants to intercept communications to detect crime if the offence was really serious, the normal methods of investigation had been tried and failed and there was good reason for thinking the investigation would result in a conviction[9]; these criteria continued substantially in force until 1980.[10]

The Home Secretary's power to authorise telephone tapping has been extremely controversial. It is frequently suggested that the criteria for issuing warrants are not adhered to[11]; the Government strongly deny this and have been supported by the reviews carried out by Lord Diplock and Lord Bridge. It also seems that telephone tapping may be more extensive and technically efficient than the authorities have admitted.[12] In *Malone* v. *MPC*[13] Sir Robert Megarry V.-C. said that "telephone tapping is a subject which cries out for legislation." The Phillips Commission recommended that the use of surveillance devices should require the specific authority of a warrant issued by a magistrates' court.[14] Nevertheless, the Government has consistently resisted putting administrative practices into a legislative framework.

The lawfulness of telephone tapping was, of course, challenged in *Malone* v. *MPC (No. 2)*.[15] Amongst the various arguments unsuccessfully deployed, it was also claimed that telephone tapping was unlawful because it was not authorised by any express power. However, Sir Robert Megarry V.-C. was unimpressed and said:

> "The underlying assumption of this contention is that nothing is lawful that is not positively authorised by law. As I have indicated, Eng-

[7] Report of Committee of Privy Councillors, appointed to inquire into the interception of communications, Cmnd. 283 (1975), para. 38.
[8] *Ibid.* para. 51.
[9] *Ibid.* para. 64.
[10] The Interception of Communications in Great Britain (1980) Cmnd. 7873, para. 3.
[11] See, *e.g.* T. Bunyon, *The History and Practice of the Political Police in Britain* at pp. 207–209.
[12] *New Statesman*, February 1 and 15, 1980.
[13] [1979] Ch. 344 at 380.
[14] Royal Commission on Criminal Procedure, Cmnd. 8092 (1981), paras. 3.56–3.60.
[15] [1979] Ch. 344.

land is not a country where everything is forbidden except what is expressly permitted. One possible illustration is smoking."[16]

He was also of the view that various statutory provisions were not inconsistent with telephone tapping being lawful.[17]

The legality of the Home Secretary's power to authorise telephone tapping came before the courts in a slightly different way in *R.* v. *Secretary of State for Home Affairs, ex p. Ruddock*.[18] An official of the Campaign for Nuclear Disarmament unsuccessfully alleged that the Home Secretary had acted unlawfully by authorising M15 to tap her telephone for party political purposes. Taylor J. rejected the submission that the court had no jurisdiction to hear the case on national security grounds and held that the Home Secretary was under a duty to act fairly and must therefore act in accordance with his published criteria when issuing warrants. The fact that the Home Secretary had publicly adopted criteria on six occasions from 1951 to 1982 gave rise to a regular practice which the applicant could reasonably expect to continue. However, Taylor J. was not prepared to infer from the evidence that the Home Secretary had issued a warrant in breach of his criteria. The effect of the Interception of Communications Act 1985 will debar a court from hearing such an application in the future.[19]

Surveillance and the European Convention

After failing in the High Court Mr. Malone brought proceedings claiming that telephone tapping violated the European Convention on Human Rights. The European Court of Human Rights unanimously decided that the British Government had breached Article 8 of the Convention[20] since telephone tapping was not "in accordance with the law."[21] It ruled that the law had to be sufficiently clear in terms to give citizens an adequate indication of the circumstances in which and the conditions under which telephone tapping could be carried out. The law had to indicate the scope of any executive discretion and the manner of its exercise in order to give the citizen protection against arbitrary interference.

It is submitted that closely analogous arguments apply to police practices of "aural" and "visual" surveillance covering matters such as the planting of "electronic bugs" and the use of video cameras to observe the activities of people in private places. Such practices are clearly violations of the rights to "respect for private life" in Article 8 and are not "in accordance with the law" being governed only by administrative guidelines. It is submitted that this is also an area which "cries out for legislation."

16 *Malone* v. *MPC (No. 2)* [1979] Ch. 344 at 366.

17 *Ibid.*; the provisions of the Post Office Act 1969 at 370; the Wireless Telegraphy Act 1949 at 379.

18 [1987] 2 All E.R. 518, Taylor J.

19 The Home Secretary in fact argued unsuccessfully that Taylor J. should not exercise his discretion to hear judicial review proceedings for this reason.

20 See Chap. 14 below at p. 430.

21 *Malone* v. *U.K.* (1984) 7 E.H.R.R. 14; see also, the European Commission on Human Rights Report on the case (1983) 5 E.H.R.R. 385.

The Interception of Communications Act 1985

In response to the decision of the European Court in the *Malone* case the Government published a white paper[22] and subsequently the Interception of Communications Act 1985 was enacted. The Bill was, with some justification, described by *The Times* as:

> "one of the Government's 'dumb insolence' measures . . . in which the minimum action possible is taken to comply with the letter of rulings under international agreements."[23]

The 1985 Act regulates interception of post as well as telephone tapping and covers any communication sent by a public[24] telecommunications system.[25] The Act created a new criminal offence where a person intentionally intercepts a communication but provides a defence where the communication is intercepted under a warrant issued by the Secretary of State (or if there are reasonable grounds to believe that the sender or recipient of the communication consented).[26] The Secretary of State cannot issue a warrant unless

> "he considers the warrant is necessary—
> (a) in the interests of national security;
> (b) for the purpose of preventing or detecting serious crime;
> (c) for the purpose of safeguarding the economic well-being of the United Kingdom."[27]

Serious crime is defined as one or more offences if:

> "(a) it involves the use of violence, results in substantial financial gain or is conduct by a large number of people in pursuance of a common purpose; or
> (b) the offence . . . is an offence for which a person who has attained the age of twenty one and has no previous convictions could reasonably be expected to be sentenced to imprisonment for a term of three years or more."[28]

When considering whether to issue a warrant, the Secretary of State must specifically take account of whether the information could be reasonably obtained by other means.[29]

The warrant which is issued will permit interceptions of communications sent to or from one or more addresses specified in it. The address (or addresses) specified in it are those which are likely to be used for communications to or from the persons or premises specified in it. However, it will also be permissible to intercept any other communication as is necessary to intercept those communications allowed under the warrant.[30] These limi-

[22] The Interception of Communications in the United Kingdom, Cmnd. 9438 (1985).
[23] *The Times*, March 6, 1985.
[24] As defined in s.9 of the Telecommunications Act 1984.
[25] As defined by s.4(1) of the Telecommunications Act 1984.
[26] s.1(1) and (2) of the Interception of Communications Act 1985.
[27] s.2(2).
[28] s.10(3).
[29] s.2(3).
[30] s.3(1).

tations can be waived for communications sent or received outside the British Isles if the Secretary of State issues a certificate.[31]

Warrants are normally issued by the Secretary of State (although there is a special procedure for urgent cases) and will last for two months.[32] Warrants issued on the grounds of national security or economic well-being can be renewed for up to six months if they are endorsed to this effect, any other warrant can only be renewed for a month.[33] The Secretary of State has the power at any time to modify the warrant.[34]

When issuing a warrant the Secretary of State must make such arrangements as he considers necessary to ensure that the following are kept to the minimum necessary:

(1) the extent to which the material is disclosed;
(2) the number of people to whom it is disclosed;
(3) the extent to which it is copied;
(4) the number of copies made.

In addition, he must make such arrangements to ensure copies of the material are destroyed as soon as its retention is no longer necessary for the purpose for which it was issued.[35]

The Act is designed to prohibit allegations of telephone tapping or interception of post being made in any court proceedings. The Government has thus ensured that information such as that disclosed to Mr Malone in his criminal trial or the civil proceedings he later instituted cannot be disclosed in the future. Section 9(1) provides that: "In any proceedings before any court or tribunal no evidence shall be adduced and no questions shall be asked which (in either case) tends to suggest" that the section 1 offence was committed or a warrant was issued.[36]

Any person who believes his communications have been intercepted can apply to a tribunal.[37] The issues which the tribunal can consider are extremely limited. Unless the complaint is thought frivolous or vexatious, it can investigate whether a warrant (or certificate) was issued and whether the authorisation requirements of the Act[38] have been followed. If no warrant was issued the tribunal cannot consider the matter further; it is a criminal offence for the police to pursue. Nor can the tribunal concern itself with how the intercepted material is handled if the warrant is properly authorised; the Act therefore does not give the complainant an effective legal remedy where, for example, intercepted material is improperly disclosed. Although the Commissioner appointed under the Act has jurisdiction to consider whether the arrangements made to prevent such abuses are adequate[39] the complainant has no right to be informed of his views.

Complaints can be investigated by the tribunal but the statute seeks to ensure that they can go no further. According to section 7(8):

[31] s.3(2) and (3).
[32] s.4(1) and (6)(*a*).
[33] s.4(6)(*c*).
[34] s.5.
[35] s.6.
[36] Except for proceedings before the tribunal (see below) or if it is relevant to the fairness of a dismissal for committing the criminal offence; s.9(3) and (4).
[37] s.7(1) and (2); Sched. 1.
[38] Under ss.2–5.
[39] See below at p. 289.

> "The decision of the Tribunal (including any decisions as to their jurisdiction) shall not be subject to appeal or liable to be reviewed in any court."

There is an argument that this section does not wholly exclude the possibility of judicial review.[40] An error of law made by the tribunal may deprive it of jurisdiction and render its decision a nullity. It will, therefore, not be a "decision" of the tribunal and will not be caught by a clause which provides that the court has no jurisdiction to review "decisions." In *Pearlman* v. *Keepers & Governors of Harrow School*[41] Lord Denning M.R. said that:

> "no court or tribunal has jurisdiction to make an error of law on which the decision of the case depends."

It appears, however, that this proposition is too broad[42] although it seems that there is a presumption that if an administrative tribunal asks the wrong question its decision is a nullity.[43] As the authorities now stand, it is unclear whether a particular error of law will take a tribunal out of its jurisdiction.[44] It is submitted that if it could be shown that the "interception of communications" tribunal had taken entirely irrelevant matters into account or reached a wholly unreasonable decision then an application judicial review of its decision could be made. Nevertheless, given the lack of a formal hearing and a reasoned decision it is highly unlikely that such an application would succeed in practice.

The complaints procedure under the Act is inadequate for a number of reasons:

(1) the investigative process which the tribunal undertakes does not permit the complainant to see any documents or information disclosed to it unless the person who gave it consents[45];
(2) the Act does not contemplate any kind of hearing and does not permit the complainant to know its findings[46];
(3) although the Prime Minister will be sent a report of the tribunal's findings if the Act is breached, the complainant is simply notified of its conclusion.[47] On the other hand, if no breach is found, the complainant will simply be told that there was no contravention of the Act[48];
(4) the principles the tribunal applies in determining whether the Act is breached are those for judicial review[49]: in other words, the tribunal must decide whether the Secretary of State misdirected himself in law, failed to act in accordance with natural justice or made

[40] See Chap. 13 below at p. 397.
[41] [1979] Q.B. 56 at 70.
[42] See *In re Racal Communications* [1981] A.C. 394.
[43] *Ibid.* at 383, *per* Lord Diplock; see also *R.* v. *Chief Immigration Officer, ex p. Kharrazi* [1980] 1 W.L.R. 1396.
[44] See *R.* v. *Greater Manchester Coroner, ex p. Tal* [1985] Q.B. 67 and see G. Aldous and J. Alder *Applications for Judicial Review* at pp. 31 *et seq.*
[45] Sched. 1, para. 4(2).
[46] *Ibid.*
[47] s.7(4).
[48] s.7(7).
[49] s.7(4).

> a decision which was so unreasonable that no reasonable Secretary of State could have made it.[50] This is rather different from adjudicating on whether the Act has been breached or not.

Nevertheless, if the tribunal decides that the Act has been contravened, it can quash a relevant warrant (or certificate), direct that copies of the intercepted material be destroyed and direct that the Secretary of State pay a specified sum as compensation.[51]

The overall responsibility for ensuring that the provisions of the act are followed lies with the Commissioner appointed under the Act. He must conduct a general review of the way in which the Secretary of State carries out his statutory duties, he must provide annual reports to the Prime Minister and will report to him in any case where the arrangements made for handling intercepted materials are inadequate.[52]

It is doubtful whether the Interception of Communications Act 1985 in fact complies with the judgment of the European Court in the *Malone* case.[53] The Act has not introduced any method of controlling the metering of telephone calls despite the European Court's ruling that the practice of recording telephone numbers of outgoing telephone calls, just as much as telephone tapping itself, must be "in accordance with the law." Although it is now an offence, *inter alia,* for a person running a public telecommunications system intentionally to disclose to another any information concerning the use of the service, no offence will be committed in relation to:

> "any disclosure which is made for the prevention or detection of crime or for the purpose of any criminal proceedings."[54]

It is accordingly submitted that none of the requirements specified by the European Court[55] have been adhered to and that the arrangements which permit the disclosure of information from metering telephone calls violate Article 8 of the Convention.

It has also been suggested that the system of control which operates outside the courts conflicts with the concurring judgment in the European Court of Judge Pettiti[56] that its legality must be tested in a judicial forum. The system for ensuring that warrants once granted are not abused depends entirely upon administrative action rather than the law and may likewise not satisfy the Convention.[57] Moreover, if the system is compared with the procedure reviewed by the European Court in the *Klass* case,[58] it is arguable that the appointment of the Commissioner and tribunal do not meet the requirement of independence and that the failure of the Act to ensure that an individual is notified of the fact of his surveillance also breaches the Convention.[59]

[50] See, Chap. 13 below at p. 400.
[51] s.7(5).
[52] s.8.
[53] (1984) 7 E.H.R.R. 14.
[54] Sched. 2, substituted for s.45 of the Telecommunications Act 1984.
[55] See above at p. 285.
[56] (1984) 7 E.H.R.R. 14 at 49–55.
[57] Feldman at p. 463.
[58] (1978) 2 E.H.R.R. 214; see Chap. 14 below at p. 431.
[59] See I. J. Lloyd "The Interception of Communications Act 1985" (1986) 49 M.L.R. 8.

5. POLICE COMPUTERS AND PERSONAL DATA

Introduction

The police now use a variety of computers to collate, process and store large quantities of personal information. Since 1972 the Police National Computer has provided a vast information base to assist with police work. Individuals can be identified by a name check using the criminal names index (which lists people with criminal convictions and those awaiting court hearings), the wanted and missing persons index and the disqualified drivers index. Individuals and their cars can be traced from the vehicle registration number through the vehicle driver index (which is linked to the Driver and Vehicle Licensing Centre in Swansea), the stolen and suspect vehicle index and the stolen chassis/engine index. Finally, the police are able to link central and regional records by means of the fingerprints index and the cross-reference index.[60]

Several criticisms have been levelled at this police facility. It appears relatively straightforward to gain access to the data base by, for example, simply pretending to be police officers.[61] The police also pass on information to public bodies without any express statutory authorisation to do so; thus, reports of current convictions are made to public and professional bodies for doctors, dentists, nurses, people employed in charge of children, youth leaders, civil servants, atomic energy and post office employees, barristers and solicitors.[62] Sometimes the information which the police rely on is very inaccurate. To a large extent the dangers posed by police computers are the same as those claimed in relation to all abuse of computerised information storage systems, that information held in large computerised stores represents a fundamental intrusion on personal privacy. However, it has been pointed out that this conventional objection is too broad to be of assistance in the detailed process of devising the necessary remedial measures.[63]

The common law provides little protection for misuse of computer information. A person who discovers that the police have disclosed untrue or misleading information may bring an action for defamation but the police could probably rely on the defence of qualified privilege.[64] The negligent disclosure of confidential information might in some circumstances give rise to a cause of action in negligence.[65] It has even been suggested that an action might lie for the tort in *Rylands* v. *Fletcher*[66] but this is, to say the least, far-fetched.[67] There will only be a potential remedy for breach of confidence if the information concerned was originally acquired "in confidence."[68]

[60] See generally, C. Pounder, *Police Computers and the Metropolitan Police.*
[61] See *The Observer*, November 8, 1981.
[62] "Computer: Safeguards for Privacy" Cmnd. 6354 (1975), para. 40.
[63] C. Tapper, *Computer Law*, Chap. 5.
[64] Chap. 10 below at p. 319.
[65] See *e.g., Furniss* v. *Fitchett* [1958] N.Z.L.R. 396, where a doctor disclosed information to an estranged husband concerning his wife without her consent.
[66] (1868) L.R. 3 H.L. 330.
[67] See C. Tapper, *Computers and the Law* at p. 64.
[68] See above at pp. 275 *et seq.*

Unsuccessful attempts were made to introduce statutory safeguards in 1969 and 1971. The Younger Committee[69] recommended legislation to keep the techniques of collecting and processing personal information on computer under review.[70] In 1975 a white paper was published proposing a permanent statutory agency to protect data subjects[71] and the Lindop Committee on Data Protection was appointed the following year.

The Lindop Committee reported in 1978.[72] It recommended a Data Protection Authority be established which would draft codes of practice for different classes of personal data handling applications which could then have the force of law. It was suggested that such an Authority should be able to require information from users of the system, maintain a register, investigate complaints, make spot checks and conduct formal hearings if there were important disagreements concerning the codes of practice. The Committee felt that all computer systems should come under the Authority's jurisdiction; in the light of the Home Office's opposition to this principle it recommended that the Home Secretary's power to grant exemptions be strictly limited to national security so that there would be exemption for police records including criminal intelligence.[73]

The proposals of the Lindop Committee were too far-reaching to win governmental approval. A further white paper was published in 1982[74] and eventually formed the basis for the Data Protection Act 1984. However, the motivation for legislating in this area had altered. A concern for protecting privacy had been superseded by the need to avoid penalties for failing to ratify the European Convention for the Protection of the Individual with regard to the Automatic Processing of Personal Data[75] which had been prepared by the Council of Europe.[76] As a result the new legislative framework will not substantially affect the storage or disclosure of personal information on police computers. Despite its impact on other areas the Data Protection Act will do little to change police practices.

The Data Protection Act 1984: general principles

The purpose of the Act is to protect personal data. However, "personal" does not mean "private"; the Act applies to data which relates to an identifiable person and includes expressions of personal opinion.[77] The Act obliges users[78] to comply with the data protection principles[79] in relation to

[69] See above at p. 274.
[70] C.N.N.D. 5012, 1972 at para. 621.
[71] "Computers and Privacy", Cmnd. 6353 (1975).
[72] "Report of the Committee on Data Protection", Cmnd. 7341 (1978).
[73] *Ibid.* Chap. 23.
[74] "Data Protection: the Government's Proposals for Legislation", Cmnd. 8539 (1982).
[75] Published as Annex A to "Data Protection: the Government's Proposals for Legislation", Cmnd. 8539 (1982).
[76] Strasbourg; Council of Europe (1981).
[77] s.1(3).
[78] As defined by s.1(5).
[79] ss.2(2), 7(2), 10, 11 and 12.

a "data subject"[80] and to register under the Act[81] with the Data Protection Registrar. The most important restriction on the application of the Act is that it only applies to personal data that is processed automatically[82]; it therefore does not regulate personal information based on manual records or on a mixed manual and automated system.

The general principles of data protection as contained in Schedule 1, Part 1 of the Act are:

(1) that information contained in personal data must be obtained and processed fairly and lawfully;
(2) that personal data must be held for one or more specified and lawful purpose;
(3) that personal data for any purpose must not be used or disclosed in any matter incompatible with the purpose for which it is held;
(4) that personal data held for any purpose must be adequate, relevant and not excessive in relation to that purpose;
(5) that personal data must be kept accurate and up to date; however, this principle is hedged round with limitations[83];
(6) that personal data should not be kept longer than is necessary for the purpose;
(7) that an individual is entitled, at reasonable intervals and without undue delay or expense to be informed by a data user that he is a subject and to be given access to the data; where appropriate, he will be entitled to have such data corrected or erased;
(8) the appropriate security measures must be taken against unauthorised access to or alteration, disclosure or destruction of, personal data and against the accidental loss or destruction of personal data.

But, where personal data is held for police purposes, only some of these principles are applicable. Information required for the purpose of safeguarding national security has a blanket exemption from the provisions of the Act; if a Minister of the Crown certifies that the exemption is required on national security grounds, this will be conclusive evidence of that fact.[84] Moreover, most information held by the police will not be subject to the non-disclosure principle nor to the obligation that access must be given to an individual concerning the data referring to him.

The non-disclosure provisions of the Act do not apply where:

(1) disclosure is for the purpose of preventing or detecting crime;
(2) disclosure is for the purpose of apprehending or prosecuting offenders;
(3) disclosure is likely to prejudice the prevention or detection of crime or the apprehension or prosecution of offenders.[85]

These exclusions from the Act are extremely widely drawn. Sir Norman Lindop said the provisions:

"will create a fraud upon the public. In respect of non-disclosure the

[80] As defined by s.1(4).
[81] s.5(5).
[82] s.1(2).
[83] See below at p. 294.
[84] s.27(1) and (2).
[85] s.28(3).

[Data Protection Act] will condone secret disclosures in contravention of a public undertaking in statutory form."[86]

In situations covered by these exclusions no remedy will lie for disclosing information to persons not listed in the register kept by the Data Protection Registrar; the Registrar will also be prevented from exercising any of his powers for breaking a data protection principle.[87] Not only does this mean that the police have a wide power to disclose personal information from their data banks; they will also be entitled to receive information from any data bank in the country which will not, by passing on such information, contravene the Act. However, the police are not confined to seeking the consent of a data user in order to have access to the information it holds; they may also invoke their powers under the Police and Criminal Evidence Act 1984 which permits them to seize computerised information under their various powers of seizure.[88]

Similarly, a data subject is denied access to any information and the Registrar cannot exercise any of his powers[89] where personal data is held for:

(1) the prevention or detection of crime;
(2) the apprehension or prosecution of offenders.[90]

In other words, there is no right of access to material held on police computers.

The Data Protection Act 1984: remedies

The Act provides various remedies for breaches of its provisions. For these purposes, constables under the direction and control of the chief officer of police[91] will be treated as his servants.[92] Nevertheless, the remedies will in general be of little practical value because the data subject has no access to information held by the police and therefore in practice, cannot make representations or obtain remedy in relation to it.

The data subject can make a complaint to the Registrar in relation to contraventions of the Act[93] but has no right of appeal from his determination.[94]

The Act also provides the following remedies:

(1) Access. The data subject can claim entitlement to access to personal data on the basis that the information is held for a purpose that does not come within the wide exemption granted to the police.[95] He must first apply to the police in writing and pay any fee required. He may then apply to

[86] *The Times*, March 26, 1984.
[87] Data Protection Act 1984, s.26(2).
[88] See Chap. 7 above at p. 214.
[89] s.26(2) of the Data Protection Act 1984.
[90] s.28(1).
[91] See Chap. 1 above at p. 30.
[92] s.38(3).
[93] s.36(3).
[94] s.13.
[95] s.21(1).

either the High Court or county court[96] complaining that the police have not complied with his request which the court can then order them to do.[97] The court may inspect the information itself but cannot order it to be made available to the data subject until it has ruled in its favour[98];

(2) Compensation. The data subject is entitled to compensation for damage and distress for the inaccuracy of the data.[99] In order to be entitled to make such a claim the data subject must prove that damage was suffered as a result of the inaccuracy.[1] The definition of "inaccuracy" and nature of the defences available further restrict the availability of this remedy. Data is inaccurate if it is "incorrect or misleading as to any matter of fact"[2] and therefore, excludes opinions, assertions or judgments. Inaccurate data received from third parties will not breach the Act if the data accurately records that it came from a third party, indicates its source and indicates any record of notification by the data subject that the information is incorrect or misleading.[3] It is also a defence under the Act for the data user to show that he took such care as in all the circumstances was reasonably required to ensure the data was accurate.[4]

(3) Rectification and erasure. If the High Court or county court[5] is satisfied that the data information is inaccurate as defined above, it can order the rectification or erasure of the data including any expression of opinion based on inaccurate data.[6] The court can correct information that comes from a third party or make such order as it thinks fit.[7] The court will only erase data if it is satisfied that the data subject has suffered damage because of unauthorised disclosure or access given to it and there is a substantial risk of it recurring.[8] As there is no right to complain about unauthorised disclosure by the police this remedy will not be available against them.

Because no duty to comply with the disclosure principle is cast upon the police in their police work the general right under the Act to compensation for unauthorised disclosure of information will not be available against them.

The Data Protection Act 1984 provides important new safeguards on the threats posed to privacy by storing and disseminating personal information. It is unfortunate that the statute effectively excludes the police from the ambit of its provisions with the result that there is no proper remedy in English law in relation to inaccurate information held on police computers.

96 s.21(1).
97 s.28(8).
98 s.25(2).
99 s.22(1).
1 *Ibid.*
2 s.22(4).
3 s.22(2).
4 s.22(3).
5 s.25.
6 s.24(1).
7 s.25(2).
8 s.25(3).

10. Negligence and Other Civil Actions

1. INTRODUCTION

In Part II of this book the "traditional tort actions" against the police were considered. These actions are by far the most important. They cover the areas where citizens will be most concerned with unlawful police activity: assault, unlawful arrest and imprisonment, interference with land and goods and unjustified prosecutions. Nevertheless, the law provides a wide range of other causes of action which may be relevant to the citizen's position in relation to the police. This chapter deals with six areas: negligence, breach of statutory duty, defamation, conspiracy, misfeasance in public office and actions after death.

2. NEGLIGENCE

Introduction

The common law action in negligence has, in recent decades, become of central importance to the law of tort. Large areas of tortious liability have been gradually redefined and assimilated to it. Nevertheless there have been very few attempts to fix the police with liability for negligence in relation to their "operational policing" functions. Complex and difficult questions arise concerning matters such as the existence of a duty of care, the policy limitations on such a duty, and the intervening acts of third parties.

The elements of the tort

The elements of the tort of negligence are clear and well established. There must be:

(1) a duty of care owed by the defendant to the plaintiff;
(2) a breach by the defendant of this duty;
(3) damage to the plaintiff;
(4) which is caused by the breach of duty.

(1) Duty of care. The generally accepted test[1] to be applied to establish whether or not a duty of care is owed by the plaintiff to the defendant is set out in the speech of Lord Wilberforce in *Anns* v. *Merton*[2]:

> "the question has to be approached in two stages. First one has to ask whether, as between the alleged wrongdoer and the person who has suffered damage there is a sufficient relationship of proximity or neighbourhood such that, in the reasonable contemplation of the former, carelessness on his part may be likely to cause damage to the latter, in which case a prima facie duty of care arises. Secondly, if the first question is answered affirmatively, it is necessary to consider whether there are any considerations which ought to negative, or to reduce or limit the scope of the duty or the class of person to whom it is owed or the damages to which a breach of it may give rise."

Thus, if it is forseeable that the plaintiff will be damaged by the defendant's lack of care, a **duty of care** will arise unless there are **policy considerations** which restrict or negative the duty. Policy considerations may "negative" a duty of care if it is not "just and reasonable" that a duty be imposed.[3]

(2) Breach of duty. The defendant will be in breach of his duty if he fails to take such care as is reasonable in all the circumstances. The standard of care is that of the reasonable man. This is a matter of law and the court will take into account matters such as the degree of risk if the duty is not fulfilled, the seriousness of the risk, the utility of the defendant's acts and the cost of avoiding the harm.[4] In police cases the standard of care will often not be a high one, because the police act under considerable pressure, with competing demands on their resources, often in situations of some danger.[5] Whether the defendant is in breach of his duty in a particular case is a question of fact and degree.

(3) Damage. Because negligence is an action on the case, there will only be a complete cause of action if the plaintiff can show some "special damage" such as personal injury, nervous shock or economic loss. If economic loss is the only damage caused then there are strict "policy limitations" on recovery. The plaintiff can only recover for "pure economic loss" if he can show a "very close proximity" to the defendant.[6] In general, the plaintiff can only recover for damage which is "reasonably foreseeable."[7]

(4) Causation. Even if the plaintiff was damaged and the defendant was in breach of a duty owed to him, there will be no action unless the damage was in fact caused by the breach. The defendant will not be liable if, on a proper

[1] But see the remarks of Oliver L.J. in *Leigh & Sillavan Ltd.* v. *Aliakmon Shipping Co.* [1985] Q.B. 350 and see also *per* Lord Brandon *ibid*; and *per* Lord Goff in *Smith* v. *Littlewoods* [1987] 2 W.L.R. 480 at 511 and *Yuen kuen-yeu* v. *Att. Gen. of Hong Kong* [1987] 2 All E.R. 705 at 710.

[2] [1978] A.C. 728 at 751–752.

[3] See *per* Lord Keith, *Governors of Peabody Donation Fund* v. *Sir Lindsay Parkinson & Co. Ltd.* [1985] A.C. 210.

[4] See Clerk & Lindsell, paras. 10–31–10–42.

[5] See, *e.g.*, *Marshall* v. *Osmond* [1983] Q.B. 1034.

[6] See *Junior Books* v. *Veitchi* [1983] 1 A.C. 520; *Muirhead* v. *International Tank Specialities Ltd.* [1985] 3 All E.R. 705.

[7] See Chap. 11 below at p. 337.

understanding of events, the plaintiff's damage was not in fact caused by the negligence of the defendant but by some intervening "new act" (*novus actus interveniens*). Human action does not, of itself, sever the connected sequence of events.[8] The basic rule was summarised by Greer L.J. in the leading case of *Haynes* v. *Harwood*[9] as follows:

> "If what is relied upon as a *novus actus interveniens* is the very kind of thing which is likely to happen if the want of care which is alleged takes place, the principle embodied in the maxim is no defence."

In police cases the first element will often be the most difficult to establish. Special considerations may arise if the police are acting under "statutory powers."[10] Even if the plaintiff can establish a prima facie duty of care this may well be negatived by "policy considerations." When it is alleged that there has been a negligent failure to carry out proper investigations special difficulties arise concerning liability for the acts of independent third parties.

Negligence liability and independent third parties

Difficult legal issues arise when the plaintiff's claim is based on damage caused by an independent third party who, it is said, was placed in a position to cause the damage by the defendant's negligence. It is clear that the simple fact that the damage was caused by a third party:

> "does not, of itself, preclude success of the claim, since breach of duty on the part of the person against whom the claim is made may also have played a part in causing the damage."[11]

Nevertheless, the situations in which such an action may succeed have been strictly limited although the precise basis and extent of this limitation have been unclear.

There is no doubt that there will be liability if there is a "special relationship" between the defendant and the third party by virtue of which the defendant is responsible for controlling the actions of the third party.[12] There will also be liability if the defendant negligently causes or permits a source of danger to be created in a situation where it is reasonably foreseeable that third parties may interfere with it.[13]

There have been, however, considerable difficulties as to liability in cases where there is no "special relationship" or situation of danger.[14] The authorities revealed two different approaches with different practical consequences. These can be called the "policy" and the "foreseeability" approaches.

The first approach treats the limitation as a question of policy. On this

[8] See *The Oropesa* [1943] P. 32 at 37.
[9] [1935] 1 K.B. 146 at 156; see also *Knightley* v. *Johns* [1982] 1 W.L.R. 349.
[10] See below at pp. 299 *et seq.*
[11] *Smith* v. *Littlewoods Ltd.* [1987] 2 W.L.R. 480 at 491H, *per* Lord Mackay; see also *Paterson Zochonis* v. *Mefarken Packaging* [1983] F.S.R. 273 at 298, *per* Goff L.J.
[12] See *Dorset Yacht* v. *Home Office* [1970] A.C. 1004.
[13] See *per* Lord Goff, *Smith* v. *Littlewoods*, [1987] 2 W.L.R. 480 at 504.
[14] *Cf. per* Goff L.J., *P. Perl (Exporters)* v. *Camden* [1984] Q.B. 342 at 359H–360A.

view, policy excludes liability in the absence of a special relationship or other special circumstances. This was the analysis of Lord Denning M.R. in *Lamb* v. *Camden*[15] and was partially supported by Oliver L.J. (as he then was).[16] In *P. Perl (Exporters)* v. *Camden*[17] Goff L.J. (as he then was) applied Lord Wilberforce's test in *Anns*[18] and suggested that "policy considerations" negatived a duty of care in the absence of a special relationship between the defendant and the third party. More recently, Lord Goff has refined his analysis of the absence of a duty of care in this area stating that the fundamental reason for it is "that the common law does not impose liability for what are called pure omissions."[19]

The second approach treats the question as being a matter of foreseeability: if the third party intervention is foreseeable with a sufficiently high degree of probability there will be a duty of care. In *Dorset Yacht* v. *Home Office*[20] Lord Reid said that there would be liability if the "intervening action" of the third party was "very likely" (or perhaps just "likely")[21] to happen. In subsequent cases it has been suggested that the defendant may be liable where third party intervention is "likely or very likely to happen,"[22] that there must be a "very high degree of foreseeability,"[23] perhaps "amounting almost to inevitability.'[24]

This conflict was resolved by the decision of the House of Lords in *Smith* v. *Littlewoods*[25] when this second approach was endorsed by a majority. It was said that "mere foreseeability of damage is certainly not a sufficient basis to found liability."[26] Nevertheless, as Lord Mackay (with whom Lord Keith and Lord Griffiths agreed, Lord Brandon taking a similar approach)[27] said:

> "what the reasonable man is bound to foresee in a case involving injury or damage by independent human agency, just as in cases where such agency plays no part, is the probable consequences of his own act or omission, but that, in such a case, a clear basis will be required on which to assert that the injury or damage is more than a mere possibility."[28]

The result must be "highly probable or very likely" and the needle that

15 [1981] Q.B. 625 at 636E–638C.

16 *Ibid.* at 643; but see Lord Mackay's analysis of their reasoning in *Smith* v. *Littlewoods* [1987] 2 W.L.R. 480 at 495E–H.

17 [1984] Q.B. 342 at 359A.

18 See above at p. 296.

19 *Smith* v. *Littlewoods* [1987] 2 W.L.R. 480 at 502H.

20 [1970] A.C. 1004 at 1030.

21 See the analysis of Lord Mackay in *Smith* v. *Littlewoods* [1987] 2 W.L.R. 480 at 492; although Lord Reid treated the question as a matter of causation, see the remarks of Goff L.J. in *Paterson Zochonis* v. *Merfarken Packaging* [1983] F.S.R. 273 at 298.

22 *Per* Oliver L.J., *P. Perl (Exporters) Ltd.* v. *Camden*, [1984] Q.B. 342 at 354A, explaining his analysis in *Lamb* v. *Camden LBC.* [1981] Q.B. 625.

23 *P. Perl (Exporters)* v. *Camden* [1984] Q.B. 342 at 352A, *per* Waller L.J.

24 *Lamb* v. *Camden LBC* [1981] Q.B. 625 at 643.

25 [1987] 2 W.L.R. 480.

26 *per* Lord Griffiths, [1987] 2 W.L.R. 480 at 484F.

27 He also treats the issue as depending on reasonable foreseeability, *Smith* v. *Littlewoods* [1987] 2 W.L.R. 480 at 483 E-F.

28 *Ibid.* at 493H–494A.

measures the probability of a particular result must be "near the top of the scale."[29] It is submitted that this is the correct approach and is in line with the older authorities which deal with the problem as one of causation. As Greer L.J. put it in a passage which has often been approved:

> "it is not true to say that where a plaintiff has suffered damage occasioned by a combination of the wrongful act of a defendant and some further conscious act by an intervening person, that of itself prevents the court coming to a conclusion in the plaintiff's favour if the accident was the natural and probable consequence of the wrongful act."[30]

The fact that the third party's acts are unlawful is no objection to liability. As Lord Reid has said:

> "Unfortunately, tortious or criminal action by a third party is often 'the very kind of thing' which is likely to happen as a result of the wrongful or careless act of the defendant."[31]

It is submitted, therefore, that in the absence of "special relationships," a person will be liable for the tortious acts of third parties if these are reasonably forseeable consequences of his own negligence. Liability will depend on the facts of each particular case.

Negligence and police "powers"

In many cases, alleged police negligence will relate to the exercise of their statutory **powers**. When a negligence action is brought against a public body or official in relation to the exercise of a power conferred by statute, special "public law" principles must be applied to decide whether or not a negligence action will lie.

The fact that a public official has a statutory power to do something means that he has a discretion whether or not to do it in a particular situation. As long as he is acting within the "limits of a discretion bona fide exercised" there is no duty of care at common law. A duty of care only arises if the official acts in a way which is *ultra vires*. As Lord Wilberforce said in *Anns* v. *Merton*[32]:

> "in the case of a power, liability cannot exist unless the act complained of lies outside the ambit of the power."

Thus, the first question to be asked in relation to potential proceedings against the police in respect of negligent exercise of their statutory powers is whether they were acting *ultra vires*. This question, in turn, depends on the type of activity involved.

In *Anns* v. *Merton*[33] Lord Wilberforce drew a distinction between the

[29] *Smith* v. *Littlewoods* [1987] 2 W.L.R. 480 at 493H.
[30] *Haynes* v. *Harwood* [1935] 1 K.B. 146 at 156.
[31] *Dorset Yacht* v. *Home Office* [1970] A.C. 1004 at 1030.
[32] [1978] A.C. 728 at 758; see also the classic exposition by Lord Diplock in *Dorset Yacht* v. *Home Office* [1970] A.C. 1004 at 1067–1068.
[33] [1978] A.C. 728 at 754.

"policy"[34] and the "operational" areas.[35] When a public official is faced with a situation in which a statutory power might be exercised he must first decide if, when, and how to exercise it. This is a decision in the "policy area." It involves the direct exercise of a "public law" discretion and will only be *ultra vires* and hence give rise to potential negligence liability if the discretion can be impugned on general "public law" grounds: illegality, procedural impropriety or irrationality.[36] If the official decides to exercise the power then he enters the "operational" area. This also involves some "discretionary" elements as to the precise manner in which it is to be exercised. In relation to these elements there will be a common law duty of care if the official acts in a way which is *ultra vires* his discretion. On the other hand, when his activities are "purely operational" ordinary lack of care will render his actions *ultra vires*. As Lord Wilberforce puts it:

> "the more 'operational' a power or duty may be, the easier it is to superimpose upon it a common law duty of care."[37]

The standard of care will depend on the precise terms of the statute which confers the power.

The application of this distinction between the "policy" and the "operational" areas to the police can be illustrated by an example. A police constable has a power to enter premises without warrant for the purpose of "saving life or limb or preventing serious damage to property."[38] When he is considering whether or not to enter particular premises he is making a decision in the "policy" area. If he decides not to act, a negligence claim will only lie if he was not acting "within the limits of his discretion bona fide exercised." This will be the case if, for example, he fails to take into account the fact that there are screams and obvious signs of an assault being committed. If, on the other hand, he decides to act then he will be within the "operational" area and, unless there are discretionary elements present, he will be potentially liable in negligence. Thus, if he enters but fails to take reasonable care in conducting a search then he may liable if damage results.

There is no doubt that a very complex reasoning process is involved here and the whole "public law" approach to the negligence of public authorities has been strongly criticised.[39] It has been suggested that the decision of the House of Lords in the case of *Governors of the Peabody Donation Fund* v. *Sir Lindsay Parkinson & Co. Ltd.*[40] shows that this approach is now no longer followed.[41] In that case the House of Lords had to consider the statutory powers of a local authority to approve a drainage system for a housing

[34] The term "discretionary" or "decision-making" is sometimes used; see *Cocks* v. *Thanet DC* [1983] 2 A.C. 286 see below at p. 311.

[35] The term "executive" is sometimes used to refer to the latter area.

[36] See *Mohammed-Holgate* v. *Duke* [1984] A.C. 437 at 442, *per* Lord Diplock and see generally, Chap. 13 below at p. 400.

[37] *Ibid* at 754.

[38] Police and Criminal Evidence Act 1984, s.17(1)(*e*).

[39] See Carol Harlow, *Compensation and Government Torts* at Part II, Chap. 2; Winfield & Jolowicz at pp. 83 *et seq.*

[40] [1985] A.C. 210; followed in *Investors in Industry* v. *South Bedfordshire DC* [1986] 2 W.L.R. 937: (C.A.).

[41] See Elias Galy, "Civil Liability of Public Authorities" (1986) 136 New L.J. 435 at 495.

development. It was held that the authority owed no duty of care in the exercise of these powers. What is striking about the argument and judgments both in the Court of Appeal and House of Lords is that there was no appeal to "public law" considerations of any kind. Nevertheless, it is submitted that such considerations did not arise on the facts of that case because the local authority inspector involved was clearly acting *ultra vires* by failing to give any consideration to the question of whether the proposals submitted to him by the plaintiff's architects were in accordance with the approved plans. It would follow that the *Peabody* case does not, in fact, contradict the "public law" approach.

It is now clearly established that special principles do apply to negligence actions against public authorities exercising statutory powers. The general principles have been usefully summarised as follows:

> "Where a plaintiff claims damages for negligence at common law against a public body or official purporting to act in pursuance of a power conferred by statute or other legislation, he can only succeed if he can show (1) that the act complained of was not within the limits of a discretion bona fide exercised under the relevant power, (2) that having regard to all the circumstances, including the legislation creating the relevant power, there was sufficient proximity to create a duty of care on the defendant to avoid damage to the plaintiff of the type complained of, and no ground for negativing (or reducing or limiting) such duty of care, (3) that it was reasonably foreseeable by the defendant, or by those for whom he was vicariously responsible, that the act complained of was likely to cause damage of the type in fact suffered by the plaintiff by reason of such act."[42]

The police have been sued for the negligent exercise of statutory powers in two reported cases. The case of *Rivers* v. *Cutting*[43] involved a police removal of a vehicle abandoned on the motorway under Regulation 4 of the Removal and Disposal of Vehicles Regulations 1968. The police had this done by a garage under their statutory powers to "arrange" the disposal of such vehicles and it had been done negligently. The Court of Appeal had to consider a police officer's duty in relation to the exercise of a statutory power. It was held that he had to exercise reasonable care when exercising such a power. It was common ground that if the police officer had decided to exercise the power himself he would have owed the owner a duty of care in relation to the manner in which the car was removed. On the facts of the case the police officer was not vicariously liable for the negligence of the independent contractor garage because he had selected the contractor with reasonable care. The case involved activities in the "executive" field and "public law" issues did not, therefore, arise.

The applicability of the special "public law" rules to an action in negligence against the police was directly considered in the case of *Rigby* v. *Chief Constable of Northamptonshire*.[44] It was alleged, *inter alia*, that the chief constable had been negligent in failing to have at his disposal a particular device for the delivery of CS gas known as the "Ferret." The chief

[42] *per* Goff L.J., *Fellowes* v. *Rother DC* [1983] 1 All E.R. 513.
[43] [1982] 1 W.L.R. 1146.
[44] [1985] 1 W.L.R. 1242; see also below at p. 303.

constable had the statutory function of advising on the purchase of equipment. Taylor J. accepted the defendant's submission that the distinction between the "policy" and "executive" spheres was applicable here. The decision not to get Ferret was in the policy field and was therefore a matter of discretion. He concluded that:

> "The chief constable was in my view exercising the discretion under his statutory powers to defer purchase of the Ferret, and I find that this policy was followed bona fide."[45]

The plaintiff's claim under this head therefore failed.

Negligence and police activities

There is no doubt that in many spheres of activity the police are liable for negligence and that no special principles of law apply. One example which lies outside the range of this book concerns "accident at work" negligence actions brought by serving police officers. Such actions are common and are governed by the same principles which cover ordinary negligence actions by employees.

Similarly, actions against the police in respect of negligent driving are common and usually uncontroversial in law. It has been held that police drivers, acting in the course of their duties owe the same duty of care as all other road users.[46] This applies even when they are answering emergency calls.

The fact that the police are engaged in "policing" activities does not exempt them from ordinary duties of care. These duties of care are not "negatived" just because the police are engaged in difficult or dangerous work—but the nature of the work is taken into account in assessing the applicable "standard of care." The principle is clearly illustrated by the case of *Marshall* v. *Osmond*[47] which involved injury to a suspected criminal at the end of a chase by a police car. The Court of Appeal reversed the trial judge on the law and held that a police officer owed the same duty of care to a criminal he was pursuing as to anyone else, namely a duty "to exercise such care and skill as is reasonable in all the circumstances."[48] They went on to support the trial judge's conclusion and held that the officer was, in fact, not in breach of this duty.

If police conduct, in all the circumstances, falls below the standard expected of "reasonable police officers" the courts will impose negligence liability. Thus, in the case of *Knightley* v. *Johns*[49] the police had been called to an accident in a tunnel. The police inspector in charge, in contravention of standing orders, had forgotten to close the tunnel to traffic. He therefore ordered the plaintiff, a police motorcyclist, to ride back down the tunnel,

45 [1985] 1 W.L.R. 1242 at 1251A.
46 See *Gaynor* v. *Allen* [1959] 2 Q.B. 403; *Woods* v. *Richards* [1977] R.T.R. 20.
47 [1983] Q.B. 1034.
48 *Ibid.* at 1038.
49 [1982] 1 W.L.R. 349.

against the flow of traffic, to close it to traffic. The plaintiff collided with a car and the Court of Appeal held that the Chief Constable was vicariously liable for the inspector's negligence. The case raised complex questions concerning *novus actus interveniens* but the point to note is that there was no discussion as to whether the police should be held liable for a negligent performance of their duties. The Court assumed that, if the inspector did not come up to the standard of the "reasonable police officer" (and there was no *novus actus*) then negligence liability followed.

In general then, when the police are **acting** (as opposed to **failing to act**) they will owe a duty of care to people who are likely to be directly affected by their actions. No policy considerations will "restrict or negative" this duty of care. This is illustrated by four cases in which such a duty of care was accepted.

The briefly reported case of *Bryson* v. *Northumbria Police Authority*[50] concerned a young man who had been arrested for drunkenness, kept in a cell to sober up for some time and then released at 4.55a.m. In the cell he had been vomiting and it seems unlikely that he had fully recovered by the time of his release. Wandering home in the wrong direction he was killed in an accident on an urban by-pass. In those circumstances Reeve J. held that the police, in exercising their discretion whether to release or detain an arrested person owe him a duty of care, but that, on the facts they had discharged that duty. No policy considerations appear to have limited the duty.

A similar approach was adopted by Taylor J. in the case of *Rigby* v. *Chief Constable of Northampton*.[51] This involved police attempts to "flush" a psychopath out of a gun shop. They did this with CS gas which was generated by a canister which got very hot and which the police knew was likely to cause a fire. The police originally had a fire engine on hand but it left and they made no attempt to replace it. A CS canister was then used with no fire fighters at the scene. The canister did in fact cause a fire which destroyed the plaintiff's shop. In these circumstances he was able to recover damages for negligence. No "policy considerations" limited the duty of care.

The county court case of *Charles Wilson Automobile Engineers* v. *Chief Constable of Greater Manchester*[52] involved a claim for the negligent release of a car from police custody. The police stopped the car and arrested the occupants on suspicion of theft. Although the occupants were of no fixed abode, with no documents and were not the registered keepers of the car they were released two hours later with the car and they disappeared. The judge held that:

> "a police officer owes a duty to the owner of goods which he has seized to take reasonable care for their safety, to make such enquiries as may be reasonable to ascertain their ownership and to take reasonable steps to return them to their owner if that is possible."[53]

The duty owed by the officer was said to be "to take such care as is reasonable **in all the circumstances**."[54] As the judge said:

[50] [1977] C.L.Y. 2042.

[51] [1985] 1 W.L.R. 1242; see also above at p. 301.

[52] January 18, 1986, Manchester County Court, unreported, H.H.J. Lord. The authors would like to thank H.H. Judge Lord for supplying a copy of his judgment.

[53] *Ibid.* at p. 4.

[54] *Ibid.* at p. 5.

> "One has to take into consideration all the circumstances of the case including, for example, the difficulty of any problem facing the officer, the nature and extent of the information available to him, the need in some circumstances perhaps to make a swift decision and the myriad of other considerations which may arise in any particular case."[55]

On the facts, it was held that the police were negligent.

The Scots law in this area is the same as that in England and the Court of Session case of *Allan (or Wilson)* v. *Chief Constable of Lothian & Borders Police*[56] provides a useful illustration of the applicability of ordinary negligence principles to the police. The pursuer (plaintiff) was a widow whose husband had died of hypothermia in a field after having been taken away in a police car. The police had been called after a domestic dispute in the middle of the night. The deceased had been drunk and aggressive and the police were removing him from the place where he had been causing trouble.

Although Lord McCluskey was not prepared to hold that the police had "deliberately decided to teach . . . (the deceased) a lesson by depositing him in the remote outskirts of Edinburgh"[57] he was of the view that:

> "there is no escape from the fact that had the police officers given any thought to the weather conditions, the deceased's condition, the deceased's clothing, the remote location in which they left him, the conditions underfoot they would have been bound to realise that he was a danger to himself."[58]

He held that the police had a choice, whether to release the deceased or to hold him and:

> "In deciding how to exercise that choice they had a duty to exercise a reasonable care to have regard to the reasonably foreseeable consequences of his being released."[59]

Although it was not reasonably foreseeable that the deceased would die of hypothermia the damage suffered by him was of a "reasonably foreseeable type"—that is harm by adverse weather conditions—and could, therefore, be recovered for.[60]

The judge concluded that "the police failed in their duty to take reasonable care for . . . (the deceased's) safety"[61] and his widow was, therefore, awarded damages of £62,537 calculated on ordinary "fatal accidents" principles.[62]

In summary when police officers **act** in a negligent way they will in general be liable according to ordinary principles. However, they will not be subject to high standards of care in situations in which there is an important discretionary element in the activity in question.

[55] January 18, 1986, Manchester County Court, unreported, H.H.J. Lord at p. 5.
[56] November 25, 1986, unreported, Lord McCluskey.
[57] *Ibid.* at p. 50.
[58] *Ibid* at pp. 31–32.
[59] *Ibid.* at p. 44.
[60] See *ibid.* at pp. 45–49; relying on *Hughes* v. *Lord Advocate* [1963] A.C. 837.
[61] November 25, 1986, unreported, Lord McCluskey at pp. 50–51.
[62] See below at p. 330.

Negligent police investigations

An important area of potential police negligence liability concerns the negligent conduct of investigations into crime which leads to a failure to apprehend a criminal who subsequently causes damage to the plaintiff. It is clearly within the reasonable contemplation of police officers that carelessness in the investigation of crime "may be likely to cause damage" to citizens. Thus, if the police fail to detain an obvious burglary suspect it is foreseeable that he will cause damage to householders by committing further burglaries. If they fail to catch a persistent rapist it is foreseeable that he may commit further offences. If they ignore a burglar alarm it may be likely that burglars will be able to escape capture. In such cases a "prima facie duty of care" will arise under the first part of Lord Wilberforce's test in *Anns* v. *Merton*.[63] There are, however, a number of "policy considerations" which may restrict or exclude this duty of care.

This area was considered by the Court of Appeal in the case of *Hill* v. *Chief Constable of West Yorkshire*.[64] The action was brought against the police by the estate of a victim of the "Yorkshire Ripper" in relation to their allegedly negligent investigation of the case. It was said that the defendant was vicariously liable for the failure of his officers "to exercise all reasonable skill, experience and care and adopt and put into effect all practical means to apprehend" the perpetrator of the offences which, it could reasonably be inferred, had been committed by the same man. The Court of Appeal upheld the striking out of the plaintiff's claim as disclosing no reasonable cause of action.

Fox L.J. pointed out that in all the usual cases of civil actions against the police "the injury suffered by the complainant is the direct consequence of the acts of the police."[65] He also noted that there appeared to be no reported case in any common law jurisdiction:

> "where the police have been made liable for the acts of a criminal on the ground that they should previously have apprehended him."[66]

Although it was foreseeable that a violent criminal who was not apprehended might injure someone "foreseeability is not necessarily the test of whether a duty of care exists."[67] In particular, if the foreseeable damage was caused by the actions of a third party there was no duty of care in the absence of a "special relationship" between the defendant and the third party.[68] It was held that:

> "The fact that the police have a general duty to the public at large to suppress crime does not mean that the police have a special relationship with all possible victims of the perpetrator of a crime which they are investigating."[69]

[63] 1978] A.C. 728.
[64] [1987] 2 W.L.R. 1126; on appeal from (1986) 136 New L.J. 238.
[65] *Ibid.* at 1133D.
[66] *Ibid.* at 1133A.
[67] *Ibid.* at 1134E.
[68] *Ibid.* at 1134–35, *per* Fox L.J.; at 1139, *per* Glidewell L.J.; *cf. Smith* v. *Leurs* (1945) 70 C.L.R. 256 at 261–262.
[69] *Hill* v. *Chief Constable of West Yorkshire* (1987) at 1137C, *per* Fox L.J.

However, the court did not expressly consider the effect of the other authorities regarding "third party intervention" in negligence.[70] It is submitted that, in this situation, the question is: was the third party intervention (in this case, the Yorkshire Ripper's continuing murders) "likely or very likely to happen" if the defendants were negligent? This, it is submitted, is pre-eminently a question of fact and not a matter to be dealt with on a striking out application. The case should then have been allowed to go to trial on this issue.

The Court of Appeal also relied on "policy considerations" to "negative" the duty of care owed by the police in their investigations. Glidewell L.J. was of the view that if such actions were allowed they might have an inhibiting effect on the exercise of police judgment and that they would "very often involve the retrial of matters which had already been tried at the Crown Court."[71] He concluded that:

> "In short, the reasons for holding that the police are immune from an action of this kind are similar to those for holding that a barrister may not be sued for negligence in his conduct of proceedings in court."[72]

It is submitted that this approach is out of line with authority and does not represent the law. The dangers of "reopening" criminal proceedings are greatly exaggerated. If a negligence action involves a "collateral attack" on a decision of a criminal court it will be struck out as an abuse of the process.[73] In practice there seem to be very few problems with actions in torts such as assault or false imprisonment which involve "retrial" of criminal cases. Glidewell L.J.'s worries about the "inhibiting" effect of negligence actions on police judgment would appear to be misconceived. There is little evidence that such actions have an inhibiting effect on the judgment of, for example, solicitors, accountants, or surgeons who can be sued for negligence. The possibility of such an "inhibiting effect" has never been regarded as sufficient to "negative" duties of care in such cases. If matters of judgment are involved then it may well be that there is no breach of duty.

The Court of Appeal relied on three further considerations to "negative" a duty of care in the investigation of crime. First, according to Fox L.J. it is not reasonable that

> "if, for example, on the day when Miss Hill was murdered, another woman . . . was murdered by a killer of whom the police have no previous knowledge, the approach to compensation would be totally different in the two cases."[74]

With the greatest respect, it is submitted that this consideration is wholly irrelevant. It is, of course, perfectly sound to argue that it is unreasonable for the law of negligence to be based on fault liability. However, given that it is so based, there is nothing unreasonable about one injured person receiving compensation when the injuries are, in law, the result of the plaintiff's negligence while another person with identical injuries receives no compensa-

[70] See above at pp. 297 *et seq.*
[71] *Hill* v. *Chief Constable of West Yorkshire* (1987) at 1140B.
[72] *Ibid.* at 1140C.
[73] See *Hunter* v. *Chief Constable* [1982] A.C. 529; and Chap. 3 above at p. 61.
[74] *Hill* v. *Chief Constable of West Yorkshire,* at 1137B.

tion because no one who is worth suing was at fault. This is the essence of fault liability.

Secondly, the Court of Appeal relied on the existence of the Criminal Injuries Compensation Scheme as, in effect, negativing the existence of a duty of care. Fox L.J. thought that the problems of compensation for injury from crimes of violence was best dealt within the framework of the scheme.[74a] However, the scheme does not prevent the victim suing the criminal himself and it is clearly intended to supplement, not replace, common law remedies.

The third point which is said by Glidewell L.J. to support the judge's decision is as follows:

> "While the police owe a duty to members of the public to enforce the law, the way in which the courts should if necessary enforce that duty . . . (is) by an order of mandamus."[75]

This point is misconceived for two reasons. First, the courts can enforce police duties by actions in private law for misfeasance in a public office.[76] But, secondly, and more importantly, two entirely different types of duty are being confused. The duties of police constables are imposed by statute or common law and are not directly relevant to the law of negligence. The duty to take reasonable care is a common law duty imposed on all citizens in appropriate circumstances. When considering whether a prima facie duty of care arises the only relevant consideration is foreseeability. If damage to a potential plaintiff from police carelessness is foreseeable then a prima facie duty arises provided that the actions can be regarded as *ultra vires*.[77] This has nothing to do with police "duties" to enforce the law.

To summarise, it is submitted that *Hill's* case is wrongly decided. The "policy" considerations suggested are not sufficient to "negative" or "restrict" the duty of care which is owed by the police in the investigation of crime. It is submitted that this duty is subject to ordinary negligence principles and is not restricted in any special way. It is, however, restricted by the general principle that, in the absence of a "special relationship," a person cannot be held liable for the actions of another unless there was a "high degree of probability" that they would happen. In most cases involving negligent investigation the actual damage will be caused by the actions of a third party, namely the criminal. Police liability for the actions of criminals will depend on the applicability of the general principles of "liability for third parties" to the facts of the particular case.

The police will be liable in respect of "negligent investigations" in the following situations:

(1) If they **act** negligently, for example, by presenting a wrongdoer with the means to commit a wrong in circumstances where it is very likely he will do so.[78] Thus, if in the course of an investigation, the police negligently surrender property into the custody of criminals then they will be liable because loss of the property through criminal acts is "foreseeable with a

[74a] *Ibid.* at 1138C.

[75] *Ibid.* at 1140E.

[76] See, below at pp. 324 *et seq.*

[77] See above at pp. 299 *et seq.*

[78] See, *e.g.*, *Ontario Hospital Services Commission* v. *Borsaski* (1975) 54 D.L.R. (3d) 339.

high degree of probability." This point was directly considered in the case of *Charles Wilson Automobile Engineers* v. *Chief Constable of Greater Manchester*[79] in which the judge rejected the argument that the police's negligence was not the "cause" of the plaintiff's loss:

> "I am satisfied that the loss of the car was attributable to the police negligence. It was a natural and probable consequence which was reasonably foreseeable. In the light of the knowledge which the police officers had when they handed the car to the youths a new loss of the car to the plaintiffs was 'The very kind of thing they ought to have seen to be likely.' "[80]

(2) If they are negligent in relation to a criminal with whom they have a "special relationship," because for example, he is in custody, they may be liable for damage caused by him. Thus, liability may arise if, for example, the third party had recently escaped from police custody[81] or had been released by the police without due consideration for what might happen. As Lord McCluskey said in the Scots case of *Allan (or Wilson)* v. *Chief Constable of Lothian & Borders Police*[82]:

> "if, on being released (a drunken, aggressive and irresponsible man) . . . does behave in a manner which is reasonably foreseeable, by breaking into (nearby) . . . premises . . . then the releasing police officers could face a claim by the proprietors of the premises."

(3) If they fail to apprehend a criminal in circumstances in which damage caused by his actions is "very likely to happen." Thus if the police receive a manifestly genuine 999 call (for example, from someone who was personally known to the officer receiving the call) indicating that a criminal is, at that moment, trying to break into the caller's house, and they negligently fail to respond (for example, because police headquarters fails to alert officers who are in the area), it is submitted that they should and would be liable in negligence if the caller was injured. Or, to take an example closer to the facts of the *Hill* case, if the police negligently fail to arrest a suspected rapist (having, for example, failed to make a proper search of his house) then they will be liable if immediately afterwards he attacked the rape victim again. It is submitted that it would be offensive to the whole spirit of the law of negligence if, in obvious situations such as these, the police were able to escape liability for manifestly careless acts.

Police negligence in relation to criminal proceedings

If the police negligently fail to make proper investigations of an alleged offence then it is foreseeable that the alleged victim may suffer loss and

[79] January 18, 1986, Manchester County Court, unreported, H.H.J. Lord, see at p. 303 above.
[80] *Ibid.* at p. 7.
[81] *Cf. Dorset Yacht* v. *Home Office*, [1970] A.C. 1004.
[82] November 25, 1986, unreported, at p. 44.

damage in bringing a private prosecution. If the police negligently fail to collect proper evidence for a criminal trial then it is foreseeable that the accused may suffer loss and damage by, for example, being convicted when further evidence would have revealed his innocence. In these situations special policy considerations may well apply to "restrict or negative" negligence liability.

The first situation, that of a negligent failure to prosecute, was considered in the county court case of *Lee* v. *MPC*.[83] The first plaintiff had been attacked by one R and the police failed to prosecute. The police admitted that proper care had not been taken. The second plaintiff therefore brought a private prosecution and sued the police in negligence. The claim was struck out on the basis that there was no duty of care. The judge stated that

> "There was not sufficient proximity to create a duty of care . . . The police had a discretion. If they refused to act the Plaintiff might have sought mandamus but there is no cause of action. Otherwise large numbers of citizens could have claims against the police and could allege that there were insufficient police available. This would hamper police activity and increase crime. It is wholly contrary to public policy."

But are the "policy" considerations relied on compelling? The duty to take care in "operational matters" would be to take such care as is "reasonable in all the circumstances." The availability of police is an important factor to be taken into account. Recent cases of high authority have cast doubt on "floodgates" arguments of this sort.[84]

It is clear that, in *Lee's* case the police were exercising a "power" within the "operational" or "policy" area. They were exercising a discretion as to the institution of criminal proceedings. The crucial question was, therefore, whether, in exercising this discretion, the police were acting *ultra vires*. The plaintiff had to show that the *Wednesbury* decision was irrational. It is unclear, whether, on the facts of that case the police were acting bona fide within the limits of their discretion.

In the second type of case, there are clear "public policy" limits on police duties of care. A witness enjoys absolute immunity in respect of evidence prepared for trial.[85] In the case of *Evans* v. *London Hospital Medical College*[86] a Statement of Claim alleging the negligent preparation of medical reports for the Director of Public Prosecutions was struck out as disclosing no cause of action. This was because of the immunity attaching to witnesses for reasons of public policy. One reason for this immunity, according to Drake J., was to prevent disgruntled convicted prisoners from seeking to have their cases retried by civil suit. If actions for negligence could be brought in respect of the collection and preparation of evidence, he says:

> "it would open the way to convicted persons seeking to have their cases re-tried in the civil courts. An action could be brought alleging negligence against police officers in their investigations and the collection of

[83] February 20, 1986, Westminster County Court, unreported H.H.J. Harris.
[84] See, *e.g.*, *Junior Books Ltd.* v. *Veitchi Ltd.* [1983] 1 A.C. 520.
[85] See *Marrinan* v. *Vibart* [1963] 1 Q.B. 528.
[86] [1981] 1 W.L.R. 184.

evidence which at some later date resulted in criminal proceedings being commenced."[87]

It is submitted that this fear is not a realistic one. Nevertheless, this immunity is well-established. Its exact ambit is unclear.[88]

The relationship between negligence and other tort actions

The relationship between actions in negligence and other tort actions such as false imprisonment, assault or malicious prosecution has not been considered in the authorities. As a matter of general principle the courts will not allow actions in negligence where this has the effect of evading restrictions placed on another cause of action because, in such cases, there are strong arguments that public policy should negative the existence of a duty of care.

The most important area in which this principle is likely to be applied is that of malicious prosecution. The restrictions on such actions have been evolved over the centuries to protect prosecutors for reasons of public policy. It would be contrary to this policy to allow a plaintiff to avoid these restrictions by framing his action in negligence, rather than malicious prosecution.[88a] Similar considerations apply to actions in defamation or misfeasance in a public office.

The problem is unlikely to arise in actions for trespass. It will almost always be more advantageous from the point of view of a plaintiff to bring an action in trespass rather than in negligence.[89]

3. BREACH OF STATUTORY DUTY

Introduction

The police have a large number of specific statutory duties under legislation such as the Police Act 1964 and the Police and Criminal Evidence Act 1984. It has been held that the general duties of the police as constables are now "statutory duties."[90]

In line with general tort principles it is possible that a breach of some of these duties may give rise to an action in damages for "breach of statutory duty." In particular, such an action may be the only possible remedy for a lawfully arrested and detained suspect who is denied his rights under Part IV of the 1984 Act.[91]

[87] *Evans* v. *London Hospital Medical College* [1981] 1 W.L.R. 184 at 190C.

[88] See *ibid.* at 191–192.

[88a] See *Business Computers International* v. *Registrar of Companies, The Times,* July 1, 1987.

[89] See Chap. 4 above at p. 108.

[90] *George* v. *Garland* [1980] R.T.R. 77; see Chap. 1 above at p. 25.

[91] See Chap. 5 above at pp. 157 *et seq.*

The right of action

An action for breach of statutory duty will only lie if the statute is one which in fact confers a right of action for damages. This is, fundamentally, a question of policy: should the breach of a particular statutory provision be compensated in damages? The court must consider whether or not the statute in question intended to give a right of action in tort.[92] There are "indications which point with more or less force to the one answer or the other."[93]

The first "indication" is whether there is, in the statute, an alternative method of enforcing compliance or penalising non-compliance.[94] The absence of any other sanction creates a presumption that there is an action for breach of the statute.[95]

The second "indication" is whether or not the duty is imposed for the benefit of a particular class of persons.[96] If the duty was imposed to benefit a particular class an action is more likely to lie.

The third "indication" which may point to the absence of a right of action is a lack of precision in the definition of the statutory right which it is sought to enforce.[97]

When a statute casts duties on a public authority such as the police, difficult questions arise as to which of the duties are "public law" ones and which give rise to "private rights." A distinction has been drawn between "decision-making" functions, which are a matter of public law, and "executive" functions which may give rise to private law rights and obligations.[98] If the public authority makes an "unlawful" decision—because the proper procedures were not followed, because an incorrect view of the law was applied or for general *Wednesbury* reasons[99] this must be challenged by the "judicial review" procedure. No action for breach of statutory duty can arise. Once the decision has been made, however, private law rights do arise and may be enforced by an action for breach of statutory duty—provided that, on a true construction of the statute, such an action is available. The precise limits of this distinction remain to be worked out. The mere fact that "public law" questions arise concurrently to a "private law" right of action will not prevent a plaintiff from bringing an action for breach of statutory duty.[99a]

[92] See, *e.g., per* Lord Halsbury L.C., *Pasmore* v. *Oswaldtwistle UDC* [1898] A.C. 387 at 397.

[93] *per* Lord Simonds, *Cutler* v. *Wandsworth Stadium Ltd.* [1949] A.C. 398 at 407; see *per* Mann J., *Bourgoin SA* v. *Ministry of Agriculture* [1985] 3 All E.R. 585.

[94] *Lonrho* v. *Shell Petroleum Co. Ltd.* [1982] A.C. 173 at 185.

[95] See, *ibid*; *Square* v. *Model Farm Dairies (Bournemouth) Ltd.* [1939] 2 K.B. 365 at 375; *Reffell* v. *Surrey CC* [1964] 1 W.L.R. 358.

[96] *Butler* v. *Fife Coal Co. Ltd.* [1912] A.C. 149 at 165; but see the remarks of Atkin L.J. in *Phillips* v. *Britannia Hygienic Laundry Co.* [1923] 2 K.B. 832 at 841.

[97] *per* Lord Reid, *Cutler* v. *Wandsworth Stadium Ltd.* [1949] A.C. 398 at 417.

[98] See *Cocks* v. *Thanet DC* [1983] 2 A.C. 286.

[99] See Chap. 13 below at p. 400.

[99a] It follows that the case of *Guevara* v. *Hounslow LBC, The Times*, April 17, 1987, was wrongly decided. Once it was accepted that the plaintiff had a right of action in breach of statutory duty the "public law" questions must have been incidental to his private law rights; see generally, Chap. 13, below at p. 398.

The elements of the tort

Even if it can be established that the statute is one which confers a right of action, three other things must be established in order for a plaintiff to be entitled to recover damages for breach of statutory duty:

(1) The duty must be owed to the plaintiff.[1] There is unlikely to be any difficulty in cases brought by suspects for breaches of duty under the Police and Criminal and Evidence Act 1984. This requirement may, however, cause considerable problems if a plaintiff seeks to base an action upon general duties cast upon the police by statutes such as the Police Act 1964.

(2) The defendant must be in breach of the statutory duty. This a question of fact and, of course, depends on the precise wording of the relevant statutory provisions. The burden of proof will be on the plaintiff.

(3) The harm must be of the kind that the statute was designed to prevent.[2] Difficulties under this head are unlikely to arise in actions for breach of statutory duty under the Police and Criminal Evidence Act 1984 as the statute is designed to prevent damage of all kinds to people who are suspected of offences.

Although an action for breach of statutory duty is an action on the case[3] it is not always necessary to prove damage as part of the cause of action. Whether or not damage is a necessary ingredient of the cause of action has been said to depend on the construction of the statute involved. Thus:

> "Where, from its context, it is clear that the statute created a right in the plaintiff so absolute in its content that the plaintiff was to be protected against violation, even though it caused no damage, then the tort is actionable *per se*."[4]

The following rights have been held to give rise to a breach actionable *per se*: the statutory right to vote,[5] the right to receive a statement of how wages were made up,[6] a person's right to have his suitability for a living as a minister of religion determined.[7] A person's rights under the Police and Criminal Evidence Act 1984 should be actionable *per se* as the interests protected by the statute—interests in receiving information and assistance while under police investigation—do not usually generate "special damage" if they are violated. As Street says:

> "The courts are most likely to interpret in this manner a statute which protects an interest of the plaintiff other than his interest in his person or his goods."[8]

[1] See, *e.g.* *Knapp* v. *Railway Executive* [1949] 2 All E.R. 508.
[2] *Gorris* v. *Scott* (1874) L.R. 9 Exch. 125.
[3] See Chap. 11 below at p. 347.
[4] Street at p. 286.
[5] *Ashby* v. *White* (1703) 2 Ld.Raym. 938.
[6] *Simmonds* v. *Newport Abercarn Black Vein Steam Coal Co.* [1921] 1 K.B. 616, *per* Atkin L.J.
[7] *Ferguson* v. *Earl Kinnoull* (1842) 9 Cl. & Fin. 251 (H.L.).
[8] Street at p. 286.

Applicability to police cases

The availability of this cause of action to police cases depends on the particular statutory provision which is being relied upon. The Police and Criminal Evidence Act 1984 gives rise to a number of rights to information and assistance. No remedies for breach of these provisions is provided by the statute. It should be noted that by section 67(10) it is expressly provided that a failure to comply with any provisions of the Codes of Practice issued under section 66 "shall not of itself render him liable to any . . . civil proceedings." The only liability that this section can be seeking to exclude is that for breach of statutory duty. It is significant that the statute does not seek to exclude liability for breach of the provisions of the Act itself, as opposed to the Codes. So, an action for breach of statutory duty must then lie if the police fail to comply with the "information and assistance" provisions of the 1984 Act. The following sections would appear to give rise to potential actions:

(1) Section 56: Right to have someone informed when arrested. This section provides that:

> "Where a person has been arrested and is being held in custody in a police station or other premises, he shall be entitled, if he so requests, to have one friend or relative or other person who is known to him or who is likely to take an interest in his welfare told, as soon as is practicable except to the extent that delay is permitted by this section, that he has been arrested and is being detained there."[9]

The section permits delay only in the case of serious arrestable offences[10] if it is authorised by an officer of at least the rank of superintendent.[11] Delay may only be authorised where there are reasonable grounds for believing that[12] telling the named person of the arrest:

> "(a) will lead to interference with or harm to evidence connected with a serious arrestable offence or interference with or physical injury to other persons; or
> (b) will lead to the alerting of other persons suspected of having committed such an offence but not yet arrested for it, or
> (c) will hinder the recovery of any property obtained as a result of such an offence."[13]

If a delay is authorised the detained person must be told the reason for it and the reason should be noted on his custody record as soon as is practicable.[14] Once the reason for authorising delay ceases to exist there may be no further delay in permitting the exercise of the right.[15] Similar considerations apply to the duty to inform the "person responsible for the welfare" of a child or a young person that he is in police detention under section 57.

[9] s.56(1).
[10] See Chap. 5 above at p. 166.
[11] s.56(2).
[12] See Chap. 5 above at pp. 145 *et seq.*
[13] s.56(5).
[14] s.56(6) and (7).
[15] s.56(9).

(2) Section 58: Access to legal advice. This section provides that:

> "(1) A person arrested and held in custody in a police station or other premises shall be entitled, if he so requests, to consult a solicitor privately at any time . . .
> (4) If a person makes such a request, he must be permitted to consult a solicitor as soon as is practicable except to the extent that delay is permitted by this section."

The section permits delay only where the person is in detention for a serious arrestable offence and the delay is authorised by an officer of at least the rank of superintendent.[16] Such delay may only be authorised where the officer has reasonable grounds for believing[17] that the exercise of the right at the time the person desires to exercise it:

> "(a) will lead to interference with or harm to evidence connected with a serious arrestable offence or interference with or physical injury to other persons; or
> (b) will lead to the alerting of other persons suspected of having committed such an offence but not yet arrested for it; or
> (c) will hinder the recovery of any property obtained as a result of such an offence."

If a delay is authorised the detained person must be told the reason for it and the reason must be noted on his custody record.[18] Special provisions apply to persons detained under the terrorism provisions.[19] It is difficult to see how, in the large majority of cases, a private consultation with a solicitor could lead to the results which would justify the delay.

(3) Section 21: Rights to access and copies. The section gives the person who had custody or control of something seized by the police the right to apply for access to it[20] or the right to obtain photographs or copies.[21] This right is subject to a number of statutory limitations.[22]

The "indications" point towards there being a right of action against the police for breach of the provisions of all these sections. The only remedy provided by the Act for breach is disciplinary action against the officers involved. This does not give any right to damages to the person deprived of his statutory entitlement. The sections are designed to protect specific classes of people, namely, those in police custody or whose property has been seized. Finally, the duties under all the sections are defined with precision. It is further submitted that breaches of sections 56, 57 or 58 will be actionable *per se*.[23]

It would follow that a detained person who was denied his rights under section 56 or section 58 will have rights of action against the police for breach of statutory duty. His damages for this breach would be "at large"[24]

[16] s.58(6).
[17] See Chap. 5 above at pp. 145 *et seq.*
[18] s.58(9).
[19] s.58(12)–(18).
[20] s.21(3).
[21] s.21(4).
[22] See Chap. 7 above at p. 219.
[23] See above at pp. 312 *et seq.*
[24] *Cf. Nicholls* v. *Ely Sugar Beet Factory Ltd.* [1936] Ch. 343.

and he would also have a potential claim for aggravated and exemplary damages. Furthermore, any "reasonably foreseeable" special damages could also be recovered. A person who was denied access to property held by the police or copies of documents would also have a right of action for breach of statutory duty under section 31.

In an unreported case[25] two firms of solicitors applied for injunctions to restrain the police from breaching their statutory duty in refusing to allow them access to clients held in police custody. Rose J. refused the application saying:

> "I am not persuaded that I have jurisdiction. Assuming I did have jurisdiction were I to make the Order sought it would be unreasonable, a hindrance to police inquiries may be caused."

It is submitted that there was, in fact, no jurisdiction to make the order as the proper plaintiffs were not the solicitors but the prisoners who, in the nature of the case, could not give instructions to make the application. The prisoner would, however, have an action for damages after his release. It is further submitted that in such a situation the solicitors would have *locus* to apply for an order of mandamus to compel the police to discharge their statutory duties under section 58.[26]

4. DEFAMATION

Introduction

One of the most important areas of harm in many cases of police malpractice will be to the citizen's reputation. The fact that a person has been arrested, prosecuted or even just investigated can give rise to substantial and continuing damage. As Lord Atkin once said "it is impossible to track down the scandal, to know what quarters the poison may reach."[27]

This kind of damage can be taken into account if the person concerned can sue for false imprisonment or malicious prosecution. A successful plaintiff in one of these actions can recover damages to compensate for the damage to his reputation caused by the arrest or prosecution. If such an action cannot be pursued—because, for example, there was no arrest or prosecution—then the only remedy is an action for defamation. It is not clear whether a successful action in defamation could be brought in addition to an action in false imprisonment or malicious prosecution. On general principles, however, the same damage to reputation cannot be recovered twice over so that in such circumstances an action in defamation would usually be superfluous in any event.

It should be noted that legal aid is not available for an action in defamation and this is likely further to limit the practical usefulness of this cause of action for victims of police malpractice.

The police themselves have not been slow to realise the potential

[25] October 26, 1985; Q.B.D.
[26] See Chap. 13 below at p. 418.
[27] *Ley* v. *Hamilton* (1935) 153 L.T. 384 at 386.

usefulness of actions in defamation. In *Conerney* v. *Jacklin*[28] a police officer brought an action in defamation in respect of the contents of a police complaint made by the defendant. On a preliminary point it was held that the contents of such a complaint were not absolutely privileged and could be relied on in a defamation action.[29]

The elements of the tort

Defamation is an important and complex area of the law. Only the briefest of sketches can be given here. To succeed in an action for defamation the plaintiff must prove that:

(1) defamatory words (or other representations);
(2) referring to the plaintiff;
(3) were "published" by the defendant.

The first question is whether or not the words used are "defamatory" of the plaintiff. According to the well-known dictum of Lord Atkin the question is: "Would the words tend to lower the plaintiff in the estimation of right-thinking members of society generally?"[30] The plaintiff can allege either that the words are defamatory in their "ordinary and natural meaning" or that they are defamatory in the light of facts and circumstances known to the people to whom they were published (or both). The latter is known as a "legal innuendo" and the facts and circumstances relied on must be pleaded and proved. It is for the judge to decide whether or not the words used are **capable** of bearing a defamatory meaning and for the jury to decide whether they were **in fact** defamatory.

In cases involving the police the words in question may be of the form: "X is under police investigation for specified crimes" or "X is helping police with their inquiries" or "X has been arrested." It is not necessary that express words be used. Thus, for example, the inclusion of a person's photograph in an album labelled "Known Criminals" would clearly be defamatory.

The question of whether it is defamatory to say that a person is under investigation by the police was considered in the well-known case of *Lewis* v. *Daily Telegraph*.[31] The defendant newspaper published an article saying that the plaintiff was being investigated by the fraud squad. It was admitted that the words were capable of bearing a defamatory meaning—namely that the plaintiff was suspected of crime—but it was denied that they carried the meaning that the plaintiff's affairs were conducted fraudulently or dishonestly. A majority of the House of Lords agreed with this contention. As Lord Devlin said:

> "If the ordinary sensible man was capable of thinking that wherever there was a police inquiry there was guilt, it would be almost imposs-

[28] [1985] Crim.L.R. 234.
[29] See Chap. 2 above at p. 58.
[30] *Sim* v. *Stretch* [1936] 2 All E.R. 1237 at 1240.
[31] [1964] A.C. 234.

ible to give accurate information about anything: but in my opinion he is not."[32]

Thus, the statement that "X is under investigation for a crime" has two possible "innuendos," that "X is suspected of the crime" and that "X is guilty of the crime." Both these innuendos are defamatory, but as a matter of law, the statement is only capable of bearing the first defamatory meaning. A jury is not entitled to infer a statement as to guilt from a statement about an investigation.

The position, it is submitted, is less clear when a person is arrested or a prosecution is actually commenced. The question is: would an ordinary, sensible, person be capable of inferring dubious conduct from the fact that the police had actually made an arrest or commenced a prosecution? It is submitted that such an inference is possible because an arrest or a prosecution implies that there is a reasonable and probable cause for believing that the suspect is guilty of the crime in question. If a person is arrested in public, within the view of others, then the fact of the arrest is capable of being a "statement" which is "published" by being done in the presence of others. The fact that someone was arrested is capable of lowering them in the estimation of right-thinking members of society generally and is, therefore, defamatory. It would, presumably, be a defence for the police to show that they had reasonable grounds for making the arrest.

An example of a defamation action based on investigations into a suspected crime is found in the case of *Steinberg* v. *Selfridges Ltd.*[33] The plaintiff was stopped outside the defendant's store by three police officers and one of the defendant's store detectives on suspicion of having stolen various items from the defendant's store. The store detective searched her handbag in "full public view." It then transpired that she had receipts for the items and the store detective apologised for the mistake. She brought an action for defamation on the grounds, *inter alia,* that the words of the store detective carried the meaning that she had been reasonably suspected of having committed theft or had committed theft. It was pleaded that "the public examination of the contents of a shopper's handbag on the pavement outside the entrance to a store under the supervision of the police is widely understood to mean that the shopper has been or is reasonably suspected of theft." The case was settled on the defendant's payment of £1500 damages for defamation.

The second element is "reference to the plaintiff." The words used must, in fact, refer to the plaintiff. In many cases involving the police the plaintiff will be named as the person arrested, under investigation and so on. It is not necessary, however, for the plaintiff to be expressly named in the "statement." It is sufficient if an ordinary sensible person, with special knowledge of the facts, might reasonably believe that the statement referred to the plaintiff.[34]

If the reference to the plaintiff is unintended then the defendant may have a defence under section 4 of the Defamation Act 1952. This provides that if the words used were not defamatory "on the face of them" and the publisher did not know of circumstances by virtue of which they might be understood to be defamatory then the words shall be treated as published

32 *Lewis* v. *Daily Telegraph* [1964] A.C. 234 at 286.
33 (1985) unreported.
34 *Morgan* v. *Odhams Press* [1971] 1 W.L.R. 1239.

innocently if the publisher "exercised all reasonable care in relation to the publication."

The third element is "publication." The police will only be potentially liable in defamation if they are responsible for the "publication" of the defamatory statements which refer to the plaintiff. Publication simply means the communication of the defamatory statement to at least one person other than the plaintiff.[35] If the statements are contained in a document then it will be publication if the document is intentionally shown to any third party or if its coming to the attention of a third party could have been foreseen.[36] It will be publication if defamatory words are said in the hearing of a third party.

Libel and slander

If the defamation is in writing or by any representation of a "permanent" character then the law presumes damage. It is "publication in permanent form" to broadcast words on television or radio, provided it is for "general reception."[37] If, however, the defamation is by spoken words then special damage must be proved before an action can be brought. There are a number of slanders which are actionable *per se*.

The most important of these for our purposes is the imputation of crime. The crime imputed must be one punishable by imprisonment. A general imputation of criminality will be enough. There is no need for there to be reference to any specific crime. Thus "I know enough to put you in gaol" is actionable *per se*.[38] It is not actionable *per se* simply to cast suspicion of a crime on a particular person.[39]

It is also actionable *per se* to "disparage" a person in his office, profession, calling, trade or business. It is now no longer necessary for the words to be spoken in relation to the office, etc.[40] Spoken words will be actionable *per se* if they impute a want of integrity or dishonest conduct in the office[41] or if they impute incompetence in an office of profit.[42]

Defences

Once it has been established that the defendant "published" a defamatory statement about the plaintiff then the defendant will be liable to pay damages in defamation unless he can establish a defence.

(1) Justification. If the defendant can establish that the statement made was in fact true then he will have a complete defence. It is immaterial, for

[35] *Bata* v. *Bata* [1948] W.N. 366.
[36] *Huth* v. *Huth* [1915] 3 K.B. 32 at 38–39.
[37] Defamation Act 1952, s.1.
[38] *Webb* v. *Beavan* (1883) 11 Q.B.D. 609.
[39] *Simmons* v. *Mitchell* (1880) 6 App.Cas.156 (P.C.).
[40] s.2 of the Defamation Act 1952.
[41] *Booth* v. *Arnold* [1895] 1 Q.B. 571.
[42] *Alexander* v. *Jenkins* [1892] 1 Q.B. 797.

these purposes, that the defendant was acting maliciously. Thus it will a defence to an action based on the defamatory statement that P is under investigation for a particular crime to show that he was, in fact, under investigation. Whether or not the police had any grounds for making such an investigation is irrelevant.

If, however, an innuendo is pleaded the matter may be more complicated. A statement to the effect that the police wished to interview P about a particular crime could be said to carry the innuendo that there were some grounds for connecting P with that crime. If no such grounds existed—because, for example, the police in fact wished to interview P about a completely different matter—then the police would be unable to justify the innuendo and this defence would fail.

The defendant does not have to justify every single detail of the statement made. If it is substantially correct then he will succeed.[43] When there are several charges and the truth of only some of them is proved these can be taken into account to determine whether the remaining, unproved, charges materially injure the plaintiff's reputation.[44] Thus, for example, if the police publish statements to the effect that a person has committed five separate burglaries, the proof of three of them can be taken into account in determining whether the plaintiff has a reputation which can be injured by falsely accusing him of two further burglaries.

(2) "Absolute privilege." Any statement made in court proceedings, of whatever kind, is absolutely privileged. This privilege extends to proceedings before other tribunals which exercise functions similar to courts.[45] It does not extend to licensing sessions.[46] Another area is that of communications made by one officer of state to another in the course of his official duty. It appears that the officers in question must be of very high rank. In the case of *Merricks* v. *Nott-Bower*[47] the Court of Appeal refused to strike out a libel claim based on a report on two police officers by a Deputy Commissioner of the Metropolitan Police to the Commissioner. In the Australian case of *Gibbons* v. *Dufell*[48] it was held that a report made by an inspector of police to his superior officer was subject to qualified but not absolute privilege.

(3) "Qualified privilege." This covers communications made in the discharge of a public or private duty or in the conduct of a person's own affairs or where his interest is concerned:

> "If fairly warranted by any reasonable occasion or exigency and honestly made such communications are protected for the common convenience and welfare of society."[49]

This defence covers information given to the police in order to detect

[43] *Alexander* v. *North Eastern Ry.* (1865) 6 B. & S. 340.
[44] Defamation Act 1952, s.5.
[45] *O'Connor* v. *Waldron* [1935] A.C. 76 at 81.
[46] *Attwood* v. *Chapman* [1914] 3 K.B. 275.
[47] [1965] 1 Q.B. 57.
[48] (1932) 47 C.L.R. 520.
[49] *per* Parke B., *Toogood* v. *Spyring* (1834) 1 Cr.M. & R. 181 at 193; see also *Adam* v. *Ward* [1917] A.C. 309 at 349.

crime.[50] Thus in the case of *Padmore* v. *Lawrence*[51] the defendant wrongly accused the plaintiff of theft in the presence of third parties. It was held that such a charge was not slanderous if made bona fide. As Coleridge J. said:

> "For the sake of public justice, charges and communications, which otherwise be slanderous, are protected if bona fide made in the prosecution of an inquiry into a suspected crime."[52]

This case was approved by the Court of Appeal in *Collins* v. *Cooper*[53] in which it was held that all material statements made by the persons interested in the detection of crime during their investigations and material thereto were subject to a qualified privilege which would, therefore, be destroyed by want of bona fides.[54]

In the case of *Wenman* v. *Ash*[55] the defendant published accusations about crimes by the plaintiff to the plaintiff's wife. This was held not to be subject to qualified privilege because the allegations were not made in the "prosecution of an inquiry" into the crime, but in the course of general letters of complaint about various other matters. It was held in the Scots case of *Malcolm* v. *Duncan*[56] that a defamation action could not be based on statements made by one police officer investigating a crime to another or to a person "mixed up" in the affair because such statements were subject to qualified privilege.[57] In general, it is submitted that statements made by the police which are bona fide and in the execution of their duties would be held to be privileged.[58]

The defence of qualified privilege will be rebutted if the statements in question were published "maliciously." The burden of proving malice is on the plaintiff. The most common way of doing this is by establishing that the defendant did not believe in the truth of his statement or was reckless as to its truth or falsity. An honest but unreasonable belief in its truth is not malicious.[59] It is also "malicious" to use the privileged occasion for an improper purpose.[60] The publisher of the statement must use the occasion of privilege in accordance with the privilege. The privilege will be lost if the improper motive was the dominant one. The defendant will also lose his privilege if he exceeds it by, for example, publishing a statement more widely than is necessary.[61]

(4) "Fair comment." This covers comment on matters of public interest. The comment must be an expression of opinion and not an assertion of fact.

[50] *Johnson* v. *Evans* (1800) 3 Esp. 32; *Lightbody* v. *Gordon* (1882) 9 R. 937 (Court of Session).

[51] (1840) 11 Ad. & El. 380.

[52] *Ibid.* at 382.

[53] [1902] 19 T.L.R. 118.

[54] *per* Collins M.R., at 119; see also *Shufflebottom* v. *Allday* (1857) 5 W.R. 315 at 316.

[55] (1853) 13 C.B. 836.

[56] (1897) 24 R. 747 (Court of Session).

[57] The statement in *Gatley on Libel and Slander* para. 486 that the privilege attaches to any statement made to the police is not supported by this case. The actual decision in *Malcolm* v. *Duncan*, which involved a striking out, is extremely dubious as the issue of malice was not properly considered.

[58] This is the view expressed in Street at p. 334.

[59] *Horrocks* v. *Lowe* [1975] A.C. 135.

[60] *Clark* v. *Molyneux* (1877) 3 Q.B.D. 237 at 246.

[61] *Adam* v. *Ward* [1917] A.C. 309.

The defendant must have been commenting on true or privileged statements of fact. This defence can be rebutted by proof that the comments were not made honestly or were made "maliciously."

It should be noted that it is no defence to a defamation action that the publisher of the statements honestly and reasonably believed them to be true.

Applicability to police cases

There is no reported case in which the police have been successfully sued for libel or slander in respect of statements made in the course of their duties. In a number of cases a slander claim has been joined to a claim in false imprisonment or malicious prosecution but the plaintiff's claim has been dismissed on all causes of action.[62]

If a plaintiff can establish that police officers "published" statements about him which were defamatory the police will usually be able to rely on one of two defences.

The first is that of justification. While statements such as "P is being sought by the police to assist with inquiries" are capable of bearing the defamatory meaning that "P is suspected of a crime" the police will have a defence if P **really was** suspected of a crime. It is unlikely that such statements would be made in any other circumstances. As has already been suggested, an action may lie if the police in fact have no grounds to connect P with the crime or if they are seeking him for an entirely different matter.[63]

Secondly, even assuming that the statements made were untrue the police will usually be able to rely on the defence of "qualified privilege." It is likely that any statements made by police officers who are acting in the course of their duties will attract "qualified privilege." Thus, even if an untrue defamatory statement about the plaintiff is made by a police officer, he will only be able to succeed in an action for defamation if he can prove that the officer in question made the statement "maliciously."

An action in defamation will, therefore, be most appropriate when it can be shown that untrue statements made about a person by police officers, which did not lead to any arrest or prosecution were made maliciously. This might apply to statements in police records or on the police computer. It is difficult to see the action having wide practical application.

5. CONSPIRACY

Introduction

The tort of conspiracy is usually applied to situations where people combine together for the purpose of damaging another's trade or business. Many

[62] See, *e.g.*, *Middleweek* v. *Chief Constable The Times*, August 1, 1985; *Bayliss* v. *Hill* [1984] unreported, except for the final paragraph of the judgment of Hirst J. which is reported at *The Times*, April 17, 1984; and see *Moberly* v. *MPC* (1987) May 13, unreported, C.A.

[63] See above at p. 319.

of the leading cases involve trade union action. Nevertheless, the tort is of general application and successful actions have been brought against the police on at least two occasions.[64]

A tortious conspiracy can take one of two forms: a combination for the purpose of damaging the plaintiff or a combination to perform an unlawful act which damages the plaintiff. Both forms of the tort may be relevant to actions against the police although the successful cases appear to have been under the second form. There are important differences between the elements of the two forms of the tort.[65]

Combination to perform an unlawful act

The elements of a tortious conspiracy which takes the form of a combination to perform an unlawful act are as follows: there must be:

(1) a combination between two or more persons;
(2) to perform an unlawful act;
(3) the dominant purpose of which is to injure the plaintiff;
(4) as a result of which combination the plaintiff suffers damage.

A combination is an understanding or agreement between two or more persons. If the existence of a combination is established the liability of a particular defendant depends on whether, having regard to his knowledge, utterances and actions, he was sufficiently a party to the combination and common design.[66] Any act which is itself tortious will be sufficient for the tort of conspiracy. Each defendant must be aware of the facts which make the combination unlawful.[67] But the overt acts must themselves be actionable.

This principle appears to be contradicted by the case of *Sam* v. *Cluney*[68] in which two police officers were successfully sued for, *inter alia*, conspiracy to give false evidence in a criminal trial. However, this case appears to have been impliedly overruled by the decision of the Court of Appeal in *Marrinan* v. *Vibart*.[69] That case concerned an alleged conspiracy to give perjured evidence at a criminal trial. It was held not to be actionable because there would have been no action in respect of the evidence itself in the absence of a conspiracy because of the absolute privilege attaching to such evidence.[70]

It is now clear, following the decision of the House of Lords in *Lonrho* v. *Shell Petroleum Co. Ltd. (No. 2)*[71] that an "unlawful act" conspiracy will only be actionable if the predominant purpose of the combination was an intent to injure the plaintiff. This qualification brings the first type of conspiracy into line with the second type but greatly limits its scope.

[64] *Sam* v. *Cluney* [1956] Crim.L.R. 271; *Selby & Firman* v. *Maclennan, The Times*, May 9, 1961.
[65] Hughes "The Tort of Conspiracy" (1952) 15 M.L.R. 209.
[66] See *per* Stamp J., *Torquay Hotel Co.* v. *Cousins* [1969] 2 Ch. 106 at 121.
[67] *Pritchard* v. *Briggs* [1980] Ch. 338 at 414 and 424.
[68] [1956] Crim.L.R. 271.
[69] [1963] 1 Q.B. 234 and 528.
[70] See also *Roy* v. *Prior* [1971] A.C. 470.
[71] [1982] A.C. 173.

Conspiracy is an action on the case and so is only actionable on proof of "special damage."[72] In other words, the combination will only be actionable if it is actually carried into effect so as to damage the plaintiff. It will, however, be sufficient damage if the plaintiff has incurred expense in investigating and counteracting the machinations of defendants.[73]

This form of the tort is severely limited in its scope because if the actions of the defendants are tortious then the plaintiff can recover damages without the necessity of suing in conspiracy. The courts are reluctant to allow the joinder of a claim based on conspiracy to commit a particular tort with a claim based on that tort. As Denning L.J. said in *Ward* v. *Lewis*[74];

> "When a tort has been committed by two or more persons an allegation of a prior conspiracy to commit the tort adds nothing. The prior agreement merges into the tort. A party is not allowed to gain an added advantage by charging conspiracy when the agreement has become merged in the tort."

Combination to injure

The second form of conspiracy is a "combination to injure." The distinguishing feature of this is that the defendants need not engage in any unlawful acts. As Lord Macnaghten put it[75] a conspiracy to injure may:

> "give rise to civil liability even though the end were brought about by conduct and acts which, by themselves and apart from the element of combination or concerted action could not be regarded as a legal wrong."

The elements of a tortious conspiracy which takes the form of a combination to injure the plaintiff are as follows: there must be

(1) a combination between two or more persons;
(2) whose dominant purpose is to cause injury to the plaintiff;
(3) which causes damage to the plaintiff.

The first and third elements are identical to the first form of the tort.

The second element does, however, present very considerable legal and practical difficulties. When considering whether there is an "intent to injure" the plaintiff a distinction must be drawn:

> "between the case where the object is the legitimate benefit of the combiners and the case where the object is deliberate damage without just cause."[76]

It is clear that if the defendants are acting in their own legitimate interests

[72] See Chap. 11 below at p. 347.
[73] *BMTA* v. *Salvadori* [1949] Ch. 556.
[74] [1955] 1 W.L.R. 9 at 11.
[75] *Quinn* v. *Leathem* [1901] A.C. 495 at 510; approved in *Crofter Hand Woven Harris Tweed Co. Ltd.* v. *Veitch* [1942] A.C. 435 at 448 and 461.
[76] *per* Lord Wright, in the *Crofter's* case [1942] A.C. 435 at 469.

the fact that disproportionate harm is caused to the plaintiff is irrelevant.[77] Neither does it matter that the defendants were acting maliciously.[78]

Applicability to police cases

In the successful cases already mentioned[79] the additional cause of action in conspiracy does not appear to have had any significant effect on the quantum of damages recovered. It is difficult to think of practical situations in which an action in conspiracy will add anything to an action in a substantive tort in a police case. Any "combination to injure" a citizen by police officers would be actionable as a misfeasance in a public office without the need to invoke the tort of conspiracy.[80] The effect of *Marrinan* v. *Vibart*[81] appears to be to eliminate any potential police liability for conspiracy to give perjured evidence.

6. MISFEASANCE IN A PUBLIC OFFICE

Introduction

A police constable holds a "public office."[82] One consequence of this is that a constable who wilfully neglects to perform his duty is guilty of a crime at common law.[83] It also entails potential civil liability in the ancient tort of misfeasance in public office.

The action for misfeasance in public office can be traced back at least to the early eighteenth century. In the famous case of *Ashby* v. *White*,[84] the House of Lords upheld an action for damages by an elector who had been wrongly refused a vote in parliamentary elections. The elements of the tort were clarified and developed in a number of nineteenth century cases. Nevertheless, for reasons which are not entirely clear, it appears to have fallen into disuse in England for a considerable period[85] and the leading textbooks in the law of tort either ignore it entirely or classify it as being "doubtful."

Such a view is now plainly untenable. In the Privy Council case of *Dunlop* v. *Woollahra Municipal Council*[86] Lord Diplock refers to the "well-established tort of misfeasance by a public officer in the discharge of his public duties." In the case of *Bourgoin SA* v. *Ministry of Agriculture*[87] Mann

[77] *Crofter's* case [1942] A.C. 435, *per* Viscount Simon, at 447.
[78] *Ibid. per* Viscount Maugham at 450, *per* Lord Wright at 471.
[79] See above at p. 322.
[80] See below.
[81] [1963] 1 Q.B. 234.
[82] See Chap. 1 above at p. 23.
[83] See *R.* v. *Dytham* [1979] Q.B. 722.
[84] (1703) 2 Ld. Raym. 938.
[85] See *Davis* v. *Bromley Corporation* [1908] 1 K.B. 170.
[86] [1982] A.C. 158.
[87] [1985] 3 All E.R. 585.

J. provided an important and detailed analysis of the tort.[88] The existence of an analogous cause of action in Scotland was confirmed by the case of *Micosta SA* v. *Shetland Islands Council.*[89]

The elements of the tort

The precise "elements" of the tort do not appear to have been set out systematically in any case or textbook. There are, it is submitted, four of them. The tort is committed when:

(1) a public officer;
(2) causes damage;
(3) to a "foreseeable" plaintiff;
(4) by acts or omissions which are a "malicious abuse" of his office.

(1) "A public officer." This term covers:

> "everyone who is appointed to discharge a public duty, and receives compensation in whatever shape, from the crown or otherwise."[90]

There can be no doubt that a police constable is a "public officer" in this sense. In *Lewis* v. *Cattle*[91] Lord Hewart C.J. said that "a police officer is a person who holds office under His Majesty." The point was conceded in *R.* v. *Dytham*[92] In the important Australian case of *Farrington* v. *Thomson & Bridgland*[93] a sergeant of police was held to be the holder of a public office.

(2) Damage. This is required because misfeasance is an action on the case. Any kind of damage will be sufficient, including, it is submitted, not only financial damage, but loss of liberty or damage to reputation.[94]

(3) A foreseeable plaintiff. This element involves the issue of limitation of the class of potential plaintiffs. In many of the old cases the defendant's acts were "aimed at " a particular person for malicious reasons. There was, therefore only one potential plaintiff and no "limitation" issue arose. In the *Bourgoin* case it was unsuccessfully argued that "intent to injure the plaintiff" ("targeted malice") was an essential ingredient of the tort. It was held that a plaintiff would be entitled to sue in either of two situations:

(1) if damage was caused to him by a malicious act which was aimed at him;
(2) if the defendant had deliberately done an act which he knew he did not have power to do—with knowledge of its consequences—and the plaintiff had suffered damage as a result.[95]

[88] This analysis was unanimously supported by the Court of Appeal.
[89] [1986] S.L.T. 193; although the action failed on the facts. For a note on this case see Colin T. Reid [1986] P.L. 380.
[90] *Henly* v. *Mayor and Burgesses of Lyme* (1828) 5 Bing. 91 at 107.
[91] [1938] 2 K.B. 454 at 457.
[92] [1979] Q.B. 722.
[93] [1959] V.R. 286 at 292; see below at p. 328.
[94] See *Beaurain* v. *Scott* (1811) 3 Camp. 387.
[95] *Bourgoin SA* v. *Ministry of Agriculture* [1985] 3 All E.R. 585 at 602, *per* Mann J.; 623–624 *per* Oliver L.J.

On this view, the class of potential plaintiffs would embrace any claimant who in fact suffers damage, provided that damage was foreseeable. The "limitation" issue was not expressly considered in the *Bourgoin* case but the class of potential plaintiffs seems dangerously large, bearing in mind the numbers of people who may be affected by the actions of public officers such as police constables. It could be argued that one possible limiting principle would be to confine plaintiffs to the class of those to whom injury from an unlawful administrative act is reasonably foreseeable. The test would, then, be the same as in negligence.

Another possibility was suggested in the Australian case of *Tampion* v. *Anderson*.[96] It was held that the plaintiff must show that:

> "he was a member of the public or one of the members of the public to whom the holder of the office owed a duty not to commit the particular abuse complained of."

Thus, it might be argued that if a police officer stood by and allowed someone to be injured by attackers (as in the *Dytham* case), the person injured (or, as in *Dytham*, his estate or dependants) could sue but, for example, his employer, could not.

The whole question of "limitation" of the class of potential plaintiffs to whom the duty to behave properly in a public office is owed awaits further judicial clarification.

(4) Act or omission. The fourth element is some act or omission, by the public officer, which constitutes a "malicious abuse" of his office. It is now clear that there does not need to be a "positive act" or "misfeasance" to produce liability. An omission, by which the officer fails to perform a public duty will be sufficient.[97] An important question arises when a police officer orders someone to do something when he has no power to do so. Is such an order an "act" for the purposes of this tort? In an Australian case a police officer ordered a hotel owner to close his hotel, knowing that he had no power to do so. It was held that this was sufficient to found liability in misfeasance.[98]

Malice

Malice has always caused the most difficulty in relation to this tort. It has often been argued that whenever damage is caused by a public officer doing something beyond his powers an action for damages should lie. This argument has been rejected in the large majority of cases.[99] The position is different, however, if the act is **knowingly** invalid. There is now no doubt that in such a case tortious liability will arise. In the *Bourgoin* case (in an analysis accepted by all the judges in the Court of Appeal)[1] Mann J. put the point like this:

[96] [1973] V.R. 715 at 749.
[97] See *Henly's* case (1828) 5 Bing. 91 at 107.
[98] See *Farrington* v. *Thomson & Bridgland* [1959] V.R. 286 at 293–294.
[99] See *Dunlop* v. *Woollahra Muncipal Council* [1982] A.C. 158; and *Takaro Properties* v. *Rowling* [1978] 2 N.Z.L.R. 314.
[1] [1985] 3 All E.R. 585 at 622j–624d, *per* Oliver L.J.

> "There is no sensible distinction between the case where an officer performs an act which he has no power to perform with the object of injuring 'A' (which the defendant accepts is actionable at the instance of 'A') and the case where an officer performs an act which he knows he has no power to perform with the object of conferring a benefit on 'B' but which has the foreseeable and actual consequence of injury to 'A'."[2]

Thus, a "misfeasance" or "malicious abuse" is committed by the police in one of two circumstances:

(1) where a police officer does something for a "malicious motive" which causes damage to the plaintiff;
(2) where damage is caused by a police officer "knowingly" doing something which he has no power to do.

(1) Improper motives. The first alternative requires "malice." As in malicious prosecution cases "malice" does not simply mean "ill will" or spite. As Lord Campbell C.J. said to the jury in *Tozer* v. *Child* (a direction upheld by the Court of the Queen's Bench)

> "malice might be proved, not only by evidence of personal hostility or spite, but by any evidence of any other corrupt or improper motive."[3]

Any "wrongful motive" will, therefore, be sufficient "malice" for these purposes. Thus, it will be a "malicious abuse of office" for a police officer to request a person to wait for him at a police station in a deliberate attempt to harm his business or to relieve him of the burden of conducting immediate inquiries to enable him to go home early. The latter motive is a "wrongful" one in law, even though no spite or hostility are involved.

If the actions of a police officer are "malicious" in this extended sense they do not have to be *ultra vires* his powers to attract liability.[4] In other words, there will be liability in damages for any loss caused by police acts or omissions based on wrongful motives. Thus a police officer who lawfully seizes goods which he has reasonable grounds for believing are evidence of an offence which it is necessary to seize to prevent them being concealed will be liable for misfeasance if his motive in seizing the goods is not the collection of evidence but some wrongful motive such as causing damage to the owner's business. Despite the lawfulness of his acts he will be liable because of the maliciousness of his motive.

The mere presence of a wrongful motive is not, in itself, sufficient to found liability. Such a motive must be determinative of the act or omission in question. The criminal case of *R.* v. *Llewellyn-Jones,*[5] provides useful guidance here. The case involved a County Court Registrar who was accused of making an order in relation to funds under his control "in the expectation that he would gain personal advantage from the making of such an order." The trial judge ruled that:

> "if the registrar of a county court when exercising his power to order payment out of court of money held on behalf of a beneficiary were to make an order in expectation of some personal benefit he hoped to

[2] *Bourgoin SA* v. *Ministry of Agriculture* [1985] 3 All E.R. 585 at 602e–f.
[3] (1857) 7 E. & B. 377 at 379.
[4] See *per* Viscount Simonds, *Smith* v. *East Elloe RDC* [1956] A.C. 736.
[5] (1966) 51 Cr.App.R. 4.

> obtain and in circumstances where, had it not been for the personal benefit, he would not have made the order, that would be an example of misconduct in a public duty . . . but I would not be prepared to say that it would be misconduct for this purpose for a registrar to make a decision which did affect his personal interests, merely because he knew that his interests were so involved, if the decision was made honestly and in a genuine belief that it was a proper exercise of his jurisdiction."[6]

(2) Knowing invalidity. The second alternative way that a police officer can "abuse" his office is by doing something which he **knows** he has no power to do. Thus the unlawfulness of his actions is a necessary precondition to liability. Under this second alternative motive is entirely irrelevant. He may act out of the best of motives but, if he knows that he has no power to act in that way then he will be liable in tort for damage caused.[7] It is clear that "actual knowledge" of invalidity is necessary. "Constructive knowledge" will not be enough.

The most famous of all recent misfeasance cases was under this second head. It concerned an order given by the prime minister and attorney-general of Quebec to a liquor licensing authority. He ordered the cancellation of the plaintiff's restaurant licence because the plaintiff had stood bail for various Jehovah's Witnesses who were at that time responsible for serious public order problems in Quebec. Nevertheless, the Supreme Court of Canada found that the defendant had abused his office and awarded the plaintiff damages of $33,123.[8]

An important example is the case of *Farrington* v. *Thomson & Bridgland.*[9] The plaintiff was the licensee of a hotel which the police ordered him to close down because they believed his licence to be forfeit. It was established that the police, in giving such orders were "intentionally purporting to exercise a power to give binding orders to the plaintiff which they were fully aware, at the time, that they did not possess."[10] It was held that this was sufficient to found a misfeasance action. Smith J. also decided that the fact that the plaintiff had obeyed the order was not sufficient to make the resultant damage too remote.[11]

Applicability to police cases

The tort of misfeasance in public office is, it is submitted, a well-established cause of action which is plainly applicable to the police. In many situations it will overlap with established torts. Thus if a police officer arrests a plaintiff knowing that he has, in fact, no power to do so he will be liable in false imprisonment as well as misfeasance. Given the fact that the burden of justifying false imprisonment is on the police the former would obviously be the simplest cause of action to pursue.

[6] *R.* v. *Llewellyn-Jones* (1966) 51 Cr.App.R. 4 at 6.

[7] See *Farrington* v. *Thomson & Bridgland* [1959] V.R. 286.

[8] See *Roncarelli* v. *Duplessis* (1959) 16 D.L.R. (2d) 689.

[9] [1959] V.R. 286.

[10] *Ibid.* at 291.

[11] *Ibid.* at 293–297.

Nevertheless, there are circumstances in which misfeasance may be the only available cause of action. Thus if a constable makes a lawful arrest with a malicious motive an action in false imprisonment will not be available but there will be a cause of action in misfeasance. To take another example, if the police give a person orders which they know they have no power to give and the person obeys and as a result suffers loss then there will be no action in trespass. There will, however, be an action in misfeasance as *Farrington's* case illustrates.

It would seem that if a police officer brings a prosecution against someone with a malicious motive but **with** reasonable and probable cause then, if the prosecution terminates in that person's favour, an action for misfeasance will lie.

If a person is caused damage by a police policy decision which is known to be *ultra vires* then damages can be recovered in misfeasance. If a policeman knowingly or maliciously neglects to carry out his duties then an action may be brought. In *R.* v. *Dytham,*[12] the police constable was accused of "wilfully omitting to take any steps to preserve the Queen's peace or to protect the person" of a man he saw being attacked. The man died and the constable was convicted of the offence of wilful neglect of his duty. It is submitted that the deceased's estate could have recovered damages in misfeasance.

7. ACTIONS AFTER DEATH

Introduction

At common law a person's death extinguished all rights of action that he might have had. In particular, if the death was a result of the tortious acts of another, the deceased's family would have no right of action in respect of the death.[13] The position is now governed by statute.

If a person dies as the result of the tortious acts of another there are two ways in which an action might be brought. First, by reason of the Law Reform (Miscellaneous Provisions) Act 1934, certain causes of action which were vested in the deceased at the time of his death survive for the benefit of his estate. Secondly, certain "dependants" of the deceased now have a right of action under the Fatal Accidents Act 1976.

Law Reform (Miscellaneous Provisions) Act 1934

By section 1(1) of the 1934 Act it is provided that all causes of action, with the exception of actions for defamation and seduction which were vested in a person on his death shall survive for the benefit of his estate.

It is expressly provided, by section 1(2)(*a*) that the damages recoverable for the benefit of the estate "shall not include any exemplary damages." Where the person's death has been caused by the act or omission which gives rise

[12] [1979] Q.B. 722.
[13] *Admiralty Commissioners* v. *SS. Amerika* [1917] A.C. 38.

to the cause of action the damages recoverable for the benefit of the estate shall be calculated without reference to any loss or gain to his estate consequent on his death, except that a sum in respect of funeral expenses may be included.[14] Damages for "loss of expectation of life" and for the "lost years" cannot be recovered if the death occurred after January 1, 1983.[15]

It follows that an action can be brought by the estate of a person who died as a result of police misconduct. Compensatory and aggravated damages can be recovered by the estate.

The Fatal Accidents Act 1976

The 1976 Act gives a right of action to "dependants" of a deceased person whose death was caused by any "wrongful act, neglect or default" such as would, if death had not ensued, have entitled the person injured to recover damages.[16]

Dependants are defined in section 1(2) and include spouses, parents and grandparents, children and grandchildren, nephews nieces and cousins and any person who had been living with the deceased in the same household for a period of at least two years immediately before death as husband or wife and any person treated by the deceased as a parent or as a "child of the family."

A husband or wife or the parents of an unmarried minor are entitled to damages for "bereavement"[17] in the sum of £3500.[18] Other damages are awarded as are proportionate to the injury resulting from the death to the dependants respectively. Such damages are assessed on the basis of the "value of the dependency," in other words, the dependants are entitled to that sum of money that will replace the "material benefits" provided to them by the deceased.[19]

It should be noted that the dependants cannot recover if the deceased earned his living by crime, because their claim would be defeated by the defence of *ex turpi causa*.[20]

The damages recoverable can be reduced to take into account any "contributory negligence" by the deceased.[21]

The dependants of anyone killed as a result of police wrongdoing will, therefore, have an action against the police under the Fatal Accidents Act.

8. LIMITATION

All the causes of action discussed in this chapter are "founded on tort." The basic tort limitation period of six years "from the date on which the cause of action accrued" therefore applies.[22]

[14] s.1(2)(*c*).
[15] Administration of Justice Act 1982, s.1.
[16] s.1(1).
[17] s.1A.
[18] s.1A(3).
[19] See generally, *Kemp & Kemp on the Quantity of Damages*, Vol. 1.
[20] *Burns* v. *Edman* [1970] 2 Q.B. 541.
[21] s.5.
[22] See Limitation Act 1980, s.2.

The cause of action accrues at the moment at which the plaintiff could first sue. When a tort is actionable *per se*, time will run from the moment at which the wrongful act was committed. Thus, a cause of action in libel will run from the moment of publication and will be time-barred six years later. On the other hand, where damage is essential to the cause of action and it will only arise when the damage actually occurs. Thus, a cause of action in negligence, misfeasance in a public office or conspiracy will only arise when the plaintiff actually suffers loss or damage as a result of the defendant's breach of duty or misfeasance. In the case of a breach of statutory duty the date of accrual of the cause of action will depend on whether the statute is construed as giving a cause of action which is actionable *per se*.[23] If a statute does give rise to a breach which is actionable *per se* then time will run from the date of the breach, otherwise time will run from the date on which damage takes place.

Where the action is "in case" the cause of action will accrue whether or not the plaintiff knows that the damage has taken place.[24] Thus, for example, if property is damaged by negligent police action time will run from the date of damage, not the date when the plaintiff discovers that it has happened.

Where the damages claimed by the plaintiff "consist of or include damages in respect of personal injuries[25] to the plaintiff or any other person" then the applicable limitation period is three years.[26] In such a case the time period runs from either the date on which the cause of action accrued or the date of knowledge (if later) of the person injured.[27] The court has a discretion to extend the limitation period under section 33 of the Limitation Act 1980.[28]

If the person injured dies before the expiration of the three year limitation period then the limitation period for a cause of action surviving for the benefit of the estate under section 1 of the Law Reform (Miscellaneous Provisions) Act 1934 is three years from the date of death or the date of the knowledge of the personal representative, whichever is the later.[29] If the person injured dies after the expiry of the limitation period then his personal representatives can ask the court to override the limitation period.[30]

An action under the Fatal Accidents Act 1976 cannot be brought if the death occurred when the person injured could no longer maintain an action in respect of the injury, whether because the action is time-barred or for any other reason.[31] Where the action would have been barred by the three year time limit in respect of personal injuries there is no statutory discretion to override the time limit under section 33.[32] No action under the Fatal Accidents Act can be brought after the expiration of three years from the date of death or the date of knowledge of the person for whose benefit the action is

[23] See above at p. 312.
[24] See *Pirelli General Cable Works* v. *Faber (Oscar) & Partners* [1983] 2 A.C. 1.
[25] As defined by the Limitation Act 1980, s.38(1).
[26] Limitation Act 1980, s.11(1).
[27] s.11(4).
[28] For a detailed discussion, see Chap. 4 above at p. 125.
[29] Limitation Act 1980, s.11(5).
[30] *Ibid.* s.33(4) and (5).
[31] Limitation Act 1980, s.12(1).
[32] *Ibid.*

brought, whichever is the later.[33] If the action was maintainable at the date of death then the court does have discretion to extend time under section 33.[34]

Where any fact relevant to the cause of action is deliberately concealed by the defendant the period of limitation does not begin to run until the plaintiff discovered the concealment or could, with reasonable diligence have discovered it.[35]

9. GENERAL DEFENCES

Introduction

There are a number of general defences which are potentially applicable to all the tort actions considered in this chapter. The most important of these are as follows:

(1) contributory negligence;
(2) consent;
(3) necessity;
(4) the plaintiff is a wrongdoer.

Contributory negligence

At common law contributory negligence was a complete defence to an action in negligence or breach of statutory duty but docs not sccm to have been applied to any other cause of action.[36] The position is now governed by the Law Reform (Contributory Negligence) Act 1945. If a plaintiff in an action for negligence suffers damage "as the result partly of his own fault" his damages are reduced "to such an extent as the court thinks just and equitable having regard to the claimant's share in the responsibility for the damage.[37]

The position when the plaintiff's claim is a tort other than negligence or breach of statutory duty is unclear. "Contributory negligence" will only be a defence to an action for defamation, conspiracy or misfeasance if it can be shown that the defendant's acts were themselves tortious; mere "carelessness" by the defendant will not be sufficient.[38]

[33] Limitation Act 1980, s.12(2).
[34] *Ibid.* s.12(3).
[35] *Ibid.* s.32(1).
[36] See Glanville Williams, *Joint Torts and Contributory Negligence* at pp. 197–222 and pp. 317–349.
[37] Law Reform (Contributory Negligence) Act 1945, s.1(1).
[38] See the full discussion in Chap. 11 below at p. 339.

Consent

The maxim *volenti non fit injuria*, that to which a man consents cannot be considered an injury, is of general application in the law of tort.[39] The defence of consent takes two forms: as consent to the invasion of interests or the willing assumption of risk of injury.[40]

No action will lie in respect of acts which were authorised by the plaintiff. The defendant must establish that the plaintiff's consent was fully and freely given. This form of the defence applies to intentional torts such as trespass to land or goods. It also applies to actions for defamation[41] and presumably to misfeasance and conspiracy.

The defence of *volenti* also applies in "non-intentional torts" when the plaintiff has agreed to "assume the risk" of suffering damage. The scope of the defence of consent as "assumption of risk" has been considerably restricted by judicial decision. It is necessary for the defendants to show that:

> "the plaintiff voluntarily and freely with full knowledge of the nature of the risk he ran impliedly agreed to incur it."[42]

It is not enough that the plaintiff had **knowledge** of the risk; he must be shown to have **consented** not to hold the defendant liable:

> "The plaintiff must agree, expressly or impliedly, to waive any claim for any injury that may befall him due to the lack of reasonable care by the defendant."[43]

The defence must be specifically pleaded.[44]

The defence of *volenti* is very rarely successful in actions for breach of statutory duty or negligence.[45] Although it was held to be applicable in *Ashton* v. *Turner*.[46] This was a negligence action by one of two burglars who had been drinking against the other who had injured him by crashing their getaway car. It was held that no duty of care was owed by the driver to the passenger in that situation but that the action failed, in any event, because the passenger had assumed the risk of such injury by taking part in the burglary and attempted escape.

Necessity

There is no doubt that "necessity" is a defence to an action in trespass, especially when human life is at stake.[47] The defence probably applies to "intentional torts." It will apply if the defendant takes "reasonable

[39] See Chap. 4 above at p. 122.
[40] See Street at p. 67.
[41] See Street at p. 317.
[42] *Letang* v. *Ottawa Ry.* [1926] A.C. 725 at 731.
[43] *per* Lord Denning M.R., *Nettleship* v. *Weston* [1971] 2 Q.B. 691 at 701.
[44] *James* v. *Wellington City* [1972] N.Z.L.R. 978.
[45] But see, *ICI* v. *Shatwell* [1965] A.C. 656.
[46] [1981] 1 Q.B. 137; see below at p. 334.
[47] See *Rigby* v. *Chief Constable* [1985] 1 W.L.R. 1242 at 1252H, 1253A.

measures" to deal with a "real and imminent danger."[48] The police may be able to rely on it to justify taking reasonably necessary steps to prevent crime.[49] The defence will not, however, be available if the necessity has arisen from the defendant's own negligence.[50]

In the case of *Rigby* v. *Chief Constable*[51] the police successfully relied on this defence to an action for trespass when they had set the plaintiff's gun shop alight by firing CS gas canisters into it to "flush out" a dangerous armed psychopath. Although the trespass was justified by necessity it was no defence to an allegation of negligence in making arrangements to deal with the consequences of the intrusion. The defendant was, therefore, found guilty of negligence for firing the gas canister when no fire fighting equipment was on hand.[52]

The plaintiff is a wrongdoer

This defence has been discussed in relation to trespass to the person[53] and interference with goods.[54] Its scope remains unclear but it seems that the plaintiff's wrongdoing may, in some circumstances extinguish any right of action in reliance on the maxim *ex turpi causa non oritur actio*; an action does not arise from a base cause. In the case of *Thackwell* v. *Barclay's Bank*[55] Hutchison J. suggested that the Court should consider whether there was any illegality of which the court should take notice and whether, if there was, giving relief to the plaintiff was contrary to public policy because it would be indirectly assisting or encouraging him in his criminal act.

The fact that the plaintiff was engaged in a criminal act may mean that he cannot recover for damage caused by the defendant's tortious conduct. In *Murphy* v. *Culhane*[56] it was held that a man who takes part in a criminal affray may be said "to have been guilty of such a wicked act as to deprive himself of a cause of action."[57]

On the other hand, the plaintiff's wrongdoing may mean that the defendant's acts were not, in the circumstance, tortious. In the case of *Ashton* v. *Turner*[58] Ewbank J. held that:

> "The law of England may in certain circumstances not recognise the existence of a duty of care by one participant in a crime to another participant in the same crime, in relation to an act done in connection with

[48] *Cresswell* v. *Sirl* [1948] 1 K.B. 241.
[49] *Hambley* v. *Shepley* (1967) 67 D.L.R. (2d) 94.
[50] See *Esso Petroleum* v. *Southport Corporation* [1956] A.C. 218 at 242; *Rigby* v. *Chief Constable* [1985] 1 W.L.R. 1242.
[51] [1985] 1 W.L.R. 1242.
[52] See above at p. 303.
[53] See Chap. 4 above at pp. 121 *et seq.*
[54] Chap. 6 above at p. 200.
[55] [1986] 1 All E.R. 676.
[56] [1977] Q.B. 94.
[57] *per* Lord Denning M.R., at 98.
[58] [1981] 1 Q.B. 137 at 145; applying the reasoning of the High Court of Australia in *Smith* v. *Jenkins* (1970) 44 A.L.J.R. 78.

> the commission of that crime. The law is based on public policy, and the application of the law depends on a consideration of all the facts."

He went on to find that, on the facts, no duty of care existed between the plaintiff and the defendants.

This defence is, however, limited in scope and "Cases where an action in tort has been defeated by [it] . . . are exceedingly rare."[59] It is submitted that it will only succeed in two situations:

(1) where, to establish his cause of action the plaintiff has to rely on criminal activity to found his claim[60];
(2) where, by giving the relief sought the court would be "indirectly assisting or encouraging" him in his criminal act.[61]

Thus, for example, a claim that the police had not shown proper care in looking after a person in police custody, would not be defeated simply because the person being held was being held for admitted wrongdoing. On the other hand, a plaintiff who was injured following a negligent failure by the police to deal with his 999 call in relation to a criminal affray which he had instigated would not succeed in a negligence claim.

[59] *per* Lord Asquith, *NCB* v. *England* [1954] A.C. 403 at 428; and see the authorities considered in *Thackwell* v. *Barclay's Bank*, [1986] 1 All E.R. 676 at 684–688.
[60] *Taylor* v. *Chester* (1869) L.R. 4 Q.B. 309; see Street at p. 89.
[61] *Thackwell* v. *Barclay's Bank* [1986] 1 All E.R. 676 at 687d, 689e; see also *Euro-Diam Ltd.* v. *Bathurst* [1987] 2 All E.R. 113.

11. Damages

1. INTRODUCTION

The various tort actions already considered establish a number of "rights" of the citizen in relation to the police. There is a right not to be unlawfully assaulted or confined, a right not to have land or goods wrongfully interfered with, and so on. Once it is established that these rights have been interfered with the court will award compensation or make some form of order to assist the successful plaintiff. In this chapter the law in relation to damages will be examined. The other remedies available when the police infringe the citizen's rights are considered in Chapter 12.

The only remedy available at common law is that of monetary compensation or damages. In relation to actions against the police the only relevant damages are those in tort. These were classically defined by Lord Blackburn as:

> "that sum of money which will put the party who has been injured, or who has suffered, in the same position as he would have been in if he had not sustained the wrong."[1]

The assessment of damages in police cases presents considerable difficulties for the practitioner. This is because the "damage" actually suffered is not usually of a financial kind. It is necessary to place money figures on essentially "intangible" matters such as loss of liberty, damage to reputation or injured feelings. Although the courts have enormous experience of quantifying intangible losses in the context of damages for pain, suffering and loss of amenity in personal injury cases, no comparable "quantification principles" have yet been evolved for cases such as trespass to the person or malicious prosecution. The resulting difficulties are compounded by the fact that many cases involve assessment of damages by juries who are, as a matter of convention, not referred to awards in previous cases.

This area of the law is in a state of flux at the time of writing and all that can be provided are rough guidelines and a large number of examples. The Appendix to this chapter gives a wide range of examples of awards of damages in assault, false imprisonment and malicious prosecution cases over the past 30 years.

[1] *Livingstone* v. *Rawyards Coal* (1880) 5 App.Cas. 25 at 39.

2. DAMAGES IN GENERAL

Definitions

Damages are monetary compensation for civil wrongs. Their object is to compensate a plaintiff for the loss, damage and injury which results from the defendant's unlawful actions. The compensation covers both financial and non-financial loss and damage. Thus a plaintiff injured by an assault can recover for direct and indirect financial losses—such as the cost of damaged clothing and loss of wages due to the injuries—for the physical injuries suffered and for shock, distress and injuries to pride and dignity. The general principle is said to be *restitutio in integrum*, restoration to the original position. In other words, the victim of a legal wrong is entitled to recover that amount of money which will, so far as money can do, put him in the position which he would have been in had the wrong never happened.

This general principle is limited by a number of general considerations of a "policy" nature. These are briefly considered under three heads: remoteness, mitigation and contributory negligence.

Remoteness

The damage suffered by the plaintiff can only be recovered for if it is not too remote a consequence of the defendant's wrong. This in turn depends on the applicable "remoteness rules." Although it is generally accepted that different "remoteness rules" apply to different causes of action in tort, only the rules in relation to negligence have received substantial judicial attention in recent years.

It is now clearly established that when a defendant is sued in negligence, damage will be too remote if it is not a "reasonably foreseeable" consequence of his wrong.[2] This is generally thought to apply to other **non-intentional** torts such as breach of statutory duty and nuisance.

This "reasonable foreseeability" principle was only firmly established in the early 1960s. There is no need for the actual damage in fact suffered by the plaintiff to be reasonably foreseeable. The damage will not be too remote if it is of a reasonably foreseeable type.[3] This preserves the important principle that a defendant must "take his victim as he finds him." Thus, the fact that the plaintiff is unusually sensitive in a particular way will not make the damage suffered too remote, provided it is of a reasonably foreseeable type. The most famous illustrations of this principle are the so-called "egg-shell skull" cases:

> "if a man is negligently . . . injured in his body, it is no answer to the sufferer's claim for damages that he would have suffered less injury . . . if he had not had an unusually thin skull or an unusually weak heart."[4]

[2] *The Wagon Mound* [1961] A.C. 388.
[3] See *Hughes* v. *Lord Advocate* [1963] A.C. 837.
[4] *per* Kennedy J., *Dulieu* v. *White* [1901] 2 K.B. 669 at 679; *Smith* v. *Leech Brain & Co.* [1962] 2 Q.B. 405.

This principle applies to "mental"[5] and "financial"[6] as well as "physical" sensitivities. A plaintiff can recover for all the nervous shock which in fact happens to him as a result of the defendant's tort, provided that **some** nervous shock was:

> "reasonably foreseeable by the tortfeasor as a natural and probable consequence of the . . . [tort]. For this purpose the plaintiff is assumed to be a person of normal disposition and phlegm."[7]

It has been held, however, that "while a tortfeasor had to take his victim as he found him, he did not have to take his family."[8] Thus, the fact that a plaintiff's family is unusually sensitive and thus aggravates his suffering is not foreseeable and renders any resultant damage too remote.

The rules are different in the case of "intentional" torts such as trespass. This is because, as Lord Lindley once said:

> "The intention to injure the plaintiff negatives all excuses and disposes of any question of remoteness of damage."[9]

Consequently in an action for deceit, the plaintiff can recover all the actual damage directly flowing from the deceit, even if this was not foreseeable.[10] Despite the lack of clear English authority it is probable that this rule also applies in trespass to the person. As was said in a Canadian case:

> "In battery . . . any and all damage is recoverable, if it results from the wrongful act, whether it is foreseeable or not. The limitation devices of foresight and remoteness are not applicable to intentional torts."[11]

Mitigation

A further limitation on "complete compensation" is the plaintiff's duty to "mitigate his loss." The plaintiff must take reasonable steps to mitigate the losses caused by the defendant's wrong.

Nevertheless, the law does not impose onerous duties on a person who has been the victim of tortious conduct. As Lord Macmillan put it in *Banco de Portugal* v. *Waterlow*,[12] in a passage which applies to tort cases, just as much as to those in contract:

> "Where the sufferer from a breach of contract finds himself in consequence of that breach placed in a position of embarrassment the measures which he may be driven to adopt in order to extricate himself

[5] *Malcolm* v. *Broadhurst* [1970] 3 All E.R. 508.

[6] *The Arpad* [1934] P. 189 at 202–203.

[7] *Brice* v. *Brown* [1984] 1 All E.R. 997 at 1006k.

[8] *per* Widgery L.J., *McClaren* v. *Bradstreet* (1969) 113 S.J. 471.

[9] *Quinn* v. *Leathem* [1901] A.C. 495 at 537.

[10] *Doyle* v. *Olby* [1969] 2 Q.B. 158.

[11] *Allan* v. *New Mount Sinai Hospital* (1980) 109 D.L.R. (3d) 635 at 643; see also *Bettel* v. *Yim* (1978) 88 D.L.R. 543. In *Williams* v. *Humphrey*, *The Times*, February 20, 1975, Talbot J. suggested that the remoteness rules in trespass and negligence are the same, but the remarks were *obiter* and the point does not appear to have been argued.

[12] [1932] A.C. 452 at 506.

ought not to be weighed in nice scales at the instance of the party whose breach of contract has occasioned the difficulty. It is often easy after an emergency has passed to criticise the steps which have been taken to meet it but such criticism does not come well from those who have themselves created the emergency. The law is satisfied if the party placed himself in a difficult situation by reason of the breach of duty owed to him has acted reasonably in the adoption of remedial measures and will not be held to be disentitled to recover the cost of such measures merely because the party in breach can suggest that other measures less burdensome to him might have been taken."

The burden of proving a failure to mitigate is on the defendant.[13] A plaintiff who takes reasonable steps but, in fact, increases his loss, will not be penalised.[14]

The duty to mitigate will be particularly relevant in cases of interference with goods. If the police wrongfully detain an income earning chattel damages will be reduced if the plaintiff can be shown to have failed to take reasonable steps to hire or buy a replacement. Whether or not this should be done will depend on all the circumstances, including matters such as how long the chattel is likely to be detained.

Contributory negligence

At common law it was a complete defence to an action in the tort of negligence to show that the plaintiff was guilty of contributory negligence.

Contributory negligence is now governed by the Law Reform (Contributory Negligence) Act 1945, section 1(1) of which reads as follows:

> "Where any person suffers damage as the result partly of his own fault and partly the fault of any other person or persons, a claim in respect of that damage shall not be defeated by reason of the fault of the person suffering the damage, but the damage recoverable in respect thereof shall be reduced to such extent as the court thinks just and equitable having regard to the claimant's share in the responsibility for the damage."

Thus, contributory negligence is no longer a complete defence, but gives rise to a reduction in the plaintiff's damages.

There is some doubt as to the way in which the 1945 Act applies to causes of action other than negligence. "Fault" is defined in section 4 as meaning:

> "negligence, breach of statutory duty or other act or omission which gives rise to a liability in tort or would, apart from this Act, give rise to the defence of contributory negligence."

This is a very wide definition which could extend the doctrine of contributory negligence to all causes of action in tort. The doctrine does not, however, extend to conversion or trespass to goods, being specifically excluded by section 11(1) of the Torts (Interference with Goods) Act 1977. In *Murphy*

[13] *Yetton* v. *Eastwoods Froy* [1967] 1 W.L.R. 104 at 115.
[14] See *Lloyd's and Scottish Finance* v. *Modern Cars* [1966] 1 Q.B. 764 at 782.

v. *Culhane*[15] the Court of Appeal, in an extempore judgment in an interlocutory appeal, appeared to say that the 1945 Act **did** apply to trespass to the person.

Nevertheless, the application of the doctrine to other causes of action is likely to be very limited. This is because the plaintiff's act or omission must be one which "gives rise to a liability in tort" **or** would give rise to a defence of contributory negligence at common law (which only applied to actions in negligence or breach of statutory duty). It follows that the doctrine can only be invoked in an action for trespass to the person if the plaintiff has suffered damage partly as a result of some act of his own which would, of itself have **given rise to liability in tort**.

In other words, the defence of contributory negligence will only apply to an action for trespass to the person if the plaintiff had done something for which the defendant could have counterclaimed. The plaintiff must, for example, have actually committed an assault or battery on the defendant. Anything short of this, for example provocation, will not be enough.[16] Mere "carelessness" by the plaintiff is no defence unless the action is in negligence or breach of statutory duty (where there would have been a defence of contributory negligence at common law).[17]

3. TYPES OF DAMAGES

The basic classification

The English law distinguishes four basic types of damages, each serving different functions. The most common type of damages are **compensatory**. In the majority of ordinary tort cases these are the only type of damages awarded. The second type of damages are **aggravated**. These are awarded when the defendant's conduct has aggravated the plaintiff's damage. The third type of damages are **exemplary** or **punitive** damages. These are now awarded only in a very limited class of cases including, however, many police cases. The final type of damages are **nominal**. These are awarded in certain types of case when the plaintiff's rights are infringed but no loss is suffered.

It is important to keep these categories distinct because there may be very large differences between the amounts of damages recovered under the different categories. Furthermore, different rules of pleading and evidence apply to damages of different types. Many reported cases, particularly older ones, fail to draw these distinctions and so can be very misleading on matters relating to damages.

In many police cases it is likely that the damages awarded will include aggravated and exemplary as well as ordinary compensatory damages. It is, nevertheless, well established that one lump sum award of damages should

[15] [1977] Q.B. 94.
[16] See Chap. 4 above at p. 122.
[17] See the remarks of Lord Denning M.R. in *Murphy* v. *Culhane* [1977] Q.B. 94 at 99.

be made to cover all the different types.[18] It is clear from the reported cases that this rule is often not applied in practice as both judges and juries commonly make separate awards. Nevertheless, in a number of cases involving wrongful eviction, the Court of Appeal have reaffirmed the "single lump sum principle." As Stephenson L.J. said in the case of *Guppys (Bridport) Ltd.* v. *Brookling*:[19]

> "It would, of course, be helpful to an appellate court in considering an award of exemplary damages if it could be split up into damages which the judge or jury would have awarded as compensation and, as it were, the additional damages that they have awarded to punish . . . But it seems doubtful whether, even in order to assist an appellate court, the judge should attempt to extricate the punitive from the non-punitive element and a study of those speeches[20] leads me to the conclusion that the judge took the right course in making an award of a single sum for exemplary damages."[21]

Compensatory damages

The paradigm case of damages are those awarded to compensate the plaintiff for losses caused by the defendant's wrongful acts. First, the plaintiff will be compensated for all non-remote **financial** losses. Such losses cover not only areas such as the replacement of damaged property and loss of earnings, but also potential future financial losses, resulting, for example from a continuing disability caused by an injury.

Secondly, the court also attempts, under this head, to provide some financial compensation for other "damage" caused to the plaintiff:

> "In addition to any pecuniary loss specifically proved the assessment of this compensation may itself involve putting a money value upon physical hurt, as in assault, upon curtailment of liberty, as in false imprisonment or malicious prosecution, upon injury to reputation, as in defamation, false imprisonment and malicious prosecution, upon inconvenience and the disturbance of the even tenor of life, as in many torts."[22]

The most familiar example of this is in personal injury cases where the courts have established fairly clear figures for almost every conceivable type of injury or illness. The court can award similar "conventional sums" to compensate for other non-financial losses. In cases where the award of damages is not limited to financial loss which can be specifically proved, damages are said to be "at large."[23] Damages for pain and suffering, for loss

[18] *per* Lord Hailsham L.C., *Broome* v. *Cassell & Co.* [1972] A.C. 1027 at 1072E; see also *per* Lord Salmon, *Att-Gen. of St Christopher, Nevis and Anguilla* v. *Reynolds* [1980] A.C. 637 at 662–663.

[19] (1984) 14 H.L.R. 1.

[20] Lord Devlin in *Rookes* v. *Barnard* [1964] A.C. 1129, at 1228 and Lord Hailsham in *Broome* v. *Cassell & Co.*, [1972] A.C. 1027 at 1072.

[21] See also *McMillan* v. *Singh* (1985) 17 H.L.R. 120 (C.A.).

[22] *per* Lord Diplock, *Broome* v. *Cassell & Co.* [1972] A.C. 1027 at 1124F.

[23] *per* Lord Hailsham L.C., *Broome* v. *Cassell & Co.* [1972] A.C. 1027 at 1073 G–H.

of liberty or for injury to reputation are "at large" in this sense. As Lord Atkin said in a defamation case:

> "It is precisely because the 'real' damage cannot be ascertained and established that the damages are at large. It is impossible to track down the scandal, to know what quarters the poison may reach: it is impossible to weigh at all closely the compensation which will recompense a man or a woman for the insult suffered or the pain of a false accusation."[24]

The fact that damages are "at large" does not mean that the court has a complete discretion as to the damages which can be awarded. The court must be guided by the sums awarded in previous cases.

Such damages may be awarded in any tort action to compensate the plaintiff for non-financial loss and damage resulting from "the whole circumstances of the tortious wrong."[25]

When damages are "at large" it is open to the court to award "contemptuous" compensatory damages to indicate its low opinion of the plaintiff's claim. Such damages are most likely in libel cases where the plaintiff is successful but the court has such a low opinion of his reputation that derisory damages of, say one halfpenny, are awarded. Contemptuous damages cannot be awarded once the plaintiff can show that he has actually suffered damage.

This is because, as a matter of general principle, "compensatory" damages cannot be reduced by reason of the plaintiff's conduct or character. This was clearly established by the Australian case of *Fontin* v. *Katapodis*.[26] As Owen J. put it:

> "the rule by which the defendant in an action in which exemplary damages are recoverable is entitled to show that the plaintiff's own conduct was responsible for the commission of the tortious act and to use this fact to mitigate damages has no application to damages awarded by way of compensation."[27]

The principle was applied by the Court of Appeal in the assault case of *Lane* v. *Holloway*.[28]

Thus, the fact that a person assaulted by the police had provoked them or had a criminal record, is not a sufficient reason to reduce his award of compensatory damages. Similarly, provocation or misconduct will not justify a reduction in malicious prosecution or false imprisonment damages. Bad character may however, justify a lower award of compensatory damages for malicious prosecution or false imprisonment because such awards always include an element for damage to reputation and the worse a plaintiff's reputation, the less the damage caused to him by wrongful imprisonment or prosecution. It is submitted that this is the proper explanation of the ruling in the case of *Lawton* v. *Charles*,[29] that a plaintiff in a malicious prosecution case can be cross-examined on his previous convictions because this goes to "the reduction of damages."

[24] *Ley* v. *Hamilton* (1935) 153 L.T. 384 at 386.
[25] See *Pratt* v. *BMA* [1919] 1 K.B. 244 at 281.
[26] (1962) 108 C.L.R. 177.
[27] *Ibid.* at 187.
[28] [1968] 1 Q.B. 379.
[29] [1957] C.L.Y. 1328.

Aggravated damages

The second kind of damages are aggravated damages. These have been judicially defined as:

> "compensation for the injured feelings of the plaintiff where his sense of injury resulting from the wrongful physical act is justifiably heightened by the manner in which or motive for which the defendant did it."[30]

Aggravated damages are, therefore, a form of compensatory damages which are awarded to compensate the plaintiff for injuries to his feelings arising out of the defendant's tortious acts. They became separated from ordinary compensatory damages because the common law viewed such "intangible damage" with suspicion.[31] The distinction remains important today because, in contrast to the position regarding ordinary "compensatory" damages, aggravated damages can be reduced to take into account the plaintiff's own conduct and the degree to which he provoked the defendant's tort. Consequently, in *O'Connor* v. *Hewitson*[32] a person in police custody was held to have provoked an assault on him by police officers and the Court of Appeal held that it was proper not to make an award of aggravated damages.

It has been said that an award of aggravated damages is not appropriate in negligence or breach of contract cases.[33] However, this may be simply a matter of terminology as a plaintiff in a negligence or breach of contract case can be awarded compensatory damages for his distress, anxiety and inconvenience.

In assessing the quantum of aggravated damages all the circumstances of the particular case must be taken into account. One crucial factor will be the character of the plaintiff. As the Court of Appeal have said:

> "The discharge of this difficult task must depend to a substantial extent upon the type of claimant."[34]

Conduct and circumstances at any time up to judgment can be taken into account. Thus, in the case of false imprisonment it is clearly established that:

> "any evidence which tends to aggravate or mitigate the damage to a man's reputation which flows naturally from his imprisonment must be admissible up to the moment when damages are assessed . . . The damage continues until it is caused to cease by an avowal that the imprisonment was false."[35]

In *Walter* v. *Alltools*[36] the plaintiff's damage was aggravated because the defendants had not expressed regret, had not notified the plaintiff's fellow employees that the plaintiff was free from suspicion and had written a letter

[30] *per* Lord Diplock, *Broome* v. *Cassell & Co.* [1972] A.C. 1027 at 1124G.
[31] See generally, Street, *Principles of the Law of Damages* at pp. 24–25.
[32] [1979] Crim.L.R. 46.
[33] *Kralj* v. *McGrath* [1986] 1 All E.R. 54 at 61E.
[34] *per* Edmund Davies L.J., *Ansell* v. *Thomas* [1973] Court of Appeal Transcript, 73–212, p. 11; briefly reported at [1974] Crim.L.R. 31.
[35] *Walter* v. *Alltools* (1944) 61 T.L.R. 39 at 40.
[36] *Ibid.*

to the effect that the imprisonment was justified. The fact that the defendant pleads that his imprisonment or prosecution of the plaintiff was justified will aggravate the damage, even if abandoned at trial,[37] The defendant's conduct of his case at trial may serve further to aggravate the plaintiff's damage.

As in nervous shock cases a person can only recover aggravated damages if the heightening of his sense of injury is "justifiable." But once this initial threshold has been crossed then the more sensitive the plaintiff, other things being equal, the greater the aggravated damages. A person of good character is likely to be thought more "sensitive to humiliation" and, therefore to recover higher aggravated damages. than someone with a criminal record.

Awards of aggravated damages are extremely common in cases involving the police as any unlawful arrest, prosecution or detention by the police is likely "justifiably" to heighten a person's sense of injury. If the police behave in a high-handed or unpleasant way then a greater award of aggravated damages can be expected. A plaintiff's damage may be aggravated by circumstances such as: a publically embarassing wrongful arrest, racial abuse, persistent and aggressive questioning, or unpleasant conditions of detention. A failure to make a prompt apology will also give rise to a potential award of aggravated damages. If the police defend a civil action and allege in their defence and at trial that the plaintiff was lawfully arrested or reasonably suspected of a crime then this will also aggravate the plaintiff's damage if he is successful on these points.

Exemplary damages

The third type of damages is known as "exemplary" or "punitive." These are the most controversial as, unusually in the civil law, they involve an element of punishment of the defendant, being awarded to teach him that "tort does not pay" and to act as deterrent. It was once thought that these damages could be awarded whenever the defendant's conduct could be described by adjectives such as "wilful," "arrogant," "oppressive" or "outrageous." This view was rejected by the House of Lords in the case of *Rookes* v. *Barnard*.[38] Lord Devlin expressly limited exemplary damages to cases where there was either "oppressive, arbitrary or unconstitutional action by the servants of the government" or where "the defendant's conduct has been calculated by him to make a profit for himself which may well exceed the compensation payable to the plaintiff."[39]

Exemplary damages cannot be awarded outside these two categories.[40] Only the first category is likely to be relevant in actions against the police. Indeed if a police officer acted in a way "calculated by him to make a profit for himself" it is difficult to see how this could be anything other than "oppressive and arbitrary."

In strict law, a police officer is not a "servant of the government." Never-

[37] *Warwick* v. *Foulkes* (1844) 12 M. & W. 506 at 508–509, *per* Lord Abinger C.B.

[38] [1964] A.C. 1129, reaffirmed in *Broome* v. *Cassell & Co.* [1972] A.C. 1027.

[39] *Rookes* v. *Barnard* [1964] A.C. 1129 at 1226.

[40] Unless expressly authorised by statute, *Rookes* v. *Barnard*, *ibid.* at 1227.

theless, the term is to be very broadly construed in this context. As Lord Reid said in *Broome* v. *Cassell & Co.*[41]

> "The contrast is between "the government" and private individuals. Local government is as much government as national government and the police and many others are exercising governmental functions."

In the view of Lord Hailsham L.C. the first category would "obviously apply to the police."[42] It was accepted by Mars-Jones J. in *White* v. *MPC*,[43] for the purposes of awards of exemplary damages police officers are "servants of the government" and the police never appear to have sought to argue the contrary. Thus when a police officer acts in an "oppressive, arbitrary or unconstitutional" manner, a wronged citizen has a potential claim for exemplary damages. Exemplary damages were awarded against the police in the *White* case and in a large number of other first instance cases, both High Court and county court.[44]

The words "oppressive, arbitrary or unconstitutional" are disjunctive and exemplary damages *may*, therefore, be awarded if police actions fall within any one of these categories. Matters such as violence, cruelty, threats or abuse may be regarded as "oppressive or arbitrary." If there is any evidence of conduct of this kind then the question of exemplary damages should be left to the jury.

Mere negligence should not be visited by an award of exemplary damages merely because it might be said to have resulted in a trespass which, from the point of view of the person affected by it, could be regarded as oppressive. The appropriate way to compensate the plaintiff in such a case would be by an award of aggravated, rather than exemplary, damages.[45]

The question as to whether police action is "unconstitutional" is more difficult. An unlawful arrest is unconstitutional[46] so that, as Purchas L.J. put it in the case of *Holden* v. *Chief Constable of Lancashire*[47]:

> "If full effect is to be given to the word "or" in the category "oppressive, arbitrary or unconstitutional" action by government servants, wrongful arrest falls with the category."

In that case a new trial was ordered because, in the absence of "oppressive or arbitrary conduct," the trial judge had refused to leave the issue of exemplary damages to the jury. This order was made with some reluctance, Purchas L.J. saying that he wished to "reserve the full ambit of this approach."[48] It was held to be "entirely proper" for the judge, in such a case, in telling the jury that they had a power to give or withhold exemplary damages, to indicate that there were no aggravating circumstances or oppression. It seems unlikely that, in practice, exemplary damages will be

[41] [1972] A.C. 1027 at 1088A.

[42] *Ibid.* at 1077H.

[43] *The Times*, April 24, 1982.

[44] See, *e.g.*, *George* v. *MPC, The Times*, March 21, 1984, Park J. (£2000); *Connor* v. *Chief Constable of Cambridgeshire, The Times*, April 11, 1984, French J. (£500); see below at pp. 367 *et seq.*

[45] *per* Leggatt J., *Barbara* v. *Home Office* (1984) 134 New L.J. 888.

[46] *per* Lord Mansfield C.J., *Huckle* v. *Money* (1763) 2 Wils.K.B. 205.

[47] [1986] 3 W.L.R. 1107 at 1113.

[48] *Ibid.* at 1112H.

awarded in cases where the only "unconstitutional action" was an unlawful arrest.

Nevertheless, an award of exemplary damages will be appropriate in other cases of "unconstitutional" action where there is no "oppression." The actual conduct of the defendant himself does not have to be such as would justify an award of exemplary damages.[49] Thus, in *Huckle* v. *Money*,[50] exemplary damages were awarded against the defendant despite the fact that his servant had treated the plaintiff with courtesy and consideration, serving him "beef steaks and beer." The award of exemplary damages was upheld to show the law's disapproval of the government's conduct. The defendant does not even need to have known that his actions were wrong.[51]

Once it is decided that an award of exemplary damages is appropriate the difficult question of quantum arises. The courts are concerned to keep these awards within reasonable limits. Lord Devlin set out three "considerations" to be taken into account when awarding exemplary damages. First, the plaintiff cannot recover exemplary damages "unless he is the victim of the punishable behaviour."[51a] As many commentators have pointed out, this rule seems to have little practical application.[52] Secondly, the courts should see that exemplary damages are used with restraint and that awards are of moderate levels.[53] Thirdly, the means of the defendant must be considered. This consideration is obviously not relevant in police cases. In general, the size of the award of exemplary damages may be influenced by the award of compensatory damages. The judge should direct the jury that:

> "if, but only if, the sum which they have in mind to award as compensation (which may of course, be a sum aggravated by the way in which the defendant has behaved to the plaintiff) is inadequate to punish him for his outrageous conduct . . . then it can award some larger sum."[54]

The conduct of the defendant up to the date of trial can also be taken into account[55] and even the conduct of his case at trial.[56] The plaintiff's conduct including matters such as provocation is also relevant to the question of whether or not an award of exemplary damages should be made.[57]

It was, at one time, suggested that exemplary damages should be reduced if the case was tried by a judge alone who severely criticised the defendant in his judgment.[58] This approach is unlikely to be followed today as the analogous rule in libel cases[59] has since been disapproved by the House of Lords.[60]

If exemplary damages are awarded to more than one plaintiff then the total sum awarded should not exceed the total amount which the defendant

[49] *per* Lord Diplock, *Broome* v. *Cassell & Co.* [1972] A.C. 1027 at 1128 G–H.
[50] (1763) 2 Wils.K.B. 205.
[51] See *Broome* v. *Cassell & Co.* [1972] A.C. 1027 at 1129A.
[51a] *Rookes* v. *Barnard* [1964] A.C. 1129 at 1226.
[52] McGregor, para. 327.
[53] *cf. Rookes* v. *Barnard* [1964] A.C. 1129 at 1227–1228.
[54] *Ibid.* at 1227–1228.
[55] *Praed* v. *Graham* (1890) 24 Q.B.D. 53.
[56] *Greenlands* v. *Wilmshurst* [1913] 3 K.B. 507.
[57] *Lane* v. *Holloway* [1968] 1 Q.B. 379 at 391.
[58] *Hook* v. *Cunard S.S. Co.* [1953] 1 All E.R. 1021.
[59] See *Rook* v. *Fairrie* [1941] 1 K.B. 507.
[60] See *Dingle* v. *Associated Newspapers* [1964] A.C. 371.

should pay by way of punishment. A total sum appropriate to punish the defendant should be determined by the judge or the jury and this sum should then be divided by the number of plaintiffs.[61]

Nominal damages

The final category of damages is "nominal" damages. These are only awarded in cases in which the defendant's tort was "actionable *per se*" and no actual damage has been proved. It is necessary to be clear about which torts are involved here.

The English law arbitrarily distinguishes between two kinds of tort action: torts actionable per se and actions on the case. In some cases an action can be brought simply upon proof of an interference with an interest of the plaintiff. It is not necessary to prove any actual loss or damage. The law is said to "presume" damage (which is sometimes known as "general damage").[62] Such torts are said to be actionable *per se* and include actions in trespass,—whether to the person, to land or to goods—libel[63] and conversion by wrongful detention.[64]

In other torts, the cause of action is only complete when actual damage to the plaintiff (often called "special damage") takes place. These are known as "actions on the case" and include negligence, malicious prosecution, many forms of slander, breach of statutory duty, conspiracy and misfeasance in public office. A plaintiff suing "in case" can recover for the actual damage which constitutes his cause of action and for non-substantial damages at large such as injured feelings.[65]

In a successful action upon the case, some compensatory damages will always be recovered because the plaintiff must have suffered some damage to get the action off the ground in the first place.[66] Matters may be different when the plaintiff is suing in a tort actionable *per se*. He may be unable to prove any actual damage and the damage "presumed" by the law may be very slight. The appropriate award of damages will be a "nominal" one. As Lord Halsbury L.C. once said:

> "you are affirming by your nominal damages that there is an infraction of a legal right which, though it gives you no right to any real damage at all, yet gives you a right to the verdict or judgment because your legal right has been infringed."[67]

Nominal damages must be distinguished from "contemptuous" or derisory compensatory damages[68] which can be awarded in actions on the case where the damages are at large as well as in relation to matters which are actionable *per se*.

[61] *Riches* v. *News Group Newspapers* [1986] Q.B 256 at 288; see below at p. 351.
[62] See *Nicholls* v. *Ely Beet* [1936] Ch. 342 at 380.
[63] *Ley* v. *Hamilton* (1935) 153 L.T. 384.
[64] *Williams* v. *The Peel River Land Co.* (1878) 55 L.T. 689.
[65] See *Pratt* v. *BMA* [1919] 1 K.B. 244.
[66] These may, however, be "contemptuous" in certain cases, see above at p. 342.
[67] *The Mediana* [1900] A.C. 113 at 116.
[68] See above at p. 324.

4. ASSESSMENT OF DAMAGES AND APPEALS

Introduction

The assessment of financial losses is usually a straightforward matter once the facts have been found and the relevant legal principles considered. There are, however, always substantial difficulties in awarding financial compensation for non-pecuniary losses such as loss of liberty or damage to reputation. These are likely to be the most common kinds of losses in police cases.

At common law damages were assessed by juries and when they were "at large" the jury was entitled to award any sum it thought fit. The only control over this was the power to order a new trial if the damages were so high or so low that no jury could reasonably have given them. The position was very different after 1873 when an increasing proportion of civil cases came to be tried by judges alone. Different principles now apply to the assessment of damages by judges and by juries.

Assessment of "at large" damages by judges

When judges began to assess "at large" damages they initially saw their function as being identical to that of juries. Thus the assessment of damages was regarded as a "factual" matter in each case. Judges did not regard themselves as being in any way bound by awards made by judges in similar cases and such awards were not usually cited to them. As late as 1955 in the case of *Waldon* v. *War Office*[69] Lloyd Jacob J. at first instance, decided that it was not right for counsel to refer him to the quantum of damages awarded in similar cases. The Court of Appeal ruled that he was wrong on this point and that judges did have a discretion to consider cases similar to the one before him as a guide to the amount of damages to be awarded although they went on to say that this discretion should be "exercised sparingly."[70]

It is now the universal practice to cite previous analogous awards to judges in personal injury cases. The courts have established "conventional figures" for all types of injuries. These figures are not to be slavishly followed by judges without further consideration. As Lord Devlin once said:

> "The conventional figure . . . is only the starting point for a voyage of assessment which may, and generally does end up at a different figure."[71]

Nevertheless, in the very unlikely event of the facts of a case being identical to those of a previous case the quantum of an "at large" damages award would also be identical. The use of conventional sums as a starting point is now axiomatic to judge assessed "at large" damages. If a judge's award of

[69] [1956] 1 W.L.R. 51.
[70] *Ibid.* at 55.
[71] *Yorkshire Electricity Board* v. *Naylor* [1968] A.C. 529 at 549.

damages strays too far from the applicable conventional sum without good reason the Court of Appeal will intervene.[72]

It would seem then, that in police cases, when damages for non-pecuniary losses are assessed by a judge sitting alone, the judges should begin from "conventional" figures. Thus, a basic hourly rate should be awarded for the loss of liberty in a false imprisonment case. A conventional figure could be fixed for malicious prosecution for different types of offences. Such figures would then form the starting point for the judge's assessment of "compensatory damages." The special factors of each case would also be taken into account. On top of the conventional compensatory sum the judge can indicate his view of the defendant's conduct in his awards—if any—of aggravated and exemplary damages.

At present, judges do not appear to be taking this course. This leads to great uncertainty in the assessment of damages in police cases. It is to be hoped that, in the future, "conventional figures" will be arrived at to form the starting point of the assessment of damages for torts such as malicious prosecution and false imprisonment.

Assessment of damages by juries

Actions against the police for false or malicious prosecution are among the few civil cases which are still regularly tried by juries. In such cases the "assessment of damages" position is very different from that in "judge only" cases. It is a fundamental principle of the common law that the assessment of damages is a matter for the jury and for the jury alone. In his summing up the judge must direct the jury as to any rule of law affecting the assessment and measure of damages.[73] He must, if appropriate, explain to them the situations in which aggravated and exemplary damages may be awarded and he must tell them to assess damages as a single figure to cover the three different types of general damages. On current practice that is as far as the judge can go.

It appears to be generally accepted that neither counsel nor the judge can mention previous damages awards to a jury. The point was dealt with, obiter, by Singleton L.J. in *Waldon* v. *War Office*[74] as follows:

> "It may be asked: 'Why should a judge have something before him which a jury would not have?' I am not sure that there is any good reason, except perhaps, that if jurors new to the task are called on to assess damages in a case such as this, the more one can keep their minds directed to the actual issues the better. If numbers of other cases are mentioned in which actual damages have been given, the danger is confusion or complication, and I would not encourage that in a jury case."[75]

So far as this refers to counsel, it is sound in both practice and principle. The citing of cases to juries has always been viewed with suspicion in both

[72] See below at p. 352.
[73] *Morgan* v. *Odhams* [1971] 1 W.L.R. 1239.
[74] [1956] 1 W.L.R. 51.
[75] *Ibid.* at 55.

criminal and civil cases. Jurors in general do not have the training or experience to analyse and distinguish previous decided cases.

But the present practice goes much further than this. It appears to be generally accepted that the judge cannot mention previous cases or indeed any **damages figures whatsoever** to the jury. When it comes to the assessment of damages they are entirely on their own.

There appears to be no binding authority for this bizarre principle. It does not appear to form the **ratio** of any reported case. The case of *Montereale* v. *Longmans, Green & Co.*[76] is sometimes cited as authority for the principle. In fact, Glyn-Jones J. was reported as directing the jury as follows:

> "His Lordship was not allowed to suggest any figure. Some people thought that that was a pity because it might be of some help to suggest, within wide limits, an appropriate amount, because the jury were not bound by what the judge said."

The matter was discussed by the Court of Appeal in the notorious case of *Ward* v. *James.*[77] Lord Denning M.R., in giving the judgment of a five judge Court of Appeal advanced "assessability," "uniformity" and "predictability" as the three most important things in the assessment of damages. He continued:

> "None of these three is achieved when the damages are left at large to the jury. Under the present practice the judge does not give them any help at all to assess the figure. The result is that awards may vary greatly, from being much too high to much too low. There is no uniformity and no predictability."[78]

He then went on to consider possible ways of "correcting" jury awards or giving the jury more guidance. "Correction" is considered below. In relation to "guidance" he considered two possible approaches: the possibility of citing comparable cases to the jury or the possibility of the judge mentioning a conventional range of figure to assist them.

First, he argued that it would not be acceptable for the judge to mention comparable cases to the jury because counsel would have to be able to refer to cases as well and then:

> "Each counsel would refer the jury to cases which he believed were comparable but which were not really so. Speeches would be taken up with the one counsel citing analogies and the other destroying them. Then the judge would have to review them all again in his summing up. The inevitable result would be that the minds of the jury would be distracted from the instant case and left in confusion."[79]

Secondly, he rejected the idea that the judge should be able to indicate to the jury the "upper and lower limits of the sum which in his view it would be reasonable to award."[80] This would, he suggested, necessitate counsel being at liberty to mention cases and then, the same danger of confusing the jury would arise.

This objection is misconceived. The judge could hear argument from

[76] *The Times*, February 23, 1965.
[77] [1966] 1 Q.B. 273.
[78] *Ibid.* at 300 B–C.
[79] *Ibid.* at 302 C–D.
[80] *Ibid.* at 302G–303A.

counsel as to a possible range of figures in the absence of the jury. He could then give a ruling on the appropriate range and direct the jury accordingly. There would be no necessity for counsel to mention either cases or figures. The range in each particular case would clearly be closely related to the conventional sum adopted in comparable "judge only" cases. The mentioning of such a conventional sum would give the jury "something to go on" and would go some way to achieving Lord Denning's three objectives.

It is submitted that Lord Denning's suggestion that if a judge could give a jury "narrow limits" for a conventional sum "there is little point in having a jury at all"[81] is based on a misconception of the role of the jury in the assessment of damages. Once the jury have been directed on the conventional range they would not, of course, be bound to award a figure within the range and could mark their assessment of the conduct of the parties by awarding a higher or lower figure. They would be performing the traditional "assessment" function of the jury but they would not be performing it blindfold as at present. A plaintiff would not be discouraged from taking advantage of his constitutional entitlement to jury trial by fears of unpredictability.

It is difficult to avoid the conclusion that the Court of Appeal in *Ward* v. *James* had taken a policy decision to do away with juries in personal injury cases and were prepared to adopt any argument which served that end. The use of conventional "range of damages" figures would enable the civil jury to assess damages in a rational manner. If the courts refuse to allow the jury to play such a role it can only be because they see the civil jury as an anachronism which should be dispensed with. There are strong policy reasons for retaining the civil jury, especially in police cases. Judges should be allowed to suggest a range of figures to them after hearing argument. The discussion in *Ward* v. *James*[82] was clearly *obiter* and there is no binding auhority to the contrary. If a judge refuses to give such a direction he could clearly be challenged in the appellate courts.

When a jury considers an award of exemplary damages Parker L.J. in the libel case of *Riches* v. *News Group Newspapers*[83] suggested a six stage process of assessment:

> "the jury should in my judgment be told that when they have decided how much each plaintiff ought to receive by way of compensation, including any elements of aggravation, they should then: (1) aggregate those sums to arrive at a total figure for compensatory damages; (2) consider whether the case is one in which exemplary damages can be awarded, being given for this purpose full and clear directions in accordance with *Rookes* v. *Barnard* and *Cassell & Co. Ltd.* v. *Broome*; (3) if they are satisfied that the case is one in which exemplary damages can be awarded, consider whether the aggregate of compensatory damages is enough to punish the defendant; (4) if it is not enough, consider what total sum the defendant ought to pay in order to do so; (5) divide the difference between the total sum the defendant ought to pay and aggregate for compensatory damages by the number of plaintiffs and add the figure so arrived at to each of the compensatory sums; (6) having done so, award each plaintiff the total so arrived at as one undivided sum but

[81] *Ward* v. *James* [1966] 1 Q.B. 273 at 303C.
[82] [1966] 1 Q.B. 273.
[83] [1986] Q.B. 256 at 288 D–F.

state, if asked to do so, whether that sum exceeds what would have been awarded for compensation (including aggravation) only and if so what would have been awarded for such compensation."

Appeals as to quantum

The principles to be applied in quantum appeals depend on whether the damages were assessed by a judge or a jury. When the damages are assessed by a judge alone the Court of Appeal can substitute its own assessment of damages for that of the judge. In theory the Court of Appeal will only interfere if the judge acted on the wrong principle or the award is "entirely erroneous."[84] The recent practice has been considerably more flexible than this.[85]

When damages are assessed by a jury the Court of Appeal has no power to reassess them without the consent of the parties. The Court's only power is to order a new trial under R.S.C., Ord. 59, r. 11. A jury's award of damages will only lead to an order for a new trial if it is so high or so low that no reasonable jury could have arrived at it. The grounds on which a new trial can be awarded are discussed in Chapter 3.

5. DAMAGES FOR TRESPASS TO THE PERSON

Introduction

Trespass to the person is actionable *per se*. The law therefore presumes that any infringement of someone's rights over his own person results in damage. Nevertheless, nominal damages are unlikely because the law regards any interference with the person as being a serious matter.[86] Substantial compensatory and aggravated damages will be recoverable in many cases depending on the nature of the infringement. Different considerations apply to assault and false imprisonment.

Assault and battery

In a case of assault there is no physical contact but the plaintiff can recover compensatory damages for the damage presumed by law.[87] In addition he may recover damages for "nervous shock." This covers any "recognisable medical condition" of a physical or psychological nature produced by the defendant's unlawful acts even when there has been no actual physical contact. The question to be asked is: would a person of normal dis-

[84] See *Flint* v. *Lovell* [1935] 1 K.B. 354; and *The Supreme Court Practice* (1988) 59/10/13; McGregor, paras. 1567 *et seq.*

[85] See McGregor, paras. 1577 *et seq.* and Chap. 3 above at p. 92.

[86] See *Kuchenmeister* v. *Home Office* [1958] 1 Q.B. 496.

[87] See *Stenant* v. *Stonehouse* (1926) 2 D.L.R. 683.

position and phelgm have suffered such shock?[88] Furthermore, the defendant's conduct may be such as to "aggravate" the insult—if, for example, the threats take place in public and cause humiliation and distress—aggravated damages are therefore potentially recoverable. The same considerations apply to a battery which does not result in actual physical injury.

If a battery does result in physical injury to the plaintiff then the starting point for damages will be general personal injury principles. Thus in the case of *Sturley* v. *MPC*[89] a police officer twisted and fractured the plaintiff's arm. Damages of £2,000 (1986 value: £2,220) for pain, suffering and loss of amenity were awarded. If there is any element of aggravation or "oppressive conduct" by the police then the damages will be greater than would be expected in a normal personal injury case.[90]

Compensatory damages for personal injury cannot be reduced by reason of the plaintiff's conduct—such as provocation of the defendant[91]—or character. As Salmon L.J. said in *Lane* v. *Holloway*:[92]

> "on principle, when considering what damages a plaintiff is entitled to as compensation for physical injury, the fact that the plaintiff may have behaved badly is irrelevant."

A plaintiff's conduct or bad character may, of course, "properly be used to take away an element of aggravation."[93] The plaintiff's good character may result in a higher award of aggravated damages.

Damages have been awarded against the police for assault and battery in numerous reported cases. Thus, in *Flavius* v. *MPC*[94] Leonard J. awarded £1,000 (1986 value: £1,220) compensatory damages and £400 aggravated damages (1986 value: £488) to a plaintiff whose leg had been broken by an assault by police officers. In *Connor* v. *Chief Constable of Cambridgeshire*[95] French J. awarded a plaintiff who had suffered injury as the result of a blow from a police truncheon £2000 general damages and £500 exemplary damages.

Awards of damages for assault and battery are, of course, relatively common in non-police cases. Thus, in the case of *Smith* v. *Perkins*[96] The Court of Appeal refused to disturb an award of £100 (1986 value: £317) compensatory damages and £400 aggravated damages (1986 value: £1,268) made to a West Indian plaintiff who was violently and wrongfully ejected from a public house. In *Moran* v. *Duffy*[97] a county court judge awarded general damages, including aggravated damages, of £1,000 (1986 value: £1,220) to a plaintiff who was punched, suffering a black eye, cuts to his nose, injuries to his hand and a slight "mallett" deformity of two fingers.

Assault damages are, of course, not only available in simple cases where

[88] See above at p. 338.
[89] *The Times*, June 27, 1984.
[90] It appears that in *Sturley* v. *MPC, The Times*, June 27, 1984, the plaintiff's conduct was such that no award of aggravated or exemplary damages was appropriate.
[91] Subject to possible defences of "contributory negligence" or "*ex turpi causa*" see above at p. 339 and p. 334.
[92] [1968] 1 Q.B. 379 at 392 C–D.
[93] *Ibid.* at 387, *per* Lord Denning M.R.; see above at p. 342.
[94] (1982) 132 New L.J. 532.
[95] *The Times*, April 11, 1984.
[96] [1975] *Kemp & Kemp* 11–555; (C.A.)
[97] [1982] C.L.Y. 883.

threats are made or blows struck. It will be an assault if undue force is used in making what is otherwise a lawful arrest. Thus in *Allen* v. *MPC*[98] the plaintiff, who was lawfully arrested for drunken driving, recovered assault damages of £1,115 (1986 value: £1,550) because the police officers had used excessive force, putting arm locks on him and carrying him to a police van causing slight personal injury.

False imprisonment—general considerations

False imprisonment involves the curtailment of a person's liberty and he will be entailed to substantial compensatory damages for this. In *Millington* v. *MPC*[99] Forbes J. approved the following statement of the relevant law from McGregor:

> "The principal heads of damage would appear to be the injury to liberty (that is loss of time considered primarily from a non-pecuniary viewpoint) and any injury to feelings (that is the indignity, mental suffering, disgrace and humiliation with any attendant loss of social status)."[1]

The crucial factors in assessing such damages will be the length of time for which the plaintiff was imprisoned and the damage to his reputation:

> "A false imprisonment does not merely affect a man's liberty; it also affects his reputation. The damage continues until it is caused to cease by an avowal that the imprisonment was false."[2]

Any evidence tending to aggravate or mitigate this damage to reputation will be admissible up to the moment of judgment.[3] This will include the pleadings and the conduct of the defendant's case at trial.[4]

In addition the plaintiff can recover as "special damages" all quantifiable pre-trial pecuniary losses which are a direct consequence of his imprisonment. These will include the costs of obtaining his release from imprisonment[5] and loss of earnings or other opportunities. For example, in *Childs* v. *Lewis*[6] a company director who was obliged to resign as a result of his arrest was able to recover his lost director's fees in a false imprisonment action.

It is submitted that, as in assault and battery cases, the plaintiff's **compensatory** damages cannot be reduced by reason of his conduct or bad character. The law makes no distinction between harming a person by injuring his body and harming a person by depriving him of his liberty. As Lord Denning M.R. said in *Lane* v. *Holloway*,[7] "Provocation by the plaintiff can properly be used to take away any element of aggravation. But not to

98 [1980] Crim.L.R. 441.
99 Reported in part 133 New L.J. 806.
1 McGregor, para. 1357.
2 *per* Lawrence L.J., *Walter* v. *Alltools* (1944) 61 T.L.R. 39 at 40.
3 *Ibid.*
4 See above at p. 344.
5 *Pritchet* v. *Boevey* (1833) 1 Cr. & M. 775.
6 (1924) 40 T.L.R. 870.
7 [1968] 1 Q.B. 379 at 387G.

reduce the real damages." Thus, the fact that he has a criminal record or "provoked" his own imprisonment cannot reduce the damages recoverable for the loss of his liberty. On the other hand, the worse a plaintiff's reputation, the less damage an imprisonment will cause to it. When assessing **aggravated** and **exemplary** damages character and conduct are, of course, relevant.

Assessing false imprisonment damages

A large number of factors must be taken into account in the assessment of false imprisonment damages. These will vary from case to case and will include matters such as the general conduct of the police during the imprisonment, their treatment of the plaintiff and the amount of publicity the imprisonment received. Nevertheless, the key element in any award of damages for false imprisonment will be the financial value which is placed on the loss of liberty itself. It follows that a rough guide to quantum can be obtained by working out an "hourly rate" for loss of liberty compensation.

Thus, when the case is tried by a judge alone it might be expected that a "conventional sum" for loss of liberty would have been established. As in cases of battery leading to personal injury such a sum could then be the starting point for a damages award. The "compensatory award" could be increased by an award of aggravated damages in appropriate circumstances. Any person falsely imprisoned would thus receive a specific "hourly rate" for his loss of liberty and special "sensitivity to humiliation" could be taken into account in the aggravated award. Up to the time of writing, however, this approach has not been adopted by the courts. Awards of damage made by judges sitting alone cover almost as great a range as those made by juries.

At one end of the scale for "judge only awards" is the case of *Beckett* v. *Walker*[8] which involved the negligent issue of a warrant by a justice's clerk. The Court of Appeal assessed damages at £500 for a total of 53 hours in custody—a rate of £9.43 per hour. At the other end of the scale is the case of *Hayward* v. *MPC*[9] in which Caulfield J., after considering *Millington's* case awarded damages of £1750 (1986 value: £1,943) for a period of five hours, an hourly rate at 1986 prices of £432. In general, judges have not taken other "judge awards" into account. This approach is wrong in principle and makes advising on quantum in false imprisonment cases extremely difficult.

If the case is to be tried by a jury then the range of likely damages awards becomes even greater. Near to the top end of the scale is the case of *Reynolds* v. *MPC*[10] in which a High Court jury awarded the plaintiff £12,000 (1986 value: £16,440)[11] for a period of 14 hours false imprisonment, an hourly rate at 1986 prices of £1,174. This award was upheld by the Court of

[8] 1986, unreported, C.A. Transcript 86–134 an appeal from [1985] 3 C.L. 16a, in which the jury had awarded only £200.

[9] *The Times*, March 24, 1984.

[10] *The Times*, February 6, 1981.

[11] The jury said that this did not include any element of exemplary damages.

Appeal who said that, although the damages were high they were not so high that no reasonable jury ought to have awarded them and, accordingly, they could not be interfered with.[12] At the other end of the scale is the case of *Bryning* v. *Oxford*[13] in which a county court jury awarded of £25 (1986 value: £31) for ten hours false imprisonment, an hourly rate at 1986 prices of £3.[14]

Damages in false imprisonment have also been recovered when the initial arrest was lawful but the period of detention was too long. Thus in *Millington* v. *MPC*[15] Forbes J. awarded the plaintiff damages of £800 (1986 value: £936) for a total period of 41 hours—an hourly rate of £23 at 1986 prices. He described the plaintiff as an "engaging scoundrel whose acquaintance with truth was minimal" and made this award of damages for:

> "loss of liberty, humiliation and so on, bearing in mind that he had already suffered these initially by his lawful arrest."

In other words, damages were reduced to take into account the fact that the plaintiff was not to be compensated for damage caused by his lawful arrest. In *Lawrence* v. *Chief Constable of Dyfed-Powys*[16] a High Court jury awarded the plaintiff £600 (1986 value: £702) after they had found that a period of 21 hours detention was unreasonably long.[17]

It is clear from these authorities that the courts are not taking the approach to "loss of liberty damages" advocated above. Both "real" and "aggravated" damages are regarded as depending on all the circumstances of each particular case. A "sympathetic" or "respectable" plaintiff can therefore expect very substantial damages, while someone who appears to be relying on technicalities or who has a criminal record can expect very much less. As Lawton L.J. put it in *Beckett* v. *Walker*[18]:

> "I take into account that, in assessing the damages as best I can, this plaintiff was not a man with a criminal record or irregular way of life. It is true that, in the distant past, he had some minor conviction, but he was leading a respectable life and he had to suffer all this indignity."

This approach cannot stand with *Lane* v. *Holloway*[19] and, it is submitted, is wrong in principle. Just as personal injury damages for pain suffering and loss of amenity cannot be reduced because the plaintiff has often suffered injury or is insensitive to pain, so his damages for loss of liberty should not be reduced because he has been in prison before or is of bad character.

When assessing compensatory damages for damage to reputation in false imprisonment the court is obviously entitled to take into account the plaintiff's character and reputation. A plaintiff with a criminal record can expect

[12] [1982] Crim.L.R. 600.
[13] [1983] C.A. Transcript 847.
[14] The appeal concerned the judge's direction to the jury and it does not appear to have been argued that the award was unreasonably low.
[15] *The Times*, May 28, 1983.
[16] [1983] C.L.Y. 973.
[17] It is not clear from the report whether the jury decided how long would have been reasonable.
[18] 1986, unreported, C.A. Transcript 86–134.
[19] [1968] 1 Q.B. 379.

to recover less damages under this head than a plaintiff with an unblemished reputation.

False imprisonment damages: a summary

False imprisonment damages should be assessed under three basic heads: special damages, general damages, aggravated and exemplary damages, as follows:

(1) Special damages. The plaintiff is entitled to recover all special damage which is a direct consequence of his imprisonment—this includes matters such as the costs of obtaining his release, loss of earnings and lost job opportunities. As false imprisonment is an intentional tort the plaintiff is entitled to recover all loss directly flowing from the defendant's acts and there should be no reduction because a particular type of loss was not "reasonably foreseeable."

(2) General damages. It is submitted that two matters should be considered here:

(a) First, "loss of liberty" damages should be considered. The starting point here is the period of the imprisonment. A judge should begin from a conventional hourly rate (say, £300 per hour at 1986 prices).[20] This should be adjusted to take into account any aggravating or mitigating factors. An unlawful arrest should lead to a higher award as should unpleasant conditions of imprisonment;

(b) Secondly, damages for loss of reputation should be considered. The quantum of this award should take into account the plaintiff's character and reputation, the amount of publicity his imprisonment received and so on.

(3) Aggravated damages. These depend on whether the plaintiff's injured feelings were "justifiably heightened" by the conduct of the police. His conduct and character are relevant here. Circumstances of aggravation should include matters such as the conditions of detention, oppressive questioning or abuse of the plaintiff, the defendant's failure to admit that the imprisonment was unlawful or to apologise, the pleading of the defence and the conduct of the case at trial.

(4) Exemplary damages. These depend on whether the conduct of the police officers involved, or of the police force itself, was "arbitrary, oppressive or unconstitutional." If there is any evidence of "oppression" or unconstitutional conduct then the issue of exemplary damages should always be considered.[21] Exemplary damages should be added to the compensatory damages awarded.

[20] See the cases in the Appendix.
[21] See *Holden* v. *Chief Constable of Lancashire* [1986] 3 W.L.R. 1107.

6. DAMAGES FOR MALICIOUS PROSECUTION

Introduction

A maliciously prosecuted plaintiff will have suffered damage of several kinds. The most important kinds will be loss of liberty and damage to reputation. In addition, there may be financial losses such as loss of earning and costs incurred in defending the prosecution.

On general principles a successful plaintiff should, in every case, recover "compensatory damages" to cover this damage. Circumstances of aggravation should give rise to additional damages. Furthermore, exemplary damages will be potentially available in the case of police prosecutions. As with false imprisonment it appears that this stage by stage approach has not been followed by judges in assessing damages for malicious prosecution, a single "overall" figure being assessed, taking in compensatory and aggravated damages.

Special damages

It is clearly established that a maliciously prosecuted plaintiff can recover financial losses which are consequential on the prosecution. Thus, in *Childs* v. *Lewis*[22] it was accepted that the plaintiff's lost director's fees could have been recovered in a malicious prosecution action. In a number of malicious prosecution cases, the plaintiff has recovered the costs of defending the prosecution.[23] Even if the plaintiff was awarded the costs of defending the prosecution he can recover the amount by which his actual costs exceed the sum in fact awarded by the court.[24]

General damages

General damages for malicious prosecution are awarded to compensate the plaintiff for the damage to his reputation and for any loss of liberty as well as the distress and inconvenience which resulted from the prosecution. There has been no discussion of quantification principles in any reported malicious prosecution case. The quantum of damages should depend on the seriousness of the offence for which the plaintiff was prosecuted.

Although the plaintiff's compensatory damages for loss of liberty due to the prosecution should not depend on his character and previous involvement with the police it is clear that the damage to his reputation will be affected by such factors.[25] A plaintiff with a criminal record will suffer less damage to his reputation than someone of previous good character.

[22] (1924) 40 T.L.R. 870.

[23] See Appendix below at pp. 374 *et seq.*

[24] *Berry* v. *British Transport Commission* [1962] 1 Q.B. 306; the rule is thus different from that in civil cases where "taxed costs" are regarded as being a full indemnity, even though they do not cover all the sums paid out.

[25] *cf. Lawton* v. *Charles* [1957] C.L.Y. 1328; see above at p. 342.

The quantum of damages will also depend on the circumstances of the prosecution—how much publicity it received, the circumstances in which the plaintiff was charged and so on. Malicious prosecution is generally regarded as an extremely serious matter and, however minor the offence for which the plaintiff was prosecuted, very substantial damages can be expected in a successful action.

Successful malicious prosecution actions have always been relatively rare. There have only been two fully reported in the past 40 years.[26] In recent years, however, there seems to have been a significant increase in this type of case, although it is difficult to assess whether the actual rate of success has in fact increased.

When malicious prosecution actions are successful, however, awards of damages are likely to be high. Thus in 1961 two plaintiffs who were maliciously prosecuted for gross indecency were awarded damages of £1,356 15s (1986 value: £10,325) and £3,000 (1986 value: £22,830) for malicious prosecution.[27] Perhaps the most famous of all police cases is *White* v. *MPC*[28] in which the plaintiffs were each awarded £2,500 (1986 values: £3,050) for having been maliciously prosecuted for assaulting the police. These awards were expressed to include aggravated damages. Each plaintiff was awarded £20,000 (1986 value: £24,400) by way of exemplary damages.[29]

Malicious prosecution damages: a summary

Malicious prosecution damages should be assessed under three basic heads: special damages, general damages, aggravated and exemplary damages, as follows:

(1) Special damages. The plaintiff is entitled to recover all his pre-trial quantifiable pecuniary losses which are a direct consequence of the prosecution. These include the costs of defending the action, any loss of earnings or lost job opportunities which result from the prosecution.

(2) General damages. It is submitted that these should be assessed in the following stages:

(a) The period of time for which the plaintiff was deprived of his liberty should be considered. This should include time spent at the police station, time spent on remand in custody and time spent during the trial. Damages for this should be awarded at an appropriate hourly rate. It is submitted that the false imprisonment rate of £300 per hour already suggested[30] should be the starting point here. Damages under this head should not be reduced because of the plaintiff's bad character[31];

[26] *Tempest* v. *Snowden* [1952] 1 K.B. 130; *Leibo* v. *Buckman* [1952] 2 All E.R. 1057.

[27] *Selby & Firman* v. *Maclennan, The Times*, May 9, 1961.

[28] *The Times*, April 24, 1982, *per* Mars-Jones J.

[29] The total damages awarded in that case, at 1986 prices, were £63,750 which is one of the highest awards ever made in a police case—although there have been higher out of court settlements.

[30] See above at p. 357.

[31] See above at p. 356.

(b) The seriousness of the offence for which the plaintiff was prosecuted should be considered. The more serious the offence, the greater the damage to the plaintiff's reputation. Thus, for example, accusations such as dishonesty or sexual misconduct will cause more damage than accusations of minor public order offences or assaults. A money figure should be placed on this "reputation damage." "Minor" offences should attract damages of at least £1000 while a prosecution for an offence such as robbery or murder should attract very substantial sums. Such a sum should be increased if the prosecution received wide publicity;

(c) The plaintiff's reputation should then be considered. If he is of good character then the "loss of reputation" sum should not be reduced. If, on the other hand, he has previous convictions then there will be reductions in his "loss of reputation" damages.[32]

(3) Aggravated damages. These depend on whether the plaintiff's injured feelings were "justifiably heightened" by the way in which the prosecution was conducted. His conduct and character are relevant to the damages awarded under this head. A plaintiff's damage may be aggravated by the defendant's conduct up to the date of judgment. This will include, for example, a failure to acknowledge that the prosecution was wrongly brought.

(4) Exemplary damages. These will be awarded if the police conduct was "arbitrary, oppressive or unconstitutional." An award of exemplary damages will almost always be appropriate in a malicious prosecution case. It is difficult to see how it could not be oppressive to prosecute someone for a wrongful motive without reasonable and probable cause. The plaintiff's conduct and character is also relevant to the amount of damages awarded under this head.

7. DAMAGES IN RELATION TO GOODS

Introduction

Tortious interference with goods can take a number of basic forms. If the goods are damaged without being taken away then the plaintiff will be seeking financial compensation to cover the necessary repairs. If the goods are destroyed then the compensation must be for the whole value of the goods. When goods are misappropriated the potential range of remedies will be greater. The plaintiff may wish to have the goods back. On the other hand, he may prefer to restrict himself to financial compensation alone. In all three cases, the plaintiff will be able to recover "consequential losses" of various sorts. Despite some reforms brought in by the Torts (Interference with Goods) Act 1977 the rules relating to the types of damage recoverable for interference with goods remain complex and technical and only a summary is given here.[33] The principles discussed apply, with a few minor

[32] See above at p. 358.
[33] For a detailed discussion see McGregor, Chaps. 30 and 31.

exceptions, to all actions for interference with goods—whether in trespass, conversion, replevin or negligence.

Plaintiff with a limited interest

The law protects not ownership but possession. Thus, if goods are bailed, for example under a hire purchase agreement, the appropriate plaintiff is not the owner but the person hiring the goods. At common law a plaintiff with a limited interest could probably recover the full value of the goods as damages.[34] The position is now governed by section 8 of the Torts (Interference with Goods) Act 1977 which requires the plaintiff to identify any other person whom he knows to have an interest in the goods and permits the defendant to apply for any other person who has an interest in the goods to be joined as a party.[35]

Orders for the redelivery of goods

At common law a plaintiff could only seek the return of his goods in an action in detinue or replevin. Orders for the redelivery of goods in relation to trespass and conversion is now governed by the Torts (Interference with Goods) Act 1977. In proceedings for wrongful interference against a person who is in possession or control of goods the following relief is available:

> "(a) an order for delivery of the goods and for payment of any consequential damages, or
> (b) an order for delivery of the goods, but giving the defendant the alternative of paying damages by reference to the value of the goods, together in either alternative with payment of any consequential damages, or
> (c) damages."[36]

Only one of the three types of relief may be given. An order for delivery of the goods under (a) is at the discretion of the court and the plaintiff can choose between an order under sub-paragraph (b) or (c).[37] An order for delivery will not usually be made in respect of an ordinary article of commerce of no special value to the plaintiff where damages would fully compensate him.[38] Orders for redelivery of goods are discussed in Chapter 12.

Damages when goods are returned

If an order for redelivery of the goods is made under section 3(2)(*a*) or (*b*) of the 1977 Act the plaintiff is still entitled to "consequential" damages to

[34] *The Winkfield* [1902] P. 42; see generally, McGregor, para. 1080.
[35] R.S.C., Ord. 15, r. 10A.
[36] s.3(2).
[37] s.3(5).
[38] See *Whiteley* v. *Hilt* [1918] 2 K.B. 808 at 819, *per* Swinfen Eady M.R.; and also *Howard Perry* v. *BRB* [1980] 1 W.L.R. 1375.

compensate him for being deprived of the goods. He is also entitled to recover such damages when the goods are returned before hearing. The fact that he has accepted redelivery of misappropriated goods before the hearing simply goes to the reduction of the damages payable by the defendant[39]: it does not bar the continuation of the action. The delivery of an equivalent article will also have the same effect.[40] "Consequential" damages are considered below. The same principles apply whether the cause of action is conversion or trespass. Damages in replevin are assessed in the same way as in trespass and consequential losses are recoverable.[41]

Damages when goods are not returned

If goods are misappropriated and are not returned or are destroyed then the plaintiff's sole remedy will be in damages. The fundamental measure of damages is the market value of the goods. In conversion this is assessed at the time and place of the conversion.[42] Thus, if there was a conversion by taking or destruction the time and place in question will be that of the taking or destruction. If the original taking was lawful but there was a conversion by keeping, the time and place of the act of keeping will be used. Although the matter is not fully considered in the cases it would appear that, unless the plaintiff was holding the goods for resale, the market value will be the cost of buying the goods in the market.[43] A plaintiff cannot recover any increases in market value between the date of the tort and the date of trial because if he has delayed his purchase of a replacement he has failed to mitigate his loss. He can, however, probably recover any increase in market value between the time of the unlawful act and the time when he gets to know of it as consequential loss.[44] If there is a decline in value between the dates of conversion and judgment the plaintiff is entitled to the value at the date of conversion.[45]

Difficult quantification problems will arise if there is no market for the goods lost. The general rule is that the plaintiff can recover the cost of replacement.[46] However, if the replacement cost is very high the courts may only allow "the reasonable cost" of goods which "reasonably meet his needs" and which are "reasonably in the same condition."[47]

Market value or its equivalent is not, however, the only loss which can be recovered for. In accordance with the *restitutio in integrum* principle the courts will compensate a property owner for the value that of the goods **to**

[39] *Edmondson* v. *Nuttall* (1864) 17 C.B.(N.S.) 280 at 294.

[40] *Solloway* v. *McLaughlin* [1938] A.C. 247 (P.C.).

[41] *Gibbs* v. *Cruikshank* (1873) L.R. 8 C.P. 454.

[42] See, *e.g.*, *General & Finance Facilities* v. *Cooks Cars (Romford) Ltd.* [1963] 1 W.L.R. 644 at 649; in detinue the value was assessed at the date of judgment *Rosenthal* v. *Alderton & Sons Ltd.* [1946] K.B. 374.

[43] See *J. & E. Hall* v. *Barclay* [1937] 3 All E.R. 620 at 623F.

[44] *Sachs* v. *Miklos* [1948] 2 K.B. 23.

[45] *Rhodes* v. *Moules* [1895] 1 Ch. 236 at 254.

[46] *J. & E. Hall* v. *Barclay* [1937] All E.R. 620 at 624C; see also *Clyde Navigation Trustees* v. *Bowring* (1929) 34 L.1.L.R. 319.

[47] *per* Ormerod J., *Uctkos* v. *Mazzetta* [1956] 1 Lloyd's Rep. 209; see also *Moss* v. *Christchurch RDC* [1925] 2 K.B. 750.

him. This may not always accord with their market value.[48] If the goods in question are profit earning then an important component of such damages will be loss of profit. Such damages in addition to market value are an important component of all wrongful interference claims and are best considered as "consequential losses."[49]

Damaged goods

A plaintiff whose goods are unlawfully damaged is entitled to recover the cost of repair[50] and any diminution in value resulting from the repair.[51] If the repair renders the goods more valuable, it appears that the defendant is not entitled to a deduction.[52] If it is not reasonable to repair the goods then the plaintiff can only recover their market value because any repair would involve a failure by the plaintiff to mitigate his loss.[53] The plaintiff can also recover damages for loss of use.[54–55] These principles apply to actions in trespass and in conversion when the goods are returned in a damaged state.

Consequential losses

In all wrongful interference cases the plaintiff can recover "consequential losses." This covers a broad range of heads of damage.

First, the plaintiff can recover the interim hire of replacements whether the goods are damaged, destroyed[56] or eventually returned.[57] General principles of mitigation apply here and the replacements hired must be no more than are adequate for the plaintiff's needs. This will not necessarily be something of as high a standard as the goods damaged.[58] If the goods are destroyed then reasonable steps in mitigation may involve buying a replacement as soon as possible.

Secondly, if no substitute is hired, the plaintiff can recover damages for loss of use of the goods. If they were used in the course of business the plaintiff can recover any resultant loss of profit.[59] If the plaintiff was in the business of hiring the goods out he can recover the full market rate of hire for the whole period during which he was deprived of the goods. No reduction will be made for the fact that the particular goods in question might not have actually been hired for the whole period. As Romer L.J. said in the leading case of *Strand Electric Co.* v. *Brisford Entertainments*[60]:

[48] See Street at pp. 192–194 and the cases cited there.
[49] See below.
[50] *Darbishire* v. *Warran* [1963] 1 W.L.R. 1067.
[51] See, *e.g.*, *Payton* v. *Brooks* [1974] R.T.R. 169.
[52] McGregor, paras. 998–1000.
[53] See, *e.g.*, *Darbishire* v. *Warran* [1963] 1 W.L.R. 1067.
[54–55] See below.
[56] *Moore* v. *DER* [1971] 1 W.L.R. 1476.
[57] *Davis* v. *Oswell* (1837) 7 C. & P. 804.
[58] *Watson Norie* v. *Shaw* (1967) 111 S.J. 117.
[59] *Liesbosch Dredger* v. *SS Edison* [1933] A.C. 449.
[60] [1952] 2 Q.B. 246 at 257—a detinue case but setting out principles of general application; see also, *Hillesden Securities* v. *Ryjack* [1983] 1 W.L.R. 959.

"A defendant who has wrongfully detained and profited from the property of someone else cannot avail himself of such a hypothesis as this. It does not lie in the mouth of such a defendant to suggest that the owner might not have found a hirer."

Thirdly, other consequential losses may be recovered for. Thus, where a carpenter was hindered in his employment through having his tools converted by the defendant, he recovered damages for the loss of his employment as well as the loss of his tools.[61] Difficulties arise when the plaintiff loses profits on specific contracts with third parties involving the goods in question. It has been said that any loss on specific contracts with third parties can only be recovered if it could have been anticipated by the defendant.[62]

Many of the reported cases involve ships but the principles are clearly applicable to ordinary goods such as motor vehicles. As Devlin J. said in a case involving a lorry, summarising the damages available in cases where misappropriated profit earning goods are not returned:

"what has to be allowed is the loss of the lorry as a profit-earning concern . . . the value of the lorry, therefore, is its value plus the profits which it would have earned under existing contracts until such time as it could be reasonably replaced."[63]

Even when the goods are not profit-earning the plaintiff will still be entitled for damages for the period he was deprived of the use of the goods. Two methods have been suggested for calculating such damages: (i) by using the figures for the cost of maintaining and operating the goods (the cases are generally concerned with motor vehicles) (ii) by taking the interest on the capital value of the goods plus depreciation. The former method was adopted by Geoffrey Lane J. in the case of *Birmingham Corp.* v. *Sowsbery*[64] but it has also been said that there is "no special sanctity about any particular method of arriving at he appropriate sum."[65] In *Strand Electric Co.* v. *Brisford Entertainments*[66] Denning L.J. suggested that if non-profit earning goods are **used** by the defendant the plaintiff is entitled to recover the reasonable cost of hire.

Fourthly, it is well established that in an action for trespass to goods a plaintiff can recover "general damages" for matters such as annoyance and injury to credit and trade reputation.[67] In *Thurston* v. *Charles*[68] damages of £400 were awarded for the loss of reputation resulting from the showing of a private letter to an unauthorised person. There is no reason to suppose that such damages are not also available in conversion actions. In *Owen &*

[61] *Bodley* v. *Reynolds* (1846) 8 Q.B. 779; see the discussion in *France* v. *Gaudet* (1871) L.R. 6 Q.B. 199 at 205, *per* Mellor J.

[62] *The Arpad* [1934] P. 189; but see dissenting judgment of Scrutton L.J. and the discussion in McGregor, para. 1088.

[63] *Jones* v. *Port of London Authority* [1954] 1 Lloyd's Rep. 489 at 490.

[64] [1970] R.T.R. 84.

[65] *per* Willmer L.J., *The Hebridean Coast* [1961] A.C. 545 at 559.

[66] [1952] 2 Q.B. 246.

[67] *Brewer* v. *Dew* (1843) 11 M. & W. 625; *Smith* v. *Enright* (1893) L.J.Q.B. 220; the remarks of Lord Esher M.R. in *Dixon* v. *Calcraft* [1892] 1 Q.B. 458 at 464 to the effect that such damages were irrecoverable in English law were *per incuriam*.

[68] (1905) 21 T.L.R. 659; see also *Borden Chemical Co.* v. *J. G. Benkers Ltd.* (1973) 29 D.L.R. (3d) 337 in which substantial damages were recovered for the conversion of a customer list.

Smith v. *Reo Motors*[69] "exemplary" damages were awarded in a conversion case although Lord Devlin has since suggested that this award was best regarded as one of aggravated damages.[70] There is no doubt that in an appropriate case both aggravated and exemplary damages could be recovered in an action against the police for wrongful interference with goods.

8. DAMAGES IN OTHER TORT ACTIONS

Damage to land—trespass and negligence

If the plaintiff's land is tortiously damaged he is, in general, only entitled to recover the diminution in the value of the land as a result of the damage:

> "unless he establishes that he intends to or has reasonably rebuilt the structure damaged or destroyed and that his is an exceptional case in which justice requires that he should be paid the cost of restoration."[71]

"Land" will include "fixtures and fittings" as well as the actual fabric of a house or flat. Thus, if trespassing police officers damage a door or a window the onwer of the building will only be able to recover the cost of repairing them if it can be shown that justice requires it. It is submitted that in the case of damage to fixture this will almost always be the case. If, on the other hand a building is destroyed by tortious police conduct (as in *Rigby* v. *Chief Constable of Northampton*[72]) diminution in value is likely to be the most appropriate measure of damages.[73]

If land is occupied by trespassers for an appreciable length of time then the plaintiff will have a claim for damages for "occupation and use." The appropriate measure will be the market rental value of the property for the period of occupation and use.[74] It is not necessary for the plaintiff to show that he would have let the building to someone else during the period in question.[75]

Most police cases will not involve such extreme situations. The most likely trespasses are those of short duration by police officers entering without lawful authority. In such cases it is clear that the occupier of the premises is not confined to an award of nominal damages. Once it is shown that the occupier's rights have been interfered with the damages are "at large."[76] An award of aggravated or exemplary damages will also be available in appropriate circumstances.[77]

[69] (1934) 151 L.T. 274.
[70] *Rookes* v. *Barnard* [1964] A.C. 1129 at 1229.
[71] *per* Kenny J., *Munnel* v. *Calcon Ltd.* [1978] I.R. 387; approved by Scott J. in *Ward* v. *Cannock Chase DC* [1985] 3 All E.R. 537 at 558.
[72] [1985] 2 All E.R. 985.
[73] See generally, McGregor, para. 1119 where a slightly different view is taken.
[74] See McGregor, para. 1136.
[75] *Swordheath Properties* v. *Tabet* [1979] 1 W.L.R. 285.
[76] *Nicholls* v. *Ely Sugar Beet Co.* [1936] Ch. 343.
[77] See above at pp. 343 *et seq.*

Personal injury damages

If personal injury is caused by an assault by a police officer or by police negligence then ordinary personal injury principles will apply to the calculation of the compensatory damages.[78] As in all police cases exemplary damages may also be available in addition. Aggravated damages will not be available in a negligence action.[79]

Other negligence damages

Police negligence will, most commonly, lead to personal injury or property damage. In addition, damages can be recovered for "pure economic loss" such as loss of business profits. It is unclear whether such loss can be recovered for when it is not consequent on any personal injury or property damage.[80]

Defamation

Defamation cases are almost always tried by juries which, according to the rule of practice which we have already discussed[81] cannot be give any guidelines as to the quantum of damages. The plaintiff can recover compensatory damages for the harm to his reputation and, in an appropriate case, aggravated damages. Exemplary damages are common in defamation actions under Lord Devlin's second head in *Rookes* v. *Barnard*—acts calculated to make the defendant a profit which may well exceed the compensation payable to the plaintiff.[82] In actions against the police for defamation it is likely that any exemplary damages would be awarded under Lord Devlin's first head because their conduct had been "arbitrary and oppressive."

Misfeasance in a public office

There is no reported English misfeasance case involving the police. Indeed there is only one reported English case this century in which the plaintiff was successful, *Wood* v. *Blair & Helmsley RDC*.[83] He appears to have recovered only his "special damage." In 1959 the Australian case of *Farrington* v. *Thomson & Bridgland*[84] the plaintiff's damages against the police were assessed at £172 by way of compensation and £100 for exemplary damages. At the other end of the scale, the Supreme Court of

[78] See *Kemp & Kemp on the Quantum of Damages*.
[79] See *Kralj* v. *McGrath* [1986] 1 All E.R. 54 at 61.
[80] See Clerk & Lindsell, paras. 10–11, 10–14.
[81] See above at p. 349.
[82] See above at p. 344.
[83] [1957] Adm.L.R. 243.
[84] [1959] V.R. 286.

Canada awarded the plaintiff in *Roncarelli* v. *Duplessis*[85] damages of $33,123 in misfeasance after his restaurant licence had been "maliciously" cancelled because of his connections with the Jehovah's Witnesses.

On general principles a successful plaintiff in a misfeasance action against the police should recover substantial compensatory damages to compensate him for any financial loss suffered and for any loss of reputation or curtailment of his liberty. In addition aggravated damages would be available. It is of the essence of misfeasance that the police have acted maliciously or knowing that they had no power to do what they did. It follows that exemplary damages should be awarded in almost all successful misfeasance cases.

APPENDIX: DAMAGES AWARDS IN CASES OF ASSAULT, FALSE IMPRISONMENT AND MALICIOUS PROSECUTION[86]

Assault

Dunwell* v. *Chief Constable of South Yorkshire* (1978) Sheffield County Court Judge, News Report, *The Times*, January 20, 1978. **Facts: P was a student who was arrested in the course of a rag stunt with unreasonable force. His arm was held up his back and he received a black eye and a split lip. **Damages**: Compensatory; £100 (1986 value: £200).

O'Connor v. *Hewitson* [1979] Crim.L.R. 46. Court of Appeal, on appeal from Boreham J. **Facts**: P lawfully arrested for being drunk and disorderly. Behaved aggressively but was struck one or two blows that had not been justified by attempts to restrain him and to remove his shoes and jacket to prevent him injuring himself. P sustained bruising of right cheek and tenderness of right side of his face. No award of exemplary or aggravated damages because of P's provocation of police. **Damages**: Compensatory £125 (1986 value: £250.)

Allen v. *MPC* [1980] Crim.L.R. 441; *The Times*, March 24, 1980; High Court, May J. **Facts**: 44 year old Jamaican P. lawfully arrested but police officers used arm lock, then carried him to police van by his arms. Grazed chin, tenderness on abdomen, small piece of bone torn from arm, likely to cause osteo arthritis later. Excessive force used in the course of the arrest. **Damages**: Compensatory; for injury £1,000 (1986 value: £1,550), loss of earnings £90, loss of spectacles £25.

Alan* v. *MPC* (1981) Westminster County Court, Judge. **Facts: P was arrested at his office on suspicion of arson. Police found to have assaulted him in the course of arrest. **Damages**: Nominal 5p.

Evans* v. *MPC* (1981) Shoreditch County Court, Jury. **Facts: Group of

[85] (1959) 16 D.L.R. (2d) 689.
[86] "Unauthenticated cases" are marked with an asterisk(*).

youths including P were questioned about a car in their possession and arrested. Car belonged to P's mother. False imprisonment claim dismissed. **Damages**: Compensatory; £20 (1986 value: £27).

Boyd* v. *MPC* (1981) High Court Jury. News Report, *The Times*, February 7, 1981. **Facts: P, 24 year old housewife, ordered to strip to her underwear in the course of a search at a police station. **Damages**: Compensatory; £300 (1986 value: £410).

Flavius v. *MPC* (1982) 132 New L.J. 532; High Court, Leonard J. **Facts**: Police were searching P's maisonette when P resisted. He was arrested and taken by police van to the police station. Constable hit P on shin and broke his leg. **Damages**: Compensatory; £1,000 pain and suffering (1986 value: £1,200) Aggravated and exemplary; £400 (1986 value: £488).

Marnoch* v. *MPC* (1983) County Court. **Facts: P assaulted at police station after arrest for motoring offences. **Damages**: Compensatory £250 (1986 value: £293).

Brown* v. *MPC* (1984) Court unknown. **Facts: P injured when officers burst into premises when conducting a search. **Damages**: Compensatory; £200 (1986 value: £222).

Knight* v. *MPC* (1984) Court unknown. **Facts: P injured when police raided a squat. He was held against the door and his face was smashed onto the lock. **Damages**: Compensatory; £600 (1986 value: £666), Aggravated; £250 (1986 value: £278).

Sturley v. *MPC The Times*, June 27, 1984; High Court, Mars-Jones J. **Facts**: P's arm twisted and fractured in the course of a lawful arrest. **Damages**: Compensatory; £2,000 pain and suffering (1986 value: £2,220).

Connor v. *Chief Constable of Cambridgeshire, The Times*, April 11, 1984; High Court, French J. **Facts**: P was struck over the head by a police officer with a truncheon at a football match. **Damages**: Compensatory; £2,000 (1986 value: £2,220). Exemplary; £500 (1986 value: £555).

Ballard, Stewart-Park, Findlay v. *MPC* (1983) 133 New L.J. 1133; Legal Action, January 1984, 10; Westminster County Court, Judge. **Facts**: P1 and P2 had been hit over the head by police officers with truncheons in the course of a demonstration, P2 carried spread eagled and dumped on ground from a height of four feet. P3 was lawfully arrested and was prodded in stomach, hit over eye with truncheon and, as a result suffered migrainous attacks. **Damages**: P1—Compensatory; £400 including small sum for aggravated damages (1986 value: £444). P2—Compensatory; £600 including aggravated damages (1986 value: £666). P3—Compensatory; £3,000 including aggravated damages (1986 value: £3,330).

Barbara v. *Home Office* (1984) 134 New L.J. 888. High Court, Leggat J. **Facts**: Whilst in custody on remand P was injected with tranquillising drug. Liability admitted. **Damages**: Compensatory; £100 (1986 value: £111) for the physical injury. Aggravated; £500 (1986 value: £555).

Wells* v. *MPC* (1984) High Court Jury. News Report, *The Daily Telegraph*, October 12, 1984. **Facts: P assaulted in the course of arrest and given a black eye. **Damages**: Compensatory; £500 (1986 value: £555). Exemplary; £50 (1986 value: $56).

Lavery v. *Ministry of Defence* [1984] 7 N.I.J.B.; [1985] C.L.Y. 2366; N.I. Court of Appeal, Kelly L.J. **Facts**: P was injured when stopped and assaulted by a member of an Army patrol. Liability admitted, no mitigation put forward. **Damages**; Compensatory & Exemplary; £2,500 (1986 value: £2,775).

Fisher* v. *MPC* (1985) Westminster County Court, Judge. **Facts: P, at a football match saw two youths in the presence of police dog. He expressed concern to police officer that one youth who was bleeding would contract disease from police dog. Arrested for obstructing police. At the police station he was physically forced to sit down by being tripped backwards. **Damages**: Compensatory; £200 (1986 value: £212) (appeal on another point dismissed C.A., May 13, 1986, Transcript: Association).

Leon v. *MPC* [1986] C.L.Y. 2538; Clerkenwell County Court, Judge. **Facts**: Rastafarian P stopped by police to search for drugs, told them he had already been searched, ran to catch a bus. Pulled off the bus by the police, punched, kicked and thrown into a police van. Suffered swollen, bruised lips, swollen nose and forehead and bruises on back. Strong suspicion that police were motivated by racial prejudice. **Damages** Compensatory; £200. Exemplary; £1,000.

Pascal* v. *MPC* (1986) Shoreditch County Court, Jury. News Report, *The Guardian*, March 20, 1986. **Facts: P assaulted at police station during questioning, including assault by means of lighted cigarettes. **Damages**: Compensatory; £2,000, Exemplary £1,000.

Reid* v. *MPC* (1986) High Court Jury. News Report, *The Times*, May 3, 1986. **Facts: Excessive force used in the course of a lawful arrest for threatening behaviour. **Damages**: Compensatory; £200.

Williams* v. *MPC* (1986) High Court Jury. News Report, *The Daily Telegraph*, July 11, 1986. **Facts: P assaulted by plain clothes officers who chased him down the road. **Damages**: Compensatory; £1,400.

False imprisonment

Kuchenmeister v. *Home Office* [1958] 1 Q.B. 496. High Court, Barry J. **Facts**: P was German citizen, in transit through London Airport. Detained unlawfully by immigration officials for two hours three minutes. **Damages**: Compensatory; £150 (1986 value: £1,178. Hourly rate; £471).

Wershof v. *MPC* [1978] 3 All E.R. 540; High Court, May J. **Facts**: P, newly qualified solicitor, refused to hand over a ring, which police suspected was stolen, without a receipt and was arrested for obstructing the police in the execution of their duty. False imprisonment of one hour eight mins.

Damages: Compensatory; £1,000 false imprisonment and assault (1986 value: £2,000).

Graves* v. *Chief Constable of Thames Valley Police* (1978) High Court, Park J. and a Jury. News Report, *The Times*, April 21, 1978. **Facts: P, a freelance photographer working for the *Sunday People*, was arrested on suspicion of being involved in a "drug deal." P was made to strip and subjected to a "humiliating search for drugs." **Damages**: Compensatory; £500 (1986 value: £1,000).

Reynolds v. *MPC The Times*, February 6, 1981; High Court, Caulfield J. and a Jury. **Facts**: P was aged 28 and was arrested because of unreasonable suspicion that she was involved with her co-habitee in criminal activity. Held in custody for 14 hours. **Damages**: Compensatory £12,000 no award of aggravated or exemplary (1986 value: £16,440; Hourly rate: £1,174). (D's appeal against quantum rejected by C.A. [1982] Crim.L.R. 600).

Ware* v. *Matthews* (1981) High Court, Ralph Gibson J. News Report, *The Times*, February 12, 1981. **Facts: P1 and P2, father and son, were in a car which was stopped by the police. They were arrested when they refused to give their address. **Damages**: Compensatory; for each P £250 (1986 value: £343).

Quinlivan* v. *MPC* (1981) Westminster County Court, Judge. **Facts: P was Heathrow baggage checker. Seen by manageress of duty free shop loitering in the vicinity. She gained the impression he had come to collect the takings but then asked for directions for leaving the area. Police called and P later arrested at his home. Initial arrest held to be unlawful but detention lawful after further inquiries. **Damages**: Compensatory (for arrest) £100 (1986 value: £137).

Hickson* v. *MPC* (1981) Shoreditch County Court, Jury. **Facts: C10 officers were keeping observation on a lock-up garage when P intervened. Arrested for obstructing the police but acquitted. **Damages**: £500 (1986 value: £685).

Smith v. *MPC* [1982] C.L.Y. 898; Bow County Court, Judge. **Facts**: P, 36 year old former police woman was held in custody for 16 hours 45 minutes while "perfunctory" inquiries were made. **Damages**: Aggravated £2,500 (1986 value: £3,050; Hourly rate: £182); Exemplary £1,750 (1986 value: £2,135).

Payne v. *Chief Constable of Sussex* (1982) Brighton County Court, Jury. News Report, *The Daily Mail*, December 9, 1982. **Facts**: P wrongfully arrested in embarrassing circumstances, in front of work colleagues, and held for two hours. **Damages**: Compensatory & Aggravated; £1,250 (1986 value: £1,525; Hourly rate: £763).

Vincent* v. *MPC* (1982) Westminster County Court, Judge. **Facts: P arrested after suspicion of evading payment on underground. Acquitted of assault and disorderly conduct. **Damages**: Compensatory; £500 (1986 value: £610).

Lawrence v. *Chief Constable of Dyfed-Powys* [1983] C.L.Y. 973; High Court, Anthony Lincoln J. and a Jury. **Facts**: P was a 40 year old lecturer who was arrested and held incommunicado for a period of 21 hours. Only spoken to twice by police. Length of detention held by jury to have been unreasonable. **Damages**: Compensatory; £600 (1986 value: £702).

Short & Hazelgreaves* v. *MPC* (1983) High Court, Caulfield J. and a Jury. **Facts: Ps arrested in public house in Whitehall. In a subsequent case the trial judge described them as "two very cultivated young men of perfect character and excellent family who had . . . spent a fair period of time, three or four hours at night, in an unattractive police station."[87] Judge directed jury to award damages. **Damages**: Compensatory; P1 £40 (1986 value: £47), P2 £60 (1986 value: £70).

Millington v. *MPC The Times*, May 28, 1983; High Court, Forbes J. **Facts**: P lawfully arrested but held for 41 hours longer than was necessary. Judge described P as "an engaging scoundrel whose regard for truth was minimal" and made an award to take into account the fact the P had already suffered injury to feelings and to liberty from his lawful arrest. **Damages**: £800 compensatory (1986 value: £936; Hourly rate: £23).

Hayward v. *MPC The Times*, March 24, 1984; High Court, Caulfield J. **Facts**: P was an "ordinary respectable Englishman" who was wrongfully arrested at Portobello Road market and held for four hours 30 mins. **Damages**: Compensatory; £1,750 (1986 value: £1,943; Hourly rate: £432).

Ward v. *Chief Constable of Avon & Somerset* (1984) Bristol County Court, Judge, *The Times*, July 17, 1985, (C.A.) (appeal on interest); *The Times*, June 26, 1986, (C.A.) (appeal on lawfulness of arrest refused). **Facts**: P arrested on suspicion of theft, period in custody unnecessarily long by about two and a half hours. **Damages**: Compensatory; £750 (1986 value: £833; Hourly rate: £333).

Murphy v. *Oxford* (1984) Liverpool County Court, Jury, February 15, 1985, (C.A.) (police appeal on lawfulness of arrest refused). **Facts**: P arrested for burglary without being given proper details of the alleged offence. Judge ruled that the arrest was wrongful and that at least three hours of the P's total detention of four hours was unlawful. **Damages**: Compensatory; £2,000 (1986 value: £2,220; Hourly rate: £740).

Marcus* v. *MPC* (1985) Wandsworth County Court Jury. News Report, *Caribbean Times*, March 29, 1985. **Facts: P, 12 year old boy, arrested on suspicion of theft of a bicycle. Locked in detention room after it had been established that he was in lawful possession of the bicycle. **Damages**: Compensatory; £600 (1986 value: £636). Exemplary £600 (1986 value: £636).

Kemp* v. *Chief Constable of Merseyside* (1985) High Court, Liverpool. News Report, *The Guardian*, March 13, 1985. **Facts: P wrongfully arrested whilst looking at burnt out car, charged two and a half hours later. **Damages**: Compensatory; £750 (1986 value: £833; Hourly rate: £333).

**Poyser* v. *Chief Constable of Greater Manchester* (1985) Manchester

[87] *per* Caulfield J., *Hayward* v. *MPC, The Times*, March 24, 1984; Transcript: Association.

County Court, Jury. *The Guardian*, April 19, 1985. **Facts**: The three Ps were stopped whilst driving home during the 1981 Moss Side, Manchester riots. Ps were searched and beaten and then arrested. They suffered cuts and bruises. Ps later acquitted of disorderly behaviour. **Damages**: £4,500—P1 (1986 value: £4,700); £3,000—P2 (1986 value: £3,180); £1,800—P3 (1986 value: £1,908).

Cooper* v. *Chief Constable of Merseyside* (1985) High Court, Liverpool, Russell J. and a Jury. News Report, *The Guardian*, July 9, 1985. **Facts: Jury found in Ps favour in relation to three out of five incidents of wrongful arrest and trespass. **Damages**: £4,041.64 (1986 value: £4,284).

Bacon* v. *MPC* (1985) High Court, Jury. **Facts: False imprisonment for a period of 26 hours. **Damages**: £300 (1986 value: £318; Hourly rate: £12).

Felicien* v. *MPC* (1985) High Court, Jury. **Facts: P arrested under expired power of arrest attached to a domestic violence injunction, held for 36 hours. **Damages**: Compensatory £300 (1986 value: £318) (Hourly rate; £8.80); Exemplary £100 (1986 value: £106).

Lawrence* v. *MPC* (1986) Court unknown. **Facts: P held in police station for 27 hours after arrest on suspicion of being involved in a robbery. Period of detention held to have been unreasonably long. **Damages**: Compensatory £750.

Beckett v. *Walker* [1986] 11 C.L. 3. Court of Appeal. **Facts**: D was a court clerk who admitted that, due to a court order not being properly drawn up, P had been wrongfully detained for 53 hours. Jury awarded damages of £200. Court of Appeal were of the view that this was an award which no reasonable jury could have made. Damages were in negligence but Court stated that damages in false imprisonment would have been the same. **Damages**: Compensatory, £500 (Hourly rate £9.43).

Houghton v. *Chief Constable of Greater Manchester, The Times*, July 24, 1986, Court of Appeal. **Facts**: P arrested for having an offensive weapon. The offence was not an arrestable one in the circumstances. After arrest P was held in a cell for over two and a half hours. **Damages**: Compensatory; £600 (assessed by the Court of Appeal) (Hourly rate: £240).

Bryant* v. *Chief Constable of Thames Valley Police* (1986) Oxford County Court. News Report, *The Times*, July 16, 1986. **Facts: P returned to former matrimonial home to pick up personal property. Her lawyers advised her that she was entitled to force an entry. She was arrested on suspicion of burglary. **Damages**: Compensatory; £1,000 False Imprisonment and wrongful arrest. Aggravated; £500.

Simmons v. *Polak* [1986] 5 C.L. 101. Willesden County Court, Judge. **Facts**: P brought action against former fiancée for return of wedding ring. P and D had met to discuss their engagement in P's car. P had been aggressive and had locked the car door, held her by the wrists and refused to allow her to leave the car for a period of five minutes. D successfully counterclaimed for false imprisonment. **Damages**: Compensatory; £250.

Holtham* v. *MPC* (1986) High Court, Peter Pain J. and Jury. (judge's ruling on lawfulness of arrest reported *The Times*, January 1, 1987). News Report, *The Guardian*, December 16, 1986. **Facts: Mr. and Mrs. Holtham (P1 and P2) wrongfully arrested in course of investigations into allegations of murder against their son on Thursday November 20, 1980 and not released until Monday November 24, 1980. **Damages**: Compensatory; P1—£2,250; P2—£5,750.

Abobaker v. *MPC* (1987) Bloomsbury County Court, Jury. **Facts**: P, a man of Somali origin aged 41 was arrested at 4.20am for being drunk and incapable of looking after himself, He was detained at Marylebone Police Station until 7.30am. Police said he accepted a caution and produced his signature on the station book under a caution. P claimed that he was told that he was told that he not be released unless he signed. **Damages**: Compensatory £950 (Hourly rate £300).

Shaper v. *Robinson* [1987] 2 C.L. 47. Bloomsbury County Court, Jury. **Facts**: P, a barrister, arrested for being drunk in a public place. Charge dismissed by magistrates. Jury found in P's favour (after there had been a re-trial because of the judge's misdirection at the first trial). **Damages**: Compensatory: £500 for the arrest; £1,000 for the false imprisonment.

Several causes of action—not including malicious prosecution

Peacock & Hoskyn v. *Musgrave & Porter* [1956] Crim.L.R. 414. High Court, Streatfeild J. and a Jury. **Facts**: Ps left their car in a village and were walking through it when they were arrested, taken to the police station. Their particulars were taken and then they were released. Streatfeild J. held that there was reasonable cause for stopping and detaining Ps, jury found that detention was unreasonably long and more force than necessary used in the case of P1. **Damages**: Compensatory; P1 and P2—£5 each for false imprisonment (1986 value: £42). P1—£1 for assault (1986 value: £8).

McKenna* v. *Chief Constable of Cheshire* (1972) Stockport County Court, Judge. News Report, *The Times*, March 29, 1972. **Facts: P arrested when officers came to his house to inquire about his road fund licence. He was hit three times in the course of his arrest. **Damages**: Compensatory £75 (1986 value: £344) for assault, £150 (1986 value: £687) for false imprisonment.

Collier* v. *MPC* (1973) High Court, Milmo J. and a Jury. News Report, *The Times*, February 7, 1973. **Facts: P was arrested in March 1969 for loitering with intent to steal and was subsequently assaulted by 4 CID officers at Poplar police station. **Damages**: Compensatory £950 (1986 value: £4,038) for assault, £100 (1986 value: £425) for unlawful arrest.

Bryning v. *Oxford* (1982) Liverpool County Court, Jury (appeal on judge's failure to direct on exemplary damages rejected by C.A., (1983) C.A. Transcript 847). **Facts**: Plaintiff repeatedly assaulted by police officers after calling them in relation to another matter. P did not sustain any injuries. P was held by the police for a period of ten hours. **Damages**: Compensatory; £100—assault (1986 value: £122). £25—false imprisonment (1986 value: £31; Hourly rate: £3).

Simper v. *MPC* [1982] C.L.Y. 3124. Uxbridge County Court, Judge. **Facts**: P1 and P2's house unlawfully searched after P1 lawfully arrested (and later convicted). Police had forced their way in and injured P2's hand in doing so. They had also forced open an attaché case belonging to P1. **Damages**: Compensatory—for trespass, damage to attaché case, injury to P2's hand and her distress—£300 (1986 value: £366).

White v. *Brown* [1983] C.L.Y. 972. York County Court, Jury. **Facts**: P, 72 year old lady, stopped in a shop by manager of D shop. Handbag snatched and kept for "a few moments." P taken back to D shop and held for 15 minutes. Taken to police station, held for a further 90 minutes. Total period of false imprisonment two hours. D responsible for police arrest and detention. **Damages**: Compensatory; £775 trespass to goods (1986 value: £907), £520 false imprisonment (1986 value: £608: Hourly rate: £304).

Hurlings v. *Chief Constable of Merseyside* [1984] C.L.Y. 1019; Liverpool County Court, Jury. **Facts**: P's nose was fractured in the course of an arrest for being drunk and disorderly. P was not in fact drunk but he was held in custody for four hours 30 mins. **Damages**: Compensatory; £500 for assault constituted by initial arrest; £250 compensatory for initial false imprisonment (1986 value: £2,775); £5,500 for use of excessive force by police officer (1986 value: £6,105); £4,000 for subsequent false imprisonment (1986 value: £4,440; Hourly rate: £987)—damages limited to county court limit of £3,000.

George v. *MPC The Times*, March 31, 1984; High Court, Park J. **Facts**: Police forcibly and unlawfully entered P's home searching for her son, hit and kicked P and ransacked house. P had suffered bruising and tenderness over a number of parts of her body. **Damages**: Compensatory: £6,000 for trespass and assault (1986 value: £6,660). Exemplary; £2,000 (1986 value: £2,220).

Stock v. *Chief Constable of Merseyside* (1987), Legal Action, May 1987, 19; Liverpool County Court, Jury. **Facts**: P, taking part in a demonstration, was injured in course of an arrest for breach of the peace by being thrown over railings. Acquitted of a public order offence. No reason given for his arrest. **Damages**: Compensatory: £500 for injuries resulting from arrest; £1,500 for wrongful arrest. Exemplary: £3,000.

Several causes of action—including malicious prosecution

Tempest v. *Snowden* [1952] 1 All E.R. 1. High Court, Cassels J. and a Jury and Court of Appeal. **Facts**: P was prosecuted for theft by D, his former employer. The magistrates found that D had no case to answer. **Damages**: Compensatory: £200 (1986 value: £2,080), Special damages, costs of defence: £5 5s.

Leibo v. *Buckman* [1952] 2 All E.R. 1057. High Court, Oliver J. and a Jury and Court of Appeal. **Facts**: D prosecuted P for theft of £27 3s when he only had reasonable and probable cause in relation to theft of £7 15s. P was acquitted and jury found that D had prosecuted him maliciously. **Damages**: Compensatory: £50 (1986 value: £475).

Sherbourne v. *Walker* [1955] Crim.L.R. 184. High Court, Sellers J. **Facts**: P arrested by D out of pique and then prosecuted for obstruction. **Damages**: Compensatory: £100 assault and false imprisonment (1986 value: £881); £50 malicious prosecution (1986 value: £441).

Sam v. *Cluney* [1956] Crim.L.R. 271. High Court, Cassels J. and a Jury. **Facts**: P arrested in public lavatory and accused of gross indecency. P was acquitted at trial and brought an action for false imprisonment, malicious prosecution and conspiracy to injure. **Damages**: Compensatory: £1,600 (1986 value: £13,472).

Selby & Firman v. *Maclennan, The Times*, May 9, 1961. High Court, Havers J. and a Jury. **Facts**: Mr Selby and Miss Firman were accused by two police officers of committing an act of gross indecency in a car. They were acquitted at the London Sessions. The jury found that the Ds had preferred a false charge and supported it with false evidence. **Damages**: Compensatory: S—£1,356 15s for malicious prosecution (1986 value: £10,325), £100 for false imprisonment (1986 value: £761); F—£3,000 for malicious prosecution (1986 value: £22,830), £100 for false imprisonment (1986 value: £761), Special damage of £643 5s, costs of defence.

Blaker v. *Weller* [1964] Crim.L.R. 311. High Court, John Stephenson J. and a Jury. **Facts**: D, a constable, arrested P on charge of indecent exposure. P was convicted by magistrates but conviction was quashed on appeal. **Damages**: Compensatory: £25 for false imprisonment (1986 value: £174); £500 for malicious prosecution (1986 value: £3,475). Special damages (costs of defending the criminal case) £363 4s 6d.

Allum & Hislop v. *Weller & Jackson, The Times*, February 25, 1966. High Court, Marshall J. and a Jury. **Facts**: Ps, who were both black and were a barrister and a schoolteacher, were arrested at 9.30pm and held in custody until 2am. They were both prosecuted for attempted theft and acquitted. **Damages**: Compensatory; £500 for each P for false imprisonment (1986 value: £3,185) (Hourly rate £708); £3,500 for each P for malicious prosecution (1986 value: £22,295).

Walker* v. *Chief Constable of Greater Manchester* (1970) Salford Hundred Court of Record. News Report, *The Times*, November 7, 1970. **Facts: P, who was West Indian, was stopped by a police officer on suspicion of stealing a car. P was slapped and kicked and then arrested and charged with breach of peace, for which he was acquitted. **Damages**: Compensatory; £500 (1986 value: £2,690) for assault, false imprisonment and malicious prosecution.

Paling* v. *MPC* (1978) High Court, May J. and a Jury. News Report, *The Times*, February 9, 1978. **Facts: P, a sergeant in the Special Branch, was arrested by two constables in a public lavatory at Picadilly Underground station for indecency. It was alleged that he had attempted to bribe the officers with a £5 note. P was acquitted of indecency and attempted bribery at the Central Criminal Court in 1974. **Damages**: Compensatory £34,000 (1986 value: £68,000); Exemplary £3,000 (1986 value: £6,000).

Daly* v. *MPC* (1980) High Court, Boreham J. and a Jury. News Report, *The Times*, July 23, 1980. **Facts: West Indian P stopped by the police at Petticoat Lane market in May 1976. He was held overnight and the only food he was given were nuts which the police threw into his cell saying "Here you are monkey." He was subsequently acquitted of assaulting the police at the time of his arrest. **Damages**: Compensatory; £1,000 for false imprisonment (1986 value: £1,550), £25 for assault (1986 value: £39), £1,000 for malicious prosecution (1986 value: £1,550). Exemplary; £500 for malicious prosecution (1986 value: £775).

Rhone v. *MPC* (1981) Bloomsbury and Marylebone County Court, Jury. **Facts**: P was arrested for alleged drunkeness and was held in police custody for two hrs 25 mins. He was charged with being drunk and disorderly and was acquitted. **Damages**: Compensatory: £100 (1986 value: £137) for false imprisonment, £500 (1986 value: £685) for malicious prosecution. Special damages: cost of defence, £73.56.

White v. *MPC, The Times*, April 24, 1982; High Court, Mars-Jones J. **Facts**: Ps were middle aged West Indian couple. Police had a search warrant but it was not in their possession when they searched. Boths Ps were assaulted by police officers—Mr White by a truncheon. Ps were then prosecuted for assault on the police and acquitted. **Damages**: Compensatory; £1,000 for each P for false imprisonment (1986 value: £1,220); £1,000 for pain and suffering for Mrs White (1986 value: £1,220), £3,000 for pain and suffering for Mr White (1986 value: £3,660); £2,500 for each P for malicious prosecution (1986 value: £3,050). Exemplary; £20,000 exemplary for each P (1986 value: £24,400).

Podlewski* v. *MPC* (1982) Westminster County Court, Jury; News Report, *The Times*, July 29, 1982. **Facts: P was a freelance photographer arrested at a party. He was acquitted of obstruction after police claimed he had jumped on constable's back. **Damages**: Compensatory; £1,850 malicious prosecution (1986 value: £2,257); £150 false imprisonment (1986 value: £183).

McCarthy & Walls* v. *Chief Constable of Merseyside* (1984) High Court, Liverpool, Jury. News Report, *The Times*, April 14, 1985. **Facts: Ps were "framed" for theft by police officers who hoped that this would improve their prospect of promotion. **Damages**: For each P—Compensatory; £250 for false arrest (1986 value: £278), £2,000 for malicious prosecution (1986 value: £2,220). Exemplary; £4,000 (1986 value: £4,440).

Barnett* v. *MPC* (1985) High Court Jury; News Report, *The Times*, March 26, 1985. **Facts: Ammunition was "planted" in P's house by the police and he was then prosecuted for firearms offences and acquitted. **Damages**: Compensatory; £5,000 malicious prosecution (1986 value: £5,300); £250 false imprisonment (1986 value: £265).

**Wilson & Farbridge* v. *MPC* (1985) High Court, Tudor Price J. and a Jury.

News Report, *The Guardian*, December 11, 1985. **Facts**: P1, who was confined to wheelchair, was assaulted by the police, dropped on the floor of a police van and then prosecuted for assaulting the police and subsequently acquitted. P2, his girlfriend, was arrested and subjected to a humiliating strip search, during which she was made to jump up and down naked. **Damages**: P1—£1,750; P2—£2,000.

Lucas* v. *MPC* (1986, High Court, Leonard J. and a Jury. News Report, *The Guardian*, February 6, 1986. **Facts: P, 46 year old West Indian woman was punched in eye and mouth and kicked in the course of an unlawful arrest. A police officer looked up her skirt and made insulting remarks. She was then held in custody overnight and unsuccessfully prosecuted for assaulting the police. **Damages**: Compensatory; £10,000 for assault; £1,000 for false imprisonment. Exemplary; £15,000 for malicious prosecution.

Docherty v. *Chief Constable of Northumbria* (1986); Legal Action, May 20, 1987; Newcastle upon Tyne County Court, Jury. **Facts**: P walked towards police officers who had arrested his son for criminal damage and was arrested for obstructing the police. Held in custody for two hours 10 mins. Acquitted of obstructing police in execution of their duty and court refused to bind him over. **Damages**: Compensatory; £2,000 for assault, false imprisonment and malicious prosecution; Exemplary: £3,000.

12. Other Remedies

1. INTRODUCTION

Monetary compensation is not the only way in which a citizen can vindicate rights infringed by the police. The courts can, in appropriate situations, order parties to do or to refrain from doing certain things in the future. They can also give "declarations" as to the legal rights of parties in particular situations. These remedies of injunctions and declarations may in the future be of great importance in cases involving the police. The courts can also make orders relating to the return of wrongfully removed or detained property. If someone is kept in police custody without lawful justification he will be able to apply for a writ of habeas corpus.

It should be noted that the courts are not in a position to provide the remedy that the citizen may be most interested in—disciplinary action against the officers involved in infringing his rights. This is the province of the Police Complaints Authority.[1] There is no route which can be taken through the courts to compel the police to discipline or dismiss one of their number who is found to have seriously infringed a citizen's rights. In a number of notorious cases officers who have been severely criticised by the civil courts appear to have escaped disciplinary action entirely.[2] The damages awarded by the courts are paid out of the public purse and a police officer may appear to escape all personal liability for what may be very serious illegality. This can lead to public confidence in the police being diminished. It is to be hoped that the new Police Complaints Authority will go some way towards dealing with this problem.

2. INJUNCTIONS

Introduction

An injunction is an order by a court that a party to a civil action refrain from doing something or that something be done by him. There has been no reported case in which an injunction has been granted against the police in respect of their "policing" functions—although unsuccessful applications have been made in a number of unreported cases.[3] There is no reason of

[1] See Chap. 2 above at p. 40.

[2] See Introduction above at p. 14.

[3] The most famous of which was the *Dartford Tunnel* case during the 1984 Miners' Strike.

principle why injunctions should not be granted against the police in appropriate cases to restrain them from acting unlawfully.

An injunction is an equitable remedy and is, therefore, discretionary. Nevertheless, such discretion must be exercised on the basis of established principles. Before discussing the court's jurisdiction to grant injunctions and the principles on which the court's discretion is exercised it is important to be clear about the applicable terminology.

There are two basic types of injunction which are granted on very different principles. The first, and most common, type is a "prohibitory" injunction which operates to restrain a party from doing some act or acts in the future. The second type is a "mandatory" injuction which is an order that a party does some specific act or acts.

It is also important to be clear about the distinction between "final" and "interlocutory" injunctions. A final (or "perpetual") injunction is one granted when an action is finally disposed of. Such an injunction will, for example, restrain the defendant from committing specific unlawful acts for the indefinite future. An interlocutory injunction, on the other hand, is designed to preserve the position of the parties pending the trial of the action. Interlocutory injunctions will also be granted to preserve property pending trial and to "freeze" the assets of a defendant.

The third distinction is between injunctions granted in relation to some past infringement of rights—to prevent it happening again, or to restore the postion before the infringement—and injunctions granted to prevent a threatened infringement of rights. Injunctions of the latter sort are known as *quia timet* ("because he fears") injunctions. Injunctions of this latter type may have some importance in police cases if, for example, a person fears that as a result of complaints made he may be harassed by the police.

The same principles and standard of proof apply to *quia timet* as to ordinary injuctions.[4] Nevertheless, the plaintiff is claiming a remedy before any wrong has taken place and it is, therefore, more difficult to show that damage is likely. It is, in the often quoted words of Lord Dunedin, not sufficient to say "timeo" ("I fear").[5] In general:

> "the plaintiff takes upon himself the burden of proving that it is reasonably certain that what the defendant is threatening and intending to do will cause imminent and substantial damage to the plaintiff."[6]

This will be very difficult to establish in the absence of threats or other indications that the tort is likely to happen without an injunction being granted.

Jurisdiction and discretion

The Judicature Acts gave the High Court the Court of Chancery's former jurisdiction to grant injunctions. It was well-established that final

[4] See Meagher, Gummow & Lehane, *Equity*, para. 2176.

[5] *Att.-Gen. for the Dominion of Canada* v. *Ritchie Contracting and Supply Co. Ltd.* [1919] A.C. 999 at 1005.

[6] *Royal Insurance Co. Ltd.* v. *Midland Insurance Co. Ltd.* (1908) 26 R.P.C. 95 at 97.

injunctions were only available in equity to protect recognised legal or equitable rights.[7] The jurisdiction of the Court of Chancery rested:

> "upon injury to property actual or prospective, and (it had) . . . no jurisdiction to prevent the commission of acts which are merely criminal or merely illegal and do not affect any rights of property."[8]

Nevertheless, it is now generally accepted that a final injunction will lie to protect **any** legal or equitable right, whether or not this is proprietary.[9]

The High Court's jurisdiction to grant interlocutory injunctions was also statutory and such injunctions could be granted "in all cases in which it appears to the court to be just and convenient."[10] Nevertheless, it was well-established that such injunctions were also only available to protect legal or equitable rights.[11]

The position is now governed by section 37(1) of the Supreme Court Act 1981 which states that:

> "The High Court may by order (whether interlocutory or final) grant an injunction . . . in all cases in which it appears to the court to be just and convenient to do so."

Despite the very wide terms of this section it is generally thought that the power of the courts to grant injunctions are limited to specific situations defined by case law.[12] Lord Brandon has summarised the position as follows:

> "the power of the High Court to grant injunctions is . . . limited to two situations. Situation (1) is when one party to an action can show that the other party has either invaded, or threatens to invade, a legal or equitable right of the former for the enforcement of which the latter is amenable to the jurisdiction of the court. Situation (2) is where one party to an action has behaved or threatens to behave, in a manner which is unconscionable."[13]

The jurisdiction of the county court to grant injunctions is more limited than that of the High Court. In general an injunction can only be granted if it is ancillary to a money claim within the jurisdiction of the court (currently any claim up to £5,000).[14] However, the county court has the same jurisdiction as the High Court to grant injunctions or declarations relating

[7] *Day* v. *Brownrigg* (1878) 10 Ch.D. 294; *Paton* v. *Trustees of BPAS* [1979] Q.B. 276.

[8] *per* Turner L.J., *Emperor of Austria* v. *Day* (1861) 3 DeG.F. & J. 217 at 253; see also, *Kerr on Injunctions* at p. 8.

[9] See below at p. 384.

[10] Supreme Court of Judicature (Consolidation) Act 1925, s.45(1).

[11] *North London Ry* v. *Great Northern Ry* (1883) 11 Q.B.D. 30 at 40; *The Siskina* [1979] A.C. 210.

[12] But see the dissent on this point of Lord Goff of Chieveley, with whom Lord Mackay of Clashfren agreed, in *South Carolina Insurance Co.* v. *Assurantie NV* [1986] 3 W.L.R. 398 at 412–413; see also *Chief Constable of Kent* v. *V* [1983] Q.B. 34 at 41F–43A, *per* Lord Denning M.R.

[13] *South Carolina* v. *Assurantie NV* [1986] 3 W.L.R. 398 at 408 F–H. Lord Brandon goes on to mention two exceptions; the grant of injunctions to restrain foreign proceedings and the *Mareva* jurisdiction, see below at p. 383.

[14] See *R.* v. *Cheshire County Court Judge* [1921] 2 K.B. 694; and *County Court Practice*, 1987, p. 35; the notes to s.38 of the County Court Act 1984.

to land provided that the rateable value of the land is less than the county court limited (currently, £1,000).[15]

Even when there is jurisdiction to grant an injunction the court has a broad discretion whether or not to grant one in a particular case. A number of factors are taken into consideration. The most important of these is the adequacy of damages because, like all equitable remedies, injunctions are only granted when the common law remedy of damages is inadequate.[16] If damages are inadequate, however, the fact that the plaintiff will only suffer a small amount of damage will not prevent him obtaining an injunction.[17] The defendant will not be allowed to "buy" an infringement of a plaintiff's rights by paying damages rather than having an injunction granted against him.[18]

Defences to an injunction claim

An injunction will be refused if the defendant can raise one of the general "equitable defences." Thus, a plaintiff will be refused an injuction if he has delayed in making his application. The period of delay which will be fatal will depend on all the circumstances. A short period of delay may be fatal to an interlocutory injunction application[19]; on the other hand a final injunction will usually not be refused if it related to a legal right and is not outside the limitation period.[20] Closely related to delay, but distinct from it, the defence of "acquiescence."

An important consideration in police cases may well be the plaintiff's conduct. According to the well-known maxim a person must come to equity with clean hands.[21] Thus, a plaintiff who has been engaged in criminal or other illegal conduct may be refused an injunction.

Interlocutory injunctions

An interlocutory injunction may be granted to a plaintiff to protect his position pending trial of an action on the merits. The plaintiff must give an "undertaking in damages"—that is, an undertaking to pay any loss to the defendant occasioned by the interlocutory injunction.[22] The "fundamental principle" governing the grant of interlocutory injunctions is that the court

[15] County Courts Act 1984, s.22.

[16] *Beswick* v. *Beswick* [1968] A.C. 58.

[17] *Woollerton & Wilson* v. *Richard Costain Ltd.* [1970] 1 W.L.R. 411.

[18] *Shelfer* v. *City of London Lighting* [1895] 1 Ch. 287; *Kennaway* v. *Thompson* [1981] Q.B. 88.

[19] *e.g.*, five months was too long in *Shepherd Homes Ltd.* v. *Sandham* [1971] Ch. 340.

[20] *e.g.*, in a trespass case, seven years was not a bar; *Kelsen* v. *Imperial Tobacco* [1957] 2 Q.B. 334.

[21] *Malone* v. *MPC* [1980] Q.B. 49 at 71.

[22] If such an undertaking is not expressly given it will be implied into an interlocutory injunction: *Colledge* v. *Crossley*, *The Times*, March 18, 1975.

should take whichever course appears to carry the lower risk of injustice.[23] Various "guidelines" have been derived from this principle.

When considering the grant of an interlocutory prohibitory injunction the court does not directly consider the question of who is likely to win at the trial but, rather, where the "balance of convenience" lies. The principles governing the grant of such injunctions were set out by the House of Lords in *American Cyanamid* v. *Ethicon*.[24] Provided that there is a "serious issue to be tried" the availability of an interlocutory prohibitory injunction depends on the "balance of convenience." This involves asking a number of questions:

(1) Are damages an adequate remedy for the plaintiff and is the defendant able to pay them? If the answer is "yes" then the injunction should be refused. In cases involving assault or imprisonment by the police, the answer will inevitably be "no." If the answer is "no," then:

(2) Is the plaintiff's undertaking as to damages adequate protection to the defendant and is the plaintiff able to pay? The fact that the plaintiff is on Legal Aid will not prejudice his position.[25] If "yes" the injunction will be granted, if "no" then:

(3) Consider the overall "balance of convenience." This will include the extent to which both parties can be compensated in damages. The counsel of prudence is to maintain the "status quo"; this is the state of affairs existing during the period immediately preceding the issue of the claim for a permanent injunction.[26]

(4) The relative strength of the parties' cases. The court will only consider this if the "balance of convenience" is evenly balanced or if the grant or refusal of the interlocutory application will, in effect dispose of the action.[27]

Interlocutory mandatory injunctions carry a greater risk of injustice and "in a normal case" the court must "feel a high degree of assurance" that at the trial it will appear that the injunction was rightly granted.[28] Nevertheless:

> "If it appears to the court that, exceptionally, the case is one in which withholding a mandatory interlocutory injunction would in fact carry a greater risk of injustice than granting it even though the court does not feel a "high degree of assurance" about the plaintiff's chances of establishing his right there cannot be any rational basis for withholding the injunction."[29]

23 *Film Rover* v. *Cannon Film Sales* [1986] 3 All E.R. 772 at 781, *per* Hoffman J.
24 [1975] A.C. 396.
25 *Allen* v. *Jambo Holdings* [1980] 1 W.L.R. 1252.
26 See *Garden Cottage Foods Ltd.* v. *Milk Marketing Board* [1984] A.C. 130.
27 *NWL* v. *Woods* [1979] 1 W.L.R. 1294.
28 *per* Megarry J., *Shepherd Homes* v. *Sandham* [1971] Ch. 340 at 351; see also, *per* Mustill L.J., *Locabail Finance Ltd.* v. *Agroexport* [1986] 1 W.L.R. 657 at 664.
29 *Films Rover* v. *Cannon Film Sales* [1986] 3 All E.R. 772 at 781 d–e; see generally, 780e–782g.

"Freezing" injunctions in police cases

In the famous *Mareva* case[30] the Court of Appeal granted a plaintiff an injunction to "freeze" the defendant's assets pending trial on the ground that there was a danger of these assets being dissipated to prevent the plaintiff's claim being satisfied. This jurisdiction is now firmly established, although the basis for it is obscure.[31] It is expressly referred to, and by implication approved, by section 37(3) of the Supreme Court Act 1981.

It is difficult to conceive of this jurisdiction being used **against** the police. It has, however, been invoked by the police in a remarkable series of cases, to "freeze" the assets of suspected criminals. The first such injunction was granted by Forbes J. in the case of *West Mercia Constabulary* v. *Wagener*[32] to restrain a defendant who was charged with fraudulently obtaining property from making withdrawals from named bank accounts.

This case was approved by the Court of Appeal in *Chief Constable of Kent* v. *V.*[33] The reasoning in this case has been described as "hard to follow." Lord Denning M.R. granted the injunction on the basis that it was "just and convenient to do so," denying that the Chief Constable needed any legal or equitable right in the funds. Donaldson L.J. disagreed, but held, in effect that the police had a legal right to detain monies which were criminally obtained. Slade L.J., in his dissenting judgement, agreed with Donaldson L.J. that an injunction could only be granted in support of a legal or equitable right vested in the plaintiff. He went on, however, to deny that police powers of search and seizure gave them any such right over the bank accounts of suspected criminals. In the subsequent case of *Chief Constable of Hampshire* v. *A Ltd.*[34] the first instance judge preferred Slade L.J.'s dissent and it is hard to disagree. When the police appealed against the refusal of the injunction a differently constituted Court of Appeal could not find any clear ratio in the *Chief Constable of Kent* case but decided that, whatever it was, it did not allow the issue of an injunction to freeze anything but the immediate proceeds of crime. As Purchas L.J. put it:

> "In order to invoke the powers of the court under section 37(1) of the Supreme Court Act 1981, the subject matter must be identifiable with the proceeds of crime rather than the civil claims of the victims of crime."[35]

In other words, if the police do have jurisdiction to obtain injunctions to freeze the assets of suspected criminals this does not go beyond the freezing of the "direct proceeds" of crime and in particular, it does not extend to the **products** of those proceeds.

Another, apparently fatal, objection to the "*Wagener*" jurisdiction is the rule that civil proceedings to enforce a criminal law obligation imposed in the public interest can only be taken by Attorney-General.[36] This point

[30] [1975] 2 Lloyd's Rep. 509.
[31] See Meagher, Gummow & Lehane, *Equity*, para. 2176.
[32] [1982] 1 W.L.R. 127.
[33] [1983] Q.B. 34.
[34] [1985] Q.B. 132.
[35] *Ibid.* at 139E–F.
[36] See *Gouriet* v. *UPW* [1978] A.C. 435.

does not appear to have been considered in any of the three reported cases on the subject.[37]

It is submitted that the *Wagener* and *Kent* cases are wrongly decided and should not be followed. As Feldman points out, the orders have no evidential value as the police can obtain an order under the Bankers' Books Evidence Act 1879 to obtain the records of a suspect's bank account. Furthermore, considerable practical problems may arise if the suspect has liabilities to third parties which cannot be discharged without use of the frozen bank account. The police should not be able to obtain orders of such potentially draconian effect without express statutory sanction.[38] This is provided in the case of a person charged with "drug trafficking offences"[38a] by the Drug Trafficking Offences Act 1986. By section 8, the High Court is empowered to make restraint orders prohibiting dealings with any property held by a person charged with or suspected of a drug trafficking offence. The Court must have "reasonable cause to believe"[38b] that the defendant has benefited from drug trafficking.[38c] It seems likely that similar provisions will be enacted in the near future to cover all indictable offences.[38d]

Injunctions in police cases

(1) Interference with the Person. It is now established that, in an appropriate case, the court will grant an injunction to restrain trespasses to the person.[39] Such an injunction could be obtained against a particular police officer in the unlikely event of the plaintiff being able to show that, without the intervention of the court, the officer was likely to assault him in the future. If police officers were proposing to carry out investigations in excess of their powers which necessarily involved assaults on the plaintiff then an injunction would lie. This appears to have been the basis of the application in the *Dartford Tunnel* case. An injunction to restrain the commission of assaults or batteries should not be framed so as to restrain the defendant from "molesting or otherwise interfering" with the plaintiff.[40] Nevertheless, if:

> "there be evidence that the health of the plaintiff is being impaired by molestation or interference calculated to create such impairment . . . relief can be granted by way of injunction to the extent that it would be necessary to avoid that impairment of health."[41]

The injunction, in these circumstances, would be granted in the tort in *Wilkinson* v. *Downton*.[42]

[37] See also *Ashby* v. *Ebdon* [1985] Ch. 394 at 405E.
[38] For a full discussion see Feldman at 13.32–13.43.
[38a] As defined by s.38(1) of the Drug Trafficking Act 1986.
[38b] See Chap. 5 above at pp. 145 *et seq.*
[38c] See *re a Defendant, The Times*, April 7, 1987; see generally, Feldman, "Freezing Defendants' Assets before Drugs Trials" (1987) 137 New L.J. 457.
[38d] Proposals to this effect were contained in the Criminal Justice Bill 1987.
[39] *Egan* v. *Egan* [1975] Ch. 218.
[40] See *Burnett* v. *George* [1986] 11 C.L. 1; Transcript Association (C.A.).
[41] *Ibid. per* Sir John Arnold P.
[42] [1897] 2 Q.B. 57; see Chap. 4, above at p. 119.

(2) Trespass to land. It is well established that an injunction will lie to restrain a threatened or existing trespass to land. No special principles apply to the grant of such injunctions against the police although it is difficult to imagine factual situations in which they might be granted.

(3) Interference with goods. In general the courts will not grant an injunction to restrain a trespass to goods or a conversion because, prima facie damages will be an adequate remedy. This will not apply, of course, if the goods are in some way unique. An order for delivery up of the goods may be available.[43]

(4) Libel. An injunction could be obtained to restrain the publication of a libel by police officers. It is well-established that an interlocutory injunction will not be granted if the defendant intends to set up the defence of justification, fair comment or privilege.[44]

(5) Breach of confidence. A court of equity will grant an injunction to restrain a breach of confidence. Thus if the police intend to publish confidential information acquired in the course of their inquiries an injunction would clearly lie.

(6) Misfeasance. If the police were proposing to carry out activities which they knew to be in excess of their powers then, presumably, a person likely to be affected could obtain a *quia timet* injunction in misfeasance in public office.

2. DECLARATIONS

Jurisdiction and discretion

The courts have jurisdiction to make declarations of existing legal rights. Under R.S.C., Ord. 15, r. 16:

> "the court may make binding declarations of right whether or not any consequential relief is or could be claimed."

This jurisdiction is not confined to cases in which the plaintiff has a complete and subsisting cause of action apart from the rule.[45]

The relief is, however, discretionary. The court will not generally decide hypothetical or "purely theoretical" questions.[46] The remedy will not be granted to a plaintiff whose claim is too indirect and insubstantial and would not give him "relief" in any real sense.[47] Furthermore, the courts will not grant a declaration that a defendant is guilty of a crime.[48] A declaration will not be granted to a defendant in a criminal case on the ground that the

[43] See below at p. 389.
[44] *Bonnard* v. *Perryman* [1891] 2 Ch. 269.
[45] *Guaranty Trust Co. of New York* v. *Hannay* [1915] 2 K.B. 536.
[46] *Tindall* v. *Wright* [1922] W.N. 124; *Re Barnato* [1949] Ch. 258.
[47] *Thorne RDC* v. *Bunting* [1972] Ch. 470.
[48] *Haley* v. *Commissioner of Corrective Services* [1975] 1 N.S.W.L.R. 118.

facts alleged by the prosecution do not prove the offence charged because this would usurp the functions of the criminal courts.[49]

A declaration cannot be granted in respect of matters which are not justiciable in the English courts. Thus, for example, a declaration cannot be granted in respect of rights under the European Convention of Human Rights.[50]

A declaration is a final and binding statement of the legal rights of the parties. It follows that there can be no such thing as an interlocutory or interim declaration.[51] Nevertheless, the court does have jurisdiction to grant a final declaration in interlocutory proceedings although this will only be exercised "sparingly and infrequently."[52]

The county court has no jurisdiction to grant a declaration unless this is ancillary to a claim for damages which is within the jurisdiction of the court.[53] However, if the declaration relates to land the county court has the same jurisdiction as the High Court.[54]

Who can obtain declarations?

In order to obtain a declaration the plaintiff must have *locus standi*. In other words, he must have had some private right of his interfered with or have suffered special damage as a result of some interference with a public right.[55]

Declarations in police cases

Despite the lack of reported cases, it is submitted that declarations could prove a very useful remedy in police cases. If the police seized documents or other items in the course of their investigations the lawfulness of the seizure could be tested by way of proceedings for a declaration. The lawfulness of an activity engaged in by the plaintiff, such as picketing in a specific situation, could perhaps be established by means of a declaration.

The only reported case in this area is *Adams* v. *Metropolitan Police Commissioner*.[56] This involved a road across a private housing estate upon which, it was alleged, a number of road traffic offences had been committed. The police had refused to intervene because they had been advised that the road in question was not a public road within the meaning of the Road Traffic Act 1972. The residents of a private estate sought declarations that the

[49] *Imperial Tobacco Ltd.* v. *Att.-Gen.* [1981] A.C. 718.
[50] *Malone* v. *Metropolitan Police Commissioner* [1979] Ch. 344.
[51] *International General Electric Co. of New York Ltd.* v. *Commissioners of Customs & Excise* [1962] Ch. 784 at 789, 790.
[52] *Clarke* v. *Chadburn* [1985] 1 W.L.R. 78—such a declaration was in fact granted in that case.
[53] *De Vries* v. *Smallridge* [1928] 1 K.B. 482; see the *County Court Practice* 1987 at p. 16; the notes to s.15 of the County Courts Act 1984.
[54] County Courts Act 1984, s.22.
[55] *Boyce* v. *Paddington BC* [1903] 1 Ch. 109; *Gouriet* v. *UPW* [1978] A.C. 435.
[56] [1980] R.T.R. 289.

Metropolitan Police Commissioner was not "precluded from prosecuting" the alleged offences. The Commissioner gave an undertaking to accept and act upon the court's view of the status of the road in question. Jupp J. held that the road was a public road in the relevant sense but refused a declaration saying:

> "The Commissioner's discretion in prosecuting offences should not, unnecessarily, be made to appear fettered, because it is an unfettered discretion and only in rare circumstances, though they can exist of course, do the courts interfere with it."[57]

Given the Commissioner's undertaking no declaration was in fact necessary. Nevertheless, it is submitted, a declaration should have been given in that case as the Commissioner would hardly have been "fettered" by being correctly informed about the law! It should be noted that, as a result of the decision in *O'Reilly* v. *Mackman*[58] this application would now have to be brought under the "judicial review" procedure.[59]

3. REMEDIES IN RELATION TO GOODS

Introduction

If a person's goods are unlawfully seized or retained by the police he will often wish to obtain their return rather than seeking his remedy in damages. At common law a plaintiff could only seek the return of his goods in an action in detinue or replevin. Although the return of the appropriated goods remains of the essence of replevin, redelivery in relation to the other torts is now governed by the Torts (Interference with Goods) Act 1977. In addition, in an action for conversion a mandatory order for the return of the goods could be obtained if damages were not an adequate remedy. The Police (Property) Act 1897 provides a potentially quick and efficient statutory remedy to claimants to property in the possession of the police. The various remedies are considered in this section.

Replevin

The purpose of the action in "replevin" is to enable the owner of wrongfully seized goods to obtain their provisional return pending the resolution of the dispute as to whether they were lawfully taken. This remedy has not been abolished by the Torts (Interference with Goods) Act 1977 and remains potentially useful in police cases.

An action in replevin will lie whenever there is a taking of goods from the possession of the plaintiff which would, of itself, amount to a trespass. The goods in question must have been taken out of the possession of the

[57] *Adams* v. *Metropolitan Police Commissioner* [1980] R.T.R. 289 at 300A–B.
[58] [1983] A.C. 120.
[59] See Chap. 13 below at p. 398.

plaintiff.[60] The plaintiff must be able to show unequivocal possession of the goods prior to the taking.[61]

The distinction between trespass and replevin has been expressed as follows:

> "The whole procedure of replevin, at common law, is distinguished from that in trespass in this, among other things: that, while the latter is intended to procure a compensation in damages for goods wrongfully taken out of the actual or constructive possession of the plaintiff, the object of the former is to procure the restitution of the goods themselves."[62]

If the plaintiff's goods are seized from his possession by the police he can, therefore, apply for the goods to be "replevied," that is, restored to him. The power to grant replevin is now given exclusively to the registrar of the county court, irrespective of the value of the goods seized.[63]

The procedure for applying for replevin is set out in Schedule 1 to the County Courts Act 1984. The person seeking replevin (the replevisor) must give "security" as proved in paragraph 2 of the Schedule. It is a condition of such "security" that the replevisor will commence an action against the seizor in the High Court within one week from the date on which the security is given or will commence an action in the county court within one month from that date. In either case:

> "(a) the replevisor shall give security, to be approved by the registrar having power in the matter, for such an amount as the registrar thinks sufficient to cover both the probable costs of the action and . . .
>
> (ii) in a case where the goods replevied have been seized otherwise than under colour of distress, the value of the goods; and
>
> (b) it shall be a further condition of the security that the replevisor will—
>
> (i) prosecute the action with effect and without delay; and
>
> (ii) make return of the goods, if a return of them is ordered in the action."

This security is known as a "replevin bond." If such a security is given the registrar may issue a warrant for return of the goods.

Subsequent to the "replevy" of the goods there will be a trial of the action in replevin. If the plaintiff is successful in this action he can, as well as retaining the goods, recover damages for the taking, assessed in trespass. Such damages may include an element for the illegal taking, annoyance and the costs of the replevin.[64]

Joinder of other causes of action with replevin has been said to be "irregular and illegal" at common law.[65]

The remedy of replevin was traditionally used in cases where goods were seized by wrongful distress or some other judicial taking but it is strongly

[60] *Shannon* v. *Shannon* (1804) 1 Sch. & Lef. 324 at 326; *Mennie* v. *Blake* (1856) 6 E. & B. 842 at 849; *Swaffer* v. *Mulcahy* [1934] 1 K.B. 608 at 636.
[61] *Shannon* v. *Shannon* (1804) 1 Sch. & Lef. 324 at 326.
[62] *per* Coleridge J., *Mennie* v. *Blake* (1856) 6 E. &. B. 842 at 846.
[63] County Courts Act 1984, s.144 and Sched. 1.
[64] *Smith* v. *Enright* (1893) 63 L.J.Q.B. 220.
[65] *per* Pollock C.B., *Mungean* v. *Wheatley* (1851) 6 Exch. 88 at 97.

arguable that it is available in all cases of wrongful taking. As Lord Campbell C.J. put it in *Mellor* v. *Leather*[66]:

> "we are of opinion, upon the authority not only of the textbooks, but of decided cases that replevin will lie when goods have been unlawfully taken, though not as distress."[67]

It was added, however, that this was an "unusual form of action."

It has been held that section 6 of the Constables Protection Act 1750[68] does not apply to such an action because it is an action *in rem*.[69] Thus, an action against the police will be available when they have seized goods under a warrant which was issued without jurisdiction. Nevertheless, it is hard to see the action being of much practical value in police cases as the police will usually set up a defence of "lawful justification" in relation to a seizure of goods and are likely to claim that the goods are required for their investigations. Unless the taking and retention of the goods was plainly unlawful it is unlikely that a Registrar will order the goods to replevied.

Orders for the redelivery of goods

In proceedings for wrongful interference with goods against a person who is in possession or control of the goods the following relief is available:

> "(a) an order for delivery of the goods and for payment of any consequential damages, or
> (b) an order for delivery of the goods, but giving the defendant the alternative of paying damages by reference to the value of the goods, together in either alternative with payment of any consequential damages, or
> (c) damages."[70]

Only one of the three types of relief may be given. An order for delivery of the goods under (a) is at the discretion of the court and the plaintiff can choose between an order under sub-paragraph (b) or (c).[71] An order for delivery will not usually be made in respect of an ordinary article of commerce of no special value to the plaintiff where damages would fully compensate him.[72] If the plaintiff chooses damages the defendant cannot satisfy the judgment by returning the goods.[73] If it is shown to the court's satisfaction that an order for delivery of the goods has not been complied with the order may be revoked and replaced by an order for the payment of damages "by reference to the value of the goods."[74]

[66] (1853) 1 E. & B. 619 at 628.
[67] See also *Shannon* v. *Shannon* (1804) 1 Sch. & Lef. 324; the point was said to be "not settled" in *Mennie* v. *Blake* (1856) 6 E.&B. 842 at 847–849 but *Mellor* v. *Leather* was not cited.
[68] See Chap. 3 above at p. 64.
[69] *Milward* v. *Cafin* (1779) 2 Wm.Bl. 1330 1331.
[70] Torts (Interference with Goods) Act 1977, s.3(2).
[71] *Ibid.*, s.3(5).
[72] See *Whiteley* v. *Hilt* [1918] 2 K.B. 808 at 819, *per* Swinfen Eady M.R.; and also *Howard Perry* v. *BRB* [1980] 1 W.L.R. 1375.
[73] Torts (Interference with Goods) Act 1977, s.3(5).
[74] s.3(4).

Under section 4 of the 1977 Act the court has power to make an order for interim delivery up of goods.[75]

Other orders in relation to goods

Under R.S.C., Ord 29, r. 2, any party to a cause or matter can apply to the court for an order for the "detention, custody or preservation" of any property which is the subject-matter of the cause or matter or "as to which any question may arise." This may be of importance if it appears that the police are proposing to deliver property claimed by the plaintiff to a third party.

A party may also apply for an order for the "inspection" of the property[76] or the taking of samples.[77] Inspection is limited to physical objects, so that an inspection of police methods in particular situations could not be ordered under this rule.[78] An application for the inspection of documents cannot be made under this provision.[79]

The Police (Property) Act 1897

The police very often take possession of property to which they make no claim, but the true ownership of which is disputed. Parliament has provided a summary remedy for the police in this situation which is now found in the Police (Property) Act 1897. By section 1(1) of the Act, when property has come into the possesion of the police in connection with their investigation of a suspected offence, a court of summary jurisdiction may, on the application of either an officer of police, or a claimant to the property:

> "make an order for the delivery of the property to the person appearing to the court to be the owner thereof, or, if the owner cannot be ascertained, make such order with respect to the property as to the magistrate or the court may seem meet."

The making of such an order does not affect the right of any person to take legal proceedings against anyone in possession of property delivered under the court order. But such proceedings must be taken within six months of the date of the order and "on the expiration of those six months the right shall cease."[80]

The "owner" to whom delivery of the goods may be ordered is:

> "a person who is entitled to the goods in question, a person whose goods they are, not simply the person who happens to have them in his hands at any given moment."[81]

In other words, the fact that a person is in actual possession of goods will

[75] See R.S.C. Ord. 29, r. 2A and *Howard Perry* v. *BRB* [1980] 1 W.L.R. 1375.
[76] *Ibid.*
[77] R.S.C., Ord. 29, r. 3.
[78] *Tudor Co.* v. *China etc. Co* [1930] W.N. 200.
[79] See *Taylor* v. *Anderton, The Times,* October 21, 1986.
[80] s.1(2).
[81] *per* Lord Widgery C.J. *Raymond Lyons* v. *MPC* [1975] Q.B. 321.

not be sufficient for him to obtain an order under section 1. He must show "ownership" in the sense of "title to the goods." However, the person who was in actual possession is entitled to resist the making of an order if he can show a "lien" over the goods for the payment of a sum of money. Thus, it was held that the innkeeper's lien attaches to stolen property received by a guest as security for payment and that the magistrates should not order its delivery to the owner.[82]

The effect of an order under section 1(1) is that the claimant to the goods has to prove that he is the **owner** and cannot rely on any possessory title he had prior to the making of the order.[83] In other words, once an order is made, the former possessor of the goods is put in a considerably worse position than before. It is submitted that this is not the position when goods are seized by the police for evidential purposes.[84]

A Police Property Act application should not be made when there is any serious dispute about the entitlement to the property. The Divisional Court have gone so far as to say that the use of the Act should be actively discouraged:

> "in cases which involve a real issue of law or any real difficulty in determining whether a particular person is or is not the owner."[85]

The Act deals with goods in the "possession" of the police. This must, it is submitted, must be understood as "lawful possession." Thus, when the goods are in the possession of the police unlawfully—having, for example, been seized under a warrant which is issued without jurisdiction[86]—the procedure under the Act would not be available. If an application was made in these circumstances an order of prohibition could be sought to prevent the magistrates from hearing the case.

It appears that an (unappealable) order for costs can be made by the magistrates in an application under this Act,[87] provided it is made by "complaint." It is, however, "inappropriate" to make such an order against the police where they do not object to the order sought.[88]

Other statutes relating to the disposal of goods in the possession of the police

Under section 43 of the Powers of Criminal Courts Act 1973, when a person has been convicted of an offence punishable on indictment with imprisonment for a term of two years or more and the court is satisfied that any property which was in his possession or under his control at the time of his apprehension has been used, or was intended for use, for the purpose of committing or facilitating the commission of any offence, the court may

[82] *Marsh* v. *MPC* [1945] K.B. 43.
[83] *Irving* v. *National Prvincial Bank* [1962] 2 Q.B. 73, approving *Buckley* v. *Gross* (1863) 3 B. & S. 566 at 572.
[84] See Chap. 6 above at p. 189.
[85] *Raymond Lyons* v. *MPC* [1975] Q.B. 321.
[86] *Quinn* v. *Pratt* [1908] 2 I.R. 69 at 82 is authority for the proposition that goods so seized are not in "the possession" of the police.
[87] *R.* v. *Uxbridge JJ ex. p. MPC* [1981] 3 All E.R. 129.
[88] See also *Mercer* v. *Oldham* [1984] Crim.L.R. 232.

make an order[89] under the section. Such an order deprives the offender of his rights, if any, in the property, which shall be taken into the possession of the police.[90]

When property is in the possession of the police under this section the Police (Property) Act applies with two modifications:

(1) no application shall be made in respect of such property after the expiration of six months from the date of the order[91];

(2) no application shall succeed unless the claimant satisfies the court "either that he had not consented to the offender having possession of the property or that he did not know, and no reason to suspect, that the property was likely to be used for the purpose mentioned in subsection (1)."[92]

This places an extremely heavy burden on the applicant and it has been held, in a Crown Court case, that a claimant to goods in police possession under the 1897 or the 1973 Acts is equally free to pursue a remedy at common law and the requirements laid down by section 43(4) do not then apply.[93]

Remedies in relation to goods: a summary

The police may be in possession of goods in a wide variety of circumstances. The following are common situations in which the police hold goods belonging to other people:

(1) where they acknowledge that the goods belong to an innocent party but are reluctant to return them to the plaintiff because of what are perceived as competing civil claims. An example of this is where a stolen car which has been sold by the thief to a bona fide purchaser has been recovered by the police;

(2) where it is not alleged that the plaintiff has any criminal involvement but the police claim that his goods in fact belong to someone else;

(3) where the goods have been taken from the plaintiff but the police claim that they are stolen;

(4) where it is claimed that the goods are being held for the purposes of an investigation or for use as evidence.

Different remedies will be appropriate to these different situations. The available remedies are, in summary, as follows:

(1) The Police (Property) Act 1897. This will be the appropriate remedy if damages are not being sought but the **owner** of goods simply wants them back as quickly and as simply as possible. An application under the Act does not prejudice the applicant's other civil remedies but, if he fails to obtain an order in his favour he must take other civil action within six months of the

[89] s.43(1).
[90] s.43(3).
[91] s.43(4)(*a*).
[92] s.43(4)(*b*).
[93] *Davis* v. *Hampshire Police Authority* [1978] C.L.Y. 3024.

order being made. This will be an appropriate remedy in situation (1) although it should be noted that if magistrates see any legal complexities they may refuse to make an order. In practice, therefore, an application under the Police (Property) Act should only be made in very straightforward cases.

(2) Replevin. This will also be appropriate when the owner of goods wants them back as quickly as possible. If goods have been seized under a warrant issued without jurisdiction then replevin will be the only action available to recover consequential damages as well as the goods themselves. Thus, an action in replevin may also be appropriate in situation (1). The advantage of an action in replevin is that damages can be claimed in the same action. The disadvantage is that the plaintiff must give a "replevin bond" for the full value of the goods. Once again, an order may be refused if there are any legal complexities regarding the ownership of the goods.

(3) Order for delivery up. In police cases it is unlikely that the police would wish to retain goods permanently and take the option of paying damages. Thus, it is likely that, subject to a plaintiff being able to show a right to return of the goods (whether by reason of a "possessory title" or something stronger) an order for delivery up would be made at trial. On the other hand, interim delivery up may be difficult to obtain if the police claim that the goods are being retained for the purposes of their investigations as in situation (4).[94] If the police are retaining goods because they believe them to belong to someone else or to be stolen—situations (2) and (3)—the plaintiff is unlikely to be able to obtain an order for interim delivery up and the question of ownership will have to be decided at a full trial. If the police are threatening to deliver the goods to someone else then the plaintiff should obtain an order for their "detention, custody or preservation" under R.S.C., Ord. 29, r. 2.

4. HABEAS CORPUS

Introduction

The writ of habeas corpus ad subjiciendum is often said to be the foundation stone of the liberties of the subject. As Lord Denman once put it:

> "The provisions made by the law for the liberty of the subject have been found for ages effectual to an extent never known in any other country through the medium of the summary right to the writ of habeas corpus."[95]

Given the modern limitations on the writ and in particular the practice of adjourning any application to give notice to the police, this statement sounds rather exaggerated today. Nevertheless, it does, at the limit, serve as a remedy for those in police detention and the threat of an application is perhaps, on occasion, sufficient to secure the early release of detained persons.

[94] See *Malone* v. *MPC* [1980] Q.B. 49.
[95] *R.* v. *Batcheldor* (1839) 1 Per. & Dav. 516 at 567.

Habeas corpus is a prerogative writ by which the Queen's Courts can inquire into the reasons for the imprisonment of any person. The purpose of the writ is to order the production of the body of the imprisoned person before the court so that inquires into the reasons for the imprisonment can be made and release from unlawful detention can be secured.

Availability of the writ

Habeas corpus is available in any case where a citizen has been wrongfully deprived of his liberty. Once a person has been convicted by a competent criminal court whether on indictment[96] or by a court of summary jurisdiction[97] habeas corpus will not be granted. The appropriate means of redress is an appeal.[98] In general, habeas corpus is, like all "administrative law" remedies, simply concerned with the question of whether the order for detention was made with jurisdiction, not whether it was correct on the merits.

Procedure

An application for a writ of habeas corpus is made *ex parte* to the Divisional Court of the Queen's Bench Division or, if no such court is sitting, to a single judge in court or, if no court is sitting, "otherwise than in court," in other words, at home or wherever a judge can be found.[99] The application should be supported by an affidavit by the person restrained or, if he is unable to make an affidavit, by someone acting on his behalf.[1] The affidavit should set out the nature of the restraint.

The application need not be in the name of the person detained but may be made by any person at his instance, or by a relative or friend on his behalf. The affidavit should set out the reasons why the person detained is not making the application. A mere stranger acting without authority will not be allowed to apply.[2] The established practice is for applications to be made by counsel and this will not be departed from "unless some sufficient ground is shown."[3]

An application which is not made to the Divisional Court may be ordered to be adjourned to the Divisional Court.[4] The Divisional Court may either make an order forthwith for the issue of a writ, or the application may be adjourned so that notice of it can be given.[5] The latter course will be adopted unless the case is an urgent one or unless justice would be defeated by the issue of a summons or a notice of motion.

[96] *ex p. Lees* (1858) E.B. & E. 828.
[97] *Re Corke* [1954] 1 W.L.R. 899.
[98] See *ex p. Hinds* [1961] 1 W.L.R. 325.
[99] R.S.C., Ord. 54, r. 1(0).
[1] R.S.C., Ord. 54, r. 1(3).
[2] *Ex. p. Child* (1854) 15 C.B. 238.
[3] *Re Greene* (1941) 57 T.L.R. 533; see, *e.g.*, *ex p. Hinds* [1961] 1 W.L.R. 325, in which the applicant's wife was heard.
[4] R.S.C., Ord. 54, r. 2(1).
[5] *Ibid.*

An application cannot be renewed in respect of the same person on the same grounds unless there is fresh evidence in support.[6] In a civil matter an appeal against a refusal to grant a writ lies to the Court of Appeal. In a criminal matter appeal lies to the House of Lords.

If a writ of habeas corpus is issued it is usually served personally on the person to whom it is directed.[7] The return to the writ must state "all the causes of the detainer of the person restrained."[8] If the return on its face shows that there is a valid authority for the detention the onus is then on the applicant to show that the detention is illegal. As Ashworth J. put it in the case of *R.* v. *Governor of Brixton Prison, ex.p. Ahsan*[9]:

> "I accept entirely the principle that the custodian is called upon to justify the detention, but he does so by making a return which is valid on the face of it . . . it is then for the person detained to place evidence before the court showing that what appears to be a valid return is in fact invalid."[10]

If the detention is unlawful the writ is granted "as of right," (*ex debito justitiae*) but not "as of course."[11] Although it may be refused where there is another remedy available whereby the validity of the detention may be questioned, the court has no discretion to refuse it if the detention is unlawful and no other remedy is available.

Applicability in police cases

The remedy of habeas corpus is used in police cases where a person is being detained by the police without having been lawfully arrested or without the proper procedures having been complied with. Police powers of detention of suspects and the relevant procedures have now been substantially clarified by Part IV of the Police and Criminal Evidence Act 1984.[12] Section 51(*d*) of the 1984 Act expressly preserves the right of a person in police detention to apply for habeas corpus. As a result of the 1984 Act the position regarding habeas corpus is now much clearer than it was at common law. If a person is held for longer than the prescribed periods[13] without the prescribed procedures being complied with[14], then habeas corpus will be available. If, however, the detention is for the periods allowed by the Act and the procedures are complied with, then it will not be available.

The appropriate person to whom the writ is directed will normally be the

[6] Administration of Justice Act 1960, s.14(2); this represents the common law position, see *Re Hastings (No. 2)* [1959] 1 Q.B. 358.

[7] R.S.C., Ord. 54, r. 6.

[8] R.S.C., Ord. 54, r. 7.

[9] [1969] 2 Q.B. 222.

[10] *per* Ashworth J. at 237; see also *R.* v. *Governor of Risley Remand Centre. ex p. Hassan* [1976] 1 W.L.R. 971.

[11] *Re Corke* [1954] 1 W.L.R. 899; *R* v. *Pentonville Prison Governor, ex p. Azam* [1974] A.C. 18 at 32.

[12] See Chap. 5 above at pp. 157 *et seq.*

[13] See Chap. 5 above at pp. 163 *et seq.*

[14] See Chap. 5 above at pp. 164 *et seq.*

appropriate chief officer of police, the custody officer and the officer in charge of the case.[15]

When an application for habeas corpus is made on behalf of a person in police detention the court's usual practice is to adjourn the application for 24 hours under R.S.C. Ord. 54, r. 2(1), so that notice may be given to the police. This usually gives the police sufficient time to remedy the "unlawfulness" of the detention.

An interesting ilustration of the use of habeas corpus in police detention cases can be found in the case of *R.* v. *Holmes, ex p. Sherman.*[16] The applicant was arrested on a Tuesday and, not having been charged by Thursday his solicitor applied for a writ of habeas corpus on his behalf. In line with the usual practice the hearing was adjourned until the Friday for notice to be given to the police. The police did not realise that they had been served with notice of the adjourned hearing so they did not turn up on the Friday. A writ was, therefore, issued. The officer in charge of the case then appeared at court and explained that he had not charged the applicants so that they could "assist police with their inquiries" because he knew that once a charge had been made bail would have to be considered. The applicant was then released on bail. The Division Court made it clear that:

> "habeas corpus is a remedy for an abuse of power and it should rarely be necessary to invoke it . . . However, it is right that all should know that the writ of habeas corpus had not fallen into disuse but is . . . a real and available remedy."[17]

It is clear however that the remedy is of extremely limited use. A person who has been unlawfully detained in police custody and does manage to have a habeas corpus application made on his behalf can, due to the practice of automatic 24 hour adjournment, be unlawfully detained for another day.[18]

[15] See *LAG Bulletin*, August 1979 at pp. 182–4; R. J. Sharpe, *Habeas Corpus.*

[16] [1981] 2 All E.R. 612.

[17] *Ibid.* at 616d–f.

[18] Only 21 habeas corpus applications of all types were made in 1984, only two of which were successful: *Judicial Statistics: Annual Report* Cmnd. 9599, (1984), p. 18.

13. Judicial Review of Police Decisions

1. INTRODUCTION

A police constable is a public officer and his activities are thus subject to the ultimate direction and control of the High Court under the "judicial review" procedure set out in R.S.C., Ord. 53. In many cases the only way that a controversial policing decision can be challenged is through this procedure.

The High Court's "judicial review" jurisdiction is "supervisory" rather than "appellate." It is concerned;

> "to ensure that the individual is given fair treatment by the authority to which he has been subjected . . . it is no part of that purpose to substitute the opinion of the judiciary or of individual judges for that of the authority constituted by law to decide the matters in question."[1]

In other words, what is reviewed is form, procedure and appearance rather than the substantive decision. A policing decision cannot be challenged simply because it was "wrong" but only because it was arrived at in some "formally improper" way.

Although there is no doubt that the actions of the police are subject to judicial review it should be noted that no application of this type against the police has ever been successful. In several cases the court has expressed considerable sympathy with the applicants but has refused to give the relief sought on general "policy grounds."[2] Actions against the police represent an important exception to the modern trend towards "judicial activism" in the public law field. The courts show little hesitation in reviewing the discretion of Ministers of the Crown, even if they are exercising the Royal Prerogative,[3] but they display great circumspection in inquiring into the actions of unelected chief constables whose actions are not subject to day to day control by any public authority.[4] While such circumspection is understandable in relation to day to day policing decisions it is less justifiable when "general policy decisions" are involved. It is submitted that the courts should not hesitate to quash "unlawful" policy decisions by police

[1] *per* Lord Hailsham L.C., *Chief Constable of North Wales* v. *Evans* [1982] 1 W.L.R. 1155 at 1160.

[2] See below at pp. 401 *et seq.* for a discussion of the cases.

[3] See, *e.g.*, *CCSU* v. *Minister for Civil Service* [1985] A.C. 374.

[4] See below at pp. 411 *et seq.*

officers. The courts need not make their own "policing decisions" but can simply direct the police to reconsider the matter as is the common practice in other spheres of judicial review.

This chapter begins with a brief consideration of the general principles which now govern judicial review. The case law is then surveyed: the six reported police judicial review cases from the first *Blackburn* case in 1968 to the *Levey* case in 1986. In the next section a possible approach to judicial review of police decisions is proposed on the basis of a distinction between three different types of decisions. The question of judicial review by police authorities is then considered, in particular, in relation to using the courts to control "operational policing decisions" by chief constables. After a discussion of the various remedies available in judicial review applications, the final section gives a brief summary of the judicial review procedure.

2. GENERAL PRINCIPLES OF REVIEW

Public and private law

English law now draws a strict distinction between "private" and "public" law rights.[5] The former depend on the established causes of action and must be pursued by the ordinary procedures. The latter can only be protected by the "judicial review" procedure. Thus if a plaintiff was falsely imprisoned or maliciously prosecuted by police officers this will be a matter of "private law" and his remedy will lie in an ordinary tort action. If, on the other hand, he is aggrieved by a "police policy" decision, for example, not to prosecute a certain class of offenders[6] then he has no cause of action in private law and must seek his remedy through judicial review.

This distinction in unclear and has yet to be fully worked out. Considerable difficulties arise, for example, when a statute casts a duty on a public authority and, through the neglect of this duty a citizen suffers damage. A distinction has been drawn between the "decision-making" functions of a public authority, which can only be challenged by "judicial review," and its "executive" functions which give rise to potential private law remedies via an action for breach of statutory duty or negligence.[7] This second distinction is also unclear and it has not been considered in any reported police case.

In any event, it is clear that attempts to challenge police **policy** decisions by someone who has not suffered direct "special damage" must be made via the judicial review procedure. If a citizen does suffer special damage then the position is more complex. If his only cause of action is for negligence or breach of statutory duty then the police are likely to raise the "public law" nature of their duties by way of defence.[8] When in doubt a plaintiff should

[5] Following the decision of the House of Lords in *O'Reilly* v. *Mackman* [1983] 2 A.C. 237.

[6] As in the various *Blackburn* cases, see below at pp. 402 *et seq.*

[7] *Cocks* v. *Thanet DC* [1983] 2 A.C. 286; see also *Guevara* v. *Hounslow L.B.C.*, *The Times*, April 17, 1987.

[8] See, *e.g.*, *Hill* v. *Chief Constable for West Yorkshire* [1987] 2 W.L.R. 1126.

go by way of judicial review and append a private law claim for damages under Ord. 53, r. 7(1)(*b*).[9]

Preconditions for review: decision and sufficient interest

For the judicial review procedure to be available to a particular person three conditions must be fulfilled:

(1) there must be a "decision" or a refusal to make a decision;
(2) The "decision-maker" must be "empowered by public law . . . to make decisions that, if validly made, will lead to administrative action or abstention from action by an authority endowed by law with executive powers."[10] These first two conditions will be fulfilled if the "decision-maker" is under a public duty to do some particular act or acts;
(3) The applicant must have a "sufficient interest"[11] in the decision. This notion has not been precisely defined but depends on all the circumstances of the case.[12] Nevertheless, it is clear that someone whose rights and obligations in private law are affected by the decision or who is deprived of a "legitimate expectation" does have a "sufficient interest."[13]

Many police powers derive from the common law and not from statute. There is, however:

> "no reason why simply because a decision-making power is derived from a common law and not a statutory source, it should *for that reason only* be immune from judicial review."[14]

In relation to police decisions the third requirement may present some difficulty. In the case of *R.* v. *Metropolitan Police Commissioner, ex p. Blackburn (No. 4)*,[15] the Court of Appeal held that Mr. Blackburn, as an ordinary private citizen, had sufficient interest to bring proceedings for mandamus against the Commissioner (*per* Lawton and Ackner LJJ.). In *R.* v. *Oxford, ex p. Levey*,[16] the applicant was seeking review of policing policy in the Toxteth district of Liverpool after having been robbed nearby. The Divisional Court held[17] that he did not have sufficient interest because he did not live there. The Court of Appeal rejected this analysis as follows:

> "It is implicit in the judgment that no member of the public living in or visiting Liverpool has a sufficient interest in complaining of an alleged failure by the Merseyside police to fulfil their duties. This I do not accept. It must depend upon the circumstances. In any event Mr Levey,

[9] See below at p. 418.
[10] *per* Lord Diplock, *CCSU* v. *Minister for the Civil Service* [1985] A.C. 374 at 409B.
[11] Ord. 53, r. 3(7).
[12] See *R.* v. *Inland Revenue Commissioners ex p. National Federation of Self Employed* [1982] A.C. 617.
[13] See *per* Lord Diplock, in the *CCSU* case, [1985] A.C. 374 at 949f–g.
[14] *Ibid.* at 410C, *per* Lord Diplock.
[15] *The Times*, March 6, 1980.
[16] *The Times*, November 1, 1986.
[17] *The Times*, December 18, 1985.

> who had been robbed in Liverpool and who was alleging that the chances of recovering his property had been much diminished by the conduct of the Merseyside police, clearly had a special interest in the matter."

If these three conditions are satisfied, an applicant is entitled to be heard on an application for judicial review. To obtain judicial review he must satisfy the court of the existence of one of the well-established "ground for review."

Ground for review

To obtain relief the applicant must show that the decision was in some sense *ultra vires* or procedurally "unfair." It is extremely difficult to provide an exhaustive classification of the grounds on which judicial review has been granted. Lord Diplock has sought to provide such a classification under three heads: "illegality," "irrationality" and "procedural impropriety."[18]

(1) "Illegality." A decision maker must "understand correctly the law that regulates his decision-making power." If he "misdirects himself in law" then his decision will be liable to review. This head of review has been invoked in a number of police cases. It will be "illegal" for a public body not to perform a public duty, whether under statute or at common law. This may arise from a "decision" not to act or it may simply involve a failure even to consider the matter. In these circumstances the High Court has jurisdiction to order the performance of public duties.

(2) "Irrationality." A decision is reviewable if it is "irrational." This is also known as "*Wednesbury* unreasonableness."[19] This covers a wide range of matters. Thus, the decision-maker must act in good faith, he must take relevant matters into account and exclude from his consideration irrelevant matters. A decision can also be challenged if it is "so unreasonable that no reasonable authority could have made it."

(3) "Procedural impropriety." The decision maker must observe the rules of natural justice and other rules of procedure which have been laid down by the courts.

Judicial review and discretion

To challenge the exercise of a public law discretion may involve both the first and the second heads of review. The courts have devoted considerable attention to the challenge of discretion over the past two decades. A public authority's discretion must be properly exercised and must not be fettered by policy or improper delegation. Most importantly, the principle that the decision-maker must take all relevant matters into account and must

[18] *CCSU* v. *Minister for the Civil Service* [1985] A.C. 374 at 410–411.

[19] See *per* Lord Greene M.R., *Associated Provincial Picture Houses Ltd.* v. *Wednesbury Corp.* [1948] 1 K.B. 233 at 230.

ignore irrelevant matters has enabled the Courts to review a whole range of activities which were previously thought to be purely "executive" matters.

It has been seen that police powers and duties contain a very substantial "discretionary element."[20] Nevertheless, it is clearly established that even 'the widest possible" discretion, expressed in wholly subjective terms, can be reviewed by the courts. The literal construction of statutory powers which once conferred unfettered and uncontrollable discretion upon the body exercising them[21] has been superseded by a more interventionist approach.[22] The analysis now favoured by the courts is illustrated by the *Tameside* case[23] where the Education Secretary attempted to reverse a Conservative council's refusal to implement a scheme for comprehensive education. He relied upon his statutory power to give such directions as "appear to him expedient" if he was satisfied that a local authority was acting unreasonably. As Lord Wilberforce put it:

> "The section is framed in a "subjective" form—if the Secretary of State "is satisfied." This form of section is quite well known, and at first sight might seem to exclude judicial review. Sections in this form may, no doubt, exclude judicial review on what is or has become a matter of pure judgment. But I do not think that they go further than that. If a judgment requires, before it can be made, the existence of some facts then, although the evaluation of those facts is for the Secretary of State alone, the court must inquire whether those facts exist, and have been taken into account, whether the judgment has been made upon a proper self-direction as to those facts, whether the judgment has not been made upon other facts which ought not to have been taken into account. If these requirements are not met, then the exercise of the discretion, however bona fide it may be becomes capable of challenge."[24]

Thus, it is submitted that although the police do have a broad discretion in the performance of their duties, this discretion is not arbitrary or unfettered. In considering how to keep the peace, prevent crime and so on the police must act bona fide, direct themselves properly on the facts and not take irrelevant facts into account. If this discretion is exercised improperly, the police will be failing in their duties and judicial review will lie.

3. THE CASE LAW

Introduction

There are only six reported cases in which applicants have sought judicial review by the Divisional Court of police actions.[25] In all but one of these

[20] See Chap. 1 above at p. 24.

[21] *e.g., Robinson* v. *Minister of Town & Country Planning* [1947] K.B. 702.

[22] *e.g., Commissioners for Customs & Excise* v. *Deeley* [1962] 1 Q.B. 340.

[23] *Secretary of State for Education* v. *Tameside Borough Council* [1977] A.C. 1014.

[24] *Ibid.* at 1047.

[25] See also *Adams* v. *MPC* [1980] R.T.R. 289; see below at p. 409, which was an action for a declaration which would now have to be brought as an application for judicial review under R.S.C., Ord. 53.

cases the applicants have sought orders of mandamus to compel the police to carry out public duties. These duties have already been considered[26] It is important to consider the facts and orders applied for in each case so that the various dicta can be properly evaluated.

Blackburn (No. 1)

The most famous and important of all police judicial review cases remains the first, reported as *R.* v. *Commissioner of Police of the Metropolis, ex p. Blackburn* ("*Blackburn (No. 1)*").[27] Mr. Blackburn, a private citizen, applied for an order of mandamus to direct the Commissioner to reverse a policy decision not to enforce certain gaming legislation. The Court of Appeal accepted that the police do owe the public a duty to enforce the law and that the courts could, if necessary, compel them to perform it. Lord Denning M.R. stated the position as follows:

> "I hold it to be the duty of the Commissioner of Police of the Metropolis, as it is of every chief constable, to enforce the law of the land. He must take steps so to post his men that crimes may be detected; and that honest citizens may go about their affairs in peace. He must decide whether or no suspected persons are to be prosecuted and, if need be, bring the prosecution or see that it is brought."[28]

However, the Court of Appeal also made it clear that the police have a very broad discretion. These dicta of Lord Denning M.R. are often quoted:

> "Although the chief officers of police are answerable to the law, there are many fields in which they have a discretion with which the law will not interfere. For instance, it is for the Commissioner of Police of the Metropolis, or the chief constable as the case may be, to decide in any particular case whether inquiries should be pursued, or whether an arrest should be made or a prosecution brought. It must be for him to decide on the disposition of his force and the concentration of his resources on any particular crime or area. No court can or should give him direction on such a matter. He can also make policy decisions and give effect to them, as for instance was often done when prosecutions were not brought for attempted suicide. But there are some policy decision with which, I think, the courts in a case can, if necessary, interfere. Suppose a chief constable were to issue a directive to his men that no person should be prosecuted for stealing any goods less than £100 in value. I should have thought that the court could countermand it. He would be failing in his duty to enforce the law."[29]

In this case the Commissioner had already undertaken to revoke his policy decision so no order of mandamus was made and the court felt it unnecessary to consider whether Mr Blackburn had sufficient interest to seek judicial review. It should be noted that these dicta of Lord Denning M.R. were *obiter* as the ratio of the Court of Appeal's decision concerned

[26] See Chap. 1 above at p. 25.
[27] [1968] 2 Q.B. 118.
[28] *Ibid.* at 136A.
[29] *Ibid.* at 136C–F.

the extent to which an admitted obligation by the police to enforce the law is subject to judicial control.[30]

Blackburn (No. 3)

In 1973 Mr Blackburn once again sought an order of mandamus against the Metropolitan Police Commissioner, this time to compel him to prosecute in pornography cases: *R.* v. *Commissioner of Police for the Metropolis ex p. Blackburn (No. 3).*[31] Mandamus was refused and the Court reiterated the principles laid down in the first *Blackburn* case. According to Lord Denning M.R. that case:

> "made it clear that, in the carrying out of their duty of enforcing the law, the police have a discretion with which the court will not interfere. There might, however, be extreme cases in which he was not carrying out his duty. And then we would."[32]

Roskill L.J., however, put the matter slightly differently, saying that in the earlier case:

> "This court held that the respondent [*i.e.* the MPC] owed a duty to the public to enforce the law which he could be compelled to perform and that while he had a discretion not to prosecute in particular cases his discretion was not an absolute discretion."[33]

It is submitted that this is the correct analysis of the position. Even regarding the decision whether or not to prosecute in **particular cases** the police do not have an "absolute discretion." "*Wednesbury* unreasonableness" will vitiate particular prosecution decisions.

The court said that Mr Blackburn had served a useful purpose in drawing the question of pornography to the court's attention, but that it was not a suitable case for an order of mandamus.

Blackburn (No. 4)

The third case again involved Mr Blackburn. He again sought mandamus to compel the Metropolitan Police Commissioner to enforce the law against obscenity. The application was refused by both the Division Court and the Court of Appeal.[34] Lawton L.J. made some general observations about the jurisdiction of the courts to review the activities of chief constables. He said that:

[30] See Geoffrey Marshall, "Police Accountability Revisited" in D. Butler and A. H. Halsey, *Policy and Politics.*

[31] [1973] Q.B. 241.

[32] *Ibid.* at 254B.

[33] *Ibid.* at 258F.

[34] *R.* v. *Metropolitan Police Commissioner, ex p. Blackburn (No. 4), The Times,* December 1, 1979, and *The Times,* March 6, 1980.

> "Mr Blackburn's appeal was misconceived. He was asking the court to tell the commissioner how to do his job in respect of the publication of obscene matter. The court might be able to make an order of mandamus if the commissioner or any chief constable made no attempt to enforce the law, but the court had no jurisdiction to tell the commissioner how he was to perform his duties . . . The commissioner should be left to decide how he was to deploy his officers how many activities they should undertake and how they should do their job . . . The intention of the relevant statutes was to leave the commissioner to do his job as he thought fit and to empower the Home Secretary to remove him if he was not doing it efficiently. There was no justification for the courts to meddle with the way he performed his duties."

It is arguable that this is too broadly stated and should not be followed. In particular, it is clearly established that the Commissioner does not have an "unfettered discretion" to do his job "as he thinks fit."[35] Lord Denning M.R. and Ackner L.J. did not support this broad statement but agreed that the Commissioner could not be criticised but suggested that the Attorney General might consider civil process to enforce the relevant criminal law.

The CND march case

In the case of *Kent* v. *Metropolitan Police Commissioner*[36] Monsignor Bruce Kent, on behalf of the Campaign for Nuclear Disarmement, applied for declarations that an order banning marches in the metropolis was null and void. The Commissioner had made this order, with the consent of the Home Secretary, under section 3 of the Public Order Act 1936, prohibiting the holding within the Metropolitan Police district of all public processions (save or those traditionally held on May 1 and those of a religious character customarily held) for a period of 28 days. Under section 3(1) the Commissioner had power to impose conditions on the organisers of processions if he had "reasonable ground for apprehending that the procession may occasion serious public disorder." If he was "of the opinion" that his powers were not sufficient "to enable him to prevent serious public disorder" he could, with the consent of the Home Secretary, make an order banning all processions for a period of up to three months.[37]

The applicant contended that the ban on all processions marches was much too wide. Lord Denning M.R. said this point "troubled him considerably," but that it was a matter of judgment for the Commissioner and he could not say that he was at fault. Ackner L.J. agreed saying that there was nothing to suggest that the Commissioner "had acted outside his powers or capriciously." Sir Denys Buckley was of the view that the Commissioner's reasons for making the order "seemed meagre" but that:

> "it was for the applicants to demonstrate that there were no or no

[35] See above at p. 403.
[36] *The Times*, May 15, 1981.
[37] s.3(3).

> reasonable grounds on which the Commissioner could have held that the CND marches would be likely to cause serious public disorders."

It is submitted that this is not the appropriate test as to whether such an order was lawful. The Commissioner had a discretion under the statute. In order to challenge the exercise of such a discretion it is not necessary to show that there are no or no reasonable grounds for its exercise, but that it was exercised in a way which was *Wednesbury* irrational.[38] Further, the width of the ban in this case was such that there was a clear inference that his discretion was not properly exercised.

The CEGB case

The fifth case was *R.* v. *Chief Constable of Devon and Cornwall ex p. CEGB* ("the *CEGB* case").[39] The applicants were the Central Electricity Generating Board who were being prevented from carrying out a survey which they were empowered by statute to do by protesters on the land. The Chief Constable refused to take action to remove the protesters because, he said, no breach of the peace had occurred or was threatened. The Court of Appeal took a strong view of the merits of the application and said that the police were plainly entitled to take action to remove the objectors as a breach of the peace was likely. Nevertheless, no order for mandamus was granted. Lord Denning M.R. said:

> "The decision of the chief constable not to intervene in this case was a policy decision with which I think the courts should not interfere."[40]

According to Templeman L.J.:

> "The police are not bound in all circumstances to act every time there is a breach of the law, criminal or civil . . . The court cannot tell the police how and when their powers should be exercised, for the court cannot judge the explosiveness of the situation or deal with the individual problems which will arise as a result of the activities of the obstructors."[41]

It is submitted that this does not represent the correct approach. The crucial question is whether or not the police policy decision is illegal or unreasonable in the requisite sense. If it is, then it should be quashed. Confusion has perhaps arisen because the order claimed was mandamus, the effect of which would have been to compel the chief constable to intervene. But if the situation is seen as a "decision" rather than a dereliction of a public duty then the way is clear for the court's intervention. The court does not have to judge the "explosiveness" of the situation in order to **quash** the chief constable's decision not to intervene. Like any other public authority whose decision is quashed the chief constable would then have to make his decision again.

[38] See above at p. 400.
[39] [1982] Q.B. 458.
[40] *Ibid.* at 472D.
[41] *Ibid.* at 480G.

The Levey case

The most recent reported case was *R.* v. *Oxford, ex p. Levey.*[42] The applicant had been robbed in Liverpool. A police car had given chase but had withdrawn on entering the Toxteth district of the city. It was said that this withdrawal was a consequence of an unreasonable police policy decision to apply lower standards of policing to Toxteth which made it, in effect a "no go" area. This decision was challenged on the ground that it involved an abdication by the chief constable of "his undoubted duty to take all reasonable measures open to him in the light of his resources to keep the peace, enforce the law and to do so even-handedly."[43] The application was refused. According to Sir John Donaldson M.R.:

> "There is no doubt about the duty of the Chief and other Constables to keep the peace and enforce the law. Nor is there any doubt about the jurisdiction and readiness of the courts to intervene by mandatory, prohibitory or declaratory orders, if it established that they are failing in their duty. Indeed such a failure can constitute a criminal offence (*R.* v. *Dytham* [1979] 3 All E.R. 641). However, Chief Constables have the widest possible discretion in their choice of methods whereby they will discharge this duty (*R.* v. *Commissioner of Police for the Metropolis, ex p. Blackburn* [1968] 2 Q.B. 118). Any police officer who finds that his chosen policing methods are ineffective will be under a duty to re-examine them and consider whether any and, if so, what alteration is required, but one incident or even several would not necessarily be a sound basis for such a re-examination or, *a fortiori*, a change. The fact has to be faced that some areas are far more difficult to police than others and Toxteth is recognised to be one of these."

He went on to hold that it was not for the courts to review the chief constable's choice of methods "provided that he does not exceed the limits of his discretion."

4. POLICE DECISIONS

Introduction

A police constable, of whatever rank, is an "officer of the Crown" and, therefore, holds a "public office." There are a whole range of circumstances in which police constables make "decisions" which affect people's rights or "legitimate expectations." Different considerations of "judicial policy" apply in different circumstances. It is useful to distinguish three separate categories of potentially reviewable decisions. These categories shade into one another but, it is submitted, are of assistance is assessing the likely reaction of the Courts to particular factual situations.

[42] *The Times*, December 18, 1985; *The Times*, November 11, 1986.

[43] This quotation and the next are from the full transcript of the case, *per* Sir John Donaldson M.R.

Decisions not to act

The first category is that of policy decisions not to do something which, it is alleged, is covered by general police duties. If it can be established that the police have decided not to do something which it is clearly their duty to do, then this decision is reviewable. There is now no doubt that, in a clear case, the courts will grant an order of mandamus.

The classic statement of the position can be found in *Blackburn (No. 1)*[44] Salmon L.J. put the point as follows:

> "In the extremely unlikely event . . . of the police failing or refusing to carry out their duty, the court would not be powerless to intervene. For example, if, as is quite unthinkable, the chief police officer in any district were to issue an instruction that as a matter of policy the police would take no steps to prosecute any housebreaker, I have little doubt but that any household in the district would be able to obtain an order of mandamus for the instruction to be withdrawn."[45]

An example of a decision under this head would be a general refusal by the police to intervene in "domestic disputes." Such a refusal would be a clear dereliction of duty.

However the availability of mandamus to compel the police to perform their duties is strictly limited. A decision of this category will only be reviewable in when there is a clear "dereliction of duty." If the police have arrived at the decision in good faith and on the basis of a proper appreciation of the applicable law, then it is extremely unlikely that a review application will be successful. Applications for judicial review of "decisions" of this type should, therefore, only be contemplated in the strongest of cases.

General policy decisions

The second category of "police decisions" are those of a "general policy nature" where it is said that the police have improperly exercised their "policing discretion" rather than failed in their duty. Thus, it is clear that a chief constable may decide on the disposition of his force or on what kind of offences to concentrate resources on. These are "general policy decisions." Whether they can be challenged in judicial review proceedings depends on the circumstances of the decision.

Decisions of this type can probably be challenged in the courts if they are "illegal" or "irrational."[46] Thus, if a Chief Officer of Police decided to allocate extra resources to a particular area solely because the chair of the police authority lived there, this decision could be challenged as irrational because "irrelevant matters" had been taken into account. Similarly, if he directed his officers to stop and search everyone of "unconventional appearance" for drugs this would be a reviewable because it would be "illegal."[47]

A policy decision of this kind was considered in the case of *R.* v. *Oxford,*

[44] [1968] 2 Q.B. 118.
[45] *Ibid.* at 138G–139B.
[46] See above at p. 400.
[47] See Chap. 5 above at p. 129.

ex p. Levey.[48] It was alleged that it was *ultra vires* for the chief constable to adopt a policy whereby Toxteth was deemed, on some occasions, to be a "no go area." The application was refused because the applicant had failed to establish that the chief constable had exceeded the limits of his discretion.

Specific police decisions

The third category of police decisions that of "specific" decisions made by individual police officers. This category is by far the largest and contains all the specific, day to day, decisions made by police officers at all levels which have effects on the rights and legitimate expectations of individuals. When the "specific" decisions are made by high ranking police officers this category shades into the second category of "general policy" decisions. Nevertheless, it is submitted that very different "judicial policy" considerations will apply to decisions made by Chief Police Officers affecting policing policy throughout a large area—the second category—and the specific decisions of individual constables regarding particular problems within their area of responsibility.

Many "specific police decisions" will, of course, have direct legal consequences, and will be most appropriately challenged in the legal process of which they form part. Thus, when the police decide to prosecute in a particular case it is clear that the defendant's only remedy is to defend himself in the criminal courts and, if successful, to sue for malicious prosecution.

There are, however, large numbers of specific police decisions which affect the rights and expectations of individuals which are not justiciable at private law. One example of such a decision is the "ban on marches" which was challenged in the case of *Kent* v. *MPC.*[49] Another example of is a decision by the police **not to prosecute** in an individual cases. A potential defendant may have been deprived of the right to clear his name. More importantly, a victim of crime, may well be aggrieved by the absence of a prosecution. It is submitted that a victim of crime who could show that the decision not to prosecute had been taken dishonestly or in bad faith would plainly have a good ground for judicial review of the decision. This contention derives some support from the county court case of *Lee* v. *MPC*[50] which was an action against the police for a negligent failure to prosecute a person who had assaulted the first plaintiff. The negligence action was dismissed on "policy grounds."[51] The judge held that:

> "The police owed no duty. They had a discretion. If they refused to act *the plaintiffs might have sought mandamus* [our emphasis]."

Thus, for example, if a chief constable decided not to prosecute a particular person on the wholly irrelevant ground that he was related to a senior politician, then this exercise of police discretion could be challenged in the courts.

Similarly, if in the exercise of their discretion, the police decide not to prosecute a particular person on the erroneous view that the law did not for-

48 *The Times*, December 18, 1985; *The Times*, November 11, 1986.
49 *The Times*, May 15, 1981.
50 Unreported, February 20, 1986, Westminster County Court, H.H. Judge Harris.
51 See the discussion in Chap. 10 above at p. 309.

bid the activities in which he was engaged then, it is submitted that judicial review would lie to quash this decision (under Lord Diplock's first head). An example of an attempt to review a police decision of this kind can be found in the case of *Adams* v. *MPC*.[52] Although this was not an application for judicial review it is clearly the kind of case which, after *O'Reilly* v. *Mackman*,[53] would have to be brought under the Order 53 procedure. The residents of a private estate sought a declaration that a road across the estate was a "public road" within the meaning of the Road Traffic Act so that the police would not be "precluded from prosecuting" alleged motoring offences which had taken place there. The Commissioner gave an undertaking to accept the court's view of the status of the road so that the declarations were unnecessary.[54]

Another example of a decision of this kind which would probably be open to judicial review would be the decision of a particular constable or police station not to take any action on a complaint of racial harassment on the grounds that "such complaints were always unsubstantiated." A victim of such harassment may well be able to apply for an order of certiorari quashing the decision and mandamus to direct reconsideration of the decision. A "general policy decision" by a high ranking police officer not to follow up such complaints would also be subject to review.

Conclusion: judicial review applications by the citizen

In general, in the case of all "non-justiciable" police decisions, the general *Wednesbury* unreasonableness principles should apply. Of course, police discretion in these cases may be extremely wide but it is a cardinal principle of the English law of judicial review, established over the past 30 years, that no public law discretion is entirely unfettered. There is no reason why this principle should not be equally applicable to the police.

In the more recent judicial review cases the question of police duty has been expressed somewhat differently. The police, it is said, have a duty to enforce the law, but this is subject to a very broad discretion in particular cases. Thus, for example, in *Blackburn (No. 1)* Salmon L.J. says that "the police owe the public a clear legal duty to enforce the law" but, he goes on, "the police have a wide discretion as to whether or not they will prosecute in any particular case."[55]

The practical effect of the "subjective test" and the "broad discretion" approaches is probably the same. In both cases the police will be allowed a large degree of latitude in the way they go about "preserving the Queen's Peace." In both cases it is plain that there are limits, otherwise, as was said by Edmund Davies L.J. in *Blackburn (No. 1)*:

> "it would mean however brazen the failure of the police, the public would be without a remedy . . . the applicant is right in his assertion that its effect would be to place the police wholly above the law."[56]

[52] [1980] R.T.R. 289.
[53] [1983] 2 A.C. 237.
[54] See the further discussion in Chap. 12 above at p. 386.
[55] [1968] 2 Q.B. 118 at 138, 139.
[56] *Ibid.* at 148.

Beyond these limits a private citizen with a "sufficient interest" could and should be able to obtain an order of certiorari to quash the decision and, in an appropriate case, an order of mandamus to compel the police to carry out their duties. The attitude of the courts as exemplified in the cases from *Blackburn (No. 1)* through to *Levey* suggests, however, that such applications are likely to be successful only in the strongest, most extreme, cases. Despite the frequent judicial dicta to the effect that the police are "subject to the law" and the almost total lack of operational police accountability, judicial review of police decisions is very much a remedy of last resort. It is difficult to see it being of appreciable practical value to the citizen. As Sir John Donaldson M.R. has said:

> "such is the necessary width of the Chief Constable's discretion as to the method of policing which he will adopt and such, in general, is the conscientiousness of such officers, that only in very rare cases will it be possible to make a convincing prima facie case of breach of duty."

The cases in which an applicant will be successful in establishing not only a prima facie case but an actual entitlement to relief will, therefore, be very rare indeed.

5. JUDICIAL REVIEW AND POLICE AUTHORITIES

Introduction

It is not just individual citizens who are able to make judicial review applications in relation to police activities. The statutory scheme of control over the police[57] gives police authorities few direct powers over the actions of their chief constables. If police authorities wish to compel their chief constables to follow a particular course of action they have to have recourse to the judicial review procedure. This procedure can be used to deal with disputes between police authorities and chief constables over their statutory functions under the Police Act 1964. Applications of this type have been very rare but may increase in the future as the arguments for democratic control over the police gain support.

More controversially, police authorities may use the judicial review procedure to try and reassert some measure of control over "operational policing policy."[58] The question of "operational control" over policing activities is a complex and controversial one. Any discussion of judicial review in this area involves an assessment of the conventional doctrine of the "operational independence" of chief constables. It was earlier suggested that there is no historical basis for claiming complete operational autonomy for chief constables.[58a] Furthermore, the legal justifications for the doctrine are extremely flimsy. It follows that there is nothing unlawful in police authorities giving chief constables advice and instructions on general policy issues. If chief constables refuse to accept such advice and instructions then, it is submitted, an application for judicial review would lie.

[57] See Chap. 1 above at pp. 30 *et seq*.

[58] For some comments on the historical position see Introduction, above at p. 7.

[58a] See Introduction above at p. 7.

Judicial review to enforce statutory responsibilities

Judicial review is available where police authorities claim that chief constables are failing in their statutory duties or are abrogating to themselves matters which belong to the authority.

The Police Act 1964 reserves very few statutory functions exclusively to police authorities.[59] Nevertheless, if chief constables do encroach upon these functions the authority may seek the appropriate declaratory judgment. The only reported instance of such proceedings is the case of *R.* v. *Secretary of State for Home Department, ex p. Northumbria Police Authority.*[60] The police authority sought a declaration that the Home Secretary had no power to issue their chief constable with plastic bullets without its consent except in situations of grave emergency. The decision turned on the nature of the express function of police authorities to provide vehicles, clothing and other equipment for police purposes under section 4(4) of the Police Act 1964. After holding that the Home Secretary's power to issue police equipment derived from the Royal Prerogative, the Divisional Court went on to reject the submission that a prerogative power to supply was inconsistent either expressly or by implication with the statutory power to equip conferred upon police authorities. According to Mann J.:

> "[Section 4(4)] is not drawn so as to create a monopoly and even granted the different statutory functions of a police authority and of the Secretary of State we see no cause to imply that the conferred power is to be a monopoly . . .
>
> The decision whether or not to use equipment supplied by the Secretary of State is for the chief constable alone to make . . . This court will not intervene to control the use which a chief constable makes of the resources available to him."[60a]

Although police authorities may consider this type of claim for judicial review more frequently following the lead of the Northumbria Authority, the approach taken by the Divisional Court is not very encouraging. Even though the statute is silent on the Home Secretary's role and functions and gives the police authority express functions in this area, the court would not intervene on its behalf. This decision is in line with the non-interventionist trend of police judicial review cases.

The doctrine of operational independence

An area of central constitutional importance which could be clarified by judicial review applications by police authorities is that of the "operational independence" of chief constables. Although there are no reported cases dealing directly with this area it is treated in some detail because of its great constitutional and political importance and its indirect importance for all

[59] See Chap. 1 above at p. 31.
[60] [1987] 2 W.L.R. 998.
[60a] *Ibid.* at 1005 C–E.

cases involving the "duties and independence" of the police. It has received scant treatment in the legal and constitutional textbooks.[61]

The conventional wisdom is that chief constables are "officers of the Crown" and "public servants," that their power are exercisable "by virtue of their offices" as constables on their own responsibility and that neither police authorities nor central government can give them operational instructions of any kind.[62]

This doctrine of "operational independence" is a startling one and does not reflect historical precedent.[63] Moreover, it suggests that chief constables have a unique status among public servants. They are paid and appointed by public authorities with very substantial resources at their disposal yet their discretion in deploying these resources is said to be unfettered. They are said to be responsible to the law and to the law alone. Nevertheless, when their decisions have been challenged in applications for judicial review the courts have, as has been seen, refused to exercise any supervisory jurisdiction.

The doctrine is claimed to be of general application. It covers not only quasi-judicial decisions about whether or not to apply for a warrant or commence a prosecution in an individual case but also the entire range of "policing policy decisions" covering matters such as what crimes to concentrate police resources on, which geographical areas to deploy police in, how they should be deployed, the policing of political marches and demonstrations and so on. The doctrine is an exorbitant one and its legal foundations are extremely slight.

It should be noted that the doctrine is only applied to chief constables and not to ordinary police constables. There has never been any suggestion that senior police officers cannot give "operational orders" to their subordinates. It will be seen that the very existence of a hierarchical police force in which senior officers give "operational orders" to constables casts considerable doubt on the doctrine.

The statutory position

By section 4(1) of the Police Act 1964 police authorities are under a general duty to "secure the maintenance of an adequate and efficient force." The precise meaning of this is unclear. It appears to create a specific sphere of responsibility for the police authority as distinct from those within which the chief constable or the Home Secretary are responsible. However, the statute is silent as to whether this positive duty gives any consequential powers of control over a chief constable's "operational functions" beyond calling for reports under section 12 or seeking the Home Secretary's approval to retire him on grounds of efficiency under section 5(4). Nevertheless, it is submitted, that the duty to secure an "efficient force" involves consideration by the police authority of policing issues, at least of a general nature.

[61] But see Marshall, Lustgarten, and Tony Jefferson & Roger Grimshaw, *Controlling the Constable*, see also Clayton and Tomlinson, "Can Police Authorities Give Orders to Chief Constables?" (1984) 134 New L.J. 880.

[62] See *Halsbury's Laws of England*, Vol. 36, paras. 230, 249.

[63] See Introduction above at p. 7.

Section 5(1) of the Police Act 1964, on the other hand, places the police under the "direction and control of the chief constable." However, it would appear that this phrase only covers immediate operational direction and control but does not bear on the question of the extent to which the chief constable is under the supervision of the police authority. The chief constable's control is not expressed to be "exclusive."[64] Nevertheless, the Police Act 1964 has imposed a very different structure of authority from that contained in previous legislation. Whereas the earlier statutes designated justices or created committees with a responsibility for policing which then appointed chief constables, the 1964 Act sets up police forces,[65] police authorities of specified composition and function[66] and a chief constable with his power defined in section 5. The structural change may seem significant and intentional but it does not necessarily follow that the 1964 Act enshrines the supremacy of the chief constable in the statue.[67]

It is, then, submitted that the statutory provisions do not provide any direct justification for the doctrine of operational independence. The Police Act 1964 does not expressly prohibit police authorities from giving operational policing instructions.

The common law position

The only basis in law for the doctrine of operational independence appears to be the common law. The statement of principle in *Halsbury's Laws of England*[68] cites three cases in support, *Fisher* v. *Oldham Corporation*,[69] *A-G for New South Wales* v. *Perpetual Trustee Co.*[70] and *R.* v *Metropolitan Police Commissioner, ex p. Blackburn*.[71]

In *Fisher* v. *Oldham Corporation* it was held that a police constable was not a servant of the local authority so that the watch committee was not vicariously liable for his tortious acts. McCardie J. ruled that he is:

> "a servant of the State, a ministerial officer of the central power though subject, in some respects, to local supervision and local regulation."[72]

The actual decision in this case is not surprising although it appears that it went beyond binding precedent[73] and was reversed by section 48 of the Police Act 1964.[74] The relationship between public authorities and those they employ is seldom a straightforward one of master and servant. Thus, for example, neither civil servants nor members of the armed forces can

64 Marshall at p. 98.
65 s.1.
66 ss.2–4.
67 But see Lustgarten at p. 75.
68 Vol. 36, para. 320.
69 [1930] 2 K.B. 364.
70 [1955] A.C. 457.
71 [1968] 2 Q.B. 118.
72 [1930] 2 K.B. 364 at 371.
73 See Marshall, Chap. 3.
74 See Chap. 1 above at p. 35.

recover damages for wrongful dismissal. They are employed as Crown Servants at the pleasure of the Crown and, at common law, can be dismissed at will.[75]

Nevertheless, it does not follow that because a constable was not a servant of the watch committee, the committee cannot give orders to him or to his chief constable. Whilst the relationship of a master and servant involves some relationship of control (although the amount of actual control necessary to justify finding a relationship of master and servant now appears fairly slight[76]) the fact that someone engages an independent contractor does not prevent him exercising any control; for example, if a householder engages a builder as an independent contractor he is plainly entitled to give the builder instructions about how to do the work or what materials to use.

The question of vicarious liability is clearly quite separate from general constitutional issues of police accountability. A particular finding in *Fisher* v. *Oldham* that insufficient control exists to prove the relationship of master and servant does not justify a wider inference of general independence on all matters pertaining to law enforcement and keeping the peace.[77]

The judgment in *Fisher* v. *Oldham Corporation*[78] also contains *obiter dicta* on which a second argument for operational independence has been based. McCardie J. said[79]:

> "Supposing that a police officer arrested a man for a serious felony? Suppose too that the watch committee passed a resolution directing that the felon be released. Of what value would such a resolution be? Not only would it be the plain duty of the police officer to disregard the resolution, but it would also be the duty of the chief constable to consider whether an information should not at once be laid against the members of the watch committee for a conspiracy to obstruct the course of criminal justice."

Nevertheless, the police would be obliged to disregard such a plainly unlawful instruction independent of any special relationship they had with the police authority.[80] Indeed, *R.* v. *MPC, ex p. Blackburn*[81] makes it clear that because the police are under a public duty to enforce the law, the court will intervene if they attempt to comply with unlawful instructions.

This argument which is based on giving unlawful instructions, rests on a fallacy. The fact that a police authority cannot give **unlawful** instructions to police officers does not mean it cannot give **any** instructions. It would be unlawful for a chief constable to direct one of his men to release a "felon" but no one doubts that he is entitled to give them lawful orders.

The third argument for the doctrine of operational independence arises from the Privy Council case of *A-G for New South Wales* v. *Perpetual Trus-*

[75] *Riordan* v. *War Office* [1961] 1 W.L.R. 210; *R.* v. *Secretary of State for Foreign & Commonwealth Affairs, ex p. Council of Civil Service Unions* [1984] I.R.L.R. 353.

[76] See *Nethermere St. Neots* v. *Taverna* [1984] I.C.R. 612.

[77] See Marshall at pp. 43–44; but see Tony Jefferson and Roger Grimshaw, *Controlling the Constable* at p. 52.

[78] [1930] 2 K.B. 364.

[79] *Ibid.* at 372–373.

[80] See Marshall at p. 37; but see Jefferson & Grimshaw, *Controlling the Constable* at p. 52.

[81] [1968] 2 Q.B. 118.

tee Co.[82] In holding that a police officer was not employed by the Government, the Privy Council ruled that the constable is the holder of a public office whose authority is original and not delegated so that it is exercised at his own discretion by virtue of his office.

However, the holding of the common law office of constable does not confer complete freedom from external control on the holder.[83] Such a contention would result in it being illegal for senior officers to give instructions to ordinary constables. The claim is also contrary to the reasoning in *Hawkins* v. *Bepey*[84] which established that a police officer laying an information before a magistrate acts in a representative capacity for the chief constable because he is obeying the chief constable's order which he is bound to follow.

Furthermore, although a constable has wide discretionary powers, subject to the orders of his superiors this need not have implications for his legal status. For example, National Health Service consultants have a wide discretion in carrying out their professional skills but do not have a special legal status as a result. It is suggested that there is a further difficulty with this view. It is assumed that the independence of an ordinary police constable in relation to his duties applies *mutatis mutandis* to the relationship between chief constables and police authorities. There is no obvious reason why the former set of principles is determinative of the latter.

The most important recent judicial exposition of the doctrine of operational independence is to be found in the case of *R.* v. *Metropolitan Police Commissioner, ex p. Blackburn.*[85] Lord Denning M.R. states that:

> "I have no hesitation in holding that, like every constable in the land, . . . [the Commissioner of the Metropolitan Police] should be and is independent of the executive. He is not subject to the orders of the Secretary of State, save that under the Police Act, the Secretary of State can call upon him to give a report or to retire in the interests of efficiency. I hold it to be the duty of the Commissioner of Police, as it is of every Chief Constable, to enforce the law of the land. He must take steps so as to post his men that crimes may be detected; and that honest citizens may go about their affairs in peace. He must decide whether or not suspected persons are to be prosecuted; and, if need be, bring the prosecution or see that it is brought. But in all these things he is not a servant of anyone, save the law itself. No minister of the Crown can tell him he must, or must not, prosecute this man or that one. The responsibility for law enforcement lies on him. He is answerable to the law and to the law alone. This appears sufficiently from *Fisher* v. *Oldham Corporation* and *A-G for New South Wales* v. *Perpetual Trustee Co.*"[86]

It has already been noted that this passage is *obiter.*[87] It has also been suggested that the authorities cited do not support the general proposition put forward.

[82] [1955] A.C. 457.

[83] See Chap. 1 above at p. 23.

[84] [1980] 1 W.L.R. 419.

[85] [1968] 2 Q.B. 118.

[86] *Ibid.* at 135–136; approved in *R* v. *Metropolitan Police Commissioner, ex p. Blackburn (No. 3)* [1973] Q.B. 241 and in *R.* v. *Chief Constable of Devon and Cornwall, ex p. CEGB* [1982] Q.B. 458.

[87] See above at p. 403.

Operational independence in general

In addition to the arguments based on the case law, supporters of the doctrine of operational independence often rely on two further general propositions. First it is said that because a chief constable has discretion regarding the disposition of his men and the prosecution of particular cases, he is therefore not subject to **any** outside interference. Secondly, "operational independence" is said to rest on a general constitutional doctrine that chief constables, like the judiciary, must be independent of the executive.

The claim that a prohibition of intervention in particular cases involves an embargo against giving general instructions is unsustainable.[88] This argument involves what has been described as the "fallacy of the seamless web": the assumption that if democratic control is recognised as legitimate in any aspect of policing it must inevitably extend to every aspect so that opposing the doctrine of operational independence involves advocating that politicians can direct the police not to arrest their supporters.[89] It is possible to accept that police authorities cannot, and should not, give directions in specific matters without conceding the entire doctrine of operational independence.

The confusion involved in the second, "constitutional" contention was revealed by Professor Wade when the Willink Commission sought his advice on the independence of chief constables.[90] The necessity for ensuring the chief constables are independent of the executive is said to arise out of the principle of the separation of powers. It is generally accepted that the judiciary and the judicial process should be independent of the government. However, Professor Wade observes that the maintenance of law and order is an executive function. Although he accepted that the quasi-judicial discretion regarding prosecutions should remain with chief constables, he concludes that a chief constable only needed to be entirely independent where technical knowledge of the law was required. However, with the advent of the Crown Prosecution Service, following the Prosecution of Offences Act 1985, the "constitutional argument" appears to be untenable.

It is, accordingly, submitted that police authorities can lawfully give operational orders of a general nature to their chief constables, for example, in areas such as (a) the types of crimes that should be concentrated upon, (b) the general methods of policing and (c) the general policy regarding the questioning of suspects. It may be argued that chief constables are in no different position from other non judicial public officials subject to the direction of the executive. If a chief constable refuses to obey lawful operational instructions from his police authority they are entitled to seek the appropriate public law remedy.[91]

It has been argued that applications for judicial review based upon the police authority's duties under section 4(1) of the Police Act 1964 would only be appropriate if judges were able to make "technical" evaluations of, for example, policing needs, the adequacy of provision and the quality of

[88] See Marshall, "Police Accountability Revisited," in D. Butler and A. H. Hadsey, *Policy and Politics.*

[89] Lustgarten at p. 65.

[90] *op. cit.*, Minutes of Evidence, II, pp. 33–34.

[91] See below at p. 417.

performance. Even the most ardent advocate of judicial review would recognise such evaluations as being outside the competence of the courts.[92] However, this argument is misconceived. If police authorities are entitled to give general "operational instructions" to their chief constables, they are entitled to orders of mandamus to ensure that chief constables take account of these instructions. The court should grant a remedy unless the chief constable can show that the orders given are "unlawful" on general public law grounds. Unless the order is "illegal," or "irrational"[93] it is submitted that the chief constable is obliged to obey it. It will be "illegal" if it relates to specific cases. It will be "irrational" if the authority is not acting bona fide, has taken irrelevant matters into account or has failed to take relevant matters into account. In order to make such an assessment the court does not need to consider "technical policing matters" any more than it needs to consider "technical housing matters" when considering the lawfulness of local authority decisions relating to homeless persons.

6. THE REMEDIES

Introduction

The traditional remedy available on an application for judicial review was one of the three "prerogative writs": certiorari, mandamus or prohibition. These remedies were subject to different technical rules of some complexity. In 1977 the Supreme Court Rules were reformed and the new R.S.C. Ord. 53 greatly simplified the position. The old cases on the availability of the different orders in particular situations must, therefore, be treated with some care.

The remedies after 1977

Under the new rules the High Court has a wider range of remedies available on a judicial review application. It can grant declarations or injunctions in place of or in addition to prerogative orders. It can also award damages, but only in situations where "private law" damages would be available. Nevertheless, the three prerogative orders remain by far the most important remedies available on judicial review. We will consider each of these in turn.

The order of certiorari has the effect of quashing the police decision. Its original function was simply to "call up the record" of the proceedings of an inferior tribunal. If the record displayed an error on its face the decision could be quashed. Matters outside the record could only be challenged if the applicant could show an excess of jurisdiction. Over the years it has become much more flexible and it can now be used to quash any decision which is "procedurally improper," "illegal" or *Wednesbury* unreasonable.

[92] Lustgarten at p. 85.
[93] See above at p. 400.

There is some authority to suggest that certiorari will only lie to quash a **written** decision.[94] But the documents constituting the "decision" have been construed very liberally in recent years. Thus, in the case of *R* v. *Knightsbridge Crown Court, ex p. The Aspinall Curzon*[95] the affidavit of the applicant's solicitor was treated as part of the record of the decision. It is clear, however, that certiorari will not lie to review purely physical acts such as the entering of premises.[96] The remedies of declaration and injunctions will be available in situations where for these "technical" reasons certiorari would be refused.

The second of the prerogative orders is **mandamus**. This is an order compelling a public authority such as the police to carry out their duties.

The third prerogative order is **prohibition**. This is issued to prevent the police from doing something which would be in excess of their jurisdiction.

It should be noted that the prerogative orders and related remedies which are sought in judicial review proceedings are **discretionary**. Even when an applicant establishes his entitlement to a remedy the court may, in its discretion refuse to grant it. As we have seen, this has, until now, been the approach of the Courts in police judicial review cases where an entitlement to relief has been established.[97]

By R.S.C., Ord. 53, r. 7 the court may, on an application for judicial review, award damages if the applicant has included a claim for damages in support of his application for leave and he could have been awarded damages if the claim had been made in an ordinary action.[98]

Choosing the remedy in police cases

The reported police cases have generally involved claims for mandamus to compel the police to do particular things. It is perhaps understandable why the courts are reluctant to grant such orders. To order in advance that the officers should carry out their duties in large numbers of specific situations is to run the risk of the Court "acting in vain," of making an order which cannot be realistically complied with.[99]

There is no such danger, however, with the other orders available under the Order 53 procedure. When a Chief Officer of Police decides not to intervene on the basis of a misapprehension of the law the most appropriate remedy may be to quash his decision by an order of certiorari. He would then simply have to consider the matter again and there would be no danger of the court "acting in vain." If the decision was an oral one a similar result could be achieved by the court granting a declaration as to the relevant law.

This may also be the appropriate remedy for other police decisions, for example, a decision **not to prosecute** in specific cases. The quashing of such decisions would mean that the police would be obliged to reconsider but, as is often the situation in relation to inferior tribunals, the specific result of

[94] *R.* v. *Newington Licensing JJ, ex p. Conrad* [1948] 1 K.B. 681.
[95] *The Times*, December 16, 1982.
[96] *R.* v. *IRC, ex. p. Rossminster* [1980] A.C. 952.
[97] See, *e.g.*, *Blackburn (No. 1)* [1968] 2 Q.B. 118; the *CEGB* case [1982] Q.B. 458.
[98] For an example of damages being awarded in a judicial review case see *R.* v. *Liverpool City Council, ex p. Coade, The Independent*, October 9, 1986.
[99] See the remarks of Templeman l.J. in the *CEGB* case, [1982] Q.B. 458 at 480G.

the new decision would not be dictated by the court. The decision-making process would have to be gone through again.

In another type of case, if the police decided to make investigations on the basis of a misapprehension of the law, then the most appropriate remedy may be prohibition or an injunction. Once again, this would not run the risk of fettering a necessary policing discretion. All these other remedies are much more flexible than mandamus. The undoubted necessity for a wide police discretion to enable complex operational decisions to be taken in line with factors such as the "explosiveness" of the situation can be preserved. At the same time, the law can assert some kind of control over the actions of police officers.

If a person has suffered special damage by reason of an alleged "illegal" police policy decision he can join a claim for damages to an application for judicial review. Thus in the case of *R.* v. *Oxford, ex p. Levey,*[1] the application for judicial review contained a claim for damages for negligence and breach of statutory duty. A finding that the police were in breach of duty will be of considerable assistance in, for example, a claim for negligence or breach of statutory duty. Another advantage will be that a judicial review claim will be heard after a matter of months rather than the years that most civil actions will take to come to trial. On the other hand, the extreme reluctance of the courts to grant judicial review of police decisions means that an applicant taking this course is unlikely to succeed in his claim for damages and so this course should only be adopted in the very clearest cases.

7. PROCEDURE

Introduction

The judicial review procedure is in two parts. First there is the application for leave. This acts as a "filter" for applications. If an applicant does not have "sufficient interest" in the decision or has a hopeless case then leave will be refused. If leave is obtained then there is a full hearing on the merits of the application before the Divisional Court of the Queen's Bench Division of the High Court.[2]

Judicial review applications are divided into "criminal" and "civil" matters. There are important procedural differences between the two types of application. The rules do not provide any definition of these categories, but a "criminal cause or matter" is widely construed. It covers "a decision by way of judicial determination of any question raised or with regard to proceedings, the subject matter of which is criminal, at whatever stage of the proceedings the question arises."[3] Nevertheless, it was held in the first

[1] *The Times,* November 1, 1986.

[2] In 1984 there were 918 judicial review applications, 215 (23 per cent.) were refused leave. Of the 401 applications which were heard relief was granted in 187 cases (47 per cent.): *Judicial Statistics:*, Cmnd. 9599, (1984), p. 18.

[3] *Ex p. Woodhall* (1888) 20 Q.B.D. 832, *per* Lord Esher.

Blackburn case[4] that the application for mandamus in relation to police prosecution policy was a "civil cause or matter." But an application for mandamus to compel the police to assist in the bringing of prosecutions may well be a "criminal cause or matter."[5] Any application for judicial review of orders made or refused under the Police and Criminal Evidence Act 1984 will involve a "criminal cause or matter."[5a]

It is submitted that an application relating to general police duties or policy—that is, to decisions in the first or second categories—will be a civil cause or matter. On the other hand, an application relating to a specific police decision—the third category—will be a "criminal cause or matter" if the ultimate outcome may effect the criminal prosecution of a specific individual.

Time limits

The first hurdle for any application for judicial review is the time limit. An application for judicial review must be made "promptly and in any event within three months from when the date when grounds for the application first arose."[6] The simple fact that an application is brought within three months does not necessarily mean that it is prompt.[7]

The court has jurisdiction to extend the period within which the application shall be made if it "considers that there is good reason" for so doing.[8] Even if there is a "good reason" for extending the time limits this does not mean that the late application must be allowed. By section 31(6) of the Supreme Court Act 1981 if the High Court considers that there has been undue delay in making an application for judicial review it may refuse to grant leave or relief if:

> "it considers that the granting of the relief sought would be likely to cause substantial hardship to, or substantially prejudice the rights of, any person or would be detrimental to good administration."

It seems that delay will be "undue" whenever there is failure to act promptly or within three months.[9]

One important cause of delay is likely to be difficulties in obtaining legal aid. The Court of Appeal made it clear in the case of *R.* v. *Stratford-upon-Avon DC, ex p. Jackson*[10] that if delay is entirely due to time taken in obtaining legal aid, (and the applicant was not at fault), this will be a "good reason" under Ord. 53, r. 4. Nevertheless, the court retains a discretion to refuse to grant leave under section 31(6).

When there is an application to extend time under Ord. 53, r. 4 notice should be given to the respondent.[11]

[4] [1968] 2 Q.B. 118.
[5] *Ibid. per* Lord Denning M.R., at 134.
[5a] See *R.* v. *Central Criminal Court, ex p. Carr, The Independent*, May 13, 1987.
[6] Ord. 53, r. 4(1).
[7] *R.* v. *Greenwich BC, ex p. Cedar Transport, The Times*, August 3, 1983.
[8] Ord. 53, r. 4(1).
[9] *R.* v. *Stratford-on-Avon DC, ex p. Jackson* [1985] 3 All E.R. 769.
[10] *Ibid.*
[11] *R.* v. *Ashford, Kent JJ, ex p. Richley* [1955] 1 W.L.R. 562.

Applying for leave

Once it has been decided that a judicial review application is appropriate and legal aid has been obtained, the first step is to apply for leave by filing a Form 86A with the Crown Office. The application must specify the name and description of the applicant, the relief sought and the grounds, the name and address of the applicant's solicitors and his address for service. It should be accompanied by an affidavit verifying the facts relied on.[12] This should exhibit the "order, warrant, commitment, conviction, inquisition or record" whose validity is being questioned.[13] This notice of application forms the basis of the full hearing and it is important to ensure that it includes all relief claimed and matters relied on.[14]

There is a choice as how the leave application is dealt with. An applicant can request an oral leave hearing on the Notice of Application. This is, however, unusual. The usual procedure, which will be gone through unless a specific request for an oral hearing is made, is for the leave application to be considered on the papers, by a single judge[15] who can order an oral hearing. If leave is refused by the single judge the application may be renewed in an oral hearing. In a civil matter this (unless otherwise directed) will be before a single judge in open court. In a criminal matter it will be before a full Divisional Court.[16] The applicant must lodge a notice of his intention to renew his application in form 86B within ten days of being served with notice of the single judge's refusal.[17]

If an oral hearing is requested on the Notice of Application, it will take place, in the first instance, before a single judge, either in chambers or in open court. It will be appropriate to ask for an oral hearing if interim relief is being sought or if there is some delay which needs oral explanation.

The judge who deals with the initial application for leave may invite the respondent to attend. In the case of *R.* v. *Oxford, ex p. Levey,*[18] Taylor J. took this course but the respondent chief constable argued that there was no jurisdiction to do this. The Court of Appeal emphatically rejected this contention:

> "The suggestion that Taylor J. had no jurisdiction to adjourn the hearing of the *ex parte* application and to invite the attendance of the Chief Constable in person or by counsel is wholly misconceived. Any court is entitled to hear someone who may be affected by a decision on an *ex parte* application and sometimes it is highly desirable that this shall be done in the interests of justice. In the context of Order 53, where the proposed respondent is by definition one who is, or who is said to be, entrusted with powers and duties under public law, it is particularly desirable that such invitations should be accepted."

If leave is refused after an oral hearing then, in a "criminal matter" the

[12] Ord. 53, r. 3(2).
[13] Ord. 53, r. 9(2).
[14] See R. J. F. Gordon, *Judicial Review: Practice and Procedure,* para. 7–12; on amendment, see *ibid.* para. 8–14.
[15] Ord. 53, r. 3(3).
[16] Ord. 53, r. 3(4) (*a*).
[17] Ord. 53, r. 3(5).
[18] *The Times,* November 1, 1986.

application may be renewed before the full Divisional Court. In a "civil matter" the applicant must renew his application before the Court of Appeal.

It is generally thought that if the Divisional Court refuses leave in a criminal matter the application cannot be renewed before the Court of Appeal,[19] In a civil matter an application for leave can be renewed before the Court of Appeal. If the Court of Appeal refuses leave, the application cannot be renewed before the House of Lords.[20]

The application proper

If leave is granted, then the next stage is to make an application for judicial review by originating motion to a Divisional Court of the Queen's Bench Division.[21] The notice of motion and a copy of the statement in support of the application for leave must be served on all persons directly affected. The notice of motion must be filed in the Crown Office within 14 days of the grant of leave.[22] An affidavit of service of the notice of motion must also be filed.[23] There must be, unless the court granting leave has otherwise directed, as least ten days between service and hearing.[24] If the respondent court wishes to file an affidavit this must be done within 21 days of the service of the notice of motion.[25] Before the full hearing interlocutory applications may be made to a judge or master for matters such as leave to cross-examine, discovery or interrogatories.[26] The rules governing discovery in judicial review proceedings are the same as in ordinary actions.[27]

The hearing of the application in a civil matter is usually by a single judge in open court, although in police cases it is likely that it will be directed that the application will be heard by a full Divisional Court.[28] In a criminal matter the hearing will be before a full Divisional Court, usually consisting of two judges. The case is opened by the applicant in person or counsel on his behalf. After the respondents (if any) are heard, the applicant has a right of reply.[29]

Where the relief sought is a declaration, an injunction or damages, the court may order the proceedings to continue as if they had been begun by writ.[30] There can be no order for transfer if certiorari and prohibition are the

[19] See *R.* v. *Bolton JJ, ex p. Graeme, The Times,* March 14, 1986; *The Supreme Court Practice,* 53/1–14/5 but see R.S.C., Ord. 59, r. 14(3) and R. J. F. Gordon, *Judicial Review: Practice and Procedure,* para. 7–18.

[20] *Re Poh* [1983] 1 W.L.R. 2.

[21] Ord. 53, r. 5.

[22] Ord. 53, r. 5(5).

[23] Ord. 53, r. 5(6).

[24] Ord. 53, r. (4)

[25] Ord. 53, r. 6(4).

[26] Ord. 53, r. 8; see generally, R. J. F. Gordon *Judicial Review: Practice and Procedure* paras. 8–10–8–15; Aldous and Alder, *Applications for Judicial Review,* Chap. 14.

[27] *R.* v. *Governor of Pentonville, ex p. Herbage (No. 2), The Times,* May 29, 1986.

[28] As, *e.g.,* in *R.* v. *Oxford, ex p. Levey, The Times,* November 1, 1986.

[29] *R.* v. *Dunne* [1943] K.B. 516.

[30] Ord. 53, r. 9(5).

only remedies sought in the notice of application[31] or if the application is struck out as disclosing no reasonable claim in public law.[31a]

Appeals

If the application is refused then the appeals position depends on whether the application is civil or criminal. In a civil matter, an appeal lies, without leave, to the Court of Appeal.[32] In criminal matters there is no appeal to the Court of Appeal.[33] There is, however, a "leapfrog" appeal to the House of Lords with the leave of the Divisional Court or the House of Lords. In the latter case the Divisional Court must certify that a point of law of general public importance is involved.[34]

[31] See *R.* v. *East Berks Health Authority, ex. p. Walsh* [1985] Q.B. 152.

[31a] See *R.* v. *Secretary of State for Home Affairs, ex p. Dew, The Times,* March 6, 1987.

[32] Supreme Court Act 1981, s.16; see R.S.C., Ord. 59, for the general procedure.

[33] Supreme Court Act 1981, s.18(1)(*a*).

[34] Administration of Justice Act 1960, s.1(2). In 1984 there were 20 applications for leave to appeal from the Divisional Court in criminal matters, seven of which were allowed. The Divisional Court itself gave leave in three cases. The House of Lords actually heard eight appeals of this type, four of which were successful, *Judicial Statistics:* Cmnd. 9599, (1984), pp. 10–11.

14. The European Convention on Human Rights

1. INTRODUCTION

The European Convention on Human Rights provides fertile ground for civil rights lawyers to challenge the conformity of the English law to certain "fundamental human rights." The United Kingdom has therefore contested more applications than any other country which is party to the Convention. A citizen who is a victim of police misconduct but finds himself without remedy in the English Courts may be able to make a successful complaint under the European Convention.

The European Convention for the Protection of Human Rights and Fundamental Freedoms[1] was signed in 1950 under the auspices of the Council of Europe. The United Kingdom is a party to the Convention and to the first,[2] second,[3] third[4] and fifth[5] protocols. The impetus for the Convention came from the movements towards unifying Europe after the Second World War. In 1948 the Brussels Treaty was signed by the United Kingdom, France, Belgium, Luxembourg and the Netherlands and established a Consultative Council consisting of foreign ministers. In 1949 the Statute of the Council of Europe[6] was signed in London establishing a Consultative Assembly. One of the first issues discussed at the first Ordinary Session of this Consultative Assembly was a convention on fundamental rights. Despite considerable disputes concerning the content of these substantive rights and the machinery for enforcing their guarantee, the convention was eventually agreed in May 1950.[7] The United Kingdom was the first government to ratify the Convention. However, the right for individuals to bring a petition was not accepted until 1966.

The Convention does not form part of the English law; thus in *Malone* v.

[1] Rome, November 4, 1950; T.S. 71 Cmd. 8969, (1953).

[2] Protocol, Paris, March 20, 1952; T.S. 46 Cmd. 9221, (1954).

[3] Protocol No. 2, Strasbourg, May 6, 1963; T.S. 104 Cmnd. 4551, (1970).

[4] Protocol No. 3, Strasbourg, May 6, 1963; T.S. 106 Cmnd. 4552, (1970).

[5] Strasbourg, January 20, 1966; T.S. 48, Cmnd. 4963 (1972).

[6] Statute of the Council of Europe, Cmd. 7776, (1949).

[7] For a discussion concerning the attitude of the British government towards the convention both at this stage and subsequently, see A. Lester "Fundamental Rights: The United Kingdom Isolated" (1984) Public Law 46.

MPC[8] it was held that the court had no power to grant a declaration that the Convention was breached since the convention was not justiciable in England. The Convention merely has the status of a treaty and its primary relevance is that it may be used as an aid to construing statutes.[9] The impact of the Convention has been most extensively discussed in immigration cases where Lord Denning's views have fluctuated considerably. In *Birdie* v. *Secretary of State for Home Affairs*[10] he declared that if an Act of Parliament did not conform to the Convention he would be inclined to rule it invalid. However, in *R.* v. *Secretary of State for Home Department ex. p. Bhajan Singh*[11] he withdrew this remark and subsequently amended his statements in the later case by saying immigration officers need not bear in mind the principles of the Convention when applying the immigration rules,[12] the general principles to be applied were stated by Scarman L.J. in *Pan American* v. *Department of Trade*[13];

> "The courts shall take no notice of treaties unless they are embodied in Acts of Parliament. However, international conventions may be looked at when Parliament require it although no express words have been used or where two courses are reasonably open to the Court but one is inconsistent with the convention which the other is not."

Any alleged violation of the European Convention must, therefore, be pursued by making a direct petition under its provisions. In the first instance this must be made to the European Commission on Human Rights. This comprises a member of every state which is party to the Convention[14] who sits in a personal capacity.[15] If the petition is ruled admissible and no friendly settlement is effected it is forwarded to the Committee of Ministers. Either the Commission or the government responding to the petition can put the case before the European Court of Human Rights. This body consists of judges equal in number to the members of the Council of Europe who must each be from a different state.[16] On the other hand, it is possible for the Committee of Ministers to itself decide that the Convention had been breached.

This procedure has the result that case law arises from several different sources. The European Commission gives decisions on the admissibility of petitions which is final and binding on the parties. The Commission also makes reports after ruling an application is admissible, investigating the facts and attempting a friendly settlement which is unsuccessful; these reports contain opinions and are therefore persuasive but not binding. On the other hand, the judgments of the European Court are binding on the states concerned.[17] Similarly, the decision of the Committee of Ministers is binding on them.[17a]

[8] [1979] Ch. 344; Chap. 9 above at p. 284.
[9] *Waddington* v. *Miah* [1974] 1 W.L.R. 683.
[10] (1975) 119 S.J. 322.
[11] [1976] Q.B. 198.
[12] *R.* v. *Chief Immigration Officer, ex. p. Bibi* [1976] 3 All E.R. 843.
[13] [1976] 1 Lloyds' Rep. 257 at 261; see also *Malone* v. *MPC* [1979] Ch. 344.
[14] Article 20.
[15] Article 23.
[16] Article 35.
[17] Article 52.
[17a] Article 32.

In this chapter the provisions of the Convention which are most relevant to policing activities are briefly discussed. The procedure in making an application based on the Convention is then considered. The intention is not to examine in detail whether and to what extent the English law on police powers confirms to the European Convention but to indicate a possible line of inquiry when a remedy for police misconduct is sought.[18]

2. POLICE ACTIVITIES AND THE EUROPEAN CONVENTION

General considerations

The Convention protects a variety of "human rights." The rights which may be relevant to police activity include the rights to life,[19] respect for private and family life,[20] home and correspondence,[21] peaceful assembly and association.[22]

These rights may only be interfered with or restricted in such a manner as is "prescribed by law." The procedure must be lawful under domestic law[23] which must be in conformity with the provisions of the Convention.[24] Furthermore, it has been held that the domestic law must comply with the following general requirements:

(1) the law must be adequately accessible, *i.e.* the citizen must be able to have an indication that is adequate in the circumstances of the legal rules applicable to a given case;

(2) a norm cannot be regarded as "law" unless formulated with sufficient precision to enable the citizen to regulate his conduct.[25]

Thus, a domestic law which allows the interference with "rights" will contravene the Convention if it is not clearly formulated and accessible.

The Convention allows various restrictions of rights and freedoms which must be applied for the purpose for which they are prescribed by it.[26] Even when restrictions are within the Convention they must comply with the general principle of "proportionality"; in other words, they "must be proportionate to the legitimate aim pursued."[27]

By Article 13 of the Convention:

> "Everyone whose rights and freedoms as set forth in this Convention are violated shall have an effective remedy before a national authority notwithstanding that the violation has been committed by persons acting in an official capacity."

[18] See also J. Alderson *Human Rights and the Police*, Council of Europe.
[19] Article 2.
[20] Article 5.
[21] Article 8.
[22] Article 11.
[23] See Application 7729/76, D.R. 7 p. 164.
[24] *Winterwerp* v. *Netherlands* (1979) 18 Yearbook H.R. 192.
[25] See *Sunday Times* v. *United Kingdom* (1979) 2 E.H.R.R. 245.
[26] Article 18.
[27] *Handyside* v. *UK* (1976) 17 Yearbook H.R. 228.

In relation to police activity it may well be that in many situations the "complaints procedure" will be "an effective remedy" for the purposes of the Convention. In holding an application from Denmark inadmissible, the Commission held that the fact that a police complaints board had taken no action in a particular case and that it refused to order investigations in 90 per cent. of cases were not sufficient reasons for holding that the remedy is ineffective.[28]

These general points must be borne in mind when particular types of police activity are considered in relation to the provisions of the Convention.

Arrest and detention

A person's rights in relation to detention and arrest are guaranteed by Article 5 of the Convention which provides as follows:

> "(1) Everyone has the right to liberty and security of person. No one shall be deprived of his liberty save in following cases and in accordance with a procedure prescribed by law
> (a) the lawful detention of a person after conviction by a competent court;
> (b) the lawful arrest or detention of a person for non compliance with the lawful order of a court or in order to secure the fulfillment of any obligations prescribed by law;
> (c) the lawful arrest or detention of a person effected for the purpose of bringing him before the competent legal authority on reasonable suspicion of having committed an offence or when it is reasonably considered necessary to prevent his committing an offence or fleeing after having done so;
> (d) the detention of a minor by lawful order for the purpose of educational supervision or his lawful detention for the purpose of bringing him before the competent lawful authority;
> (e) the lawful detention of persons for the prevention of the spreading of infectious diseases, or persons of unsound mind, alcoholics or drug addicts, or vagrants;
> (f) the lawful arrest or detention of a person to prevent his effecting an unauthorised entry into the country or of a person against whom action is being taken with a view to deportation or extradition;
> (2) Everyone who is arrested shall be informed promptly, in a language which he understands, of the reasons for his arrest.
> (3) Everyone arrested or detained in accordance with the provisions of paragraph 1(c) of this Article shall be brought promptly before a judge or other officer authorised by law to exercise judicial power and shall be entitled to trial within a reasonable time or to release pending trial. Release may be conditioned by guarantees to appear for trial.
> (4) Everyone who is deprived of his liberty by arrest or detention shall be entitled to take proceedings by which the lawfulness of his detention

[28] Application 8828/79; *X* v. *Denmark* (1983) 5 E.H.R.R. 278.

shall be decided speedily by a court and his release ordered if the detention is not lawful.
(5) Everyone who has been the victim of arrest or detention in contravention of the provisions of this Article shall have an enforceable right to compensation."

If police arrest and detention procedures are not defined by clear and accessible rules then may be challenged as not being in accordance with Article 5.

The limitations on police powers of arrest imposed by the Convention do not differ to any appreciable extent to those contained in English law.[29] The Commission has held that good reasons to believe a suspect has committed the offence are sufficient to justify his arrest or detention since there is no need at this stage to prove the reality and nature of the offence.[30] It has also ruled that to establish reasonable suspicion, it is essential to consider the circumstances existing at the time of arrest.[31]

Article 5(2) is closely analogous to common law principles regarding the statement of reasons for an arrest.[32] It does not require the suspect to be given the necessary information in a particular form nor need it consist in a complete list of the charges against him.[33] It is sufficient if a person who is arrested is informed of the reason for his arrest in broad terms and given proper reasons later.[34] Article 5(2) provides no guarantee of the right to contact a lawyer.[35]

Under Article 5(3) a person must be "brought promptly" before a court. The Commission has held that the maximum delay which can occur is four days[36] although a delay of five days was acceptable in an exceptional case where the prisoner had to receive medical treatment.[37] It is unlikely, therefore, that the detention provisions of the Police and Criminal Evidence Act 1984 will be found to contravene the Convention.

The use of force on arrest

The use of force may potentially violate the Convention's guarantee of the right to life or the right not to be subject to torture or inhuman or degrading treatment. The "right to life" is protected by Article 2 which provides as follows:

"(1) Everyone's right to life shall be protected by law. No one shall be deprived of his life intentionally save in the execution of a sentence of a court following his conviction of a crime for which this penalty is provided by law.

[29] See Chap. 5 above at pp. 138 *et seq.*
[30] Application 8224/78, D.R. 15 at 211.
[31] Application 7755/77, D.R. 9 at 210.
[32] See Chap. 5 above at pp. 133 *et seq.*
[33] Application 8098/77, D.R. 16 at 111.
[34] Application 8828/79; *X.* v. *Denmark* (1983) 5 E.H.R.R. 278; Article 5(2) was complied with when the suspect was given proper reasons six hours after arrest.
[35] *Ibid.*
[36] Application 2394/66; Coll. 21 at 69.
[37] Application 4960/71; Coll. 42 at 49.

(2) Deprivation of life shall not be regarded as inflicted in contravention of the article when it results from force which is no more than absolutely necessary:

(a) in defence of any person from unlawful violence;
(b) in order to effect a lawful arrest or prevent the escape of a person lawfully detained;
(c) in action lawfully taken for the purpose of quelling riot or insurrection."

The use of force is subject to the principle of proportionality.[38] It has been suggested that the Convention only licences the minimum force necessary to achieve the desired objective.[39] Nevertheless, if this principle is observed, the Convention allows the use of lethal force in appropriate circumstances. Thus, a police officer who fired a fatal shot in a riot has been considered as acting in lawful self-defence.[40] A soldier who accidentally killed a young child with a plastic bullet has been held to have used such force as was absolutely necessary to quell a riot.[41]

By Article 3 of the Convention "No one shall be subjected to torture or inhuman or degrading treatment." It has been held that where a complainant alleged he was twice assaulted by police officers when arrested whilst his hands were handcuffed behind his back and then savaged by a police dog this (even had it been proved), did not amount to sufficiently serious treatment to constitute inhuman or degrading treatment contrary to Article 3.[42] It is submitted that the restrictions imposed by the English law on the use of force on arrest[43] are in accordance with the Convention.

The treatment of suspects

By Article 3 of the convention no one shall be subjected to torture or to inhuman or degrading treatment. These notions have been explained by the Commission as follows[44]:

> "It is plain that there may be treatment to which all these descriptions apply, for all torture may be inhuman or degrading, and inhuman treatment is also degrading. The notion of inhuman treatment covers at least such treatment as deliberately causes severe suffering, mental or physical, which in a particular situation is unjustifiable. The word "torture" is often used to describe inhuman treatment which has a purpose, such as obtaining information or confessions or the infliction of punishment, and it is generally an aggravated form of inhuman treatment, Treatment or punishment or an individual may be such to be degrading if it grossly humiliates him before others or drives him to act against his will or conscience."

[38] See above at p. 426.
[39] See J. Alderson, *Human Rights and the Police*, Council of Europe at p. 68.
[40] Application 2758/66; *X.* v. *Belgium* 12 Yearbook H.R. 174.
[41] Application 10044/84; (1984) 7 E.H.R.R. 409.
[42] Application 4220/69; Coll. 37 at 51.
[43] See Chap. 4 above at p. 123.
[44] Applications 3321, 3322, 3323 and 3344/67; *Denmark* v. *Greece* 12 Yearbook H.R. (special volume) 690.

The Commission, therefore, held that solitary confinement, isolation in a police cell without food or access to toilets, mock executions, threats to throw a person out of the window, the used of insulting language, rubbing the head with vomit, being forced to strip naked and being present at the torture of friends and relatives were all torture. Sensory deprivation such as wall standing, hooding, subjection to noise and deprivation of sleep, food and drink when taken together contravened Article 3.[45] Solitary confinement of a dangerous prisoner does not breach the Convention[46] but refusal of proper medical care may do so.[47] In some circumstances force feeding may violate the Convention.[48] Considerable jurisprudence has developed around prisoner's rights based upon Article 3 but it is outside the scope of this book. A failure to allow suspects detained under the prevention of terrorism legislation to communicate with their spouses cannot be justified as a denial of the right to private and family life being necessary for the prevention of crime[49] unless there is a danger of accomplices being warned.[50]

Search and seizure

Police powers of search and seizure will breach the Convention if they do not comply with Article 8 which provides:

> "(1) Everyone has the right to respect for his private and family life, his home and his correspondence.
> (2) There shall be no interference by a public authority with the exercise of this right except such as is in accordance with the law and is necessary in a democratic society in the interests of national security, public safety or the economic well-being of the country, for the prevention of disorder or crime, for the protection of health or moral, or for the protection of the rights and freedoms of others."

Any interference with a person's private and family life, home and correspondence must, therefore, be "in accordance" with clearly defined rules of domestic law.[51] Any interferences which may be justified under Article 8(2) must be "proportionate" to the legitimate aim pursued.[52]

The seizure of a private document required for a criminal investigation interfered with respect for private life but may be justified as being necessary for the prevention of crime or disorder.[53]

Furthermore, Article 1 of the First Protocol[54] states that:

> "every natural or legal person is entitled to peaceful enjoyment of his possessions. No one shall be deprived of his possessions except in the

[45] *Ireland* v. *United Kingdom* (1978) 2 E.H.R.R. 25.
[46] Application 9907/82; (1984) 7 E.H.R.R. 533.
[47] Application 44165/70; 38 Collection H.R. 18.
[48] Application 10565/83; (1984) 7 E.H.R.R. 152.
[49] *i.e.* justified under Article 8(2).
[50] Applications 8022, 8025, 8027/77; *McVeigh* v. *United Kingdom* (1981) 5 E.H.R.R. 71.
[51] See above at p. 426.
[52] See above at p. 426.
[53] Application 530/59; *X.* v. *Germany* C.D. 2.
[54] Protocol, Paris, March 20, 1952; T.S. 46 (1954) Cmd. 9221.

public interest and subject to the conditions provided by law and by the general principles of international law.

The preceding paragraph shall not, however, impair the right of a state to enforce such laws as it deems necessary to control the use of property in accordance with the general interest . . ."

Possessions for these purposes include both moveable and immoveable property.[55] In enforcing laws to control the use of property a state enjoys "a wide margin of appreciation" both in choosing the method of enforcement and in ascertaining whether the consequences enforcement are justified in general interest.[56] Where a complaint was made because copies of an obscene book were held following a search of premises by the police, it was found that the seizure was only provisional since he would have been entitled to their return if acquitted. Moreover, seizure aimed at the protection of morals was justified and being within the meaning of "general interest."[57]

Body samples, photographs and fingerprinting

Taking body samples may amount to "inhuman and degrading treatment" contrary to Article 3.[58] It might also breach the right of respect to private life under Article 8(1) unless justified by Article 8(2). However, taking and retaining photographs of a demonstration will not mean that the police are guilty of invading privacy.[59] Producing intimate photographs during a trial or keeping records including documents, photographs and fingerprints relating to previous criminal cases were found to be necessary in a democratic society.[60]

Surveillance

Police surveillance may also breach the guarantee of privacy contained in Article 8.[61] In the *Klass* case[62] the European Court took judicial notice both of the technical advances made in surveillance and of the development of terrorism. The state is entitled to counter terrorism with secret surveillance of mail, post and telecommunications under exceptional circumstances although it cannot adopt whatever measures it thinks appropriate in the name of the struggle against espionage and terrorism.

In the *Klass* case the Court gave some general guidance as to the application of Article 8 to legislation authorising surveillance:

(1) the legislation must be designed to ensure surveillance is not ordered haphazardly, irregularly or without due and proper care;

[55] Application 7456/76; D.R. 13 at 40.
[56] *Allgemein Gollund Silberschecdean* v. *United Kingdom* (1986) 9 E.H.R.R. 1.
[57] Application 5493/72; *Handyside* v. *United Kingdom* 19 Yearbook H.R. 506.
[58] See above at p. 429.
[59] Application 5877/72; *X.* v. *United Kingdom* Coll. H.R. 90.
[60] Application 1307/61; *X.* v. *Germany* 5 Yearbook H.R. 230.
[61] See above at p. 430.
[62] Application 5029/71; *Klass* v. *Germany* (1978) 2 E.H.R.R. 214.

(2) surveillance must be reviewed and must be accompanied by procedures which guarantee individual rights;
(3) it is in principle desireable to entrust the supervisory control to a judge in accordance with the rule of law, but other safeguards might suffice if they are independent and vested with sufficient powers to exercise an effective and continuous control;
(4) if the surveillance was justified under Article 8(2) the a failure to inform the individual under surveillance of this fact afterwards is in principle justified.[63]

However, the Court upheld the validity of the legislation under review. Similarly, a telephone tap of a lawyer who supported terrorist activities was justified for the purpose of "national security and the prevention of crime."[64]

Nevertheless, any justification with the right to privacy must be "in accordance with the law" with the result that the telephone tapping and metering in the *Malone* case[65] was in breach of the convention.[66] The Commission in the *Malone* case were of the view that the existence of adequate legal sageguards was an essential guarantee against the abuse of a system of secret surveillance. They suggested that the existence of rules of law binding the authorities not to misuse the system was an important safeguard even if there was little or no possibility of recourse to the courts.[67]

The disclosure of information from a secret police register to prospective employers will constitute a violation of the Convention unless it is justified as being in accordance with the law and in the interests of one of the grounds stipulated in Article 8(2)[68]

Police practices of "visual and aural surveillance" are clearly in breach of Article 8 as they are not "in accordance with the law," being regulated only by administrative guidelines.[69]

Article 8 is likely to provide fertile ground for applications in relation to the police because it guarantees rights which receive almost no protection under English law. Applications under this Article will often be the only remedy available to those who have been subject to unreasonable surveillance.[70]

3. PRACTICE AND PROCEDURE

Making an application

Although one state which is a party to the Convention may refer another which is party to the Commission for an alleged breach[71] only the right of

[63] *Klass* v. *Germany* (1978) 2 E.H.R.R. 214 at 232–236.
[64] Application 8290/78; D.R. 18 at 176.
[65] See Chap. 9 above at p. 285.
[66] Application 8691/79; *Malone* v. *United Kingdom* (1984) 7 E.H.R.R. 14.
[67] *Malone* v. *United Kingdom* (1983) 5 E.H.R.R. 385.
[68] Application 9248/81; *Leander* v. *Sweden* (1984) 7 E.H.R.R. 57.
[69] See Chap. 9 above at p. 285.
[70] See generally, Chap. 9 above at pp. 282 *et seq.*
[71] Under Article 24.

individuals to present applications will be examined. In fact, the Commission may receive an application from any individual, non-governmental organisation or group of individuals who claim to be a victim of a violation of the Convention.[72]

Although a group which has a separate and artificial legal personality like a company or a church cannot prove that it is a person who could enjoy the rights conferred by the Convention[73] a direct victim for these purposes includes a wife complaining about treatment to her husband[74] and parents complaining about treatment to their children.[75] The petition itself must allege that the petitioner is a victim of a violation or it will be rejected. So, for example, the Commission rejected an application of ill-treatment in relation to a fellow prisoner.[76] The Commission cannot examine as an abstract question whether domestic law conforms to the Convention.[77]

The Commission has drawn up its own rules of procedure.[78] Proceedings for breach of the Convention are initiated by an application in writing signed by the applicant or his representative.[79] No special form is required but the application must include[80]:

(1) the applicant's name;
(2) the name of the state complained against;
(3) the object of the claim;
(4) the provision of the Convention relied on;
(5) a statement of facts and arguments.

Any documentation relied on must be attached. If applicable, evidence must be provided that all domestic remedies have been exhausted.[81] The application should be submitted to the Secretary-General of the Council of Europe who will transmit it to the President of the Commission[82] but in practice most applications are made by writing to the Secretary of the European Commission of Human Rights whose address is: Council of Europe, Palais de l'Europe, F67006 Strasbourg Cedex, France.

The applicant may request, or the Commission may grant on its own initiative, free legal aid for the presentation of his case in the following situations:

(1) where observations in writing on the admissability of the application have been received from the respondent government or the time limit for their submission has expired[83];
(2) where the application is declared admissible[84];

[72] Article 25, para. 1.
[73] Application 742/60; *X.* v. *Germany*; 7 Coll. H.R. 104.
[74] Applications 9214/80, 9473/81, 9474/81; *X, Cabales and Balkandale* v. *United Kingdom* (1982) 5 E.H.R.R. 132.
[75] Application 8811/79; *X, Y and Z* v. *Sweden* (1982) 5 E.H.R.R. 147.
[76] Application 2300/64; *X.* v. *Germany*; 22 Coll. H.R. 73.
[77] Application 332/57; *"Lawless" Case (Merits)* 4 Yearbook H.R. 438 (European Court).
[78] "The European Commission of Human Rights Rules of Procedure" 17 Yearbook H.R. 34.
[79] *Ibid.* r. 40(1).
[80] *Ibid.* r. 44.
[81] *Ibid.* r. 41(2); see below at p. 434.
[82] *Ibid.* r. 42.
[83] *Ibid.* Addendum. r. 1(*a*).
[84] *Ibid.* Addendum. r. 1(*b*).

(3) in any other case where the Commission is satisfied that legal representation is essential for the proper presentation of his case and he does not have sufficient means to pay the costs.[85] The applicant can prove his lack of means by completing a form of declaration of means[86] and an ordinary legal aid certificate will be acceptable.

The rejection of applications

The Commission will reject an application in the following circumstances:

(1) where the applicant has not exhausted his domestic remedies[87];
(2) where the application is not presented within six months of the final decision being taken[88];
(3) where the application is anonymous[89];
(4) where an application is substantially the same as a matter which has already been examined by the Commission[90];
(5) where the application has already been submitted to another procedure of international investigation or settlement and it contains no relevant new information[91];
(6) where the Commission considers the application to be incompatible with the provisions of the Convention[92];
(7) where the Commission considers the application manifestly ill-founded[93];
(8) where the Commission considers it an abuse of the right to petition.[94]

The need to exhaust domestic remedies has meant that applications have been rejected by the Commission where the applicant failed to appeal to the Court of Appeal[95] or failed to appeal to the Court of Appeal from a single judge's failure to grant leave.[96] In the *Malone* case, the UK government did not insist that there should have been an appeal from the decision of Sir Robert Megarry V.-C. A failure to bring civil proceedings against the police where the application alleged an unlawful arrest also resulted in the application being rejected.[97] If proceedings are commenced out of time or appealed out of time, domestic remedies will not have been exhausted.[98] The application will also be rejected if the applicant fails to exhaust rem-

[85] "The European Commission of Human Rights Rules of Procedure" 17 Yearbook H.R. 34, Addendum, r. 2.
[86] *Ibid.* Addendum. r. 3(*a*).
[87] Article 27, para. 3; Article 26.
[88] Article 27, para. 3; Article 26.
[89] Article 27, para. 1(*a*).
[90] Article 27, para. 1(*b*).
[91] Article 27, para. 1(*b*).
[92] Article 27, para. 2.
[93] Article 27, para. 2.
[94] Article 27, para. 2.
[95] Application 4789/71; *X.* v. *United Kingdom* 40 Coll.H.R. 31.
[96] Application 3485/68; 12 Yearbook H.R. 288.
[97] Application 5197/71; *X.* v. *United Kingdom* 42 Coll.H.R. 138.
[98] Application 325/58; *X.* v. *Germany*; 2 Yearbook H.R. 342, at 344.

edies because of his lawyer's advice that they are ineffective[99] and if there is any real doubt as to whether the remedy is effective, it should be sought[1] On the other hand, a complaint concerning legislation as such does not require domestic remedies to be exhausted[2] so, for example, it would not be necessary to take court proceedings if a challenge was mounted to one of the provisions of the Police and Criminal Evidence Act 1984.

An application will not be rejected as being substantially the same as a previous one if it is presented by a different petitioner from the initial application[3] or if it is the same petitioner who has his application earlier rejected because of his failure to exhaust his domestic remedies.[4] However, the petitioner cannot represent an application unless the new one contains a new fact which would have required a different decision had it previously been known by the Commission.[5]

Procedure on admissible applications

Every application is referred to a member of the Commission who acts as a rapporteur[6] and may request information about the facts from the respondent government.[7] He reports to the Commission in order to give his opinion whether the application is admissible[8] and the Commission will either declare it admissible and examine the facts complained of further and ask for observations from the respondent government.[9]

Once the Commission has accepted the application, it must examine the petition with the representatives of the parties for the purpose of ascertaining the facts and may undertake an investigation for which the respondent government must furnish all necessary facilities after exchanging views with the Commission. The Commission then takes on a conciliatory role to bring about a friendly settlement on the basis of respect for the rights as defined in the Convention.[10] If a friendly settlement is reached, the Commission will publish a brief report on the case.

If no friendly settlement is achieved, the Commission must draw up a full report on the facts of the application and state its opinion as to whether the facts found disclose a breach of the Convention.[11] The report is transmitted to the Committee of Ministers and to the state concerned.[12]

The Commission may bring the application before the European Court or the respondent government may do so.[13] Rather oddly, however, the

[99] Application 1488/62; *X.* v. *Belgium* 13 Coll.H.R. 93.
[1] Application 1661/62; *X & Y* v. *Belgium* 6 Yearbook 360.
[2] Application 5493/72; *Handyside* v. *United Kingdom* 45 Coll.H.R. 23.
[3] Application 493/59; *X* v. *Ireland* 4 Yearbook 302.
[4] Application 3448/67; *Wernhoff* v. *Germany* 30 Coll.H.R. 56.
[5] Application 3780/68; *X* v. *Belgium* 37 Coll.H.R. 6.
[6] European Commission of Human Rights Rules of Procedure, r. 45(1).
[7] *Ibid.* r. 45(2).
[8] *Ibid.* r. 45(3).
[9] *Ibid.* r. 46(2).
[10] Article 28.
[11] Article 31, para. 1.
[12] Article 31, para. 2.
[13] Article 48.

complainant himself cannot. If the Commission decides to put the case before the European Court, its report is sent to the applicant for his written observations.[14] However, if the application is not referred to the European Court within three months of its transmission to the Committee of Ministers, the Committee itself will decide if there is a violation of the Convention by a two-thirds majority.[15]

A case heard before the European Court is heard by seven judges.[16] Its hearings are in public. The Court has drawn up its own rules of procedure.[17] The judgment of the Court is binding[18] and the parties to any case have undertaken to abide by its decision.[19] The Court's decision is transmitted to the Committee of Ministers who supervise its execution.[20] Moreover, the Court has an inherent jurisdiction to interpret its own judgments and that interpretation is binding on the parties.[21]

14 European Commission of Human Rights Rules of Procedure, r. 76.
15 Article 32.
16 Article 43.
17 Rules of Procedure of the European Court of Human Rights, 5 E.H.R.R. 647.
18 Article 52.
19 Article 53.
20 Article 54.
21 *Ringeisen* v. *Austria (No. 3)* 1 E.H.R.R. 513.

Index